DESIGNING AND PROGRAMMING MODERN COMPUTER SYSTEMS
MODERN COMPUTER SYSTEMS
Volume II
SUPERCOMPUTING SYSTEMS: RECONFIGURABLE ARCHITECTURES

Svetlana P. Kartashev
International Supercomputing Institute

Steven I. Kartashev
International Supercomputing Institute

PRENTICE HALL, Englewood Cliffs, New Jersey 07632

Library of Congress Cataloging-in-Publication Data
(Revised for vol. 2)

Designing and programming modern computers and systems.

Vol. 2 — has title: Designing and programming
modern computer systems.
  Includes bibliographies and indexes.
  Contents: v. 1. LSI modular computer systems—
v. 2 Supercomputing systems.
  1. Computer engineering.   2. Computer architecture.
I. Kartashev, Svetlana. II. Kartashev, Steven I.
III. Title: Designing and programming modern computer
systems.
TK7885.D474   1982   004   81-21078

Editorial/production supervision: *Raeia Maes*
Manufacturing buyer: *Mary Ann Gloriande*

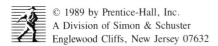

Printed in the United States of America

10 9 8 7 6 5 4 3 2 1

ISBN   0-13-201435-1

Prentice-Hall International (UK) Limited, *London*
Prentice-Hall of Australia Pty. Limited, *Sydney*
Prentice-Hall Canada Inc., *Toronto*
Prentice-Hall Hispanoamericana, S.A., *Mexico*
Prentice-Hall of India Private Limited, *New Delhi*
Prentice-Hall of Japan, Inc., *Tokyo*
Simon & Schuster Asia Pte. Ltd., *Singapore*
Editora Prentice-Hall do Brasil, Ltda., *Rio de Janeiro*

Contents

FOREWORD xiii

by

Gene Myron Amdahl

PREFACE xvii

Chapter I

MOTIVATION: MISSION-CRITICAL COMPUTING,
PROBLEMS AND SOLUTIONS 1

Chapter II

RECONFIGURATION SOFTWARE: RECONFIGURATION
METHODOLOGY   19

Chapter III

RECONFIGURATION FLOW CHART   145

Chapter IV

DYNAMIC COMPILER   249

Chapter V

ALGORITHM DEVELOPMENT   309

Foreword

BY

GENE MYRON AMDAHL

This is the second volume in the series, *Designing and Programming Modern Computer Systems*, initiated by Prentice Hall in 1982.

This volume deals with supercomputing in the context of reconfigurable architectures. The important class of these architectures, called dynamic architectures and invented by Svetlana P. Kartashev and Steven I. Kartashev in the 1970s, allows dynamic partitioning of the resources into different sets of computers with varied word sizes and automatic assumption of various computer architectures under the software control.

The authors' vision is to define a dynamic architecture as given hardware box assembled from processor and memory units that can be formed into differing computing structures under the program control. These structures are: multicomputers/multiprocessors, arrays, pipelines, networks, and mixed. Each structure is characterized by parameters variability extended to the architectural type of the structure (multicomputer, array, pipeline, network, mixed), the word sizes of its units (dynamic computers, processor elements, pipeline stages, network nodes), the number of units included in the structure, and the interconnections between concurrent structures formed dynamically.

The major objective of this approach is to improve performance through more extensive utilization of the available hardware resources than is possible to achieve in modern computer systems. Currently, available supercomputers achieve peak performance only for particular portions of computations being underutilized a significant portion of their time.

There are many reasons for this performance degradation, but the major one is associated with the **mismatch** between the hardware computing structure and the task being computed.

Sources of this mismatch are:

- **Bit size mismatch:** The bit size requirements of the program are smaller or larger than that of the hardware resources that compute this program. If these requirements are smaller, the difference in bit sizes extended to the processor and memory resources becomes unused and leads to **performance degradation** caused by the failure of the computer hardware to utilize it. If these requirements are larger, the computation should proceed in a much slower and less precise floating-point form, leading again to a performance degradation as a result.
- **Concurrency mismatch:** The program requirements on the number of parallel instruction and data streams are smaller or larger than those of the hardware resources. If these requirements are smaller, the idleness of the unused portion of the hardware leads to slowing the time of the execution of other concurrent programs (tasks) in the mix. If these requirements are larger, parallel information streams (instruction and/or data) must be computed sequentially, again leading to an increase in the overall computation time.
- **Interconnection mismatch:** The program requirements on the interconnection of the used resource units (processor and memory resources involved in computations) mismatch the available interconnections in a computer system.

As a result, the data exchanges among engaged resources take much longer than if these resources were connected optimally.

The only way to overcome mismatches that create a nonoptimal use of the hardware resources is through reconfigurable interconnections when the resources are partitioned dynamically into a varied number of computing structures each of which has the bit size also varied via software.

Another problem that must be solved is the development of very fast reconfiguration from one computing structure to another in order to eliminate any reconfiguration overhead from the total computation time. This radical departure from the conventional computation process requires development of program preprocessing techniques aimed at finding the optimal architectural structures that can be used in computations. Thereafter, these structures will be assumed automatically via software with the use of developed reconfiguration methodology.

What will happen as a result is that the same hardware resource will perform automatic switches from one architectural configuration to another in order to achieve a significant performance improvement because of the creation of tightly fitted computer structures and the release of redundant resources into computations of new programs.

Therefore, development of the software which, on the one hand, accomplishes actual system reconfigurations and which, on the other hand, finds a sequence of matching hardware computing structures that must be assumed in computations becomes the cornerstone of this approach.

The authors' solution to this formidable task involves developing the following:

- **Comprehensive reconfiguration methodology** which allows the authors to perform very fast reconfigurations in dynamic multicomputer systems/multicomputer networks and fault-tolerant reconfigurations. The latter are aimed at turning off the faulty modules from computations. The structure used previously is preserved. Its performance is organized on a reduced level with faulty modules being turned off.
- **Program preprocessing techniques** for dynamic multicomputer systems and multicomputer networks. The algorithms are developed to allow automatic construction of the sequence of architectural states that can be assumed during computations. The authors call this sequence the **reconfiguration flow chart**. Each state of the reconfiguration flow chart is understood as a set of concurrent dynamic computers with the word sizes selected by the programmer via software. The authors present techniques to accommodate both static programs and those arriving during computations (dynamic programs). For the dynamic programs, the flow chart constructed for static programs is modified by inserting dynamically created states that take into account the resource requirements of dynamic programs.

All in all, this volume contains highly original research material on supercomputing systems with dynamic architecture for use by hardware and software engineers in designing such systems and in performing their extensive software development.

The end result is to take advantage of the reconfigurability of the hardware for unlocking a new and heretofore unused source of performance improvement for the applications with very demanding requirements on supercomputer power, of which mission critical computations is a particular case.

Preface

This book is dedicated to the description of the principal software tools for dynamic architectures, which are called **reconfiguration software**. We will discuss the two categories of reconfiguration software:

    I. reconfiguration methodology

    II. reconfiguration flow chart

Another major subject of this book is associated with extensive algorithm development aimed at performing comprehensive comparison computation made by dynamic architectures with those performed by conventional systems having similar resource complexity. The results of these comparisons are either in concrete speed-up figures expressed in percentages or in other valid demonstrations of superior computations shown by dynamic architectures, if concrete numerical percentages cannot be obtained due to the multiplicity of alternative ways computations can be exhibited by conventional systems.

The composition of this book is as follows. Chapter I, **Motivation**:

    a. Introduces the problem of mission-critical Supercomputing systems which can be resolved only with the use of dynamic architectures.

    b. Finds desirable characteristics for dynamic architectures in mission-critical applications.

    c. Shows that dynamic architectures possess powerful capabilities for implementing most useful architectural features for reconfigurable architectures in mission-critical applications.

Chapter II, **Reconfiguration Software**, discusses the two categories of reconfiguration software introduced above. It gives a comprehensive description of the reconfiguration methodology applicable for architectural and fault-tolerant reconfigurations. General problems of these reconfigurations are presented in Sec. 1. For the architectural reconfigurations introduced in Sec. 2, the following techniques are introduced:

a. Multicomputer reconfigurations

b. Network reconfigurations

For fault-tolerant reconfiguration (Secs. 5 through 7), we discuss the formation of gracefully degraded reconfigurable binary trees with the use of reconfigurations.

Chapter III introduces the software techniques leading to an automatic construction of the **reconfiguration flow chart** for two types of systems; (a) **dynamic multicomputer systems** (Secs. 3 and 5) and (b) **dynamic networks organized as reconfigurable binary trees** (Sec. 4).

For dynamic multicomputer systems, the construction of a reconfiguration flow chart leads toward the minimization of program delays and the total time of executing all programs from a given program mix. For reconfigurable binary trees, the construction of such a flow chart leads to a significant data-exchange optimization, because it is possible to select such tree configurations as consecutive states in this flow chart in which each pair of nodes with large data exchanges can be connected with the minimal communication path of length 1 (i.e., these two nodes become adjacent in a selected tree configuration).

Also, for dynamic multicomputer systems, we discuss two types of reconfiguration flow charts: **static**, in Sec. 3, and **dynamic**, in Sec. 5. A **static reconfiguration flow chart** takes into account the reconfiguration requests of those programs called **static** that are available in the system before the beginning of the procedures aimed at automatic construction of this flow chart.

A **dynamic reconfiguration flow chart** considers reconfiguration requests of those programs called **dynamic** that arrive at the system when it is executing a reconfiguration flow chart. Thus a dynamic reconfiguration flow chart can be conceived as a modified static flow chart with newly added architectural states created dynamically that take into account reconfiguration requests of dynamic programs.

The objectives of Chapter IV are:

1. To outline the effect of dynamic reconfiguration on some popular ADA constructs

2. To give memory management techniques for data structures in relational data bases that are created dynamically

Section 1 is dedicated to handling, in dynamic architectures, such well-known ADA constructs as:

a. ADA packages (Sec. 1.1)

b. Task rendezvous (Sec. 1.2)

c. Exceptions handling (Sec. 1.3)

Section 2 introduces the topic of memory allocation in a relational data base implemented as a dynamically reconfigurable multiprocessor system including content-addressable memories. The description of such a relational data base is made in Sec. 2.2. Section 2.3 performs the classification of all allocation schemes. Section 2.4 addresses the problem of file interference and Secs. 2.5 and 2.6 devise optimal allocations for various types of files introduced in Sec. 2.3.

Chapter V, **Algorithm Development**, discusses the organization of computations in dynamic architectures for the following classes of algorithms:

a. General-purpose program mix made of concurrent programs with no data dependencies (Sec. 2.1)

b. Parallel construct fork–join (Sec. 2.2)

c. Producer–consumer algorithms (Sec. 3)

d. Array computations encountered in the solution of relaxation equations and pulse deinterleaving algorithms (Sec. 4)

e. Data-base management in tree data bases (Sec. 5)

f. Real-time sorting (Sec. 6)

g. Tree-structured algorithms (Sec. 7)

Finally, following Chapter V we present the conclusions to this volume. Overall conclusions are divided into the following topical areas presented in respective sections:

a. Conclusions on the reconfiguration flow chart and reconfiguration methodology

b. Conclusions on algorithm development

Svetlana P. Kartashev
Steven I. Kartashev

Chapter I

Motivation: Mission-Critical Computing, Problems and Solutions

1 ADAPTABLE SOFTWARE FOR MISSION-CRITICAL COMPUTERS

A Supercomputing system whose performance is based on successful execution of its mission, which is specified by the concrete mission-critical requirements defined quantitatively, is now called a *mission-critical Supercomputing system* [5].†

As was shown in [1], the performance requirements of most mission-critical Supercomputing systems greatly exceed those that can now be obtained by commercially available computer systems. The reason for this is that mission-critical computers must accommodate a large number of highly complex and dynamically changing requirements of defense systems.

These requirements originate from the following important characteristics of modern defense systems: deep penetration and wide range; quick and flexible response; great precision; versatility of missions and conditions; high reliability; long endurance and easy and fast mobility.

Currently, the most popular way of meeting these requirements consists of designing a massively parallel architecture made of p processors where p is a very large number ($p \geq 10,000$). This approach however, is prone to significant performance degradation because of the following factors:

F1. Amdahl's law [2], which establishes considerable performance degradation if a parallel program contains even a small fraction of sequential computation, becomes far more severe for large p. Indeed, in accordance with this law, the speed-up, S, caus-

---

† Number in brackets refer to references given at the end of this volume.

1

ed by computation of the same parallel program in p processors where f is a fraction of serial computation in this program, is determined as follows:

$$S = \frac{1}{f + (1 - f)/p} = \frac{p}{f \bullet (p - 1) + 1}$$

Since f ranges from $f = 0$ if the program is entirely parallel to $f = 1$, if the program is entirely serial the following ranges of S can be obtained:

For $f = 0$, $S = p$, i.e., S achieves its maximum and there is no performance degradation in a parallel computer with p processors. For $f = 1$, $S = 1$, i.e., a computer with p processors acts as a serial computer containing one processor. Since for this case, all other processors are wasted, there is no sense in computing this program in parallel. Therefore, speed-up function S declines monotonically from $S = p$ to $S = 1$, and the larger p is, the steeper the decline of S is for the same interval domain taken by the fraction f of sequential computation present in the program. It then follows that massively parallel architectures are affected more strongly than parallel architectures with smaller p by (even smaller) insertions of serial computations.

F2. Massively parallel architectures introduce **far greater delays in data exchanges between cooperating processors** than the architectures with smaller p [3]. Indeed, for a massively parallel architecture, because of the complexity and bandwidth restrictions, two processors are interconnected together (via an interconnection network or directly) only if they belong to the same processors' cluster. Thus, if processors PE_i and PE_j are from different clusters, data exchanges among them take a significant amount of time which results in considerable performance degradation.

F3. Massively parallel architectures feature **gross underutilization of resources** because it is almost impossible to perform a balanced task assignment to thousands of processors during which all processors are not idle and engaged in computations continuously.

As a result of these factors, such architectural approaches must be tried for mission-critical computations which (a) are not so prone to the devastating effect of Amdahl's law, (b) are capable of minimizing data exchange delays, and (c) maintain the high utilization factor of the used hardware resources.

Let us establish what types of architectures should be used for a mission-critical supercomputing system in order to satisfy the severe requirements of mission-critical applications on the following:

1. **computer response time** to a given set of input information;
2. **increased sophistication and complexity** of real-time application algorithms; and
3. **absolute software and hardware reliability** required to identify every real-time target.

1.1 Dedicated and Adaptable Supercomputing Systems

The types of architectures used in mission-critical Supercomputing systems are defined by the characteristics of the missions a Supercomputing system is destined to compute.

Complex real-time missions can undergo rapid or continuous changes or they can be fixed for the Supercomputing system life cycle. The first type of mission requires that the Supercomputing system's architecture be able to adapt to the algorithms in order to compute them within the minimal times which are needed; we will call these Supercomputing systems *adaptable or reconfigurable* † [5, 7]. The second type of mission is most effectively solved by *dedicated* (real-time) Supercomputing systems that contain dedicated hardware circuits which speed up execution of mission-critical algorithms [1].

1.2 Two Types of Adaptable Software

Both types of Supercomputing systems require that their software be adaptable. However, the types of adaptations to be performed by an adaptable software depend on the Supercomputing system type. For adaptable Supercomputing systems, the software must take advantage of the additional performance gains that can be achieved via reconfiguration [4]. We will call this type of adaptable software *reconfiguration software.*

For dedicated Supercomputing systems, the adaptable software must serve not a single but multiple and dedicated (target) Supercomputing systems, i.e., be *retargetable* in order to defray the huge software development costs which are introduced into the software development of every dedicated Supercomputing system [5].

A description of both types of adaptations that have to be performed by an adaptable software follows.

1.2.1 Reconfiguration Software for Adaptable Supercomputing Systems: Classification

By *reconfiguration software* for adaptable Supercomputing systems, we understand a collection of software tools that possesses the following attributes:

a. They provide for extensive use of the reconfigurability concept implemented in the hardware of any such system.

b. They must be included into a software package of any adaptable Supercomputing system to enable it to compute mission-critical programs written in ADA programming language.

While attribute **a** follows from the principal function that must be implemented in the reconfiguration software for an adaptable Supercomputing system, attribute **b** originates from the fact that ADA was adopted in 1982 as the standard high-level language for mission-critical applications, requiring that all executing programs be written in ADA.

In all, reconfiguration software can now be divided into the following categories:

† Throughout this volume the terms ''adaptable'' and ''reconfigurable'' are interchangeable, since they are equivalent and mean the adaptation of the architecture to an algorithm with the use of dynamic reconfiguration.

Category 1: Reconfiguration Flow Chart [4]

The major objective of these tools can be formulated as follows: Given a set of concurrent application programs presented in ADA:

- Find the flow chart of Supercomputing system configurations, otherwise called *reconfiguration flow chart,* assumed by an adaptable Supercomputing system in the execution of these programs.
- Monitor the correct execution of the reconfiguration flow chart when the program requests on reconfigurations are (a) static, or known in advance, and (b) dynamic, or not known in advance.

For case b, a static flow chart created for a static program mix should be corrected by the new requests of newly arriving programs not known at the time of construction of a static flow chart.

Therefore, the **reconfiguration flow chart** is a set of software tools aimed at automatic construction of the reconfiguration flow chart of an adaptable Supercomputing system. It improves the performance of the system by allowing its reconfiguration in accordance with static or dynamic reconfiguration requests of a set of concurrent programs [4].

Category 2: Reconfiguration Methodology

This is a second set of software tools that must be included into reconfiguration software. It is directed toward the development of fast and concurrent reconfiguration techniques aimed at switching a current architectural configuration or a *current architectural state* into the next architectural state. Since a set of possible architectural states of an adaptable Supercomputing system may include five architectures (array, pipeline, network, multicomputer/multiprocessor, mixed), this set of tools is understood as comprehensive reconfiguration methodology aimed at changing either a current architecture and/or parameters in the same architecture [6, 7]. An example of a Supercomputing system changing its architecture includes a system transition from, say, pipeline to multicomputer or network architecture.

However, since each architectural type may also be dynamically reconfigurable, there can be a number of architectural states of the same type that are characterized by different parameters of formed computer structures with the same dedication [8]. For instance, a multicomputer system including 64 bits of memory and processor resources may function as a single 64-bit computer (one state) or two 32-bit computers (second state), or one 16-bit and one 48-bit computer, etc. [9].

Therefore, the importance of the development of viable reconfiguration methodology consists of improving the Supercomputing system performance by maximizing the time $\Delta = \Delta T - \Delta t$, where ΔT is the time of program speed-up because of the Supercomputing system reconfigurability; Δt is the reconfiguration overhead, measured as the time lost during reconfiguration when no computation can be performed. Thus, a viable reconfiguration methodology improves Δ by the minimization of Δt.

It then follows from this analysis, with the fast reconfiguration methodology being developed, that an adaptable Supercomputing system will be able to execute its reconfiguration flow chart quickly and efficiently, introducing minimal delays in architectural transitions (when no computation can be performed) from one architectural state to another [8].

Category 3: Dynamic Compiler Software

This is a set of software tools that reconfigures an adaptable Supercomputing system into architectural states that facilitate the execution of the following ADA constructs: dynamic multitasking, task rendezvous, packages, exception handling, dynamic data types, etc. Therefore, this set of software tools also improves Supercomputing system performance by a significant compiler optimization that can be achieved via reconfiguration.

1.2.2 Assessment of Different Categories of Reconfiguration Software

Although all three categories of reconfiguration software use the reconfigurability of an adaptable Supercomputing system, the difference between them is as follows: the first two categories must be present in any software environment created for an adaptable Supercomputing system, since they allow the programmer to improve the performance of his or her programs by taking advantage of the reconfigurability of the hardware.

On the other hand, the dynamic compiler software will be present only in the software environment of an adaptable Supercomputing system that is created for ADA programming language. Thus, it is language-dependent software. It improves program performance by creating *dynamically* the hardware constructs that have their match in ADA language constructs. Therefore, it is the software that also uses reconfigurability of hardware. In this respect, it differs from standard ADA compilers created elsewhere [10, 11].

It should be noted that all three categories of reconfiguration software are of equal importance.

The *reconfiguration flow chart* and *reconfiguration methodology* will allow the automatic computation of complex programs on an adaptable Supercomputing system that creates additional parallelism, in comparison with static systems, at the expense of reconfigurability of the system. Therefore, the first two categories of reconfiguration software unlock for the programmer all the benefits of adaptable Supercomputing systems aimed at speeding up execution of programs and minimization of program delays.

On the other hand, the *dynamic compiler software* will improve performance by creating architectural constructs which facilitate both program compilation and execution of ADA language constructs via extensive use of the modularity and reconfigurability concepts of an adaptable Supercomputing system.

Note: The importance of dynamic compiler software cannot be underestimated since some important concepts of ADA language have direct support from similar features exhibited by adaptable Supercomputing systems on the hardware level.

For instance, consider such distinguishing ADA features as static and dynamic multitasking and the organization of task rendezvous [10–13]. These ADA features have a direct analogy in the property of an adaptable Supercomputing system:

1. To create in the system the number of concurrent computers dynamically to conform to the current number of tasks. [8]
2. To organize very fast data exchanges between concurrent computers formed dynamically conforming to simple and easy organization of task rendezvous [15, 17, 18].

Another ADA feature aimed at the creation of data types with dynamic structure is also supported by the capability of an adaptable Supercomputing system to form various network configurations [6, 15, 16]. These networks can be used as dynamic data structures of complex data bases that have a form of reconfigurable binary trees (single and multirooted) or reconfigurable stars (single and multirooted), etc. [6].

Or the fundamental ADA package construct also has its close analogy with the ability of an adaptable Supercomputing system (1) to form a computing module or memory module with varying degree of complexity, and (2) to have this module change its bit size and/or to include any combination of processor and memory modules in it [7, 8, 9]. This formation of a computing or memory module that supports an ADA package can be made by an adaptable Supercomputing system via software with the use of one machine instruction, etc. [8].

1.2.3 Retargetable Software

By *retargetable software,* we understand a set of software tools created for ADA and its environment that allows the use of these tools by a set of dedicated Supercomputing systems [11, 12, 20–23]. The major objective of retargetable software is to reduce enormous software development costs for dedicated mission-critical Supercomputing systems, which originate from the popular practice of building a dedicated Supercomputing system for a dedicated mission-critical application.

Indeed, the past way of overcoming the problems of stressing timing requirements for mission-critical computers (before the appearance of an adaptable Supercomputing system approach) was to build dedicated computers and systems (arrays, pipelines, systolic architectures, dedicated multiprocessors, etc.) that were oriented only to the solution of certain (often narrow) classes of mission-critical algorithms.

However, this approach to building a dedicated computer system was also combined with building dedicated software for such a system in order that it take into account special hardware features implemented in the system, types of computations that are encountered in the tasks designated for this system, etc. Therefore, past experience in building dedicated mission-critical Supercomputing systems led to the following undesirable consequences:

1. Rapid expansion and growth in complexity of a class of mission-critical applications have led to extreme diversity and a variety of dedicated computer systems. This, in turn, has led to enormous investments in software, since the software costs usually greatly exceed the hardware costs.
2. The exponential growth of software costs would have continued if defense algorithms had continued to be solved only with the dedicated computer systems that featured a double dedication on the hardware and software levels.

Indeed, it is expected that by 1990 software will cost $32.1 billion and hardware $5.2 billion if the past approach of constructing dedicated software for dedicated Supercomputing systems continues.

A current approach to reducing the software costs for dedicated Supercomputing systems consists of using a unique programming language, ADA, for all DOD embedded systems and is pointed at creating a portable, retargetable, integrated software environment that is able to meet the rigorous requirements of program standardization and modularity [10-13, 19-29].

Therefore, work on retargetable software is aimed at the following directions:

a. Standardization of ADA compilers [11, 13, 26, 27-29]
b. Creation of standard portable ADA language systems, otherwise called ADA environments [10, 11]
c. Development of direct execution architectures that support ADA language constructs, etc. [30]

1.2.4 Summary: Merger of Two Types of Adaptable Software

Therefore, the objective of reconfiguration software is to improve the performance of mission-critical Supercomputing systems via extensive use of reconfiguration, whereas the objective of retargetable software is to reduce software costs by applying the concepts of standardization, portability, and modularity to software development for Supercomputing systems. Although these two objectives are not conflicting but complementary, they were developed independently in two different research communities, with practically no interaction with each other. However, their most lasting effect will be accomplished if they converge, because software modularity alone is not the only method for reducing software costs. Another method consists of reducing the number of different types of dedicated computers and systems used for mission-critical algorithms.

Indeed, since a dynamic architecture may form various types of architecture, it may be used for assembling different types of dedicated systems: arrays, pipelines, multicomputers, networks [7]. Thus, the same system software can be used with no changes in all dedicated subsystems that are assembled from a single building block.

To achieve the most lasting effect, the approach of using dynamic architectures as a means of creating standard modular and reconfigurable hardware has to be combined with the same efforts performed on the level of software. That is, the task of reducing software costs must be attacked from the two fronts, *software* and *hard-*

ware, whereby current research efforts aimed at software standardization, portability, and retargetability must merge with analogous efforts in the area of creating standard modular and reconfigurable hardware and reconfiguration software. Such a combined approach not only overcomes the problem of creating a mission-critical supercomputer that satisfies given real-time requirements, but will greatly simplify the solution of the software modularity problem itself since the standard modular and reconfigurable hardware provides a natural hardware support for the creation of standard software modules — the main target of software standardization.

Therefore, to be most effective for mission-critical applications, the modularity and portability concept developed and implemented in software has to merge with a similar concept developed on a hardware level. The objective of standardization and portability when applied to mission-critical computer architectures means creation of modular computer systems assembled from a minimal number of different module types and provided with standard and reconfigurable modular interfaces. Meeting severe real-time restrictions in such systems is achieved via dynamic reconfiguration of the available interconnections, when the system forms its architectural configurations dynamically in response to the computational needs of executing algorithms.

2 DESIRABLE ARCHITECTURAL CHARACTERISTICS OF MISSION-CRITICAL SUPERCOMPUTING SYSTEMS

Let us now establish the useful architectural reconfigurations that must be included in a mission-critical Supercomputing system in order to satisfy all the stressing needs of mission-critical applications. It is essential that a mission-critical Supercomputing system be provided with the following characteristics:

2.1 Dynamic Precision of Operation

The requirement of deep penetration, quick response, and great precision of intercepting a target necessitates that a mission-critical computer have a dynamically changeable word size that assumes a far larger value than is used nowadays (more than 64 bits) in order to sustain continuous work in a fixed-point operation.

Indeed, a fixed-point operation is far more precise and at least twice as fast as a floating-point operation. Furthermore, in view of the versatility of the missions to be performed by the same mission-critical computer, both the precision requirements and the ranges of computed results may significantly vary.

To implement both demands on the changeable precision and range of computed results in the most timely fashion specified by very stressing timing characteristics of a mission-critical application, a Supercomputing system must be provided with a dynamic precision property, which is interpreted as the computer capability of changing its word size via software in response to variant precision demands of a diversified spectrum of algorithms.

2.2 Dynamic Instruction and Data Parallelism

The requirement of quick and flexible responses dictates that a computer system be provided with the capability of meeting specific and changing time requirements by changing via software the number of computers, arrays, and pipelines that are formed in the system. This capability will allow adaptation to a changeable instruction and the data parallelism that can be encountered in mission-critical algorithms. Below is a justification of this architectural characteristic.

Presently, the computational parallelism in instruction and data execution is regarded as a principal technique of improving the performance of a computer system. However, to be used in a most cost-efficient fashion, this parallelism must be dynamic, i.e., specified by the requirements of particular applications.

For instance, consider 64 bits of processor and memory resources. These resources must be capable of functioning as a single 64-bit computer executing one program with 64-bit words or as four 16-bit computers executing concurrently four programs each of which operates with 16-bit data words; or as two 32-bit computers; or as one 16-bit and one 48-bit computer, etc. Therefore, to meet the dynamic requirements of mission-critical algorithms on instruction and data parallelism, a computer system must be capable of dynamically partitioning its resources into a variable number of computers and/or arrays to satisfy the timing requirements on quick and flexible responses.

Since the entire bit size of any computer system is permanent, the feature of dynamic instruction and data parallelism is accompanied by dynamic precision of operation, i.e., the capability of a programmer to form a variant number of dynamic computers with selectable word sizes (precision). Thus, the architectural feature of having dynamic instruction and data parallelism not only will improve the specific response time of a computer system but also its precision needed by the deep penetration and wide-range requirements discussed in Sec. 2.1.

2.3 Capability of Changing the Type of Architecture

There is great variety in the computational missions to be performed by mission-critical computers in a cost-efficient manner, i.e., satisfying dynamic response and precision requirements necessitated by these missions. Since each mission is characterized by its most effective computer architecture, a computer system must be capable of switching its current architecture dynamically to provide the best performance characteristics that are required for any given mission.

2.4 Enhanced Fault-Tolerance Accomplished via Dynamic Replacement and Graceful Degradation

To implement high reliability and long endurance, a computer system must be capable of performing the following fault-tolerant reconfigurations:

a. *dynamic-replacement strategy* aimed at replacing each faulty module with a spare from the available spare bank without decrease in system throughput.

b. *graceful-degradation strategy* aimed at turning off each faulty module from computation and maintaining adequate performance using the fault-free modules that remain in the system.

Usually, the graceful-degradation strategy follows that of dynamic replacement when the entire bank of spares is emptied.

Implementation of dynamic-replacement and graceful-degradation capabilities will allow an adaptable Supercomputing system to achieve a high reliability and long endurance in performance, since the system will operate correctly in spite of faults and will perform an adequate function at a reduced level even when all spares are taken from the bank.

2.5 Summary: Modularity and Reconfigurability of the System Architecture

To implement dynamic precision, dynamic instruction, and data parallelism, and enhanced fault tolerance, the architecture of a mission-critical Supercomputing system must be modular and dynamically reconfigurable, since all these useful capabilities can be realized only via architectural reconfigurations in modular computer hardware. In addition, the modular architecture will implement the mobility requirement of modern defense systems, since it will allow simple microminiaturization by taking advantage of a new generation of LSI components.

3 DYNAMIC ARCHITECTURE AS A POWERFUL MEANS OF IMPLEMENTING MOST USEFUL ARCHITECTURAL FEATURES OF MISSION-CRITICAL SUPERCOMPUTING SYSTEMS

As was shown above, a computer architecture that implements the above architectural characteristics must possess the following attributes:

- It must be modular.
- It must be dynamically reconfigurable.
- It must be capable of forming a variable number of computers with selectable word sizes.
- It must switch its type of architecture by transforming a multicomputer system into an array or pipeline system or by forming a network architecture or a mixed architecture that incorporates any combination of possible architectures.

A computer system that possesses these attributes is called *dynamic architecture* [9, 31]. In general, a computer system with dynamic architecture can be viewed as an advanced reconfigurable architecture which may change via software the type of architecture and the number and word sizes of operating computers that are formed in the system [7, 8, 14, 32].

Dynamic architecture can assume the following types of architecture: multicomputer/multiprocessor, array, pipeline, network, and mixed. It can make transitions via software from one type of architecture to another. Furthermore, it can partition the available resources into a variable number of computers with selectable word sizes. Thus, a programmer may select both the number and word sizes of concurrent computers that can be formed in the system via software and the type of architecture that can be used for a current mission-critical computation.

A transition from one architecture to another, as well as from one set of concurrent computers to another, is performed practically instantaneously (during several clock periods) and using a single program instruction [8].

3.1 Major Drawbacks of Commercial Supercomputing Systems

The major obstacle which prevents modern high-performance commercial Supercomputing systems from becoming successful mission-critical computers is in their inability to implement dynamic instruction and data parallelism and the accompanying dynamic precision of operation.

Indeed, to accommodate a large range of computed results, these computers operate in floating-point form. This leads to a significant deterioration of their precision capabilities, which may be adequate for commercial applications and may become inadequate for mission-critical requirements.

Furthermore, since the number of instruction and data paths in these systems is fixed, they are incapable of meeting the most demanding response times via dynamic increase in the number of data and instructions that can be computed at a time in the system. Thus, because of fixed architecture, these systems will be incapable of meeting more stressing and changing mission-critical requirements other than those they have been designed for.

The problems with these supersystems typify those that are usually encountered when a commercial Supercomputing system is used for variant real-time applications. Any throughput growth in a commercial Supercomputing system can be accomplished only via the modular expansion of existing systems with new equipment. Thus, it is out of reach for many mission-critical applications (space, etc.) that eliminate the factor of manual interference into a computer operation.

Since a commercial Supercomputer cannot increase its throughput dynamically via reconfiguration, to meet a particular very stressing response time, the computer system must have a very demanding and permanent throughput rate (in terms of MIPS or BIPS), although in other less critical situations, some portions of the system equipment become idle, leading to a significant underutilization of system resources. Thus, the existing practice of building a Supercomputing system with permanent throughput that satisfies maximum response requirements leads to a much more complex system than the one designed for the same requirements and possessing dynamic throughput implemented via dynamic instruction and data parallelism. Also, when the response times change because of technological progress, a system with fixed throughput will be incapable of meeting new and more demanding throughput requirements. Thus, an expensive mission-critical computer with fixed throughput becomes dead for the application.

3.2 Classes of Cost-Effective Applications for Dynamic Architectures

The ability of dynamic architectures to achieve a higher throughput than that of conventional systems with the same hardware complexity is demonstrated in Chapter V, *Algorithm Development.*

Special features of a dynamic architecture such as a multitude of various architectural states and fast transitions from one state to another make these architectures applicable to a broad spectrum of mission critical applications. Below we outline briefly the classes of algorithms that can be effectively computed by a system with dynamic architecture. A detailed analysis of sampled computations performed by dynamic architecture for typical algorithms from these classes is given in Chapter V.

CI. The algorithms that vary between broad scope (high parallelism) and coarse detail (small precision) and narrow scope (low parallelism) and fine detail (high precision) are prime candidates for the dynamic architectures. Examples of such algorithms would be root finding in multidimensional space, feature finding in a picture for all real-time image processing, and division by mutiplicative iteration. The reason for this is the capability of dynamic architectures to provide a dynamically variable trade-off between the number of information streams (both instruction and/or data) being processed in parallel and the word sizes of those streams.

- Root finding in a multidimensional function starts with crude evaluations of the function at many points and becomes more precise as it converges on the solution set.
- Feature analysis and object identification often start with bulk processing of an input array to find interesting regions which are then analyzed with much more care.
- Parallel division algorithms (Newton-Rapheson or Anderson-Earle-Goldschmidt-Powers methods) can calculate initial approximations with truncated terms, performing only the last iteration using full data width.

Since root finding, feature analysis, and division algorithms are popular features of many signal-processing algorithms (such as fast Fourier transforms, solutions of quadratic equations, and spectral analysis), the system becomes cost effective in solving all these algorithms.

CII. Parallel algorithms that have a high degree of data dependencies between instruction streams whereby one instruction stream needs data words computed by another instruction stream are another class of applications well suited for dynamic architectures. This class of problems falls under the category of *producer-consumer algorithms,* whereby one instruction stream *produces* data words that are *consumed* by another instruction stream.

Indeed, consider as an example a dynamic architecture having been built by these authors and their co-workers for Ballistic Missile Defense Applications (Figure I.1). This system can move data between processors either in large numbers via a slower I/O bus or in smaller numbers via a fast DC bus with practically no degradation of the tasks being computed concurrently with these moves. Relatively slow broadcasts are provided by the I/O elements GE and the fast broadcasts are provided by the direct memory-to-memory transfers via the DC bus. Virtual moves are also made possible by the ability of one PE to borrow a page of memory from another PE. Computers also have the ability to communicate with each other directly, via their PEs, by means of the shift bus available in the system.

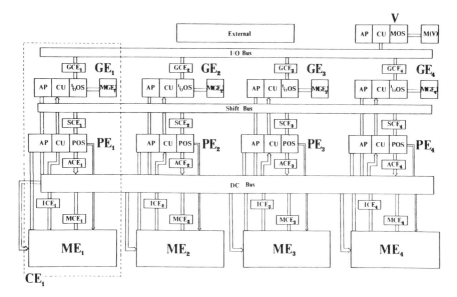

FIGURE I.1

The following classes of algorithms belong to the producer-consumer type:

Parallel searching and sorting requires a great deal of overlap and communication of information between subsets of data.

Relaxation methods (including meteorological processing and aerodynamic simulation) usually involve the estimation of the value of one point as a function of all the points surrounding it.

Elimination of hidden surfaces when displaying views of solid objects and scenes usually requires that many planes or edges be considered as the candidate for visibility in each region of the screen. Thus, the data words that characterize each plane or edge need to be broadcast for the analysis of possible elimination.

CIII. Algorithms requiring different types of computations (multicomputer/multiprocessor, array, pipeline, network) are also well suited for dynamic architectures. Indeed, an architectural capability to assume various architectural states (multicomputer, array, network) and to perform fast reconfigurations from one state to another makes these architectures suitable for the algorithms encountered in multiple-user development work, computer-aided design, picture processing, scene analysis, etc. Let us show the suitability of dynamic architectures in all such computations:

- During *multiple-user development work* (algorithm and program testing), different users may require different machine configurations for their work or co-residence of several configurations in the same system. Thus, the ability of the dynamic architectures to assume different configurations will greatly facilitate algorithm development for a diversified spectrum of users.

- *Computer-aided design* includes flexible graphics, sophisticated data-base use, component placement and connection routing optimization, and simulation of the operation of the system being designed. Each phase makes different demands on computational resources and is best processed by a differently structured computer.
- *Picture processing and scene analysis,* whether the raw input is visual, radar, sonic, or from some other form of sensor, all require some form of bulk processing of the input for potentially interesting data, filtering out of noise, selection of objects, and identification of those that are of interest. Each of these stages is dealt with differently and requires a different type of processing in order to be efficiently computed.

3.3 Comparative Evaluation Figures

In Chapter 5 a comparative performance evaluation for dynamic architectures has been performed for the following classes of algorithms:

   I. General-purpose program mix consisting of an arbitrary mix of programs with no data dependencies

  II. Parallel construct fork-join

 III. Producer-consumer algorithms, or algorithms with data dependencies

 IV. Relaxation algorithms

  V. Pulse deinterleaving algorithms

 VI. Data management in tree data bases

VII. Real-time sorting

VIII. Tree-structured algorithms

The following performance figures have been obtained for these classes of algorithms.

I. For a typical general-purpose program mix consisting of 14 programs, a dynamic architecture achieves a 42% speed-up in comparison with a fixed multicomputer system having the same complexity of resources (see pages 311-312).

II. For the fork-join construct, the performance improvement is 42% in comparison with conventional computations (see pages 318-327).

Note: It is shown that the only source of both these speed-ups is in dynamic reconfiguration implemented via dynamic instruction and data parallelism, since it becomes possible to compute each program in a minimal-size computer and release the redundant resources into additional computations. Thus, dynamic architecture maximizes the number of programs computed by the available resources with due regard to program precision requirements.

III. Although for the evaluated producer-consumer algorithm no comparative performance figures could be obtained (in terms of speed-up percent) due to the variability of possible ways the analyzed algorithm can be computed conventionally, the obtained performance gains are also impressive. It is shown that for dynamic architectures the extensive data exchanges required by producer-consumer algorithms are optimal from the following viewpoints:

1. Because of the variety of alternative routes, the interference of operating systems into data exchanges can be reduced to a minimum.
2. Each data exchange takes the minimal time since it takes only a few levels of gates in the memory-processor bus.
3. All data exchanges are made in parallel for variable-size data words (see pages 327-344).

IV. For the typical relaxation algorithms, the accomplished speed-up is 33% in comparison with static array systems having the same resource complexity. The only source of this speed-up is reconfiguration, which allows formation of the dynamic array system (pages 347-357).

V. For a typical pulse deinterleaving algorithm that consists of forming separate pulse trains out of arriving interleaving pulses, the accomplished speed-up is 37%. The origin of this speed-up is only due to dynamic reconfiguration, which releases redundant resources into additional computations (pages 357-367).

VI. Especially efficient is the use of dynamic reconfiguration in reconfigurable tree-structured data bases. It is shown that, due to the capability of dynamic architectures to perform data-base reconfigurations that allow each pair of tree nodes that exchange information to be connected with a much shorter communication path than that organized in any static tree data base, the performance improvement in data-base operation is 370% (pages 367-368).

That is, instead of the time $1430T_0$ spent by a static tree data base to perform a given assortment of data exchanges among its nodes, the reconfigurable tree data base organizes the same data exchanges in $300T_0$; i.e., it improves performance by 370%.

VII. Although no performance evaluation figures for real-time sorting could be obtained due to the variability of sorting algorithms and their execution in conventional systems, the extreme effectiveness of dynamic architectures in real-time sorting is also proved beyond any reasonable doubt. This is true because of the following reasons [6, 15]:

It is shown that most effective architectural configurations that sustain real-time sorting are single or multirooted binary trees or stars whereby the number of roots in a multiple tree-star structure specifies the number of sorting classes that must be distinguished; the number of levels in each tree or star (interconnected into a multiple structure via their roots) shows the number of steps in a sorting algorithm; the number of outcomes for each sorting step specifies what type of tree or star structure should be used. For a tree structure there are only two outcomes for each sorting step (T, true, or F, false). For a star structure, the number of possible outcomes becomes larger than two.

The capability of dynamic architectures to assume various multirooted tree and star structures makes them indispensable computing structures for real-time sorting (pages 54-69). Also, as shown in this chapter, each such reconfiguration can be performed practically instantaneously, since it requires that only one reconfiguration instruction and two control codes (bias B and reconfiguration code RC) be received by all network nodes requested for reconfiguration.

To form each new single or multirooted sorting structure, all network nodes perform a single concurrent logical operation (mod 2 add) taking the time of $2t_d$. Therefore, each network reconfiguration can be organized during one clock period.

Thus, dynamic architecture may perform very fast reconfigurations from one sorting structure to another and achieve significant improvements in performance because of architectural adaptation to a particular sorting algorithm.

VIII. For tree-structured algorithms, the performance gains are similar to those obtained for data management in tree data bases (class VI), because a typical tree-structured algorithm also requires extensive data exchanges among tree nodes. Thus, as follows from evaluation of class VI, dynamic architectures become extremely effective in executing all tree-structured algorithms because of their capability to assume 2^n various binary tree structures and to perform fast reconfigurations from one tree structure to another.

3.4 Summary: Brief Analysis of Cost-Efficient Applications for Dynamic Architecture

As follows from the performance evaluation of a diversified spectrum of general-purpose and signal-processing algorithms performed in Chapter 5, dynamic reconfiguration becomes an extremely important factor in improving the performance of a computer system. No conventional general-purpose architecture can accomplish such performance gains as can be done with the use of reconfiguration.

As for dedicated signal-processing architectures used in mission-critical computers now, although their gains in performance are considerable because of the dedicated hardware circuits present in these systems, their major drawbacks are:

a. Narrow area of applications

b. Significant software costs in system development

Therefore, both conventional systems (general purpose and dedicated) become unsuitable for real-time applications (satellites, space, etc.) that are characterized by:

a. Extreme versatility and unpredictability of possible mission-critical computations

b. Inability to interfere manually into space-borne computer systems

For such applications, dynamic architecture becomes the only viable alternative for possible use because of the following factors:

F1. A system with dynamic architecture may reconfigure itself automatically into the new architectural configuration most suitable for the new application.

F2. Since the time of such reconfiguration is very small, a system with dynamic architecture may achieve a cost-efficient performance for each given mission, because an ideal hardware structure can be created for computation during the negligible amount of time that is taken by the reconfiguration process.

F3. The life cycle (field life) of a system with dynamic architecture becomes much longer than that for any conventional architecture, general purpose or dedicated. The reason for this is that a dynamic architecture creates a given throughput with much smaller complexity of resources than that of conventional general-purpose architectures, or the same resource complexity in dynamic architectures creates a higher throughput than in conventional systems because of reconfiguration. Using these features, a dynamic mission-critical computer may reconfigure itself into these hardware structures that are cost-efficient for computing new missions characterized by extremely demanding response and precision requirements not taken into account during the architectural design of the computer.

On the other hand, both fixed architectures (general purpose and dedicated) may fail in execution of such new missions if they have far more stressing time and precision requirements than those implemented in existing systems, since their architectures are static and cannot be changed via ground command. Therefore, both conventional systems may become dead for the application, whereas a system with dynamic architecture continues its adequate performance in computing new missions characterized by more demanding response characteristics.

F4. Because of enhanced fault-tolerance (dynamic replacement and graceful degradation) implemented via dynamic reconfiguration, a system with dynamic architecture is provided with much greater reliability, robustness, and longevity than existing architectures. These factors are of extreme importance for all missions in view of the critical nature of the applications.

As follows from the above, dynamic architectures become extremely effective for mission-critical applications since they allow the realization of throughputs comparable with those of dedicated Supersystems without paying the heavy price of a narrow area of applications and incurring significant software costs into the system development, which characterizes a dedicated Supercomputing system approach.

Reconfiguration Software: Reconfiguration Methodology

1 INTRODUCTION

Reconfiguration methodology is the first set of tools that forms a part of the reconfiguration software. It includes a set of reconfiguration algorithms aimed at achieving:

1. *Architectural reconfiguration* from one architectural state to another
2. *Fault-tolerant reconfiguration* aimed at purging out faulty modules from the system (Fig. II.1)

For the architectural reconfiguration, comprehensive reconfiguration methodology should include reconfiguration algorithms in the following types of architecture: (1) multicomputer, (2) array, (3) pipeline, (4) network, and (5) mixed, which means a combination of the above architectures.

For fault-tolerant reconfigurations, two strategies should be included in the reconfiguration methodology:

a. *Dynamic replacement* aimed at replacing faulty modules with available spares. Thus, dynamic replacement retains the system throughput.
b. *Graceful degradation* aimed at forming a subsystem with smaller throughput using fault-free modules that still remain.

The graceful degradation strategy goes into effect when the dynamic replacement comes to an end; i.e., no spare modules remain in the system that could have maintained unimpaired system performance. The task of the reconfiguration is to continue fault-

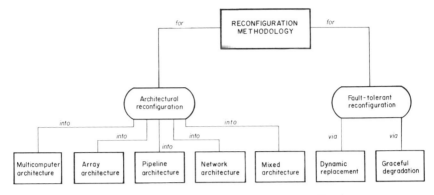

FIGURE II.1 Reconfiguration methodology: classification

free operation in a system at a reduced level, continuously turning off all faulty modules from the operation until the entire system resource is exhausted.

This chapter addresses the following aspects of the overall reconfiguration methodology presented in Figure II.1. For architectural reconfiguration, we introduce the techniques for multicomputer and network reconfigurations. For fault-tolerant reconfigurations, we concentrate on designing fault-tolerant reconfigurable binary trees with graceful degradation. That is, the reconfiguration techniques to be presented will be aimed at the concurrent purging of faulty modules out of binary trees and the formation of gracefully degraded trees from the remaining modules.

2 ARCHITECTURAL RECONFIGURATION

In general, architectural reconfiguration is supervised by the system monitor, since:

a. The monitor must find the moment of time when such reconfiguration is possible.

b. The monitor should resolve conflicts among programs with conflicting reconfiguration requests.

Having performed steps a and b, the monitor allows the system reconfiguration, which includes:

1. Accessing a set of new control codes by each computing module of the next architectural state formed dynamically

2. Establishment of new interconnections in the system

3. Start-up of programs assigned to the next architectural state.

Therefore, any architectural reconfiguration $N \rightarrow N^*$, where N is a current architectural state and N^* is the next state, includes the following steps:

Step 1. Conflict resolution.   Since programs computed in state N are asynchronous and independent, they may feature conflicting needs for the next architectural state N^*. The monitor must resolve these conflicts on the basis of priorities assigned to the programs. Therefore, one must organize the procedure for conflict resolution during which the monitor allows or denies an architectural reconfiguration requested by a program.

Step 2. Task Synchronization.   All programs assigned in state N to the hardware resources that are requested for forming new computing structures in state N^* must finish their computations in N and inform the monitor of this finish.

Step 3. Access of variable control codes and establishment of new interconnections in the network.   Each architectural state is characterized by its own set of control codes. For instance, as was shown in Volume I, Chapter III, this series, to reconfigure into a new multicomputer state requires writing four control codes with changeable values into each computer element of the requested resources. On the other hand, to establish a new network state (rings, trees, and stars) requires only two invariant control codes to be written to all CEs of requested resources.

Therefore, required control codes can be either stored as an array in the memory, or if their number is small (as is true for network reconfigurations), it is beneficial to store them in the architectural switch instruction, $N \rightarrow N^*$. For the first case, storage of the array of control codes should be organized to minimize the time of their sorting and accessing to requested computer elements. For the second case, organization of the architectural switch instruction should be developed that allows these codes to be sent (possibly via monitor) to requested computing resources that will be using these codes for formation of N^*.

Finally, establishment of new interconnections in the interconnection network is performed following the access of variable control codes. This establishment finalizes the act of forming new computing structures of the next architectural state. Such interconnections should be established that allow correct formation of (a) *reconfigurable instruction buses,* which broadcast each instruction only to the modules of a newly formed computing structure and prevent this broadcast to all other computing structures that coexist concurrently, and (b) *reconfigurable data buses,* which allow fast and concurrent data exchanges within each newly formed computing structure and between different computing structures, either existing concurrently or sequentially.

Step 4. Program start-up.   Each program must start its execution in state N^*. The following cases of this start-up should be considered.

Case 1.   Program P is assigned to both states N and N^*, and

a. P requests transition $N \rightarrow N^*$, or in other words, P is *active;* or
b. P does not request $N \rightarrow N^*$ transition (P is *passive*).

Case 2.   Program P is assigned only to N^* and

a. It is active by performing transition $N \rightarrow N^*$; or
b. It is passive by not performing transition $N \rightarrow N^*$.

3 DYNAMIC RECONFIGURATIONS IN MULTICOMPUTER SYSTEMS

Let us consider how the general sequence of Steps 1 through 4 is interpreted for the case of multicomputer reconfiguration.

3.1 Sequence of Reconfiguration Steps for Multicomputer Systems

A multicomputer reconfiguration is performed with the use of a reconfiguration instruction, $N \rightarrow N^*$. Each instruction $N \rightarrow N^*$ belongs to a program that needs a new dynamic computer and/or executes a reconfiguration request on behalf of other programs. Therefore, from the reconfiguration viewpoint, a program may be *active* by executing reconfiguration request $N \rightarrow N^*$ or *passive* by granting execution of personal reconfiguration requests to other program(s).

Such division of programs into the two types, active and passive, allows each active program to represent not only individual reconfiguration needs but those of other programs with nonconflicting needs on new dynamic computers. The results of such collective reconfigurations performed by one program on behalf of several others are a much better utilization of the CE resources than that affordable for any alternative reconfiguration scheme based on the individual resource requests.

For a *static reconfiguration flow chart,* the formation of each collective reconfiguration request represented by the active program is performed during preprocessing aimed at the construction of the static resource scheduling diagram. For a *dynamic reconfiguration flow chart,* such a formation is performed upon the arrival of a new reconfiguration request message, $\widetilde{RRM}$, issued by the dynamic program, since a dynamic program cannot know in advance about the nonconflicting reconfiguration needs of other passive programs that can be concurrent with the arriving $\widetilde{RRM}$.

Usually, the flow chart executed by the system with dynamic architecture is a combination of static and dynamic reconfiguration flow charts, whereby a static reconfiguration flow chart is modified by new architectural states created dynamically and included in the dynamic reconfiguration flow chart.

In all, for both types of the reconfiguration flow chart the sequence of reconfiguration steps for multicomputer reconfiguration is governed by the algorithm of Fig. II.2. Accordingly, when the $N \rightarrow N^*$ instruction is fetched by the dynamic computer, it forms the reconfiguration request message, $\widetilde{RRM}$, which is sent to the monitor (see Step 1, Fig. II.2). The monitor first checks whether or not the arriving $\widetilde{RRM}$ is in conflict with the current RRM or next RRM* available in the monitor that represent current state N or next state N^* (Fig. II.5). If it is in a conflict, the monitor initiates the conflict resolution (Step 2; see Fig. II.2). Otherwise, the monitor initiates the task synchronization (Step 7) to start the reconfiguration process specified with $\widetilde{RRM}$.

The actions performed by the monitor during conflict resolution depend on the relationship between the priority code, $\widetilde{PC}$, of arriving message, $\widetilde{RRM}$, with those already in the monitor, PC for current RRM and PC* for the next RRM* (Fig. II.4). If $\widetilde{PC} \leq PC^*$ and PC, the arriving $\widetilde{RRM}$ requests for the state $\widetilde{N}$ with a priority not

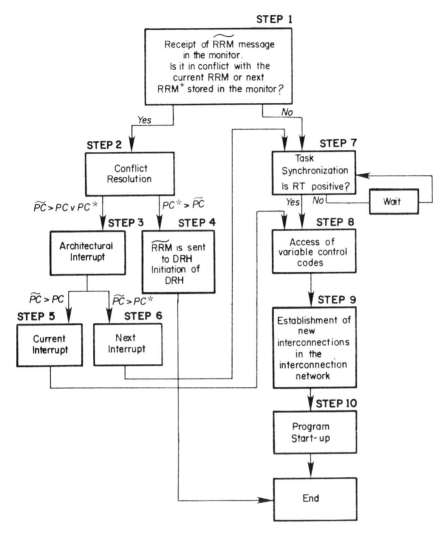

FIGURE II.2 Algorithm for multicomputer reconfiguration

higher than those of current state N and next state N^* stored in the monitor. In this case, no reconfiguration actions are performed, and the denied $\widetilde{RRM}$ is sent to the denied resource handler, DRH (see Step 4, Figs. II.2 and II.5a).

If the arriving $\widetilde{PC} > PC$ or PC^*, the monitor initiates the architectural interrupt of either the current or next state (Step 5 or 6). Program computations associated with the current state interrupt are performed immediately. As for the next state interrupt, they are performed upon completion of the current state N. The fact of completion of N is established during Step 7 of task synchronization with the use of special synchronization instruction *Stop N*, which concludes each task computed in N.

During task synchronization (Step 7), to find the readiness of requested resources to perform reconfiguration, the monitor performs a special readiness test, RT. If the requested resources are ready, the monitor signals the accessing of variant control codes by all requested computing resources (Step 8). Otherwise, a special waiting loop is initialized of which each iteration is ended with the readiness test, RT. This waiting loop is ended when RT gives positive results. The access of variant control codes is followed by the establishment of new interconnections in the used interconnection network (Step 9). This process is followed by program start-up in the new dynamic computer of the next architectural state (Step 10).

Below is a detailed description of all software organizations involved in a multicomputer reconfiguration.

3.2 Resolution of Reconfiguration Conflicts for Multicomputer Architecture

In general, reconfiguration conflicts arise during those reconfiguration requests of independent programs that cannot be met in the same architectural state.

3.2.1 Condition for Reconfiguration Conflict

If two concurrent programs P_i and P_j request transitions into two different architectural states, N_i and N_j, such that N_i and N_j cannot merge into a single architectural state, N, as $N = N_i \cup N_j$, then P_i and P_j are said to be *in conflict*.

Example.   Suppose that a current architectural state $N_3 = 0011$ features three concurrent computers: (a) $C_1(3) = [CE_1, CE_2, CE_3]$ executing program P_3; (b) $C_4(1) = [CE_4]$ executing program P_2, and (c) $C_5(1) = [CE_5]$ executing P_1 [Fig. II.3 (a)]. Suppose that P_3 requires a 32-bit computer $C_1(2) = [CE_1, CE_2]$ for its next task. This computer can work together with computer $C_3(3) = [CE_3, CE_4, CE_5]$, which will execute P_4. Also assume that program P_2 needs the 64-bit computer $C_1(4)$ that can be concur-

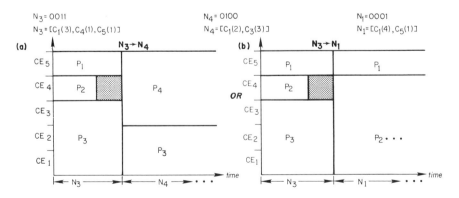

FIGURE II.3   Reconfiguration conflicts, $N_3 \rightarrow N_4$ and $N_3 \rightarrow N_1$.

rent with computer $C_5(1)$ designated for P_1. Thus, reconfiguration requests of P_3 and P_2 are conflicting since they cannot merge into the same architectural state: P_3 needs the $N_3 \rightarrow N_4$ transition, where $N_4 = [C_1(2), C_3(3)]$, whereas P_2 needs the $N_3 \rightarrow N_1$ transition, where $N_1 = [C_1(4), C_5(1)]$.

As follows from these observations, two reconfiguration requests RRM´ and RRM″ are conflicting if $RE' \wedge RE'' \neq 0$, where RE is the requested equipment code specified for each request.

For instance, for the above example, to form N_4 requested by P_3 takes $RE_3 = 11111$ since the entire system resource is requested. To form N_1 requested by P_2 takes $RE_2 = 11110$. As follows, $RE_3 \wedge RE_2 = 11111 \wedge 11110 = 11110 \neq 0$. On the other hand, if $RE' \wedge RE'' = 0$, then programs P´ and P″ request different sets of equipment for forming their states N´ and N″. Thus, there exists an architectural state $N = N' \cup N''$, which is a merger of individual states requested by P″ and P″. For this case, P´ and P″ are not in conflict, and any of these programs may perform not only its own reconfiguration request, but the one of another nonconflicting program(s). ∎

Generally, reconfiguration conflicts appear only during dynamic resource scheduling when a static reconfiguration flow chart constructed for stored programs is modified because of new arrivals with reconfiguration needs that have not been taken into account.

Indeed, as shown in [4] and Sec. 3, Chapter III, for static resource scheduling, when all the reconfiguration requests of the program mix are known in advance, it is always possible to assign the hardware resources to programs in a nonconflicting manner on the basis of program priorities. That is, if two concurrent programs P_i and P_j request transitions into different architectural states N_i and N_j that cannot merge into a single architectural state N, then such resource scheduling is possible that the reconfiguration request of the program with a lower priority (P_i or P_j) is delayed in execution until this program becomes the highest-priority program making this request.

However, dynamic resource scheduling may feature significant detours from the static reconfiguration flow chart because of the arrival of new programs with higher priorities than those currently being executed. As a result, reconfiguration conflicts appear, whereby a higher-priority reconfiguration request of a newly arriving program may be in conflict with either the current or the next architectural state of the static reconfiguration flow chart.

3.2.2 Conflict Resolution: Overall Organization

Resolution of reconfiguration conflicts is performed by the monitor upon receipt of reconfiguration request messages of individual programs. In general, each reconfiguration request message, RRM, is formed by the program that needs reconfiguration into a new dynamic computer. Therefore, the RRM message is created by the reconfiguration instruction, $N \rightarrow N^*$, belonging to the user program.

There are two types of RRM messages: *complete* and *incomplete*. A *complete RRM* requests the architectural reconfiguration $N \rightarrow N^*$ whereby a nonrequested equipment, NRE, is not idle for the duration of state N^*, where $NRE = \overline{SR \wedge RE}$, and SR is the system resource. The SR code is the n-bit code consisting of all ones, where n is the number of CEs in the system. Therefore, the meaning of this definition is: a complete RRM requests either the entire system resource for forming N* (SR = RE), or there is no idleness in the nonrequested equipment if RE is a subset of SR. An *incomplete RRM* requests an architectural reconfiguration, $N \rightarrow N*$, in which a portion or the totality of nonrequested equipment is idle for the duration of N*.

Typically, an incomplete RRM can be issued by a dynamic program which does not know in advance of the nonconflicting needs of other programs that can be executed concurrently with this incomplete RRM. Upon request of an arriving RRM, the monitor finds what class this RRM belongs to: I (incomplete) or C (complete). If it is I, the monitor transforms this RRM into the complete RRM and then initiates the conflict resolution procedure. If it is C, the monitor initiates conflict resolution. Therefore, from now on we will be dealing only with the complete RRM and the adjective "complete" will be omitted for simplicity.

The issues associated with the transformation of an incomplete RRM into the complete one will be discussed in Sec. 5, Chapter III, dealing with dynamic resource assignment and scheduling.

The RRM message includes the following codes [Fig. II.4(a)]:

1. Program user code (PUC) for finding the program priority
2. Requested equipment code (RE) for finding the moment of time when the requested resource is ready
3. Requested state code (N) for accessing required control codes and establishing desired interconnections in the network

There are some other codes which are not considered here for simplicity since they are associated with more complex issues of dynamic resource assignment.

Having received a new reconfiguration request message, $\widetilde{RRM}$, storing codes $\widetilde{PUC}$, $\widetilde{RE}$, and $\tilde{N}$, the monitor fetches priority code, $\widetilde{PC}$, of the requesting program and compares $\widetilde{PC}$ with the priority codes PC(N) and PC(N)* of the current and next architectural states already stored in monitor registers [Fig. II.4(b)]. Depending on the results of the comparisons, the following actions are initiated.

Action 1. No change in reconfiguration flow chart: Current architectural state N is sustained; next architectural state N* is sustained; arriving $\widetilde{RRM}$ is denied architectural reconfiguration into a new state $\tilde{N}$[Fig. II.4(c)].

Action 2. Architectural interrupt of the next state; N is the same; N* is swapped into $\tilde{N}$ requested by $\widetilde{RRM}$; former next state N* is denied system reconfiguration.

Action 3. Architectural interrupt of the current state: N is changed into $\tilde{N}$ requested by $\widetilde{RRM}$; former current state N is moved into the next state position; former next state N* is denied reconfiguration [Fig. II.4(c)].

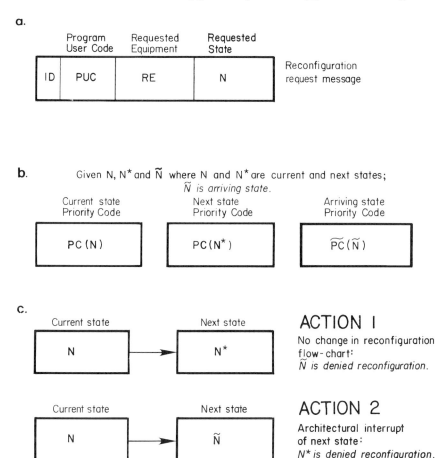

FIGURE II.4 (a) Format of reconfiguration request message; (b) priority codes for N, N*, and Ñ ; (c) Actions in reconfiguration flow chart caused by arriving RRM

Note: For all three cases, the denied architectural states are always either Ñ (arriving state) or N* (next state available in the monitor). As for N, current architectural state, it cannot be denied reconfiguration completely (current or next) because its priority is always higher than that for N*, available next state. Thus, if $\widetilde{PC}(\widetilde{N}) > PC(N)$, N becomes the next architectural state, because $PC(N) > PC(N^*)$ a priori.

Consider now concrete software organizations that lead to the implementation of Actions 1, 2, and 3.

For each newly arriving $\widehat{RRM}$ message, its $\widehat{PUC}$-$\tilde{N}$ portion can be used as the address of the monitor priority table that stores current priority codes of the programs to perform reconfiguration into state $\tilde{N}$. The advantage of having a separate priority table in the monitor is in the capability of organizing dynamic or changeable priorities that can be beneficial for a number of computational situations.

Therefore, when a new $\widehat{RRM}$ message arrives, its concatenated code $\widehat{PUC}$-$\tilde{N}$ fetches from the priority memory the priority code $PC(\tilde{N})$ of this message. Thereafter, $PC(\tilde{N})$ is compared with the two stored priority codes, $PC(N)$ for the current state, and $PC(N^*)$ for the next state, leading to the implementation of Actions 1, 2, or 3 considered below with greater detail.

3.2.2.1 Action 1: No change in reconfiguration flow chart

If $PC(N) > PC(N^*) > PC(\tilde{N})$, the arriving message $\widehat{RRM}$ is denied in its reconfiguration request and is sent to the denied resource handler, DRH [Fig. II.5(a)]. This unit is triggered into operation by each newly arriving and denied $\widehat{RRM}$. The task of DRH is to find a denied RRM with the highest priority among those stored in DRH and prefetch a selected RRM into prefetch register, R3.

Therefore, for Action 1 there is no dynamic change in the stored sequence of computation assigned with architectural states N and N*. Completion of the current architectural state N is followed by the start of N*, which is triggered with the following register-to-register transfers:

1. $R2 \rightarrow R1$, where R2 and R1 store the current and next RRM with their priorities.
2. $R3 \rightarrow R2$ and DRH is initiated again.

The advantages of such organization are as follows:

1. The contents of registers that store $PC(N)$ and $PC(N^*)$ are established immediately without a long selection process aimed at finding the highest-in-value codes that are qualified to fill them in.
2. The DRH unit can be greatly simplified, since it can now perform only sequential comparisons aimed at fetching a denied RRM with the highest priority code $PC(P)$ into the prefetch register, R3.
3. Selection of prefetched RRM does not delay current architectural reconfiguration since it is determined only by $PC(N)$ and $PC(N^*)$ already in registers R1 and R2.

3.2.2.2 Action 2: Architectural interrupt of the next state

This occurs when $PC(N) > PC(\tilde{N}) > PC(N^*)$. As a result, the arriving message RRM concatenated with $PC(\tilde{N})$ will fill in the R2 register, occupied before by the former

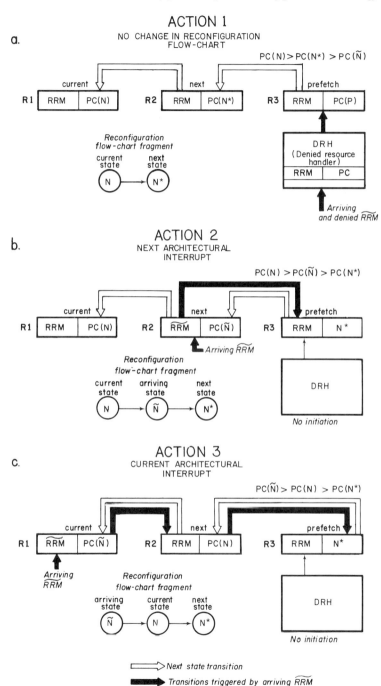

FIGURE II.5 Possible modifications in reconfiguration flow chart: (a) No modification; (b) interrupt of the next state; (c) interrupt of the current state

next RRM* [see Fig. II.5(b)]. Since of all denied RRMs, the former next RRM–PC(N*) becomes the highest in priority, it is sent to prefetch register, R3 (R2 → R3). The denied resource handler is not initiated. Therefore, for this case the change in the static reconfiguration flow chart is as follows: the N → N* transition of the static reconfiguration flow chart is changed into N → $\widetilde{N}$ → N*, where $\widetilde{N}$ is a dynamically created state.

3.2.2.3 Action 3: Architectural interrupt of the current state

This occurs when PC($\widetilde{N}$) > PC(N) > PC(N*). The arriving concatenated message $\overline{RRM}$ – PC($\widetilde{N}$) is written into R1 following the following sequential register-to-register transfers: R2 → R3, R1 → R2. These transfers save current RRM and next RRM* in R2 and R3. The static reconfiguration flow chart is switched into $\widetilde{N}$ → N → N*, and the system executes the architectural interrupt considered below [Fig. II.5(c)]. The DRH is not initiated.

3.2.3 Organization of Architectural Interrupt

Actions 2 and 3 feature next and current architectural interrupts. The difference between them is as follows. Since current architectural interrupt means immediate interruption of the current architectural state, each interrupted program has already achieved a nontrivial computational status that must be saved. Therefore, the entire system status, as well as that of each program, should be saved in order to allow future resumption of computations from the saving points that were interrupted. Thus, the monitor has to form an interrupt message and send it to any interrupted program in order that it save its current computational status.

On the other hand, since the next architectural interrupt should execute N → N instead of N → N*, anticipated in the static reconfiguration flow chart, there is no need for the monitor to interfere in the functioning of dynamic computers of the current architectural state N, provided these computers are task synchronized at the completion of N. If they are not, each of them is scheduled to execute the same program assigned to N and N* with no task synchronization. Therefore, each such program accumulates a nontrivial computational status upon completion of N. This status must be saved using the techniques for organization of saving points that are valid for current state interrupts.

Therefore, for the next state interrupts, if program P is executed in N and N* in the same dynamic computer, its computational status should be saved. If P is executed in N and N* in two different computers, there is no need to save its computational status. Nor is it necessary to save the computational status of P if it is executed only in N*, since no such status has been accumulated.

To save the computational status of each qualified program (every program for the current architectural interrupt and a nontask synchronized program for the next architectural interrupt), the monitor should form a special interrupt message (IM) and send it to all dynamic computers that should be interrupted.

3.2.3.1 Format of the interrupt messages

Each interrupt message, IM, is divided into two zones, I and II, w
the message identification and zone II shows the interrupt status (Fig

Designation of Zone I. This division of IM into I and II allows efficie.
handling for such architectural states N which have been requested several ι
the same program P and each such request has featured computation of P with a ι

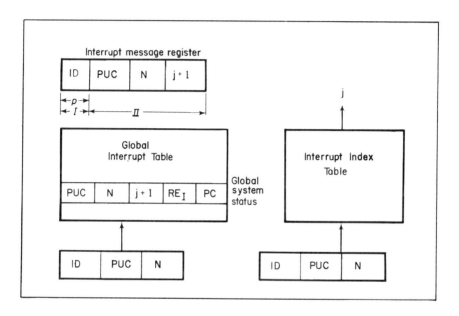

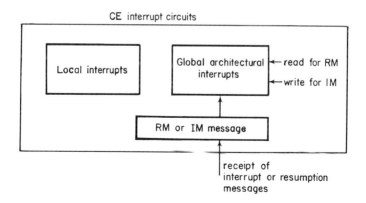

FIGURE II.6   Monitor interrupt circuits

set of other concurrent programs. Indeed, if the reconfiguration flow chart features to m appearances of the same pair (P,N), where P requests reconfiguration into N, then the number of bits in zone I is $p = \log_2 m$.

For $m = 8$, $p = \log_2 8 = 3$, and the same program P may feature up to eight differing transitions into the same architectural state N each of which is characterized by a new set of programs computed together with P. All these states N can be interrupted using a unique identification ID (zone I) of each interrupted message IM that can be formed during each interrupt.

Example. Figure II.7 considers two fragments of the reconfiguration flow chart constructed for dynamic architecture made of 5CE. In Fig. II.7, since $N_2 = [C_1(3),C_4(2)]$, the first request initiated by P_1 features concurrent computation of programs P_1 and P_2 in computers $C_1(3)$ and $C_4(2)$; the second request also made by P_1 features concurrent computation of P_1 and P_4 in $C_1(3)$ and $C_4(2)$. If $m = 2$, the reconfiguration flow chart may not have more than two such requests. This gives 1 bit for ID, where ID $= 1$ can be used for interrupting N_2 when P_1 is computed together with P_2, and ID $= 0$ can be used for interrupting N_2 during the time when P_1 is computed together with P_4. Therefore, introduction of zone I (ID) allows a reconfiguration flow chart to be much more responsive to a multitude of practical programming situations. ∎

Designation of Zone II. Zone II encodes the current interrupt status made of the following codes (Fig. II.6):

1. The program user code (PUC) of the program which has requested state N.
2. The code N of the interrupted architectural state.
3. Interrupt index $j + 1$, which shows how many times the architectural state N (when requested by the same program PUC) has been interrupted including a current interrupt.

Therefore, zone II $=$ PUC-N-$(j + 1)$ allows organization of multiple interrupts of the same state N with such formation of saving points that allows an immediate resumption of interrupted computations with no roll-back of the programs to the beginning of the architectural state N.

Formation and Destinations of the Interrupt Messages. Each IM message is formed by the monitor as follows. The monitor takes the ID-PUC-N portion of this

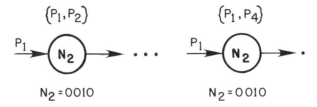

FIGURE II.7   Differing sets of programs assigned to the same state N_2

message from the current reconfiguration request message, RRM, stored in the R1 register [Fig. II.5(a)]. The index portion j is fetched from a special small *interrupt index table* in the monitor accessed with the address ID-PUC-N (Fig. II.6) and is updated as $j = j + 1$ before being included into the message. The ID-PUC-N address of the message accesses the *global interrupt table* in the monitor and writes the global system status (GSS) for the current interrupt made of the following components:

$$\text{GSS} = \text{PUC} \mid \text{N} \mid (j + 1) \mid \text{RE}_I \mid \text{PC}$$

where the different components of GSS are formed as follows:

a. The PUC-N-PC component is received with the RRM message generated by the program.

b. The RE_I code is formed, as follows:

RE_I shows the code of dynamic computers that must be interrupted as a result of this architectural interrupt. To find these computers, the monitor performs the following actions. The monitor takes the RE code of the current state, N, and the $\widehat{\text{RE}}$ code of the arriving state that is going to interrupt N. Next it finds the requested equipment RE_I affected by the interrupt as $\text{RE}_I = \text{RE} \vee \widehat{\text{RE}}$. The one's positions of RE_I show the positions of all CEs that should receive the interrupt messages in order to save the computational status of their programs.

Every such CE, upon receipt of the interrupt message, uses this message as the address of the local interrupt table destined to save the local computational status during a current state interrupt in the reconfiguration flow chart. It should be noted that it is desirable that each CE feature two types of interrupt tables: (1) for interrupts of local programs that do not involve changes in the reconfiguration flow chart, and (2) for interrupts of local programs that do involve changes in the reconfiguration flow chart (Fig. II.6).

3.2.3.2 Resumption of interrupted computations

As follows from the above organization, during current or next interrupts, if the dynamically assigned arriving architectural state Ñ interrupts N or N*, its $\widehat{\text{RRM}}$ message is either in R1 register if Ñ interrupts N or in R2 register if N interrupts N*. When Ñ is executed by the system, $\widehat{\text{RRM}}$ is in R1 [Fig. II.5(b, c)]. Completion of Ñ means resumption of the interrupted architectural state N (case 3) or N* (case 2).

Let us discuss the software organizations that feature such a resumption. Each completion of Ñ is signaled by sequential transfers R2 → R1 and R3 → R2 and initiation of denied resource handler, DRH, to fill in R3, where for all cases 1, 2, and 3, the R2 and R1 registers always store the next and currently executed RRM [Fig. II.5(a, b, c)].

To restore a current system status, the ID-PUC-N portion of the RRM message stored in R1 is sent to the global interrupt table to fetch the system status saved during this interrupt (Fig. II.6). The memory cell with this status is always cleared after this fetch. As a result, each interrupted ID-PUC-N is assigned only one cell of the global interrupt table. On the other hand, interrupt index j should be updated and saved. This justifies the use of two interrupt tables: the larger one for temporary saving of the global system status during each interrupt and a smaller one for permanent saving of the current interrupt index, j, that specifies given architectural interrupt (ID-PUC-N).

To restore the current status of each interrupted program run on every interrupted dynamic computer, the monitor forms the resumption message, RM, of which the format is similar to the interrupt message. (For a task-synchronized program affected by the next interrupt, no RM message needs to be formed.) The RM message stores the same codes, ID, PUC, N, and $j + 1$. The only difference between IM and RM is in their functions aimed, respectively, at writing and reading local computational statuses. Using the ones of requested equipment code, RE_l, the monitor sends the RM message to all CEs of interrupted dynamic computers to carry out their restarts from saving points. Each dynamic computer fetches the computational status of the local interrupted program using RM as the address of the global architectural interrupts memory that stores this status in its entirety.

3.2.3.3 Example of a current architectural interrupt caused by resolution of a reconfiguration conflict

As an example, consider the resolution of the reconfiguration conflict specified with the current architectural interrupt (Action 3). Action 2 is a subcase of this more complex organization (Fig. II.8).

Suppose that a dynamic architecture consisting of 5CE is in N_2 state, requested by program P_2, and the next state is N_1 requested by P_2.

Moment t_1. At the moment t_1, the R1 and R2 registers of the monitor store reconfiguration request messages RRM_3 formed by program P_3 and RRM_2 formed by program P_2. Register R1 stores RRM_3 concatenated with the priority code, $PC(N_3)$; RRM_3 stores the following codes: PUC_3; $RE = 11111$, since the entire resources of five CEs are requested; and $N_3 = 0011$, since $N_3 = [C_1(3), C_4(1), C_5(1)]$. The priority code, $PC(N_3)$, of this program for state N_3 is fetched upon the arrival of RRM_3, using PUC_3N_3 as the address of the priority memory.

Register R2 stores RRM_2 concatenated with $PC(N_1)$. (For more information on selecting state codes for multicomputer states, see Chapter III, Volume I, this series, pages 314–317.)

Moment t_2. Suppose that at the moment t_2 there arrives a new message, RRM_4, formed by program P_4 that requests reconfiguration into state $N_4 = 0100$. Having found priority code $PC(N_4)$, the monitor establishes that $PC(N_4) > PC(N_3)$, and there must be a current interrupt of N_3 and reconfiguration into N_4.

Moment t_3. The processor signal that finds that $PC(N_4) > PC(N_3)$ triggers new register-to-register transfers, shown in Fig. II.8 at the moment t_3. Current R1 register now stores RRM_4 concatenated with $PC(N_4)$. Register R2 saves RRM_3 concatenated with $PC(N_3)$. Register R3 saves RRM_2 concatenated with $PC(N_1)$. Therefore, the system initiates the current architectural interrupt of state N_3:

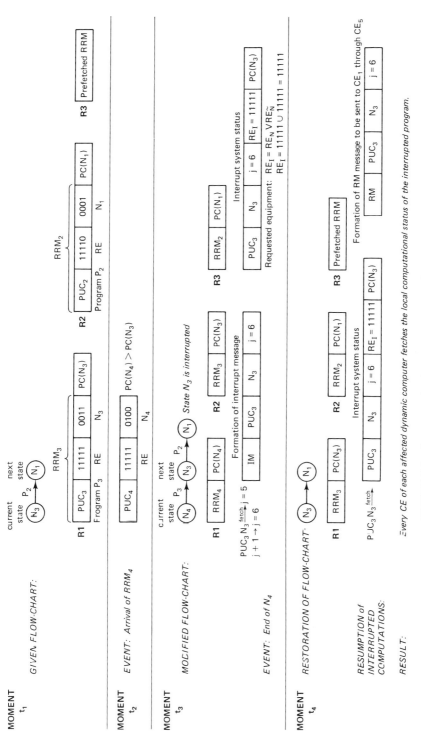

FIGURE II.8 One example of current architectural interrupt

35

a. The address PUC_3N_3 fetches the current interrupt index j. Suppose $j = 5$, giving $j + 1 = 6$.

b. Thereafter, the monitor forms the interrupt message, IM, consisting of PUC_3, N_3, and $j = 6$, and finds the requested interrupted equipment $RE_I = RE_N$ V $RE_{\tilde{N}}$, where RE_N is the requested equipment of arriving state $\tilde{N}$. Since RE_N = 11111 and $RE_{\tilde{N}}$ = 11111, RE_I = 11111. Thus, the monitor forms the interrupt system status and sends it to the cell PUC_3N_3.

c. Concurrently, the monitor sends the IM message to every CE having one in the RE_I code. Since RE_I is made of all ones, every CE of the system receives the interrupt message issued by the monitor.

d. In every CE, the portion of this message made of PUC_3, N_3 and $j = 6$ is used as the address of the local status information table for each interrupted program. Therefore, the system has interrupted the current state N_3 and can perform computations in the arriving state N_4.

Moment t_4. The end of N_4 triggers sequential transfers R2 → R1, R3 → R2, and DRH → R3. Since N_3 now occupies R1, it initiates interrupted computations by fetching an interrupted system status and sending RM resumption messages to all interrupted CEs. Each interrupted CE uses RM for fetching its local computational status which was saved during this interrupt (Fig. II.8).

3.2.3.4 Assessment of the introduced interrupt organization

The introduced organization of architectural interrupt is optimal from the following viewpoints:

01. It introduces the minimal time overhead.

02. It allows a considerable simplification of the hardware circuits responsible for an architectural interrupt.

03. It allows considerable programming flexibility.

Minimal time overhead.

I. Because the introduced interrupt organization stores a current interrupt index j, it is possible to have immediate multiple interrupts of the current architectural state. Each interrupt allows fast and immediate organization of one global and several local saving points, where:

    a. The global saving point saves a current computational status for the system in general.

    b. Each local saving point saves the computational status of each interrupted program run on the individual dynamic computer of the interrupted state N.

The interrupted computations can resume from the latest saving point, requiring no time-consuming programming associated with roll-backs of interrupted programs.

II. Each architectural interrupt may start immediately if it is current. If it is next, it waits for the completion of the current architectural state. In both cases it introduces no additional time overhead aimed at finding the highest-priority architectural state that should be executed next, since this state is always available in the R2 register in the monitor. Nor does it require any waiting time to be spent during the selection process in the denied resource handler. As a matter of fact, during both types of interrupts (current and next), the DRH unit needs no initiation because all three registers R1, R2, and R3 are filled with corresponding RRM messages. Also, the adopted organization with the interrupt messages allows immediate saving of the system status, as well as that of all local statuses associated with the *j*th interrupt of state N.

Simplification of interrupt circuits.

1. The size of the global interrupt table stored in the monitor is minimal, since only one memory word is required for storing every global system status identified with the address ID-PUC-N, in spite of the fact that this global system status may have *j* different values, where *j* is the interrupt index.

2. The circuits of the denied resource handler can be simplified by introducing sequential memory search, because the DRH unit introduces no time overhead which is additive to reconfiguration or interrupt time and aimed at finding the denied RRM message that should be prefetched into R3 register. As a matter of fact, DRH is initiated neither for the current nor next interrupt. In all cases considered, this unit selects neither current nor next RRM. Thus it can be made cheap and slow.

Program flexibility. The introduced interrupt organization allows considerable programming flexibility because of the following factors:

1. Each architectural state N requested by program P may be interrupted *j* times, where *j* is an arbitrary integer. Each interrupt results in forming one saving point for the global system status and *k* local saving points for local program statuses, where *k* is the number of interrupted concurrent programs computed in state N. There is no restriction on *j* and *k*. The formation of global and local saving points is very simple.

2. The introduced interrupt organization allows simple handling of a frequent programming situation when the same active program requests several transitions into the same architectural state in which, during each transition, this program is computed with a new set of other concurrent programs. This situation is handled by introducing a special ID field into the interrupt message which allows a unique encoding of each such case. The size of the ID field is minimal and equal to $\log_2 m$, where m is the maximal allowable number of such situations.

3.3 Task Synchronization

The objective of task synchronization is to establish the moment of time when the CE resources requested by RRM are ready for reconfiguration. The task synchronization step is performed under the following circumstances (Fig. II.2).

a. If there are no conflicts in the system, it is initiated with each arriving RRM message.
b. If there are conflicts in the system, it is performed following the stage of successful conflict resolution.

3.3.1 No Conflict Reconfiguration

If the system features no reconfiguration conflicts, it either executes a static reconfiguration flow chart in which each current state is succeeded with the unique next state or the system is idle. Therefore, the arriving $\widehat{RRM}$ message is either the one that requests the only next state N* or the one that requests the current state N in the event of the total system idleness.

If $\widehat{RRM}$ requests the next state N*, there must be the process of task synchronization aimed at finding the moment of time when the requested equipment is ready. If $\widehat{RRM}$ requests the current state, the system is idle and requested equipment is ready a priori. Thus, reconfiguration can start immediately.

3.3.2 Conflict Reconfiguration

As was shown above, for every architectural transition N $\rightarrow$ N*, the adopted organization of conflict resolution may lead to one of the following outcomes:

S1. No changes in a static reconfiguration flow chart.
S2. Two possible changes in a static reconfiguration flow chart specified with the current or next architectural interrupt.

For outcome S1, the task synchronization becomes similar to the one described in Section 3.3.1. For outcome S2, the task synchronization is warranted only for the next architectural interrupt.

Indeed, for the next interrupt, the anticipated N $\rightarrow$ N* transition of a static reconfiguration flow chart is replaced with the N $\rightarrow$ Ñ $\rightarrow$ N* transition, where Ñ is the dynamically assigned state. Therefore, computation of Ñ should wait for completion of N. This requires the task synchronization to determine the moment of this completion and the associated readiness of requested equipment. For the current interrupt, it never requires any task synchronization by definition, because the requested equipment becomes ready as a result of this interrupt.

3.3.3 Software Organization

If a user program is computed by a sequence of different-sized computers, it must be partitioned into tasks, TA, where each task is computed in a $C_i(k)$ computer [Fig. II.9(a)]. Here, i is the position of the most significant CE; k is the number of CEs.

Each task is concluded by a special synchronization instruction, Stop-N, which stores the n-bit synchronization code SC [Fig. II.9(b, c)]. The SC code is formed as follows: bit $j = 1$ if CE_j is integrated into $C_1(k)$; otherwise, bit $j = 0$ [Fig. II.9(c)]. For instance, for $n = 5$, dynamic computer $C_2(3)$ is represented with the synchronization code SC found as follows.

Since $C_2(3) = \{C2_2, CE_3, CE_4\}$, SC will have ones in positions $j = 2$, 3, and 4. The remaining two positions of SC are zeros ($2 = 5 - 3$), giving SC $= 01110$, etc. Each time the Stop N instruction is fetched by the dynamic computer $C_i(k)$, its SC code is sent to the monitor, which updates with an arriving SC its own idle equipment code, IEC. For the IEC code, its one's positions show what CEs in the system are idle. The new status of IEC is formed as follows:

$$IEC \lor SC \rightarrow IEC$$

If the program is active, its Stop-N instruction is followed by the reconfiguration instruction, $N \rightarrow N^*$ [Fig. II.9(b)]. When fetched by the dynamic computer, $C_i(k)$, the instruction $N \rightarrow N^*$ forms and sends to the monitor the reconfiguration request message, RRM, that stores the requested equipment code, RE.

For RE code, bit $j = 1$, if CE_j is requested to form a new computer in state N^*. Otherwise, $j = 0$. As was indicated above, to minimize the idleness of CEs, it is reasonable to form such requested equipment codes stored in $N \rightarrow N^*$ instructions which reflect not only the needs on a new dynamic computer of the active program P, which performs reconfiguration, but also the nonconflicting needs of other concurrent programs that can be executed together with P.

To find the moment of time when the requested equipment RE is ready for reconfiguration, the monitor performs the following readiness test:

Readiness Test: Is RE $\land$ IEC $=$ RE?

a. If yes, the requested equipment is ready.

b. If no, the requested equipment is not ready.

For case a, the monitor allows execution of Step 8 of the Multicomputer Reconfiguration Algorithm and updates again the status of the IEC register an $\overline{IEC \land RE} \rightarrow IEC$ (Fig. II.2).

For case b, the monitor initiates a waiting loop which is ended by the new iteration of the readiness test. This loop is repeated until the RT test gives a positive result.

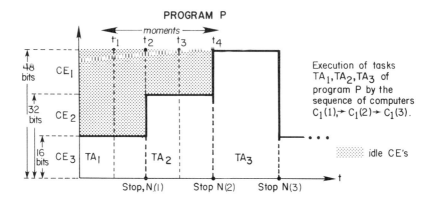

PROGRAM P

Execution of tasks TA_1, TA_2, TA_3 of program P by the sequence of computers $C_1(1), \rightarrow C_1(2) \rightarrow C_1(3)$.

:::::::: idle CE's

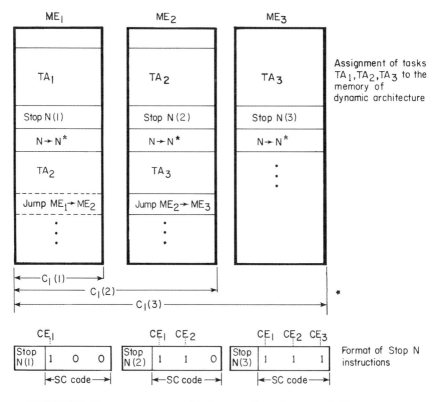

Assignment of tasks TA_1, TA_2, TA_3 to the memory of dynamic architecture

Format of Stop N instructions

FIGURE II.9 Memory management during reconfiguration requested by program Γ: (a) Execution of tasks TA_1, TA_2, and TA_3 of Program P by the sequence of computers $C_1(1)$, $C_1(2)$ and $C_1(3)$, respectively; (b) assignment of tasks TA_1, TA_2, and TA_3 to the memory of dynamic architecture; (c) format of Stop-N instructions

CONSECUTIVE STATUS OF IDLE EQUIPMENT
REGISTER IN THE MONITOR

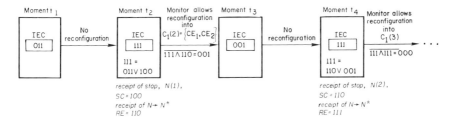

FIGURE II.10   Finding the idle equipment status in the monitor

Therefore, with the receipt of SC and RE codes the status of the IEC register in the monitor is updated. If the monitor receives a new SC code, new IEC is found as IEC V SC $\rightarrow$ IEC (Fig. II.10). If the monitor receives a new RE code and two other reconfiguration conditions are satisfied whereby (1) reconfiguration is allowed and (2) the readiness test gives a Yes answer, the new IEC is

$$\overline{\text{IEC} \wedge \text{RE}} \rightarrow \text{IEC}$$

Obtaining a new IEC update with the use of the RE code concludes the synchronization state of the multicomputer reconfiguration algorithm (Fig. II.2).

3.4 Access of Variable Codes and Establishment of New Interconnections in the Network

Both the significance of control codes to be written into each CE and the techniques used for activating new interconnections of the interconnection network depend on the adopted organization of dynamic architecture and the type of interconnection network used to partition the system into a variable number of dynamic computers with selectable word sizes.

Therefore, as an illustration, let us use one dynamic computer organization and show how one can organize in it the access of variable control codes and establishment of new interconnections in the network.

3.4.1 Description of a Dynamic Architecture with Minimal Complexity

This dynamic architecture contains n computer elements (CEs), $n - 1$ connecting elements (MSEs), and one monitor (V) [see Fig. II.11(a)]. One CE processes h-bit words in parallel. Assume $h - 16$. A pair of adjacent CEs is separated by one connecting unit, which may assume the following modes: right transfer, left transfer, and no transfer. For the right-transfer mode, a 16-bit byte is transferred from pins a^1 to a^2; for left transfer, it is transferred from pins a^2 to a^1; and for no transfer, there is no data patch between them.

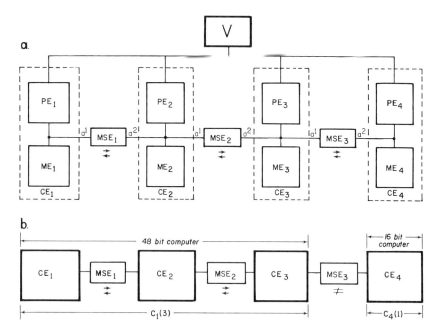

FIGURE II.11 (a) The resource of dynamic architecture containing 4CE's; (b) architectural state $N_1 = [C_1(3), C_4(1)]$

This dynamic architecture may form computers of variable size labeled $C_i(k)$. Each $C_i(k)$ computer $(k = 1, 2, ..., n)$ integrates k computer elements and $k - 1$ connecting elements. The i shows the position of the computer's most significant CE. This computer handles $16 \cdot k$ bit words and has a primary memory $16 \cdot k$ bits wide. By changing the number of computer elements in $C_i(k)$, one obtains $16, 32, 48, ..., 16 \cdot n$ bit computers. This dynamic architecture may assume 2^{n-1} states, $N_0, N_1, ..., N_{2^{(n-1)}}$. The difference between states is in the sizes, positions, and numbers of computers operating concurrently.

For instance, dynamic architecture with n CEs, where $n = 4$, forms the $2^{4-1} = 8$ different states. For state N_1, the $C_1(3)$ computer (48 bits) and the $C_4(1)$ computer (16 bits) function concurrently, i.e., $N_1 = (1 \times 48, 1 \times 16)$. The two connecting elements, MSE_1 and MSE_2 integrated by $C_1(3)$ [Fig. II.11(b)] are in a transfer mode ($\rightleftharpoons$), which may be either left or right. The instruction fetched by one CE is transferred to all the others. MSE_3 is in the no-transfer mode ($\neq$) and it separates program and data computed by $C_1(3)$ from that computer by $C_4(1)$. For the $C_1(3)$ computer, the transfer mode of its connecting units depends on which CE stores a currently executed program segment. If the instruction is fetched from CE_1, the two MSEs (MSE_1 and MSE_2) assume the right transfer mode; if it is fetched from CE_2, MSE_1 must transfer left, while MSE_2 retains its right transfers, etc.

3.4.2 Storage of Control Codes

The control codes to be stored in each CE are divided into the two categories: *variant* and *invariant*. The variant codes are reconfiguration-dependent; i.e., they change during each system reconfiguration. The invariant codes are written to each CE forever during the assembly stage. Their origin is due to the modular nature of dynamic architectures and the necessity to minimize the number of module types that are used in system implementation.

For the purposes of this discussion, we will consider storage of variant codes only, since invariant control codes are written to the PE of each CE and thus do not need to be accessed. (More information on invariant control codes can be found in Chapter III, Volume 1, this series, pages 284-286.)

To form a new dynamic computer, $C_i(k) = [CE_i, CE_{i+1}, \ldots, CE_{i+k-1}]$, one has to write four variant control codes to all its CEs: (1) k (computer size code) that shows how many CEs are included into $C_i(k)$; (2) data fetch code, m_E, that shows the time of fetching a $16 \cdot k$-bit data word from k ME in parallel; (3) significance code, b, that marks most significant, least significant, and middle computer elements contained in the dynamic computer and (4) the processor code, p, that sets the time for a processor-dependent operation.

For all modules of one CE, the same values of each variable control code should be written. To store them requires N bits, where

$$N = 2 \log_2 n + 3 + \log_2 S$$

and $2 \log_2 n + 1$ is the number of bits required to store k and p codes, because $p \leq 2k$; 2 bits are required to store $b = b_1 b_2$, where $b_1 = 1$ marks the most significant CE and $b_2 = 1$ marks the least significant CE; St_0 is the speed of the slowest ME in dynamic architecture. If $n \leq 16$, $S \leq 16$, $N = 8 + 3 + 4 = 15$ bits; i.e., storage of all variable control codes for one CE takes one 16-bit cell.

Since this dynamic architecture contains n CEs, the control codes for an architectural state may be stored in a single $16 \cdot n$-bit cell composed of n 16-bit memory bytes, where each byte stores control codes for one CE. Because this dynamic architecture may assume 2^{n-1} states, to store the control codes for all architectural states requires an array of 2^{n-1} cells of the size $16 \cdot n$ bits each. This array may be mapped either into I/O memory or primary memory. If it is stored in the initial cells of the I/O memory, $M(I/O)$, then the effective address of one $16 \cdot n$-bit cell may be made the code of the architectural state.

Example. As an example, consider the filling of one $16 \cdot n$-bit cell for the architectural state $N_9 = \{ C_1(1), C_2(3), C_5(1) \}$, having $n = 5$. The speeds of five MEs are $13t_0$ for ME_1, $12t_0$ for ME_2, $3t_0$ for ME_3, $2t_0$ for ME_4, and t_0 for MF_5. Assume that fast CLA circuits are used in the adder where the size of one group is 4 bits and it introduces $2t_d$ delay, where t_d is one gate delay. Also assume that one clock period time is $6t_d$, roughly equal to the time of 8-bit addition.

Architectural state	Dynamic computers	M(I/O$_1$) k p b m$_E$	M(I/O$_2$) k p b m$_E$	M(I/O$_3$) k p b m$_E$	M(I/O$_4$) k n h m$_E$	M(I/O$_5$) k p b m$_E$
N$_9$	C$_1$(1),Ĉ$_2$(3),C$_5$(1)	1 2 3 13	3 4 2 12	3 4 0 12	3 4 1 12	1 2 3 1

|← C$_1$(1) →|← ———————— C$_2$(3) ———————— →|← C$_5$(1) →|

FIGURE II.12   Control codes that cause reconfiguration into state N$_9$ = [C$_1$(1), C$_2$(3), C$_5$(1)]

Consider how one can find all these codes for each C$_i$(k) computer of state N$_9$ (Fig. II.12) Code $k = 1$ for C$_1$(1) and C$_5$(1), and $k = 3$ for C$_2$(3). Code p is found as follows:

$$p = \frac{16 \cdot k \cdot 2t_d}{4} \div 6t_d = \lceil 4k/3 \rceil$$

where $16 \cdot k/4$ is the number of CLA groups, and $\lceil\ \ \rceil$ means rounding to the least integer that exceeds the expression inside. Therefore, for C$_1$(1) and C$_5$(1), $p = 4 \cdot 1/3 = 2$; for C$_2$(3), $p = \lceil 4 \cdot 3/3 \rceil = 4$.

Code $b = 11 = 3$ for C$_1$(1) and C$_5$(1) since these two computers are made of one CE that is the most and least significant. For C$_2$(3) = [CE$_2$, CE$_3$, CE$_4$], $b = 10 = 2$ for CE$_2$, since it is the most significant: $b = 00$ for CE$_3$ because it is neither most nor least significant; and $b = 01 = 1$ for CE$_4$, since it is the least significant.

Code m_E shows the speed of the slowest memory unit in the primary memory of the dynamic computer. Thus for C$_1$(1), $m_E = 13t_0$, since the primary memory of this computer includes only ME$_1$; for C$_2$(3), $m_E = \max(12, 3, 2) = 12$; for C$_5$(1), $m_E = \max(1) = 1$. ∎

3.4.3 Establishment of New Interconnections of the Interconnection Network

Establishment of new transfer modes in connecting elements is performed by the monitor. The task of the monitor is to identify the connecting elements that should switch and the transfer mode each of them should assume.

To find the connecting elements that should switch, the monitor uses the code RE of requested computer elements. Since every computer element CE$_i$ is followed by connecting unit MSE$_i$ except for CE$_n$, the least significant which has no MSE$_n$ following it [Fig. II.11(a)], the first $n - 1$ bits of the RE code form code RE*, which shows the positions of the MSEs that should switch their modes. That is, if MSE has a one in RE*, it should switch because it corresponds to a requested CE in the RE code. If MSE has a zero in RE*, it should be left unchanged, because the respective CE continues to be integrated into the same computer existing for both states N and N*.

The V monitor uses the N* code to find the transfer mode that should be assumed by each MSE which is to be switched. This may be done if a special state-assignment technique is used. Since this dynamic architecture has 2^{n-1} states, and in each state separation of two adjacent computers is made by the MSE between them assuming the no-transfer mode, and integration of k CEs into one $C_i(k)$ is made by $k - 1$ connecting elements assuming a transfer mode, assigning a transfer or no-transfer mode for the MSE_i in the ith position ($i = 1, ..., n - 1$) with an 0 or 1, respectively, yields an $(n - 1)$-bit code. This code shows the positions and the number of independent computers functioning in this state. Furthermore, for each computer $C_i(k)$, this code shows the positions of all the CEs which it integrates.

Example. For this dynamic architecture with $n \cdot$ CE, where $n = 5$, all states can be assigned with a 4-bit code. Each state is represented by the decimal value of its code. For N_{11}, code 1011 shows three connecting elements, MSE_1, MSE_3, and MSE_4, in the no-transfer mode and one, MSE_2, in a transfer mode. Since MSE_1 contains 1, it separates CE_1 and CE_2; CE_1 functions as $C_1(1)$, and CE_2 is integrated by another computer. Since MSE_2 contains 0, it ties CE_2 and CE_3 together, forming computer $C_2(2)$. Since MSE_3 and MSE_4 contain 1, they separate CE_3 from CE_4 and CE_4 from CE_5; therefore, CE_4 and CE_5 function, respectively, as $C_4(1)$ and $C_5(1)$. Thus, $N_{11} = 1101$ specifies $C_1(1)$, $C_2(2)$, $C_4(1)$, and $C_5(1)$ functioning concurrently. Such a state assignment allows the V monitor to specify the mode of operation (transfer or no-transfer) that should be assumed by each MSE which should switch. To this end, it performs a bitwise comparison of RE* and N* which establishes

If bit $i = 1$ for both RE* and N*, MSE_i switches to a no-transfer mode.

If $i = 1$ for RE* and $i = 0$ for N*, MSE_i switches to a transfer mode.

If $i = 0$ for RE*, MSE_i remains unchanged.

Establishment of the proper transfer modes in the connecting elements concludes the switch of the architecture to state N*. As shown above, the technique considered requires that the N → N* instruction store the following codes: program user code, PUC for priority analysis, n-bit code, RE of requested equipment, and $(n - 1)$-bit code N* of the requested architectural state. All these codes may be mapped into one program instruction made of two 16-bit cells. ∎

3.5 General Observations about Program Start-Up

Program start-up forms Step 10 of the overall multicomputer reconfiguration algorithm (Fig. II.2). Every user program is started up in a new dynamic computer of the next architectural state with the use of a special start-up message (SUM). Therefore, to start all programs assigned to the allowed architectural state N, this state should fetch the respective *start-up state*, M(N), (N→M(N)), which is understood as a set of SUM messages *assigned* to N. Thus the entire queue, AQ, of assigned SUM messages is stored in the monitor as a table of M(N) states in order (1) to maintain the one-to-one correspondence with the reconfiguration flow chart and (2) to uphold a possible restructuring of the assigned queue for dynamic programs. Each start-up state M(N) of the assigned queue is either available in the start-up table for static programs or created dynamically for dynamic programs.

Indeed, for a static program its SUM is always assigned to the architectural state during the stage of resource assignment; for a dynamic program, as a rule, its SUM is not assigned to the architectural state, since typically a SUM message of a dynamic program may know only of the individual resource needs of this program. If these needs are smaller than the entire system resources, the respective SUM becomes *nonassigned* to the architectural state since there may exist several architectural states that contain a dynamic computer(s) required by the program represented with this SUM.

Therefore, for a dynamic program to be executed, its nonassigned SUM must first be assigned to the architectural state. This means that the monitor must either (1) find other concurrent and compatible nonassigned programs that can be assigned to the same architectural state, or (2) swap a nonassigned higher-priority program with another one having a lower priority and assigned to the existing architectural state. The action 1 leads to the *creation* and the action 2 leads to the *reassignment* of architectural states. Therefore, any nonassigned program becomes ready for computation only following the state of dynamic assignment which includes creation and reassignment of architectural states.

Note: Whereas the importance of the creation operation seems obvious, the necessity of the reassignment operation needs additional justification.

The reassignment of existing states is also an important ingredient of the dynamic assignment process, since it allows a high-priority dynamic program P_H to be reassigned to an existing architectural state N_H with higher priority while purging from this state a lower priority program P_L with compatible resource needs. Thus, because of reassignment, the execution of P_H will not be delayed, as would have happened otherwise if the monitor were not provided with this procedure.

As follows from the above, static and dynamic programs are specified with different start-up techniques. For static programs, the program start-up proceeds immediately following the preceding Step 9 of the reconfiguration algorithm (Fig. II.2), since the respective start-up state M(N) is available in the monitor. For dynamic programs, the program start-up may be delayed by the dynamic assignment process, if no architectural state is available that can integrate this program. In both cases of static and dynamic programs, the issues of program start-up become closely intertwined with the issues of resource assignment, either static or dynamic. Thus, in view of the above, start-up techniques will be discussed following procedures of dynamic assignment (see Sec. 5.7, Chapter III).

4 DYNAMIC RECONFIGURATIONS FOR MULTICOMPUTER NETWORKS

Generally, by a *multicomputer network* we mean a collection of computer elements interconnected together via an interconnection network [33]. A dynamically reconfigurable interconnection network defines a *dynamic multicomputer network*, DMN, that can assume a set of configurations during program(s) execution time and improve performance by executing each algorithm(s) in the most appropriate network configuration or sequence of configurations.

In this section we discuss the problem of the *analysis* and *synthesis* of a DMN that can reconfigure into various sets of rings with selectable periods and single and multiple trees and stars. *Analysis of DMN* means finding and quantification of all possible network structures that can be generated with these techniques. *Synthesis of DMN* means finding specific control codes that can generate a given network structure, describing a particular application.

Another closely related area discussed is associated with the development of efficient *communication* techniques in a DMN organized as a reconfigurable binary tree.

4.1 Difference between Network and Multicomputer Reconfigurations

Consider now the modifications that should be introduced into a general multicomputer reconfiguration algorithm because of the specificity offered by a DMN. In all, for a DMN, not only separate nodes can be reconfigured into variable dynamic computers, but the interconnections among separate dynamic computers are also a subject of reconfiguration via formation of variable topological structures, where each dynamic computer acts as a separate node in the network.

In general, for a DMN, the sequence of reconfiguration steps remains the same as for a multicomputer reconfiguration (Fig. II.2) since this sequence is determined by the requirement to provide correct computations in the environment of (1) conflicts and (2) reconfigurable and distributed computing resources interconnected together with an interconnection network (single staged or multistaged). Indeed, for a DMN to implement feature (1) of a multicomputer reconfiguration requires the conflict resolution process (Step 2) and its implied outcomes consisting of an architectural interrupt (current or next, Steps 3 and 5) or no interrupt (Step 4). If there are no conflicts or no architectural interrupts caused by conflicts, there is the task-synchronization step (Step 7) aimed at finding the moment of completion for programs computed in a previous computing structure.

To implement feature (2) requires accessing an array of control code (Step 8) and writing this array to the requested resource modules of the DMN, in order to establish required interconnections in the interconnection network which will then identify a new computing structure created with the use of reconfiguration.

Therefore, the difference between network and multicomputer reconfiguration is not in the overall sequence of steps to be performed in general reconfiguration algorithm (Fig. II.2), but in the set of control codes that have to be accessed and in the techniques of data paths activations.

To form a new dynamic computer will take the set of control codes considered above for a multicomputer reconfiguration. However, to form a new network structure requires not only a *node reconfiguration* aimed at formation of dynamic computers, but also the *network reconfiguration* aimed at formation of a new topology of activated interconnections among separate dynamic computers. Therefore, the network reconfiguration is accomplished with an additional set of control codes and special techniques of data-path activations in the interconnection network used.

In this section we will discuss what control codes should be selected and what techniques of data-patch activations should be used to effect concurrent network reconfigurations into rings, trees, and stars applicable for both types of interconnection networks (single staged and multiple staged).

The reconfiguraiton methodology introduced is optimal because of the following reasons:

1. This is a concurrent reconfiguration performed by all network nodes.
2. Each node concurrently with other nodes activates the new interconnections in the network during a simple mod-2 addition operation aimed at finding the successor of this node in a new network structure.
3. The entire set of new interconnections in the network is activated with the use of *only one n-bit code,* called bias, where $n = \log_2 K$ and K is the number of nodes in the network; this activation takes the time of simple logical operation of mod-2 addition.

Therefore, this methodology achieves time and memory optimization by taking the absolutely minimal time and the minimal number of bits ($\log_2 K$) to establish each network structure among the wide range of structures than can be assumed with the use of these reconfiguration techniques.

This section not only solves analysis and synthesis problems for a wide range of computing structures assumed by a DMN, but for a particular case of such structures (reconfigurable binary trees), it solves the problem of node-to-node communication by introducing efficient communication algorithms that are optimal from both viewpoints:

a. Bit size of the *routing information code,* BS(RI), that routes the message among various transit nodes of the communication path
b. *Total time of communication*

It is shown that

$$BS(RI) \leq n + 2 \log_2 \log_2 n$$

The RI code achieves an absolute theoretical minimum because of the following. Its first addend, taking n bits, uses only 1 bit per node for selecting either the right or left successor of the current node in a communication subpath directed from the root to the leaves; the second addend ($2 \log_2 \log_2 n$ bits) extends such an optimal selection to every tree configuration (out of 2^n possible) and to every communication path, ranging from a minimal path taking one node to a maximal path taking $2n - 1$ nodes in a tree made of n levels.

Therefore, since, for any n, $2n - 1 \geq n + 2 \log_2 \log_2 n$, the introduced communication algorithms may require less than one routing bit per node in the maximal communication path that includes $2n - 1$ nodes in a reconfigurable n-level binary tree made of 2^n nodes. For instance, $n = 9$ defines a binary tree with 512 nodes; in this tree the maximal communication path takes 17 nodes, where $17 = 2 \cdot 9 - 1$. If one uses a minimal routing information code, RI, that takes only 1 bit per node in the path, one obtains BS(RI) = 17 bits. However, with the introduced communication techniques, BS(RI) = 13 bits, where BS(RI) = $9 + 2 \log_2 \log_2 9 = 9 + 2 \log_2 4 = 9 + 2 \cdot 2 = 13$. Thus, the BS(RI) that can be obtained is 4 bits less than the code that takes only 1 bit per node of the communication path! Furthermore, since each transit node, N, selects its next successor in the communication path via simple logical operation taking the time of one gate delay, the total time of the node-to-node communication also becomes the theoretical minimum.

These communication techniques are applicable for reconfigurable binary trees interconnected with either multistaged or single-staged networks.

When a single- or multiple-staged interconnection network employs our techniques of optimal reconfiguration-communication in binary trees, it will take full advantage of the following:

a. The number of required control codes necessary to establish a new tree configuration is *only one* (n-bit code, B).

b. The required routing information code is of *minimal size* $(n + 2 \log_2 \log_2 n)$.

c. The speed of reconfiguration is the *time of a simple logical operation of mod-2 addition*.

d. The speed of internode communication is *one gate delay per node in the communication path*.

These advantages remain the same for both types of interconnection networks. The difference between the networks is in the time of a message transit between every pair of nodes of the communication path and the overall complexity of realization expressed in the total number of connecting elements in the network.

4.2 Contribution and Composition

The contribution of the research reported in Sec. 4 is as follows:

I. Here we devise original and simple techniques on a network reconfiguration into the structures (rings, trees and stars) that proved to be applicable for a large class of control and computational algorithms. The time of such reconfiguration achieves the theoretical minimum. These reconfiguration techniques fall under the category of the analysis and synthesis of DMN introduced above.

II. This section expands the state-of-the-art findings of shift register theory [35–39] by developing a special shift register called *shift register with the variable bias* (SRVB) as a reconfiguration tool that can be used for generating rings, trees, and stars during the time of one logical operation of mod-2 addition. This shift register overcomes the problem of complexity that arises during the synthesis and analysis of computing structures generated by traditional (linear) shift registers [35–39]. Such complexity makes prohibitive the use of linear shift registers for cost-effective network reconfigurations. More discussion on the differences between SRVB and linear shift registers can be found in [6].

In [41–43], the classical shift register theory was applied by the authors for obtaining modular implementations of sequential and logical circuits [41, 42] and dedicated computer networks [43]. Thus, the current section is a product of our long-term association with shift registers and perennial attempts to apply the results of this beautiful mathematical theory for solving important problems of computer technology at various historical stages of their appearance.

III. This section is also associated with other works on reorganizations and reconfigurations in distributed computer systems whereby a system is restructured for obtaining various types of performance optimization [44–55].

While [44–50] consider mainly hardware issues of such restructuring dealing with development and/or activation of the interconnection networks used, and [51–55] are concerned mostly with pertinent purely software issues associated with elections of new monitors, organization of communication protocols, improvement of software reliability, etc., this section is more concerned with the combination of concrete hardware–software solutions that fall under the category of reconfiguration and communication algorithms in distributed and reconfigurable computer systems.

IV. Since this section not only solves analysis and synthesis problems for a wide range of computing structures, but for a particular case of such structures (reconfigurable binary trees) also develops efficient communication algorithms, it has association with [56, 57, 58] dealing with optimal routing algorithms for multistaged networks [56, 57] and single-staged networks [58]. Because of these contributions, the communication algorithms developed in this section for reconfigurable binary trees are applicable for these trees interconnected together with either multistaged or single-staged networks.

Section 4 covers the following topics:

Section 4.3 provides the motivation for the research presented and introduces the basic idea of a SRVB. It also shows how this shift register can reconfigure a DMN into rings, trees, and stars.

Section 4.4 classifies all the network structures that can be generated with the SRVB and gives the techniques for finding a special reconfiguration code which is used for reconfiguring a SRVB into a shifting format that generates a given DMN. It also presents an overview of all network structures that can be formed, such as (1) single ring structures, (2) single tree structures, (3) composite ring structures, (4) single composite star structures, (5) multiple tree structues, and (6) multiple composite star structures.

Section 4.5 presents the solution of the analysis and synthesis problem for single ring structures generated by single and circular shift registers, SRVB. The significance of single ring structures is in providing an insight into the fundamental mathematical properties of all ring structures, either single or composite.

Section 4.6 solves the problem of analysis for composite ring structures.

Section 4.7 presents the solution of the synthesis problem alone for reconfigurable binary trees since the problem of analysis is trivial; synthesis of a binary tree consists of finding the expressions for root, leaves, and nonleaves for any given binary tree generated by the network that receives the same n-bit control code (bias). In all, it is possible to generate 2^n different tree configurations using these techniques, where n is the size of the bias. (This is true for every computing structure that can be established with these reconfiguration techniques.)

Section 4.8 develops optimal *communication algorithms* for internode communication in every tree configuration.

Section 4.9 presents conclusions on the importance of the reported research on network reconfigurations and communications.

A current scientific pursuit of these authors is in solving analysis and synthesis problems for the remaining composite structures (composite stars, multiple trees, and multiple stars) that can be generated by SRVB, and in developing efficient communication algorithms for all multiple structures obtained with the use of this reconfiguration.

4.3 Motivation

In this section we describe the area of cost-efficient applications for rings, trees, and stars and give the nature of performance improvement that can be achieved with the use of dynamic reconfiguration. Next we present the overall idea of generating various network structures with the use of SRVB and outline the essence of analysis and synthesis problems for the resulting DMNs.

4.3.1 Overall Outline of Cost-Effective Computations for DMN, Assuming Rings, Trees, and Stars

There are a number of computational and control algorithms that lend themselves to cost-effective computation in a multicomputer network [44–50]. Among the most useful network configurations are rings, trees, and stars since these describe a broad spectrum of structures assumed by a variety of computational and control algorithms.

Rings are quite useful for pipeline computations where each node of the ring fetches one operand from its local memory and receives a second operand from its predecessor in the ring. Therefore, reconfiguration into a set of rings with selectable periods alleviates the most typical problem of nonreconfigurable pipeline systems which feature a mismatch in a variety of computations between the number of resource units that are connected into a pipeline and the number of operations in a pipelined arithmetic expression(s) creating time and resource overhead in pipelined computation [3].

Trees and stars are convenient structures for a variety of computational algorithms of the "divide-and-conquer" type (sorting, evaluation of arithmetic expressions, inference algorithms for knowledge-based data bases, etc.), where the entire computation can be partitioned into portions assigned to nodes of a tree or star.

Control algorithms yielding a tree or star implementation typically describe a tree or star hierarchical management configuration where each higher level node, (1) manages

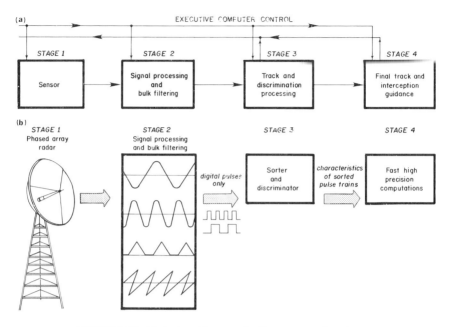

FIGURE II.13   Typical real-time application, consecutive stages

and distributes information among all lower-level nodes that follow it in a tree or star, and (2) receives completion signals from all lower-level nodes indicating that all jobs assigned for execution have been completed.

Especially efficient is the use of rings, stars, and trees in fast real-time computations, shown in Fig. II.13, since typically the structures of such computations closely match those of rings, trees, and stars (Fig. II.14). Therefore, reconfiguration into such structures allows a software-controlled adaptation to particular algorithm parameters, yielding significant performance improvement in computations. More information on the suitability of rings, trees, and stars to fast real-time computations is given in Sec. 6, Chapter V.

4.3.2 Two Factors of Performance Optimization

In general, a dynamic architecture improves performance Δ, where $\Delta = \Delta T - \Delta t$, and ΔT is the *program speed-up* caused by system reconfigurability and Δt is the *reconfiguration overhead* when no computation can be performed. Therefore, to increase Δ, one has to maximize ΔT and minimize Δt. In dynamic architectures the program speed-up, ΔT, is maximized at the expense of the following factors:

  a. *Creation of additional concurrency* in a system: This is accomplished via its dynamic reconfiguration into closely fitted (minimal) hardware structures whose parameters match those of the executing algorithm(s) and the accompanied release of redundant computer elements into additional computations. Such

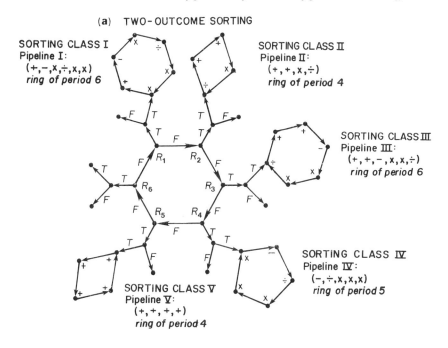

(a) TWO-OUTCOME SORTING

SORTING CLASS I
Pipeline I:
(+,−,×,÷,×,×)
ring of period 6

SORTING CLASS II
Pipeline II:
(+,+,×,÷)
ring of period 4

SORTING CLASS III
Pipeline III:
(+,+,−,×,×,÷)
ring of period 6

SORTING CLASS IV
Pipeline IV:
(−,÷,×,×,×)
ring of period 5

SORTING CLASS V
Pipeline V:
(+,+,+,+)
ring of period 4

(b) MULTIPLE- OUTCOME SORTING

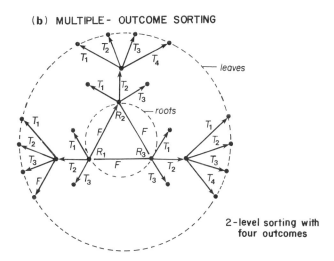

2-level sorting with
four outcomes

FIGURE II.14 Application of ring-trees and ring-stars structures for real-time sorting

a release always creates an additional parallelism in execution in comparison
with nonreconfigurable systems having the same complexity of resources. For
example, as is shown in [4], in the execution of a general-purpose program mix
made 14 programs with no data dependencies, a dynamic architecture achieves
a 42% speed-up in comparison with a static system having the same complexi-

ty of resources. The only source of this speed-up is in a dynamic reconfigurability which minimizes the word sizes of concurrent computers and starts nonused CEs into additional parallel computations that cannot be organized in any static system.

b. *Data-exchange optimization* in the system: This is accomplished via dynamic reconfiguration into hardware structures (in particular trees and stars) in which node pairs with a large number of data exchanges are connected via communication paths of minimal length.

For instance, as was shown in [63] and Sec. 4.1, due to the capability of dynamic architectures to perform such reconfigurations in tree data bases that allow each pair of communicating nodes to be connected with a very short communication path, the performance improvement in data-base transactions can approach 370%. That is, for a sampled assortment of node-to-node data exchanges, a static tree data base spends the time of $1430T_0$ to execute all exchanges among its nodes, whereas a reconfigurable tree data base organizes the same data exchanges in $300T_0$.

Therefore, the major motivation behind the use of the dynamic multicomputer network is twofold:

A1. By reconfiguring the DMN into the structure(s) that most closely approximate(s) the executing algorithm(s), one achieves performance improvement ΔT at the expense of added executional concurrency and data-exchange optimization.

A2. By developing fast and concurrent reconfiguration techniques, an additional performance improvement is achieved at the expense of minimization or total elimination of any reconfiguration overhead that accompanies a conventional reconfiguration process.

Therefore, the benefits of fast reconfiguration methodology are in the capability of a dynamic multicomputer network to execute all the necessary reconfigurations quickly and efficiently, introducing minimal delays in architectural transitions from one architectural state to another, and in optimizing system performance because of the close match between the structures of algorithms and the configurations of the computing network that can be accomplished via reconfiguration.

4.3.3 Concurrent Reconfiguration

A dynamic multicomputer network that reconfigures into trees, stars, and rings can be organized if its nodes identified with computer elements, CE, are interconnected with either the memory-processor bus (or DC bus), described in [7], or with any multistaged interconnection network in which, to organize a data broadcast between a pair of nodes N and N*, it is sufficient for a network node N to generate the position code or address code of N* [56, 57].

Activation of a data path between N and N* will be denoted as the *connection* $N \to N^*$, meaning that:

1. N generates the position code of N* and establishes a data path between N and N*.
2. The data path between N and N* is bidirectional: either from N to N* or from N* to N. It can be one of the four types PE-ME*, PE-PE*, ME-PE*, ME-ME*, where the first element belongs to node N and the second element belongs to node N*, and PE stands for the processor element and ME stands for the memory element.

To minimize the time of reconfiguration, it is reasonable to assume that for each network structure:

a. All connections $N \to N^*$ are established concurrently.
b. The rule of succession $N \to N^*$ is maintained *during reconfiguration* such that each node N has the minimal number of immediate successors N* in this structure.

The assumptions a and b lead to the overall minimization of the reconfiguration time by implementing the concept of *concurrent reconfiguration* and spending the minimal number of pins and minimal time in each CE for implementing this concept.

Note: Both assumptions a and b make contributions toward implementation of the concurrent reconfiguration concept. While the contribution of assumption a is obvious, assumption b needs additional explanations, presented below.

For any alternative organization requiring node N to have *p* successors during reconfiguration, the following two cases must be distinguished:

Case 1. Node N maintains parallel (dedicated) connections with all its *p* successors.

Case 2. Node N maintains sequential (shared) connections with all its successors.

Case 1 is infeasible due to the pin count limitation in each CE identified with one node N, since to activate *p* parallel and *controllable* connections with *p* successors of node N will take $p(h + n)$ pins in each CE, where $p \cdot n$ is the number of address pins. [For $p = 4$, $h = 16$, $n = 4$, each CE will have 80 pins only for external node-to-node data broadcast, not to mention other (local) pins that must be present in each CE to support its operation as a computing module.] Case 2 is also infeasible, since to activate all shared connections of node N with its *p* successors will take *p* time intervals, where one interval is the time to activate one connection $N \to N^*$.

For rings, the rule of minimal number of successors is trivial; for trees and stars, to hold this rule during reconfiguration requires that the direction of succession be maintained from the leaves to the root(s). This will transform trees and stars into *single successor structures,* since each node N will have only one successor in this structure.

4.3.4 Contribution of Shift-Register Theory

In this section the following procedure will be used to activate each connection N → N* belonging to a new network structure. Assume that a special shift register of length *n* resides in each node N, where *n* is the length of its position code [Fig. II.15(a)]. Suppose that, in the given network structure to be assumed, node N has to be connected with node N* via the PE-PE*, PE-ME*, ME-ME*, or ME-PE* data path. Then for each type of communication between N and N*, node N generates position code N* using a left-shifted shift register that generates N* as follows:

$$N* = 1[N] + B \tag{1}$$

where 1[N] is a 1-bit shift of the binary representation of N to the left and B is an *n*-bit reconfiguration constant brought with the reconfiguration instruction to *all network nodes that are requested for reconfiguration.* Reconfiguration constant B will be called *bias,* and the shift register of Fig. II.15(a) is called a *shift register with variable bias* (SRVB).

In Fig. II.15(a), with the use of bias B = 101, the network of six nodes reconfigures into two rings of period 3 (2 • 3 = 6), while the remaining two nodes receiving the same B = 101 will function independently of any other nodes and each form a ring of period 1. For instance, consider the establishment of the $N_5 \rightarrow N_6$ connection for this network: N_5 stores N = 101 in its SRVB. Thus, it generates N* = 1[101] + 101 = 011 + 101 = 110. As shown in [7], for a single-staged network, generation of N* = 110 in N_5 is sufficient to establish the $N_5 \rightarrow N_6$ connection of any given type (PE-PE*, PE-ME*, ME-ME*, ME-PE*), since N* = 6 generated inside node N_5 selects the connecting element MSE_6 that establishes a data path with N_5 [Fig II.15(b)]. Similarly, for the Omega multistaged network described in [57], generation of code N* is sufficient to activate the data path N → N*. This data path will contain *n* connecting elements for the PE → ME* connection or 2*n* connecting elements for the PE → PE* or ME → ME* connections, where *n* is the size of the node position code ($n = \log_2 K$).

As follows from the above examples, this reconfiguration methodology is applicable to single- and multi-staged networks. The difference between these two networks is in (1) the time of message transit between two adjacent nodes, N → N*, of the communication path, and (2) the overall complexity of realization, expressed with the number of connecting elements in the network.

This difference is expressed by the following time–cost trade-off. If all network nodes are interconnected with an interconnection network that connects the entire processor resource made of *K* PE with the entire memory resource made of *K* ME, then for a more complex and faster single-staged network a message transit between every pair of nodes of the communication path will be delayed by a pair of consecutive connecting elements in the path, whereas for a multistaged interconnection network, this transit will be delayed by $2n = 2 \log_2 K$ consecutive connecting elements. At the same

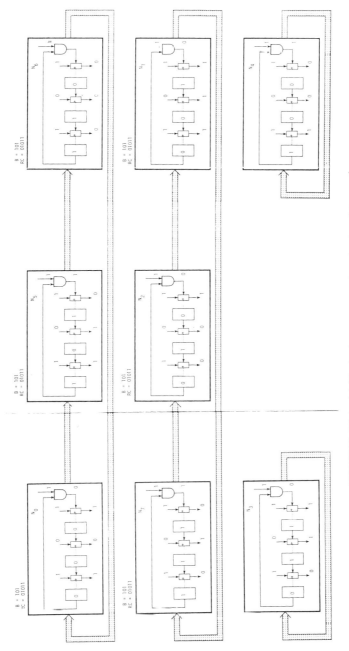

FIGURE II.15(a) (a) Single ring structure, described by $SF_1 = [3^1]$

57

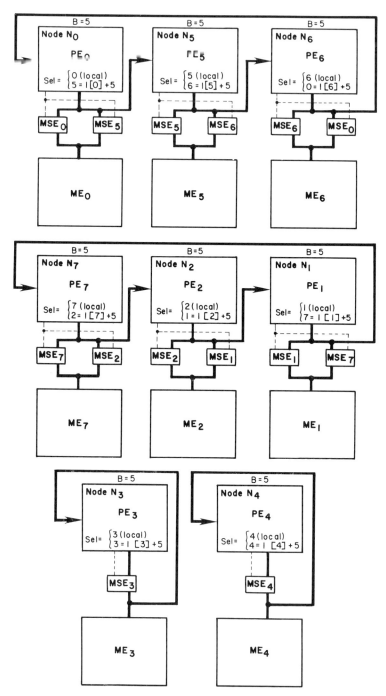

FIGURE II.15(b) Interconnections in the bus that support single ring structure, $SF_1 = [3^1]$

time, a single-staged network will require K_2 connecting elements with a single-port bidirectional broadcast, whereas a multiple-staged network will take $K/2 \cdot \log_2 K$ connecting elements with a four-port bidirectional broadcast or $2K \cdot \log_2 K$ connecting elements with single-port bidirectional broadcast.

Note: If each N → N* connection will take only one connecting element for a single-staged network or n connecting elements for a multiple-staged network, then for every node N it becomes impossible to perform either local or nonlocal memory-processor data exchanges (PE → ME, PE → ME*, or ME → PE*).

The only allowable exchange for such a network becomes PE → PE*. Since this network will have only PE → PE* communications, it will have neither local nor nonlocal PE → ME communications. It will thus become merely infeasible, since any processor PE will be incapable of sending a data array to a memory (local or nonlocal).

For the single-staged network of Fig. II.15(b), since all nodes receive the same bias B = 101, all of them establish N → N* connections concurrently. Therefore, the network reconfigures into the structure of Fig. II.15(b) during the time of one bit shift (one gate delay, t_d) and one mod-2 addition ($2t_d$). Thus, the entire reconfiguration time takes the time of $3t_d$ delay and can be executed during one clock period.

This is true for reconfiguration into any network structure, since different network structures are distinguished only by different biases and different types of SRVB that may be activated in each network node. To this end, each shift register SRVB is classified as follows:

a. It can be either *single* or *composite*, where a composite SRVB consists of $k > 1$ single SRVBs.

b. Each component shift register of a composite SRVB may perform either circular or noncircular shifts, denoted as $1[N]_1$ and $1[N]_0$, respectively.

In Fig. II.15(a), each SRVB is *single*, since each shift register performs a circular shift. In Fig. II.16(b), there is a composite SRVB having size $n = 5$ and consisting of three single shift registers, of which the one leftmost performs noncircular shift and the two rightmost perform circular shifts, respectively. The network structure generated with the SRVB and receiving bias B = 00011 is shown in Fig. II.16(a). It consists of two four-rooted binary trees.

Reconfiguration of any SRVB into any given type (single, composite, circular, noncircular) is performed with the special reconfiguration code RC that is brought to each network node requested for reconfiguration with the special reconfiguration instruction described in [6]. Therefore, concurrent reconfiguration into any network structure is accomplished with the following two codes: (1) bias B and (2) reconfiguration code RC. Techniques for selecting these codes are presented below in this Section.

4.3.5 Problem of Network Analysis and Synthesis

When we apply our shift-register theory for generating multicomputer networks, the following problems of consequence must be solved.

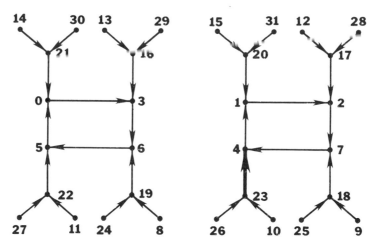

FIGURE II.16(a) Multiple tree structure

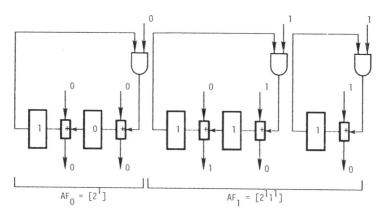

FIGURE II.16(b) Configuration of the SRVB which generates the multiple tree structure of Fig. 11.16(a)

Network Analysis. Given a type of SRVB and bias B, find the network structure that is generated with this SRVB.

Network Synthesis. Given the configuration of a network structure, find the SRVB and bias B that can generate either this structure or a larger one that properly contains the given configuration as a substructure.

It should be noted that the network analysis and synthesis are complementary inasmuch as a solution of the analysis problem provides an insight into all possible network structures that can be obtained. This will give a programmer an invaluable insight into how many structures are nonisomorphic and what biases must be selected to generate nonisomorphic structures. Thus, the solution of the analysis problem will lead to a minimization of the total memory space required to store a table of different network structures and the different SRVBs and biases that can generate them.

On the other hand, solution of the synthesis problem is of extreme practical necessity to a programmer. Indeed, the task of the programmer is to reconfigure a multicomputer network into a given network structure obtained from the analysis of a complex algorithm. To do so he or she must select the type of SRVB and bias B that generate this structure. Thus, he or she needs the solution of the synthesis problem.

4.4 Classification Among Network Structures: Overview and Examples

This subsection will classify all network structures that can be generated by concurrent SRVBs residing in each network node. Assume that network nodes are interconnected with the DC-bus described in Chapter 3, Vol. 1, this series and also in [6-8]. Thus, due to space considerations, the description of this bus is not repeated in this Chapter. Each reconfiguration is concurrent and carried out by all affected network nodes with the use of only two codes: reconfiguration code, RC, and bias B, where RC reconfigures a SRVB into a specific *shifting format* and B generates a unique successor N* of N in the new network structure that will be formed.

This subsection will also present a technique for finding the RC code. Techniques for finding biases for single, ring and tree structures and composite ring structures are given in subsections 4.5, 4.6, 4.7, and 4.8, Chapter II. In general, classification among network structures as well as finding the RC code are contingent on the types of SRVB that can be formed via reconfiguration.

4.4.1 Single and Composite SRVB

As was indicated above, each SRVB can be either a single or a composite shift register consisting of several single SRVBs. Thus, reconfiguration of an n-bit SRVB into a composite shift register is understood as its partitioning into p single shift registers, of size k_i ($i = 1, \ldots, p$). Therefore, each composite SRVB will be described with the *shifting format*,

$$SF = [k_1, k_2, \ldots, k_p]$$

where $n = k_1 + \ldots, + k_p$.

Since the formulas that describe generated network structures depend on the number, r_i, of shift registers having size i, it will be convenient to represent shifting formats in the following form:

$$SF = [1^{r_1}, 2^{r_2}, \ldots, t^{r_t}]$$

where r_i ($r_i \geq 0$) will be called the *multiplicity* of the i-bit shift register. Thus,

$$n = r_1 + 2r_2 + \ldots, + t \cdot r_t.$$

Since each single shift register of the shifting format SF may perform either circular shift if feedback input FI $= 1$ or noncircular shift if FI $= 0$, the shifting format SF may be divided into the following categories:

    a. *Circular* SF_1, when all its single shift registers perform circular shifts.

    b. *Noncircular* SF_0, when all its single shift registers perform noncircular shifts.

    c. *Mixed* SF_{10}, when single shift registers described by it perform circular and noncircular shifts.

It will be convenient to represent mixed SF_{10} as a union of circular and noncircular SF; i.e., $SF_{10} = SF_1 \cup SF_0$, where SF_1 includes all circular single shift registers and SF_0 includes all noncircular ones. For instance, if $SF_{10} = [3_0^1, 4_1^2, 5_1^1, 2_0^2]$, then $SF_1 = [4^2, 5^1]$ and $SF_0 = [3^1, 2^2]$; i.e., $SF_{10} = SF_1 \cup SF_0$.

4.4.2 Reconfiguration of a SRVB Into a Given Shifting Format, SF

Reconfiguration of the SRVB into any given shifting format will be performed with the reconfiguration code, RC. The code RC is stored in the reconfiguration instruction and described as follows: RC is a $(2n - 1)$-bit code, where n is the size of each SRVB. It consists of $(n - 1)$ 2-bit zones, Z_i, consisting of bits F_i and S_i, and one 1-bit zone, Z_0, including only 1 bit, F_0. Thus, RC $= (Z_{n-1}, Z_{n-2}, \ldots, Z_1, Z_0)$, where $Z_i = (F_i, \ S_i)$ if $i \neq 0$ and $Z_0 = F_0$ (Fig. II.17).

Each zone Z_i encodes, respectively, feedback and shifting paths for the two bits, b_i and b_{i-1}, of the SRVB, where b_i is more significant than b_{i-1}. For instance, in Fig. II.17, for $n = 5$, RC $= (Z_4, Z_3, Z_2, Z_1, Z_0)$, and zone Z_4 encodes the feedback path ending in b_4 (bit F_4) and the shift path from b_3 to b_4 (bit S_4); zone Z_3 encodes the feedback path ending in b_3 (bit F_3) and the shift path from b_2 to b_3 (bit S_3), etc. Finally, the least significant zone, Z_0, has only 1 bit, F_0, associated with the feedback path routed to bit b_0 and no shift path from the next less significant bit since b_0 is the LSB of the SRVB.

For each zone, $Z_i = (F_i, S_i)$, the values of F_i and S_i show what type of path is activated for every pair of consecutive bits, b_i and b_{i-1}. If $F_i = 1$, the respective feedback input, FI, is activated. This means that b_i receives circular feedback information controlled by bit F_i and receives no shift information controlled by bit S_i from the next less signficant bit, b_{i-1}. If $F_i = 0$, feedback input is deactivated. This means that either bit b_i receives no feedback controlled by F_i and only shift controlled by S_i, or bit b_i receives a noncircular feedback (for trees and stars).

Bit $S_i = 1$ of zone Z_i stands for left shift from b_{i-1} to b_i and $S_i = 0$ stands for no shift from b_{i-1}. Therefore, together F_i and S_i show what type of path is activated between b_i and b_{i-1}: shift path ($F_i = 0$, $S_i = 1$) or feedback path to b_i and no shift from b_{i-1} ($F_i = 0$ or 1, $S_i = 0$). Therefore, for zone Z_i, if $S_i = 1$, $F_i = 0$; if $S_i = 0$, $F_i = 0$ or 1.

Since $S_i = 1$ means that bits b_i and b_{i-1} belong to the same shift register and $S_i = 0$ means that they belong to different shift registers, each $\overline{S}_i$ is sent to activate a new feedback path initiated in the next less significant bit b_{i-1}. Likewise, each S_i is

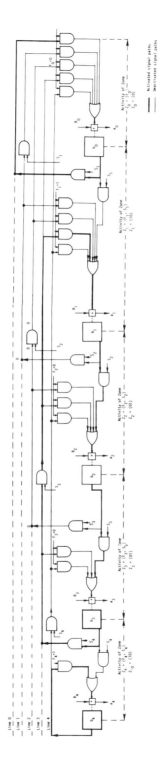

FIGURE II.17 Activation of the shifting format $SF = [1_1, 3_1, 1_0] = [1, 3]_1 \cup [1]_0$ in the 5-bit SRVB

63

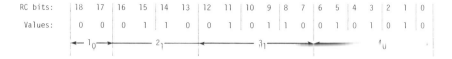

FIGURE II.18   Formation of the reconfiguration code RC for the shifting format $SF_{10} = [1_0, 2_1, 3, 4_0]$

sent not only to a shift path between b_i and b_{i-1}, but also to the feedback path initiated in b_i, either to maintain both paths ($S_i = 1$) or block the unwanted transfer of either b_i to less significant bits of the shift register or b_{i-1} to b_i ($S_i = 0$).

As follows from the above, reconfiguration code RC can be easily selected by a programmer given a shifting format SF.

Example.   Consider formation of the RC code for $SF = [1_0, 2_1, 3_1, 4_0]$, where $n = 1 + 2 + 3 + 4 = 10$. The number of bits in the RC code is $2n - 1 = 19$. For the leftmost significant shift register, 1_0, since $k_1 = 1$, the number of 01 zones is $k_1 - 1 = 0$.

Two adjacent shift registers, 1_0 and 2_1, are separated by zone 00, since 1_0 performs noncircular shift. Thus, bits 18 and 17 store 00 (Fig. II.18). For the 2_1 shift register, the number of 01 zones is $k_2 - 1 = 2 - 1 = 1$. Thus, bits 16 and 15 store 01. Two adjacent shift registers, 2_1 and 3_1, are separated with zone 10 (bits 14 and 13), since 2_1 performs circular shift. For the 3_1 register, the number of 01 zones is $3 - 1 = 2$. They are in bits 12, 11 and 10, 9. Adjacent registers, 3_1 and 4_0, are separated with the 10 zone (bits 8, 7), since 3_1 performs circular shift. Finally, for the 4_0 shift register, the number of 01 zones is $4 - 1 = 3$, and the least significant bit is 0, since 4_0 performs noncircular shift.   ∎

4.4.3 Types of Network Structures

Before attacking the general analysis and synthesis problem introduced in Sec. 4.3.5, one must establish a classification of the network structures that can be generated by SRVBs. Since shifting formats describing a SRVB can be (1) single and composite and (2) circular, noncircular, and mixed, the classification below is based on the attributes 1 and 2 and is shown in Fig. II.19.

Accordingly, the network structures are divided into single and composite if they are generated by single and composite SRVBs, respectively. Single structures are further subdivided into single tree structures, STSs, generated by single SF_0 and single ring structures, SRS, generated by single SF_1.

Composite structures are divided into composite ring structures, CRS, generated by composite SF_1; composite stars, CS, generated by composite SF_0; and mixed structures generated by mixed $SF_{10} = SF_1 \cup SF_0$. The mixed structure is a composite multiple-tree structure, CMTS, if SF_0 is single, or it is a composite multiple-star structure, MSS, if SF_0 is composite. Below is an illustration of each type of structure which is described by this classification.

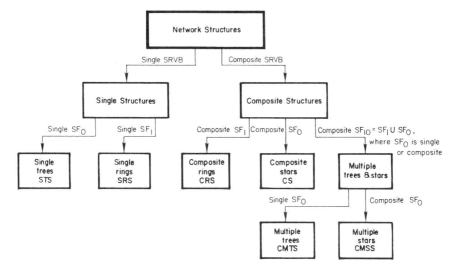

FIGURE II.19 Classification among network structures generated with the use of SRVB

4.4.3.1 Single ring structures, SRS, generated by single SRVB with circular shifting formats, $SF_1 = [n^1]$

Figure II.15 shows a single ring structure generated by $SF_1 = [3^1]$ receiving bias $B = 101$.

4.4.3.2 Single tree structures, STS, generated by single SRVB with noncircular shifting formats, $SF_0 = [n^1]$

Figure II.20(a, b) shows the STS described by the $SF_0 = [4^1]$ and generated by bias $B = 1001$. As seen, it is a four-level binary tree having a single root, $R = 0111$; R forms a cycle of period 1 since it succeeds itself in this tree. Indeed, the successor $N*$ of R is $N* = 1[R]_0 + B = 1[0111]_0 + 1001 = 1110 + 1001 = 0111$.

4.4.3.3 Composite ring structures, CRS, generated by composite SRVB with circular arithmetic formats, $AF_1 = [1^{r_1}, 2^{r_2}, \ldots, n^{r_n}]$

Figure II.21(a) and II.21(b) show a CRS structure generated by $SF_1 = [2^1, 3^1]$ and the SRVB receiving bias $B = 10010$ that generates this structure.

4.4.3.4 Composite star structures, CSS, generated by composite SRVB with noncircular shifting formats, $SF_0 = [1^{r_1}, 2^{r_2}, \ldots, n_{r_n}]$

Figure II.22 features a composite star described by $SF_0 = [3^1, 2^1]$. This star is generated by the SRVB given by $SF_0 = [2^1, 3^1]$ and receiving bias $B = 00101$.

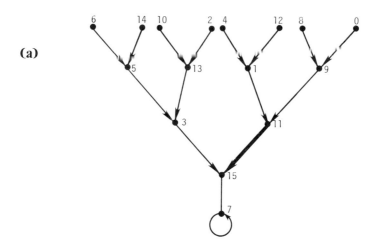

(a)

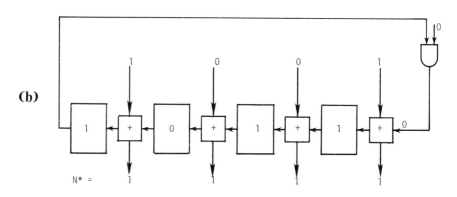

(b)

FIGURE II.20(a, b) The STS described by the $SF_0 = [4^1]$

4.4.3.5 Multiple tree structures, MTS, generated by composite SRVB with mixed $SF_{10} = SF_1$ or SF_0, where SF_0 describes single noncircular SRVB

$SF_{10} = [1^{r_n}, 2^{r_2}, \ldots, n^{r_n}]_1 \cup [p^1]_0$, where p is the number of levels in an MTS. Fig. II.16(b) shows a composite shift register with $SF_{10} = [2^1]_0 \cup [2^1, 1^1]_1$. The MTS structure generated with it is shown in Fig. II.16(a). Since $p = 2$, we obtain a two-level MTS.

4.4.3.6 Multiple star structures, MSS, generated by composite SRVB with mixed $SF_{10} = SF_1 \times SF_0$, where SF_0 described composite noncircular SRVB

$$SF = [1^{r_1}, 2^{r_2}, \ldots, N^{r_n}]_1 \cup [1^{k_1}, 2^{k_2}, \ldots, p^{k_p}]_0$$

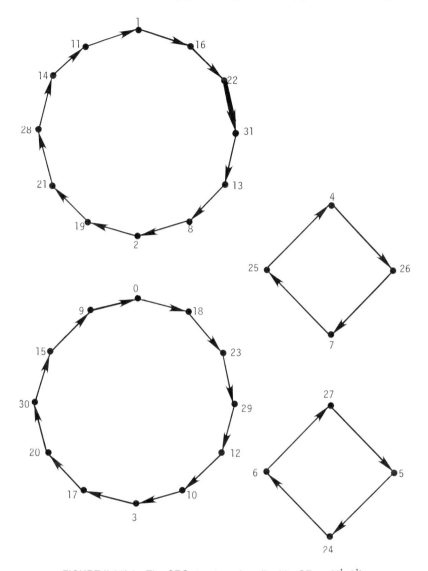

FIGURE II.21(a) The CRS structure described by $SF_1 = [2^1, 3^1]$

Figure II.23 shows an MSS structure described by $SF_{10} = [2^1]_1 \cup [2^1, 1^1]_0$; the shift register that generates this structure is shown in Fig. II.24. It receives $B = 01101$.

To solve the analysis problem for a general case of an SRVB described with an arbitrary shifting format, SF, consider single structures (trees and rings) generated with single shift registers, i.e., those identified by $SF = [n^1]$, circular or noncircular. These will be discussed in Subsections 4.5 and 4.6.

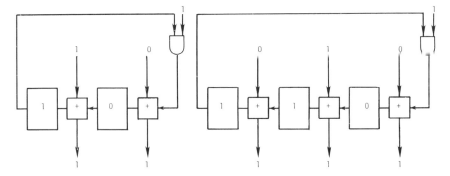

FIGURE II.21(b) Configuration of the SRVB which generates the CRS of Fig. II.21(a)

(a)

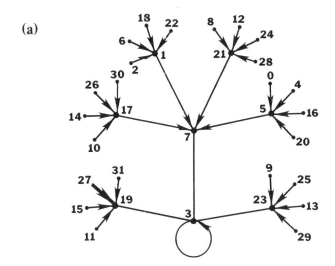

(b)

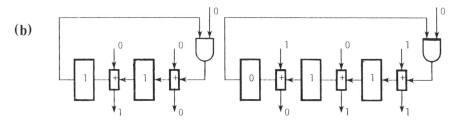

FIGURE II.22 Composite star structure (CSS) described by $SF_0 = [2^1, 3^1]$

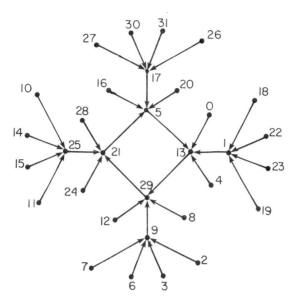

FIGURE II.23 Multiple star structure (MSS) described by $SF_{10} = [2^1], U[2^1, 1^1]_0$

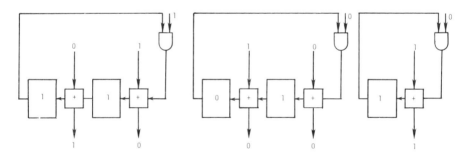

FIGURE II.24 Configuration of the SRVB which generates the MSS of Fig. II.23

4.5 Single Ring Structures: Analysis and Synthesis

A *single ring structure*, SRS, is a set of rings that is generated by single shift registers available in network nodes. An SRS is defined as follows:

a. A set of periods, $SP = \{T\}$, where T is the period of a ring generated in the SRS.
b. The number $D(T)$ of rings having the same period, T.

Therefore, we define SRS as SRS $= \{D(T):T \in SP\}$.

To introduce formulas that show how to find sets SP and SRS, respectively, we have to consider a *generic ring (GRI)* produced by bias B

4.5.1 Generic Ring

A *generic ring* is a ring that is generated by a circular SRVB ($SF_1 = [n^1]$) storing bias B. Thus bias B is always the first node of GRI and 0 is its last node because 0 is succeeded by B. In other words, GRI $= \{A_0 = B, A_1, \ldots, A_{T-1} = 0\}$, where T is the period of GRI.

Figure II.25 shows GRI $= \{4, 5, 7, 3, 2, 0\}$ of period $T = 6$ generated by a 3-bit circular shift register receiving bias B $= 4$. The same shift register receiving B $= 101$ generates GRI of period T $= 3$ (Fig. II.15). Therefore, it is necessary to study more closely the structure of bias B in order to find the period of a generic ring.

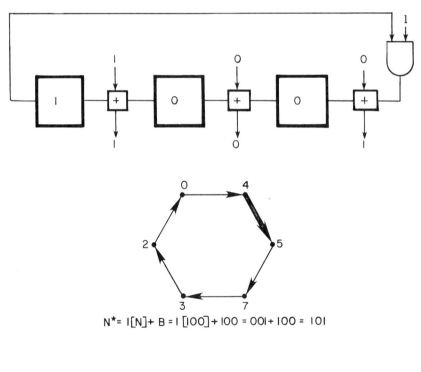

$$N^* = I[N] + B = I[100] + 100 = 001 + 100 = 101$$

$$N^* = I[N] + B = I[110] + 100 = 101 + 100 = 001$$

FIGURE II.25 Generic ring of period T $= 6$

4.5.2 Bias Structure

Since bias B is a binary number, it can be given by its *one's positions,* hereafter called *generating position, GP,* as

$$B = GP_1 + GP_2 \ldots + GP_t$$

where t is called the *bias weight.*

Since a SRVB receives bias B, then the SRVB bits can be divided into two categories:

a . *Generating positions,* GP_i ($i = 1, \ldots, t$), where each GP_i immediately follows the mod-2 adder fed with the respective generating position of the bias.

b. *Propagating positions,* PP, where each PP propagates the value of the preceding bit of the SRVB.

Each propagating position located between GP_i and GP_{i+1} is assigned the same index i, such as $PP(i)$, of the immediate less significant GP_i, because every $PP(i)$ propagates the value of this GP_i with no modifications.

Example. In Fig. II.26(a), generating bits of the 9-bit SRVB receiving bias B = 000110010 are $GP_1 = 2$, $GP_2 = 16$, and $GP_3 = 32$. There are two propagating positions, $PP_1(1)$ and $PP_2(1)$, that follow GP_1. Between GP_2 and GP_3, there are no propagating positions. Finally, between GP_3 and GP_1 there are four propagating positions: $PP_1(3)$, $PP_2(3)$, $PP_3(3)$, and $PP_4(3)$. ■

Bias distance, a_i ($i = 1, \ldots, t$), represents the number of shifts between two generating positions, GP_i and GP_{i+1}, i.e., $GP_{i+1} = a_i[GP_i]$. Since for a single ring structure, SRVB performs a circular shift, then $GP_1 = a_t[GP_t]$. Obviously,

$$a_1 + a_2 + \ldots + a_t = n$$

If such a_i's are selected that n given by the above expression can be factorized as $n = p \bullet m = p(b_1 + b_2 + \ldots + b_d)$, where

$$m = b_1 + b_2 + \ldots + b_d \qquad (2)$$

is called the *bias period,* and p is the number of such identical sums, called the *bias index,* then bias B will be called *m-reducible.*

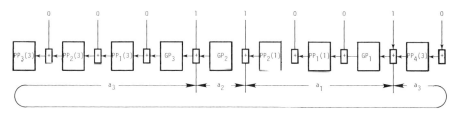

FIGURE II.26(a) Generating and propagating positions of the SRVB receiving bias
B = 000110010

For an m-reducible bias, since

$$p \cdot m = n, \quad p \cdot d = t, \tag{3}$$

because each addend b_i in the bias period represents p identical distances: $b_i = a_i = a_{d+i} = a_{2d+i} = \ldots = a_{(p-1)+i}$, where $i = 1, \ldots, d$. Integer d is called the *bias dimension*. Bias B is called *even-weighted* if t is an even integer and *odd-weighted* if t is an odd integer.

Example.   Bias B = 00111   00111   00111   is 5-reducible since the bias distances,
$\quad\quad\quad\quad\quad\quad\quad\quad m \quad\quad\quad m \quad\quad\quad m$

a_1 through a_9, form three bias periods, $m = 5$, giving bias index $p = 3$ and bias dimension $d = 3$. Therefore, $n = m \cdot p = 15$ and $t = p \cdot d = 3 \cdot 3 = 9$ [Fig. II.26(b)].

From this definition, if $p = 1$ and $n = m$, bias B becomes *n-reducible* or *irreducible*. For the n-reducible bias, $t = d$, i.e., the bias dimension d coincides with the bias weight t; for the m-reducible bias, d is a divisor of t, not coincident with t.

If t is odd, then both the bias index p and the bias dimension d are odd, because $t = p \cdot d$. If t is even, then either d is even and/or p is even. As will be shown below, if t is odd, the period of the generic ring is always $2m$, where $m \cdot p = n$. If t is even, then the period of the generic ring is $2m$ if d is odd, or it is m if d is even. Thus, m, p, d, and t are crucial parameters for finding the period of the generic ring. The next section finds the period of the generic ring is found in Sec. 4.5.3.1 for an odd-weighted bias and in Sec. 4.5.3.2 for an even-weighted bias. ∎

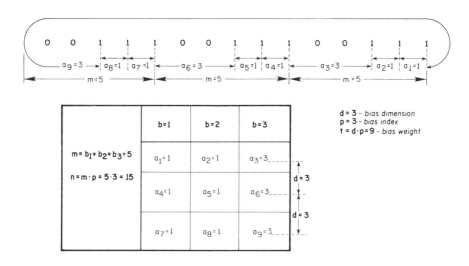

FIGURE II.26(b) Structure of the 5-reducible bias: B = 00111   00111   00111

4.5.3 Period of Generic Ring

Given the generic ring GRI = $\{A_0 = B, A_1, A_2, \ldots, A^{T-1} = 0\}$.

Let SGP_i be a set that includes the same generating position, GP_i, taken out from the words, $A_0, A_1, \ldots, A_{T-1}$, of the generic ring; i.e., $SGP_1 = \{GP_1(A_0), GP_1(A_1), GP_1(A_2), \ldots, GP_1(A_{T-1})\}$, $SGP_2 = \{GP_2(A_0), GP_2(A_1), GP_2(A_2), \ldots, GP_2(A_{T-1})\}$, $\ldots, SGP^t = \{GP_t(A_0), GP_t(A_1), GP_t(A_2), \ldots, GP_t(A_{T-1})\}$. Then one can establish the following interesting properties for the sets $SGP_1, SGP_2, \ldots, SGP_t$, for case 1 when bias weight is odd (odd-weighted bias) and case 2 when bias weight is even (even-weighted bias).

4.5.3.1 Generic ring period for an odd-weighted bias

For an odd-weighted bias $B = GR_1 + GP_2 + \ldots + GP_t$ having $GP_2 = a_1[GP_1]$, $GP_3 = a_2[GP_2], \ldots, GP_t = a_{t-1}[GP_{t-1}]$ and $GP_1 = a_t[GP_t]$, the sets of generating positions have the following structure, which is given with greater detail for SGP_1 and then generalized for SGP_i .

In other words, SGP_1 consists of two half-sets, HGP and $\overline{\text{HGP}}$, respectively. Each half-set includes alternating ones and zeros fields consisting of consecutive ones and zeros, respectively. The size of each field is a bias distance a_j $(j = t, t - 1, \ldots, a_1)$. Since t is odd, in each half-set the values of the two boundary fields (leftmost and rightmost) with sizes a_t and a_1, respectively, are always the same. In the HGP half-set, a_t and a_1 define the one's fields. In the $\overline{\text{HGP}}$ half-set, a_t and a_1 define the zero's fields. A shorter notation for SGH_1 is

$$(4)$$

where 1 or 0 show the value of the field, and the subscript below shows its size. Thus, $1_4 = 1111, 0_2 = 00$, etc.

Similarly, one can find all the other sets of generating positions, SGP. In general, for SGP_i, since GP_i is a_{i-1}bit shifted from GP_{i-1}, as $GP_i = a_{i-1}[GP_i]$, the sequence of bias distances that specify the sizes of alternating fields is $a_{i-1}, a_{i-2}, \ldots, a_1, a_t, \ldots, a_i$ and

$$\overset{\overset{\displaystyle\longleftarrow\text{—HGP—}\quad\overline{\text{HGP}}\text{—}\longrightarrow}{}}{SGP_1} = \{1_{a_{i-1}}, 0_{a_{1-2}}, 1_{a_{i-3}}, \ldots, 1_{a_i}, \cup\, 0_{a_{i-1}}, 1_{a_{i-2}}, 0_{a_{i-3}}, \ldots, 0_{a_i}\}$$ (5)

If $i = t$, then, for the most significant GP_t, the set SGP_t, is

$$SGP_1 = \{1_{a_{t-1}}, 0_{a_{t-2}}, 1_{a_{t-3}}, \ldots, 0_{a_1}, 1_{a_t}\, \cup\, 0_{a_{t-1}}, 1_{a_{t-2}}, 0_{a_{t-3}}, \ldots, 1_{a_1}, 0_{a_t}\}$$

In general, the physical explanation of this interesting structure of each SGP set is as follows: this structure is determined by the ability of each generating position of an SRVB to set its value into 1 if the preceding bit is 0 and to reset its value into 0 if the preceding bit is 1 (Fig. II.27).

On the other hand, propagating positions only propagate the values of preceding bits of SRVB. Thus, for a GP_i of an SRVB that produces a generating ring, if all the preceding propagating positions store 1, GP_i will assume consecutive zeros in SGP_i. The number of such consecutive zeros in the set SGP_i is a_{i-1}, which is the distance between GP_i and GP_{i-1}. If all the preceding propagating positions store 0 (as in $A_0 = B$), GP_i assumes consecutive ones in SGP_i. The number of such consecutive ones is also a_{i-1}. This property ensures alternation of ones and zeros fields in each set of generating position, SGP.

Example. For the 6-bit SRVB receiving bias $B = \underset{a_3}{001}\ \underset{a_2}{01}\ \underset{a_1}{1}$, the generating positions are $GP1 = 1$, $GP_2 = 2$, and $GP_3 = 8$. The bias distances are $a_1 = 1$, $a_2 = 2$, and $a_3 = 3$. When this SRVB stores B, it forms the following generating ring, GRI, of period 12 (Fig. II.28). GRI = {11, 29, 49, 40, 26, 63, 52, 34, 14, 23, 37, 0} = {001011, 011101, 110001, 101000, 011010, 111111, 110100, 100010, 001110, 010111, 100101, 000000}. Thus, we obtain the following sets SGP_i $(i = 1, 2, 3)$:

$$SGP_1 = \overset{\overset{\displaystyle\longleftarrow n\longrightarrow\!\!\longleftarrow n\longrightarrow}{}}{\{\underset{\leftarrow a_3\rightarrow}{111}\ \underset{\leftarrow a_2\rightarrow}{00}\ \underset{\leftarrow a_1\rightarrow}{1}\ \underset{\leftarrow a_3\rightarrow}{000}\ \underset{\leftarrow a_2\rightarrow}{11}\ \underset{a_1}{0}\,\}} = \{1_3, 0_2, 1_1, \cup\, 0_3, 1_2, 0_1\}$$

$$SGP_2 = \overset{\overset{\displaystyle\longleftarrow n\longrightarrow\!\!\longleftarrow n\longrightarrow}{}}{\{\underset{\leftarrow a_1\rightarrow}{1}\ \underset{\leftarrow a_3\rightarrow}{000}\ \underset{\leftarrow a_2\rightarrow}{11}\ \underset{a_1}{0}\ \underset{\leftarrow a_3\rightarrow}{111}\ \underset{a_2}{00}\,|\}} = \{1_1, 0_3, 1_2, \cup\, 0_3, 1_2, 0_1\}$$

$$SGP_3 = \overset{\overset{\displaystyle\longleftarrow n\longrightarrow\!\!\longleftarrow n\longrightarrow}{}}{\{\underset{\leftarrow a_2\rightarrow}{11}\ \underset{\leftarrow a_1\rightarrow}{0}\ \underset{\leftarrow a_3\rightarrow}{111}\ \underset{a_2}{00}\ \underset{\leftarrow a_1\rightarrow}{1}\ \underset{a_3}{000}\,\}} = \{1_3, 0_2, 1_1, \cup\, 0_1, 1_3, 0_2\}$$

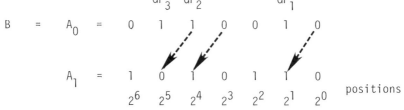

FIGURE II.27 Set-reset property of generating positions

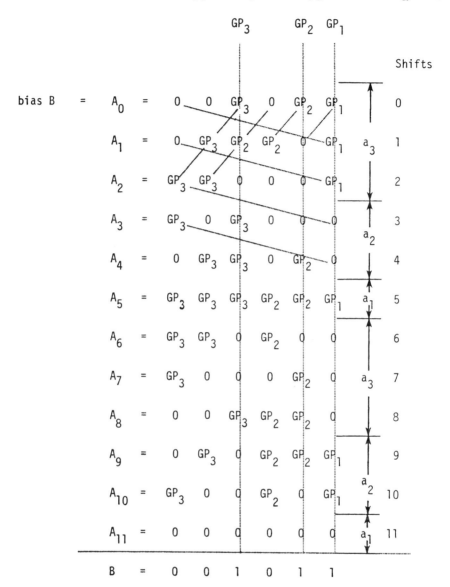

FIGURE II.28 Formation of GRI with period T = 12 receiving bias B = 001011

As follows, in each SGP the two half-sets, HGP and $\overline{\text{HGP}}$, are complements; i.e., SGP = HGP ∪ $\overline{\text{HGP}}$. As follows from the structure of each SGP_i, if bias B is *m*-reducible, then the period of each SGP_i is 2*m*; that is, following 2*m* words in generic ring GRI, the meanings of generating position GP_i are repeated. If bias B is *n*-reducible, the period of each SGP_i is 2*n*. ∎

Example. Let

$$
\begin{array}{ccc}
GP_3 & GP_2 & GP_1 \\
\downarrow & \downarrow & \downarrow \\
\text{bias } B = \quad 100 & 100 & 100
\end{array}
$$

Since $a_1 = a_2 = a_3 = 3$ and $n = 9$, $m = 3$ and $p = 3$; that is, $m \cdot p = 3 \cdot 3 = 9$. Therefore, this bias is 3-reducible. Let us build SGP_1, SGP_2, and SGP_3 for generating positions GP_1, GP_2, and GP_3, respectively.

For GP_1, since GP_1 is obtained via the a_3-bit shift of GP_3, $GP_1 = a_3[GP_3] = 3[GP_3]$, the sequence of bias distances that specify the field sizes is a_3, a_2, a_1. Thus,

$$
SGP_1 = \{ \underbrace{111}_{a_3} \; \underbrace{000}_{a_2} \; \underbrace{111}_{a_1} \; \cup \; \underbrace{000}_{a_3} \; \underbrace{111}_{a_2} \; \underbrace{000}_{a_1} \} = \{111 \; \cup \; 000\}
$$

As follows, the period of SGP_1 is $2m = 6$, since, following the six words of generic GRI, the values of SGP_1 are repeated (Fig. II.29). Similarly, for SGP_2, since $GP_2 = a_1[GP_1]$, we have the following sequence of ones and zeros fields alternation in SGP_2: a_1, a_3, a_2 That is,

$$
SGP_1 = \{ \underbrace{111}_{a_1} \; \underbrace{000}_{a_3} \; \underbrace{111}_{a_2} \; \cup \; \underbrace{000}_{a_1} \; \underbrace{111}_{a_3} \; \underbrace{000}_{a_2} \} = \{111 \; \cup \; 000\}
$$

			GP_3			GP_2			GP_1		
B	=	A_0 =	1	0	0	1	0	0	1	0	0
		A_1 =	1	0	1	1	0	1	1	0	1
		A_2 =	1	1	1	1	1	1	1	1	1
		A_3 =	0	1	1	0	1	1	0	1	1
		A_4 =	0	1	0	0	1	0	0	1	0
		A_5 =	0	0	0	0	0	0	0	0	0
B	=	A_0 =	1	0	0	1	0	0	1	0	0

FIGURE II.29 Generic ring of period T = 6 formed with 3-reducible bias B = 100100100

and

$$SGP_3 = \{111 \cup 000\}$$

We now construct a set of propagating position, SPP*(i), where a PP(i) follows the generating position, GP_i .

Clearly, SPP$_j(i)$ is a j-bit shift of SGP$_i$, where j changes from $j = 1$ to $j = a_i-1$ since any propagating position only propagates the information received from the preceding bit. Thus, SPP$_1(i) = 1[SGP_i]$; SPP$_2(i) = 2[SGP_i]$, . . . , SPP$_{a_{i-1}}(i) = (a_i - 1)$ [SGP$_i$]. Therefore, if $2m$ is the period of SGP$_i$, it is also the period of any SPP$_j(i)$, where $j = 1, \ldots, a_i-1, i = 1, \ldots, t$. Thus, $2m$ is the period of the generic ring. ■

We can now formulate this result as follows:

Theorem 1. For an odd-weighted m-reducible bias B, the period of the generic ring is always $2m$, where $m \cdot p = n$ and m is the bias period and n is the size of the SRVB.

Corollary. For an n-reducible or irreducible bias having $m \cdot p = n \cdot 1 = n$, the period of the generic ring is $2n$.

4.5.3.2 An even-weighted bias B

Let us now discuss the structures of the sets of generating and propagating positions for an even-weighted bias B. The next step is to determine the period of the generic ring produced by an even-weighted bias B.

For an even-weighted bias $B = GP_1 + GP_2 + \ldots + GP_t$, the sets of generating positions have the same structure of alternating ones and zeros fields as for an odd-weighted bias B, because this property of SGP$_i$ is caused by the fundamental ability of each GP$_i$ to complement the value of a_{i-1} positions ($a_i - 1$ propagating and one generating) that precede GP$_i$ in the SRVB and are shifted into the GP$_i$ location in the generic ring.

Therefore, if bias is m-reducible, where $m = b_1 + b_2 + \ldots + b_d$, the period of alternation of ones and zeros fields in each SGP$_i$ becomes m if d is even and $2m$ if d is odd. This establishes the following theorem that specifies the period of generic ring produced by an even-weighted bias.

Theorem 2. For an even-weighted m-reducible bias B, the period of the generic ring $T = m$ if bias dimension d is even, and $T = 2m$ if bias dimension d is odd, where $m = b_1 + b_2 + \ldots + b_d$.

Corollary. An even-weighted irreducible bias generates GRI with period n, since $d = t$ is even.

4.5.4 Transforming a Generic Ring Into Another Ring of Single Ring Structure

The material below is aimed at developing a transformation technique that modifies a generic ring into any other ring, RI, that can be generated by a single and circular SRVB. Thus the procedures that are developed are aimed at the solution of the following problem: Given generic ring GRI or period T and bias B. Let T^* be the period of another ring in single ring structure. Find a generic state A_0^* that generates this ring if the bias B is the same,

The significance of solving this problem is as follows. First, we will be able to specify a single ring structure, SRS, for given size, n, of SRVB that receives bias B. Thus, we will solve the analysis problem for SRS. Alternately, if an SRS configuration is given, we can find out how this configuration can be generated with SRVB. This will solve the synthesis problem for SRS. Second, one can find out what bias should be selected in order that a given ring include a selectable node.

4.5.4.1 Approach outline

To find a generic state, A_0^*, of a new ring, we will modify bias B with the special modification code, MC, that will constructed below to give $A_0^* = B + MC$. Since by condition, a new ring, RI, with period T^* is generated with the same bias B that has created generic ring GRI, this ring has the same generating positions, GP_1, GP_2, ..., GP_t, that characterize bias B. In this ring, these positions also form sets of generating positions, SGP_1^*, SGP_2^*, ..., SGP_t^*. The period of these sets, however, is T^*, since T^* is the period of the ring RI.

Thus, for each SGP_i with period T of the generic ring, there exists SGP_i^* with period T^* of a new ring, RI. Therefore, the transforms techniques will be aimed at modifying SGP_i into SGP_i^*. Since each SGP_i is formed of shifted bias digits modified by GP_i, GP_{i-1}, ..., GP_1, the modification of SGP_i^* will give us *bias modifiable positions,* i.e., those that will be modified with the MC code to yield A_0^*. (The MC code will thus have ones in these positions.) Since an odd-weighted and even-weighted bias generate two different types of GRI, the SRS structure depends only on two factors: the size n of SRVB and the type of bias selected (even-weighted or odd-weighted). Thus, we will develop these techniques for an odd-weighted bias in Sec. 4.5.4.2 and for even-weighted biases in Sec. 4.5.4.3.

4.5.4.2 Ring transform techniques for an odd-weighted bias B

First we illustrate these transform techniques via a special example. Thereafter, we develop them as algorithmic procedures.

Example. Given the following bias B:

	a_5		a_4		a_3	a_2	a_1	
Bias B =	0 1		0 0 0 1		0 0 0 1	0 0 1	0 1	(6)
bias digits	14 13		12 11 10 9		8 7 6 5	4 3 2	1 0	

with generating positions, $GP_1 = 1$, $GP_2 = 4$, $GP_3 = 32$, $GP_4 = 512$, and $GP_5 = 2^{13} = 4096$. Thus, bias weight $t = 5$ is odd. Bias distances are $a_1 = 2$, $a_2 = 3$, $a_3 = 4$, $a_4 = 4$, and $a_5 = 2$. Since $n = 2 + 3 + 4 + 4 + 2 = 15$, bias is irreducible. According to Theorem 1, it generates the GRI of period $2 \cdot n = 2 \cdot 15 = 30$. Let us construct the SGP_1 set for generating position GP_1: Since $GP_1 = a_t[GP_t] = a_5[GP_5]$, the sequence of bias distances that specifies the sizes of ones and zeros fields in SGP_1 set is a_5, a_4, a_3, a_2, a_1, and

$$SGP_1 = \{1_{a5}, 0_{a4}, 1_{a3}, 0_{a2}, 1_{a1}\} \cup \{0_{a5}, 1_{a4}, 0_{a3}, 1_{a2}, 0_{a1}\}$$
$$= \{1_2, 0_4, 1_4, 0_3, 1_2\} \cup \{0_2, 1_4, 0_4, 1_3, 0_2\}$$

where the half-set $HGP_1 = \{1_2, 0_4, 1_4, 0_3, 1_2\}$ and $\overline{HGP_1} = \{0_2, 1_4, 0_4, 1_3, 0_2\}$. As seen, the period of SGP_1 is $2 + 4 + 4 + 3 + 2 + 2 + 4 + 4 + 3 + 2 = 30$. Assume that this GRI is transformed into the new ring, RI, with period $T^* = 2m = 10$ and identified with the following set of generating positions: $SGP_1^* = \{1_5, 0_5\}$. The new ring will also have five SGP_i^*, since in generating it the SRVB will get the same bias that produced the GRI ring. Thus, the techniques to be developed are applicable to any SGP_i–SGP_i^* pair, where SGP_i is from the GRI and SGP_i^* is from a new ring belonging to a single ring structure.

Let us apply them to an SGP_1–SGP_1^* pair to find the bias positions that have to be modified to generate $SGP_1^* = \{1_5, 0_5\}$, since SGP_1^* has period $2m = 10$. Our procedures will be illustrated by the table in Fig. II.30. This table consists of eight columns. Column 1 identifies the states of GRI having period $T = 30$ and $A_0 = B$, where B is given by Eq. (6). Column 2 shows consecutive states of the GRI. Column 3 specifies

Col. 1		Col. 2														Col.3	Col.4	Col.5	Col.6	Col.7	Col.8
	GP_5				GP_4			GP_3			GP_2		GP_1		SGP_1*	Shifted Bias positions	MD	MC	A_0*		
GRI Nodes / Binary digits	14	13	12	11	10	9	8	7	6	5	4	3	2	1	0						
$A_0 = B$	0	1	0	0	0	1	0	0	0	1	0	0	1	0	1	1	0			
$A_1 =$	1	1	0	0	1	1	0	0	1	1	0	1	1	1	1	1	14	0	0
$A_2 =$	1	1	0	1	1	1	0	1	1	1	1	1	0	1	0	1	13	13	1	0
$A_3 =$	1	1	1	1	1	1	0	1	0	1	1	0	0	0	0	1	12	12	1	0
$A_4 =$	1	0	1	1	0	1	1	0	0	0	0	1	0	0	1	11	11	1	1
$A_5 =$	0	0	1	1	0	0	1	0	0	1	0	1	1	0	0	0	10	0		
$A_6 =$	0	0	0	0	0	0	0	1	1	1	1	0	1	0	9	9	1	0
$A_7 =$	0	0	0	0	0	1	0	1	1	0	1	1	1	1	0	8	8	1	1
$A_8 =$	0	1	0	0	1	1	1	1	0	0	1	1	0	1	1	0	7	7	1	1
$A_9 =$	1	1	0	1	1	0	1	0	0	0	1	0	0	1	1	0	6	6	1	1
$A_{10} =$	1	1	1	1	0	0	0	0	0	0	0	0	1	0	1	5	5	1	0
$A_{11} =$	1	0	1	0	0	0	0	0	1	0	0	0	0	0	1	4	4	1	1
$A_{12} =$	0	0	0	0	1	0	0	1	1	0	0	1	0	0	1	3	3	1	1
$A_{13} =$	0	1	0	1	1	1	0	1	1	1	0	1	1	0	1	1	2	0	1
$A_{14} =$	1	1	1	1	1	1	1	1	1	1	1	1	1	1	1	1	0	0
$A_{15} =$	1	0	1	1	1	0	1	1	0	1	1	0	1	0	0	0	0	1
$A_{16} =$	0	0	1	1	0	0	1	1	0	0	1	0	0	0	0	0	14	
$A_{17} =$	0	0	1	0	0	0	1	0	0	0	0	0	1	0	1	0	13	
$A_{18} =$	0	0	0	0	0	0	0	0	1	0	1	1	1	0	12	
$A_{19} =$	0	1	0	0	0	1	0	0	1	1	1	0	1	1	0	11	
$A_{20} =$	1	1	0	0	1	1	0	1	1	0	1	0	0	1	1	1	10	
$A_{21} =$	1	1	0	1	1	1	1	1	0	0	0	0	0	1	0	1	9	
$A_{22} =$	1	1	1	1	1	0	0	1	0	0	0	0	0	0	1	8	
$A_{23} =$	1	0	1	1	0	0	0	1	1	0	0	1	0	0	1	7	
$A_{24} =$	0	0	1	0	0	1	0	1	1	1	0	1	1	0	0	1	6	
$A_{25} =$	0	0	0	0	1	1	1	1	1	0	1	1	1	0	1	0	5	
$A_{26} =$	0	1	0	1	0	1	1	1	1	0	1	1	1	1	0	4	
$A_{27} =$	1	1	1	1	0	0	1	1	0	0	1	1	0	1	0	3	
$A_{28} =$	1	0	1	0	0	0	0	0	0	0	1	0	0	1	0	2	
$A_{29} =$	0	0	0	0	0	0	0	0	0	0	0	0	0	0	1	

FIGURE II.30 Ring transform technique

the set SGP_1 of generating position GP_1 of this ring. Column 4 shows the SGP_i^* set of a new ring with period $2m = 10$. Column 5 specifies shifted bias positions that appear in the SGP_1 set. (For instance, for state A_0, this position is 0, since $GP_1 = 2^0$ for state A_1, SRVB performs first circular shift, and bias position 14 appears in SGP_1. For state A_2, bias position 13 appears in SGP_1, etc.)

Column 6 finds the modifiable bias digits, MD, that have to be modified to obtain A_0^*. The MD digits are found as follows: each MD digit corresponds to such a pair (GP_1, GP_i^*) that $GP_1 \neq GP_i^*$, where GP_1 is in col. 3 and GP_i^* is in col. 4. To achieve the equality $GP_1 = GP_i^*$, a respective bias digit that is fed to GP_1 via the mod-2 adder has to be modified. Thus, col. 6 is filled as follows: if $GP_1 = GP_i^*$, MD is empty. If $GP_1 \neq GP_i^*$, MD is the shifted bias position shown in col. 5. For instance, for shifted bias positions 0 and 14 (col. 5), $GP_1 = GP_i^* = 1$. Thus, MD is empty. For shifted bias position 13 (Col. 5), $GP_1 = 0$ and $GP_i^* = 1$. Thus $GP_1 \neq GP_i^*$ and MD = 13, meaning that bias digit 13 should be modified. Similarly, one finds all the other modifiable bias digits. They are 3, 4, 5, 6, 7, 8, 9, 11, 12, 13, since $GP_i \neq GP_i^*$ for each MD.

Thus, the modification code,

$$\begin{array}{ccccccccccccccc}
 & 14 & 13 & 12 & 11 & 10 & 9 & 8 & 7 & 6 & 5 & 4 & 3 & 2 & 1 & 0 \\
MC = & 0 & 1 & 1 & 1 & 0 & 1 & 1 & 1 & 1 & 1 & 1 & 1 & 0 & 0 & 0 \quad \text{of col. 7}
\end{array}$$

is formed of nonempty MD digits. Therefore,

$$\begin{array}{ccccccccccccccc}
 & 14 & 13 & 12 & 11 & 10 & 9 & 8 & 7 & 6 & 5 & 4 & 3 & 2 & 1 & 0 \\
A_0^* = B + MC = & 0 & 0 & 1 & 1 & 0 & 0 & 1 & 1 & 1 & 0 & 1 & 1 & 1 & 0 & 1
\end{array}$$

By construction, A_0^* will generate a ring of period 10, since its SGP_i^* set is given as $SGP_1^* = \{1_5, 0_5\}$. This ring is shown in Fig. II.31. ■

All these findings can be generalized in the following ring transform procedures formulated for an odd-weighted bias B.

Ring Transform Procedures for an Odd-Weighted Bias B

Rule 1. For any odd-weighted bias B, one can find a generic word, A_0^*, that generates the ring of period $2m$, where $m \cdot p = n$ and p is an odd integer. To find A_0^*, one has to find the modification code, MC, giving $A^* = B + MC$.

Rule 2. The following procedure may be used to find the MC code:

1. Construct an arbitrary SGP_i^* set having period $2m$.
2. Select arbitrarily a matching SGP_i set produced by generating position GP_i of GRI and match SGP_i and SGP_i^* digit by digit as $GP_i = GP_i^*$? If for a k entry, where $k = 0, 1, \ldots, T - 1$, $GP_i = GP_i^*$, the respective bias position is unmodifiable. If $GP_i \neq GP_i^*$, the respective bias position is modifiable.

Rule 3. The location of each modifiable bias digit, MD, is found as follows: Let k ($k = 0, 1, 2, \ldots, T - 1$) be a position of such a pair $(GP_i, GP_i^*)_k$, that $GP_i \neq GP_i^*$.

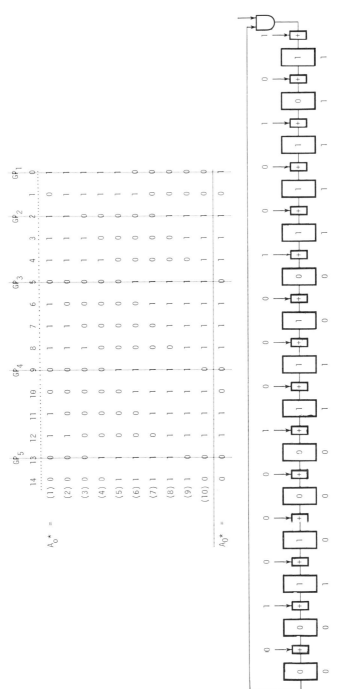

FIGURE II.31 Generation of the ring of period T = 10 using the ring transform technique of Fig. II.30

81

Since $GP_i \neq GP_i^*$ occurs during the kth shift of the MD digit in the bias, $k[MD] = GP_i$. Thus, $MD = k^{-1}[GP_i] = GP_i - k \pmod{n}$. Thus, if $GP_i - k > 0$, $MD = GP_i - k$; if $GP_i - k < 0$, $MD = GP_i + n - k$; if $GP_i - k = 0$, $MD = GP_i$.

Rule 4. The modification code, MC, is found as follows. Each position MD is 1 in MC. All other positions are zeros.

Rules 1 through 4 formulate the algorithm for creating a ring of period $2m$, provided bias is given and odd-weighted. Thus, these rules acquire significance since they allow a deterministic selection by programmer of the network nodes that can or cannot be included into a ring of desired period, or what bias B must be selected in order that a desired node be in the ring. The rules of such converse selection are a simple extension of rules 1 through 4.

4.5.4.3 Ring transforms for an even-weighted bias

These are simple extensions of the techniques described above for an odd-weighted bias. The only difference is for an even-weighted bias having even dimension d. This bias will generate GRI with period m, which is a divisor of n. Thus, every set of generating positions SGP is also of period m and not $2m$ as was the case for an odd-weighted bias or for an even-weighted bias having d odd. Therefore, for any new ring RI, every set of generating positions, SGP, also has the period $m \in SD_n$, where SD_n is a set of divisors of n.

4.5.5 Quantitative Characterization of a Single Ring Structure

The material below is aimed at finding the quantitative parameters of SRS, which are understood as the number of rings, $D(T)$, with period T, where $T \in SP$ and SP is the set of periods, i.e., $SRS = \{D(T): T \in SP\}$. Thus, to solve this problem one has to find SP. This depends on the type of bias used (odd-weighted or even-weighted).

Theorem 3. A single ring structure receiving an odd-weighted bias has the following set of ring periods: $SP \text{ (odd)} = \overline{SD}_{2n} = SD_{2_n} - SD_n$. An SRS receiving an even-weighted bias has the set of ring periods $SP \text{ (even)} = SD_n$, where n is the size of SRVB, and SD_n is a set of divisors of n.

Since these are the two types of single ring structures generated by odd and even biases, respectively, let us first define SRS quantitatively, with an odd-weighted bias B.

4.5.5.1 Odd-weighted bias

For an SRS receiving an odd-weighted bias, the following properties characterize any ring of period $2m$, where $2m \in \overline{SD}_{2n}$.

1. $m \cdot p = n$ and p is odd.
2. Each generating position in this ring forms the set $SGP = HGP \cup \overline{HGP}$ of period $2m$.

3. The number of bits in each half-set HGP is m.

4. The number d of ones and zeros fields in $\overline{\text{HGP}}$ (HGP) is odd and they alternate (although a ones field does not necessarily go first for SGP_i as was the case for GRI); the sizes of ones and zeros fields are added to give $m = b_1 + b_2 + \ldots + b_d$.

Since for an odd-weighted bias any ring half-period, m, will necessarily have an odd number of addends, d, where $d \leq t$, expression of m via d addends will be called an *odd representation of number m*, ORS(m). In other words, ORS(m) = $b_1 + b_2 + \ldots + b_d$, if d is odd.

Since each ORS(m) specifies one ring of period $T = 2m$, the number $D(T)$ of rings with the same period $T = 2m$ is completely specified by the number of ORSs that can be found for a given integer m.

Obviously, for a ring period $T = 2m$ the number of odd representations, ORS(m), is independent of the size n of the shift register. This leads to the independence of the $D(T)$-number of size n. Therefore, we can use a recursive procedure for finding $D(T)$.

We start with $n = 2^s$, where $s = 0, 1, 2, \ldots, n$. This n contains only one odd divisor, $p = 1$; i.e., $n = 1 \cdot n$. Therefore, the set of the ring periods generated by this SRVB, SP, has only one member, $2n$; i.e., SP = $\{2n\}$. Thus, only rings of period $2n$ are generated, and $2n \cdot D(2n) = 2^n$ or $T \cdot D(T) = 2^{T/2}$.

Let $n = 2^s \cdot \text{PD}$, where PD is a prime divisor. For this case, n has two odd divisors, $p_1 = 1$ and $p_2 = \text{PD}$. For $p_1 = 1$, $m = 2^s \cdot \text{PD}$ and the SRVB generates the rings with period $2m = 2$. For $p_2 = \text{PD}$, $m = 2^s$ and the SRVB generates the rings with period $2m = 2 \cdot 2^s = 2^{s+1}$. The number $D(2^{s+1})$ of rings of period $T = 2^{s+1}$ is $T \cdot D(T) = 2^{T/2}$. Therefore, for this case, $2n \cdot D(2n) + T \cdot D(T) = 2^n$ and $T \cdot D(T) = 2^{T/2}$, where $T = 2^{s+1}$. This gives $D(2n) = (2^n) = (2^{T/2})/2_n$, etc.

Continuing this procedure further, we find all $D(T')$ for all $T' \in \overline{\text{SD}}_T$, where T is an arbitrary (even) number, since it is impossible for a ring period T to be odd if bias is odd-weighted. Following the determination of $D(T')$ for all divisors, $T' \in \overline{\text{SD}}_T$, one can use the same binary space, $2^{T/2}$, for finding $D(T)$.

This gives Theorem 4, which quantifies a single ring structure generated by an odd-weighted bias B.

Theorem 4. For any ring period $T \in$ SP generated by single ring structure with an odd-weighted bias B, the number $D(T)$ of rings with the same period T is determined as follows:

$$2^{T/2} = \sum_{T' \in \overline{\text{SD}}_T} T' \cdot D(T') \qquad (7)$$

Example: Let us quantify the SRS generated by the 15-bit SRVB receiving an even-weighted bias B. For $n = 15$, $\overline{\text{SD}}_{30} = \text{SD}_{30} - \text{SD}_{15} = \{30, 15, 10, 6, 5, 3, 2, 1\} - \{15, 3, 5, 1\} = \{30, 10, 6, 2\}$. For $T = 2$, $\overline{\text{SD}}_2 = \{2, 1\} - \{1\} = \{2\}$. Thus, $2^1 = 2 \cdot D(2)$ and $D(2) = 1$. For $T = 6$, $\overline{\text{SD}}_6 = \{6, 3, 2, 1\} - \{3, 1\} = \{6, 2\}$ and $2^3 = 6 \cdot D(6) + 2 \cdot D(2) = 6 \cdot D(6) + 2 \cdot 1$; $D(6) = \dfrac{8 - 2}{6} = 1$. For $T = 10$, $\overline{\text{SD}}_{10}$

$= \{10, 5, 2, 1\} - \{5, 1\} = \{10, 2\}$ and $2^5 = 10 \cdot D(10) + 2 \cdot D(2) = 10 \cdot D(10) + 2 \cdot 1$; $D(10) = \dfrac{32 - 2}{10} = 3$. For $T = 30$,

$$D(30) = \frac{2^{15} - 10 \cdot D(10) - 6 \cdot D(6) - 2 \cdot D(2)}{30} = \frac{32{,}768 - 30 - 6 - 2}{30}$$

$$= \frac{32{,}730}{30} = 1{,}091$$

Therefore, a quantification technique that is specified with Eq. (7) is very simple and can be applied for arbitrary n.   ∎

4.5.5.2 Even-weighted bias

Quantification of an SRS specified with an even-weighted bias can also be performed via recursive procedure, because any period T is expressed as either $T = m$ or $T = 2m$, where $m = b_1 + b_2 + \cdots + b_d$. Since, for any T, $D(T)$ is independent of the size n of the shift register and is generated in T-ary binary space, we can introduce Theorem 5, which quantifies a single ring structure generated by an even-weighted bias B.

Theorem 5. For any period $T \in SP$ generated by SRS receiving an even-weighted bias B, the number of rings, $D(T)$, with period T is determined as follows:

$$2^T = \sum_{T' \in SD_T} T' \cdot D(T') \tag{8}$$

Example. Let us quantify the SRS generated by the 15-bit SRVB receiving an even-weighted bias B. For $n = 15$, $SD_{15} = \{1, 3, 5, 15\}$. For $T = 1$, $SD_1 = \{1\}$. Therefore, $2^1 = 1 \cdot D(1)$, giving $D(1) = 2$. For $T = 3$, $SD_3 = \{3, 1\}$. Therefore, $2^3 = 1 \cdot D(1) + 3 \cdot D(3)$ and $D(3) = (2^3 - D(1))/3 = (8 - 2)/3 = 2$. For $T = 5$, $SD_5 = \{5, 1\}$. Thus, $2^5 = 1 \cdot D(1) + 5 \cdot D(5)$ and $D(5) = (32 - 2)/5 = 6$. For $T = 15$, $SD_{15} = \{1, 3, 5, 15\}$. Thus, $2^{15} = 1 \cdot D(1) + 3 \cdot D(3) + 5 \cdot D(5) + 15 \cdot D(15)$ and $D(15) = (2^{15} - 1 \cdot D(1) - 3 \cdot D(3) - 5 \cdot D(5))/15 = (32{,}768 - 2 \cdot 3 - 5 \cdot 6 - 2)/15 = 2182$.   ∎

4.5.6   Analysis and Synthesis of Single Ring Structures

Theorems 4 and 5 provide one with a general solution of analysis and synthesis problems for single ring structures. Below are analysis and synthesis techniques developed on the basis of Theorems 4 and 5.

4.5.6.1   Analysis of single ring structures

Given: size n of SRVB. Find all the SRSs that can be generated with it. There are only two SRS structures that can be generated by this SRVB:

1. SRS (odd) generated by an odd-weighted bias. Its quantification is given in Theorems 3 and 4.
2. SRS (even) generated by an even-weighted bias. Its quanitification is given in Theorems 3 and 5.

The result is the SRS table (Table II.1) constructed below for the synthesis so that both procedures can share this table.

4.5.6.2 Synthesis of SRS

Given an SRS configuration, SRS(G), find the minimal size n and bias B that can generate all the rings of this SRS.

Step 1. Construct the SRS table that specifies all possible SRSs that can be generated by shift registers having size $n = 2, 3, 4 \ldots$.

Example: Table II.1 specifies the SRS table for $n = 2, \ldots, 20$. This table consists of five columns. Column 0 gives the size n of the shift register. Column 1 specifies the set of ring periods, SP (even), for an SRS receiving an even-weighted bias B (Theorem 3). Column 2 specifies the set, SRS (even), found for an even-weighted bias B. The values of $D(T)$ were found using Eq. (8) of Theorem 5. Column 3 specifies the set of periods, SP (odd), for an SRS receiving an odd-weighted bias B (Theorem 3). Column 4 specifies the set, SRS (odd), found for an odd-weighted bias B. The values of $D(T)$ were found using Eq. (7) of Theorem 4.

As an example, consider how one can fill in the row $n = 12$ of the table. Using Theorem 3, find the set of ring periods, SP (even), generated by the SRS receiving an even-weighted bias. SP (even) $= SD_{12} = \{12, 6, 4, 3, 2, 1\}$. Using Theorem 5, quantify the SRS (even) as follows:

For $T = 1$, $2^1 = 1 \cdot \underline{D(1)}$, $\underline{D(1)} = 2(1)$; for $T = 2$, $2^2 = 2 \cdot \underline{D(2)} + 1 \cdot D(1)$, $\underline{D(2)} = 1(2)$; for $T = 3$, $2^3 = 3 \cdot \underline{D(3)} + 1 \cdot D(1)$, $\underline{D(3)} = 2(3)$; for $T = 4$, $2^4 = 4 \cdot \underline{D(4)} + 2 \cdot D(2) + 1 \cdot D(1)$, $\underline{D(4)} = 3(4)$; for $T = 6$, $2^6 = 6 \cdot \underline{D(6)} + 3 \cdot D(3) + 2 \cdot D(2) + 1 \cdot D(1)$, $\underline{D(6)} = 9(6)$; for $T = 12$, $2^{12} = 12 \cdot \underline{D(12)} \pm 6 \cdot D(6) + 3 \cdot D(3) + 4 \cdot D(4) + 2 \cdot D(2) + 1 \cdot D(1)$, $\underline{D(12)} = 335\,(12)$.

Next, we find the set of ring periods, SP (odd), generated by an odd-weighted bias: SP (odd) $= SD_{2 \cdot 12} - SD_{12} = \{24, 8, 6, 4, 12, 3, 2, 1\} - \{12, 6, 4, 3, 2, 1\} = \{24, 8\}$.

Using Theorem 4, we quantify SRS (odd) as follows. For $T = 8$, $2^{8/2} = 8 \cdot \underline{D(8)}$, $\underline{D(8)} = 2(8)$. For $T = 24$, $2^{24/2} = 8 \cdot D(8) + 24 \cdot D(24)$, $\underline{D(24)} = 170\,(24)$. ∎

Step 2. Find the minimal n such that a given SRS configuration [SRS(G)] is a subset of the standard one [SRS(S)] specified for this row. Find what category the standard SRS(S) belongs to: odd or even. If it is odd, select an arbitrary odd-weighted bias to generate it. If it is even, select an arbitrary even-weighted bias to generate it.

Let us evaluate an upper bound n_m of size n of SRVB that can generate SRS(G). Find T_m, the maximal period of a ring, RI $\in$ SRS(G). If T_m is even and SRS(G) is a subset of SRS (odd), $n_m = T_m/2$, since this ring structure can be generated by the SRVB of size $n_m = T_m/2$ receiving an odd-weighted bias. If T_m is odd and/or SRS(G) is a subset of SRS (even), $n_m = T_m$ since this ring structure can be generated by the SRVB of size

TABLE II.1

SRS Table

| | Bias B is even-weighted | | Bias B is odd-weighted | |
Col. 0 Size n of SR.B n	Col. 1 SP(even)	Col. 2 SRS (even) = {D(T)} $T \in$ SP (even)	Col. 3 SP (odd)	Col. 4 SRS (odd) = {D(T)} $T \in$ SP (odd)
2	1,2	2(1), 1(2)	4	1(4)
3	3, 1	2(1), 2(3)	6, 2	1(2), 1(6)
4	4, 2, 1	2(1), 1(2), 3(4)	8	2(8)
5	5, 1	2(1), 6(5)	2, 10	1(2), 3(10)
6	6, 3, 2, 1	2(1), 1(2), 2(3), 9(6)	4, 12	1(4), 5(12)
7	7, 1	2(1), 18(7)	2, 14	1(2), 9(14)
8	8, 4, 2, 1	2(1), 1(2), 3(4), 30(8)	16	16(16)
9	9, 3, 1	2(1), 2(3), 56(9)	18, 6, 2	1(2), 1(6), 28(18)
10	10, 5, 2, 1	2(1), 1(2), 6(5), 99(10)	20, 4	1(4), 51(20)
11	11, 1	2(1), 186(11)	22, 2	1(2), 93(22)
12	12, 6, 4, 3, 2, 1	2(1), 1(2), 2(3), 3(4), 9(6), 335(12)	24, 8	2(8), 170(24)
13	1, 13	2(1), 630(13)	2, 26	1(2), 315(26)
14	1, 2, 7, 14	2(1), 1(2), 18(7), 1161(14)	4, 28	1(4), 585(28)
15	1, 2, 5, 15	2(1), 2(3), 6(5), 2182(15)	2, 6, 10, 30	1(2), 1(6), 5(10), 1091(30)
16	1, 2, 4, 8, 16	2(1), 1(2), 3(4), 30(8), 4080(16)	32	2048(32)
17	1, 17	2(1), 7710(17)	2, 34	1(2), 3855(34)
18	1, 2, 3, 6, 9, 18	2(1), 1(2), 2(3), 9(6), 56(9), 14532(18)	4, 12, 36	1(4), 5(12), 7280(36)
19	1, 19	2(1), 27594(19)	2, 38	1(2), 1279(38)
20	1, 2, 4, 5, 10, 20	2(1), 1(2), 3(4), 6(5), 99(10), 52377(20)	8, 40	2(8), 2621(40)

$n_m = T_m$ receiving an even-weighted bias. It should be noted that these upper bounds work only for such (given) sets of rings that are properly contained in some standard SRS(S). Otherwise, a given set of rings should be generated with a composite shift register; i.e., it will be *properly contained* in a composite ring structure, discussed in Sec. 4.6.

For instance, if given SRS(G) = {4, 12}, $T_m = 12$, giving $n_m = T_m/2 = 6$. Thus, this SRS(G) can be generated in a 6-bit SRVB receiving an odd-weighted bias (see row 6, Table II.1). If the given SRS(G) = {4, 12}, $n_m = 4$, since {4, 2} ⊂ {4, 2, 1}, which specifies standard even ring structure that can be generated with single SRVB.

The next procedure is divided into two concurrent steps, Step 3 and Step 4, depending on whether the given SRS(G) coincides with standard SRS(S) [SRS(G) = SRS(S)] or it is a proper subset of it [SRS(G) < SRS(S)]. If SRS(G) = SRS(S), go to Step 3. If SRS(G) < SRS(S), go to Step 4.

Step 3. This step generates a complete SRS using a simplified algorithm that cannot distinguish among rings. Thus, if a complete SRS is generated, it can be produced very easily using the predecessor-successor rule, $N \rightarrow N^*$, as follows: $N^* = 1[N] + B$, where bias B was selected in Step 2. Thus, Step 3 selects a given binary number, N, of size n and generates its successor as $N^* = 1[N] + B$.

Step 4. This step generates incomplete SRS as follows. Since Step 2 has determined a standard SRS that properly contains a given SRS(G), select in standard SRS(S) those rings that are members of the given SRS(G). Generate each ring using the ring-transform techniques specified in Sec. 4.5.4.

Example. Since Step 3 is very simple, let us illustrate the synthesis procedure (Step 2 and Step 4) for a partial network, SRS(G) = {3(12)}, containing three rings of period 12. Using Table II.1, we find that the smallest n that can generate this SRS is $n = 6$. For $n = 6$, SRS(G) is a proper subset of SRS (odd) generated in 6-bit SRVB with an odd-weighted bias.

Select

$$GP_3 \qquad GP_2 \qquad GP_1$$

$$B = 1 \quad 0 \qquad 0 \quad 1 \qquad 0 \quad 1$$

having $t = 3$ (odd) and $a_1 = 2$, $a_2 = 3$ and $a_3 = 1$. This bias is irreducible and it forms generating ring GRI of period $T = 12$. Generate this ring using the $N \rightarrow N^*$ rule, where $N^* = 1[N] + B$, and B is the initial state of this ring. For $m = 6$, select arbitrarily two odd representations of m that produce rings of period 12: $m_1 = 1 + 2 + 3$ and $m_2 = 1 + 1 + 4$. Generate two remaining rings, RI_1 and RI_2, using the ring-transform techniques comprehensively specified in Sec. 4.5.4 (Fig. II.32). ■

4.6 Composite Ring Structures

As was shown in Sec. 4.4, composite structures are composite rings (CRS), composite stars (CS), composite multiple trees (CMTS), and composite multiple stars (CMSS)

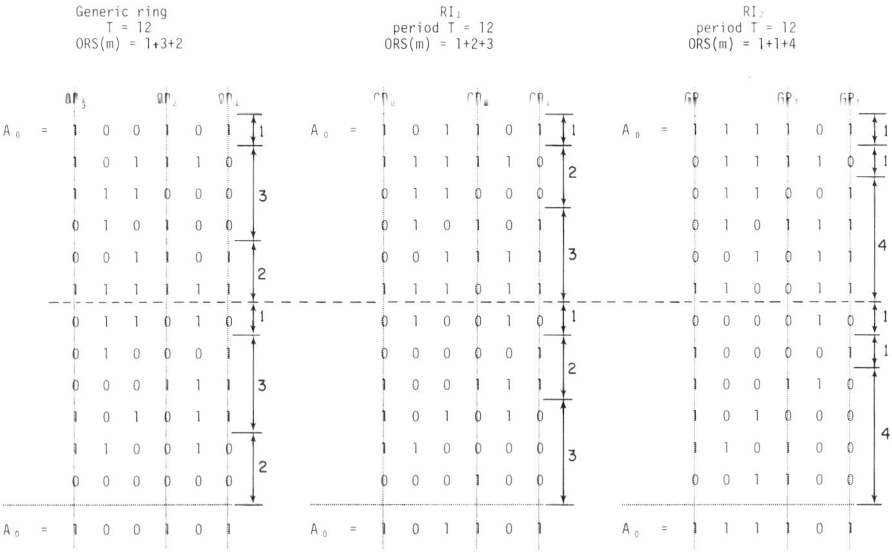

```
Generic ring                    RI₁                          RI₂
    T = 12                  period T = 12               period T = 12
ORS(m) = 1+3+2              ORS(m) = 1+2+3               ORS(m) = 1+1+4

     DP₃   DP₂   DP₁           CP_u  CP_a  CP_l            GP    GP    GP₁

A₀ = 1 0 0 | 1 0 1 | 1   A₀ = 1 0 1 | 1 0 1 | 1      A₀ = 1 1 1 | 1 0 1 | 1
     1 0 1 | 1 1 0            1 1 1 | 1 1 0 | 2            0 1 1 | 1 1 0 | 1
     1 1 1 | 0 0 0 | 3        0 1 1 | 0 0 0              0 1 1 | 0 0 1
     0 1 0 | 1 0 0            0 1 0 | 1 0 1              0 1 0 | 1 1 1
     0 0 1 | 1 0 0            0 0 1 | 1 1 1 | 3          0 0 1 | 0 1 1 | 4
     1 1 1 | 1 1 1 | 2        1 1 0 | 1 1 1              1 1 0 | 0 1 1
    ------------------       ------------------         ------------------
     0 1 1 | 0 1 0 | 1        0 1 0 | 0 1 0 | 1          0 0 0 | 0 1 0 | 1
     0 1 0 | 0 0 1            0 0 0 | 0 0 1 | 2          1 0 0 | 0 0 1 | 1
     0 0 0 | 1 1 1 | 3        1 0 0 | 1 1 1              1 0 0 | 1 1 0
     1 0 1 | 0 1 1            1 0 1 | 0 1 0              1 0 1 | 0 0 0
     1 1 0 | 0 1 0            1 1 0 | 0 0 0 | 3          1 1 0 | 1 0 0 | 4
     0 0 0 | 0 0 0 | 2        0 0 0 | 1 0 0              0 0 1 | 1 0 0

A₀ = 1 0 0 | 1 0 1       A₀ = 1 0 1 | 1 0 1          A₀ = 1 1 1 | 1 0 1
```

FIGURE II.32   Synthesis of a partial network SRS(G) = {3(12)}

(Fig. II.19). In this subsection we will develop simple analysis formulas for composite rings. Other composite structures are the subject of our current studies.

Since general composite ring structure, CRSs are specified with composite shifting formats, $SF_1 = [1^{r_1}, 2^{r_2}, ..., t^{r_t}]$, containing components i_{r_i} $(i = 1, ..., t)$, our first task is to specify the CRSs generated by $SF_1 = [i^{r_i}]$. Thereafter, a general CRS specified with an arbitrary shifting formal will be found using simple multiplicative laws that govern the formation of rings in composite binary spaces from component rings specified for subspaces $[i^{r_i}]$.

4.6.1 Multiple Single Rings

In general, a composite ring structure specified with shifting format $SF = [i^{r_i}]$ and generated with such a bias B that maintains either oddness or evenness within this format will be called a *multiple single CRS* or, symbolically, *ms-CRS*.

Example. Let $SF_1 = [5^3]$, having $i = 5$, $r_i = 3$, and $n = 3 \cdot 5 = 15$, and the SRVB receives an odd-weighted bias,

$$B^{(1)} = \begin{array}{ccc} \overset{\leftarrow 5 \rightarrow}{01101} & \overset{\leftarrow 5 \rightarrow}{01101} & \overset{\leftarrow 5 \rightarrow}{10000} \\ \leftarrow B_1 \rightarrow & \leftarrow B_2 \rightarrow & \leftarrow B_3 \rightarrow \end{array}$$

having $t = 7$. This bias is split into B_1, B_2 and B_3, where $B_1 = 01101$, $B_2 = 01101$, and $B_3 = 10000$. This bias maintains oddness for all its components, since each B_i is odd-weighted. (For B_1, $t_1 = 3$, for B_2, $t_2 = 3$, and for B_3, $t_3 = 1$).

This shifting format, when fed with B $^{(1)}$, generates ms-CRS. For bias B$^{(2)}$ = 01101 01111 10100 feeding the same SF$_1$ = [5^3], t = 9. Thus, this bias is odd-weighted. However, oddness or evenness of a bias components is not maintained, because B$_1$ = 01101, t_1 = 3, B$_2$ = 01111, t_2 = 4, and B$_3$ = 10100, t_3 = 2; i.e., this bias has a switch from odd-weighted component B$_1$ to even-weighted B$_2$. As a result, shifting format SF = [5^3] fed with the bias B$^{(2)}$ does not generate the ms-CRS. ∎

Bias B for a ms-CRS that maintains either the oddness or evenness of its components within SF = [i^{r_i}] will be called *odd-composite* and *even-composite* respectively. Any other bias will be called *mixed*. As follows from this definition for a mixed bias, some bias components are odd-weighted and some are even-weighted.

Since SF$_1$ = [i^{r_i}] that specifies ms-CRS differs from single SF$_1$ =[i^1] only by a multiplicity factor $r_i > 1$, the set of periods, SP, for a multiple single ring structure, ms-CRS, is the same as that for a single ring structure, SRS. That is, there are two types of multiple single ring structures, odd and even, generated by odd-composite and even-composite biases, respectively, where SP (odd) specifies the set of ring periods for an odd-composite structure and SP (even) specifies the set of ring periods for an even-composite structure. Therefore, for an odd ms-CRS, SP (odd) =$\overline{SD}_{2i}$ = SD$_{2i}$ - SD$_i$. For an even ms-CRS, SP (even) = SD$_i$, where SD$_i$ is the set of divisors for integer i.

With these definitions in order, specification of ms-CRS is accomplished in the following two theorems (Theorems 6 and 7) developed for odd- and even-composite biases, respectively. (These theorems are simple extensions of Theorems 4 and 5 developed for single ring structures.)

Theorem 6. For a multiple SF$_1$ = [i^{r_i}] and any odd-composite bias B, any 2s ∈ SP (odd) induces the following recursive procedure that gives consecutive numbers $D(T)$ of rings with period T, where T ∈ $\overline{SD}_{2s}$:

$$2^{s \cdot r_i} = \sum_{T \in \overline{SD}_{2s}} T \cdot D(T)$$

Example. Let SF$_1$ = [5^3], having i = 5 and r_i = 3, and shifting register SRVB receives an odd-composite bias B, say (B = 01101 01101 10110), having t = 9. This specifies an odd-composite ring structure as follows:

SP (odd) = $\overline{SD}_{2i}$ = SD$_{10}$ - SD$_5$ = {10, 5, 2, 1} − {5, 1} = {10, 2},
   $\overline{SD}_2$ = SD$_2$ − SD$_1$ = {2, 1} - {1} = {2}.
For 2s = 2, 2$^{s \cdot r_i}$ = 2$^{1 \cdot 3}$ = 2 • D(2); D(2) = 8/2 = 4.
For 2s = 10, 2$^{s \cdot r_i}$ = 2$^{5 \cdot 3}$ = 10 •D(10) + 2 • D(2) = 10 • D(10) + 2 •4;
   D(10) = (2^{12} − 8)/10 = (32,768 - 8)/10 = 3276.

Theorem 7. For a multiple SF$_1$ = [i^{r_i}] and any even-composite bias B, any s ∈ SP (even) induces the following recursive procedure that gives consecutive $D(T)$, T ∈ SD$_s$:

$$2^{s \cdot r_i} = \sum_{T \in \overline{SD}_s} T \cdot D(T)$$

Example: Let the SRVB be the same as in the previous example ($SF_1 = [5^3]$), with the only difference being that bias B be an even-composite. This gives an even-composite ring structure as follows:

SF (even) $= SD_s = \{5, 1\}$.
For $s = 1$, $2^{s \cdot r_i} = 2^{1 \cdot 3} = 1 \cdot D(1)$; $D(1) = 8$.
For $s = 5$, $^{s \cdot r_i} = 2^{5 \cdot 3} = 5 \cdot D(5) + 1 \cdot D(1) = 5 \cdot D(5) + 8$.
$D(5) = (2^{15} - 8)/5 = 6552$.

4.6.2 Arbitrary Shifting Formats

With the specification of the ms-CRS, we can specify composite ring structures generated by arbitrary shifting formats, $SF = [1^{r_1}, 2^{r_2}, \ldots, t^{r_t}]$, and biases B.

First, for each component format $[i^{r_i}]$, we specify what type of bias B_i is induced: odd-composite, even-composite, or mixed. If it is an odd-composite, we mark it with O_i; if it is an even-composite, we mark it with E_i; if it is mixed, we split this component format into two smaller ones that are specified with O-composite or E-composite biases, respectively, and use the same notation O_i or E_i for smaller formats that are obtained during such splitting.

As a result of this procedure, the original shifting format, $SF = [1^{r_1}, 2^{r_2}, \ldots, t^{r_t}]$, is specified with a *characterization format*, $CF = [m_1, m_2, \ldots, m_t]$, where $m_1, m_2, \ldots, m_t \in \{O, E\}$. The total number of nodes in the network is

$$2^{r_1 + 2r_2 + \cdots + t \cdot r_t}$$

(9)

Each factor $2^{i \cdot r_i}$ of this expression is replaced with either

$$\sum_{T \in \overline{SD}_{2i}} T \bullet D(T), \quad \text{if } m_i = 0_i$$

or

$$\sum_{T \in \overline{SD}_i} T \bullet D(T), \quad \text{if } m_i = E_i$$

Having performed this replacement for all factors of Eq. (9), we obtain a multiplicative polynomial that allows us to characterize all composite ring structures quantitatively.

Consider the following cases of this characterization.

Case 1.   All bias components of characterization format CF are odd-composite, specifying an *odd-composite ring structure:* $CF = [O_1, O_2, \ldots, O_t]$.

Case 2.   All bias components of CF are even composite, specifying an *even-composite ring structure:* $CF = [E_1, E_2, \ldots, E_t]$.

Case 3.   CF is made of O- or E-composite bias components specifying a *mixed composite ring structure:* $CF = [m_1, m_2, \ldots, m_t]$, $m_1, m_2, \ldots, m_t \in \{O, E\}$.

4.6.2.1 Odd-composite ring structures

Given $SF_1 = [1^{r_1}, 2^{r_2}, \ldots t^{r_t}]$ and $CF = [O_1, O_2, \ldots, O_t]$, let $S_O = \{i: r_i \geq 1\}$. For each integer $i \in S_O$, find the set $\overline{SD}_{2i}$. Let $(b_1, b_2, \ldots, b_t)$ be an arbitrary vector such that $b_i \in \overline{SD}_{2i}$. Then the set of ring periods for an odd-composite ring structure is specified as follows.

Theorem 8. If $v = \text{lcm}(b_2, b_2, \ldots, b_t)$, then $v \in SP$, where lcm is the least common multiple of integers $b_1, b_2, \ldots, b_t$.

Corollary. For odd-composite ring structure SP is made of even numbers.

As follows from Theorem 8, the set of periods for an odd-composite ring structure is specified as the set of least common multiples (lcm) found for all members of the Cartesian product, constructed from $\overline{SD}_{2i}$ sets, where $i \in S_O$.

Example. Let $SF_1 = [3^2, 4^2, 5^1]$ and $CF = O_3, O_4, O_5]; S_O = \{3,4,5\}$. For every integer $i \in S_O$, let us construct sets $\overline{SD}_{2i}$: for $i = 3$, $\overline{SD}_{2i} = \overline{SD}_6 = SD_6, - SD_3 = \{6, 3, 2, 1\} - \{3, 1\} = \{6, 2\}$; for $i = 4$, $\overline{SD}_8 = SD_8 - SD_4 = \{8\}$; for $i = 5$, $\overline{SD}_{10} = SD_{10} - SD_5 = \{10, 2\}$. Find the Cartesian product, CP, formed from $\overline{SD}_{2i}$ sets, where $i \in S_O$: $CP = \overline{SD}_6 \times \overline{SD}_8 \times \overline{SD}_{10} = \{(6, 8, 10), (6, 8, 2), (2, 8, 10), (2, 8, 2)\}$. The set of ring periods for this odd-composite ring structure is

$$SP = \{\text{lcm}(6, 8, 10), \text{lcm}(6, 8, 2), \text{lcm}(2, 8, 10), \text{lcm}(2, 8, 2)\} = \{120, 24, 40, 8\} \quad \blacksquare$$

We can now formulate the following theorem that performs specification for the entire class of odd-composite ring structures.

Theorem 9. For any $2b \in SP$,

$$\prod_{i \in S_o} 2^{gcd[b,i] \cdot r_i} = \sum_{T \in \overline{SD}_{2b}} T \cdot D(T)$$

This theorem allows quantization of any odd-composite ring structure specified with shifting format $SF = [1^{r_1}, 2^{r_2}, \ldots, t^{r_t}]$ and characterization format $CF = [O_2, O_2, \ldots, O_t]$.

Example. Consider the SRVB of Fig. II.21(b) fed with bias $B = 10010$. This SRVB is specified with shifting format $SF = [2^1, 3^1]$ and odd-composite bias $B = B_1, B_2$, where $B_1 = 10$ ($t_1 = 1$) and $B_2 = 010$ ($t_2 = 1$). Since each B_i is odd-weighted, characterization format $CF = [O_2, O_3]$. Using Theorems 8 and 9, let us quantify this odd-composite ring structure. First we will find the set SP of ring periods using the techniques of Theorems 8 and 9. $S_O = \{2, 3\}$; for any $i \in S_o$, find $\overline{SD}_{2i}$. For $i = 2$, $\overline{SD}_4 = SD_4 - SD_2 = \{4, 2, 1\} - \{2, 1\} = \{4\}$; for $i = 3$, $\overline{SD}_6 = \{6, 3, 2, 1\} - \{3, 1\} = \{6, 2\}$. Find the Cartesian product of $\overline{SD}_{2i}$ sets: $CP = \overline{SD}_4 \times \overline{SD}_6 = \{(4,$

6), (4, 2)}; the set of ring periods SP = {ℓcm(4, 6), ℓcm(4, 2)} = {12, 4}. Using Theorem 9, let us find $D(12)$ and $D(4)$.

For $4 \in$ SP, $2^{gcd(2, 2)} r_2 + gcd(2, 3) r_3 = 4 \cdot D(4)$; $2^{2+1} = 2^3 = 4 \cdot D(4)$; $D(4) = 8/4 = 2$. For $12 \in$ SP, $2^{gcd(6, 2)} r_2 + gcd(6, 3) r_3 = 12 \cdot D(12) + 4 \cdot D(4) = 12 \cdot D(12) + 4 \cdot 2$; $D(12) = (2^5 - 8)/12 = 2$.

Therefore, this odd-composite ring structure contains two rings with period 4 and two rings with period 12: CRS = {2(4), 2(12),} [See Fig. II.21(a)]. As we have seen, this technique of quantization of odd-composite ring structures is very simple and can be performed for binary spaces of arbitrary dimension.

As an illustration, let us specify the odd-composite ring structure given by the SF_0 = $[3^2, 4^2, 5^1]$ in the n-dimensional binary space, where $n = 3 \cdot 2 + 4 \cdot 2 + 5 = 19$. Earlier we obtained the set of ring periods SP = {120, 24, 40, 8} for this SF_0. Let us find $D(T)$ for every $T \in$ SP. For $T = 8$, $\overline{SD}_8 = \{8, 4, 2, 1\} - \{4, 2, 1\} = \{8\}$. $2^{gcd(4, 3)r_3 + gcd(4, 4)r_4 + gcd(4, 5)r_5} = 8 \cdot D(8)$; $2^{1 \cdot r_3 + 4 \cdot r_4 + 1 \cdot r_5} = 8 \cdot D(8)$, where $r_2 = 2$, $r_4 = 2$, and $r_5 = 1$. Therefore, $D(8) = 256$.

For $T = 40$, $\overline{SD}_{40} = \{40, 20, 8, 5, 4, 2, 1\} - \{20, 5, 4, 2, 1\} = \{40, 8\}$. $2^{gcd(20 \cdot 3) \cdot r_3 + gcd(20, 4) \cdot r_4 + gcd(20, 5) \cdot r_5} = 40 \cdot D(40) + 8 \cdot D(40) + 8 \cdot D(8)$; $2^{15} = 40 \cdot D(40) + 2048$; $D(40) = (2^{15} - 2048)/40 = 768$.

For $T = 24$, $\overline{SD}_{24} = SD_{24} - SD_{12} = \{24, 8\}$. $2^{gcd(12, 3) \cdot r_3 + gcd (12, 4)r_4 + gcd(12, 5)r_5} = 24 \cdot D(24) + 8 \cdot D(8)$. $2^{3 \cdot 2 + 4 \cdot 2 + 1 \cdot 1} = 24 \cdot D(24) + 2048$. $D(24) = (2^{15} - 2048)/24 = 1280$.

Finally, $120 \cdot D(120) = 2^{19} - 24 \cdot D(24) - 40 \cdot D(40) - 8 \cdot D(8)$. $D(120) = (524, 288, - 30,720 - 30,720 - 2,048)/120 = 3,840$. ■

4.6.2.2 Even-composite ring structures

This structure is quantified similarly to the odd-composite ring structure considered in Sec. 4.6.2.1 except for the fact that, for every i, instead of set $\overline{SD}_{2i} = SD_{2i} - SD_i$ we are using set SD_i. The set of periods, SP, is found as follows: Given $SF_1 = [1^{r_1}, 2^{r_2}, \ldots, t^{r_t}]$, CF = $[E_1, E_2, \ldots, E_t]$. Let $S_E = \{i : r_i \geq 1\}$. For each integer $i \in S_E$, find the set of divisors SD_i. Let $(b_1, b_2, \ldots, b_t)$ be an arbitrary vector such that $b_i \in SD_i$. Then the set of periods, SP, is defined as follows:

Theorem 10. If $v = $ lcm $(b_1, b_2, \ldots, b_t)$, $v \in$ SP. Therefore, SP is the set of lcm's found for all members of the Cartesian product constructed from SD_i sets where $i \in S_E$.

Theorem 11. For any $b \in$ SP

$$\prod_{i \in S_E} 2^{gcd(b, i)r_i} = \sum_{T \in SD_b} T \cdot D(T)$$

Theorems 10 and 11 allow quantization of any even-composite ring structure specified with $SF_1 = [1^{r_1}, 2^{r_2}, \ldots, t^{r_t}]$, CF = $[E_1, E_2, \ldots, E_t]$.

Example. Let $SF_1 = [1^1, 2^1, 3^1, 4^1, 6^1]$; $n = 1 + 2 + 3 + 4 + 6 = 16$; $S_E = \{1, 2, 3, 4, 6\}$; $SD_1 = \{1\}$; $SD_2 = \{2, 1\}$; $SD_3 = \{3, 1\}$; $SD_4 = \{4, 2, 1\}$; $SD_6 = \{6, 3, 2, 1\}$. Find $CP = SD_1 \times SD_2 \times SD_3 \times SD_4 \times SD_6 = \{(1, 2, 3, 4, 6), (1, 2, 1, 1, 1), (1, 1, 3, 1, 1), (1, 2, 1, 4, 1), (1, 2, 3, 2, 1), (1, 1, 1, 1, 1)\}$. (We included only those members in the CP that give different lcm's.) $SP = \{\mathrm{lcm}(1, 2, 3, 4, 6), \mathrm{lcm}(1, 2, 1, 1, 1), \mathrm{lcm}(1, 1, 3, 1, 1), \mathrm{lcm}(1, 2, 1, 4, 1), \mathrm{lcm}(1, 2, 3, 2, 1), \mathrm{lcm}(1, 1, 1, 1, 1)\} = \{12, 2, 3, 4, 6, 1\}$. $D(1) = 2^{1+1+1+1+1} = 32$; $2D(2) + D(1) = 2^{1+2+1+2+2} = 256$; $D(2) = 112$; $3D(3) + D(1) = 2^{1+1+3+1+3}$; $D(3) = 160$; $4D(4) + 2D(2) + D(1) = 2^{1+2+1+4+2}$; $D(4) = 192$; $6D(6) + 3D(3) + 2D(2) + D(1) = 2^{1+2+3+2+6}$; $D(6) = 2608$; $12 \cdot D(12) + 6D(6) + 4 \cdot D(4) + 3 \cdot D(3) + 2 \cdot D(2) + D(1) = 2^{1+2+3+4+6}$; $D(12) = 4032$. ∎

4.6.2.3 Mixed composite ring structures

Given $SF_1 = [1^{r_1}, 2^{r_2}, \ldots, t^{r_t}]$, $CF = [m_1, m_2, \ldots, m_t]$, where $m_1, m_2, \ldots, m_t \in \{O, E\}$. Let us form S_O and S_E sets: $S_O = \{i : r_i \geq 1 \text{ and } m_i = O_i\}$; $S_E = \{j : r_j \geq 1 \text{ and } m_j = E_j\}$. For any integer $i \in S_O$, let us form $\overline{SD}_{2i} = SD_{2i} - SD_i$. For any integer $j \in S_E$, let us form SD_j. Form the Cartesian product, CP_{OE} from all sets $\overline{SD}_{2i}$ ($i \in S_O$) and SD_j ($j \in S_E$). Let $(b_1, b_2, \ldots, b_t)$ be an arbitrary member of CP_{OE}.

Theorem 12. If $v = \mathrm{lcm}(b_1, b_2, \ldots, b_t)$, $v \in SP$.

Corollary. For mixed composite ring structures, the set of periods, SP, includes only even numbers.

Theorem 13. For any $2b \in SP$,

$$\prod_{i \in S_O} 2^{\gcd(b,\, i)r_i} \qquad \prod_{j \in S_E} 2^{\gcd(2b,\, j)\,\cdot\, r_j} = \sum_{T \in \overline{SD}_{2j} \cap SP} T \cdot D(T)$$

Theorems 12 and 13 allow specification of an arbitrary composite ring structure.

Example. $SF_1 = [3^{r_3}, 5^{r_5}, 6^{r_6}]$, $r_3 = r_5 = r_6 = 1$. $CF = [O_3, E_5, E_6]$; $S_O = \{3\}$, $S_E = \{5, 6\}$. For $i \in S_O$, find $\overline{SD}_{2i} = \overline{SD}_6 = SD_6 - SD_3 = \{6, 2\}$. For $j \in S_E$, find SD_j; for $j = 5$, $SD_5 = \{5, 1\}$; for $j = 6$, $SD_6 = \{6, 3, 2, 1\}$. Find the Cartesian product, $CP_{OE} = \overline{SD}_6 \times SD_5 \times SD_6$. Since full CP_{OE} contains 16 members, many of which have the same lcm's, we will include in CP_{OE} only those members that have different lcm's: $CP_{OE} = \{(6, 5, 6), (2, 5, 1), (6, 1, 1), (2, 1, 2)\}$. Thus, the set of periods for this ring structure is $SP = \mathrm{lcm}(6, 5, 6), \mathrm{lcm}(2, 5, 1), \mathrm{lcm}(6, 1, 1), \mathrm{lcm}(2, 1, 2)\} = \{30, 10, 6, 2\}$.

$$2D(2) - 2^{\gcd(3,\, 1)\,\cdot\,1 + \gcd(5,\, 2)\,\cdot\,1 + \gcd(6,\, 2)\,\cdot\,1} = 2^{1+1+2} = 2^4$$
$$D(2) = 8$$
$$6 \cdot D(6) + 2 \cdot D(2) = 2^{\gcd(3,\, 3)\,\cdot\,1 + \gcd(5,\, 6)\,\cdot\,1 + \gcd(6,\, 6)\,\cdot\,1} = 2^{3+1+6} = 2^{10}$$
$$D(6) = 168$$

$$10 \cdot D(10) + 2 \cdot D(2) = 2^{gcd(3, 5) \cdot 1 + gcd(5, 10) \cdot 1 + gcd(6, 10) \cdot 1} = 2^{1 + 5 + 2} = 256$$
$$D(10) = 24$$
$$30 \cdot D(30) + 10 \cdot D(10) + 6 \cdot D(6) + 2 \cdot D(2) =$$
$$2^{14}; \ D(30) = 504 \quad \blacksquare$$

4.7 Single Tree Structures

As was indicated in Subsection 4.4, a *single tree structure* is generated by a single SRVB described by a noncircular shifting format, $SF_0 = [n^1]$ [Fig. II.33(a)]. For the same size n of SRVB, the difference between different single trees is in the relative positions of their roots, leaves, and nonleaves, although structurally they are isomorphic to each other [Fig. II.33(b)]. Thus, the task of reconfiguration is to reconfigure the network from one tree to another to optimize the time of data exchanges in tree data bases [63].

To distinguish among single and multirooted trees, we will tabulate all possible tree structures as follows: since a tree structure, TS (single, STS, or multirooted, MTS), is always generated by a noncircular SRVB with shifting format $SF_0 = [n^1]$, then TS $= k(n^1, \vec{p})$ shows that TS contains k p-rooted trees; for each p-rooted tree, its roots form a ring of period p (i.e., $\vec{p}$) and each tree has n levels (i.e., n^1). For instance, TS $= 1(n^1, \vec{1})$ shows that this is a single tree of n levels with the root forming a cycle of period 1. The multirooted tree structure of Fig. II.16 is described as TS $= 2(2^1, \vec{4})$, etc.

Since in a single tree structure its root may store important information that needs to be transferred to other nodes (deactivation of some tree nodes from computation

3-LEVEL TREE

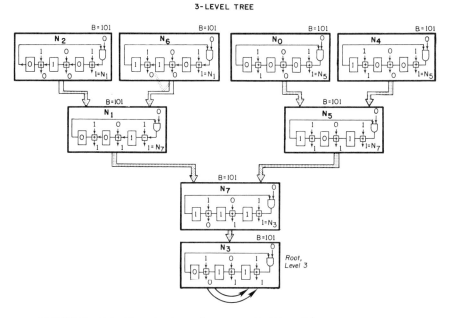

FIGURE II.33(a)   Three-level tree described with $SF_0 = [3^1]$

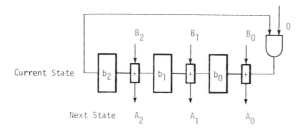

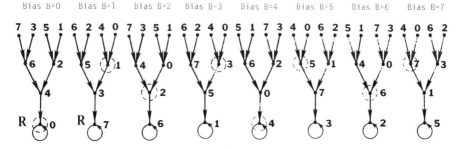

FIGURE II.33(b) Assortment of different trees that can be generated with $SF_0 = [3^1]$

or other managerial information), it is desirable to develop simple formulas that define the root, R, without actual construction of STS. Also, it is important that the programmer be provided with a simple technique to find out what nodes form leaves and nonleaves for the given bias B, or, more generally, if bias B is given, what nodes are the nodes of the ith level ($i = 0, \ldots, n$). This feature will greatly facilitate communication among nodes inside the binary tree generated with given bias B [65].

Indeed, using this technique, each node may form the position code of the destination node in a tree and establish a communication path with the destination. Theorems 14 and 15 provide the solution to this important problem stated as follows:

Given a noncircular shifting format, $SF_0 = [n^1]$, and bias B. Find the nodes of the ith level, where $i = 0, \ldots, n$.

While Theorem 14 gives a solution for the root (the node of level n), the more general Theorem 15 gives a solution for any node of the level i ($i = 0, \ldots, n$). To establish these theorems, let us first look again into the bias structure for noncircular shifting formats, $SF_0 = [n^1]$, since these SFs generate binary trees.

4.7.1 Bias Structure for a Noncircular Shifting Format

Given bias $B = GP_1 + GP_2 + \ldots + GP_t$, where t is the bias weight, GP_i is its generating position ($i = 1, \ldots, t$). As with circular shifting format, let $a_1, a_2, \ldots, a_t$ be *bias distances* defined as follows. $GP_{i+1} = a_i[GP_i]$; i.e., a_i shows the number of

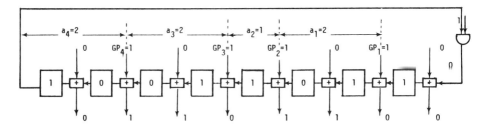

FIGURE II.34 Bias structure for a noncircular shifting format SF_0

left-hand shifts between GP_i and GP_{i+1}, where i changes from 1 to $t-1$. For GP_t, $a_t[GP_t]$ = 0; since we are having a noncircular shift (Fig. II.34). Thus, for a noncircular SRVB, $a_t[GP_t] = 0$; for a circular SRVB, $a_t[GP_t] = GP_1$. This small distinction among circular and noncircular SRVB leads to a fundamental distinction among the network structures that are generated.

For each generating position, GP_i, let us form a mod-2 sum of all left j-bit shifts of GP_i ranging from $j = 0$ to $j = a_i - 1$, where a_i is the bias distance such that $a_i[GP_i]$ = GP_{i+1}. Denote this sum as $BL(GP_i) = GP_i + 1[GP_i] + \ldots + (a_1 - 1)[GP_i]$. By construction, GP_i is an addend of $BL(GP_i)$ and GP_{i+1} is not an addend of $BL(GP_i)$.

Example.

	GP_5			GP_4		GP_3	GP_2		GP_1	
Let bias B =	1	0	0	1	0	1	1	0	1	0
Bias digits	9	8	7	6	5	4	3	2	1	0

(10)

Bias GPs are $GP_1 = 2^1$, $GP_2 = 2^3$, $GP_3 = 2^4$, $GP_4 = 2^6$, and $GP_5 = 2^8$. Bias distances are $a_1 = 2$, since a 2-bit shift of GP_1 gives GP_2; $a_2 = 1$, since $1[GP_2] = GP_3$; $a_3 = 2$, since $2[GP_3] = GP_4$; $a_4 = 3$, since $3[GP_4] = GP_5$; and $a_5 = 1$, since $1[GP_5]$ = 0, because SRVB performs a noncircular shift.

Let us form $BL(GP_i)$ sums:

$$
\begin{array}{ccccccccccc}
 & & & & & & & & & GP_1 & \\
BL(GP_1) = GP_1 + 1[GP_1] = 0 & 0 & 0 & 0 & 0 & 0 & 0 & 1 & 1 & 0 \\
 & 9 & 8 & 7 & 6 & 5 & 4 & 3 & 2 & 1 & 0
\end{array}
$$

where $a_1 - 1 = 2 - 1 = 1$ and

$$
\begin{array}{l}
BL(GP_2) = GP_2 = 0 \quad 0 \quad 0 \quad 0 \quad 0 \quad 0 \quad 1 \quad 0 \quad 0 \quad 0, \quad \text{since } a_2 - 1 = 0 \\
 9 \quad 8 \quad 7 \quad 6 \quad 5 \quad 4 \quad 3 \quad 2 \quad 1 \quad 0
\end{array}
$$

$$
\begin{array}{l}
BL(GP_3) = GP_3 + 1[GP_3] = 0 \quad 0 \quad 0 \quad 0 \quad 1 \quad 1 \quad 0 \quad 0 \quad 0 \quad 0, \quad \text{since} \\
 9 \quad 8 \quad 7 \quad 6 \quad 5 \quad 4 \quad 3 \quad 2 \quad 1 \quad 0
\end{array}
$$

$a_3 - 1 = 1$ (11)

$$
\begin{array}{l}
BL(GP_4) = GP_4 + 1[GP_4] + 2[GP_4] = 0 \quad 1 \quad 1 \quad 1 \quad 0 \quad 0 \quad 0 \quad 0 \quad 0 \quad 0, \\
 9 \quad 8 \quad 7 \quad 6 \quad 5 \quad 4 \quad 3 \quad 2 \quad 1 \quad 0
\end{array}
$$

since $a_4 - 1 = 2$

$$BL(GP_5) = GP_5 = 1 \quad 0 \quad 0 \quad 0 \quad 0 \quad 0 \quad 0 \quad 0 \quad 0 \quad 0 \quad \blacksquare$$
$$ 9 \quad 8 \quad 7 \quad 6 \quad 5 \quad 4 \quad 3 \quad 2 \quad 1 \quad 0$$

4.7.2 Synthesis of the Root

With the introduction of BL sums, we can establish the theorem which constructs the root.

Theorem 14. For a binary tree generated by SRVB receiving bias $B = GP_1 + GP_2 + \ldots + GP_t$, let GP_1, GP_3, GP_5, ..., GP_k be odd generating positions of the bias, where $k = t$ if t is odd and $k = t - 1$ if t is even.

Form BL sums for odd generating positions of the bias as $BL(GP_1)$, $BL(GP_3)$, ..., $BL(GP_k)$. The root, R is:

$$R = BL(GP_1) + BL(GP_3) + \cdots + BL(GP_k)$$

Proof. To prove this theorem is to form the successor N^* of R as $N^* = 1[R] + B$ and show that $N^* = R$. To do so, let us first find a 1-bit shift of a $BL(GP_i)$, where $i = 1, \ldots, t - 1$: $1[BL(GP_i)] = 1[GP_i + 1[GP_i] + \cdots + (a_i - 1) [GP_i]] = 1[GP_i] + 2[GP_i] + \ldots + a_i - 1[GP_i] + a_i[GP_i]$. Since $a_i[GP_i] = GP_{i+1}$

$$1[BL(GP_i)] = 1[GP_i] + 2[GP_i] + \cdots + (a_i - 1) [GP_i] + GP_{i+1}$$

Let us add $GP_i + GP_i = 0$ to the above expression as $1[BL(GP_i)] + 0 = 1[BL(GP_i)] + GP_i + GP_i = GP_i + BL(GP_i) + GP_{i+1}$, because

$$GP_i + 1[BL(GP_i)] = \underline{GP_i + 1[GP_1] + \cdots + (a_i - 1)[GP_i] + GP_{i+1}} = BL(GP_i) + GP_{i+1}$$
$$ BL(GP_i)$$

Now let us find $1[BL(GP_t)]$ for the case $i = t$: $1[BL(GP_t)] = GP_t + BL(GP_t)$, because $a_t[GP_t] = 0$, since SRVB performs a noncircular shift. Thus, for $i \le t - 1$,

$$1[BL(GP_i)] = GP_i + BL(GP_i) + GP_{i+1}$$

For $i = t$,

$$1[BL(GP_t)] = GP_t + BL(GP_t)$$

These findings are crucial for specifying the successor of the root R:

$$N^* = 1[R] + B = 1[BL(GP_1) + BL(GP_3) + BL(GP_5) + \cdots + BL(GP_k)] + GP_1 + GP_2 + \cdots + GP_t = 1[BL(GP_1)] + \cdots + 1(BL(GP_k)] + GP_1 + \cdots + GP_t$$

Let us find N^* for an even t: since t is even, the last addend in the root is $BL(GP_{t-1})$, because the root is formed of odd BL sums Thus,

$$1[BL(GP_1)] = GP_1 + BL(GP_1) + GP_2$$
$$1[BL(GP_3)] = GP_3 + BL(GP_3) + GP_4$$
$$1[BL(GP_{t-1})] = BP_{t-1} + BL(GP_{t-1}) + GP_t$$

Substituting these expressions into the expression for N* gives

$$N* = \frac{GP_1 + BL(GP_1) + GP_2}{1[DL(GP_i)]} + \frac{GP_3 + BL(GP_3) + GP_4 + \cdots}{1[BL(GP_3)]}$$

$$+ \frac{GP_{t-1} + BL(GP_{t-1}) + GP_t}{1[BL(GP_{t-1})]} + \frac{GP_1 + GP_3 + GP_4 + \cdots + GP_{t-1} + GP_t}{B}$$

$$= BL(GP_1) + BL(GP_3 + \cdots + BL(GP_{t-1}) = R$$

Thus, R succeeds itself, which proves the theorem for an even weighed bias. For an odd-weighted bias, it is proved similarly by taking into account that $BL(GP_t)$ is the last odd addend of the root R, and we use the expression developed for $i = t$ to find the 1-bit shift of $BL(GP_t)$. ∎QED

Example. Let us form the root R for bias B given by Eq. (10).

$$R = BL(GP_1) + BL(GP_3) + BL(GP_5) = \overset{GP_5}{\underset{\overline{BL(GP_5)}}{1}} \; 0 \; 0 \; \overset{GP_4 \; GP_3}{\underset{\overline{BL(GP_3)}}{0 \; 1 \; 1}} \; \overset{GP_2}{0} \; \overset{GP_1}{\underset{\overline{BL(GP_1)}}{1 \; 1}} \; 0$$

where BL sums for odd-generating positions are specified in Eq. (11).
Find the successor N* of R:

$$N* = 1[R] + B = \overset{9\;8\;7\;6\;5\;4\;3\;2\;1\;0}{0\;0\;0\;1\;1\;0\;1\;1\;0\;0} + \overset{9\;8\;7\;6\;5\;4\;3\;2\;1\;0}{1\;0\;0\;1\;0\;1\;1\;0\;1\;0}$$

$$= \overset{9\;8\;7\;6\;5\;4\;3\;2\;1\;0}{1\;0\;0\;0\;1\;1\;0\;1\;1\;0} = R \quad ■$$

As we have seen, the technique for constructing the root is very simple and can be easily performed by the programmer who can find the root for the given bias B and then store it in the instruction that reconfigures the network in the given single binary tree, or the root R can be formed inside each code N by the hardware circuits containing two shifters interconnected with a mod-2 counter that generates two outputs, even and odd.

Example. Consider a logical diagram that forms the root for bias B = 100101000100100. Since bias B is 15 bit, the circuit includes two 15-bit shifters, shifter 1 and shifter 2, connected together serially via a mod-2 counter, CO [Fig. II.35(a)]. Initial settings of these devices are shifter 1 stores bias B, CO stores 0, and shifter 2 stores zeros. At each clock period, CO performs mod 2 counting of ones shifted out from shifter 1. Thus, it generates the signal $Q_{odd} = 1$ if the number of counted ones is odd. Otherwise, it generates Q_{even} if the number of counted ones is even. Therefore, CO is switched into generating signal Q_{odd} each time when the least significant bit of shifter 1 stores either an odd-generating position G_i or $(a_i - 1)$ consecutive zero bits that follow G_i in the bias B. The CO is triggered into generating signal Q_{even} by an even-

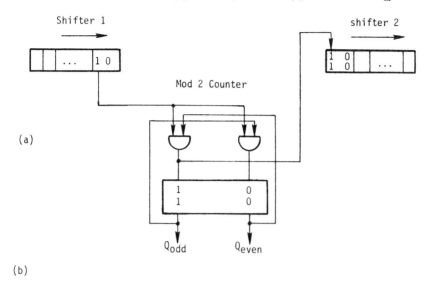

(a)

(b)

Col. 1	Col. 2	Col. 3	Col. 4
Initial Setting	Shifter 1 100101000100100	Mod Counter 2 0	Shifter 2 000000000000000
Clocks:			
T_0	010010100010010	0	000000000000000
T_1	001001010001001	0	000000000000000
T_2	000100101000100	1	100000000000000
T_3	000010010100010	1	110000000000000
T_4	000001001010001	1	111000000000000
T_5	000000100101000	0	011100000000000
T_6	000000010010100	0	001110000000000
T_7	000000001001010	0	000111000000000
T_8	000000000100101	0	000011100000000
T_9	000000000010010	1	100001110000000
T_{10}	000000000001001	1	110000111000000
T_{11}	000000000000100	0	011000011100000
T_{12}	000000000000010	0	001100001110000
T_{13}	000000000000001	0	000110000111000
T_{14}	000000000000000	1	100011000011100

FIGURE II.35 Logical diagram for forming the root: (a) Connection of two shifters with mod 2 counter; (b) timing diagram

generating position G_j and all the $(a_j - 1)$ consecutive zeros that follow G_j. Thus, during n-bit shifting of shifter 1, Q_{odd} generates consecutive bits of the root R, which are written to shifter 2. After n shifting iterations, shifter 2 stores the root R obtained for the given bias B. Hardware formation of the root, R, for bias B = 100101000100100 is shown in Fig. II.35(b), where col. 1 gives clock periods and col. 2 shows the content of shifter 1 during clock period T_i. Similarly, cols. 3 and 4 show the contents of CO and shifter 2 during clock periods T_i. The root R is formed during the clock period T_{14}. ∎

Therefore, each tree node N is capable either of receiving root R via program instruction that reconfigures the network into a given binary tree or node N can generate root R via hardware circuits that receive bias B. Root R can be used for forming codes of other tree node(s) with which a given node wishes to communicate. This formation of the tree nodes from the root can be accomplished using the synthesis technique present in the next section.

4.7.3 Synthesis of an Arbitrary Tree Node (Nonleaves or Leaves)

In this section, we will develop a synthesis procedure for constructing a tree node of the jth level ($j = 0, \ldots, n$) if bias B is given. The node of the nth level (root) was constructed in Theorem 14. Here we present a more general result which extends our findings to any ith-level node ($i = n, n - 1, n - 2, \ldots, 0$). To establish this result, let us introduce the notion of recursive sum, $RS_i(k)$, where $k \leq i, i \geq 0$

Basis: $RS_0(0) = 0, i = 0, k = 0$.
Inductive Step: $RS_i(k) = X_i + RS_m(k - 1)$, where $k \leq i, X_i = 2^{n-i}$, and $m < i$.
Therefore, if SRVB stores $RS_i(k)$, its position b_{n-i} is always 1, and $k - 1$ is the total number of other more significant ones positions.

Example. Consider storage of various recursive sums in a 5-bit SRVB (Fig. II.36). The 5-bit code $10111 = X_1 + X_3 + X_4 + X_5$ has four ones and X_5 is the least significant variable, giving $i = 5$ and $k = 4$. Therefore, $RS_i(k) = RS_5(4) = X_5 + RS_4(3)$, because X_4 is the next least significant variable; $RS_4(3) = X_4 + RS_3(2), RS_3(2) = X_3 + RS_1(1)$, $RS_1(1) = X_1$, etc. ∎

For a recursive sum, $RS_i(k) = X_i + RS_m(k - 1)$, X_i will be called a *level variable.* As shown below, level variable $X_i = 1$ uniquely specifies all tree nodes of level $n - i$. Once we have introduced the notion of recursive sum $RS_i(k)$, we can develop the synthesis technique for constructing the node of level $n - i (i = n, n - 1, \ldots, 0)$.

Theorem 15. In a single binary tree formed with bias B, any tree node, $N(n - i)$, of level $n - i(i = 0, \ldots, n)$ can be found as follows:

$$N(n - i) = R + RS_i(k),$$

where $k \leq i$, R is the root, and $RS_i(k)$ is a recursive sum with level variable X_i.

Example. Given bias B = $\overset{6\ \ 5\ \ 4\ \ 3\ \ 2\ \ 1\ \ 0}{1\ 0\ 1\ 1\ 0\ 1\ 1}$. Let us construct all the nodes of levels $n - i = 7, 6, 5$, and 4 (Fig. II.37). Here $n = 7$. Therefore, the root is of level 7: R = $BL(GP_1) + BL(GP_3) + BL(GP_5)$ and $GP_1 = 2^0 = 1, GP_3 = 2^3 = 8$, and $GP_5 = 2^6$

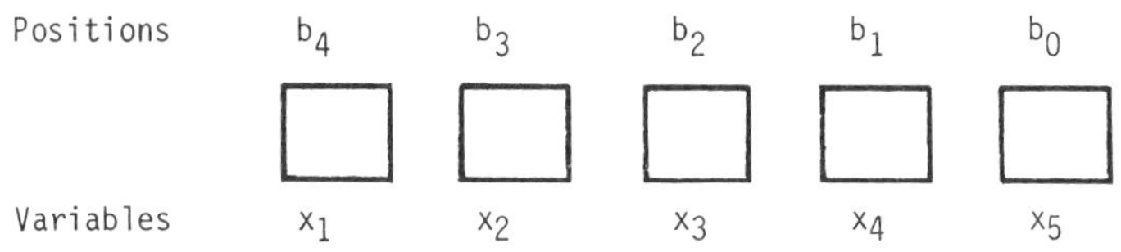

Positions	b_4	b_3	b_2	b_1	b_0
	□	□	□	□	□
Variables	x_1	x_2	x_3	x_4	x_5

Code	1	0	1	1	1
Variables	x_1		x_3	x_4	x_5

Least Significant Variable X_5 $i = 5$	Number of Ones $k = 4$	$RS_5(4) = X_5 + RS_4(3)$ $RS_4(3) = X_4 + RS_3(2)$ $RS_3(2) = X_3 + RS_1(1)$ $RS_1(1) = X1$

Code	0	1	1	1	0
Variables		x_2	x_3	x_4	
$i = 4$	$k = 3$	$RS_i(k) = RS_4(3) = X_4 + RS_3(2)$ $RS_3(2) = X_3 + RS_2(1)$ $RS_2(1) = X1$

FIGURE II.36 Formation of various recusive sums in the two 5-bit registers storing codes 10111 and 01110, respectively

$= 64$; $BL(GP_1) = GP_1$, since $a_1 = 1$; $BL(GP_3) = GP_3$, since $a_3 = 1$ and $BL(GP_5) =$
$$GP_5 \quad GP_3 \quad GP_1$$
GP_5, since $a_5 = 1$. Thus, $R = 1 0\ \ 0 1\ \ 0\ \ 0 1$. Indeed, the successor N^* of R is N^*
$= 1[R] + B = 1[1001001] + 1011011 = 0010010 + 1011011 = 1001001 = R = X_1 +$
$X_4 + X_7$.

The node of level 6 is $N(n - 1) = R + RS_1(1) = R + X_1 = 0001001 = X_4 +$
X_7. This node is succeeded by the root because $N^* = 1[N(6)] + B = 0010010 + 1011011$
$= 1001001 = R$.

There are two nodes of level $n - 2 = 5$: $N_1(5) = R + RS_2(1) = R + X_2 = 1101001$
$= 105$ and $N_2(5) = R + RS_2(2) = R + X_1 + X_2 = X_2 + X_4 + X_7 = 0101001$. Indeed,
$N_1(5)$ is succeeded by $N^* = 1[N_1(5)] + B = 1010010 + 1011011 = 0001001 = N(6)$
$= 9$. Likewise, $N_2(5)$ is succeeded by $N^* = 1[N_2(5)] + B = 1010010 + 1011011 = 0001001$
$= 9$, etc. ■

Proof. To prove this theorem is to establish that any node $N(s) = R + RS_i(k)$ of
level $s = n - i$ is succeeded by the node $N(s + 1) = R + RS_{i+1}(m)$ of level $s + 1$. The
reconfiguration successor N^* of $N(s)$ is $N^* = 1[N(s)] + B = 1[R + RS_i(k)] + B =$
$1[R] + 1[RS_i(k)] + B$. In accordance with Theorem 14, the successor of R is R.

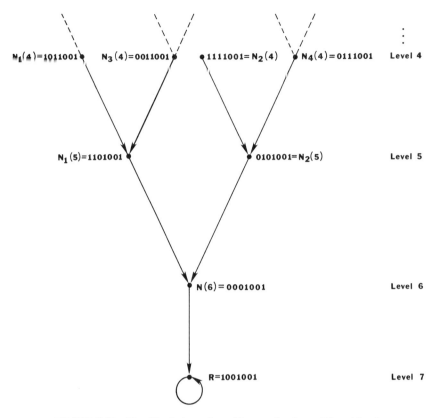

FIGURE II.37 Algorithmic formation of tree nodes from different levels

Therefore, $R = 1[R] + B$. Thus, $N^* = 1[R] + B + 1[RS_i(k)] = R + 1[RS_i(k)]$. By definition, $RS_i(k) = 2^s + RS_j(k - 1)$. Thus, $1[RS_i(k)] = 1[2^s] + 1[RS_j(k - 1)] = 2^{s+1} + RS_{j+1}(\ell)$, where $\ell = k - 1$ if $RS_j(k - 1)$ does not have 2^{n-1}, and $1 = k - 2$ if $RS_j(k - 1)$ does have 2^{n-1} because $1[2^{n-1}] = 0$, since SRVB performs a noncircular shift. Therefore, $1[RS_i(k)] = RS_{i+1}(m)$, where $m = k \vee k - 1$ and $N^* = R + RS_{i+1}(m)$, which shows that N^* is the node of the next level $s + 1$.   ■QED

In this section we presented very simple techniques that allow synthesis of any node of level i in a binary tree generated in SRVB receiving bias B. As follows, the fastest distribution of the root to other nodes occurs if the root is stored in the reconfiguration instruction and then broadcast to each tree node. Having received the root, each given tree node may form the code of an sth-level destination node via the mod-2 addition of the root with a corresponding recursive sum, $RS_i(k)$ where $s = n - i$. Since formation of each $RS_i(k)$ can be made by a very simple logical circuit, the destination node, $N(s) = R + RS_i(k)$, can be created during one clock period.

4.8 Efficient Internode Communications in Reconfigurable Binary Trees

In any reconfigurable binary tree, organization of efficient communication among tree nodes presents a major problem because, during reconfiguration, position of tree nodes change. Therefore, to route a communication message from a source node, N_s, to a destination node, N_d, requires storage of the position codes of all transit nodes of the $N_s \rightarrow N_d$ communication path. This routing information (RI) can be either stored in a communication message (CM) or distributed among transit nodes so that each transit node stores the position code of its successor in the $N_s \rightarrow N_d$ communication path. Both these alternatives are infeasible since they lead to a large bit size of the RI code and a long time of internode communication associated with the large size of RI.

In this subsection we will develop optimal communication techniques that allow taking full advantage of the fine mathematical properties of SRVB. To develop these techniques, we use the following approach:

1. We specify the communication circuits that must be placed inside each tree node so that this node is equipped with the efficient and minimal time transit functions, whereby it merely transmits a received message to the next node of communication path, introducing a minimal communication delay in such a transit.

2. Using the root and node formulas specified in Theorems 14 and 15 of Sec. 4.7, we find a routing information code for a root → node communication in the given tree configuration.

3. Using these findings, we then attack the general problem of an arbitrary node → node communication.

4.8.1 Communication Circuits Inside a Transit Node

Each transit node N has three closest neighbors in the binary tree: the left node (LN), the right node (RN), and the reconfiguration successor N* [Fig. II.38(a)]. To perform efficient communication transit, node N must be capable of generating inside the position codes of LN, RN and N*. While generation of N* is done with the use of the reconfiguration equation as $N^* = 1[N]_0 + B$, generation of LN and RN can be done using the techniques presented below.†

4.8.1.1 Generation inside node N of its closest neighbors

To select efficiently LN and RN, we have to fix their positions within the same level. That is, LN and RN must be ordered with respect to the current root, R, which is the most significant node in the tree. Assume that $R > LN > RN$.

---

†Since in this section we will always deal with noncircular shifts, the 0 subscript in $1[N]_0$ will be omitted for the sake of simplicity.

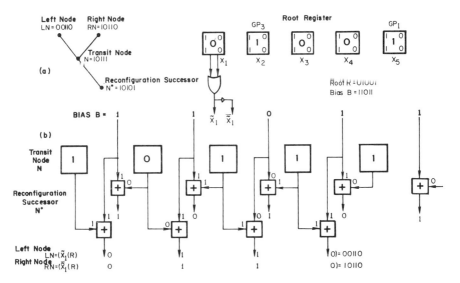

FIGURE II.38 Generation inside node N of its three adjacent neighbors, LN, RN, and $\tilde{N}$ in the binary tree

Since LN and RN are on the same level, they are specified by the two recursive sums with the same level variable X_i. Thus, to establish the order among LN and RN, we have to order recursive sums.

Assume that any two recursive sums RS_i and RS_j are ordered as follows:

P1. $RS_i > RS_j$ if $X_i > X_j$, where $X_i = 2^{n-i}$ and $X_j = 2^{n-j}$.

P2. $RS_i > RS_i'$ if $RS_i + X_i > RS_i' + X_i$.

Using P1 and P2, we can generate LN and RN as follows: $N = 1[LN] + B = 1[RN] + B$, where $1[\ldots]$ is a 1-bit shift to the left. Thus. $1[LN] = 1[RN]$ or $RN = LN + X_1$, since a 1-bit shift of X_1 to the left is 0; i.e., $1[X_i] = 0$ and $1[LN + X_1] = 1[LN] + 1[X_1] = 1[LN]$. Therefore, since $LN > RN$, $LN = R + RS_i$; $RN = R + RS_i + X_1$. Thus, two nodes LN and RN differ only in position X_1. Therefore, the left node LN necessarily has the same meaning for the $\tilde{X}_1$ variable as $\tilde{X}_1$ of the root R. On the other hand, the right node RN always has its $\tilde{X}_1$ variable reversed, i.e., opposite the one of the root [Fig. II.38(b)]. Thus,

$$LN = \tilde{X}_1(R) + 1^{-1}[N + B]$$

where $1^{1-1}[\ldots]$ is a noncircular shift to the right and $\tilde{X}_1(R)$ is the meaning of the most significant variable in the node LN. Similarly, since $1[RN] = N + B$,

$$RN = \overline{\tilde{X}}_1(R) + 1^{-1}[N + B]$$

Thus, for a given tree configuration, LN and RN are obtained inside node N via the *right-shifted noncircular* SRVB receiving bias B, whereas N* is obtained conventionally inside node N using the left-shifted noncircular SRVB receiving the same bias B [Fig. II.38(b)].

Example. Figure II.38(b) shows the generation inside N = 10111 of its closest neighbors N*, LN, and RN for the binary tree having bias B = 11011 and rote R = 01001.

$$LN = X_1(R) + 1^{-1}[10111 + 11011] = 00110$$

$$RN = \overline{X}_1(R) + 1^{-1}[10111 + 11011] = 10110$$

$$N* = 1[N] + B = 01110 + 11011 = 10101 \quad \blacksquare$$

4.8.1.2 Transit functions of the node

To perform fast internode communications, each tree node N must be provided with the transit circuits that allow its effective functioning as a transit node, i.e., the one which is provided with three immediate neighbors LN, RN, and N* (Fig. II.38) or which merely passes communication messages to one of its neighbors LN, RN, or N*. Since messages may flow in the two directions, TOR and TOL, where TOR means to the root and TOL mean to the leaves, each transit node has T and D terminals, respectively, designated for TOR broadcast if the message passes from T to D or for TOL broadcast, otherwise.

To maintain concurrent communications whereby a message received by the D terminal is allowed to flow concurrently to the left and right neighbors of the given node N, each transit node is provided with the two T terminals, LT and RT, that connect given node N with the LN and RN nodes, respectively (Fig. II.39).

In this subsection, each connection of the transit node N with its successor N* and the two predecessors LN and RN in the tree is performed via a pair of connecting elements, MSE, selected during reconfiguration, since a single staged interconnection network will be used as an illustration [58] (Fig. II.40).

For the N → N* broadcast, the (MSE_N - MSE_{N^*}) pair belongs to N; for the N → LN broadcast, the (MSE_N - MSE_{LN}) pair belongs to LN; for the N → RN broadcast, the (MSE_N - MSE_{RN}) pair belongs to RN. The mode of transfer of each pair of connecting elements depends on the direction of broadcast. For the TOR communication N → N*, from N to its successor, N*, connecting element MSE_N should be activated in the *write* direction (w(MSE_N)) and MSE_{N^*} should be activated in the *read* direction (r(MSE_{N^*})). For the TOL communication N → LN, the direction of transfer in MSE_N and MSE_{LN} reverses to read for MSE_N and write for MSE_{LN} (Fig. II.39). Similar directions are true for the N → RN broadcast.

Since at each clock period, a transit node N may change the direction of broadcast, we assume that the modes of transfer in connecting elements will be activated dynamically by the messages that are allowed to pass through a given output terminal.

For the TOR broadcast via the D terminal, such activation will be performed by the L_1 logic which receives several *static inputs* and one *dynamic* input from the allowed message (saved or current). Static inputs are code N for selecting MSE_N, code N* for selecting MSE_{N^*}, r-signal for r(MSE_{N^*}), and w-signal for w(MSE_N). The L_1 logic is activated concurrently during TOR message transit via N; thus, it introduces no additional delay into a message transit. For the TOL left broadcast via the LT terminal or RT terminal, this dynamic activation is performed by the L_2 logic or L_3 logic,

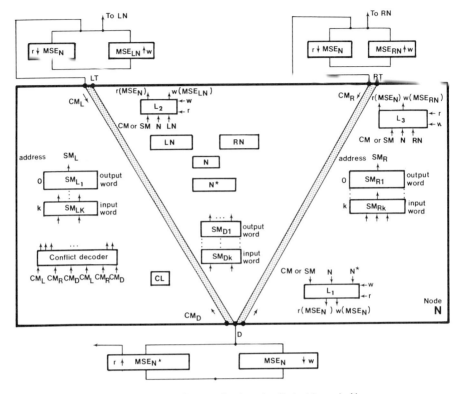

FIGURE II.39 Communication circuits inside node N

which issue, respectively, $r(MSE_N)$ and $w(MSE_{LN})$ for L_2 or $r(MSE_N)$ and $w(MSE_{RN})$ for L_3.

4.8.1.3 Conflict resolution among concurrent messages

Since there are three independent terminals in each transit node, it may receive up to three concurrent messages at a time: CM_L, CM_R, and CM_D. Since it may pass in transit only one message at a time, the node performs the conflict resolution via special logic called a *conflict decoder,* CD (Fig. II.39). The conflict decoder is a logical circuit that has a separate output for each conflict situation.

The decisions made by the conflict decoder are based on the following rules:

1. Of several messages that must use node N in transit, only one message is allowed to pass at each clock period. The remaining messages are saved. Since a transit node has three terminals (LT, RT, D), each terminal is provided with the individual push-down stack of save registers used to store saved messages, SM.

2. If a saved message, SM, is concurrent with a current message, CM, a decision to pass is given to a SM message and a CM message is saved.

3. If a message received via D terminal (saved SM_D, or current, CM_D) is concurrent with left or right messages, a decision to pass is in favor of a message received via D terminal. The remaining messages are saved.

4. Of the two concurrent left and right messages, the decision to pass favors the left message at even clock periods and the right message at odd clock periods.

Example. Suppose that a transit node N has six concurrent messages competing for transit: CM_L, CM_R, CM_D, SM_L^0, SM_R^0, and SM_D^0, where the superscript for saved messages shows their addresses in the register stacks. We assume that each stack has only one saved message, and no current message arrives until all messages are passed. At moment T_0, conflict decoder allows SM_D^0 to pass; CM_D is saved as new SM_D^0. CM_L is saved as SM_L^1; CM_R is saved as SM_R^1; at moment T_1, SM_D^0 is allowed to pass; the down stack has no saved messages; the left and right stacks store two messages each (Table II.2). At even moment T_2, SM_L^0 passes; the left stack retains one saved message; the right stack retains two messages; at odd moment T_3, SM_R^0 passes; the left and right stacks retain one message each, etc. The entire message transit ends at T_5. ∎

Another conflict situation may occur in connecting elments MSE_N and MSE_{N^*} that connect N and N*. Since they may be activated in opposite directions for N → N* and N* → N broadcasts, respectively, MSE_N and MSE_{N^*} are also provided with a simple logic for the conflict resolution. This logic is much simpler than the conflict decoder of node N, since the number of possible conflicts is smaller.

TABLE II.2

Time	Passed Messages	Saved Messages			Current Messages
		Left Stack	Right Stack	Down Stack	
Initial condition	—	SM_L^0	SM_R^0	SM_D^0	CM_L, CM_R, CM_D
T_0	SM_D^0	SM_L^0, SM_L^1	SM_R^0, SM_R^1	SM_D^0	—
T_1	SM_D^0	SM_L^0, SM_L^1	SM_R^0, SM_R^1	—	—
T_2	SM_L^0	SM_L^0	SM_R^0, SM_R^1	—	—
T_3	SM_R^0	SM_L^0	SM_R^0	—	—
T_4	SM_L^0	—	SM_R^0	—	—
T_5	SM_R^0	—	—	—	—

Below, we will introduce communication algorithms which allow efficient inter-node communications. Two types of communication will be considered:

1. Node-root communication
2. Node-node communication.

4.8.2 Node-root Communications

There are two types of node-root communication: (1) node $\rightarrow$ root, and (2) root $\rightarrow$ node.

4.8.2.1 Node-root communcations $N_s \rightarrow R$

For the $N_s \rightarrow R$ communication, N_s is the source and R is the destination; N_s generates communication message CM that stores the position code of the root, R, defined in Theorem 14. In passing this message, each transit node, N, compares R with its own position code, N. If $N = R$, the message reaches the destination. If $N \neq R$, it is passed top down from one of the top terminals (LT or RT) to the only one D terminal (Fig. II.40).

4.8.2.2 Root-node communication, $R \rightarrow N_d$

For this case, the message is generated by the root; i.e., R is the source and N_d is the destination. Message, CM, stores an address code of N_d defined as follows:

By the *address code,* AC_N of the node N, we define a binary word which contains all the routing information that allows a communication message to reach node N from the root via the minimal communication path (i.e., the one which includes each node of the tree only once).

Below, we define a procedure which allows one to obtain the address code, AC, of node N_d via a simple logical operation performed over its recursive sum, RS_i, introduced in Theorem 15. As will be shown below, the bit size of AC does not exceed n, the number of levels in the tree, where $n = \log_2 K$ and K is the number of tree nodes.

As was specified by Theorem 15, node N_d of level $n - i$ is defined as follows:

$$N_d = R + RS_i$$

where RS_i is the recursive sum. The immediate more significant successor of this node in the tree, otherwise called the reconfiguration 1-successor, can be found via the reconfigruation equation as

$$N^* = 1[N_d] + B = 1[R] + [RS_i] + B$$

Since for the root, R, $R = 1[R] + B$,

$$N^* = 1[R] + 1[RS_i] + B = R + 1[RS_i]$$

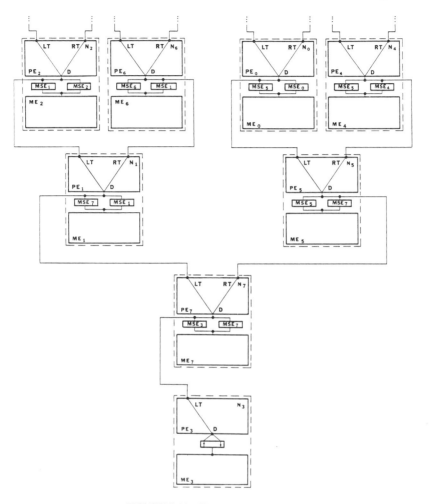

FIGURE II.40 Tree interconnections

Since $RS_i = X_i + RS_m$,

$$1[RS_i] = 1[X_i] + RS_{m-1} = X_{i-1} + RS_{m-1} = RS_{i-1}$$

Thus, $N^* = R + RS_{i-1}$.

Therefore, N^* (the reconfiguration 1-successor of N_d) is the node of the next more significant level, $n - (i - 1)$, defined via recursive sum $RS_i - 1$, which is a 1-bit shift to the left of the original recursive sum RS_i that specifies node N_d. Similarily, it is easy to show that a reconfiguration 2-successor of node N_d in the communication path with the root is specified by the recursive sum RS_{i-2}, which is 2-bit shift of RS_i: $RS_{i-2} = 2[RS_i]$, where RS_i specifies node N.

Since the destination node N_d is on the level $n - i$, it is connected with the root by minimal path having i other nodes. As we have established, consecutive nodes in this path are specified by consecutive shifts of the recursive sum RS_i that identifies given node N_d: $1[RS_i]$, $2[RS_i]$, ..., $i[RS_i]$.

Since by definition, level variable $Y_i = 1$ specifies the least significant position of RS_i of the node N_d, it will be the last one which will be shifted out during consecutive shifts of RS_i. Furthermore, since $X_i = 1$ in RS_i, it will always specify the only routing alternative from the root R to the next less signifcant node $R + X_1$ of level $n - 1$ (Fig. II.41).

The value of X_{i-1} in RS_i which is next to X_i specifies the route from level $n - 1$ to level $n - 2$. If $X_{i-1} = 1$, the only node $R + X_1$ of level n $- 1$ is followed by the right node, $RN = R + X_1 + X_2$ of level $n - 2$. If $X_{i-1} = 0$, node $R + X_1$ is followed by the left node $LN = R + X_2$ of level $n - 2$. Similarly, it is easy to show that variable X_{i-2} is responsible for selecting the route from level $n - 2$ to level $n - 3$, etc. Therefore, as follows from this analysis, consecutive variables X_i, $\widetilde{X}_{i-1}$, $\widetilde{X}_{i-2}$, ..., $\widetilde{X}_1$ that are present in RS_i, where $X_i = 1$ and $\widetilde{X}_j = 0$ or 1, are responsible for the entire route selection from one level to the next in the minimal communication path from the root R to the destination node N_d. As follows, $X_i = 1$ selects the route from level n to level $n - 1$; $\widetilde{X}_{i+1}$ selects the route from level $n - 1$ to level $n - 2$; ..., $\widetilde{X}_1$ selects the route from level $n - (i - 1)$ to the least significant level $n - 1$ of the TOL communication path, where TOL means to the leaves (Fig. II.41). Therefore, the recursive sum RS_i $= R + N_d$ contains all the routing information necessary to forward the message issued by the root to the destination node N_d. That is, the address code AC_d may be obtained from $RS_i = N_d + R$ by moving its bit X_i to the bit 1 of AC; $\widetilde{X}_{i-1}$ has to be moved to bit 2, ..., X_1 to bit i of AC [Fig. II.42(a)]. This simple logical operation will be called *rotate* or, symbolically, $AC = \mathrm{rot}(RS_i)$.

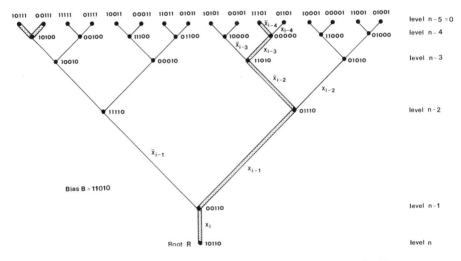

FIGURE II.41   The use of recursive sums for finding the path, $R \rightarrow N_d$

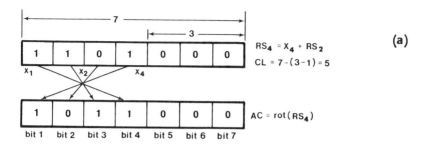

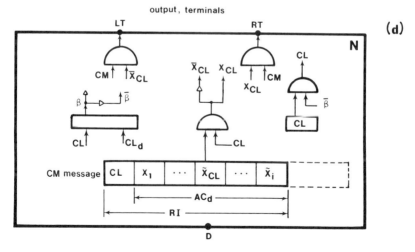

FIGURE II.42 (a) Formation of AC = rot(RS$_4$); (b) the route in the tree specified by AC = 1101; (c) routing information code; (d) message transit inside each transit mode

Example. Consider generation of the address code AC for the node N = 11101 in the binary tree with the root R = 10110. First, find the recursive sum RS_i for node N as RS_i = 11101 + 10110 = 01011; i.e., it is specified with level variable X_5 and has three ones. This identifies $i = 5$ and $k = 3$: i,e,, $RS_5(3) = X_5 + RS_4(2)$. The rotation operation performed over this recursive sum gives the address code AC_N = 11010 of the node N = 11101. As will be shown below, this code contains all the necessary routing information to route the message from the root R to node N.

However, to reduce the routing algorithm to execution of a simple logical operation in each transit node, we will stipulate that each node of level $n - j$ will store a *complemented level value,* CL [Fig. II.42(b)] of the size $\log_2 n = \log_2 \log_2 K$ that shows which bit of the address code must be selected for finding the route from the given node to the next node in the path. To find CL, each node finds its individual recursive sum as $RS_i = R + N$, then shifts RS_i to the LSB until LSB = 1, and counts the number of shifts k; CL $= n - (k - 1)$, where n is the number of levels in the tree.

Each node finds its CL when a new tree configuration is established. Thereafter, it is stored in a special register CL of size $\log_2 n$, since it will select the routing bit in all communications that will pass through a given transit node (Fig. II.39). ■

Example. For the tree of Fig. II.41 having root R = 10110, let us find the route from the root R to the node N_d = 11101 of level $n - 5 = 5 - 5 = 0$. Using the previous example, we find the recursive sum, $RS_i = R + N_d$ = 10110 + 11101 = 01011, and rotation of RS_i gives the address code AC_d = 11010. The following CL codes are stored in the nodes of this tree.

Level n: $RS_0 = 0$; $k = n$; CL $= n - (k - 1) = 1$ [Fig. II.42(b)]
Level $n - 1$: $RS_1 = X_1$; $k = n - 1 = 4$; CL $= n - (k - 1) = 5 - 3 = 2$
Level $n - 2$: $RS_2 = X_2$ or $RS_2 = X_1 + X_2$; $k = n - 2 = 3$; CL $= n - (k - 1) = 5 - 2 = 3$
Level $n - 3$: $RS_3 = X_3 + RS_2$ or $RS_3 = X_3 + RS_1$; $k = n - 3 = 2$; CL $= 4$
Level $n - 4$: $RS_4 = X_4 + RS_m$; $k = n - 4 = 1$; CL $= 5$
Level $n - 5$: $RS_5 = X_5 + RS_i$; $k = n - 5 = 0$; Cl $= 6$

The root formed communication message is shown in Fig. II.42(c); it selects the first bit of AC ($X_1 \equiv 1$) and forwards the message to the node N $(n - 1)$ of level $n - 1$ [Fig. II.42(b)]. This node stores CL = 2. Thus, it selects bit 2 of AC. Since $X_2 = 1$, CM is forwarded to the RN of level $n - 2$. This node stores CL = 3. It selects bit 3 of AC. Since $X_3 = 0$, CM is forwarded to the LN of level $n - 3$, etc. The entire communication path is shown in Fig. II.42(b). ■

Therefore, the following routing algorithm can be used for R → N_d communication.

Routing algorithm for R → N_d communication   Given root R, destination node N_d, CL value stored in each node of the tree. The algorithm routes the message issued by R to a destination node N_d. The algorithm contains two steps: *root step* and *transit* *step.* The root step is aimed at finding the address code, AC_d, of the desination node, forming the RI code for the communication message, CM, and passing CM to the only node of level $n - 1$. The transit step is executed iteratively in each transit node of the communcation path. It is aimed at finding the next transit node of the communication path and moving the CM message to this node.

Root Step: Find $AC_d = \text{rot}(R + N_d)$. Find destination code CL_d by shifting RS_i = $R + N_d$ to the right and counting the number k of consecutive zeros until LSB = 1. Then $CL_d = n - (k - 1)$. Form the routing information code RI = $CL_d AC_d$. Select bit 1 of AC_d and move the message to the next transit node.

Transit Step. Compare CL_d in the message with the local CL. If CL = CL_d, the destination N_d is reached. If CL $\neq CL_d$, select the X_{CL}-bit of the AC_d code brought with the message, where CL is the value of the local CL code [Fig. II.42(d)]. If X_{CL} = 0, route the message to the left terminal LT. If X_{CL} = 1, route the message to the right terminal RT. The entire execution of this algorithm was discussed in the previous example.

4.8.3 Node-node Communication, $N_s \rightarrow N_d$

Node-to-node communication is a more general case of $N_s \rightarrow R$ and $R \rightarrow N_d$ communications already considered, where N_s is the source node and N_d is the destination node. Indeed, for any $N_s \rightarrow N_d$ communication, the task of an optimal routing technique is to find the *closest intermediate root,* CIR, which is understood as the tree node that connects N_s and N_d with the minimal communcation path $N_s \rightarrow \text{CIR}$, CIR $\rightarrow N_d$ (Fig. II.43); i.e., for $N_s \rightarrow R$ and $R \rightarrow N_d$, CIR = R. Thus, by developing efficient node-to-node communication techniques that bypass the absolute root, R, we will reduce the amount of traffic that goes to and from the root, R, and minimize the total length and total delay of the communication path that connects N_s and N_d.

A particular case of the $N_s \rightarrow N_d$ communication occurs when:

1. N_s is a transit node on the path that connects the root, R, with N_d; or
2. N_d is a transit node on the path that connects the N_s with the root, R.

The first case is reduced to the $R \rightarrow N_d$ communication, whereas the second case is reduced to the $N_s \rightarrow R$ communication. These two particular cases are not considered here since they are obvious extensions of the $N_s \rightarrow R$ and $R \rightarrow N_d$ techniques presented in Sec. 4.8.2. Therefore, our discussion will concentrate on finding the minimal $N_s \rightarrow N_d$ communication path in which neither N_s nor N_d is on the subpath that connects the root with another node (N_d or N_s).

4.8.3.1 Closest intermediate root

To find the minimal $N_s \rightarrow N_d$ communication path, we have to find first the closest intermediate root, CIR. Since CIR is on the subpath that connects the root, R, with both N_s and N_d (Fig. II.43), the address code, AC_{CIR}, of the CIR is a left prefix of the

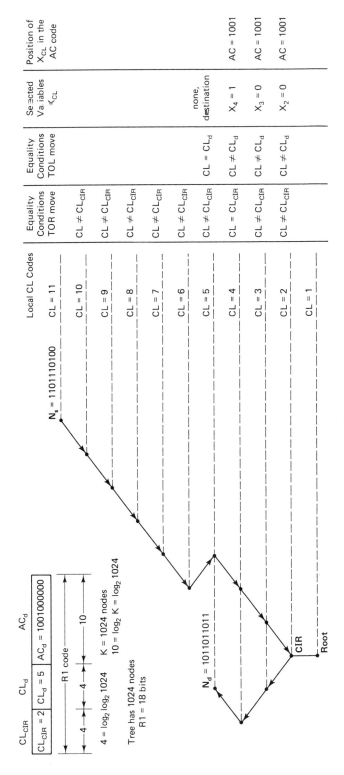

The following table appears within the figure:

Local CL Codes	Equality Conditions TOR move	Equality Conditions TOL move	Selected Variables X_{CL}	Position of X_{CL} in the AC code
CL = 11	$CL \neq CL_{CIR}$			
CL = 10	$CL \neq CL_{CIR}$			
CL = 9	$CL \neq CL_{CIR}$			
CL = 8	$CL \neq CL_{CIR}$			
CL = 7	$CL \neq CL_{CIR}$			
CL = 6	$CL \neq CL_{CIR}$	$CL = CL_d$	none, destination	
CL = 5	$CL = CL_{CIR}$	$CL \neq CL_d$	$X_4 = 1$	AC = 1001
CL = 4	$CL \neq CL_{CIR}$	$CL \neq CL_d$	$X_3 = 0$	AC = 1001
CL = 3	$CL \neq CL_{CIR}$	$CL \neq CL_d$	$X_2 = 0$	AC = 1001
CL = 2	$CL \neq CL_{CIR}$			
CL = 1				

$N_s = 1101110100$

$N_d = 1011011011$

CIR

Root

CL_{CIR} | CL_d | AC_d

| $CL_{CIR} = 2$ | $CL_d = 5$ | $AC_d = 1001000000$ |

R1 code

4 | 4 | 10

$4 = \log_2 \log_2 1024$ K = 1024 nodes
$10 = \log_2 K = \log_2 1024$

Tree has 1024 nodes
R1 = 18 bits

FIGURE II.43 The $N_s \rightarrow N_d$ communication path

114

two address codes, AC_s and AC_d, because if root, R, generates a communication message to N_s or N_d, then the CIR is the transit node on both paths, $R \rightarrow N_s$, $R \rightarrow N_d$. Thus, every message issued by the R root passes CIR before it reaches N_s and N_d. Therefore, the address code of CIR, AC_{CIR}, is the common most significant portion or the *common left prefix* of AC_s and AC_d; or $AC_{CIR} = LP_{x_i=y_i}(AC_s \wedge AC_d)$, where X_i and Y_i are binary positions of AC_s and AC_d.

To find CL_{CIR}, we find $MS = AC_s + AC_d$, and the number of *consecutive most significant zeros* LO in MS. The complemented level value of CIR is $CL_{CIR} = LO + 1$.

Example. Let us find AC_{CIR} and CL_{CIR} for N_s and N_d given by the following position codes: $N_s = 1101110100$ and $N_d = 1011011011$. Assume that these are tree nodes in a binary tree having root $R = 0010011011$ and bias $B = 0110101101$ (Fig. II.43). First, we find address codes AC_s and AC_d. To do so, we have to find recursive sums $RS(N_s)$ and $RS(N_d)$:

$$RS(N_s) = N_s + R = 1101110100 + 0010011011 = 1111101111$$

$$RS(N_d) = N_d + R = 1011011011 + 0010011011 = 1001000000$$

The address code of N_s is found by rotation of $RS(N_s)$:

$$AC_s = rot(RS(N_s)) = 1111011111$$

Similarly,

$$AC_d = rot(RS(N_d)) = 1001$$

$$AC_{CIR} = LP(1111011111 \wedge 1001) = 1, \quad \text{since } X_1 = Y_1$$

Let us find $MS = AC_s + AC_d = 1111011111 + 1001000000 = 0110111111$. In the MS, the number of consecutive most significant zeros, LO = 1; thus $CL_{CIR} = LO + 1 = 1 + 1 = 2$.

The position code of CIR can be found by rotating its address code to obtain its recursive sum: $RS(CIR) = rot(AC_{CIR}) = 1000000000$. Thereafter, the CIR position code is $CIR = R + RS(CIR) = 0010011011 + 1000000000 = 1010011011$. ∎

4.8.3.2 $N_s \rightarrow N_d$ communication path

To reach destination node N_d, the source node N_s has to form a communication message that contains the following routing information code: $RI = CL_{CIR} CL_d AC_d$ (Fig. II.43), where CL_{CIR} is the complemented-level value for the CIR node; CL_d is the complemented-level value for destination node, N_d, and AC_d is the address code for N_d. All these values can be found using the techniques presented above.

Each communication path from N_s to N_d includes two subpaths $N_s \rightarrow$ CIR and CIR $\rightarrow N_d$, where $N_s \rightarrow$ CIR is the direction of TOR (toward the root R) and CIR $\rightarrow N_d$ is the direction of TOL (toward the leaves) (Fig. II.43). In moving in the TOR direction from N_s to CIR, a communication message uses the code CL_{CIR} to reach CIR. That is, in each transit node N of the $N_s \rightarrow$ CIR subpath, CL_{CIR} stored in the message is compared with the local CL_N. If $CL_{CIR} \neq CL_N$, the communication message is forwarded to the next node in the path. If $CL_{CIR} = CL_N$, the destination node, CIR, of the $N_s \rightarrow$ CIR path is reached. Having reached CIR, the message begins the TOL movement (toward the leaves) using AC_d and CL_d portions of the RI code (Fig. II.43). That is, in each transit node, N, of the CIR $\rightarrow N_d$ path, CL_d is compared with the local CL_n. If $CL_d \neq CL_N$, the node N finds the value X_{CL} of the address code, AC_d, brought with the message, where CL is the local level value code. If $X_{CL} = 1$, the message is forwarded to the next right node. If $X_{CL} = 0$, the message is forwarded to the next left node. If $CL_d = CL_N$, $N = N_d$; i.e., destination is reached.

Example: For the $N_s \rightarrow N_d$ communication path of Fig. II.43, the routing information code, RI, of the communication message is shown in Fig. II.43. As seen, $CL_{CIR} = 2$, $CL_d = 5$, and $AC_d = 1001$. For the TOR broadcast $N_s \rightarrow$ CIR, the message reaches CIR having CL = 2. Thereafter, it starts the TOL transfer, CIR $\rightarrow N_d$. For the CIR node, $CL_{CIR} = 2$. Therefore, the second bit of the $AC_d = 1\underline{0}01$ shows what node of the tree follows the CIR node. Since $X_2 = 0$, CIR is followed by the left node LN. In the LN node, $CL_{LN} = 3$ and $X_3 = 0$ in $AC_d = 10\underline{0}1$. Thus, LN is followed by the next left node, LN, of the path, etc. The destination is achieved in the node N having $CL_N = CL_d$. ∎

As follows for the $N_s \rightarrow N_d$ communication, the bit size of the routing information code, RI, is upperbounded as follows:

$$BS(RI) \leq n + 2 \log_2 n = \log_2 K + 2 \log_2 \log_2 K$$

where n is the number of tree levels and K is the number of tree nodes.

4.9 Conclusions on Introduced Techniques for Network Reconfigurations and Communications

Section II.4 has introduced the following subjects:

S1. Analysis and synthesis methodology for dynamic multicomputer networks, DMN, that can assume rings, trees, and star configurations.

S2. Efficient communication algorithms for DMN organized as reconfigurable binary trees.

Thus, the overall conclusions will be divided into the two subjects dealing with reconfigurations and communications in DMN.

4.9.1 Assessment of Introduced Reconfiguration Methodology

The most important feature of the reconfiguration methodology presented is in the fact that it is very fast and concurrent. Indeed, to reconfigure a DMN into any of these structures requires only that two control codes (bias and reconfiguration code) be received by all network nodes and the execution of a simple logical operation in each network node. Once a new structure is established dynamically, a DMN can greatly improve performance, in comparison with any static multicomputer network, by computing an application algorithm in a closely fitted structure made of the minimal number of nodes and releasing all the unneeded nodes into additional computations.

Section II.4 presented the techniques for selecting biases and reconfiguration codes and showed that such a selection can be performed by a programmer very easily because of the fine mathematical properties that are exhibited by such networks. In this section, analysis and synthesis problems are solved for single ring and single tree structures. Also, the problem of analysis alone is solved for composite ring structures. The remaining network structures continue to be a subject of intensive studies performed by these authors.

Once all the network structures that can be generated with these techniques are known, the benefits of their use in computing will be enormous, since they possess two important factors for improving performance in a system.

F1. Considerable program speed-up attained because of system reconfiguration into the best structure for a given application(s).

F2. Additional program speed-up attained because of minimizing the time of reconfiguration overhead.

Therefore, a DMN that implements this reconfiguration methodology can greatly enhance its computational efficiency via instantaneous reconfiguration into a new advantageous network structure without paying the price of considerable reconfiguration overhead, which is introduced with conventional reconfiguration techniques.

4.9.2 Assessment of Introduced Communication Techniques

We discussed efficient communication algorithms for multicomputer networks organized as reconfigurable binary trees. The algorithms allow organization of optimal node-to-node communications, $N_s \rightarrow N_d$, where N_s is an arbitrary source node and N_d is an arbitrary destination node.

Communication between N_s and N_d is organized via the minimal communication path; i.e., the destination node N_d is achieved in such a way that each transit node of the communication path is included only once in the path $N_s \rightarrow N_d$. The communication techniques introduced are optimal from both viewpoints: the total bit size of the routing information code, BS(RI), that routes the message among various transit nodes of the communication path and the total time of communication, CD.

It is shown that BS(RI) $\leq \log_2 K + 2 \log_2 \log_2 K$, where K is the total number of nodes in a binary tree. Also, since only 1 bit of the RI code is responsible for selecting the next node in the path of the two possible alternatives LN or RN, the BS(RI) achieves the absolute theoretical minimum, because it is impossible to have 0 bits assigned for such a selection. Furthermore, since each transit node N selects its successor

RN or LN in the communication path via a logical operation that takes time of one t_d, the total time of $N_s \to N_d$ communication also approaches the theoretical minimum.

Therefore, one can utilize the broadly unique properties of these reconfigurable binary trees for various computational and control algorithms without paying the price of considerable reconfiguration overhead (when no computation can be performed) and large size for the address portion of the communication message for conventional reconfigurable binary trees.

These benefits include (1) a comprehensive fault tolerance whereby, during one clock period and using only one control code (bias), a tree with multiple faulty nodes can reconfigure itself into a fault-free gracefully degraded tree in which all faulty nodes become leaves (i.e., the connectivity of the tree structure is restored [16]), and (2) for the given assignment of tasks to the nodes of the binary tree, one can select a single (or a sequence of) tree configuration(s) in which the total length of communcation paths is optimized; i.e., all frequently exchanging nodes are connected with minimal paths of length 1 [63].

As an illustration, Sec. III.4 demonstrates the execution of a sampled data exchange table of node-to-node communications using two alternative techniques: (1) a single static tree structure, and (2) a sequence made of three tree structures $TS_1 \to TS_2 \to TS_3$, where each TS_i minimizes the duration and maximizes the concurrency of a portion of the node-to-node communications represented by a sampled data-exchange table and assigned to this TS_i. The obtained performance improvement was 370%. That is, a single static tree configuration has executed the entire table during $1430T_0$, whereas a sequence $TS_1 \to TS_2 \to TS_3$ has executed the same table during $300T_0$.

Therefore, data-exchange optimization achieved with the use of reconfiguration is an extremely powerful source for improving the performance of a reconfigurable binary tree, because by using reconfiguration one can minimize the duration and maximize the concurrency of the requested data exchanges in comparison with those performed in a static tree configuration.

5 FAULT-TOLERANT RECONFIGURATION IN A RECONFIGURABLE BINARY TREE: OVERVIEW

As indicated in Sec II.4, the overall objective of any fault-tolerant reconfiguration is to provide unimpaired performance in a computer system in the presence of faults.

5.1 Circuit- and Module-Level Reconfigurations

The fault-tolerant reconfiguration can be performed at the following levels:

a. *Circuit-level,* aimed at isolating faulty devices inside a computing module

b. *Module-level,* aimed at isolating every faulty computing module from other modules of the computer system that remain fault-free

The module-level reconfiguration is performed if and when (1) all circuit-level reconfigurations fail in the sense that they are incapable of restoring correct computations inside the faulty module, and/or (2) a faulty circuit inside the module is or becomes unique and thus nonreconfigurable, and as such it prevents fault-free performance of the entire module.

Example. A failure in a register connected with the adder of the computing module, CM, is a circuit fault that can be eliminated with the use of circuit reconfiguration. The objective of this reconfiguration is to isolate this register from receiving results or operands for computation. However, if a fault occurs in a nonreconfigurable adder of the same module, then the entire computing module becomes faulty and must be turned off from the operation.   ∎

Usually there is always a complexity trade-off between the circuit-level and module-level reconfiguration. To sustain fault-free operation of a computing module in the presence of faults requires a considerable duplication of all its circuits. Thus, if a fault occurs in a unique nonduplicated circuit, or all duplicates of this circuit have been exhausted through the previous circuit reconfigurations, this module becomes faulty, and it must be isolated from system operation using a module-level reconfiguration.

In this section we will discuss a module-level reconfiguration for reconfigurable binary trees, which were formed in Sec. 4.7 with the use of a shift register, SRVB, and one control code, bias B [see Fig. II.33(a, b)].

The following types of module-level fault-tolerant reconfigurations can be distinguished: *dynamic replacement* and *graceful degradation.* For dynamic replacement, each faulty node in a tree is replaced with a spare assigned with the same position code. Therefore, for dynamic replacement, a current tree structure remains unchanged as long as there are spare nodes in the bank. When the bank of spares becomes empty, dynamic replacement strategy is followed by graceful degradation.

5.2 Gracefully Degraded Binary Trees

For a graceful degradation, reconfiguration in a binary tree was developed by the authors in [16]. It is applicable for multiple faults in a tree when bypassing techniques may no longer work. Our technique was aimed at a concurrent formation of a gracefully degraded tree, GDT, out of fault-free nodes that remain in a system. Faulty nodes are reconfigured into those tree positions which do not disrupt the connectivity of the fault-free nodes in a selected tree configuration. Such reconfiguration allows a simple purge of all faulty nodes from the network.

Two types of gracefully degraded trees can be formed via reconfiguration:

1. Type 1, or *1-truncated GDT,* in which all faulty nodes are reconfigured into leaves. A gracefully degraded tree will have $n - 1$ levels of fault-free nodes, where n is the number of levels in the original tree [Fig. II.44(a, b)].

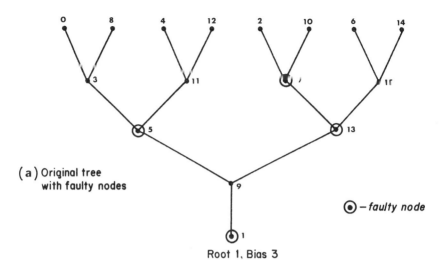

(a) Original tree
with faulty nodes

⊙ – faulty node

Root 1, Bias 3

(b) 1 - truncated GDT

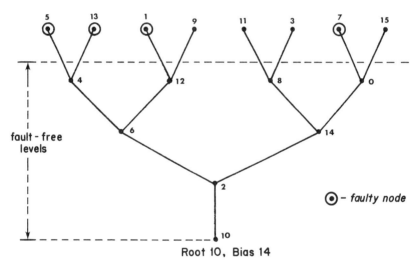

fault - free
levels

⊙ - faulty node

Root 10, Bias 14

FIGURE II.44 Type-1 graceful degradation: (a) original tree with faulty nodes; (b) 1-truncated GDT

2. Type 2, or *i-truncated GDT,* in which $i > 1$ and all faulty nodes are recon-figured into i-level tree branches, otherwise called i-end trees. Each i-end tree is made out of $(2^i - 1)$ faulty nodes. A gracefully degraded tree will have then *$n - i$ highest levels composed entirely of fault-free nodes [Fig. II.45(a)].* As *for i* lowest levels, since all faulty end trees are disconnected via reconfigura-tion, there remain only fault-free i-end trees that contain no faulty nodes.

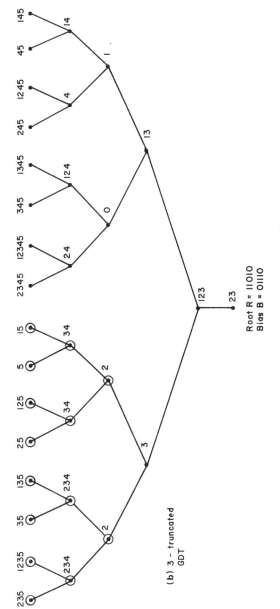

Root R = 11010
Bias B = 01110

FIGURE II.45(a)   The 3-truncated GDT

(b) 3 - truncated
GDT

121

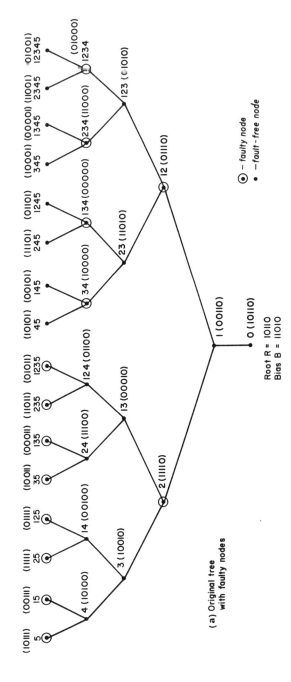

FIGURE II.45(b) Original tree with 14 faulty nodes

(a) Original tree
with faulty nodes

Root R = 10110
Bias B = 11010

⊙ – faulty node
● – fault-free node

The figures illustrate two types of graceful degradation in a binary tree that can be accomplished via reconfiguration.

5.2.1 Type 1 Graceful Degradation

Type 1 graceful degradation is illustrated in Fig. II.44 (a, b): An original tree with four faulty nodes 1, 5, 7, and 13 is reconfigured into type 1 or 1-truncated GDT in which all faulty nodes become leaves. Thus, they can be safely disconnected from the computer network without violation of its connectivity. This reconfiguration is performed with bias B = 14 and takes only one clock period to purge all four faulty nodes out of the network.

Each fault-free node N performs the following operation to form the node N* of its successor in the GDT:

$$N* = 1[N] + B, \quad \text{where } B = 14$$

For instance, if N = 4 = 0100, then N = 4 is succeeded by the following N*:

$$N* = 1[N] + B = 1[0100] + 1110 = 1000 + 1110 = 0110 = 6, \quad \text{etc.}$$

Note: For this binary tree, since there are four faulty nodes in the original tree, no bypassing of faulty nodes is applicable inasmuch as the fault-free structure left in the tree is deprived of the root and other managers of high levels; i.e., it can no longer function as a tree. The only alternative that remains is to form the 1-truncated GDT using either bias B = 14 or other biases that perform similar reconfigurations. The techniques for finding these suitable biases are given below.

5.2.2 Type 2 Graceful Degradation

Type 2 graceful degradation is illustrated in Fig. II.45(a, b): The original tree with 14 faulty nodes shown in Fig. II.45(b) is reconfigured into 3-truncated GDT [Fig. II.45(a)] in which all faulty nodes are grouped into two 3-end subtrees. Such tree reconfiguration can be performed during one clock period once the new bias B = 01110 is found. To find this bias requires $i = 3$ mod-2 additions performed sequentially, where i is the dimension of the faulty end subtree.

In Fig. II.45(a, b), all tree nodes are specified with two notations, binary and relative, where a binary notation is used to identify the position codes of tree nodes and a realtive notation is formed with respect to the root of the original tree. For instance, if root R = $x_1 + x_3 + x_4$ = 10110 [Fig. II.45(b)], the node N_{35} = R + x_3 + $x_5 = x_1 + x_3 + x_4 + x_3 + x_5 = x_1 + x_4 + x_5$ = 10011; i.e., the result of this operation is the binary code of this node. The usefulness of such relative numbering for the purposes of fault-tolerant reconfiguration will be explained in Sec. II.6.

Theretore, as follows from these examples, the fault-tolerant reconfiguration illustrated above is a very powerful technique for enhancing fault tolerance of a binary tree for a binary tree with multiple faulty nodes. During one clock period a tree with multiple faulty nodes can reconfigure into a fault-free gracefully degraded tree structure purged of all faulty nodes. This GDT maintains the fault-free status for the maximal number of high-level nodes, since all faulty nodes are purged into the lowest positions that do not disrupt the tree-type connectivity of the remaining nodes in the network. To perform such reconfiguration requires only one control code, bias B, sent concurrently to all fault-free nodes of the multicomputer network. A new gracefully degraded tree is formed as a result of one mod-2 addition operation

$$N^* = 1[N] + B$$

performed in each tree node N that forms the code N^* of its successor in the GDT. To find bias B of GDT takes one mod-2 addition for a type 1 GDT and i mod-2 additions for a type 2 GDT, where i is the dimension of the faulty end subtree [16].

5.3 Two Approaches for Tree Reconfiguration

In a distributed computing system organized as a reconfigurable binary tree, there are two approaches for performing tree reconfiguration:

1. Monitor approach
2. Root approach

Monitor approach. For the monitor approach, all fault-tolerant reconfigurations are performed by a system monitor connected to each tree node. The major advantage of this approach is that it can be performed very rapidly, since, on finding out a status of each node, the monitor, using the techniques presented in the next section, finds the best bias B that restores connectivity in the tree. Then it sends this bias to each tree node, thus effecting the tree reconfiguration into a new connected tree structure. Major disadvantages of this approach are:

1. It requires the monitor to be connected with every tree node. This requires a complex interconnection network to perform these connections.
2. The monitor may become faulty, making the monitor approach totally inapplicable.

Thus consideration of the root approach is required.

Root approach. For the root approach, a fault-tolerant reconfiguration is performed by the root, the tree's connectivity having first been temporarily restored. However, this requires that some fault-free leaves change their position codes (or addresses) and assume the position code or vacancies created by all faulty nonleaves. Such node reassignment should be temporary; permanent reassignment requires extensive modification in all program jump addresses for data exchanges with the nodes that have changed addresses, which becomes practically infeasible.

Once the tree's connectivity is temporarily restored, its temporary root receives all information on the status of all tree nodes. Next, using the techniques presented in the next section, it finds the new tree's bias B and reconfigures this tree into one in which connectivity is restored for all fault-free nodes. Also, these nodes reassume the position codes that they had in the original or source tree.

The major advantage of this approach is that it is universal, that is, independent of the fault status of the monitor. Also, it requires no interconnections that are not available in the network. Its disadvantage is that it takes a longer time than the monitor approach, since it requires two steps: (1) temporary restoration of connectivity by changing nodes' addresses and (2) reconfiguration. Of these two, the first step is more time consuming than the second, since to restore connectivity in a tree requires polling all successor nonleaves in a tree and assuming by leaves all the vacancies created by faulty nonleaves.

Therefore, the monitor and root approaches are complementary; the advantages of one approach are the disadvantages of the other. Thus, both have their own areas of application. As we will show, both approaches involve tree reconfiguration in which faulty nonleaves become leaves. This requires proper selection of the bias B to accomplish this reconfiguration.

6 SOFTWARE RECONFIGURATION METHODOLOGY FOR FAULT-TOLERANT RECONFIGURABLE BINARY TREES

In this section we describe a software reconfiguration methodology aimed at selecting a bias B that transforms the tree with multiple faulty nodes into a connected fault-free GDT requiring no node reassignment. This GDT is either 1-truncated if all faulty nodes are nonleaves or i-truncated if faulty nodes are both leaves and nonleaves.

The relationship of this research with other work in the area is as follows:

1. Since it introduces original fault-tolerant reconfiguration techniques for distributed computing systems organized as binary trees, it is connected with other works on fault-tolerant reorganizations and reconfigurations [51-55].

2. Since it uses the shift-register theory to develop reconfigurations of binary trees, it is connected with the literature on shift-register sequences [35-39].

3. Since it discusses distributed computing systems organized as binary trees, it is associated with references [44-50] dealing with distributed and reconfigurable multicomputer networks.

6.1 Section Composition

This section is organized as follows. Based on the material on reconfigurable binary trees presented previously (Sec. 4.7.2, "Synthesis of the Root" and Sec. 4.7.3, "Synthesis of an Arbitrary Tree Node"), Sec. 6.2 introduces possible types of reconfigurations in this type of tree; it shows that all possible reconfigurations are divided into two categories: (1) level reconfigurations specified with a single level variable, X_i

$(i = 1, \ldots, n)$, and (2) mixed reconfigurations, where each mixed reconfiguration is a combination of several level reconfigurations.

Section 6.3 applies the interesting properties of level and mixed reconfigurations to improving the fault tolerance in a tree.

Section 6.4 presents reconfiguration methodology aimed at finding the bias $B(r)$ of a reconfigured GDT in which all fault-free nodes become connected into a new tree structure and faulty nodes are reconfigured into i-end branches, where $i > 1$. The GDT thus reconfigured may function again, although its performance will be degraded by disconnection of all faulty nodes.

The two types of gracefully degraded trees can be generated with the bias $B(r)$: 1-truncated GDT, if $B(r)$ specifies the level reconfiguration, and i-intruncated GDT, if $B(r)$ specifies the mixed reconfiguration. To find $B(r)$ for level reconfiguration takes one mod-2 addition operation. To find $B(r)$ for i-truncated GDT takes i mod-2 additionals performed sequentially. Once the bias $B(r)$ is found, the fault-free GDT with disconnected multiple faulty nodes can be generated during one clock period, during which every fault-free node N finds its new fault-free successor N* in the tree as N* $= 1[N] + B(r)$.

6.2 Level and Mixed Reconfigurations in a Binary Tree

To solve the problem of fault-tolerant reconfiguration in a binary tree, let us introduce one recursive and successor-preserving structure, P_i, of tree nodes generated with the bias B.

6.2.1 Recursive and Successor-preserving Structure, P_i, of Tree Nodes Generated with SRVB

As we saw in Sec. 4.7.3, a node N of level $n - i$ is given as follows:

$$N(n - i) = R + RS_i \, (k)$$

where each $RS_i \, (k) = X_i + RS_m \, (k-1)$, and X_i is the level variable. Thus, all tree nodes belonging to the same level $n - i$ are identified with the same level variable $X_i = 2^{n-i}$, and a binary tree having n levels of nodes is characterized by n-level vairables X_1, X_2, ..., X_n.

Since recursive sum $RS_i \, (k) = X_i + RS_m \, (k - 1)$, each RS_i can be represented as follows using level variables X_1, X_2, ..., X_n:

$$RS_i = a_1 \cdot X_1 + a_2 \cdot X_2 + \ldots + a_{i-1} \cdot X_{i-1} + X_i$$

where $RS_0 \equiv 0$, $i \leq n$, and a_1, a_2, ..., a_{i-1} are binary coefficients. The binary coefficients a_1, a_2, ..., a_i of each recursive sum RS_i are characterized as follows:

1. For each RS_i, $a_i \equiv 1$ and $a_{i+1} \equiv 0$.
2. All coefficients a_1, ..., a_{i-1} for level variables X_1, ..., $X_{i-1} > X_i$ can assume arbitrary values 0 or 1.

As in Sec. 4.8.1, to establish the node ordering in each level of the tree, we assume that recursive sums are ordered as follows:

P1. $RS_i > RS_j$ iff $X_i > X_j$, where $X_i = 2^{n-i}$, $X_j = 2^{n-j}$
P2. $RS_i > RS_i'$ iff $RS_i + X_i > RS_i' + X_i$

Example. Consider $RS_1 = X_1$, $RS_4 = X_1 + X_3 + X_4$, and $RS_4' = X_1 + X_2 + X_4$. In accordance with P1, $RS_1 > RS_4$ and $RS_1 > RS_4'$ because $X_1 > X_4$. In accordance with P2, $RS_4' > RS_4$, because $RS_4' + X_4 = X_1 + X_2 = RS_2$; $RS_4 + X_4 = X_1 + X_3 = RS_3$ and $RS_2 > RS_3$. † ∎

With these preliminary observations, we introduce the P_i structure as follows.
Basis i $= 1$: $P_1 = (N_0, N_0 + X_1)$, where N_0 is an arbitrary tree node called *basis node*; X_1 is the level variable, $X_1 = 2^{n-1}$.
Inductive step i ≥ 1: $P_i = (P_{i-1}, P_{i-1} + X_i)$, where P_{i-1} is the $(i - 1)$-dimensional structure, and $P_{i-1} + X_i$ is obtained from P_{i-1} by complementing the X_i variable in all nodes of P_{i-1}.

Example. Construct $P_i = (P_{i-1}, P_{i-1} + X_i)$ if $i \leq 3$ and $P_1 = (R, R + X_1)$, where R is the root; that is, $N_0 = R$; assume that the root R is generated by bias $B = 10001$. Using Theorem 14 (Sec. 4.7.2), $R = X_2 + X_3 + X_4 + X_5 = 01111$ (see Fig. II.46).

$$P_1 = (R, R + X_1) = (01111, 11111)$$

$$P_2 = (\overline{P_1}, \overline{P_1 + X_2}) = (\overline{R, R + X_1}, \overline{R + X_2, R + X_1 + X_2}) = (\overline{01111, 11111}, \overline{00111, 10111})$$

$$P_3 = (P_2, P_2 + X_3) = \overline{(R, R + X_1, R + X_2, R + X_1 + X_2,}$$
$$\overline{R + X_3, R + X_1 + X_3, R + X_2 + X_3, R + X_1 + X_2 + X_3)}$$

Here and throughout a bar is extended over nodes belonging to the same substructure, P_{i-1}, where $i = 2$ and 3. ∎

Vertical and horizontal properties of the P_i structure. The P_i structure may describe both vertical and horizontal ordering among tree nodes depending on the selection of *basis* node N_0 in basis structure $P_1 = (N_0, N_0, + X_1)$. If the basis node N_0 is the root $R (N_0 = R)$ of the tree, then P_i describes the vertical ordering of the tree nodes belonging to levels $n, n-1, \ldots, n-i$ with respect to the root, which is considered the most significant node of the tree because $R = R + RS_0(0)$ and $RS_0 > RS_i$. If basis node $N_0 = R + X_i$, then $P_{i-1} + X_i$ describes the horizontal ordering of the tree nodes belonging to the same level $n-i$ (see Fig. II.46).

---

†Sometimes property P2 must be applied several times to find $RS_j > RS_j'$. For instance, $RS_4' = X_1 + X_2 + X_3 + X_4$; $RS_4'' = X_2 + X_3 + X_4$; $RS_4' + X_4 = X_1 + X_2 + X_3 = RS_3'$; $RS_4'' + X_4 = X_2 + X_3 = RS_3''$; $RS_3' + X_3 = RS_2'$; $RS_3'' + X_3 = RS_2''$, where $RS_2' = X_1 + X_2$ and $RS_2'' = X_2$; $RS_2' + X_2 = X_1 = RS_1'$; $RS_2'' + X_2 = RS_0'' = X_0$. Since $X_0 > X_1$, $RS_4' > RS_4'$.

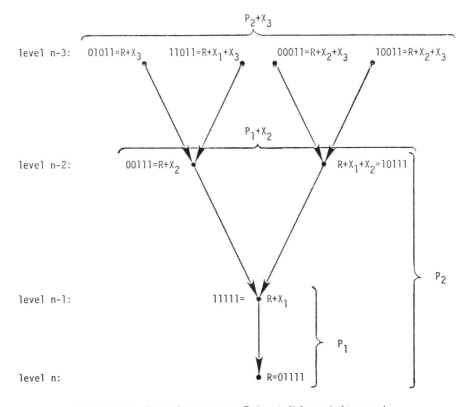

FIGURE II.46 Recursive structures P_i ($i = 1, 2$) formed of tree nodes

Relative numbering of tree structures. Since in each P_i structure the position of a tree node is specified with respect to root R with the use of level variables X_1, X_2, $\ldots$, X_i, it is convenient to represent each P_i by the positions so specified. That is, we assume that $R \equiv 0$ and $X_i \equiv i$. Then the relative numbering of each P_i is given as follows:

$$P_0 = (\bar{0}), \quad P_1 = (\bar{0}, \bar{1}), \quad P_2 = (\bar{0}, \bar{1}, \bar{2}, \overline{12})$$

$$P_3 = (\overline{\overline{0, 1, 2, 12}}, \overline{3, 13, 23, 123})$$

$$P_4 = (\overline{\overline{\overline{0, 1, 2, 12}, 3, 13, 23, 123}}, \overline{4, 14, 24, 124}, \overline{34, 134, 234, 1234})$$

and so forth, where each collection of integers $i_1, i_2, \ldots, i_k$ is understood as the node $N = R + X_{i_1} + X_{i_2} + \ldots + X_{i_k}$. For instance, $124 \equiv R + X_1 + X_2 + X_4$, where R is determined through bias B using the technique of Theorem 14. For instance, for B $= 11010$, $R = 10110 = X_1 + X_3 + X_4$. Thus

$$\text{node } 124 \equiv R + X_1 + X_2 + X_4$$
$$= X_1 + X_3 + X_4 + X_1 + X_2 + X_4$$
$$= X_2 + X_3 = 01100$$

and so on (see Fig. II.45)

6.2.2 Reconfigurations in a Binary Tree

As will be shown below, with the introduction of recursive structures P_0, P_1, P_2, ..., P_k, one can describe very easily all the reconfigurations that may occur in a binary tree. For each reconfiguration, we will be dealing with two types of trees:

1. The source tree, TS, or original tree
2. The reconfigured tree, TS(r)

The nodes of the source tree, TS, are called source nodes. The nodes of the reconfigured tree are called reconfigured nodes.

Although reconfiguration into a new tree is performed with the reconfigured bias B, interesting structural properties of the tree reconfiguration are more easily understood if one introduces a special map code MC that maps each node N of the source tree TS into the reconfigured node $N' = N + MC$ of the reconfigured tree TS(r). Thus, the MC is conceived as the mod-2 sum of level variables that may change both the levels of tree nodes and the positions of nodes within each P_i. Since $MC + MC = 0$, and 0 has no level of variables, $R + MC$ becomes the new root, R(r), in the reconfigured tree; $R(r) = R + MC$. Therefore, the types of reconfigurations that can be performed over the given tree depends on what level variables are in MC.

To describe all the possible types of reconfigurations, let us introduce the concepts of level and mixed configurations.

Level reconfigurations. By the X_i-level reconfiguration or X_i reconfiguration, we mean the reconfiguration determined by mapping code $MC = X_i$ ($i = 1, ..., n$). The X_i reconfiguration is performed on the level of all structures $P_i = (P_{i-1}, P_{i-1} + X_i)$ in the tree. It consists of exchanging P_{i-1} with $P_{i-1} + X_i$ as $P_{i-1} \leftrightarrows P_{i-1} + X_i$. Each reconfigured structure $P_i(r)$ obtained as a result of this reconfiguration is specified as follows:

$$P_i(r) = (P_{i-1} + X_i, P_{i-1})$$

In a new tree TS(r), the root R(r) becomes $R(r) = R + MC = R + X_i$. All source nodes of the level $n-i$ specified with level variable X_i become the reconfigured nodes of levels n, $n - 1$, $n - 2$, ..., $n - (i - 1)$. On the other hand, all the source nodes of higher levels n, $n - 1$, ..., $n - (i - 1)$, become the reconfigured nodes of level $n - i$. Thus the change in levels occurs only for source nodes with levels n, $n - 1$, ..., $n - i$. All source nodes of lower levels, $n - (i + 1)$, $n - (i + 2)$, ..., $n - n = 0$, described by structures P_{i+1}, P_{i+2}, ..., P_n retain their levels. Instead, in each P_{i+k} structure each reconfiguration exchange is performed on the level of P_i, whereby each left element P_{i-1} of P_i is exchanged with its right element $P_{i-1} + X_i$.

Example. For the source tree of Fig. II.47(a), let us consider all the exchanges effected by X_1 reconfiguration. This reconfiguration is restricted to all P_1 pairs of this tree, which exchange their left and right components. This source tree has the following P_1 structures:

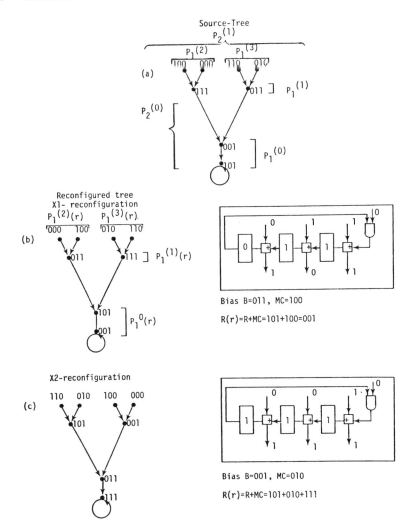

FIGURE II.47   Illustration of the two-level reconfigurations X_1 and X_2

Source P_1 structures	Reconfigured $P_1(r)$
$P_1^{(0)} = (\bar{0}, \bar{1}) = (101, 001)$	$P_1^{(0)}(r) = (\bar{1}, \bar{0}) = (001, 101)$
$P_1^{(1)} = (\bar{2}, \overline{12}) = (111, 011)$	$P_1^{(1)}(r) = (\overline{12}, \bar{2}) = (011, 111)$
$P_1^{(2)} = (\bar{3}, \overline{13}) = (100, 000)$	$P_1^{(2)}(r) = (\overline{13}, \bar{3}) = (000, 100)$
$P_1^{(3)} = (\overline{23}, \overline{123}) = (110, 010)$	$P_1^{(3)}(r) = (\overline{123}, \overline{23}) = (010, 110)$

A reconfigured tree is shown in Fig. II.47(b). It has root $R(r) = 101 + X_1 = 001$ and is generated with reconfigured $B(r) = R(r) + 1[R(r)] = 001 + 010 = 011$. Indeed,

R(r) is succeeded by itself since $1[R(r)] + B(r) = 010 + 011 = 001$. Reconfigured node $N = 101$ of level $n - 1$ is succeeded by R(r):

$$1[101] + 011 = 010 + 011 = 001$$

and so on. Similarly, one can find all the exchanges caused by the X_2 reconfiguration and performed on the level of P_2 structures. The source tree has the following P_2 structures:

$$P_2{}^{(0)} = (\overline{0, 1, 2, 12}) \quad \text{and} \quad P_2{}^{(1)} = (\overline{3, 13, 23, 123})$$

and reconfigured $P_2(r)$ are

$$P_2{}^{(0)}(r) = (\overline{2, 12, 0, 1}) = (\overline{R + X_2, R + X_1 + X_2, R, R + X_1}) = (\overline{111, 011, 101, 001})$$

$$P_2{}^{(1)}(r) = (\overline{23, 123, 3, 13}) = (\overline{R + X_2 + X_3, R + X_1 + X_2 + X_3, R + X_3, R + X_1 + X_3})$$

$$= (\overline{101 + 011, 101 + 111, 101 + 001, 101 + 101}) = (\overline{110, 010, 100, 000})$$

The X_2-reconfigured tree is shown in Fig. II.47(c). As seen, its new root $R(r) = R + X_2 = 111$, which is generated with the following bias: $B(r) = R(r) + 1[R(r)] = 111 + 110 = 001$. ∎

Mixed reconfigurations. By mixed reconfigurations or $X_{j1}, X_{j2}, \ldots, X_{jk}$ reconfigurations, we mean reconfigurations that are determined by the mapping code MC $= X_{j1} + X_{j2} + \ldots + X_{jk}$. The $X_{j1}, X_{j2}, \ldots, X_{jk}$- reconfigured tree can be found by applying concurrently $X_{j1}, X_{j2}, \ldots, X_{jk}$-level reconfigurations to the source tree.

Example. For the source tree of Fig. II.48(a), let us apply the concurrent $X_2 X_3$ reconfiguration using the mapping code MC$= X_2 + X_3$. Although this reconfiguration can be made in one step, it is interesting to show its execution in two steps that perform 3 and 32 reconfigurations, respectively, and to see that the tree obtained in two steps is coincident with the one obtained following application of MC$=011$.

Step 1. Take the X_{32} reconfiguration

$$P_3 = (P_2, P_2 + X_3)$$
$$P_3(r) = (P_2 + X_3, P_2) = (\overline{3, 13, 23, 123}, \overline{0, 1, 2, 12})$$
$$R = X_1 + X_3, \quad MC = X_3$$
$$R(r) = R + X_3 = 100, \quad B = 100$$

Thus

$$P_3(r) = (\overline{100, 000, 110, 010}, \overline{101, 001, 111, 011})$$

Step 2. Let us form all P_2 structures for the X_3 reconfigured tree, since to perform $X_3 X_2$ reconfiguration of the source tree it is sufficient to perform X_2 reconfiguration of the X_3 reconfigured tree of Fig. II.48(b).

$$P_2{}^{(0)} = (\overline{0, 1, 2, 12}) \rightarrow P_2{}^{(0)}(r) = (\overline{2, 12, 0, 1})$$

Source Tree

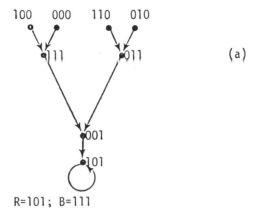

100   000   110   010

111   011

001

101

(a)

R=101; B=111

Step 1: X_3-reconfiguration

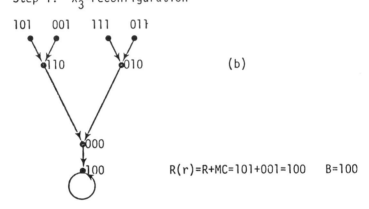

101   001   111   011

110   010

(b)

000

100   R(r)=R+MC=101+001=100   B=100

Step 2: $X_3 \cdot X_2$-reconfiguration

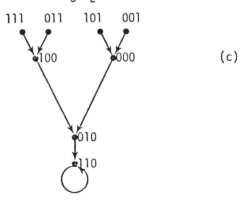

111   011   101   001

100   000

(c)

010

110

R(r)=R+MC=101+011+110   B=010

FIGURE II.48   Mixed reconfiguration $X_2 X_3$

Thus, since

$$P_2{}^{(0)} = (\overline{100, 000}, \overline{110, 010}), \quad P_2{}^{(0)}(r) = (\overline{110, 010}, \overline{100, 000})$$

The second

$$P_2{}^{(1)} = (\overline{3, 13}, \overline{23, 123})$$

is mapped into

$$P_2{}^{(1)}(r) = (\overline{23, 123}, \overline{3, 13}) = (\overline{111, 011}, \overline{101, 001}) \quad \blacksquare$$

6.3 Fault-Tolerant Reconfigurations

The interesting properties of level and mixed reconfigurations can be applied to faulty trees to restore connectivity in them. First, we note that if a tree has only faulty leaves then no connectivity is lost, since no leaf has any predecessors in a tree. Therefore, any loss of connectivity in a tree results from faulty nonleaves.

The material that follows is aimed at describing two cases that result in lost connectivity in a tree:

1. All faulty nodes are nonleaves. All leaves are fault free.
2. Both leaves and nonleaves are faulty.

6.3.1 Faulty Nonleaves and Fault-Free Leaves

If all leaves are fault free, then to restore connectivity in a tree it is sufficient to perform either a level or a mixed reconfiguration that includes the level variable X_n applicable to pair $P_n = (P_{n-1}, P_{n-1} + X_b)$. Since variable X_n exchanges the left P_{n-1} with the right $P_{n-1} + X_n$, the postreconfiguration tree TS(r) has the following changes in nodes positions: fault-free source leaves of $P_{n-1} + X_n$ become reconfigured nonleaves. Faulty source nonleaves of P_{n-1} become reconfigured leaves. Thus, the entire tree connectivity is restored via reconfiguration, requiring no node reassignments.

Example. Consider a three-level tree having root R = 001 and bias B = 011, as shown in Fig. II.49(a). Suppose that in this tree all nonleaves are faulty; that is, nodes 001, 101, 011, and 111 are faulty. The resulting network with lost connectivity is shown in Fig. II.49(b); it consists of four disjoint nodes which cannot be connected into a tree via a node bypass, as used conventionally. Restoration of connectivity may be accomplished with any reconfiguration that contains variable X_3, since X_3 exchanges P_2 and $P_2 + X_3$ within the P_3 structure where

$$P_3 = (P_2, P_2 + X_3)$$

$$P_2 = (\overline{001, 101}, \overline{011, 111})$$

$$P_2 + X_3 = (\overline{000, 100}, \overline{010, 110})$$

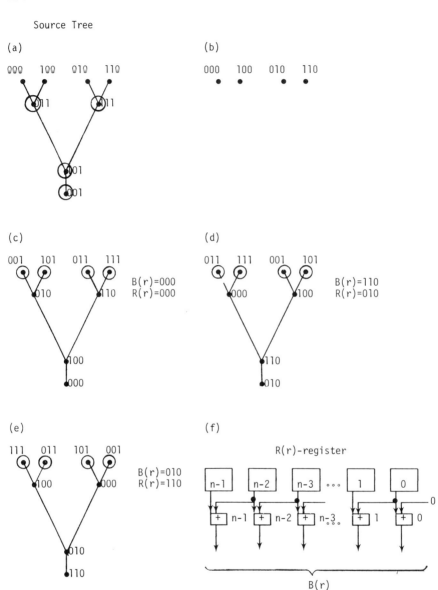

FIGURE II.49   Restoration of connectivity in the tree with the use of several X_3-reconfigurations (level) and mixed)

Thus, the lost connectivity can be restored with reconfigurations identified with the mapping codes

$$MC_1 = X_3, \quad MC_2 = X_2 + X_3, \quad MC_3 = X_1 + X_2 + X_3$$

If $MC_1 = X_3$, the reconfigured root is

$$R_1(r) = R + MC_1 = 001 + 001 = 000$$

and the bias is

$$B_1(r) = 1[R(r)] + R(r) = 0$$

[see Fig. II.49(c)]. If $MC_2 = X_2 + X_3$,

$$R_2(r) = R + MC_2 = 001 + 011 = 010$$

$$B_2 = 1[R_2(r)] + R_2(r) = 100 + 010 = 110$$

[see Fig. II.49(d)]. If $MC_3 = X_1 + X_2 + X_3$

$$R_3(r) = R + MC_3 = 001 + 111 = 110$$

$$B_3 = 1[R_3(r)] + R_3(r) = 100 + 110 = 010$$

[See Fig. II.49(e)]. As may be seen from the Fig. II.49, all these reconfigurations restore connectivity in the tree. A new bias $B(r)$ is found very easily via code MC, which is an arbitrary binary word with level variable X_n: $B(r) = 1[R(r)] + R(r)$ and $R(r) = R + MC$.

To form the reconfigured tree $TS(r)$ that contains 1-truncated GDT takes one mod-2 addition operation $1[N] + B(r)$ performed by every fault-free node N in this tree. ∎

6.3.2 Faulty Leaves and Nonleaves

If in a tree faulty nodes are leaves and nonleaves, then the reconfiguration to be performed is described by the following steps.

1. Find the number of faulty leaves, #(L), and the number of faulty nonleaves #(NL).
   If #(NL) > #(L), perform any level or mixed reconfiguration having variable X_n.
   If #(NL) < #(L), perform no X_n reconfiguration.
2. Reconfigure the source tree into a tree in which all faulty nodes are grouped into an *end subtree*, defined as follows.

By the i-dimensional *end-subtree*, we mean a tree formed of structures P_i, P_{i-1}, ..., P_0, where P_i includes only leaves and P_{i-1}, P_{i-2}, ..., P_0 are all j successors of P_i in this tree ($j = 1, 2, ..., i$). Since $P_0 = N^*$, P_0 is the unique i successor of P_i. Figure II.50 shows a tree with two two-dimensional end subtrees formed entirely of faulty nodes; faulty nodes are circled. The entire reconfigured tree is given with its relative notation (introduced in Sec. 6.2.1) with respect to the root $R \equiv 0$ of the source tree; i.e.,

$$R(r) = R + MC \equiv 0 + X_2 + X_3 = 23$$

where $MC = X_2 + X_3$.

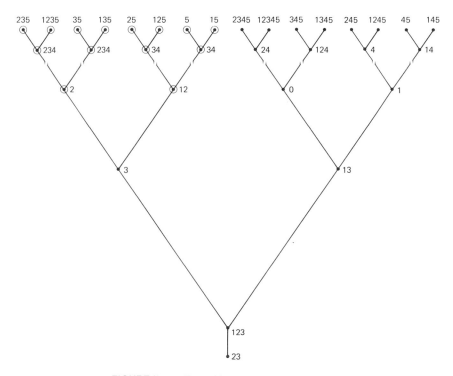

FIGURE II.50. Tree with the two faulty end-subtrees

Therefore, for the case of faulty leaves and nonleaves, one executes Step 1 to reduce the number of faulty nonleaves and then selects a reconfiguration of the tree that groups all faulty nodes into one or several end subtrees. The effectiveness of such a reconfiguration is illustrated in the following example.

Example. A source tree with faulty leaves and nonleaves is shown in Fig. II.51(a) with its relative notation. As is seen from Fig. II.51(b), without reconfiguration the fault-free nodes of this tree function as disjoint components. Assume that this source tree is generated with source bias $B = 11010$. Using Theorem 14, we find the source root $R = 10110$, because $R = 1[R] + B = 01100 + 11010 = 10110$. In Fig. II.51, position codes of all tree nodes generated with $B = 11010$ are shown in parentheses. Each node code in parentheses can be obtained by adding the root R to the relative number of this node. For instance, node $N_{35} = X_3 + X_5$ has the following position code: $N_{35} = R + X_3 + X_5 = 10110 + 00101 = 10011$, and so on. As can be seen from Fig. II.51, this source tree has eight faulty leaves and six faulty nonleaves. Therefore, in accordance with Step 1, no X_5 reconfiguration is necessary. The best reconfigured tree is obtained with mapping code $MC = X_2 + X_3$. It gives reconfigured root $R(r) = R + MC = 10110 + 01100 = 11010$. This tree can be generated with bias $B(r) = 1[R(r)] + R(r) = 10100 + 11010 = 01110$; Fig. II.52(a) shows the fault-free, gracefully degraded tree, and Fig. II.52(b) shows generation of the $N_{24} \rightarrow N_0$ transition by the SRVB receiving

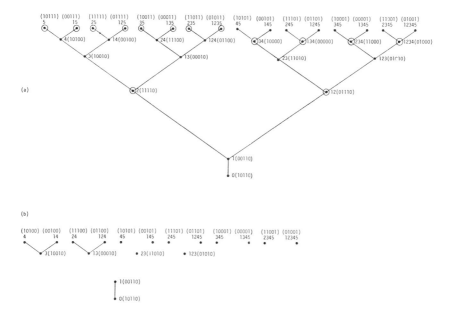

FIGURE II.51 Tree with faulty leaves and nonleaves

$B(r)$, where $N_{24} = 11100$ and $N_0 = 10110$. As seen, the reconfigured tree is gracefully degraded and without faulty components. The latter are grouped into two end subtrees and disconnected. The complete reconfigured tree with faulty and fault-free components is shown in Fig. II.50. This reconfiguration takes only one clock period if one finds bias $B(r)$. The material below gives algorithmic procedures aimed at selecting $B(r)$. ∎

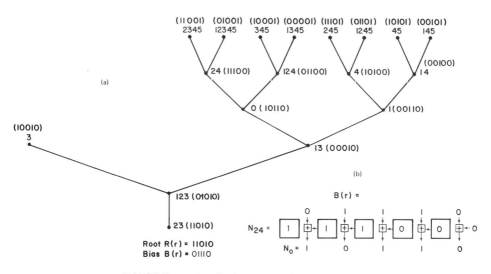

FIGURE II.52(a,b) Fault-free gracefully degraded tree

6.3.2.1 Faulty end subtree: basis step

The objective of the best reconfiguration is to assemble as many faulty nodes as possible into end subtrees that can be disconnected from the system. The procedure for finding the maximal i-dimensional faulty end tree must start by finding a complete faulty structure P_i formed of leaves, where i is a maximal integer. The next step is iterative. It consists of finding a complete faulty structure P_{i-1} somewhere in the tree and performing a tree reconfiguration that allows P_{i-1} to become the immediate successor of P_i. If P_{i-1} is complete, the process is continued for P_{i-2}. If P_{i-1} is partial, the process stops.

To perform this step, however, we must establish a *closure of succession* between P_i and P_{i-1} in the reconfigured tree TS(r). This property is formulated as follows.

Theorem 16. For any two structures P_i and P_{i-1} in the source tree, where P_i is made of leaves and P_{i-1} is any other structure of dimension $i-1$ that does not necessarily succeed P_i in this tree, it is possible to find a bias B(r) that generates a reconfigured tree TS(r) in which P_{i-1} immediately succeeds P_i and P_i retains its leaf status.

The following algorithm finds the bias B(r) that allows P_{i-1} to immediately succeed P_i. Let N and N* be two arbitrary nodes from P_i and P_{i-1}, respectively. Form the succession equation

$$N^* = 1[N] + B(r)$$
$$B(r) = N^* + 1[N]$$

Example. Consider the five-level source tree in Fig. II.52(c) given by the relative notation of its nodes with respect to root R. In this tree, there are two complete faulty pairs, $P_2 = (\overline{5}, \overline{15}, \overline{25}, \overline{125})$ and $P_1 = (\overline{3}, \overline{13})$, where P_1 does not immediately succeed P_2. Find the bias B(r) that allows P_1 to be the immediate successor of P_2. Select arbitrarily $N \in P_2$ and $N^* \in P_1$;

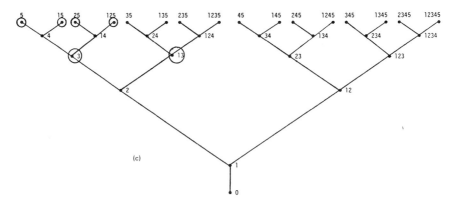

FIGURE II.52(c)   The five-level source tree with faulty leaves and nonleaves

$$N_5 = R + X_5, \quad N_{13}^* = R + X_1 + X_3$$

$$B(r) = N_{13}^* + 1[N_5]$$

$$= R + X_1 + X_3 + 1[R + X_5]$$

$$= R + X_1 + X_3 + 1[R] + 1[X_5]$$

$$= R + 1[R] + X_1 + X_3 + X_4$$

because $1[X_5] = X_4$. Since, for the source, $R = 1[R] + B$, source bias $B = R + 1[R]$. Therefore, reconfigured bias $B(r) = B + X_1 + X_3 + X_4$. Thus, by selecting any bias B of the source tree, we can find the bias $B(r)$ of the reconfigured tree in which P_2 is made of faulty leaves and is immediately succeeded by P_1.

Assume that source bias $B = 10111 = X_1 + X_3 + X_4 + X_5$, giving source root $R = 01101$. Then reconfigured bias $B(r) = B + X_1 + X_3 + X_4 = X_5 = 00001$ and the reconfigured root $R(r) = 11111$. This reconfigured tree is shown in Fig. II.52(d). It differs from the source tree by $MC = R + R(r) = 01101 + 11111 = 10010 = X_1 + X_4$. Each node is given by its relative notation with respect to the source root and by its absolute code generated by $B(r)$. As can be seen, all faulty nodes are grouped into two 2-end subtrees, requiring no node reassignment. Figure II.52(e) shows how the SRVB that stores faulty $N_{125} = R + X_1 + X_2 + X_5 = 01101 + 11001 = 10100$ and receives $B(r) = 00001$ generates its faulty successor N_3 in this tree. ■

6.3.2.2 Faulty end subtree: iterative step

Since Theorem 16 establishes the succession closure between P_i and P_{i-1} in a reconfigured tree generated with bias $B(r)$, and two nodes $N \in P_i$ and $N^* \in P_{i-1}$ were selected arbitrarily for finding $B(r)$, we will have 2^{i-1} different reconfigured trees generated with as many different biases that maintain the succession between P_i and P_{i-1}.

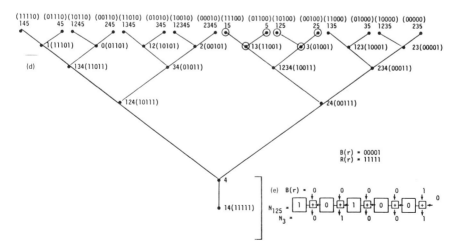

FIGURE II.52(d,e) Fault-free reconfigured GDT

These biases form the allowable bias set ABS $= \{B_0(r), B_1(r), ..., B_m(r)\}$ such that $m = 2^{i-1} - 1$ and any $B_j(r) \in$ ABS generates a tree in which the leaf-faulty structure P_i is immediately succeeded by faulty P_{i-1}. This set ABS can be found by fixing node $N \subseteq P_i$ and varying node $N^* \subseteq P_{i-1}$.

Therefore, if there are two arbitrary complete faulty structures P_i and P_{i-1} in a tree where P_{i-1} does not necessarily succeed P_i, and P_i is not a leaf structure:

1.   We can always perform X_n reconfiguration to make P_i a faulty leaf pair.

2.   We can always perform a reconfiguration whereby the leaf-faulty structure P_i is succeeded by faulty P_{i-1}.

An enlargement of the end subtree with the next faulty structure P_{i-2} depends on the location of faulty P_{i-2} in the tree, because a reconfigured tree in which P_{i-2} succeeds P_{i-1} must be such that the established succession between P_i and P_{i-1} has not been violated.

The following important property of allowable biases simplifies selection of the reconfigured bias that maintains succession between P_i, P_{i-1}, and P_{i-2}. Let $B_1(r)$ and $B_2(r)$ be two biases that maintain succession between P_i and P_{i-1}; if bias $B_1(r)$ is allowable, $B_2(r)$ is also allowable only if $B_1(r) + B_2(r)$ includes a combination of level variables $X_1, ..., X_{i-1}$ of structure P_{i-1}, where P_{i-1} succeeds P_i. Otherwise, $B_2(r)$ is not allowable.

Therefore, to find the allowable bias $B_2(r)$ that maintains the succession between P_i, P_{i-1}, and P_{i-2}, we have to find a candidate $B_2'(r)$ that maintains succession between P_{i-1} and P_{i-2}; it is understood that during the previous iterative step we found $B_1(r)$ that maintains succession between P_i and P_{i-1}. Next, we have to find $B_1(r) + B_2'(r)$ $= S$. If S contains only the level variables $X_1, X_2, ..., X_{i-1}$ that specify structure P_{i-1}, $B_2'(r)$ is an allowable bias; that is, $B_2'(r) = B_2(r)$. Thus, there exists a reconfigured tree generated by $B_2(r)$ in which the faulty end subtree includes P_i, P_{i-1}, and P_{i-2}. If S contains other level variables, $B_2'(r)$ is not an allowable bias and no allowable $B_2(r)$ can be found. Thus, the iterative process stops.

Example. Consider the binary tree with faulty nodes shown in Fig. II.51(a), in which there are the following faulty structures:

$$P_3 = (\overline{5,\ 15},\ \overline{25,\ 125},\ \overline{35,\ 135},\ \overline{235,\ 1235})$$

$$P_2 = (\overline{34,\ 134},\ \overline{234,\ 1234})$$

$$P_1 = (\overline{2,\ 12})$$

For this tree, P_2 does not succeed P_3, and P_1 does not succeed P_2. Let us find a reconfiguration of this tree that forms the faulty end tree of maximal dimension.

For the basic step, find the bias $B_1(r)$ that maintains succession between P_3 and P_2. Select $N_5 = R + X_5$ from P_3 and $N_{34} = R + X_3 + X_4$ from P_2. Form a successor equation that allows N_5 to be succeeded by N_{34}:

$$N_{34} = 1(N_5] + B_1(r)$$

$$B_1(r) = 1[N_5] + N_{34}$$

$$= 1[R + X_5] + R + X_3 + X_4$$

$$= 1[R] + X_4 + R + X_3 + X_4$$

$$= 1[R] + R + X_3$$

$$= B + X_3$$

Thus, if source bias $B = 11010$, $B_1(r) = B + X_3 = 11110$.

The iterative step proceeds as follows. In the first iteration, let us attempt to include P_1 in the end tree that includes P_3 and P_2. Assume that N_{34} is succeeded by N_{12}. Find $B_2(r)$ that allows such succession:

$$N_{12} = 1[N_{34}] + B_2(r)$$

$$= 1[R + X_3 + X_4] + B_2(r)$$

$$= R + X_1 + X_2$$

$$B_2(r) = 1[R] + X_2 + X_3 + R + X_2 + X_1$$

$$= B + X_3 + X_1$$

Find

$$B_1(r) + B_2(r) = B + X_3 + B + X_3 + X_1 = X_1$$

Since X_1 belongs to the set of level variables $[X_1, X_2]$ that specifies P_2, $B_2(r) = B + X_1 + X_3$ is an allowable bias that maintains the succession between P_3, P_2, and P_1. Thus, $B_2(r) = B + X_1 + X_3$ generates a tree in which P_3, P_2, and P_1 will be included in the faulty end tree.

The bias that accomplishes the tree reconfiguration in which P_3, P_2, and P_1 are grouped together is $B_2(r) = B + X_1 + X_3$, where B is the source bias. Since $B_2(r) = R_2(r) + 1[R_2(r)]$, where $R_2(r)$ is the root of this reconfigured tree, and $B = 1[R] + R$, where R is the root of the source tree, $R_2(r) + 1[R_2(r)] + R + 1[R] = X_1 + X_3$. Taking into account that $R_2(r) + R = MC$, where MC is the map code, one obtains $MC + 1[MC] = X_1 + X_3$. This leads to $MC = X_2 + X_3$ because $1[MC] = 1[X_2 + X_3] = X_1 + X_2$. Thus $MC + 1[MC] = X_2 + X_3 + X_1 + X_2 = X_1 + X_3$. The reconfigured tree generated with $B_2(r) = B + X_1 + X_3$ and the root $R_2(r) = R + MC = R + X_2 + X_3$ is shown in Figs. II.50 and II.52(a). As seen in this tree, all faulty nodes are grouped into a partial faulty end tree of the maximum dimension. This tree can be generated with $B_2(r) = B + X_1 + X_3$. If one assumes that the source bias $B = 11010$, then $B_2(r) = 11010 + 10100 = 01110$ (see Fig. II.52). ∎

6.3.3 Conclusions

In this section, we have studied a software methodology for fault-tolerant reconfigurations in a multicomputer network organized as a reconfigurable binary tree. We have shown how to reconfigure a binary tree with faulty nonleaves and lost connectivity into a binary tree in which all faulty nodes become leaves or form a more complex end-tree structure of a higher dimension. In both cases, these faulty nodes may be safely disconnected from the reconfigured fault-tolerant tree, which continues to function as a gracefully degraded tree made completely out of fault-free nodes. For the case where all faulty nodes become leaves, bias $B(r)$ of the reconfigured tree is found very easily during a one-step logical operation. For the case when all faulty nodes form an i-dimensional end tree, the bias $B(r)$ of the reconfigured tree can be found by a simple process that includes i mod-2 addditions performed sequentially. Once the bias $B(r)$ of the reconfigured tree is found, reconfiguration into a fault-tolerant tree (in which all faulty nodes can be safely disconnected) can be performed during the time of one clock period, since to perform this reconfiguration requires (1) the reception of the same code $B(r)$ by all tree nodes, and (2) the formation of the new successor equation $N^*(r)$ = $1[N] + B(r)$ in each fault-free node N. Such a formation includes only two logical operations: 1-bit shift and mod-2 addition. Thus, the fault-tolerant reconfiguration can be performed during one clock period.

7   CONCLUSIONS TO CHAPTER II

This chapter has presented the research accomplished in reconfiguration methodology for dynamically reconfigurable computer systems. The problem of reconfiguration methodology was divided into two planes:

1.   Architectural reconfiguration
2.   Fault-tolerant reconfiguration

The task of architectural reconfiguration is to organize an architectural transition from one state to another in the flow chart of architectural transitions, otherwise called the reconfiguration flow chart. The task of fault-tolerant reconfiguration is either (1) to organize a dynamic replacement of a faulty module(s) with the identical spare(s) or (2) to organize graceful degradation by turning off all faulty modules from computations and forming a connected and gracefully degraded architectural state from the set of remaining fault-free modules.

Therefore, the fault-tolerant reconfiguration enhances the architectural reconfiguration flow chart by adding the element of fault tolerance into it. Also, while dynamic replacement does not alter the original architectural flow chart, graceful degradation results in obtaining a reduced or gracefully degraded flow chart that reflects the system performance and functioning at a reduced level caused by turning off faulty modules from the operation.

7.1 Architectural Reconfiguration

The research completed on architectural reconfiguration focused on the solution of the following problems:

- Architectural reconfigurations in dynamic multicomputer systems
- An approach to network reconfigurations

The technique described reflects the cost efficiency of the solutions that have been obtained.

It is shown that each type of architectural reconfiguration introduced can be organized practically instantaneously with the use of only one program instruction, provided the requested resources have completed execution and the priority of the requested program warrants such reconfiguration. Therefore, an adopted architectural organization can act as fast as possible once the priority and computational status of programs warrant such actions.

For the multicomputer reconfiguration, the duration of this instruction takes the time of 64-bit addition. For the network reconfiguration, the duration of this instruction becomes even shorter: the entire reconfiguration process is reduced to executing a simple mod-2 addition ($2t_d$ delay) and can be effected with the use of only two control codes of size n and $2n - 1$, respectively, where $n = \log_2 K$ and K is the number of CE in the system. (These codes can be stored in the reconfiguration instruction, since their total bit size is $3n - 1$.)

The objectives of current research for these authors in the domain of architectural reconfiguration are aimed at developing comprehensive reconfiguration methodologies for all five architectures (multicomputer/multiprocessor, array, pipeline, network, and mixed) that can be assumed by dynamic architectures. Also, on the basis of our past involvement into this topic, we believe that the complexity of the entire algorithmic process for each type of reconfiguration will not be significantly changed and will not depart from the time of multicomputer reconfiguration. As a result, multiple system reconfigurations, which will become possible because of well-developed reconfiguration methodologies, can be performed as frequently as necessary for enhancing mission-critical computations with the introduction of almost no reconfiguration overhead into the system performance.

7.2 Fault-Tolerant Reconfigurations

The research completed on fault-tolerant reconfigurations was focused on developing graceful-degradation techniques for reconfigurable binary trees having multiple fault status. This chapter has demonstrated the high cost efficiency of the adopted solutions. It is shown that the entire graceful degradation in a reconfigurable binary tree can be accomplished:

a. During the time of mod-2 addition and using only one control code, if all faulty modules can be reconfigured into tree leaves.

b. During the time of i sequential mod-2 additions and using i control codes if all faulty modules are reconfigured into an end subtree having 2^i nodes. For instance, if $i = 2$, then the end subtree is formed out of four faulty modules ($4 = 2^2$) which are reconfigured out from the system during the time of two mod-2 additions performed sequentially. Thus, the entire reconfiguration process takes the time of $4t_d$, where $2t_d$ is the time of one mod-2 addition.

In both cases, the fault-tolerant reconfiguration will accomplish the formation of a gracefully degraded tree without faulty modules. For case a, this tree will function without some old leaves; that is, instead of an n-level original tree, it will act for some nodes as an $(n - 1)$-level tree, and for others it will remain an n-level tree. For case b, this tree will function without one or several of the i-dimensional end subtrees. Thus for cases a and b, the fault-tolerant reconfiguration preserves the connectedness of the original tree but organizes its performance at a reduced level without violating the connectivity of the remaining fault-free nodes. This type of performance is impossible to obtain via any bypassing organized in the presence of multiple faults.

The objectives of current research of these authors for fault-tolerant reconfigurations are aimed at developing comprehensive graceful-degradation and dynamic-replacement strategies for the entire set of possible architectural states and not only for reconfigurable binary trees.

Chapter III

Reconfiguraton
Flow Chart

1 INTRODUCTION

As was defined in Chapter I, Sec. 1.2.1, by *reconfiguration flow chart* we mean a set of software tools that allows an automatic construction of the sequence of architectural states given the resource requests of participating programs which form a *program mix* executed by the system.

Each state of the reconfiguration flow chart is understood as a set of nonconflicting computing structures (dynamic computers, trees, stars, pipelines, arrays, etc.) formed in the system with the use of reconfiguration. Every $N_i \rightarrow N_j$ transition of the reconfiguration flow chart from the current architectural state N_i to the next architectural state N_j is performed by the active program with the highest priority which either needs a new computing structure included into N_j or represents a set of other concurrent and nonconflicting programs assigned to N_j. Therefore, to construct reconfiguration flow chart is to assign reconfigurable hardware resources to the programs of the program mix. Henceforth, the problem of the reconfiguration flow chart is equivalent to the problem of the resource assignment in which the resources can perform dynamic reconfigurations.

In general, dynamically reconfigurable resources feature two types of resource assignments: static and dynamic. By *static resource assignment,* we understand an assignment process for which all reconfiguration needs of participating programs are given in advance before the assignment starts. For static assignment, it is always possible to assign these programs to the available system resources in a nonconflicting manner since all reconfiguration requests and program priorities are known. This leads to the total absence of conflicts in execution.

By *dynamic resource assignment,* we understand an assignment process for which all resource needs of participating programs are not given in advance. For dynamic assignment, the entire program mix consists of two types of programs: *static* with stored requests on reconfigurable resources (processor and/or memory) and *dynamic or arriving programs,* which requests on reconfigurable resources have not been considered during static assignment. The arrivals of such programs may change the constructed (static) reconfiguration flow chart since the priorities of dynamic programs may be higher than those for static ones. Therefore, dynamic assignments, as a rule, feature reconfiguration conflicts since a dynamic program may compete for the reconfigurable resources assigned to either a static program during static assignments or another dynamic program during a preceding dynamic assignment.

2 STATIC RESOURCE ASSIGNMENTS

Two types of static resource assignments will be discussed: for dynamic multicomputer systems and for reconfigurable binary trees. For dynamic multicomputer systems, the major objective of the static resource assignment is to minimize all possible program delays, via enhanced resource utilization, and to complete each program of the program mix at the earliest moment of time that is possible under the circumstances.

For reconfigurable binary trees, the major objective of the static resource assignment is to minimize the total time of node-to-node data exchanges, which can be accomplished by minimizing the path durations and maximizing path concurrencies for all node-to-node communications assigned to each tree configuration.

3 RESOURCE ASSIGNMENT FOR DYNAMIC MULTICOMPUTER SYSTEMS

To solve the problem of resource assignment for dynamic multicomputer systems requires the solution of the following problem: for every user program one has to find a sequence of minimal-size computers which may execute it. Next, the available hardware resources have to be assigned among user programs, each of which is executed by a sequence of the minimal-size computers found earlier. The hardware resource assignment is then reduced to finding a flow chart of architectural states which gives the maximal concurrency in execution of the given set of user programs.

This type of assignment is called an *adaptive assignment.* It differs from the traditional assignment for which the objective is to minimize the cost of communication between different processors (computers) involved in communication [66-70].

In general, an adaptive assignment is applicable for a computer system that has the following features:

1. Its bus structure introduces a permanent communication delay either internally (between local processor and memory belonging to the same computer)

or externally (between processor and memory of two different computers that are available in the system).

2. A computer system may adapt to executing algorithms via reconfigurable and/or dynamic adaptations [4].

For such systems, the resource assignment must reflect specific attributes of the respective architectures, i.e., be adaptive rather than minimal cost, since, due to the permanency of communication delays within a system, there is no sense in their minimization.

In addition to the system with dynamic architecture described in this chapter, one can cite here other adaptable computer systems described in [60] for which one must use adaptive resource assignment rather than the one that minimizes communication cost.

On the other hand, the resource assignment that minimizes communication costs is applied for systems assembled from different subsystems in such a way that the cost of communication between subsystems greatly exceeds that within a subsystem. Examples of such systems are conventional multicomputer systems and geographically dispersed networks.

Therefore, both types of resource assignment have different areas of application. While there are a number of research works dedicated to the resource assignment that minimizes communication cost, the literature on the adaptive assignment is still inadequate since fast reconfigurable and dynamic systems with permanent communication delays started to appear only recently. For dynamic architectures, adaptive assignment means minimization of the amount of processor and memory resources involved in computations, because only such an assignment may realize the capability of dynamic architectures to maximize the number of programs executed concurrently.

Overall assignment of the processor and memory resources for dynamic architectures is performed by the reconfiguration software system rather than by the same operating system that performs management and monitoring of the resources in the system. The reason for this functional separation between the reconfiguration software and operating systems is in excessive complexity of new functions for a distributed operating system for dynamic architectures [17, 18] that has to participate in system reconfiguration and organize parallel data exchanges.

The next subsections will introduce basic principles of Reconfiguration Software on adaptive static resource assignment and task scheduling. To perform such an assignment requires finding the individual program needs of processor and memory resources, which can be done via analysis of bit sizes and array dimensions of computed variables.

3.1 Analysis of Bit Sizes and Array Dimensions of Computed Variables

This section presents an analysis technique aimed at finding the bit sizes and array dimensions of computed results. This analysis is done by the reconfiguration software system, which then finds the diagram of computer sizes used in the computation of each program. Since a multicomputer system with dynamic architecture executes several independent programs, their computer-size diagrams then are merged into a diagram showing the static assignment of the resources among user programs. This diagram serves as a basis for the construction of a static architectural flow chart, i.e., the assignment subsystem constructs the flow chart of transitions showing what sequence of architectural states is formed and which program is allowed to perform each transition. Using this flow chart, the reconfiguration software subsystem performs memory scheduling.

Therefore, the first stage of resource assignment consists of finding for each program written in a high-level language the word sizes for a sequence of computers which could execute this program. Finding word sizes for computed variables is greatly simplified if one constructs a *program graph* in which each node includes one or more statements and the arrows show sequencing. For each node, one finds a minimal computer size in which this node may be executed. Next, one constructs a diagram of bit sizes for all graph nodes, which serves as a basis for finding a diagram of the computer sizes required for executing a given user program. This diagram will partition the program into tasks where each task is composed of the sequence of nodes requiring the same computer size.

To perform efficient assignment of the hardware resource, it is necessary to estimate the duration of each task. This will allow one to perform a resources assignment among taks which will minimize the time of idleness of executed programs. Below we introduce a technique for finding the number of clock periods, t_0, required for the execution of each task. Since all computers formed by a dynamic architecture may use the same clock period, t_0, expressing the duration of all tasks in terms of the same t_0 shows the relative timing in their executions.

The analysis of each user program ends with the construction of its resource diagram, which shows the computer sizes and memory volumes requested by every task in this program.

3.1.1 Classification of Nodes in a Program Graph

A program, P, written in a high-level language is transformed into a *P program graph* in which each node is assigned one or several statements and arrows show sequencing of nodes. There exist two types of nodes in the graph: *simple* and *complex*. A *simple node* has one outgoing arrow, which means unconditional transition to its immediate successor. A *complex node* has several outgoing arrows. Selection of its immediate successor depends on a conditional test executed by the control statement in this node.

Nodes in the graph may be *iterative* and *noniterative*. Each *iterative node* is specified with the parameter, Z, which is the maximal number of iterations it may go through in a program loop. Parameter Z may be given as follows:

1. It can be presented explicitly in the program.
2. It can be defined via analysis of a control statement which specifies an exit from the program loop,

3. In case it cannot be defined via method 1 or 2, its statistical value can be given based on experiences with past computations of the same program.

A program's transformation into a program graph is formalized and specified in the following section.

3.1.2 Algorithm for Constructing a Program Graph (Algorithm 1)

The objective of this algorithm is to assign high-level statements to graph nodes and to determine sequencing among those nodes. The algorithm assumes that the program is stripped of all the unnecessary references and that all referencing is done for conditional or unconditional branching or for looping. This algorithm includes several separate sequences of steps aimed at handling the following types of statements:

Type 1. A noncontrol statement that is not referenced by any other statement

Type 2. A statement referenced by another control statement

Type 3. All control statements (but the DO statement)

Type 4. The DO statement

Type 5. The DO reference statement or the DO object

The flow chart of the algorithm is shown in Fig. III.1. Let us show how this algorithm handles the five types of statements mentioned above. Let A* be the statement under analysis.

Handling noncontrol and nonreferenced statements of type 1. If A* is a statement of type 1, it is assigned to the same node that includes the preceding statement, B, unless B is a control statement. If B is a control statement, A* is assigned a separate node. This procedure is established in Steps 2, 3, 4, 5, 25, and 6 (Fig. III.1). The tests in Steps 2 and 3 identify statement A* as type 1; Steps 4 and 5 find whether or not the preceding statement, B, is a control statement; Step 25 creates a new node for A* if B is a control statement; and, if B is not, Step 6 includes A* into the same node that includes B.

Handling referenced statements of type 2. If A* is a type 2 statement, it must be assigned a separate node, NA*, since it is the destination of one or more control statements. This is done in Steps 2, 3, and 18.

If a control statement, B, that references A* has been assigned to the node, NB, nodes NB and NA* should be connected by the arc, NB → NA* (Step 22).

If control statement B has not yet been assgined to a node since it follows (not necessarily immediately) statement A* in the program, the NB → NA* connection between the current node NA* and the not yet created node NB should be established in the future, during the formation of node NB. Therefore, this connection must be remembered in a special table, comprised of two columns. Column 1 contains graph nodes already assigned with statements; and col. 2 contains source or destination

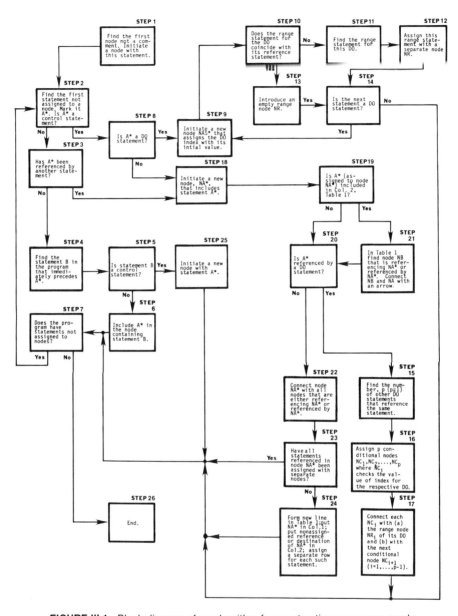

FIGURE III.1 Block diagram of an algorithm for constructing a program graph

statements not yet formed into nodes (Step 24) (Fig. III.4). (Here, by a *source state-ment* we mean a statement that references another statement. By a *destination state-ment* we mean a statement that is referenced by another statement.) Therefore, each time a new node, NA*, is formed that includes a statement A* of type 2, a test is made to check if A* is in Table 1, col. 2 (Step 19). If it is, the newly formed node NA* is connected to the source node(s), NB, of col. 1 that was formed previously and reference A* (Step 21). All these actions that handle type 2 statements are performed by Steps 2, 3, 18, 20, 19, 21, 22, 23, and 24.

Handling control statements of type 3. If A* is a type 3 statement, it must be assigned to a separate node, NA* (Steps 2, 8, 18), that will be connected with all other nodes that are destinations of NA* (Step 22). Also, A* must be tested for inclusion in Table 1, col. 2. If A* is in col. 2, it references node NB formed previously, where node NB is located in col. 1, Table 1 of Step 24. Thus the NA* → NB connection must be formed (Steps 20 and 21).

Since at the time of the formation of node NA* some of its destinations may not be assigned to separate nodes, those that are not yet assigned must be put in the col. 2 entries of Table 1, where the col. 1 entries contain node NA* (Step 24).

Handling the DO construct of types 4 and 5. If A* is a DO statement, it must be treated as follows: Each DO must be assigned a separate node, NAS, that assigns the DO index to its initial value (Step 9). The NAS node must be followed by the range node NR, which includes the DO's range statement(s). If the range statement for the DO coincides with its reference statement, then the range node should be an empty node. Therefore, steps 10, 11, 12, and 13 are aimed at finding out what type of node should be assigned as the DO range—empty or nonempty.

Example. In the program sequence that follows the following assignment of NAS and NR nodes is performed:

$$\text{DO 2} \quad I = 1, 100$$
$$\text{DO 1} \quad J = 1, 100$$
$$1 \quad A[I,J] = 0$$
$$2 \quad A[I,I] = 1$$

First we form the assignment node NAS2 for the statement DO 2 that performs the initialization $I = 1$ (Fig. III.2). NAS2 is followed by an empty range node NR2, since the range and reference statements for this DO coincide. Next, during a second iteration of Step 9 we form a second initial assignment node NAS1 for the statement DO 1 that sets $J = 1$. The range node NR1 is also empty since the reference and range statements for this DO match as well. ■

Following the formation of the range nodes, the algorithm begins a new loop in Step 2 aimed at locating the DO reference and assigning it to a separate node, NA* (Steps 18 and 20). Node NA* may be referenced by p other DO's, where $p \geq 1$. In this case it must be succeeded by p conditional nodes NC_1, NC_2, ..., NC_p, each of which checks the index of the respective DO associated with it. For the case that the DO loop terminates, NC_i is connected with NC_{i+1}. If the DO does not terminate, NC_1 is connected with its range node, NR_i.

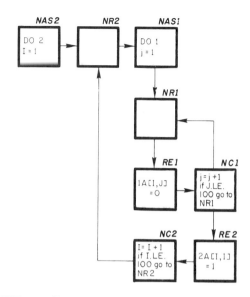

FIGURE III.2 Program graph for the two nested DO statements

Example. Let us illustrate the entire procedure for the program sequence of the previous example. Following the formation of assignment nodes NAS2 and NAS 1 and the empty range nodes NR2 and NR1, the algorithm creates the reference node RE1 for the statement DO 1 and assigns to it RE1 = 1 A[I, J] = 0 (Step 18). It next follows RE1 by the conditional node NC1, which increments the DO index J and checks whether its value terminates the DO loop. Thus, NC 1 is connected with its range node NR1 and with the reference node for the statement DO 2 I = 1, 100, etc. ∎

Example. Let us illustrate the algorithm for the FORTRAN program in Fig. III.3. The program graph for this program is shown in Fig. III.4. Step 1 assigns the statement IFLAG = 1 to node NA_0. It is followed by a comment that is omitted. Next, Steps 2 and 8 determine that DO 10 I = 1, N is a DO statement. Step 9 assigns the DO index I = 1 in the node NAS_1. NAS_1 is followed by the range node, NR_1, that includes IPIVOT(1) = 1, ROWMAX = 0. NR_1 is followed by a second assignment node, NAS_2, that assigns the DO index for DO 9. The node NAS_2 is followed by the range node NR_2. Next, the reference for DO 9 is placed into node RE_2. This node is followed by the conditional node, NC_2, that branches to the range node NR_2, forming an inner DO loop. Node NC_2 is followed by a conventional conditional branch node NA_1. Since the reference of this branch, 999, is not assigned to a node yet, we form the first entry of Table 1, which contains node NA_1 in col. 1 and 999 in col. 2. Node NA_1 is followed by the reference node RE_1 for DO 10. RE_1 is followed by the conditional node NC_1 that branches to the range node NR_1, etc. ∎

```
        SUBROUTINE FACTOR(A,W,PIVOT,D,N,IFLAG)
        DIMENSION A(N,N),W(N,N),IPIVOT(N),D(N)
        IFLAG = 1
C       INITIALIZE W, IPIVOT, D
        DO 10 I = 1,N
        IPIVOT(I) = I
        ROWMAX = 0.
        DO 9 J = 1,N
        W(I,J) = A(I,J)
    9   ROWMAX = AMAX1(ROWMAX,ABS(W(I,J)))
        IF (ROWMAX .EQ. 0.)              GO TO 999
   10   D(I) = ROWMAX
C       GAUSS ELIMINATION WITH SCALED PARTIAL PIVOTING.
        NM1 = N - 1
        IF(NM1 .EQ. 0)                  RETURN
        DO 20 K = 1,NM1
        J = K
        KP1 = K + 1
        IP = IPIVOT(K)
        COLMAX = ABS(W(IP,K))/D(IP)
        DO 11 I = KP1,N
        IP = IPIVOT(I)
        AWIKOV = ABS(W(IP,K))/D(IP)
        IF (AWIKOV .LE. COLMAX)         GO TO 11
        COLMAX = AWIKOV
        J = I
   11   CONTINUE
        IF (COLMAX .EQ. 0.)             GO TO 999
C
        IPK = IPIVOT(J)
        IPIVOT(J) = IPIVOT(K)
        IPIVOT(K) = IPK
        DO 20 I = KP1,N
        IP = IPIVOT(I)
        W(IP,K) = W(IP,K)/W(IPK,K)
        RATIO = -W(IP,K)
        DO 20 J = KP1,N
   20   W(IP,J) = RATIO*W(IPK,J) + W(IP,J)
        IF (W(IP,N) .EQ. 0.)            GO TO 999
                                        RETURN
  999   IFLAG = 2
                                        RETURN
        END
```

FIGURE III.3 FORTRAN program

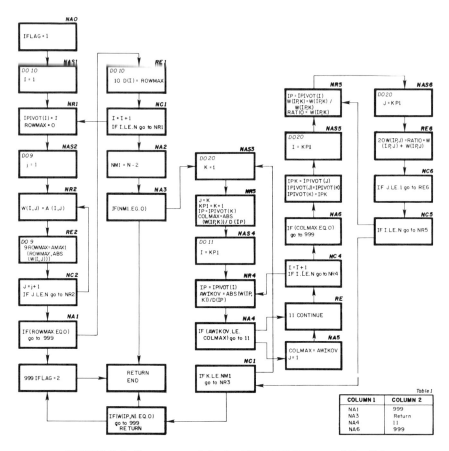

FIGURE III.4 Program graph for the FORTRAN Program of Fig. III.3

3.1.3 Number of Loop Iterations

Each variable computed in a node of the program graph ought to be analyzed to obtain its maximal bit size and the dimension of the data array required for its storage. To this end, one first specifies for each node its *parameter of iteration, Z*, showing the maximal number of iterations this node can execute. To find Z, one has to mark all nodes in the graph which belong to one program loop. (This can be done with a simple algorithm which checks the successor-predecessor relationship among nodes, which is not discussed in this chapter due to its simplicity.) For each such node, i, one finds the maximal number of iterations, Z_i, of the respective loop, and this number is assigned to all nodes included in the loop. If node b belongs to several program loops which iterate Z_a, Z_c, ..., Z_n times, respectively, then the parameter of iteration, Z_b, of this node is

$$Z_b = Z_a \cdot Z_c \cdot \ldots \cdot Z_n$$

Typically, for a program loop, the number of its iterations, Z, may be given either explicitly or determined via analysis of a control statement IF which specifies an exit from the loop. Usually this statement performs a conditional test between two variables X and Y: $X > Y$, $X < Y$, $X \geq Y$, $X \leq Y$, $X = Y$, $X \neq Y$, etc. X and Y may be computed variables which are changed during each iteration. (If one variable is a 0 or a constant, it is a particular case of a more general condition that X and Y change.)

Let Δ_1 and Δ_2 be additive increments for X and Y; i.e., $X_i = X_{i-1} + \Delta_1$ and $Y_i = Y_{i-1} + \Delta_2$. Assume that the control statement specifying exit from the loop is IF (X. GT. Y) GO TO N. (Similar techniques may be used for other types of IF.) Since the loop has to iterate Z times until $X > Y$, if $Z > 0$ then in the beginning of the iterative process (during the first iteration) $X_0 < Y_0$. Also, in order that X be greater than Y sometime in the future (after Z iterations), $\Delta_1 > \Delta_2$. After Z iterations, the following statement will become true for the first time:

$$X_0 + Z \cdot \Delta_1 > Y_0 + Z \cdot \Delta_2 \tag{1}$$

If X and Y are changed via mutiplication, i.e., $X_i = X_{i-1} * \Delta_1$ and $Y_i = Y_{i-1} * \Delta_2$, then after Z iterations

$$X_0 * \Delta_1^Z > Y_0 * \Delta_2^Z \tag{2}$$

It follows from (1) that after $Z - 1$ iterations $X_0 + (Z - 1) \cdot \Delta_1 \leq Y_0 + (Z - 1) \cdot \Delta_2$, or

$$Z \leq \frac{Y_0 - X_0}{\Delta_1 - \Delta_2} + 1 \tag{3}$$

If X and Y are changed via multiplication, after $Z - 1$ iterations,

$$X_0 * \Delta_1^{Z-1} \leq Y_0 * \Delta_2^{Z-1}, \left(\frac{\Delta_1}{\Delta_2}\right)^{Z-1} \leq \frac{Y_0}{X_0}$$

and

$$(Z - 1) \cdot (\log_2 \Delta_1 - \log_2 \Delta_2) \leq \log_2 Y_0 - \log_2 X_0$$

$$Z \leq \frac{\log_2 Y_0 - \log_2 X_0}{\log_2 \Delta_1 - log_2 \Delta_2} + 1 \tag{4}$$

For both expressions (3) and (4), X_0 and Y_0 are the initial values of variables X and Y in the control statement If (X. GT. Y) GO TO N, and Δ_1 and Δ_2 are their increments during iteration. IF Y is constant, then $\Delta_2 = 0$, and instead of (3) one obtains

$$Z \leq \frac{Y_0 - X_0}{\Delta_1} + 1 \tag{5}$$

and instead of (4) one obtains

$$Z \leq \frac{\log_2 Y_0 - \log_2 X_0}{\log_2 \Delta_1} + 1 \tag{6}$$

Similar formulas can be developed for other IF statements and for other changes in the X and Y variables during iteration.

Example. Assume that in IF (X. GT.Y), X and Y change via addition, $X = X + \Delta_1$ and $Y = Y + \Delta_2$, and $X_0 = 4$, $Y_0 = 16$, $\Delta_1 = 2$, and $\Delta_2 = 1$. Applying Eq. (3), one obtains $Z = (16 - 4) / (2 - 1) + 1 = 13$. Indeed, condition X. GT. Y is true after 13 iterations because the value of X is $X = X_0 + \Delta_1 \cdot Z = 4 + 2 \cdot 13 = 30$ and $Y = Y_0 + \Delta_2 \cdot Z = 16 + 1 \cdot 13 = 29$; i.e., $X > Y$. After 12 iterations, $X > Y$ is false because $X = 4 + 2 \cdot 12 = 28$ and $Y = 16 + 1 \cdot 12 = 28$; i.e., $X = Y$. ∎

Example. Let X and Y change via multiplication and $X_0 = 3$, $Y_0 = 35$, $\Delta_1 = 5$, and $\Delta_2 = 2$. Applying Eq. (4), one obtains

$$Z \le \frac{\log_2 35 - \log_2 3}{\log_2 5 - \log_2 2} + 1 = \frac{6 - 2}{3 - 1} + 1 = \frac{4}{2} + 1 = 3$$

Indeed, after three iterations $X = 3 \cdot 5^2 = 75$ and $Y = 35 \cdot 2^2 = 140$; i.e., $X > Y$ is false. ∎

3.1.4 Undefined Parameter of Iterations

There are instances when the parameter of iteration Z is not given explicitly, nor can it be determined analytically. This is true for the case when a loop containing node b operates with initial variables, X_0 and Y_0, which are computed in another loop, etc. All such cases can be handled by assuming that Z is a maximum of the statistical values observed during previous computations of the algorithm. Also if a loop, L_2, uses an initial variable, A_0, computed in another loop, L_1, then one may first find the bit size of the variable A_0 via analysis of loop L_1 and then assume that A_0 is the maximal word that can be stored in the bit size that was found. This word can then be taken as an initial variable for loop L_2. One can treat a sequence of loops, $L_1, L_2, \ldots, L_k$, in which loop L_i computed initial variables for loop L_{i+1} in a similar way.

If the actual number of iterations is larger than its statistical estimates, then the actual bit size, BS, of node b may exceed the analytical bit size BS′, obtained during bit-size analysis. Since a selected computer size may coincide with BS′, the actual bit size, BS, must be reduced to BS′ using the special floating-point operator discussed below.

Note. The assignment system that is under discussion is designated for real-time programs which run repeatedly over new data sets. Thus the history of past program computations is available and provided by the user. The user also provides a statistical number of iterations for those portions of a program that cannot be evaluated via software techniques. Thus the assignment system starts its work when all iteration numbers can be made available; either defined via software algorithms discussed in this section, given explicitly in the program, or provided by the user.

3.1.5 Maximal and Intermediate Bit Sizes of Computed Variables

After finding the iteration parameter of each node, one examines all nodes which contain *computed variables,* i.e., those which are assigned by the program to changeable values. For each computed variable, X, belonging to a node, one defines two parameters:

1. Its *maximal bit size*, $BS(X)$, which shows the maximal number of bits required to store X.

2. Its *maximal intermediate bit size,* $BS(X^*)$, which shows the maximal bit size of all the intermediate results, which the computer forms in calculating X.

Note that for complex arithmetic expressions, the bit size of intermediate results, $BS(X^*)$, may exceed that of the final result, $BS(X)$. For this case $BS(X^*)$ identifies the bit size of the computer which may compute the corresponding computed variable X.

$BS(X)$ is increased when the computer executes addition, multiplication, and shifts toward the most significant bit during its processing (squares, cubes, etc., are executed by the computer as iterative multiplications), whereas divisions and subtrations reduce the bit size of computer variables. Therefore, for bit size increasing operations the bit size of the computer coincides with $BS(X)$, and for bit size decreasing operations it coincides with $BS(X^*)$.

The techniques for the determination of bit sizes of integers and floating-point numbers are presented in the Appendix.

3.1.6 Finding Bit Sizes of Graph Nodes

For each variable X computed in the node d of the program graph, one finds $BS(X)$ and $BS(X^*)$ using the techniques outlined in the Appendix. Then the bit size of a node d, BSN_d, is obtained as a maximum of all bit sizes assumed by variables computed in this node; i.e., $BSN_d = \max BS(X)$. Likewise $BSN_d^* = \max[BS(X^*)]$. Therefore, each node d is specified by 2-bit parameters, BSN_d and BSN^*_d, which will be used for finding the hardware resource required by the P program.

Example. Consider a program to tabulate the function $B = (C^2 + 3C + 2) \cdot (C - 8)$ for $C = 0, 4, \ldots , 16$, but B skips the value when $C - 8 = 0$. Figure III.5(a) shows an expression of this program in FORTRAN. Figure III.5(b) shows the respective program graph built in accordance with Algorithm 1. The algorithm assigns node 1 to the first IF. Statements 2 and 3 referenced by IF are also assigned separate nodes 2 and 3. Statement Print, B, C is included in node 2, since it is not a control statement nor is it referenced by other nodes. Statement IF $(C - 16)$, 1, 1, 4 is assigned node 4, since it is a control statement. It is followed by statement Stop, assigned to node 5, since it is referenced by node 4.

(a) FORTRAN PROGRAM
for
TABULATING B FUNCTION

```
        C - 0

1   IF(C -8.)2,3,2

2   B = (C * C + 3. * C + 2.) * (C - 8.)
    PRINT, B, C

3   C = C + 4.

    IF (C - 16.)1,1,4

4   STOP
    END
```

(b) PROGRAM GRAPH
for the
FORTRAN PROGRAM

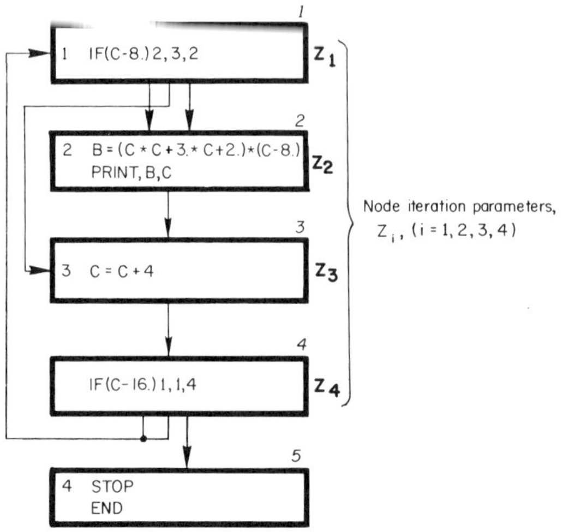

Node iteration parameters,
Z_i, $(i = 1, 2, 3, 4)$

FIGURE III.5 FORTRAN program and its program graph

Let us find the bit size of the computed variable, B. Since variable B changes during the iterative process, first we find the number of iterations, Z_2, of node 2 which computes B. Node 2 is contained in the iterative loop made of nodes 1, 2, 3, and 4. Since the exit of this loop is specified by the control statement IF $(C - 16)$ 1, 1, 4 assigned to node 4, $Z_2 = Z_4$. To find Z_4, we use Eq. (5), since the value of $Y = 16$ is not changed during iterations. Thus $Y_0 = 16$, $X_0 = 0$, $\Delta_1 = 4$, $\Delta_2 = 0$, and

$$Z_4 \le \frac{Y_0 - X_0}{\Delta_1} + 1 = \frac{16 - 0}{4} + 1 = 5$$

Therefore, the program loop made of nodes 1, 2, 3, and 4 iterates $Z_4 = 5$ times. Since the expression for B uses no bit size decreasing operations which reduce BS(B) as compared to BS(B^*), we obtain BS(B) $\ge$ BS(B^*). Thus the bit size of the computer is BS(B) and there is no need to find BS(B^*). To find BS(B) we will use the equations in the Appendix. Variable B is obtained as a result of multiplication, $B = D * E$, with complex changeable factors D and E, where $D = (C * C + 3 * C + 2)$ and $E = (C - 8)$.

Variable D is changed via bit increasing operations, and variable E is changed via bit decreasing operations. First, find BS(D) after Z iterations. Since D contains a computed variable C involved in $C * C$ and $3 * C$, to find BS(D), one has to find the bit size of a temporary result BS(D^*), where BS(D^*) $\le$ max[BS($C * C$), BS $(3 * C)$] + 1; BS($C * C$) is found via Eq. (A13), as BS($C * C$) $\le$ 2BS[max (C_0, Δ)] + 2 log$_2$ (1 + Z), where $C_0 = 0$ $\Delta = 4$, and $Z = 5$. Therefore, BS($C*C$) $\le$ 2BS[max(0, 4)] + 2 log$_2$ (1 + 5) = 2BS(4) + 2• log$_2$ 6 = 2 • 3 + 2 • 3 = 12. BS($3*C$) is found via

Eq. (A16), since the multiplicand 3 is not changed: BS $(3*C) \leq 2BS$ max$(3, C_0, \Delta)$ + log2 $(1 + Z) = 2BS[$max$(3, 0, 4)] + \log_2 (1 + 5) = 2BS(4) + \log_2 6 = 2 \cdot 3 + 3 = 9$. BS$(D^*) \leq$ max$[BS(C * C), BS (3 * C)] + 1 =$ max$(12, 9) + 1 = 13$ bits, and BS$(D) \leq$ max$[BS(D^*)] + 1 =$ max$(13, 2) + 1 = 14$ bits.

Let us find BS(E), where $E = (C - 8)$ is a multiplier of $B = D * E$. BS$(E) =$ max$[BS(C = C + 4), BS(8)]$, where C is involved in recursive addition $C = C + 4$; BS$(C = C + 4)$ is obtained via Eq. (A2): BS$(C = C + 4) \leq$ max$[BS(C_0),$ BS $(4)]$ + $\log_2 (1 + Z) =$ max$[BS(0), BS(4)] + \log_2 (1 + Z) = 3 + \log_2 (1 + 5) = 6$ bits. Thus, BS$(E) =$ max$[6, 4] = 6$ bits.

Next, since we found the upper bounds on bit sizes assumed by D and E with due regard of iterative process, we may use Eq. (A12) to find BS(B): BS$(B) \leq$ BS(D) + BS$(E) = 14 + 6 = 20$ bits. Thus, for node 2, $BSN_2 = BSN_2^* = 20$ bits.

Nodes 1, 3, and 4 use variable C involved in recursive addition $C = C + 4$. Since BS$(C = C + 4) \leq 6$, for nodes 1, 3, and 4, BSN = BSN* = 6 bits. ■

As follows from the above, finding the bit sizes for computed variables is a simple process which uses the bit sizes of the variables before iteration, the number of iterations, and the bit sizes of other variables which were computed previously.

3.1.7 Array Dimensions of Variables Computed in Graph Nodes

During the analysis of each graph node, one has to specify the dimensions of data arrays, DA, for all computed variables. To this end, in a node one finds a statement which provides for storage of a computed variable or variables. Let this statement specify that v computed variables, $X_1, X_2, \dots , X_v$, be stored and the iteration parameter for the node be Z. Then the required dimension of the array to store variables $X_1, X_2, \dots , X_v$ is DA $= v \times Z$. The dimension of the data array for all variables computed in the node, DAN, is the sum of the DAs obtained for all statements: DAN $= \Sigma$ DA.

Example. Using the program graph of Fig. III.5, we find that node 2 prints B and C variables; i.e., $v = 2$. Since node 1 iterates $Z_2 = 5$ times, the dimension of the data array which contains all B and C variables is DA $= v \times Z = 2 \times 5 = 10$ data words. Since no other variables of node 2 have to be stored, $DAN_2 = 10$. ■

As a result of the analysis introduced above, each node is characterized by the following parameters: iteration paramenter Z, 2-bit size parameters BSN and BSN*, and data array dimension parameter DAN.

3.2 Resource Diagrams for Individual Programs

Analysis of the program nodes is succeeded by construction of the diagram of the hardware resource required by a program, or *P-resource diagram,* which is made in the following stages.

3.2.1 Bit-size Diagram of a Program Graph

Having found bit sizes for all nodes in a program graph, one constructs its bit-size diagram in which the horizontal axis specifies the nodes of the program graph, and the vertical axis shows the two bit-size parameters, BSN and BSN*, found for each node. Figure III.6 shows a bit-size diagram built for a program graph containing 15 nodes. Vertical dotted and solid lines show the respective BSN* and BSN parameters for the case, BSN* > BSN. For example, for node 7, $BSN*_7 = 64$ bits and $BSN_7 = 32$ bits. The bit-size diagram serves as a basis for finding the computer-size diagram required by the program.

3.2.2 Alignment of the Bit-size Diagram

The bit-size diagram is aligned next by the assignment system in order to exclude excessive changes in computer sizes. This means that for a sequence of nodes requiring approximately the same bit size a statistically dominant bit size is found. It is then accepted as the size of the computer which will compute this sequence. If a node in the sequence requires an exceptionally large bit size for a fixed-point operation, then it is necessary to replace it using a floating-point operation. For instance, Fig. III.6 shows a bit-size diagram for 15 nodes. The dominant size for this sequence is 48 bits. However, for node 7, the maximal intermediary bit size BSN* = 64 bits.

Suppose that in analyzing node 7 one finds that this size is obtained for a fixed-point multiplication operation. Reduction to 48 bits may be accomplished by replacing a fixed-point by a floating-point multiplication. Let us introduce some techniques which allow such a replacement.

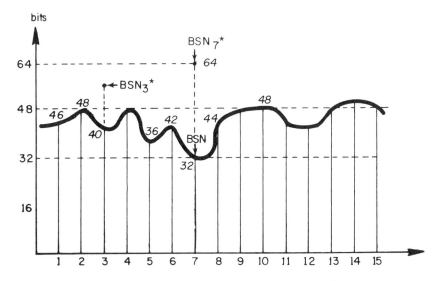

FIGURE III.6 Bit-size diagram of a program graph

3.2.2.1 Alignment in bit sizes

Let the bit size of the node for a fixed-point operation (FI bits) have to be reduced to a smaller bit size for a floating-point operation (FL bits). First we find a fixed-point variable, X, computed in the node which requires FI bits; i.e., $BS(X) = FI$. When X is transformed into a floating-point form, it includes exponent, XE, and mantissa, XM, i.e., $X = XE \times XM$. Since XE and XM have to be stored in a new and smaller bit size FL, $FL = BS(XE) + BS(XM)$.

Let us find the number of bits, $BS(XE)$, to be assigned for XE. When X is a fixed-point number, it cannot be larger than $2^{FI} - 1$. Thus $X \le 2^{FI} - 1$ and $XE \le FI$. Consequently, $BS(XE) \le BS(FI)$, and $FL \le BS(FI) + BS(XM)$.

Therefore, for a floating-point number, $X = XE \times XM$, stored in FL bits, one has to assign for the exponent $BS(FI)$ bits, where FI is the bit size of the same number in fixed-point form. Then the remaining bits may be assigned for mantissa, XM: $BS(XM) = FL - BS(FI)$.

Example. Let a fixed-point form of a variable X take 64 bits. Suppose that X has to be converted into a floating-point form taking 48 bits. Thus, $FI = 64$ and $FL = 48$. Since a 64-bit number cannot be larger than $2^{64} - 1$, exponent XE of the X number is bounded above as $XE \le 64$ and $BS(XE) \le BS(64) = 7$ bits. Therefore, in a floating-point register taking $FL = 48$ bits, one has to assign $BS(64) = 7$ bits for XE. The remaining bits may be assigned for the mantissa: $BS(XM) = 48 - 7 = 41$ bits. ∎

If a node in the graph is specified with a smaller number of bits than the dominant bit size, its size is increased. This increase may be performed by introducing additional precision bits if all operations in the node are fixed point or by converting a floating-point number taking FL bits into a fixed-point form taking FI bits, where $FL < FI$. Both types of alignment are described by simple and well-known procedures.

Alignment of all graph nodes to the dominant bit sizes results in finding the computer-size diagram which specifies the sequence of computer sizes required for computation of the program. This diagram partitions the program into tasks, where each task is composed of nodes requiring the same computer size. Figure III.7(a) shows the computer-size diagram (dotted lines) obtained from the bit-size diagram (curved line) and built for a program containing 800 nodes. This diagrams partitions the program into four tasks computed by 48, 32, 16, and 32 bit computers, respectively [Fig. III.7(b)].

3.2.3 Time to Execute One Task in a Dynamic Computer

The adaptive assignment of the resources of a dynamic architecture among independent programs must be based on the execution time of each task in a given-size computer. Indeed, since a system with dynamic architecture may compute several concurrent programs, one architectural state may feature several independent tasks computed in concurrent computers. The problem is in deciding which task should switch the ar-

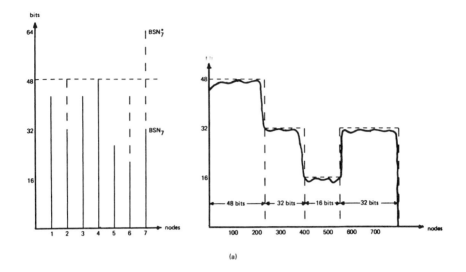

(a)

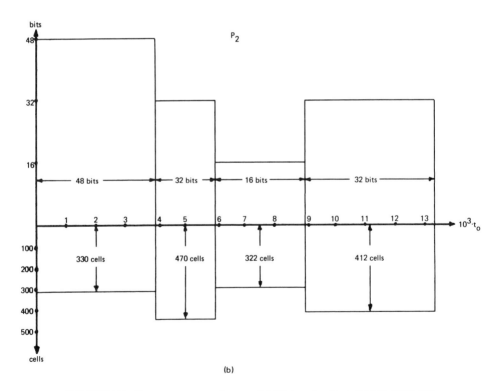

(b)

FIGURE III.7   Program resource diagram: (a) Bit size alignment; (b) processor and memory resources required by program P

chitecture into the next state. If it is done by the task requiring the longest execution, the remaining tasks will finish their executions earlier and will await the end of the longest task. Therefore, performance will deteriorate. Thus, it is expedient that the longest task be executed in several states using the same computer. In this case, the shorter tasks may switch architecture and continue their execution without waiting for the end of the longest task. The system will perform correctly because the resource of the longest task will not be requested for reconfiguration. Therefore, if one assigns the hardware resource on the basis of time, the idle time of the computed programs will be minimized.

However, the diagram of computer sizes has been built for program nodes. This is why it is necessary to find a tentative time for executing a task in a given-size computer. Since all computers of dynamic architecture use the same clock period, t_0, the time to execute a task may be expressed in terms of t_0. To this end, one first finds the number of clock periods, t_0, required for each node included in the task. This is done with due regard to iterative execution as specified by the iteration parameter Z of the node.

Having found the time for each node, one finds the time of the task as the sum of times for the nodes included in the task. Therefore, to find the time of one task, one has to find the time to execute one node. This may be accomplished if one finds the time to execute one machine instruction, since each statement in the node may be interpreted as a sequence of machine instructions.

3.2.3.1 One instruction time

Since all computers of dynamic architecture use modular control organization, MCD [8], the number of clock periods, t_0, required to execute one instruction may be determined as follows. Each instruction is executed during one instruction cycle (IC), which consists of d intervals: $IC = T_1 + T_2 + \ldots + T_d$. Since the control organization must generate variable time intervals which are functions of operand word size for processor-dependent operations and memory speed for memory access operations, the MCD generates a variable time interval, T, in the following way: T contains b clock periods, t_0; i.e., $T = b \cdot t_0$, where t_0 is the time of the longest operation (8-bit addition) in one LSI module used for assembling each computer. Variation of T is achieved by variation of b, which for different types of operations assumes the value of one of several control codes stored in each LSI module of the computer.

For an interval in which a processor dependent operation is executed, b assumes the value of *processor code p,* where p is the number of clock periods, t_0, that a processor-dependent operation requires to execute in a given-size computer. For an interval in which an instruction is fetched, b assumes the value of *fetch instruction code* m_I, where m_I is the number of clock periods required to fetch an instruction from a given memory element. For an interval in which a data word is fetched, b assumes the value of *fetch data code* m_E, where m_E specifies the speed of the slowest memory element contained in the primary memory of the computer.

For one instruction, sequencing of the intervals is defined by an interval sequencer which is included in the MCD of every LSI module. In this sequencer, each interval is identified with one state, and a sequence of states is selected by the instruction op code. For each interval, variation of its duration is achieved with the *operation sequencer.* This sequencer is controlled by one of three codes (p, m_E, m_I) considered above. This is achieved by executing a loop which lasts either p, or $m_I \div$ or m_E clock periods, t_0. If the interval sequencer initiates the operation sequencer, the interval sequencer retains its state (interval) until the operation sequencer completes its operation. Therefore, the interval duration is a function of one of three codes stored in an LSI module of the computer.

When a new computer is formed, it is sufficient to write new values of codes p, m_E, and m_I into all its LSI modules for the control unit to start generation of new time intervals.

Example. Let us find the clock periods, t_0, required for an addition instruction. It is executed during the following time intervals: $T_1 = m_I \cdot t_0$ performs instruction fetch, where m_I is the fetch instruction code; $T_2 = t_o$ performs instruction decoding; $T_3 = m_E \cdot t_o$ fetches the operand, where m_E is the fetch data code; $T_4 = 2t_0 \cdot p$ *performs the addition, where p is the processor code.* Assume that $m_I = m_E = 2$, and for a 16-bit computer, $p = 1$; for a 32-bit computer, $p = 2$; for a 48-bit computer, $p = 3$, etc. Then, for a 16-bit computer, the time to execute this instruction is $T = T_1 + T_2 + T_3 + T_4 = 2t_0 + t_0 + 2t_0 + 2t_0 \cdot 1 = 7t_0$. In a 32-bit computer, this instruction is executed during time $T = 2t_0 + t_0 + 2t_0 + 2t_0 \cdot 2 = 9t_0$, etc. ∎

3.2.3.2 One graph node time

Having found the times to execute all instructions of the instruction set, one constructs a special table in which rows correspond to machine instructions. An entry in a row shows the number of clock periods required for the execution of that instruction. A processor-dependent instruction is assigned n rows, each showing the instruction time in a computer of given size ranging from 16 to $16 \cdot n$ bits, respectively. A processor-independent instruction is assigned a single row since its execution time does not depend on the computer size. Therefore, if a statement is interpreted as f machine instructions, then its time is found as the sum of the times of all its instructions. If this statement belongs to a node with iteration parameter Z, then the number of clock periods thus obtained is multiplied by Z. Having obtained the time of each statement, one may find the time of the node and the time of the task.

Example. For the program graph of Fig. III.5, let us find the time to execute node 2. This node computes $B = (C * C + 3 * C + 2) + (C - 8)$ and prints B and C variables. Execution of B takes four machine instructions: (1) addition instruction, I_+, which fetches one operand from the memory; (2) modified addition instruction, I_+^*, which adds two operands stored in processor registers; (3) multiplication instruction, $I_\times$, which fetches one operand from the memory; and (4) modified multiplication instruction, $I_\times^*$, which multiplies two operands stored in processor registers.

Since for computation of B one needs variables C and $C - 8$ used in the preceding node 1, assume that current C and $C - 8$ are stored in registers R1 and R2 of the processor. Then the following instruction sequence computes B:

1. I_x^* computes $C \times C \rightarrow$ R3 (i.e., product is sent to a double-precision register, R3).
2. I_x computes $3 \times C \rightarrow$ R4.
3. I_s^* finds R3 + R3 $\rightarrow$ R5 (R5 stores $C * C + 3 * C$).
4. I_+ finds R5 + 2 $\rightarrow$ R6 (R6 stores $C * C + 3 * C + 2$).
5. I_x^* computes R6 $\times$ R2 $\rightarrow$ R7 (R7 stores a current variable, B). Statement "Print, B, C" is interpreted as two print instructions, I_p.
6. I_p sends the R7 register content to a cache register of the I/O device.
7. I_p also sends the R1 register content to the I/O device.

As was found earlier, the bit size of node 2 is $BSN_2 = 20$ bits. Assume that this node is executed in a 32-bit computer storing the following control codes: processor code, $p = 2$; instruction fetch code, $m_I = 2$; data fetch code, $m_E = 3$. Using the technique illustrated above, we find that the time to execute I_+ in a 32-bit computer is $T(I_+) = 10t_0$; for the modified addition instruction, $T(I_+^*) = 7t_0$, since the time of operand fetch ($T_3 = 3t_0$) is eliminated.

Let us find the time, $T(I_x)$, of the multiplication instruction in a 32-bit computer. For simplicity, assume that no fast multiplication schemes are used and the multiplication operation takes the time of 32 additions (each taking the time $2t_0 \cdot p = 4t_0$) and 32 shifts (one t_0 per shift). $T(I_x) = T_1 + T_2 + T_3 + T_4$, where $T_1 = m_I \cdot t_0 = 2t_0$ fetches the instruction; $T_2 = t_0$ decodes I_x; $T_3 = m_E \cdot t_0 = 3t_0$ fetches the multiplicand; $T_4 = 32 \cdot t_0 p + 32t_0 = 160t_0$ performs multiplication as 32 additions and 32 shifts. Therefore, $T(I_x) = 2t_0 + t_0 + 3t_0 + 160t_0 = 166t_0$.

For the modified multiplication instruction, $T(I_x^*) = 163t_0$, since the time of the operand fetch is eliminated. For the print instruction, $T(I_p) = T_1 + T_2 + T_3$, where $T_1 = m_I \cdot t_0 = 2t_0$, $T_2 = t_0$, and $T_3 = 2t_0$ since T_3 sends the result of R3 to a local cache and the I/O device; therefore, $T(I_p) = 2t_0 + t_0 + 2t_0 = 5t_0$.

Find the time of one interation of node 2. $T_0(N_2) = T(I_x^*) + T(I_x) + T(I_x^*) + T(I_+) + T(I_+^*) + T(I_p) + T(I_p) = 163t_0 + 166t_0 + 7t_0 + 10t_0 + 163t_0 + 5t_0 + 5t_0 = 519t_0$.

Earlier we found that node 2 iterates $Z = 5$ times. Therefore, the total time to execute node 2 during Z iterations is $T_Z(N_2) = 519 \cdot t_0 \cdot Z = 519 \cdot 5t_0 = 2595t_0$. ∎

3.2.4 P-Resource Diagram

After finding the time to execute each task in a given-size computer, one constructs the hardware resource diagram for the entire program, P, otherwise called the *P-resource diagram*. In this diagram the horizontal axis shows the time of functioning of each task, and the vertical axis contains two portions: the upper portion shows computer sizes, and the lower portion shows dimensions of data arrays. Figure III.7(b) shows the P-resource diagram constructed on the basis of an aligned diagram of Fig. III.7(a). The horizontal axis indicates the number of clock periods, t_0, which execute each task in a given-size computer. In accordance with Fig. III.7(a), the first and second tasks executed by 18-bit and 32-bit computers take 220 and 180 nodes, respectively; however, the first task takes around $4 \cdot 10^3 t_0$, whereas the second one is executed in about $2 \cdot 10^3 t_0$ [Fig. III.7(b)]. Although the two tasks take approximately the same number of nodes, the first one requires twice as long as the second one to execute.

Each task above was specified by a unique computer size. To find the space required by its data, one adds all the DAN dimensions found earlier for the task nodes to the dimension of the array of initial data, which lists all the initial words used in computation of all the task nodes.

Having constructed a P-resource diagram for each program P, one performs the overall assignment of the system resources among user programs. This assignment takes into account specific attributes of dynamic architectures discussed in [2, 3, 7, 8, 9].

3.3 Adaptive Assignment of System Resources

To find a sequence of states assumed by a dynamic architecture computing a set of user programs, one has to perform a hardware resource assignment among tasks to identify which computer elements should be assigned to each task of any given program, P. This may be done by using all the P-resource diagrams obtained in Sec. 3.2.4. The reconfiguration software system maps all such diagrams onto the following two diagrams showing the distribution of the DC group resource:

1. *CE resource diagram,* which charts the computer elements assigned to each task and defines the flow chart of architectural transitions.

2. *ME resource diagram,* which indicates the allocation of the DC group primary memory among various user programs.

3.3.1 Priority Assignment

To obtain the CE resources diagram, one has to map all P-resource diagrams on the DC group *assignable resources* defined below.

3.3.1.1 DC group resources

Generally, by the *resource* of one dynamic computer group (DC group) we mean n computer elements CE (interconnected together via a reconfigurable memory-processor bus) and one monitor V (Fig. III.8). Since a detailed organization of this bus was given in Chapter 3, Volume 1, here it is introduced only as a point of reference.

Each CE includes h-bit processor element PE, h-bit-wide memory element ME, and h-bit I/O element GE. Accept that $h = 16$. A reconfigurable bus includes two types of connecting elements: address-connecting element ASE and memory-connecting element MSE.

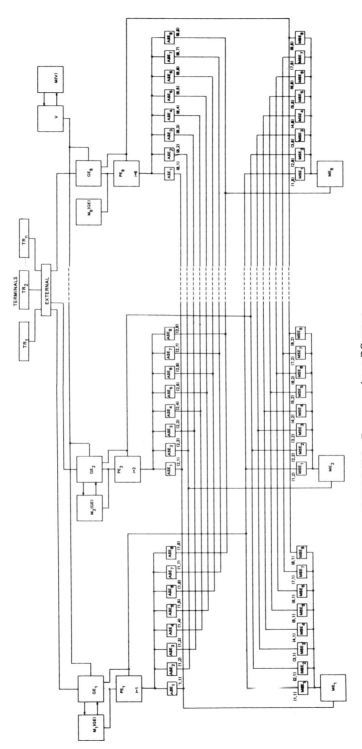

FIGURE III.8 Resource of one DC group

167

Since each P-resource diagram contains PE and ME portions showing the requested needs on PE and ME resources, mapping P-resource diagrams onto DC group computing resources means allocation of the processor resource containing n PE and memory resource containing n ME. The engagement of all other resources (GE, ASE, MSE) in executions is automatically determined by the processor and memory allocation. As for the V monitor, its main function is to monitor DC group reconfiguration from one state to another. Thus, it is not involved in assignment.

Therefore, if the DC group executes p concurrent and sequential programs during the total execution time T, the total *assignable resource* R that is distributed among programs is

$$R = n \cdot CE \cdot T \tag{7}$$

The DC group forms dynamic computers, $C_i(k)$, via software, where k shows the number of integrated CEs and i shows the position of its most significant CE. This computer handles $16 \cdot k$-bit words and has a primary memory $16 \cdot k$-bit wide; thus each word is stored in a single parallel cell made of k 16-bit bytes. To reduce the complexity and increase the speed of the reconfigurable processor bus destined to transmit processor signals such as carries, overflows, and equalities among PEs, each $C_i(k)$ *must include* only adjacent CEs for which positions are fixed as CE_i, CE_{i+1}, ... , CE_{i+k-1}. For instance, dynamic computer $C_3(3)$ contains CE_3, CE_4, and CE_5, and it handles $16 \cdot 3$-bit words; its CE_3 is the most significant; its CE_5 is the least significant.

3.3.1.2 Program priorities

To prevent the idleness of the total assignable resource R, assume that at any moment of time the number of computers that can be formed dynamically is smaller than the number of concurrent programs that need resources. For this case, both assigning resources and monitoring program executions are made with due regard for the *program priorities,* PR. These are integers assigned to the programs by the operating system on the basis of their relative importance.

To prevent indeterminate assignments whereby the software system does not know which program must be given a computational time, priorities PR_1, ... , PR_p, assigned to p programs P_1, P_2, ... , P_p, respectively, form a well-ordered sequence of integers

$$PR_1 > PR_2 > \ldots > PR_p$$

where PR_i is the priority of program P_i. Once priorities are introduced, the following rule governs resource assignment and monitor actions of the operating system.

Assignment Priority. IF $PR_i > PR_j$, then P_i-resource diagram is mapped first onto the available resource $R' \leq R$, where R is given by Eq. (7); the P_j-resource diagram is then mapped onto the remaining resource $R' - P_i$, where

$$P_i = k_1 \cdot CE \cdot t(TA_1) + k_2 \cdot CE \cdot t(TA_2) + \cdots + k_t \cdot CE \cdot t(TA_t) \tag{8}$$

and $t(TA_i)$ is the duration of task TA_i requiring k_i computer elements CE.

3.3.1.3 Interruptible and noninterruptible programs

Since, by condition, the resource needs of p programs exceed the maximal number n of dynamic computers that can be formed in the DC group, some programs will be computed in an interrupted mode of operation. In general, computer programs may be divided into two classes: *noninterruptible* and *interruptible.* Program P is *noninterruptible* if it cannot be interrupted either because of the specificities of its algorithm (for instance, real-time control) or due to the requirement that its computational time be kept minimal so it cannot tolerate delays caused by program interrupts. All the remaining programs will be called *interruptible.*

Obviously, to satisfy the condition of noninterruption, the following rules must be obeyed:

1. If d noninterruptible programs P_1, P_2, ... , P_d are executed concurrently and m_i is the maximal number of CEs required by P_i ($i = 1$, ... , d), then

$$m_1 + m_2 + \ldots + m_d \leq n \qquad (9)$$

where n is the total number of CEs in the system. Conversely, if n is given, then using Eq. (9) one can define the maximal number of concurrent noninterruptible programs inasmuch as each m_i can be found from a P-resource diagram.

2. If the total number r of noninterruptible programs exceeds d defined via Eq. (9), then their executions must be organized sequentially during l periods of time so that

$$r = d_1 + d_2 + \ldots d_l \qquad (10)$$

where d_i is the number of concurrent noninterruptible programs computed during the ith period and defined via Eq. (9).

3. If there is a concurrent execution of a program mix made of d noninterruptible programs and t interruptible programs, then to satisfy the condition of noninterruption for each noninterruptible program, its priority, PR, must be higher than that of any concurrent interruptible program. Otherwise, the CE resource used by a noninterruptible program may be given to an interruptible program with a higher priority which will interrupt the computation of a noninterruptible program. That is inadmissible.

As for the distribution of priorities among d concurrent noninterruptible programs, this can be done arbitrarily, since by definition they cannot be interrupted.

3.3.2 Construction of the CE Resource Diagram

This is done in two stages:

Stage 1. Allocate assignable resource R $= n \cdot$ CE $\cdot$ T to noninterruptible programs. Find the resource R$'$ $\leq$ R left.

Stage 2. Assign resource R' to all interruptible programs.

Before outlining the assigning procedures for Stages 1 and 2, let us introduce the rule of left and right prefix, which will be used in both stages of constructing the CE resource diagram.

3.3.2.1 Rule of left and right prefixes

Dynamic computer $C(k)$ is called a *right prefix* of dynamic computer $C'(k')$ if $C(k)$ is formed of k least significant CE belonging to computer $C'(k')$, where $k \leq k'$. Obviously, it is assumed that $C(k)$ and $C'(k')$ do not exist concurrently. Similar definition can be made for a *left prefix*; the only requirement is that $C(k)$ be made of k most significant CE belonging to computer $C'(k')$ and $k \leq k'$.

The significance of these definitions will become clear in the context of an adopted technique for storing $16 \cdot k$-bit words that was described in [8]. Accordingly, for a dynamic computer $C(k)$ assembled from k CE, a $16k$-bit data word is stored in a parallel cell of k ME made of k 16-bit bytes specified with the same address.

Therefore, if two consecutive tasks are computed by two computers $C(k)$ and $C'(k')$, and $C(k)$ is a right prefix of $C'(k')$, then a larger computer, $C'(k')$, can easily access all data words that were computed earlier by the smaller computer, $C(k)$, since these are stored in k least significant bytes of the primary memory of the larger computer, $C'(k')$.

Example. In Fig. III.9, dynamic 32-bit computer $C_9(2)$ is a right prefix of 48-bit computer $C_8(3)$. Thus, 32-bit data words computed by $C_9(2)$ are stored in 32-bit cells of ME_9 and ME_{10}. Computer $C_8(3)$ can easily access these data since ME_9 and ME_{10} are least significant bytes of its primary memory made of ME_8, ME_9, and ME_{10}.

If a computer $C(k)$ is a left prefix of $C'(k')$, then $C'(k')$ can also access data words computer by $C(k)$ using a special fetch-shift instruction which shifts each such data word by $(k' - k)$ bytes in order that it be received by the least significant portion of computer $C'(k')$. Organization of this instruction was discussed in [8].

In all, if $C(k)$ is a left or right prefix of computer $C'(k')$, then $C'(k')$ can easily access data words computed by $C(k)$ without any interference of the operating system, since these data words are stored in the local primary memory of the $C'(k')$ computer.

It then follows that if two sequential tasks TA_1 and TA_2 of the same program are computed in computer $C(k)$ and $C'(k')$, a data exchange between TA_1 and TA_2 (whereby TA_2 receives data words computed before by TA_1) is performed without memory contention and associated interference of the operating system, provided the computer $C(k)$ is a left or right prefix of computer $C'(k')$. ■

Now that the significance of left and right prefix is established, let us present the rule of left and right prefixes that will be used in assignment procedures for both noninterruptible and interruptible programs.

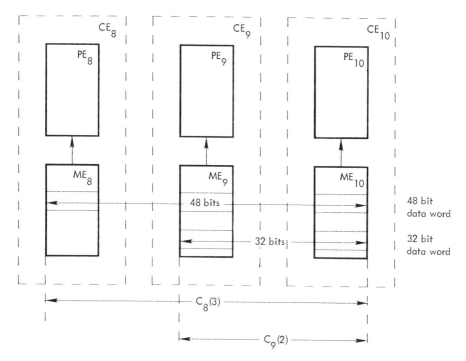

FIGURE III.9 Right prefix rule for data storage

Rule of left and right prefixes during assignment. For any two sequential tasks of the same P-resource diagram requiring the dynamic computers $C(k)$ and $C'(k')$, where $k < k'$, the resource assignment will provide that $C(k)$ be a left or right prefix of $C'(k')$. Such an assignment will eliminate any memory contention that arises each time when $C'(k')$ should access the primary memory of another concurrent computer, say $C''(k'')$, for the data words computed by $C(k)$ that existed earlier. Each such accessing would have required the activation of the local operating system of $C''(k'')$, which is designated to check the priority of a program run on $C'(k')$ to perform a nonlocal memory access to the primary memory or separate MEs of the computer $C''(k'')$.

3.3.2.2 Assignment of CE resources for noninterruptible programs

Given a set of noninterruptible programs P_1, P_2, ... , P_r specified with ordered priorities $PR_1 > PR_2 > \ldots > PR_r$ and the assignable resource $R = n \cdot CE \cdot T$. Construct a two-axis CE diagram in which the vertical line is assigned for n CE and the horizontal line shows time T of the total system engagement in computation.

Step 1. For each noninterruptible program P_i, use its P_i-resource diagram to find the following *program parameters*: (a) the maximal number, m_i, of CE it needs, and (b) the time, T_i, of its total execution.

Step 2. Find d_1 programs with highest priorities such that $m_1 + m_2 + \cdots + m_{d_1} \leq n$. Form the first set of concurrent programs, CNS_1, from these programs. Consider one program $P^* \in CNS_1$. Find its program parameters, m^* and T^*. On the CE resource diagram allocate m^* CEs for computing P^* during the time, T^*. Do this procedure for all programs from the set CNS_1.

Step 3.   This step is iterative. It assumes that the CE resource has been allocated for all programs from the set CNS_i, where Step 2 allocated all programs from the set CNS_1 (i.e., it did allocation for basis $i = 1$). Using this assumption, Step 3 performs two iterative actions: (a) it forms set CNS_{i+1} and (b) it allocates the CE resource for programs from set CNS_{i+1}. The following procedures are used:

Action 1.   Select a program P^* with the highest priority not allocated with the resources yet. Find its m^* and T^* program parameters.

Action 2.   On the CE resource diagram find the moment of time when m^* consecutive CEs assigned to a program(s) from the preceding CNS_i finish their execution. Allocate these CEs for program P^* during time T^*. Mark the end of their engagement on the time axis. Introduce this P^* into CNS_{i+1}.

Action 3.   Perform the following check: add all m^* parameters of programs P^* already in CNS_{i+1}; i.e., find

$$n_{i+1} = \sum_{P^* \in CNS_{i+1}} m^*$$

(11)

Find

$$n - n_{i+1} = \Delta$$

Find

$$T_{max}(i + 1) = \max_{P^* \in CNS_{i+1}} (T^*)$$

(12)

If $\Delta = 0$, set CNS_{i+1} has been formed. Repeat Step 3 for the next set CNS_{i+2}. If no programs are left, go to Step 4.

If $\Delta > 0$, find if there is a noninterruptible program left not assigned with resources. If no such program is left, the procedure ends. If there are such programs, select a highest-priority program P^* left and find its T^* and m^* parameters. Find $\Delta - m^*$. If $\Delta - m^* \geq 0$, go to Action 2, Step 3, for this program. If $\Delta - m^* < 0$, find if there is a program P' next highest in priority with the following m' and T' parameters: $m' < \Delta$ and $T' < T_{max}(i + 1)$, where $T_{max}(i + 1)$ is defined in Eq. (12). If such a program is available include it into CNS_{i+1} and go to Action 2, Step 3, for this program. If no such program is available, set CNS_{i+1} is completed. Go to Step 3 to form the next set CNS_{i+2}.

Note: By construction, n_{i+1} defined in Eq. (11) cannot be larger than n, the total number of CEs in the resource; thus this step does not branch on $n_{i+1} > n$.

Step 4. For each program P* allocated with m^* CEs during the time T^*, chart on the CE diagram its specific PE resource requirements defined by the PE portion of its P* resource diagram. Use the rule of right prefix (defined in Sec. 3.3.2.1) during this charting. This completes the mapping of P* needs onto the CE resource diagram.

It should be noted that since, for each noninterruptible P*, m^* CEs are allocated during the entire time T^*, we can use either left or right prefix for charting the specific needs of this P*. However, right prefix is preferable since its use requires no shifting during fetch. Thus, it can be performed faster.

Example. Given eight noninterruptible programs, P_1 through P_8 (Table III.1) with ordered priorities. Maximal needs of these programs on the CE resource are in col. 2, whereas col. 3 shows their times of execution. Using the assignment procedures outlined above, let us allocate assignable resource $R = n \cdot CE \cdot T = 5 \cdot CE \cdot T$ for these programs.

Step 1. Table III.1 already shows execution of Step 1.

Step 2. Form set CNS_1 (Fig. III.10), as follows: Since $n = 5$, $n_1 = m_1 + m_2 = 2 + 3 = 5$; i.e., $CNS_1 = \{P_1, P_2\}$. In Fig. III.10, allocate $m_1 = 2$ CE (CE_1 and CE_2) for P_1 for 10 sec and $m_2 = 3$ CE (CE_3, CE_4, and CE_5) for P_2 for 20 sec.

Find $n = n_1 = 5 - 5 = 0$. Set $CNS_1 = \{P_1, P_2\}$ has been formed.

Table III.1

Col. 1	Col. 2	Col. 3
Priority-Ordered Sequence of Noninterrupt Programs	Maximal Number of CE Required by Each P_i m_i	Time of Execution of Each P_i (sec)
P_1	2	10
P_2	3	20
P_3	4	30
P_4	4	20
P_5	3	10
P_6	2	30
P_7	1	20
P_8	1	40

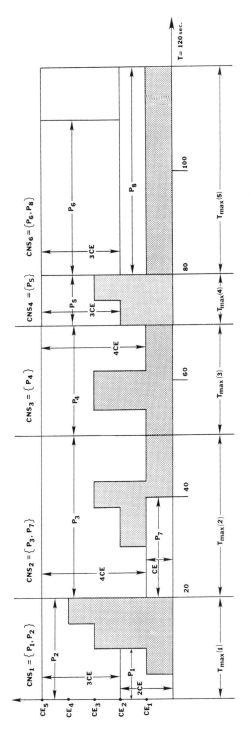

FIGURE III.10 Allocation of assignable resources for eight noninterruptible programs P_1 through P_8

174

Step 3. Select P_3, $m_3 = 4$, $T_3 = 30$. On the CE resource diagram $m_3 = 4$, the four CEs are free at $T = 20$ sec. Allocate four consecutive CEs (CE_2 through CE_5) for P_3 during $T_3 = 30$ sec. Using Eq. (11), find current $n_2 = 4$. Since $n - n_2 > 0$, select next P_4, $m_4 = 4$, $T_4 = 20$. Find $n - n_2 = \Delta = 1$. Since $\Delta - m_4 = 1 - 4 < 0$, P_4 cannot be mapped onto the CE resource left. Find $T_{max}(2) = T_3 = 30$. In Table III.1, find program P_7 that has $m_7 = \Delta = 1$ and $T_7 = 20 < T_{max}(2)$. Map P_7 on the CE_1 during $T_7 = 20$. Therefore, $CNS_2 = \{P_3, P_7\}$, etc.

In applying the Step 3 procedure, the algorithm forms five sets for CNS_i ($i = 1, \ldots, 5$). Figure III.10 shows each CNS_i and its $T_{max}(i)$.

Step 4. This step charts the actual CE needs of each noninterruptible program P^* and m^* CEs allocated during Step 3. These are shown with light areas on the CE resource diagram of Fig. III.10. Shaded areas show free resources left for mapping interruptible programs. As follows, the total time of execution of noninterruptible programs is $T = 120$ sec.

3.3.2.3 Assignment of CE resources for interruptible programs

As follows from the procedures introduced in the previous section, as a result of mapping noninterruptible programs on the CE resource diagram, some CEs are idle. To eliminate their idleness, interruptible programs are first mapped onto these idle CEs. The remaining portions of interruptible programs are then mapped onto those CE resources that are released after execution of a noninterruptible program(s).

Each interruptible program P_i is given by its P_i-resource diagram for which the PE portion is specified as

$$P_i = k_1 \cdot CE \cdot t(TA_1) + k_2 \cdot CE \cdot t(TA_2) + \cdots + k_p \cdot CE \cdot t(TA_p) \quad (13)$$

where $t(TA_j)$ is the time of the task TA_j requiring k_j CEs.

Therefore, the minimal time $T_{min}(p_i)$ to execute P_i without interrupt is

$$T_{min}(P_i) = \sum_{j=1}^{j=p} t(TA_j) \quad (14)$$

Mapping P_i onto the CE diagram thus consists of finding such time slots TS_j of q_j CEs ($j = 1, \ldots, p$) that the following conditions are satisfied:

a. $TS_1 \geq t(TA_1)$, $q_1 \geq k_1$
       $TS_2 \geq t(TA_2)$, $q_2 \geq k_2$
       .   .
       .   .
       .   .
       $TS_p \geq t(TA_p)$, $q_p \geq k_p$

b.   The rule of left and/or right prefix is satisfied.

Note: Time slot TS_j may be continuous or it may consist of several smaller slots during which at least k_j CEs are free. Consequently, not only tasks may be separated by interrupts, but interrupts may occur within some tasks.

If the program is interrupted m times with the time $t(INT_l)$ of the ℓth interrupt ($\ell = 1, ..., m$), then the actual execution time of this program is

$$T_{act}(P_i) = T_{min}(P_i) + \sum_{l=1}^{l=m} t(INT_l) \tag{15}$$

Obviously, there may be several assignment strategies for an interruptible program P_i, each of which is specified by its own value of $T_{act}(P_i)$ because of the variability of $t(INT_l)$ times, as well as the number of interrupts for each strategy.

The best assignment strategy should minimize the second addend in Eq. (15); i.e., it will be able to complete execution of P_i at the earliest possible moment of time on the the time axis. Therefore, mapping of each interruptible P_i is reduced to (1) comparing its resource needs for each task with the idle resources that are left, (2) finding the total execution time $T_{act}(P_i)$ for each strategy of mapping, and (3) selecting such mapping that leads to the earliest execution of P_i.

Example.   Let the CE portions of the P-resource diagrams of six interruptible programs be shown on Fig. III.11. Using the procedures outlined above, let us map these diagrams onto the CE-resource diagram of Fig. III.10, which shows the assignment of the CE resources for eight noninterruptible programs given by Table III.1. Since the priorities of P_9 through P_{14} are ordered as $PR_9 > PR_{10} > ... > PR_{14}$, let us first map P_9.

As follows from Fig. III.11(a), minimal execution time for P_9 is $T_{min}(P_9) = 5 + 17.5 + 15 = 37.5$. Figure III.12 shows the mapping of P_9 onto the time slots that are available. As follows from Fig. III.12, there exists only one strategy of mapping during time slots $TS_1 = 15$, $TS_2 = 2.5$, and $TS_3 = 20$. The time slot TS_1 accommodates task TA_1 requiring a 16-bit computer and a portion of task TA_2 requiring a 48-bit computer. Since $t(TA_1) = 5$ and $t(TA_2) = 17.5$, during time slots TS_1 only a 10-sec portion of TA_2 is computed. The entire TA_2 is executed during $TS_2 = 5$ and $TS_3 = 20$. During time slot TS_3, 15 sec of TA_3 is also executed. Complete execution of P_9 ends during $TS_3 = 20$. The actual time of executing P_9 in an interrupted mode is:

$$T_{act}(P_9) = T_{min}(P_9) + t(INT_1) + t(INT_2) = 37.5 + 20 + 12.5 = 70$$

It occurs at the moment $t = 75$, where $t(INT_1)$ is the interrupt in P_9 caused by noninterruptible program P_3. Although P_3 releases the resource needed by P_9 at $t = 37.5$, P_9 cannot use it, since a portion of the resource of the 48-bit computer needed by P_9 is still used by P_7, which is a noninterruptible program whose priority is higher than that of P_9. The second interrupt $t(INT_2)$ in P_9 execution is again caused by P_3, which again needs the resource used by P_9. When P_4 releases this resource at time $t = 55$, P_9 uses it during $TS_3 = 20$.

For the next interruptible program, P_{10}, there exists two strategies of assignment. Let us evaluate the expedience of using each of them.

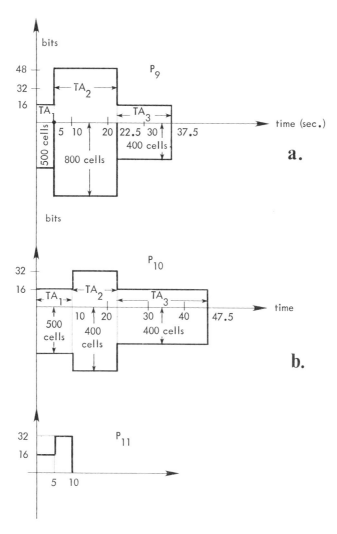

FIGURE III.11(a, b) P-resource diagrams of three interruptible programs P_9 through P_{11}

Strategy 1. Execution of P_{10} starts at $t^{(1)} = 15$ and proceeds during two time slots, $TS_1^{(1)}(P_{10}) = 5$ and $TS_2^{(1)}(P_{10}) = 42.5$, separated by a single interrupt, $t(INT_1^{(1)}) = 115$, leading to the moment $t = 177.5$ when execution of P_{10} ends. The total execution time for P_{10} is equal to $T_{act}^{(1)}(P_{10}) = 47.5 + 115 = 162.5$.

Strategy 2. Execution of P_{10} starts at $t^{(2)} = 30$ and is accomplished in three time slots, $TS_1^{(2)}(P_{10}) = 10$, $TS_2^{(2)}(P_{10}) = 2.5$, and $TS_3^{(2)}(P_{10}) = 35$, separated from each other by the following interrupt times: $t(INT_1^{(2)}) = 20$ and $t(INT_2^{(2)}) = 57.5$, leading to the following execution time for P_{10}: $T_{act}^{(2)}(P_{10}) = 47.5 + 77.5 = 125.0$ that ends at time $t = 155$.

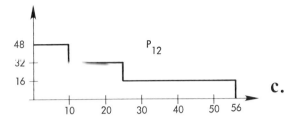

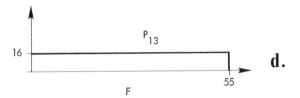

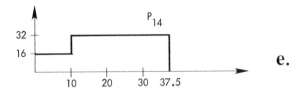

FIGURE III.11(c, d, e)   P-resource diagrams of three interruptible programs P_{12}
through P_{14}

Therefore, the second strategy is preferable, since it gives a smaller time $T_{act}^{(2)}(P_{10})$ = 125.0 and the earliest moment $t = 155$ of completing P_{10}. Similarly, one maps all other interruptible programs onto the CE resource diagram (Fig. III.12). ■

3.3.2.4 Minimization of computation delays

The assignment procedures introduced in Secs. 3.3.2.2 and 3.3.2.3 for noninterruptible and interruptible programs lead to minimization of computational delays in program execution because of the following reasons.

1. The procedures specify that all the highest-priority programs be executed in the noninterrupted mode of operation (i.e., during the minimal execution times required by them).

2. The use of the rule of right and left prefix applied during assignment eliminates all memory contentions in data exchanges of consecutive tasks.

3. The fundamental ability of dynamic architecture to minimize the amount of CE resource involved in the computation of each program P by computing

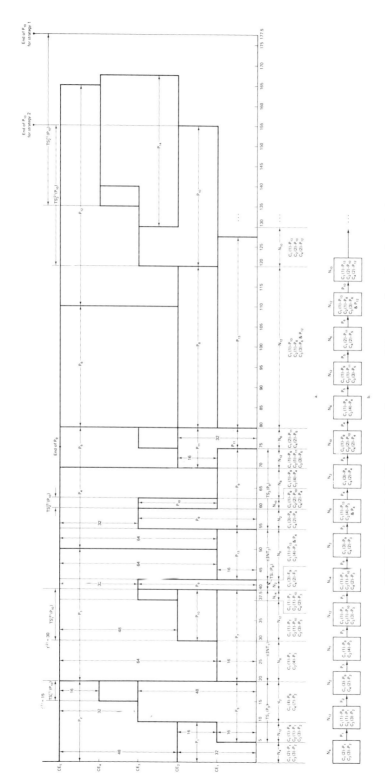

FIGURE III.12 Joint CE-resource diagram and the reconfiguration flow chart obtained from it

179

it by a sequence of dynamic computers releases the following amount of CE (i.e., PE and ME) resources. Let CE needs of P be given by Eq. (13) as follows:

$$p = k_1 \cdot CE \cdot t(TA_1) + k_2 \cdot CE \cdot t(TA_2) + \cdots + k_p \cdot CE \cdot t(TA_p)$$

Find the m parameter of this program:

$$m = \max(k_1, k_2, \ldots, k_p)$$

In conventional architectures, a computer that may compute this program will contain at least m CE. This means that during the entire time $T = t(TA_1) + \cdots + t(TA_p)$ of P computation these m CEs will be busy and will not be able to compute any other program. On the other hand, dynamic architecture releases the following resources, RR(P), involved in the computation of P:

$$RR(P) = (m - k_1) \cdot CE \cdot t(TA_1) + (m - k_2) \cdot CE \cdot t(TA_2) + \cdots + \\ (m - k_p) \cdot CE \cdot t(TA_p) \qquad (16)$$

All released resources, RR(P), can be used for computing interruptible programs, resulting in minimizing the duration of each interrupt. This leads to a lessening of the problem of program delays when a program should wait until the resource it requests becomes available.

Thus, the actual time of program P execution $T_{act}(P)$ given by Eq. (15) will be minimized due to the capability of a dynamic architecture to free the resource, RR(P), while computing each program P. In conventional architectures, minimization in Eq. (15) is accomplished only via adding additional resources to the system. In dynamic architectures it is accomplished by existing resources because of their adaptation capabilities.

Example.   Let us evaluate the amount of additional concurrency gained on the CE resource diagram in Fig. III.12 and obtained through the introduced techniques of mapping noninterruptible and interruptible programs. First, let us find the released resources, RR(P), for each of the eight noninterruptible programs, P_1 through P_8 which are mapped by Stage 1 onto the CE resource diagram.

Using Table III.1, we find that, for P_1, $m_1 = 2$ and $T_1 = 10$ sec. Using Fig. III.12, we find that during the time $t(TA_1)$ of the first task, where $t(TA_1) = 5$ sec, P_1 is executed by 2 CE (i.e., $k_1 = 2$); during the time $t(TA_2)$ of the second task, where $t(TA_2) = 5$ sec, P_1 is executed by 1 CE (i.e., $k_2 = 1$). Thus, $RR(P_1) = (2 - 2) \cdot CE \cdot 5$ sec $+ (2 - 1) \cdot CE \cdot 5$ sec $= 1 \cdot CE \cdot 5$ sec; i.e., the assignment procedure releases one CE during 5 sec in the course of executing program P_1. We use this CE to start executing the interruptible program P_9. Thus, $RR(P_1)$ is used for other computations.

For P_2, having $m_2 = 3$ and $T_2 = 20$ sec, $k_1 = 3$, $t(TA_1) = 10$; $k_2 = 2$, $t(TA_2) = 10$. Therefore,

$$RR(P_2) = (3 - 3) \cdot CE \cdot 10 \text{ sec} + (3 - 2) \cdot CE \cdot 10 \text{ sec} = 1 \cdot CE \cdot 10 \text{ sec}$$

$RR(P_2)$ is also used for executing P_9; $RR(P_3) = (4 - 4) \cdot CE \cdot 10$ sec $+ (4 - 3) \cdot CE \cdot 7.5$ sec $+ (4 - 2) \cdot CE \cdot 5$ sec $+ (4 - 4) \cdot CE = 1 \cdot CE \cdot 7.5$ sec $+ 2 \cdot CE \cdot 5$ sec, etc.

As follows from Fig. III.12, the following programs release resources in computations: P_1, P_2, P_3, P_4, P_5, and P_{12}. The remaining programs either do not release resources (P_6, P_7, P_8, P_{13}), since they are computed by the same-size computers, or they are computed by released resources in the interrupted mode of operation (P_9, P_{10}) and in the uninterrupted mode of operation (P_{11}, P_{14}). Table III.2 shows the RR(P_i) for each qualified program and the amount of used RR(P_i) that is used for other computations. As follows, each used RR(P_i) specifies an additional concurrency gained by the system via proper use of its adaptation capabilities.

The total additional concurrency is understood as the total time of freeing r CE, where $r = 1, 2, \ldots.$ Thus, the total time of freeing one CE is FT(CE) = 5 + 10 + 10 + 20 = 45 sec, where the first addened (5 sec) is the time of using one CE released by P_1 and is found on line 2 of Table III.2; 10 sec is the time of using one CE released by P_2 and is found on line 4 of Table III.2; etc.

The total time of freeing two CEs is

$$FT(2CE) = 7.5 + 2.5 + 25 = 35$$

Therefore, the total additional concurrency of the resources is

$$ACR = 1 \cdot CE \cdot 45 \text{ sec} + 2 \cdot CE \cdot 35 \text{ sec}$$

This concurrency results in the minimization of the total engagement time, T, of the assignable resources, R, consisting of 5 CEs and executing 14 programs. As follows from Fig. III.12, $R = n \cdot CE \cdot T = 5 \cdot CE \cdot 167.5$ sec ∎

3.4 DC Group Flow Chart

Construction of the CE resource diagram gives an architectural flow chart of the system transitions from one architectural state to another, where each architectural state N_i is specified by the number and sizes of dynamic computers working concurrently.

In general, an architectural flow chart is a directed graph in which a node means an architectural state, and an arrow is marked by a program which is allowed execution of the transition. This program is found on the CE resource diagram and it is conceived as the highest-priority program that needs to form a new dynamic computer. The architectural states are assigned with binary codes using the assignment technique that minimizes the time of architectural reconfiguration. This assignment and organization of the architectural reconfiguration were described in Chapter II (Sec. 3.1 and Sec. 3.4.3).

Example.   Let us describe the constructing procedures used to build the flow chart of Fig. III.12(b), which describes the CE-resource diagram of Fig. III.12(a). Accordingly, in Fig. III.12(a), two programs, P_1 and P_2, are computed in the following dynamic computers: P_1 is in $C_1(2)$ that includes CE_1 and CE_2, i.e., $C_1(2) = \{CE_1, CE_2\}$; P_2 is in $C_3(3) = \{CE_3, CE_4, CE_5\}$, which includes CE_3, CE_4, and CE_5.

Using Table III.3 of the dynamic computers that was constructed with the use of the assignment technique described in Chapter II, Sec. 3.4.3, and in [7, 8], which shows

Table III.2

	No. of Tasks	m_i/T_i	Task$_1$		Task$_2$		Task$_3$		Task$_4$	
			m_i-k_1	$t(TA_1)$	m_i-k_2	$t(TA_2)$	m_i-k_3	$t(TA_3)$	m_i-k_4	$t(TA_4)$
1 RR(P$_1$)	2	2 10	$\frac{1}{M}$	5	1	5				
2 Used RR(P$_1$)		-	$\frac{1}{M}$	1		5				
3 RR(P$_2$)	2	3 20	-	10	1	10				
4 Used RR(P$_2$)		-	-	-	1	10				
5 RR(P$_3$)	4	4 30	-	10	1	7.5	2	5	$\frac{1}{M}$	7.5
6 Used RR(P$_3$)			-	-	1	10	2	2.5		
7 RR(P$_3$)	3	4 20		5	2	7.5	$\frac{1}{M}$	7.5		
8 Used RR(P$_4$)					2	7.5				
9 RR(P$_5$)	2	3 10	-	5	1	5				
10 Used RR(P$_5$)			-		$\frac{1}{M}$	5				
11 RR(P$_{12}$)	3	3 56	-	10	1	15	2	31		
12 Used RR(P$_{12}$)					1	20	2	25		
13 — Total Time of Freeing One CE	1 · CE(5 + 10 + 10+ 20)						45 sec			
14 — Total Time of Freeing Two CE	2 · CE(7.5 + 2.5 +25)						35 sec			
Total Additional Concurrency	1 · CE 45 sec + 2CE · 35 sec									

Table III.3

States	Position of Concurrent Computers	Bit Sizes of Computers
N_0	$C_1(5)$	1×80
N_1	$C_1(4)$, $C_5(1)$	1×64, 1×16
N_2	$C_1(3)$, $C_4(2)$	1×48, 1×32
N_3	$C_1(2)$, $C_4(1)$, $C_5(1)$	1×48, 2×16
N_4	$C_1(2)$, $C_3(3)$	1×32, 1×48
N_5	$C_1(2)$, $C_3(2)$, $C_5(1)$	2×32, 1×16
N_6	$C_1(2)$, $C_3(1)$, $C_4(2)$	1×32, 1×16, 1×32
N_7	$C_1(2)$, $C_3(1)$, $C_4(1)$, $C_5(1)$	1×32, 3×16
N_8	$C_1(1)$, $C_2(4)$	1×16, 1×64
N_9	$C_1(1)$, $C_2(3)$, $C_5(1)$	1×16, 1×48, 1×16
N_{10}	$C_1(1)$, $C_2(2)$, $C_4(2)$	1×16, 2×32
N_{11}	$C_1(1)$, $C_2(2)$, $C_4(1)$, $C_5(1)$	1×16, 1×32, 2×16
N_{12}	$C_1(1)$, $C_2(1)$, $C_3(3)$	2×16, 1×48
N_{13}	$C_1(1)$, $C_2(1)$, $C_3(2)$, $C_5(1)$	2×16, 1×32, 1×16
N_{14}	$C_1(1)$, $C_2(1)$, $C_3(1)$, $C_4(2)$	3×16, 1×32
N_{15}	$C_1(1)$, $C_2(1)$, $C_3(1)$, $C_4(1)$, $C_5(1)$	5×16

the architectural state assignment for $n = 5$, we see that $C_1(2)$ and $C_3(3)$ specify architectural state N_4. This states exists during 5 sec. Transition to the next state is made by P_1, since this is the highest-priority program that needs the new dynamic computer $C_2(1)$. The released resource of CE_1 is used to form $C_1(1)$, which computes P_9. Thus, the next architectural state is $N_{12} = [C_1(1), C_2(1), C_3(3)]$. This state computes three programs: P_9 in $C_1(1) = \{CE_1\}$, P_1 in $C_2(1) = \{CE_2\}$, and P_2 in $C_3(3) = \{CE_3, CE_4, CE_5\}$. State N_{12} exists during 5 sec.

The next state is $N_2 = [C_1(3), C_4(2)]$. The $N_{12} \rightarrow N_2$ transition is performed by P_2, since this is the highest-priority program that needs new dynamic computer $C_4(2) = \{CE_4, CE_5\}$. Program P_1 ends execution. Its resource is used by P_9, which is computed in $C_1(3) = \{CE_1, CE_2, CE_3\}$.

Note: Although P_2 needs a smaller computer, there is no need to reconfigure into a new state since the resource of CE_4 is idle.

The next state is $N_8 = [C_1(1), C_2(4)]$, where $C_1(1) = \{CE_1\}$ computes P_8 and $C_2(4) = \{CE_2, CE_3, CE_4, CE_5\}$ computes P_3. $N_2 \rightarrow N_8$ transition is performed by P_3, which starts computation at $t = 20$.

Note: The first instruction segment of P_3 is stored continuously following the last instruction of P_2, so its initial address is obtained via program counter increment. Program P_3 starts execution by requesting $N_2 \rightarrow N_8$ transition, etc. ∎

3.5 ME Resource Diagram

Construction of the ME resource diagram is equivalent to distributing the DC group primary memory among various user programs. To construct the ME resource diagram, one has to use the memory size portions of all the P-resource diagrams and the DC group flow chart. Since the ME resource diagram shows the scheduling of primary memory for accessing in different states of the DC group flow chart, for each architectural state the procedure has to find two memory spaces which store, respectively, the data and instruction arrays of one user program.

In constructing the ME resource diagram, we are using the following principles (1 and 2) of memory management, which implement universality of executed programs and achieve a complete filling of the DC group primary memory. These principles were introduced in [8, 9].

Principle 1. In any $C_i(k)$ computer that includes k CE (CE_i, CE_{i+1}, ..., CE_{i+k-1}), one $16 \cdot k$-bit word is stored in a single parallel cell of k MEs, all with the same address. For instance, for the 48-bit computer $C_1(3)$, a 48-bit word is stored in ME_1, ME_2, and ME_3 under the same address A_p. Consequently, a data array containing d $16 \cdot k$-bit words will take d parallel cells for its storage in different-size computers, resulting in the independence of the data array size d from the computer size k. This leads to the independence of a data address from the computer size. When a $16 \cdot k$-bit word is accessed, each of k CE generates the same address, which results in a concurrent fetch of all k 16-bit bytes comprising the data word.

Principle 2. Since the minimal-size computer is equivalent to one CE, the instruction size has been made coincident with that of one CE. The instruction sequences are stored in consecutive cells of one ME, and complex programs may be stored in several MEs. The instruction fetched from one ME would then be sent concurrently to all modules of the $C(k)$ computer. Therefore, the same program occupies the same number of cells in any size of computer, achieving independence of the sizes of instruction arrays from computer sizes. This leads to the independence of the instruction address (jump address, etc.) of the computer size.

Therefore, these two principles provide for the independence of both a data address and an instruction address from computer sizes. This accomplishes the independence of programs from computer sizes, otherwise called *universality of programs*. These principles are used in the overall strategy of constructing the ME resource diagram that is presented below.

The primary memory is first assigned for all data arrays used by computers functioning in different states. Positions of computer elements included in each $C_i(k)$ computer give those of the memory elements which should store the data array of $16 \cdot k$-bit words used by this computer. For instance, since computer $C_1(2)$ consists of CE_1 and CE_2, its data array, made of d 32-bit words, should be stored in d parallel cells of ME_1

and ME_2, specified with the same addresses. The sizes of data arrays are taken from the memory portion of each P-resource diagram. Since construction of the CE resource diagram has specified which computer elements execute each program, we use the memory portions of these CEs to map data arrays onto them.

3.5.1 Procedures for Mapping Data Arrays onto Primary Memory of a DC Group

These procedures are iterative and applied to every task TA of P. Let us formulate one iteration of mapping.

Given the P-resource diagram of program P and the CE resource diagram (constructed in Sec. 3.3.2).

Step 1. Using the P-resource diagram, select task TA* that data array has not been assigned to the memory. Find its size d^*. Using the CE resource diagram, find CEs that execute TA*. [Let TA* be executed in $C_i(k) = (CE_i, CE_{i+1}, ..., CE_{i+k-1}.]$ Find the MEs having the same positions, i.e., $ME_i, ME_{i+1}, ..., ME_{i+k-1}$.

Step 2. Select arbitrarily d^* consecutive addresses $A_0^*, A_1^*, ..., A_{d-1}^*$ that specify empty cells in $ME_i, ME_{i+1}, ..., ME_{i+k-1}$. Map d^* $16k$-bit words of TA* onto parallel cells of $ME_i, ME_{i+1}, ..., ME_{i+k-1}$ under the same addresses $A_0^*, A_1^*, ..., A_{d-1}^*$.

Do Steps 1 and 2 for all tasks of program P.

Example. Let us use these procedures to map data arrays of program P_9 onto the primary memory. Using the P_9-resource diagram [Fig.III.11(a)], we find that P_9 consists of three tasks: TA_1, TA_2, and TA_3 executed in 16-bit, 48-bit, and 16-bit computers, respectively. The TA_1 needs 500 16-bit words, TA_2 needs 800 48-bit words, and TA_3 needs 400 16-bit words. Using the CE-resource diagram [Fig. III.12(a)], we see that TA_1 is executed in CE_1; TA_2 is executed in CE_1, CE_2, CE_3; and TA_3 is executed in CE_1. Thus, the first data array is mapped onto 500 arbitrary cells of ME_1 (Fig. III.13). The second data array containing 800 48-bit words is mapped onto 800 free 48-bit cells of ME_1, ME_2, and ME_3. Each 48-bit cell is formed of three 16-bit bytes (the first from ME_1, the second from ME_2, the third from ME_3) under the same address. The third array of 400 16-bit cells is mapped onto free cells of ME_1. ∎

3.5.2 Procedures for Mapping Instruction Arrays onto Primary Memory of a DC Group

In accordance with principle 2, the instructions are stored in consecutive cells of one ME. It can be any ME of the primary memory M of the dynamic computer, inasmuch as the organizations introduced in [8, 9] have shown how an instruction stored in this ME can be fetched to all CEs of the computer.

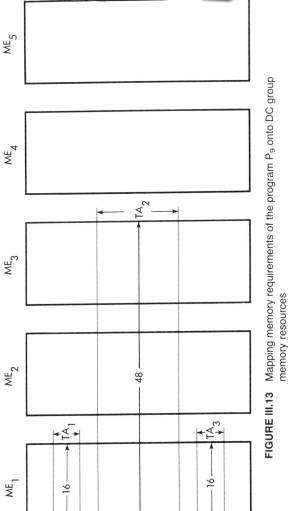

FIGURE III.13 Mapping memory requirements of the program P_9 onto DC group memory resources

186

Sequencing of the program within one architectural state. If program P is large enough, it can be stored in several MEs of the dynamic computer by concluding each portion of this program by a special *Jump $ME_i \rightarrow ME_j$* instruction discussed in [8], which stops instruction fetches from the ME_i and activates instruction fetches from the ME_j.

Therefore, instruction *Jump $ME_i \rightarrow ME_j$* performs sequencing of one program among different MEs when the program is computed in a single architectural state.

Example. Consider execution of P_1 by $C_1(2)$ computer in state N_4 of the architectural flow chart. Since $C_1(2)$ includes CE_1 and CE_2, P_1 can be stored in ME_1 and/or ME_2 (Fig. III.14). Let P_1 be partitioned into three segments: P_1 -1, P_1 -2, and P_1 -3, so that P_1 -1 and P_1 -3 are stored in ME_1 and P_1 -2 is stored in ME_2. This requires that

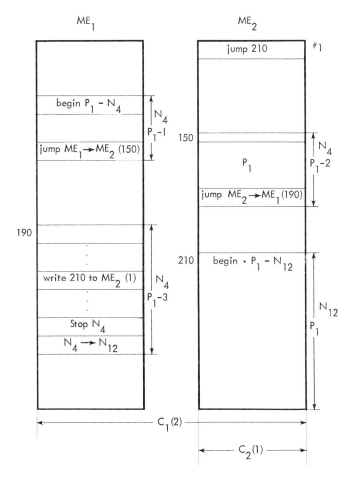

FIGURE III.14 Mapping instruction array of program P_1 onto available memory resources of ME_1 and ME_2

P_1 -1 be concluded by *Jump* $ME_1 \rightarrow ME_2(A_p)$ that organizes fetches of P_1 -2 beginning at address A_p of ME_2. (In Fig. III.14, $A_p = 150$.) Task P_1 -2 is concluded by instruction *Jump* $ME_2 \rightarrow ME_1(190)$ that organizes fetches of P_1 -3 beginning at address 190 of ME_1, etc. Thus, all empty spaces of ME_1 and ME_2 can be filled.   ■

Sequencing of one program computed by several architectural states.   Let program P be computed in the two architectural states N and N*, such that the DC group performs the N → N* reconfiguration. The problem that has to be solved consists of finding the addressing procedures for generation of instruction addresses for program P in states N and N*, respectively. There are three cases of such computation.

Case 1.   Program P is computed in the same computer, $C(k)$, that exists in both states N and N*. As was shown in [8, 9] for this case, computation of P is not affected by reconfiguration since the resource of $C(k)$ is not used for forming N*. Thus, program P ignores reconfiguration and its computation in two states proceeds as if no reconfiguration is performed.

Case 2.   Program P is computed by two different computers, $C(k)$ and $C^*(k^*)$, where $C(k)$ belongs to N and $C^*(k^*)$ belongs to N* and

a.   P performs N → N* transition, or
b.   P does not perform N → N* transition.

Case 3.   Of the two consecutive states N and N* such that N → N*, P is executed only in N*, and

a.   P performs N → N* transition, or
b.   P does not perform N → N* transition.

Since case 1 does not affect computation of P, it requires no special addressing, Thus, we will consider cases 2 and 3 only.

Case 2.   As was shown in [8, 9], the resource of $C(k)$ computer that has computed program P in state N forms a portion of the requested resource that is used to form new computers of state N*. Therefore, before reconfiguration N → N*, all requested resources of CEs must end executions in state N and inform the monitor of this moment. It then follows that each program that is run on two different computers in states N and N* must be concluded by a special synchronization instruction, *Stop N*, that informs the monitor that the resource of $C(k)$ has ended its execution in N. The *Stop N* instruction stores an n-bit resource code that has ones in those positions that correspond to CEs of $C(k)$ computer. Organization of the *Stop N* instruction was introduced in Chapter II, Sec. 3.3. The subcases (a) and (b) of case 2 are distinguished as follows. If program P performs the N → N* transition, then its *Stop N* instruction is concluded by the reconfiguration instruction N → N* discussed in Chapter II, Sec. 3. If program P does not perform N → N*, then *Stop N* is the end instruction of its task computed in state N.

Example.   Case 2 can be illustrated by the $N_4 \rightarrow N_{12}$ transition of the architectural flow chart performed by P_1 (Fig. III.12). In N_4, P_1 is computed by $C_1(2) = \{CE_1, CE_2\}$. In N_{12}, it is computed by $C_2(1) = \{CE_2\}$. Since $C_1(2)$ is split to form $C_2(1)$, the last portion of P_1 run on $C_1(2)$ is concluded by a *Stop-N_4* instruction that sends to the monitor the *n*-bit code 11000, which shows that $C_1(2)$ ended its operation (Fig. III.14). Since P_1 performs reconfiguration, *Stop-N_4* is concluded by reconfiguration instruction $N_4 \rightarrow N_{12}$.   ■

Consider the issue of address generation for case 2. Generation of addresses for P in state $N*$ can be performed using one of the following addressing techiques.

Addressing technique AT1: The first segment of P in computer $C*(k*)$ is stored in its most significant CE.

Addressing technique AT2: The first segment of P in computer $C*(k*)$ is stored continuously in the same CE that stored it in computer $C(k)$; i.e., instruction addresses form a continuous sequence for $C(k)$ and $C*(k*)$.

Technique AT1 is preferable, since it excludes from the $N \rightarrow N*$ instruction the code of the initial CE. However, it requires that the computer successor, $C*(k*)$, be a left or right prefix of the computer predecessor, $C(k)$, in order that $C(k)$ be capable of writing to the most significant ME of $C*(k*)$ the base address of program P in $C*(k*)$. Usually, this address is written to cell 1. Thus, $C*(k*)$ performs a +1 increment of its counter to fetch the base address of P. If this condition is not satisfied, then the AT2 technique is used and computer $C*(k*)$ continues the address generation that was stopped in $C(k)$. Since the last portion of P may be stored in any ME_j of $C(k)$, the $N \rightarrow N*$ instruction should store the code j of ME_j in order that this code be received by all CEs of $C*(k*)$.

Example.   The use of the AT1 technique is shown in Fig. III.14, whereby the last portion of $P_1 - 3$ of P_1 in state N_4 has an instruction that writes the base address (210) of P_1 in state N_{12} to cell 1 of ME_2. Since, in state N_{12}, P_1 is executed by $C_2(1)$ computer, ME_2 is its most significant ME. When $C_2(1)$ begins operation, it fetches cell +1, obtained by a simple counter increment. Thus, it fetches base address 210 and may jump to executing P_1 in state N_{12}.   ■

Case 3.   For case 3(a), P is executed only in the successor state $N*$ of the $N \rightarrow N*$ transition and P performs reconfiguration $N \rightarrow N*$. The following addressing is used. Using the CE resource diagram constructed in Sec. 3.3.2, one finds:

a.   The program P', for which computation ends in state N and which shares its CE resources with the program P.

b.   The computer $C'(k')$ that executes P' in state N. Since the resource of $C'(k')$ is used to form a new computer for program P, program P' is concluded by the synchronization instruction *Stop N*. The *Stop N* instruction is followed by the reconfiguration instruction, $N \rightarrow N*$, which stores, however, the priority of program P and not that of its predecessor P'. The first segment of P is stored in the same ME that stored the last segment of P'; i.e., one uses the addressing technique AT2 to generate addresses of P in state N*.

Example. Case 3(a) is exemplified by the first $N_2 \rightarrow N_8$ transition requested by P_3 [Fig. III.12(b)]. Program P_3 is executed in state N_8 and on. On the CE resource diagram, we find that P_3 is preceded by P_2 program, which finished its execution in state N_2. P_2 is executed by $C_4(2) = \{CE_4, CE_5\}$; P_3 is executed by $C_2(4) = \{CE_2, CE_3, CE_4, CE_5\}$. Suppose that the last segment of P_2 is in ME_4 (Fig. III.15). It is concluded by instruction *Stop* N_2, which is followed by reconfiguration instruction $N_2 \rightarrow N_8$ that stores the priority of P_3. The first segment of P_3 immediately follows instruction $N_2 \rightarrow N_8$. Instruction $N_2 \rightarrow N_8$ stores code $i = 4$ of ME_4, which during reconfiguration is transferred to all CEs of $C_2(4)$ in order to organize instruction fetches from ME_4. The program counter of CE_4 proceeds to generation of the addresses for the instructions stored in ME_4 as if no reconfiguration is performed. This is possible because, in acordance with the organization of instruction fetches described in [8], during an instruction fetch the instruction address is generated only in one PE_j that is local to the ME_j in which a current program segment is stored. An instruction is fetched, however, to all PEs of the dynamic computer since all of them store the same position code j of the ME_j. ■

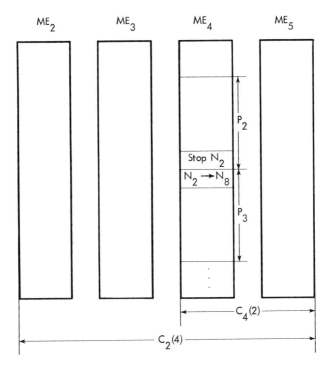

FIGURE III.15 Insertion of synchronization and reconfiguration instructions into the reconfiguration flow chart

For case 3(b), P is executed only in the successor state N* of the $N \rightarrow N^*$ transition and P performs no $N \rightarrow N^*$ reconfiguration. This means that P is an interruptible program and its base address is stored in a local CE$_j$. The position code j of CE$_j$ is stored in reconfiguration instruction $N \rightarrow N^*$ and is transferred during reconfiguration to all CEs of the computer that executes P in state N*. The processor element PE$_j$ stores the base address of the interruptible P and initiates generation of instruction addresses for ME$_j$.

Case 3(b) concludes consideration for all cases of sequencing which may occur during execution of the architectural flow chart.

3.6 Conclusions

This section presented a complete methodology for the adaptive assignment of hardware resources required by dynamic computer architectures. The techniques start with the bit-size analysis of an executing program written in FORTRAN aimed at selecting a sequence of computers that will execute this program and end with the construction of CE resource and ME resource diagrams.

This section shows that the methodology presented leads to the absolute minimization of the total time of execution required by a set of concurrent programs due to the capability of dynamic architectures to minimize the amount of processor and memory resources used in executing each user program. The consequences of this minimization are in additional concurrency gained on the same resouce complexity, which allows one to minimize program delays due to the unavailability of hardware resources and thus leads to the overall minimization of the time of computation.

4   STATIC RESOURCE ASSIGNMENTS IN RECONFIGURABLE BINARY TREE

As was indicated in Sec. 2 for reconfigurable binary trees, the major objective of static resource assignment is to minimize the total time of node-to-node data exchanges by minimizing the path durations and maximizing path concurrencies for all node-to-node communications assigned to each tree configuration. This performance optimization can be made especially efficient if the reconfiguration process is very fast and carried out with the minimal number of control codes. For this case, one can take full advantage of significant performance improvement achieved via instantaneous reconfiguration into a new and better tree structure, TS, without paying the price of considerable reconfiguration overhead expressed in terms of the time of reconfiguration and the memory space for storing required control codes that accompany conventional reconfiguration techniques.

Earlier (see Chapter II, Secs. 4.3.3 through 4.3.5) we introduced *optimal reconfiguration techniques* that carry out an instantaneous reconfiguration into a new tree structure, TS$_i$, during the time of a simple logical operation and using only one control code of size n, where $n = \log_2 K$ and K is the number of nodes in a tree [Fig. II.33(a)].

In all, it is possible to generate 2^n tree structures with this reconfiguration technique [Fig. II.33(b)]. In this section we will make a detailed performance assessment of possible data-exchange benefits that can be obtained from the use of these reconfigurable binary trees. This is done by computing a given collection of data exchanges using two alternatives:

1. A single (static) tree configuration
2. A sequence of three dynamic configurations (structures), $TS_1 \rightarrow TS_2 \rightarrow TS_3$, each of which can be assumed instantaneously

The obtained performance improvement is 370%; i.e., a sequence of three tree configurations executes the same assortment of data exchanges 370% faster than a single (static) tree configuration.

Also, later in this section we will give the overall structure of a data exchange optimization algorithm aimed at finding the best sequence S of tree structures ($S = TS_1 \rightarrow TS_2 \rightarrow ... \rightarrow TS_k$) that can minimize the total time of data exchanges (Fig. III.16). One iteration of this algorithm consists of sequential computation of process 1 and process 2. Process 1 is aimed at selecting a current tree structure TS_i; process 2 is aimed at assigning all qualified exchange pairs to TS_i.

Section 4 will conclude with the overall evaluation of the complexity of the data-exchange optimization algorithm. We will develop the upper bounds of the algorithm

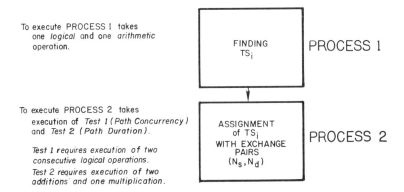

GIVEN: A data exchange table, T
FIND: A sequence S of tree structures TS_i,
that can execute T during the minimal time,
where $S = TS_1 \rightarrow TS_2 \rightarrow ... TS_k$.

ONE ITERATION OF
DATA EXCHANGE OPTIMIZATION ALGORITHM

To execute PROCESS 1 takes one *logical* and one *arithmetic* operation.

FINDING TS_i

PROCESS 1

To execute PROCESS 2 takes execution of *Test 1 (Path Concurrency)* and *Test 2 (Path Duration)*.

Test 1 requires execution of two consecutive logical operations.
Test 2 requires execution of two additions and one multiplication.

ASSIGNMENT of TS_i WITH EXCHANGE PAIRS (N_s, N_d)

PROCESS 2

FIGURE III.16 Data exchange optimization algorithm for a reconfigurable binary tree

complexity and show the extreme amenability of the introduced techniques of data-exchange optimization for computerization. Using the upper bounds obtained, we will find that for a reconfigurable binary tree having 512 nodes, finding a sequence (flow chart) of tree configurations, $S = TS_1 \rightarrow TS_2 \rightarrow ... \rightarrow TS_{20}$, having 20 TS_i will take not more than 1 minute of computer time in a computer that executes 2 million operations per second. Therefore, the preprocessing overhead introduced with finding the flow chart of tree structures is very insignificant compared to an enormous performance improvement that can be obtained because of such reconfiguration.

4.1 Data-Exchange Optimization: Overview and Examples

In general, the introduced data-exchange optimization algorithm is aimed at improving performance by reconfiguring the reconfigurable binary tree into a sequence of tree configurations in which for each tree configuration:

a. Every pair of tree nodes with a large number of data exchanges is connected with the path of length 1.

b. The maximal number of node pairs can perform concurrent exchanges in each tree configuration because there is no path sharing among them.

These two objectives can be accomplished if all data exchanges between communicating node pairs can be performed not in a single tree configuration (tree structure) but in a sequence of tree structures, $TS_1 \rightarrow TS_2 \rightarrow ... \rightarrow TS_k$.

Assignment of communicating node pairs (N_s, N_d), where N_s is the source node and N_d is the destination node, to each tree structure TS_i is performed with the use of the iterative procedure given below, which describes one iterative step:

Assume that for the binary tree we have already found the sequence of tree structures $TS_1 \rightarrow TS_2 \rightarrow ... \rightarrow TS_{i-1}$. Our task is to find a current TS_i. Such finding is performed as follows.

Of all node pairs that remain nonassigned, select the pair (N_s^*, N_d^*) that exchanges the largest number of words. This pair is called the *main pair* for TS_i. We select such a tree structure TS_i where N_s^* and N_d^* are adjacent; i.e., they are connected via the minimal communication path of length 1 (Fig. III.17). Thus the time of data exchange $TE(N_s^*, N_d^*)$ between N_s^* and N_d^* achieves the absolute minimum since it is impossible to connect these nodes with a smaller communication path. We assume that the time $TE(N_s^*, N_d^*)$ of data exchange for the main pair is the time of the holding tree structure, TS_i; i.e., $TE(N_s^*, N_d^*) = T(TS_i)$.

Next we assign to tree structure TS_i all other communicating pairs (N_s', N_d'), (N_s'', N_d''), etc. that do not increase $T(TS_i)$ and can be performed concurrently with each other and with the main pair (N_s^*, N_d^*). This completes the iterative step, and the assignment iteration is repeated again for the next iteration. The effectiveness of such data-exchange optimization can be illustrated via the following example.

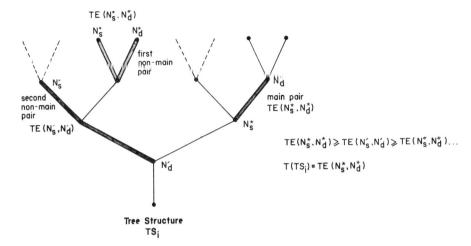

FIGURE III.17 Assignment of the main pair of nodes and several nonmain pairs of those to the tree structure TS$_i$

Example. Given a data-exchange table made of all data-exchanging pairs (N_s, N_d), where each N_s is in col. 1 and each N_d is in col. 2; col. 3 shows the number of data words that must be transferred (see Table III.4). Let this table be executed using two alternative techniques:

a. A single static tree configuration [Fig. III.18(a)]

b. A sequence of dynamic tree configurations, $TS_1 \rightarrow TS_2 \rightarrow TS_3$ [Fig. III.18(b)]. ∎

4.1.1 Execution of Table III.4 in a Static Binary Tree

For a static binary tree, we select the only possible tree configuration that can be obtained without the use of SRVB which optimizes the node-to-node routing by assigning only 1 bit of the address, AC, for selecting the left or right successor of any transit node in a communication path from the root. This configuration can be found via the following assignment process. Let AC be the address code from the root to the node N of level $n - i$. Obviously, AC contains i binary positions because the communciation path to N from the root R has i edges. The n-bit code N is found as follows:

$$N = \underbrace{\lfloor \text{rot(AC)} \rfloor}_{i} \quad \underbrace{\lfloor 00 \cdots 0 \rfloor}_{n - i}$$

where rot is a simple logical operation called *rotation* extended to AC made of i positions. The remaining $(n - i)$ positions of N are filled with 0's [Fig. III.18(a)].

For instance, if AC $= 1$, then the node N $= \underbrace{\lfloor \text{rot(1)} \rfloor}_{1} \underbrace{\lfloor 00 \rfloor}_{2} = 100$; if AC $= \underbrace{100}_{3}$,

TABLE III.4

DATA-EXCHANGE TABLE

Communication Path Numbers, NN	Column 1 Source Node, N_s	Column 2 Destination Node, N_d	Column 3 Number of Words to Be Transferred, DAN	Column 4 Length of Minimal Communication Path in Static Binary Tree, PL	Column 5 Time of Exchange in Static Tree, $TE = PL \cdot DAN \cdot T_o$
1	3	2	50	3	$150T_o$
2	7	1	100	4	$400T_o$
3	6	4	20	1	$20T_o$
4	5	2	100	1	$100T_o$
5	4	0	50	1	$50T_o$
6	6	2	30	2	$60T_o$
7	3	5	100	4	$400T_o$
8	1	3	100	4	$400T_o$

195

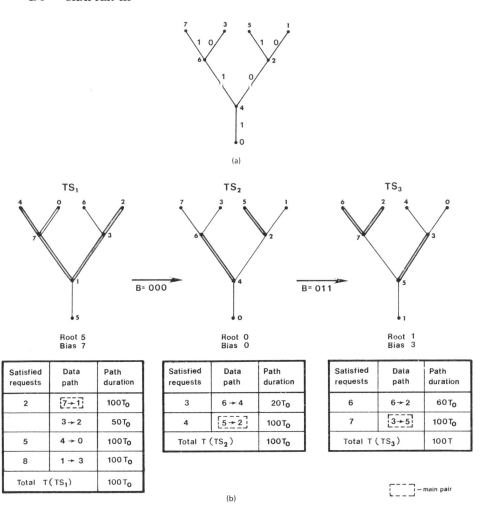

(a)

(b)

FIGURE III.18 (a) An optimal static tree configuration; (b) a sequence of dynamic tree configurations

then the node $N = \text{rot}(100) = 001$; for $AC = 110$, $N = \text{rot}(110) = 011$, etc. For the root, R, its address code $AC_R = \underbrace{0}_{1}$, giving $R = \underbrace{\text{rot}(0)}_{1}\,\underbrace{00}_{2} = 000$. This justifies encoding $R = 000$.

However, when Table III.4 is executed in the static tree structure of Fig. III.18(a) in which positions of tree nodes inside a static tree do not change, the length of each communication path, PL, is shown in col. 4. As seen, some of the communication requests can be performed concurrently, since the respective communication paths are not shared. Otherwise, they must be performed sequentially.

For instance, communication requests 1, 4, and 5 are concurrent, since their paths are not shared [Fig. III.19(a)]. On the other hand, requests 2, 3, 6, 7, and 8 are sequen-

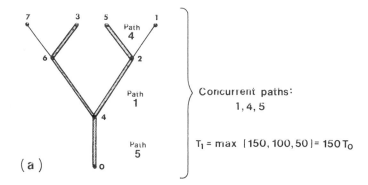

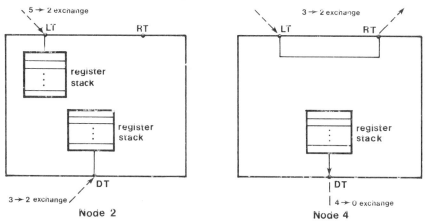

FIGURE III.19(a) Mapping concurrent data paths onto the optimal static tree configuration

tial, since they use shared communication paths. Let T_0 be the time of word transit via single node. To execute all the data exchanges of Table III.4 in the static tree configurations of Fig. III.18(a) requires time $T_{ST} = 1430T_0$, where $T_{ST} = T_1(1, 4, 5) + T_2(2) + T_3(3) + T_4(6) + T_5(7) + T_6(8) = 150T_0 + 400T_0 + 20T_0 + 60T_0 + 400T_0 + 400T_0 = 1430T_0$, and $T_1(1, 4, 5) = 150T_0$ is the time to execute concurrent requests 1, 4, and 5 [Fig. III.19(a)]; $T_2(2) = 400T_0$ is the time for request 2; $T_3(3) = 20T_0$ is the time of request 3, etc. [Fig. III.19(b, c, d, e, f)].

4.1.2 Execution of Table III.4 in Dynamic Tree Configurations

To execute the same table in dynamic tree configurations (alternative b) takes only $300T_0$ [Fig. III.18(b)]. Thus, the accomplished performance improvement is 370%. Con-

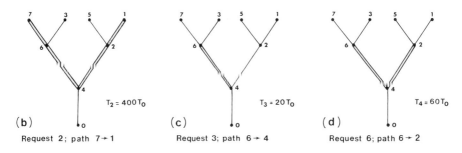

(b) Request 2; path 7→1 $T_2 = 400 T_0$

(c) Request 3; path 6→4 $T_3 = 20 T_0$

(d) Request 6; path 6→2 $T_4 = 60 T_0$

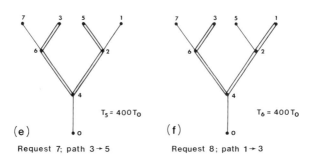

(e) Request 7; path 3→5 $T_5 = 400 T_0$

(f) Request 8; path 1→3 $T_6 = 400 T_0$

FIGURE III.19(b, c, d, e, f)   Mapping shared data paths onto the optimal static tree configuration

sider now Fig. III.18(b) with more detail. TS_1 is the first tree configuration that is generated with bias $B = 7$. Node pair (7, 1) is the main pair since nodes 7 and 1 are the first in Table III.4 that exchange the maximal number of words. The path length, PL, for $7 \rightarrow 1$ data path is PL = 1. Since 100 words must be transferred, path duration TE(7, 1) = $100 T_0$.

Thus, the time $T(TS_1)$ of holding this structure is the time of the $7 \rightarrow 1$ exchange, or $T(TS_1) = 100 T_0$. Of all data exchanges, we assign the $3 \rightarrow 2$ exchange to this tree, since nodes 3 and 2 are also adjacent in this tree. Since, during the $3 \rightarrow 2$ exchange, 50 data words are transferred, the duration of this exchange in TS_1 is $50 T_0$ etc. In all, the exchange pairs that are assigned to TS_1 are shown in Fig. III.18(b).

Next, the tree reconfigures into TS_2 using bias $B = 0$. Here the main pair is $5 \rightarrow 2$, giving $T(TS_2) = 100 T_0$. The only other exchange that is executed concurrently with $5 \rightarrow 2$ is $6 \rightarrow 4$. The final configuration is TS_3. Its main pair is $3 \rightarrow 5$. The only other exchange is $6 \rightarrow 2$. The time of TS_3 is $T(TS_3) = 100 T_0$. Thus, the entire Table III.4 is executed during $300 T_0$ if the binary tree assumes a sequence of tree configurations $TS_1 \rightarrow TS_2 \rightarrow TS_3$ versus $1430 T_0$ required for the same table in a single tree configuration.

4.1.3 Summary

As follows from this example, data-exchange optimization achieved with the use of reconfiguration in a tree is an extremely powerful source of improving the performance of the binary tree because, using reconfiguration, one can minimize the duration and maximize the concurrency of the requested data exchanges in comparison with those performed in a static tree configuration.

4.2 Data-Exchange Optimization Algorithm: Overall Structure

As was shown above, data-exchange optimization can be accomplished by finding a sequence, S, of consecutive tree configurations that must be assumed in the execution of all the required node-to-node data exchanges, where $S = TS_1 \rightarrow TS_2 \rightarrow \cdots \rightarrow TS_k$. Since this process is iterative, below we will introduce a reconfiguration technique aimed at performing one iteration of data-exchange optimization.

4.2.1 Description of One Iteration of Data-Exchange Optimization

Given the data-exchange table that inlcudes all the required node-to-node data exchanges (cols. 1, 2, and 3 of Table III.4). One iteration of data-exchange optimization includes the following processes (Fig. III.16).

Process 1.   Selection of the main pair (N_s^*, N_d^*) for the tree structure TS_i; finding the bias B (TS_i) that can generate TS_i, and finding the time $T(TS_i)$ of holding TS_i.

Process 2.   Finding all other **concurrent** communicating pairs (N_s', N_d') that can be assigned to TS_i; i.e., those pairs will be found whose communication times in TS_i do not increase the time $T(TS_i)$ found during process 1.

Process 1.   As the main pair for TS_i, such tree nodes N_s^*, N_d^* are selected that exchange the largest number of words, DAN*. If there are several candidates with the same DAN, one of them with the smallest index in the table is selected. The remaining pairs are left in the table.

Once the main pair (N_s^*, N_d^*) is selected, the following reconfiguration equation is formed:

$$N_d^* = 1[N_s^*] + B(TS_i)$$

Using this equation, one can find bias $B(TS_i)$ of TS_i in which N_s^* and N_d^* are adjacent:

$$B(TS_i) = N_d^* + 1[N_s^*] \tag{16}$$

Using col. 3 of the data-exchange table, find the DAN* parameter for the main pair N_s^*, N_d^*. The time of holding tree structure TS_i, $T(TS_i) = DAN^* \cdot T_0$, where T_0

is the time of one word transit via one node. Indeed, since N_s^* and N_d^* are connected in TS_i with the path of length 1, each word is delayed by one T_0 to reach destination N_d.

Example. Let us apply the constructive procedures of process 1 for generating tree structure TS_1 for the data-exchange table represented by Table III.4. There are four pairs (N_s, N_d) in Table III.4 that exchange the largest number of words. These pairs are $(7, 1)$, $(5, 2)$, $(3, 5)$, and $(1, 3)$.

Select the $(7, 1)$ pair as the main pair of TS_1, since it is assigned the smallest index; i.e., $N_s^* = 7$ and $N_d^* = 1$. Using Eq. (16), find the bias $B(TS_1)$: $B(TS_1) = 1 + 1[7] = 001 + 1[111] = 001 + 110 = 111$ [Fig. III.18(b)]. Since for the $7 \rightarrow 1$ data exchange, DAN $= 100$, the time of holding TS_1 is $T(TS_1) = 100T_0$. ∎

Process 2. This algorithm consists of finding all other concurrent communicating pairs, N_s', N_d', that can be assigned to the tree structure, TS_i. To find such pairs, the following problems need solution:

Problem 1:   *Path concurrency:* Given two exchanging pairs (N_s, N_d) and (N_s', N_d'). Can these two pairs be executed concurrently in the tree structure, TS_i?

Problem 2:   *Path duration:* Given a data-exchange path (N_s, N_d) assigned to TS_i. Find the duration of this path in TS_i, where duration of the path is understood as the duration of a data exchange that is performed via this path.

Solutions to these problems will allow an assignment of each node pair (N_s, N_d) to tree structure TS_i only if (N_s, N_d) is concurrent with all other pairs already assigned to TS_i and its path duration TE $\leq T(TS_i)$. Below are the solutions to Problem 1 (Sec. 4.3) and Problem 2 (Sec. 4.4).

4.3 General Concurrency Test between Two Data Paths in a Reconfigurable Binary Tree

In general, two communicating pairs (N_s, N_d) and (N_s', N_d') are concurrent if their data exchanges can be performed in parallel via nonshared communication paths.

4.3.1 Paths Concurrency in a Reconfigurable Binary Tree

It is easy to show that the two data paths are nonshared if their intersection contains not more than one node. Indeed, if the intersection of two paths is empty, then these paths are totally separated spatially. Thus they can be activated concurrently.

If the intersection of the two paths is made only of one common node, this node can serve only in one of the following functions [Fig. III.20(a)]:

(a)

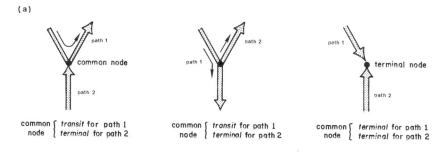

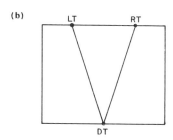

FIGURE III.20 The case of two intersecting paths with one common node achieves total terminal separation

a . Transit node for one path and terminal node (source or destination) for another path

b. Terminal node for both paths

As was shown in Chapter II, Sec. 4.8.1.2, to improve concurrency of communication, each tree node must be provided with the three terminals LT, RT, and DT (Figs. II.39 and III.20). Therefore, implementation of the transit function inside this node requires connection of only two terminals out of three (LT-RT, or LT-DT, or RT-DT); implementation of the source or destination functions requires only one remaining terminal that is left unused in this node. Thus, if the two paths have only one common node, these paths can be activated concurrently since there is a complete terminal separation in the only common node which they have.

It is easy to show that, in order to be activated concurrently, the two paths cannot have more than one common node. Indeed, if they have at least two common nodes, no terminal separation can be accomplished in the sequence of common nodes and each common node shares at least one terminal between the two paths [Fig. III.21(a, b)]. This proves our proposition about concurrency condition for two data paths in a binary tree.

Example. In Fig. III.19(a), the following three concurrent data exchanges can be mapped onto a single tree configuration:

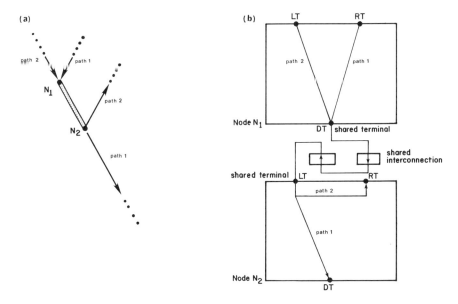

FIGURE III.21   The case of two intersecting paths with at least two common nodes achieves terminal and interconnection sharing

a. $3 \to 2$, taking path $1 = (3 \to 6 \to 4 \to 2)$ of length 3
b. $5 \to 2$, taking path $4 = (5 \to 2)$ of length 1
c. $4 \to 0$, taking path $5 = (4 \to 0)$ of length 1

Paths 1 and 4 have one common node 2, which is the destination node for both paths. These two paths are concurrent since for the $5 \to 2$ exchange the LT terminal is used, and for the $3 \to 2$ exchange the DT terminal is used. Similarly, paths 1 and 5 also have one common node 4, which is a transit node for path 1 via transit connection of the LT and RT terminals and the source node for path 5 via the DT terminal. ■

4.3.2 Fast Path Concurrency Test

Once the paths' concurrency condition is found, our task is to develop a fast algorithm that can perform a simple concurrency test aimed at finding out whether or not two data paths, PA1 and PA2, can be activated concurrently in the tree structure TS_i. Using fine mathematical properties of SRVB, we will develop a test that will feature no path building aimed at checking the path concurrency condition. Instead, this test will be described by a two-step algorithm in which each step executes a simple logical operation of prefix comparison. To develop such a test, we will use the concepts of address code, AC_N, and the closest intermediate root, CIR, introduced in Chapter II, Sec. 4.8.2.2.

Left Prefix of the Address Code of Node N. In general, by the address code AC_N of the node N we define such a binary word which contains all the routing information which allows a data word to reach node N from the current root R of TS_i using the minimal communication path. The length, ℓ, of AC_N is restricted by n, the number of levels in the tree, where $\ell = n$ for leaves located on the level 0 and, for a tree node of level i, $\ell = n - i$.

Therefore, if the two tree nodes N and N' having levels i and i', where $i < i'$, are on the same communication path from the root, R, then their addressing codes AC_N and AC_N' are related as follows:

a. AC_N has $\ell = n - i$ binary digits, AC_N' has $\ell' = n - i'$ binary digits, where $n - i > n - i'$.

b. AC_N' is a left prefix of AC_N, because to reach N from the root, R, a communication message must pass node N' in transit. Thus, it must use the address information of AC_N' before it reaches N. We will denote the operation of left prefix as LP, meaning that $AC_N' = LP(AC_N)$.

In general, as was shown in Sec. 4.8.2.2, to find AC_N, we have to:

a. Find the recursive sum RS_i for N as $RS_i = N + R$, where R is the root,
b. Perform logical operation rot $(RS_i) = AC_N$.

Example. Let N' = 01110 be on the subpath to N = 11101 from the root R = 10110 in a binary tree configuration generated with bias B = 11010 (Fig. III.22). Using the technique of Chapter II, Sec. 4.8.2.2, let us find AC_N' and AC_N:

$$AC_N = \text{rot}(R + N) = \text{rot}(10110 + 11101) = \text{rot}\ \overset{x_1x_2x_3x_4x_5}{(01011)} = \text{rot}(RS_5) = 11010, \quad \ell_N = 5$$

$$AC_{N'} = \text{rot}(R + N') = \text{rot}(10110 + 01110) = \text{rot}\ \overset{x_1x_2}{(11000)} = \text{rot}(RS_2) = 11, \quad \ell_N' = 2$$

Here **rot** is the rotation operation defined in Sec. 4.8.2.2. As seen, AC_N has the length $l_N = 5$, since the rotation is performed over recursive sum RS_5 having $x_5 = 1$. On the other hand, AC_N' has length $\ell_N' = 2$, since the least significant position which is rotated in RS_2 is $x_2 = 1$. Also, AC_N' is a left prefix of AC_N because, to reach N, a message must pass N' in transit. Thus, $AC_N' = LP(AC_N)$ or $11 = LP(\underline{11}010)$. ∎

4.3.2.1 First left prefix test for closest intermediate roots

The left prefix operation defined above is crucial for performing the concurrency test between two communication paths in the TS_i, PA $- N_s \rightarrow N_d$ and PA' = $N_s' \rightarrow N_d'$, constructed for two communicating node pairs (N_s, N_d) and (N_s', N_d'). First, we note that each path in the tree is specified with its own *closest intermediate root*, CIR, that connects the root R with both N_s and N_d. In particular, CIR can coincide with

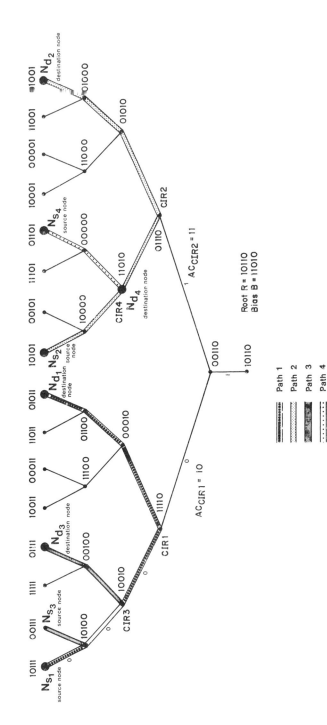

FIGURE III.22 Reconfigurable binary tree with four different paths

204

either N_s or N_d (see Sec. 4.8.3.1, Chapter II). Let CIR1 and CIR2 be defined for paths PA1 $= N_{s1} \rightarrow N_{d1}$ and PA2 $= N_{s2} \rightarrow N_{d2}$, respectively.

If the address codes of CIR1 and CIR2 are neither related via left prefix operation nor are they coincident, then neither CIR1 nor CIR2 is on each other's subpaths. Therefore, the two paths they represent are separated spatially and can always be activated concurrently.

Example. Consider the binary tree of Fig. III.22 generated with bias B = 11010. Its root is R = 10110. This tree contains two spatially separated paths, PA1 and PA2, where PA = $N_s \rightarrow N_d$ and N_{s1} = 10111, N_{d1} = 01011, and PA2 = $N_{s2} \rightarrow N_{d2}$ and N_{s2} = 10101, N_{d2} = 01001. It is easy to show that the address codes for two CIRs that represent these two paths are not related via LP operation to each other. This specifies a complete spatial separation of these two paths, which allows their concurrent activation.

Using the techniques of Chapter II, Sec. 4.8.3, let us find the address codes for the CIRs for these two paths:

Path PA1. To find AC_{CIR1}, we find the address code of the source node, AC_{s1} = rot(R + N_{s1}) = rot (10110 ÷ 10111) = rot (00001) = 10000; next we find the address code of the destination node AC_{d1} = rot (R + N_{d1}) = rot (10110 + 01011) = rot (11101) = 10111.

$$AC_{CIR1} = \underset{x_i = y_i}{LP} (AC_{s1} \wedge AC_{d1}) = LP(10000 \wedge 10111) = 10$$

where x_i and y_i are binary positions of AC_{s1} and AC_{d1}, respectively.

Path PA2. To find AC_{CIR2}, we find AC_{s2} = rot (R + N_{s2}) = rot (10110 + 10101) = rot (00011) = 11000; AC_{d2} = rot (R + N_{d2}) = rot (10110 + 01001) = rot (11111) = 11111.

$$AC_{CIR2} = \underset{x_i = y_i}{LP} (AC_{s2} \wedge AC_{d2}) = LP(11000 \wedge 11111) = 11$$

Since AC_{CIR1} = 10 and AC_{CIR2} = 11, these two codes are not related via LP operations and the paths they specify are always concurrent. Therefore, if two paths PA1 and PA2 in the tree have address codes AC_{CIR1} and AC_{CIR2} for their closest immediate roots, and neither of them is a left prefix of another, then PA1 and PA2 can be activated concurrently.

However, the LP test for closest intermediate roots does not define alone all concurrent paths in the tree: that is, two paths can be activated concurrently without the requirements for nonleft prefix condition between the address codes of their CIRs. Therefore, the left prefix test forms Step 1 of a general concurrency test which includes other steps discussed below (Fig. III.23). ◼

4.3.2.2 Second left prefix test for cross-CIRs

Those paths that do satisfy the first left prefix test must be tested further for left prefixes of their cross-CIRs. By a *cross-CIR* of the two paths PA1 = $N_{s1} \rightarrow N_{d1}$ and PA2 = $N_{s2} \rightarrow N_{d2}$, we mean the closest intermediate root of a cross-path, C-PA, that

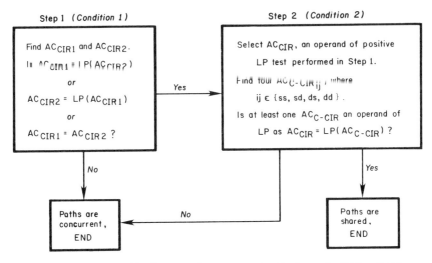

Step 1 *(Condition 1)*

Find AC_{CIR1} and AC_{CIR2}.

Is $AC_{CIR1} = LP(AC_{CIR2})$

or

$AC_{CIR2} = LP(AC_{CIR1})$

or

$AC_{CIR1} = AC_{CIR2}$?

Step 2 *(Condition 2)*

Select AC_{CIR}, an operand of positive

LP test performed in Step 1.

Find four $AC_{C\text{-}CIR_{ij}}$, where

$ij \in \{ss, sd, ds, dd\}$.

Is at least one $AC_{C\text{-}CIR}$ an operand of

LP as $AC_{CIR} = LP(AC_{C\text{-}CIR})$?

Yes

No

Yes

No

Paths are
concurrent,
END

Paths are
shared,
END

FIGURE III.23 Algorithm for general concurrency test for two paths PA1 and PA2
in reconfigurable binary tree

has a source node identified with one of the terminal nodes from $PA(N_{s1}$ or $N_{d1})$ and
the destination node identified with one of the terminal nodes (N_{s2} or N_{d2}) from PA_2.

Since PA1 and PA2 have two terminal nodes each, it is possible to construct four
cross-paths for them that are specified with four cross-CIRs (C-CIR). These paths are

$$C\text{-}PA_{ss} = N_{s1} \rightarrow N_{s2}, \; C\text{-}PA_{sd} = N_{s1} \rightarrow N_{d2}, \; C\text{-}PA_{ds} = N_{d1} \rightarrow N_{s2} \; C\text{-}PA_{dd} = N_{d1} \rightarrow N_{d2}$$

This gives four cross CIRs for these paths: ss cross CIR C-CIR$_{ss}$ for C-PA$_{ss}$, sd cross
CIR C-CIR$_{sd}$ for C-PA$_{sd}$, ds cross CIR C-CIR$_{ds}$ for C-PA$_{ds}$, and dd cross CIR C-CIR$_{dd}$
for C-PA$_{dd}$ (Fig. III.24).

Thus, the second left prefix test is aimed at checking the left prefix condition for
the address code of the respective cross-CIR, which is created for every cross-path.
That is, of the two address codes for two original CIRs, AC_{CIR1} and AC_{CIR2} found for
path 1 and path 2, we select the one which is the operand for the first left prefix test,
since this CIR2 can be reached from CIR1 if the journey starts from the root. (If CIR1
= CIR2, either of them is selected.) In other words, if $AC_{CIR1} = LP(AC_{CIR2})$, select
the right operand AC_{CIR2}, which identifies a longer path from the root than AC_{CIR1}.

Next we find the address code for each cross-CIR, $AC_{C\text{-}CIRij}$, where $i, j \in \{ss,$
sd, ds, dd$\}$. Following these findings, the second left prefix test can be formulated as
follows: If there exists one $AC_{C\text{-}CIRij}$ such that $AC_{CIR2} = LP(AC_{C\text{-}CIRij})$, then two
paths, PA1 and PA2, are not concurrent, since they contain more than one common
node. Otherwise, these two paths are concurrent in a sense that, at most, they share
only one node.

Therefore, in a reconfigurable binary tree generated with bias B, the following two
conditions must be satisfied in order that any two paths, PA1 and PA2, in this tree be
shared, where path sharing is understood as the availability of at least two common
nodes in these paths:

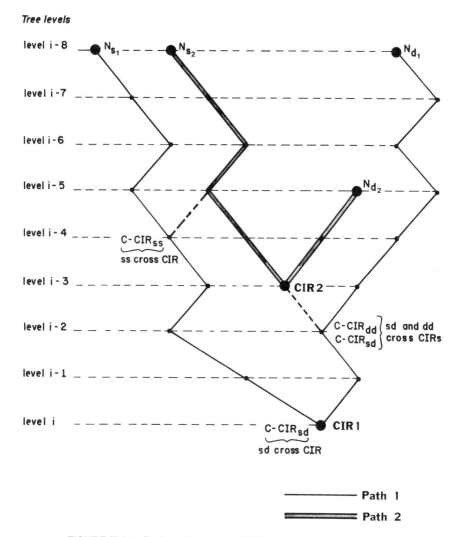

FIGURE III.24 Finding of four cross-CIR's for the two paths 1 and 2

Condition 1. $\text{AC}_{CIR1} = \text{LP}(\text{AC}_{CIR2})$ or $\text{AC}_{CIR1} = \text{AC}_{CIR2}$

Condition 2. $\text{AC}_{CIR2} = \text{LP}(\text{AC}_{C\text{-}CIR})$ (Fig. III.23)

Note: If for condition 1 the requirement is that the two address codes for two CIRs be either coincident or related via LP, for condition 2 the only requirement is that one CIR be on the subpath to one of the cross-CIRs. Thus, no coincidence requirement between CIR2 and C-CIR is necessary for condition 2, since two cross-paths may have such coincidence and still be concurrent [see Fig. III.25(a)].

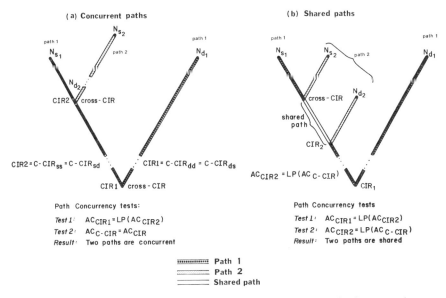

FIGURE III.25(a, b) The results of the path concurrency tests for the two paths having a common CIR

Below is an intuitive explanation of condition 2. (*Note:* A formal proof of condition 2 can be easily derived using the ideas of this explanation.)

If of the two CIRs (CIR1 and CIR2), CIR2 is reached only by transit via CIR1, then there are the following two cases of such transit [Fig. III.25(a, b, c)].

Case 1. CIR2 is a common node for the two paths, PA1 and PA2 [Fig. III.25(a, b)].

Case 2. CIR2 is not a common node for the two paths [Fig. III.25(c)]. Consider these two cases in the order of their appearance.

Case 1. If CIR2 is a common node for the two paths, there are two alternatives for path location in the tree.
Alternative 1. If CIR2 is the only common node of the two paths PA1 and PA2, then it is either (a) a terminal node for one path and a transit node for another path, or (b) a terminal node for both paths [see Fig. III.20(a)]. Since in both instances (a, b) there is a path (PA1 and/or PA2) for which CIR2 is a terminal node, CIR2 coincides with the two cross-CIRs: CIR2 = C-CIR$_{ij}$. Likewise, CIR1 coincides with another two cross-CIRs [Fig. III.25(a)].

Thus, the address codes for CIRs and cross-CIRs are coincident, yielding no left prefix condition (condition 2) between them. It then follows that the two paths PA1 and PA2 can be activated concurrently.
Alternative 2. CIR2 is not the only common node in the two paths PA1 and PA2. This means that there exists a sequence of common nodes (which contains at least two nodes) that starts with one cross-CIR node and ends with CIR2 [Fig. III.25(b)]. Thus,

(c) Concurrent paths

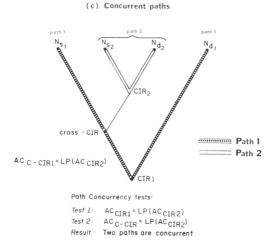

Path Concurrency tests:

Test 1: $AC_{CIR1} = LP(AC_{CIR2})$
Test 2: $AC_{C-CIR} = LP(AC_{CIR2})$
Result: Two paths are concurrent

FIGURE III.25(c)   The results of the path concurrency test for the two paths with no common CIR

this cross-CIR can be reached only via CIR2 if the journey starts from the root, since CIR2 is the closest intermediate root by definition. Therefore, the address code for CIR2 becomes a left prefix of this cross-CIR address code, yielding the validity of condition 2.

Case 2. If CIR2 is not a common node between the two paths, but can be reached from CIR1, then all the cross-CIRs are on path 1 [Fig. III.25(c)]. Thus, CIR2 can be reached from all cross-CIRs, leading to the condition that the address codes for all cross-CIRs become left prefixes of CIR 2. Then the paths are concurrent. An opposite case of path sharing as specified by condition 2 requires that AC of CIR2 be a left prefix of the AC found for at least one cross-CIR.

Example.   Let us illustrate the validity of conditions 1 and 2 for the following path pairs: (1) PA1 and PA3 and (2) PA2 and PA4 (Fig. III.22). As seen from this figure, PA1 and PA3 are shared; PA2 and PA4 are concurrent. Therefore, PA1 and PA3 must satisfy conditions 1 and 2 (yes, yes), whereas PA2 and PA4 must satisfy condition 1 and must not satisfy condition 2 (yes, no) of the general path concurrency test (Fig. III.23). Let us check these theoretical findings with experimental results developed for path pairs (1) and (2).

Paths 1 and 3. For path 1, using an earlier example, we find that $AC_{CIR1} = 10$. For path 3, let us find the address code of its CIR3. Since $N_{s3} = 00111$ and $N_{d3} = 01111$, $AC_{s3} = \text{rot}(R + N_{s3}) = \text{rot}(10110 + 00111) = 10001$ $AC_{d3} = \text{rot}(R + N_{d3}) = \text{rot}(10110 + 01111) = 10011$. Since $AC_{s3} + AC_{d3} = \underset{L0=3}{\underline{00010}}$, $L0 = 3$, giving $AC_{CIR3} = 100$. Therefore, condition 1 gives a *yes* answer because $AC_{CIR1} = LP(AC_{CIR3})$, inasmuch $10 = LP(100)$.

Let us check condition 2 for these paths: Find first the address code for the ss cross-CIR, where N_{s1} = 10111 and N_{s3} = 00111. Since AC_{s1} = 10000, AC_{s3} = 10001 and AC_{s1} + AC_{s3} = $\underset{10=4}{00001}$; giving L0 = 4 and $AC_{C\text{-}CIRss}$ = 1000. Thus, AC_{CIR3} = LP($AC_{C\text{-}CIRss}$), since 100 = LP(1000); therefore, condition 2 also gives a *yes* answer. As a result, paths 1 and 3 are shared and must be executed sequentially.

Paths 2 and 4. For path 2, AC_{CIR2} = 11. For path 4, CIR4 coincides with terminal node N_{d4}, giving CIR4 = 11010, AC_{CIR4} = rot(R + CIR4) = rot (01100) = 110. Condition 1 gives *yes*, since AC_{CIR2} = 11 = LP(AC_{CIR4}) = 110.

Application of condition 2 gives a *no* answer, since CIR4 = C-CIR$_{ss}$ = C-CIR$_{sd}$ and CIR2 = C-CIR$_{dd}$ = C-CIR$_{ds}$. Therefore, for paths 2 and 4 the entire answer is *yes, no,* which allows them to be concurrent (see Fig. III.23). ∎

4.4 Path Durations in a Reconfigurable Binary Tree

Finding the path duration for the path PA = $N_s \rightarrow N_d$ is the second portion of process 2. It is performed for each data path of the data-exchange table that has passed through the path concurrency test.

As with the path concurrency test, path duration can be found by actually building each path in TS$_i$. However, this procedure becomes quite unattractive for large data-exchange tables since it introduces complex processing. A much more interesting procedure is to find path durations analytically using a simple formula based on complemented level codes, CL, found for source node, N_s, destination node, N_d, and the CIR-code. See Chapter II, Sec. 4.8.2.2, where it was shown that a CL code defines the 2's complement of the node level in the tree structure, TS$_i$, generated with bias B and having root R.

To find CL_N, we have to find its recursive sum as RS = N + R and then find the number k of least significant zeros in this RS: $CL_N = n - k + 1$. That is, if k is the actual level of N, then $n - k + 1$ is its CL level. Therefore, for the data path specified with the nodes N_s, N_d, CIR, the total path length PL = PL$_1$ + PL$_2$, where each PL$_i$ (i = 1, 2) defines the difference between the two CLs, specified for the terminal node (s or d) and the CIR node (Fig. III.26). That is, PL$_1$ = CL$_s$ − CL$_{CIR}$ and PL$_2$ = CL$_d$ − CL$_{CIR}$. Therefore,

$$PL = CL_s + CL_d - 2CL_{CIR} \tag{17}$$

Once the path length is found, the path duration, TE, can be defined as follows:

$$TE = PL \cdot DAN \cdot T_0 \tag{18}$$

where DAN is the number of data words to be transferred.

Example. Let us find the path length PL and path duration TE between two nodes, N_s and N_d, in the tree structure TS$_i$ generated with bias B = 110111, where N_s = 001001 and N_d = 110110, and N_s has to send to N_d DAN data words, where DAN = 100 (Fig. III.26). Using the techniques of Chapter II, Sec. 4.7.2, we find the root of this tree as R = 101101.

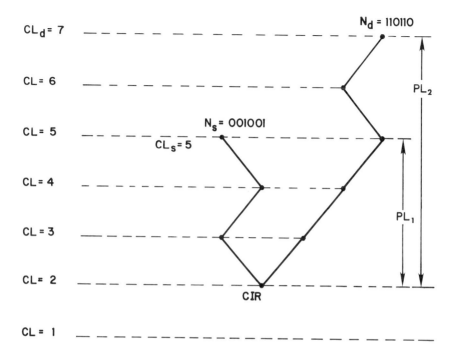

$$PL = CL_s - CL_{CIR} + CL_d - CL_{CIR} = CL_s + CL_d - 2CL_{CIR} = 5 + 7 - 2 \cdot 2 = 12 - 4 = 8$$

FIGURE III.26   Finding the path duration in a reconfigurable binary tree

Find CL_s and CL_d via two recursive sums, RS_s and RS_d: $RS_s = N_s + R = 001001 + 101101 = 100\underset{k}{10}0$, giving $k = 2$ and $CL_s = n - k + 1 = 6 - 2 + 1 = 5$; the second $RS_d = N_d + R = 110110 + 101101 = 011011$, giving $k = 0$ and $CL_d = n - k + 1 = 6 - 0 + 1 = 7$.

Find the CL code for the CIR. To do this we have to first find AC codes for N_s and N_d: $AC_s = \text{rot}(RS_s) = \text{rot}(100100) = 1001$ and $AC_d = \text{rot}(011011) = 110110$, and $AC_s + AC_d = 1001 + 110110 = \underset{LO=1}{010010}$, giving $LO = 1$ and $CL_{CIR} = LO + 1 = 2$

Therefore, the path length for this path is

$$PL = CL_s + CL_d - 2CL_{CIR} = 5 + 7 - 2 \cdot 2 = 12 - 4 = 8$$

and the path duration $TE = PL \cdot DAN \cdot T_0 = 8 \cdot 100 \cdot T_0 = 800T_0$. ∎

4.5 Handling the Data-Exchange Table with the Use of Process 2

In this section we will show how the path concurrency and path duration test should be applied to the data-exchange table (Table III.4) in order to perform assignment of

TABLE III.5

Derivative Table for TS₁

Col. 1	Col. 2	Col. 3 Source Node, N_s			Col. 4 Destination Node, N_d			Col. 5 CIR		Col. 6 Address Codes for Cross-CIRs					
Tree Structure	Communication Paths	RS_s	AC_s	CL_s	RS_d	AC_d	CL_d	AC_{CIR}	CL_{CIR}	Cross-Path Pair	Path Type	ss	sd	ds	dd
TS₁ Main Pair (7, 1) of path 2:	1(3 →2) $N_s = 011$ $N_d = 010$	110	11	3	111	111	4	11	3	2, 1		1	1	1	1
	3(6 →4) $N_s = 110$ $N_d = 100$	011	110	4	0 1	100	4	1	2	2, 3		1	10	1	1A
B = 111 R = 101 $T(TS_1) = 100T_0$	4(5 → 2) $N_s = 101$ $n_d = 010$	0	∅	1	111	111	4	∅	1	2, 4		∅1	1	∅	1
$AC_7 = 10$ $AC_1 = 1$ $AC_{CIR2} = 1$	5(4 → 0) $N_s = 100$ $N_d = 000$	001	100	4	101	101	4	10	3	2, 5		10	10	1	1
	6(6 → 2) $N_s = 110$ $N_d = 010$	011	110	4	111	111	4	11	3	2, 6		1	1	1	1
	6(6 →2)	—	—	—	—	—	—	—	—	1, 6		11	11	11	111
	7(3 → 5) $N_s = 011$ $N_d = 101$	110	11	3	0	∅	1	∅	1	2, 7		1	∅	1	∅
	8(1 ∅ 3)	100	1	2	110	11	3	1	2	N/N		N/N	N/N	N/N	N/N

∅ means no digits.
N/N means no need to find.

Col. 7			Col. 8					Col. 9	Col. 10	Col. 11		
Condition 1			Condition 2							Assignment Status		
Path Pair	Status of CIRs	Cond. 1 Status	ss	sd	ds	dd	Cond. 2 Status	PL	TE	Test 1 Shrd. Paths Pair	Test 2 TE > T(TS)?	Assignment Status
1, 2	$AC_{CIR2} = 1$ is LP of $AC_{CIR1} = 11$ $1 = LP(11)$	Yes	$11 \neq LP(1)$	$11 \neq LP(1)$	$11 \neq LP(1)$	$11 \neq LP(1)$	No	1	$50T_o$	No	No	Yes
2, 3	$AC_{CIR2} = 1$ $AC_{CIR1} = 1$ $1 = 1$	Yes	$1 \neq LP(1)$	$1 = LP(10)$	$1 \neq LP(1)$	$1 \neq LP(1)$	Yes	N/N	N/N	Yes	N N	No
2, 4	$L = LP(1)$	Yes	$1 \neq LP(\varnothing)$	$1 \neq LP(1)$	$1 \neq LP(\varnothing)$	$1 \neq LP(1)$	No	3	$300T_o$	No	Yes	No
2, 5	$1 = LP(10)$	Yes	$10 \neq LP(10)$	$10 \neq LP(10)$	$10 \neq LP(1)$	$10 \neq LP(1)$	No	2	$100T_o$	No	No	Yes
2, 6	$1 = LP(11)$	Yes	$11 \neq LP(1)$	$11 \neq LP(1)$	$II \neq LP(1)$	$11 \neq LP(1)$	No	2	$60T_o$	No	No	No
1, 6	$11 \sim 11$	Yes	$11 \neq LP(11)$	$11 \neq LP(11)$	$11 \neq LP(11)$	$11 \neq LP(111)$	Yes	2	$60T_o$	Yes	No	
2, 7	$\varnothing = LP)1)$	Yes	$1 \neq LP(1)$	$1 \neq LP(\varnothing)$	$1 \neq LP(1)$	$1 \neq LP(\varnothing)$	No	2	$200T_o$	No	Yes	No
N/N	N/N	N/N	N/N	N/N	N/N	N/N	N/N	1	$100T_o$	No	No	Yes

node pairs (N_s, N_d) to TS_i. Process 2 starts with handling Table III.4 which includes *nonassigned node pairs*. Therefore, those communicating pairs (N_s, N_d) that have been assigned to previous TS_j ($j = 1, ..., i - 1$) are crossed out from Table III.4. Also, for process 2, the bias B, the root R, the main pair, and the time $T(TS_i)$ of TS_i are given since these were found by process 1.

Process 2 forms a derivative table (Table III.5), which construction is illustrated for TS_1 obtained earlier [see Fig. III.18(b)]. As follows from this example, for TS_1 the main pair is (7, 1); the time $T(TS_1) = 100T_0$; nodes (7, 1) are connected with the path having path length PE = 1; root R = 5 and bias B = 7.

In general, the derivative table for TS_i consists of 11 columns, where col. 1 defines TS_i; col. 2 shows nonassigned communication path j ($N_s \rightarrow N_d$), where j is the path number and N_s and N_d are its terminal nodes; col. 3 forms recursive sum RS_s, address code AC_s, and complemented level code, CL_s, for the source node; col. 4 forms RS_d, AC_d, and CL_d for the destination node; col. 5 finds AC_{CIR} and CL_{CIR}; col. 6 finds four cross-CIRs for each path pair (PA_i, PA_j), where PA_j is the given path, and PA_i was already assigned to TS_i (in the beginning, PA_i is the main pair of TS_i); col. 6 finds address codes for all cross-CIRs found for the (PA_i, PA_j) path pair; col. 7 checks the validity of condition 1; col. 8 checks the validity of condition 2; col. 9 finds the path length PL; col. 10 finds the path duration, TE; and col. 11 performs a decision process on whether or not given path $PA_j = N_s \rightarrow N_d$ should be assigned to tree structure TS_i. This decision is based on the two tests.

Test 1. Is path PA_j shared with other paths already assigned to TS_i?

Test 2. Does the path duration, TE_j, for the path $PA_j = N_s \rightarrow N_d$ exceed the time $T(TS_i)$?

If there are two no's for these tests, the path PA_j is assigned to TS_i yielding *yes* assignment status. Otherwise, the path is not assigned to TS_i.

Note: If at least one test of the assignment process gives a yes answer, there is no need (N/N) to perform another test, since the assignment decision becomes negative by having at least one yes in a two-variable combination.

Thus, the assignment decision can be implemented via a 2-input NAND-gate, where the first input is the output of test 1 and the second input is the output of test 2.

Let us illustrate now filling the entries of the derivative table for TS_1 for two communicating paths: (a) 4 → 0, which is assigned to TS_1, and (b) 5 → 2, which is not assigned to TS_1.

Path 5 (4 → 0): $N_s = 100$, $N_d = 000$.

Col. 3: $RS_s = N_s + R = 100 + 101 = 001$
$AC_s = \text{rot}(RS_s) = \text{rot}(001) = 100$
$CL_s = n - k + 1 = 3 - 0 + 1 = 4$

Col. 4: $RS_d = N_d + R = 000 + 101 = 101$
$AC_d = \text{rot}(RS_d) = \text{rot}(101) = 101$
$CL_d = n - k + 1 = 3 - 0 + 1 = 4$

Col. 5: $AC_{CIR} = \mathop{LP}\limits_{x_r = y_i \, (i = 1, ..., n)} (AC_s \wedge AC_d) = LP \, (\overset{x_1 x_2 \quad y_1 y_2}{100 \wedge 101}) = \dfrac{10}{LO}$

$CL_{CIR} = LO + 1 = 2 + 1 = 3$

Col. 6: Since the main path is path 2 ($7 \rightarrow 1$) and the given path is path 5 ($4 \rightarrow 0$), the tested path pair is 2, 5.

$$AC(C\text{-}CIR_{ss}) = \underset{x_i = y_i}{LP} \ (AC_7 \wedge AC_4) = LP \ (\overset{x_1 x_2}{10} \ \wedge \ \overset{y_1 y_2}{100}) = 10$$

$$AC(C\text{-}CIR_{sd}) = \underset{x_i = y_i}{LP} \ (AC_7 \wedge AC_0) = LP \ (10 \wedge 101) = 10$$

$$AC(C\text{-}CIR_{ds}) = \underset{x_i = y_i}{LP} \ (AC_1 \wedge AC_4) = LP \ (1 \wedge 100) = 1$$

$$AC(C\text{-}CIR_{dd}) = \underset{x_i = y_i}{LP} \ (AC_1 \wedge AC_0) = LP \ (1 \wedge 101) = 1$$

Col. 7: $AC_{CIR2} = 1$; $AC_{CIR5} = 10$, $1 = LP(10)$, giving a *yes* answer for condition 1 status.

Col. 8: Since $AC(C\text{-}CIR_{ss}) = 10$ and $AC_{CIR5} = 10$, these two address codes coincide, giving $10 \neq LP(10)$; similarly, for the sd test, $10 \neq LP(10)$; for the ds test, $10 \neq LP(1)$; for the dd test, $10 \neq LP(1)$. Thus, the overall status of condition 2 is *no*.

Col. 9: $PL = PL_1 + PL_2 = Cl_s + CL_d - 2CL_{CIR} = 4 + 4 - 2 \cdot 3 = 2$

Col. 10: $TE = DAN \cdot PL \cdot T_0 = 50 \cdot 2 \cdot T_0 = 100 T_0$

Col. 11: Test 1 gives a *no* anser, since condition 2 is negative for all cross-CIRs. Test 2 also gives a *no* answer, since $TE = 100T_0 = T(TS_1) = 100T_0$. Therefore, this path is assigned to TS_1.

Path 4 ($5 \rightarrow 2$): $N_s = 5$, $N_d = 2$.

Col. 3: $RS_s = R + N_s = 101 + 101 = 000$
$AC_s = AC_5 = rot(0) = \varnothing$ (empty symbol)
$CL_s = CL_5 = n - k + 1 = 3 - 3 + 1 = 1$

Col. 4: $RS_d = R + N_d = 101 + 010 = 111$
$AC_d = AC_2 = rot(111) = 111$
$CL_d = CL_2 = n - k + 1 = 3 - 0 + 1 = 4$

Col. 5: $AC_{CIR} = LP(AC_s \wedge AC_d) = LP(\varnothing \wedge 111) = \varnothing$
$CL_{CIR} = LO + 1 = 0 + 1 = 1$

Col. 6: Tested path pair is 2, 4, where 2 is the main path number and 4 is the given path number.
ss-cross path is $7 \rightarrow 5$
$$AC(C\text{-}CIR_{ss}) = \underset{x_i = y_i}{LP} \ (AC_7 \wedge AC_5) - LP(10 \wedge \varnothing) = \varnothing$$
sd cross path is $7 \rightarrow 2$
$$AC(C\text{-}CIR_{sd}) = \underset{x_i = y_i}{LP} \ (AC_7 \wedge AC_2) = LP(\overset{x_1}{10} \wedge \overset{y_1}{111}) = 1$$

ds cross path is $1 \to 5$

$$AC(C\text{-}CIR_{ds}) = \quad LP \quad (AC_1 \wedge AC_5) = LP(1 \wedge \varnothing) = \varnothing$$

$$x_i = y_i$$

dd cross path is $1 \to 2$

$$AC(C\text{-}CIR_{dd}) = LP(AC_1 \wedge AC_2) = LP(1 \wedge 111) = 1$$

Col. 7: Tested path pair is 2, 4

$$AC_{CIR2} = 1; \; AC_{CIR4} = \varnothing, \; \varnothing = LP(1)$$

Condition 1 status is *yes*

Col. 8: For ss cross path, $1 \neq LP \; (\varnothing)$; giving a *no* answer

For sd cross path, $1 \neq LP \; (1)$; giving a *no* answer

For ds cross path, $1 \neq LP \; (\varnothing)$; giving a *no* answer

For dd cross path, $1 \neq LP \; (1)$; giving a *no* answer

Therefore, the overall status of condition 2 is *no* and the $5 \to 2$ path is concurrent with the main path.

We do not compare $5 \to 2$ with $3 \to 2$ already assigned for the following reasons. The length of $5 \to 2$ is $PL = CL_5 + CL_2 - 2CL_{CIR} = 1 + 4 - 2 \cdot 1 = 3$, giving $TE = PL \cdot DAN \cdot T_0 = 3 \cdot 100T_0 = 300T_0$. Thus, $TE = 300T_0 > T(TS_1) = 100T_0$ and no concurrency test is required. However, as follows from Fig. III.18(b) for TS_1, $5 \to 2$ is concurrent with $7 \to 1$, which was established above; however, $5 \to 2$ is not concurrent with $3 \to 2$.

As a matter of fact, to eliminate unnecessary concurrency tests, cols. 9 and 10 of the derivative table can be computed following col. 5; i.e., they can precede execution of col. 6. In this case, if test 2 gives a *yes* answer $[TE > T(TS_i)]$, there is no need to perform concurrency tests.

4.6 Complexity of the Two Processes (Processes 1 and 2)

In this section, we will develop upper bounds for the complexity of the two processes (process 1 and process 2) aimed at formation of TS_i (process 1) and assignment of node pairs to this TS_i (process 2), given a data-exchange table having DP data-exchange pairs, N_s, N_d.

4.6.1 Complexity of Process 1

To form TS_i, requires:

a. Selection of the main pair

b. Finding bias B for TS_i

c. Finding root R for TS_i

d. Finding address codes AC_s and AC_d

To perform step a requires DP comparisons, $A > B$, where DP is the number of exchanging pairs. To find B requires one logical operation (mod-2 add). To find R takes

n shifting steps, where n is the number of levels in the tree. To find AC_s and AC_d requires two logical operations, rot$(N + R)$.

Therefore, if the unit of process complexity, CM is one operation, OP, taking the time of not more than one clock period, then CM (process 1) $\leq$ (DP $+ 1 + n + 2$) • OP $=$ (DP $+ 3 + n$) • OP.

4.6.2 Complexity of Process 2

Consider the worst complexity case. It occurs for the data-exchange table having all exchanging pairs assigned to a single tree structure, TS_1, since for this case condition 2 must be tested for all possible cross paths, giving the number of path pairs that must be tested for path concurrency as C_{DP}^2.

On the other hand, if the data-exchange table is executed by a sequence, $S = TS_1 \rightarrow TS_2 \rightarrow \cdots \rightarrow TS_k$ of tree structures, then the complexity of process 2 for each TS_i becomes much smaller, since many possible path pairs will be eliminated from the concurrency test for each TS_i. Therefore, we assume that CM (process 2) is upper bounded by such a CM_{DP} that tests C_{DP}^2 possible paths pairs:

$$CM \text{ (process 2)} \leq CM_{DP}$$

Let us now evaluate CM_{DP}. Formation of the derivative table is reduced to finding:

a. The entries of cols. 3, 4, 5, 9, and 10 for DP data exchange pairs
b. The entries of cols. 6, 7, 8, and 11 for C_{DP}^2 cross data pairs.

Let the $CM_{DP}(1)$ be the complexity of the process a and $CM_{DP}(2)$ be the complexity of the process b. Clearly, $CM_{DP} = CM_{DP}(1) + CM_{DP}(2)$. Let us evaluate both addends $CM_{DP}(1)$ and $CM_{DP}(2)$.

Evaluation of $CM_{DP}(1)$. For each data path to compute, each of the cols. 3 and 4 requires 3 • OP; computation of col. 5 takes 2 • OP, computation of col. 9 takes 2 • OP $(+, -)$; and computation of col. 10 takes one OP. Thus, $CM_{DP}(1) = (3 + 3 + 2 + 2 + 1)$ • DP • OP $= 11$ • DP • OP.

Evaluation of $CM_{DP}(2)$. For each path's pair, one performs the following computations:

a. Entries of col. 6 take 4 • OP.
b. Entries of col. 7 take one OP.
c. Entries of col. 8 take 4 • OP.
d. Entries of col. 11 take one OP.

Therefore, $CM_{DP}(2) = C_{DP}^2$ • $(4 + 1 + 4 + 1) = 10C_{DP}^2$ • OP. Therefore, the total complexity of process 2 is upper bounded as follows: CM (process 2) ≤ 11 • DP • OP $+ 5$DP • (DP $- 1$) • OP $= 5$DP^2 • OP $+ 6$DP • OP $=$ DP • OP$(5$DP $+ 6)$

Overall Complexity Evaluation. As follows from the above material, the overall complexity, CM, of processes 1 and 2 is upper bounded as follows:

$$CM \leq (DP + 3 + n) \cdot OP + DP \cdot OP (5DP + 6)$$

Let us find the meaning of this upper bound for concrete numbers of exchanging pairs, DP: If DP = 1024 and n = 9, which characterize tree structures having 512 nodes and 1024 data exchanging pairs, to find each tree structure takes the following time T:

$$T \leq (1024 + 3 + 9)OP + 1024(5 \cdot 1024 + 6)OP \simeq 5,251,000 \ OP$$

For an average computer having 2 million OPs per second, the task of finding each TS_i requires not more than 3 seconds. Therefore, if there are k = 20 tree structures that should be assumed, the entire preprocessing algorithm aimed at finding $20TS_i$ will take not more than 1 minute of computer time.

Note: What was found in this example was the overall time of preprocessing aimed at finding the flow chart $S = TS_1 \rightarrow TS_2 \rightarrow ... \rightarrow TS_{20}$ of tree configurations for a realistic data-exchange table mapped onto a sequence containing 20 binary trees, each of which has 512 nodes.

As was shown, this time cannot exceed 1 minute of computer time aimed at automatic preprocessing. Once the flow chart S is found, the time of reconfiguration from one tree structure to another is negligibly small, since it takes only one OP and is carried out with the use of one control code, which is found during preprocessing.

4.7 Conclusions

Section 4 has conclusively demonstrated that the use of reconfigurable binary trees achieves a dramatic effect on improving the performance of reconfigurable tree data bases. Implementation of a reconfigurable data base effects about 370% improvement in performance, since it is always possible to perform such data-base reconfigurations for which every pair of communicating nodes with a long communication request is connected with the path of length 1.

Also, since such a given data base will feature limited path sharing inasmuch as it assumes such configurations having major paths are of length 1, it is possible to improve significantly the concurrency of data-base operations. Furthermore, each reconfiguration is accomplished with the use of only one control code (bias) and takes the time of one logical operation. Thus it takes only one instruction and introduces no reconfiguration overhead into data-base performance.

Therefore, reconfiguration in tree data bases becomes a major factor of improving their performance since:

1. Data-base reconfiguration may considerably minimize the length of the communication path between each pair of nodes with long communication exchanges.

2. Data-base reconfiguration dramatically increases the concurrency of communication since the number of common links shared among various paths is significantly reduced in view of minimization of path lengths.

3. The time of data-base reconfiguration is negligibly small since it takes only one logical operation (mod-2 addition) and requires only one n-bit control code, bias B, to be received by all tree nodes, where n is the number of levels in a tree.

The time of obtaining a flow chart (sequence) of tree data-base reconfigurations is also very inconsequential if one bears in mind the tremendous performance advantages of such reconfigurations. To obtain a flow chart made of 20 tree structures in a data base made of 512 tree nodes requires not more than 1 minute of automatic processing. Once this flow chart is obtained, the benefits for improved performance are immeasurable and cannot be obtained in any alternative static data base.

Therefore, tree data-base reconfiguration is an extremely powerful source of performance improvement, which must be used in those data bases (real-time data bases) in which the speed of data exchanges is the major factor of performance evaluation.

5 DYNAMIC RESOURCE ASSIGNMENTS

As was indicated above (see Sec. 1 this chapter) by *dynamic resource assignment* we understand a process of assigning arriving program P_D to the available hardware resources, for which the resource needs of program P_D are given only with the arrival of the reconfiguration request message that represents P_D.

5.1 Static and Dynamic Programs

As follows from the above definition, all computed programs can be divided into the two classes: *dynamic* or arriving programs, P_D, and *static* or nonarriving programs P_s.

Any dynamic program P_D possesses the following attributes:

A1. Its assignment to hardware resources proceeds during system execution.

A2. Program P_D represents only the individual resource needs. It does not represent the resource needs of other programs that can be executed concurrently in the same architectural state.

A3. Program P_D, as a rule, is nonassigned to an architectural state if its resource needs form a portion (not totality) of the system assignable resource.

On the other hand, static programs, P_s, possess the opposite attributes, $\overline{A1}$, $\overline{A2}$, $\overline{A3}$, where each $\overline{Ai}$ ($i = 1, 2, 3$) is a complement of Ai:

$\overline{A1}$. For a static program, P_s, its assignment to hardware resources is made during compilation, i.e., during preprocessing, and not during computation.

$\overline{A2}$. Any qualified static program, P_s, represents the reconfiguration needs of other programs that can be satisfied in the same architectural state. Indeed, as was shown above (Chapter II, Sec. 3), static programs can be *active* and *passive*, where an active program requests an architectural reconfiguration (N → N*) and a passive program does not request any architectural reconfiguration.

If a static program, P_s , is active, then P_s represents not only the individual resource needs, but also those of other programs that can be executed in the architectural state N*, since N* has been formed in advance during static resource assignment. If a static program, P_s , is passive, it requests no reconfiguration by definition, since all reconfiguration requests are made only by active programs. Therefore, we established principle $\overline{A2}$.

$\overline{A3}$.   Any static program, P_s , is always assigned to the architectural state N by the static assignment process which precedes computation.

5.2 Dynamic Assignment: Brief Overview and Material Composition

As follows from attributes A1 to A3 for dynamic programs and $\overline{A1}$ to $\overline{A3}$ for static programs, all the architectural states for static programs are stored; for dynamic programs, they must be either created or reassigned during dynamic assignment, where the significance of these two operations will be given below.

To eliminate gross underutilization of the hardware resources, we will stipulate that any program can be computed in the system only if it is assigned to the architectural state. Therefore, a static program is always ready for computation; a dynamic program must first be assigned to an architectural state before its computation can start.

To start each program assigned to the architectural state N, the monitor must possess its start-up message, SUM, which must be sent from the monitor to the hardware resources assigned to this program whenever the computation of N is allowed. For static programs an assigned queue, AQ, of start-up messages, assigned to the architectural states, is stored in the monitor.

Dynamic programs are also represented by a queue, NAQ, of nonassigned messages, otherwise called *nonassigned queue.* The task of the dynamic assignment is thus reduced to the *absorption* of the nonassigned queue NAQ with the assigned queue AQ. This absorption can be implemented via the following two operations, discussed below:

- *Creation,* aimed at creation of a new architectural state,
- *Reassignment,* aimed at reassigning a new high-priority program to an existing architectural state, while deleting from this state an old program with a lower priority status with compatible time and resource needs. This deleted program acquires a status of nonassigned program, and its SUM is sent back to the nonassigned queue, NAQ.

With these preliminary observations and definitions, the material on dynamic assignment in Section 5 will be organized as follows. First, we specify what program attributes warrant program division into assigned and nonassigned (Sec. 5.3). Next, we introduce the main conditions of dynamic assignment (Sec. 5.4) and specify the two types of queues of start-up messages, *assigned* and *nonassigned,* that can be formed in the monitor (Sec. 5.5). Thereafter, we define the procedures of *assignment and creation of architectural states* that lead to the absorption of the nonassigned queue with the assigned one (Sec. 5.6).

This will prepare us for a discussion of the specific program start-up techniques for static and dynamic programs in Sec. 5.7, which will be reduced to maintaining a one-to-one correspondence between a restructurable reconfiguration flow chart and the assigned dynamic queue of SUM messages.

Note: The material of Sec. 5 is closely related with that of Chapter II, Sec. 3, and Sec. 3 of this chapter.

5.3 Assigned and Nonassigned Programs

There are two types of programs represented with their SUM messages: *assigned* (bit A = 1) and *nonassigned* (A = 0) (Fig. III.27). An assigned SUM is assigned to the architectural state N. A nonassigned SUM is free. It is the task of the monitor to select an architectural state N that can execute a nonassigned SUM.

A program belongs to the A class, if it is static (S) or it requests the total system resource (T) for its reconfiguration into state N. This defines $A = S \vee T$. Otherwise, a program is attributed to the $\overline{A}$ class. Therefore, the $\overline{A}$ class is made of those user programs that are dynamic $(\overline{S})$ and request a portion (not totality) of the available CE resources, giving $\overline{A} = \overline{S \vee T} = \overline{S} \wedge \overline{T}$. Let us show that this formal partition of all user programs into A and $\overline{A}$ classes is well supported by simple intuitive observations.

If a program P is static $(P = P_s)$, then the state N that executes P_s can be determined during preliminary static resource assignment. Therefore, P_s becomes assigned to this N. In view of the arbitrariness of selecting P_s and N, any static program P_s belongs to the A class. Likewise, if the dynamic program P_D requests the entire system resource $(T = 1)$ for its reconfiguration into N, it also becomes assigned to this N.

All other programs belong to $\overline{A}$. These programs are nonstatic (i.e., they are dynamic), and they do not request the totality of the resources. Indeed, a typical dynamic program P_D may know only of the individual resource needs. If these needs become nontotal $(\overline{T} = 1)$, there are a number or architectural states than can execute this P_D.

Therefore, programs division into A and $\overline{A}$ classes specifies the division of all start messages SUM into the two zones A and $\overline{A}$, where the A zone stores all the codes that

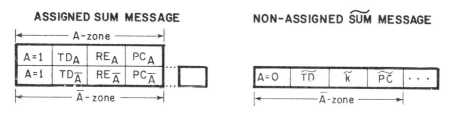

FIGURE III.27 Assigned and nonassigned start-up messages, SUM

associate this SUM with the respective architectural state N, and the $\overline{A}$ zone stores all the individual program codes that allow program start-up in a new dynamic computer and a possible (re)assignment of this program to a (new) architectural state.

For any assigned program, the start-up message SUM contains two zones A and $\overline{A}$. For any nonassigned program, the SUM message contains only $\overline{A}$ zone (Fig. III 77) The codes to be stored in zones A and $\overline{A}$ will be introduced in the order of their necessity.

5.4 Conditions of Dynamic Assignment

If a dynamic program, P_D, arrives with nonassigned SUM (bit A = 0), the task of the monitor is to perform a dynamic assignment of this SUM to the architectural state N so that the following conditions are satisfied:

C1. *Fulfillment of the program resource needs:* A selected architectural state N must contain a dynamic computer(s) which is needed by dynamic program P_D.

C2. *Minimal delay in computations:* A selected architectural state N must be assumed by the system earlier than any possible alternative state N' which can also satisfy the resource needs of program P_D.

Implementation of principle C2 requires that dynamic programs be assigned to architectural states on the basis of their priorities using the following rule.

Rule for Dynamic Assignment. For any two architectural states N and N', where N' follows N in the architectural flow chart (not necessarily immediately), none of the programs assigned to N' has a higher priority than any of those assigned to N if:

* N can satisfy the resource needs of each such program.
* The reconfiguration flow chart can assume N and N' with such an assignment; i.e., none of the existing architectural states becomes unreachable or dead because of a particular dynamic assignment.
* Unwarranted idleness of equipment during computation of N is not created with such an assignment.
* All programs to be assigned to N and N' are available before the system assumes N and N'.

Therefore, the implementation of both principles C1 and C2 in a dynamic situation characterized by the unpredictable arrival of dynamic programs with the priorities unknown in advance requires (1) a continuous reassignment of existing architectural states, and (2) continuous creation of new architectural states. Only perennial execution of these two operations in the system will guarantee that:

* Each architectural state assumed by the system is assigned with the set of highest-priority programs from those currently available.
* Each such program will meet its individual resource needs in this state and

will not introduce unwarranted delays in the execution of other programs computed by the system.

5.5 Two Types of Queues of Start-Up Messages

A dynamic architecture that executes a given program mix made of static and dynamic programs must necessarily have a queue of SUM messages. Since any nonassigned SUM message must first be assigned to the architectural state N before it can be executed in a system, there are two types of SUM queues: assigned, AQ, and nonassigned, NAQ. An assigned queue is made of assigned SUMs and is ready for computation. A nonassigned queue is made of nonassigned SUMs that should be absorbed by the assigned queue before they can be computed in the system.

5.5.1 Assigned Queue

An assigned queue, AQ, is understood as a sequence of start states M(N), where each state M(N) is represented by such a set of SUM messages that are assigned to the same architectural state N.

Any assigned queue, AQ, must possess the following attributes:

A1. *Synchronization attribute:* Since each start-up state M(N) is one to one with the architectural state N, the system must perform the M(N) $\rightarrow$ M(N*) transition synchronously with the N $\rightarrow$ N* transition of the reconfiguration flow chart.

A2. *Restructuring attribute:* To implement the minimal delay condition of the dynamic assignment (C2), any assigned queue must be capable of restructuring itself perennially by performing a continuous reassignment of existing architectural states and a continuous creation of the new architectural states.

Since each assigned SUM is specified with the two zones A and $\overline{A}$ (Fig. III.27), where A stores the necessary attributes of the architectural state N and $\overline{A}$ stores the individual start-up attributes of the respective program P, each state M(N) is made of those SUM messages that are identified with the same A zone, called in future the A *header.* Thus, M(N) is understood as a set consisting of one A zone (A header), which specifies the architectural state N, and m $\overline{A}_i$ zones, which identify m programs P_i assigned to N.

Example.   In Fig. III.28, there is a fragment of the resource assignment diagram for transition $N_5 \rightarrow N_8$ of the architectural flow chart, where state N_5 is assigned with programs P_1, P_2, and P_3; and state N_8 is assigned with programs P_1 and P_2, since P_3 is interrupted for the duration of N_8. State N_5 is one to one with the start state $M(N_5)$, which includes one A zone and three $\overline{A}$ zones $(\overline{A}_1, \overline{A}_2, \overline{A}_3)$ for SUM_1, SUM_2, and SUM_3 representing P_1, P_2, and P_3. The A zone stores all the global information associated with the start-up of the architectural state, N_5. Each $\overline{A}_i$ zone stores the in-

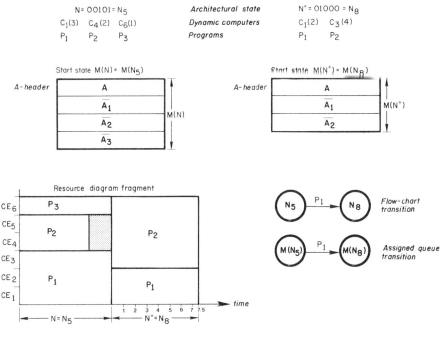

FIGURE III.28 Matching assigned queue transitions with those of reconfiguration flow chart

dividual information which allows start-up of the respective program P_i ($i = 1, 2, 3$). Start state $M(N_8)$ can be formed similarly. ■

5.5.2 Nonassigned Queue of Start-Up Messages

A nonassigned SUM queue, NAQ, is understood as a sequence of arriving and nonassigned SUM messages. For simplicity of recognition, they will be marked with waves as SUM = $\widetilde{SUM}$. In order that a $\widetilde{SUM}$ from this queue be computed by the system, it must be assigned to some start state of the assigned queue, AQ. As was indicated above, any $\widetilde{SUM}$ belonging to the NAQ is specified only with its individual $\overline{A}$ zone.

For static resource assignment, NAQ is always empty since all static programs are assigned. For dynamic resource assignment, NAQ may not be empty. In this case, NAQ begins an immediate interaction with AQ aimed at assigning $\widetilde{SUM}$s to existing or new states of AQ.

5.6 Interaction between Assigned and Nonassigned Queues

The state N of AQ that accepts an arriving $\widetilde{SUM}$ from NAQ belongs to one of the following categories: it is either an *existing state* or it is a *newly created state*. † If state N

---

†Since there is a 1-1 correspondence between start-up state $M(N)$ and architectural state N, for simplicity of notation, heretofore a start-up state $M(N)$ will be referred to as N.

is an existing state of AQ and it accepts new $\widetilde{\text{SUM}}$, this state becomes reassigned as RE(N). If state N is a new state of AQ, the assignment of one or several nonassigned $\widetilde{\text{SUM}}$s to this state means *creation*, CR(N). Thus, a new state has been created that did not exist in the original queue, AQ.

Let us now specify the conditions for reassignment and creation operations.

5.6.1 Reassignment of Architectural States

The reassignment, RE(N), allows a qualified $\widetilde{\text{SUM}}$ to be executed in the architectural state N assigned with other programs having higher priorities, provided there exists a SUM_L already assigned to N:

a. Whose priority is lower than that of $\widetilde{\text{SUM}}$.
b. Whose resource needs match those of $\widetilde{\text{SUM}}$.

If these conditions are true, the start-up message, SUM_L, exchanges its location with $\widetilde{\text{SUM}}$. That is, SUM_L becomes nonassigned and goes back to NAQ, whereas $\widetilde{\text{SUM}}$ takes its location in N.

Therefore, the RE operation allows implementation of both criteria C1 and C2 of dynamic assignment by selecting a state N which contains a dynamic computer needed by arriving $\widetilde{\text{SUM}}$ and by computing the program P_D identified with this $\widetilde{\text{SUM}}$ together with other higher-priority programs. Therefore, the moment of time, T_C, when the arriving dynamic program, P_D, can be completed occurs at the earliest convenience, which minimizes a delay in computing P_D.

Surely, the RE operation should not delay the computation of state N, since N may contain higher-priority programs than that of the newly reassigned. Nor should the equipment given to reassigned $\widetilde{\text{SUM}}$ be idle in RE(N) during a longer time than that warranted in a given computational situation. Therefore, RE(N) is performed if the following conditions are satisfied.

Conditions for the Architectural Reassignment. Given architectural state N specified with its A header and zones $\overline{A}_1$, $\overline{A}_2$, ..., $\overline{A}_m$, suppose that there arrives a nonassigned $\widetilde{\text{SUM}}$ that can be integrated into N using the RE(N) operation. State N can be reassigned as RE(N) if the following conditions are satisfied:

REC 1. State N is not delayed in its execution because of such reassignment:

$$TD_A > \widetilde{\text{TD}}$$

where TD_A is the tentative duration of state N stored in the A header, which is the duration of the active and/or highest-priority program that performs reconfiguration into N and/or assigned to N; $\widetilde{\text{TD}}$ is the tentative duration of the dynamic program represented with this SUM which is tested for reassignment to this N.

Note: If N is an architectural state of the static reconfiguration flow chart, the active program P which performs reconfiguration into N may be nonassigned to N. In this case, the A header stores the basic parameters (TD, PC, etc.) of the highest-priority program assigned to N. If N is a dynamically created state, then the A header always stores the basic parameters of the active program since this program is always assigned to N, and its priority in N is the highest.

REC 2. A tested program represented with this $\widetilde{SUM}$ should not finish its computation in N earlier than at the moment $T_C = TD_A - D_0$, since otherwise such a finish will create unwarranted idleness among k CEs that will be assigned to this program, where D_0 is a maximal admissible delay selected by the programmer and stored in the monitor. Therefore, REC 2 finds the difference

$$\Delta = \widetilde{TD} - TD_A = \{ {}_0^{-D}$$

If $\Delta = -D$, Δ is compared with D_0. If $|\Delta| \leq D_0$, REC 2 is positive. Otherwise, it is negative. If $\Delta = 0$, REC 2 is positive (Fig. III.29).

Note: Since REC 2 is tested after REC 1, Δ cannot be positive, since, if $\Delta = +D$, REC 1 is negative.

REC 3. There exists such an individual zone $\overline{A}_L$ in N whose priority is lower than that of tested $\widetilde{SUM}$ and whose resource needs match those of $\widetilde{SUM}$:

$$PC(\overline{A}_L) < PC(\widetilde{SUM})$$

$$RE(\overline{A}_L) = RE(\widetilde{SUM})$$

Refinement 1. The tested $\widetilde{SUM}$ does not need to store the code RE of the needed dynamic computer $C_i(k)$ which specifies the position of all CEs integrated into this computer, since in a nonassigned $\widetilde{SUM}$ the availability of the RE code will impose an unnecessary restriction which will prevent many useful optimizations that can be performed with the reassignment operation.

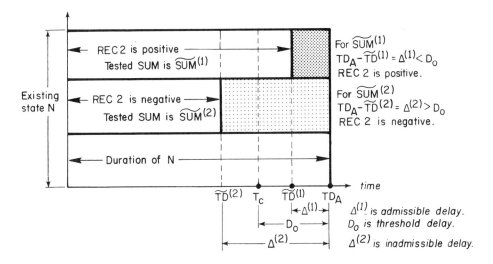

FIGURE III.29 Illustration of the REC2 condition of architectural reassignment

Instead, the tested $\widetilde{\text{SUM}}$ may store the computer size code $\widetilde{k}$, which shows how many CEs have to be integrated into this computer. On the other hand, since the replaced $\overline{A}_L$ specifies the assigned program, its code $\text{RE}(\overline{A}_L)$ shows which CEs are assigned to its dynamic computer. For instance, if $\text{RE}(\overline{A}_L) = 01110$, this means that this program is executed by dynamic computer $C_2(3) = [CE_2, CE_3, CE_4]$ made of 3 CEs. In this case, the resource match between $\overline{A}_L$ and $\widetilde{\text{SUM}}$ can be established as a result of a simple decoding operation whereby $\text{RE}(\overline{A}_L)$ is first decoded into respective computer-size codes k_L (for our case, $k_L = 3$) and only then compared with $\widetilde{k}$ as $k_L = \widetilde{k}$.

Refinement 2. Another useful refinement of the reassignment condition REC 3 is as follows: One assigned zone $\overline{A}_L$ may be replaced with several (t) nonassigned $\widetilde{\text{SUM}}$s $(\widetilde{\text{SUM}}_{i_1}, \widetilde{\text{SUM}}_{i_2}, \ldots, \widetilde{\text{SUM}}_{i_t})$ if its priority is lower than that of every $\widetilde{\text{SUM}}_{i_j}$ ($j = 1, \ldots, t$) and $k_L = \widetilde{k}_{i_1} + \widetilde{k}_{i_2} + \ldots + \widetilde{k}_{i_t}$, where $\widetilde{k}_{i_j}$ is the computer-size code of nonassigned $\widetilde{\text{SUM}}_{i_j}$.

REC 4: The priority of the tested $\widetilde{\text{SUM}}$ must not be higher than that of the A header that stores the priority of the active or highest in priority program assigned to N.

The significance of REC 4 is that this condition prevents the tested $\widetilde{\text{SUM}}$ from becoming the A header. Otherwise, if $\widetilde{\text{SUM}}$ becomes the A header, it will create a new architectural state, and the RE-operation will become confused with the CR operation.

Therefore, to perform the RE operation the following codes should be stored in the A and $\overline{A}$ zones (Fig. III.27):

1. *Tentative duration code, TD:* In the A zone this code shows the tentative duration of state N, which is identical to that of the highest-priority program that is computed in N. In the $\overline{A}$ zone this code shows the tentative duration of the individual program that is represented with this $\overline{A}$.

2. *Priority code, PC:* In the A zone this code shows the priority of the highest-priority program that is computed in N; in the $\overline{A}$ zone this code shows the priority of the program that is represented with this $\overline{A}$.

3. *Requested equipment code, RE:* In the A zone the RE_A code shows the entire equipment requested for reconfiguration into state N; in the $\overline{A}$ zone the RE_A gives the individual code of the dynamic computer needed by this $\overline{A}$.

4. *Computer-size code, k:* This code is stored only in the nonassigned $\widetilde{\text{SUM}}$ (Fig. III.27). When this $\widetilde{\text{SUM}}$ becomes assigned to the architectural state N, this code becomes exchanged with the matching $\text{RE}(\overline{A}_L)$ of the displaced $\overline{A}_L$ zone, whereas the displaced A_L zone will receive $\widetilde{k}$ from $\widetilde{\text{SUM}}$ before going back to the nonassigned queue.

Example. Consider the reassignment of the architectural state N_8 requested by program P_1 (Fig. III.28). State N_8 was originally assigned to P_1 and P_2, where P_1 was computed in the $C_1(2)$ computer and P_2 was computed in the $C_3(4)$ computer.

Suppose that the start state $M(N_8)$ for N_8 is as given in Fig. III.30(a). Here the A header is filled with the following codes. Since P_1 performs transition into N_8, it is the active program with the highest priority ($PC = 7$). Thus, for the A header, $PC = 7$; $TD = 7.5$, since this is the time of P_1 duration; and $RE = 111111$, since the

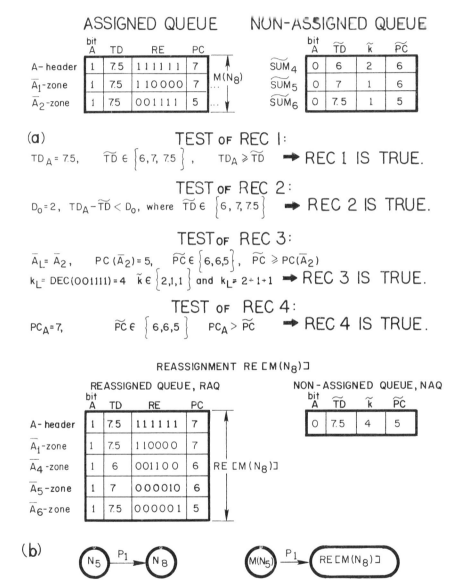

FIGURE III.30 Reassignment of architectural states

entire resources of six CEs are requested to form N_8. The two $\overline{A}$ zones ($\overline{A}_1$ and $\overline{A}_2$) of $M(N_8)$ represent programs P_1 and P_2, in a sense that they store individual codes (ID, RE, PC) for P_1 and P_2.

Suppose that this assigned queue, AQ, coexists dynamically with the nonempty nonassigned queue made of three dynamic $\widetilde{SUM}$s: $\widetilde{SUM}_4$, $\widetilde{SUM}_5$, and $\widetilde{SUM}_6$ [Fig. III.30(a)]. Execution of four reassignment conditions, REC 1, REC 2, REC 3, and REC 4, gives positive results. This warrants reassignment. This means that there exists zone $\bar{A}_L$ ($\bar{A}_L = \bar{A}_2$) that can be replaced with these nonassigned $\widetilde{SUM}$s. The status of these two queues after the reassignment, $RE[M(N_8)]$, is shown in Fig. III.30(b). As seen, the reassigned queue, RAQ, now has the same header and four $\bar{A}$ zones ($\bar{A} \in \{\bar{A}_1, \bar{A}_4, \bar{A}_5, \bar{A}_6\}$). The nonassigned queue, NAQ, is now made of only one displaced SUM_L message that becomes nonassigned ($SUM_L = \widetilde{SUM} = \bar{A}_2$).

Note: The only changes in this $\bar{A}_2$ are:

a. It has acquired a nonassigned status (bit $A = 0$).

b. Its $RE = 001111$ is transformed into $\widetilde{k} = 4$, since there is no need to fix the positions of CEs that are needed by this program. ∎

5.6.2 Creation of a New Architectural State

The creation of a new architectural state, CR(N), is performed by the nonassigned program P (represented with its $\widetilde{SUM}$) whose priority is either higher or lower than those of all other programs already assigned to the architectural states. The program P that creates CR(N) will be called the *program generator*, $\widetilde{P} = \widetilde{P}_{gen}$. Its $\widetilde{SUM}$ will be denoted $\widetilde{SUM}_{gen}$.

Indeed, if the priority of $\widetilde{P}_{gen}$ is higher than those of all assigned programs, the $\widetilde{SUM}_{gen}$ cannot be integrated (reassigned) into any existing architectural state, because such a reassignment will violate the reassignment condition RED 4 inasmuch as the header priority will become lower than that of $\widetilde{SUM}_{gen}$. If the priority of $\widetilde{P}_{gen}$ is lower than those of all assigned programs, then P_{gen} cannot be reassigned to existing states either, since there exists no zone $\bar{A}_L$ that can exchange its location with the $\widetilde{SUM}_{gen}$, because, by definition, the priority of each assigned $\bar{A}$ is higher than that of $\widetilde{SUM}_{gen}$.

Therefore, the only option which is left for $\widetilde{P}_{gen}$ is to create a new architectural state, CR(N). This operation is iterative and includes the following Steps (Fig. III.31).

Step 1. Generation of the A-header.

Step 2. Selection of the qualified program, called *program joiner,* that can join CR(N).

Each iteration of Step 2 is concluded by the following test:

Is $\Delta = 0$?

If $\Delta = 0$, the creation is completed.

If $\Delta > 0$, Step 2 is iterated again.

Here $\Delta = n - k_i$; n is the total number of CEs in the system, and k_i is the cumulative number of CEs integrated into dynamic computers during i iterations of Step 2, where

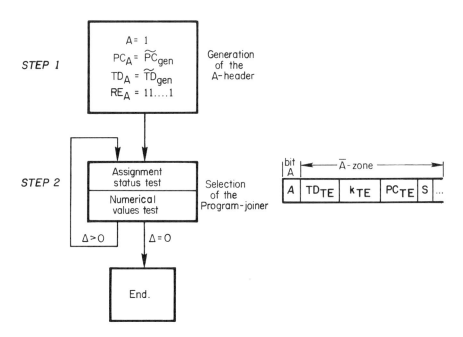

FIGURE III.31 Algorithm for creating a new architectural state

$i \geq 1$. Obviously, $k_i = k_{i-1} + k(\text{TE}_i)$, where $k(\text{TE}_i)$ is the number of CEs required by the program that is tested for join during the ith iteration of Step 2. As follows, $k_0 = k_{gen}$ and $k_1 = k_{gen} + k(\text{TE}_1)$. Let us now describe the processes of Steps 1 and 2.

5.6.2.1 Generation of the A header

When $\widetilde{\text{SUM}}_{gen}$ creates new state CR[N], its priority code becomes the priority code of the newly created state stored in the A header ($\widetilde{\text{PC}}_{gen} = \text{PC}_A$). Likewise, its duration time $\widetilde{\text{TD}}_{gen}$ becomes the time of duration for the newly created state, CR[N]: $\widetilde{\text{TD}}_{gen} = \text{TD}_A$. As for RE_A, $\text{RE}_A = 111 \ldots 1$.

There are several things to note about requested equipment code, RE (Fig. III.27). For every newly created state, $\text{RE} = \underbrace{11 \ldots 1}_{n}$, since there should be no unused equip-

ment during CR[N] computation and every program assigned to CR[N] starts execution of the new task in this state.† (Thus, its preceding task, if any, assigned to the predecessor of CR[N] in the architectural flow chart always ends with the synchronization instruction *Stop N.*)

Note: Since $\widetilde{\mathrm{SUM}}_{gen}$ is nonassigned, its computer-size code $\widetilde{k}_{gen} < n$. Therefore, a newly created architectural state will always have at least one program joiner. Thus, the creation operation will always have at least one iteration of the next Step 2 aimed at finding a qualified program that can join CR[N].

5.6.2.2 Selection of the program joiner

Let us now discuss what programs may join a newly created state CR[N]. The following qualifications of every tested program, P_{TE}, must be tested:

Q1. Its assignment status
Q2. Numerical values of its $\overline{A}$ zone

Assignment Status Test. Program P_{TE} which may join CR[N] can be assigned and nonassigned. If program P_{TE} is assigned, it must be *passive*. If program P_{TE} is nonassigned, it is always *active*.

Indeed, if P_{TE} was assigned to some other state N′ before it joins CR[N], it could not be active in N′. Otherwise, if P_{TE} joins CR[N], state N′ may become deprived of the only active program that requests reconfiguration into N′ for the case P_{TE} is active and computed in N′. For this case, state N′ becomes unreachable or dead in the reconfiguration flow chart.

If P_{TE} is nonassigned, P_{TE} is the dynamic program that makes all its individual reconfiguration requests. Therefore, this program contains all reconfiguration instructions that generate these requests. This defines the active status for every P_{TE} if it is nonassigned. Thus, to perform the assignment status test, the $\overline{A}$ zone of every program must be added with a special bit S that recognizes the active or passive status of this program: S = 0 if the program is active; S = 1 if the program is passive (Fig. III.31).

For assigned programs, recognized by bit A = 1, if S = 1, the assignment status test is followed by the numerical values test; if S = 0, end. For nonassigned programs (bit A = 0), S ≡ 0; thus there is no need to make the assignment status test.

Numerical Value Tests. There are four numerical value tests that can qualify program P_{TE} for joining CR[N].

Test 1. If P_{TE} was assigned to state N′, the priority of state N′ stored in its A′ header must be lower than that of CR[N] and stored in its A header; otherwise, execution of tested program P_{TE} in CR(N) will be delayed in comparison with that in N′, leading to violation of principle C2 of dynamic assignment. Thus test 1 performs the following comparison:

†If there is a created sequence of new architectural states that includes more than one state, the RE may not have all ones. See Sec. 5.6.4.

Is $PC_A > PC_{A'}$?

Is yes, test 1 is positive; go to test 2.

If no, test 1 is negative; end.

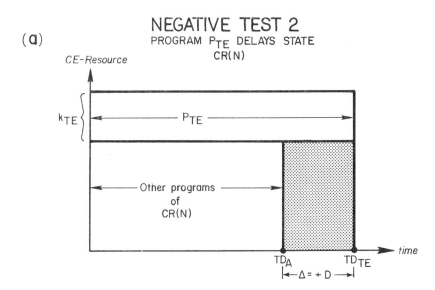

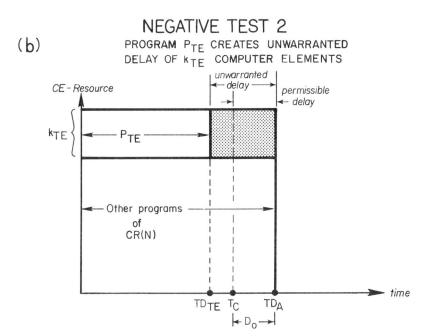

FIGURE III.32   Illustration of Test 2

Test 2. Execution of program P_{TE} should not delay the architectural state CR(N) (Fig. III.32). Nor should the program P_{TE} finish its computation earlier than at the moment $T_c = TD_A - D_0$, since such a finish will create unwarranted idleness among k_{TE} computer elements that execute this program, where D_0 is the maximal delay, selected by the programmer and stored in the monitor [Fig. III.32(b)].

Therefore, test 2 finds the difference

$$\Delta = TD_{TE} - TD_A = \begin{cases} +D \\ -D \\ 0 \end{cases}$$

where TD_{TE} and TD_A are the tentative durations of program P_{TE} and state CR(N); TD_{TE} is stored in $\widetilde{SUM}$; TD_A is stored in the A header.

If $\Delta = +D$, tests 2 is negative; end.

If $\Delta = -D$, Δ is compared with D_0. If $|\Delta| \le D_0$,   test 2 is positive.
Otherwise, it is negative; end.

If $\Delta = 0$, test 2 is positive.

Test 3. Since program P_{TE} joins CR[N], the priority PC_{TE} should not be higher than that of CR[N]. Thus test 3 checks:

Is $PC_{TE} \le PC_A$?

If yes, test 3 is positive; go to test 4.

If no, test 3 is negative; end.

Test 4. State CR[N] must have enough equipment to compute P_{TE}. Therefore, during every (*i*th) iteration of Step 2, the following *equipment equation* should be formed:

$k_i = k_{i-1} + k(TE_i)$ where $i \ge 1$ and $k_1 = k_{gen} + k(TE_1)$. Find $n - k_i$:

If $n - k_i \ge 0$, test 4 is positive.

If $n - k_i < 0$, test 4 is negative.

Program P_{TE} joins state CR[N] if the assignment test and all four numerical value tests give positive results. Otherwise, P_{TE} is dropped from consideration and a new candidate is selected for testing. [The example of creating CR(N) will be discussed in the next section.]

5.6.3 Absorption of the NAQ Queue

Each time the NAQ queue is not empty it begins the *absorption process* (Fig. III.33). The absorption process leads to either complete or incomplete absorption of the current NAQ by the assigned queue, AQ. If absorption is complete, AQ − NAQ = 0. If

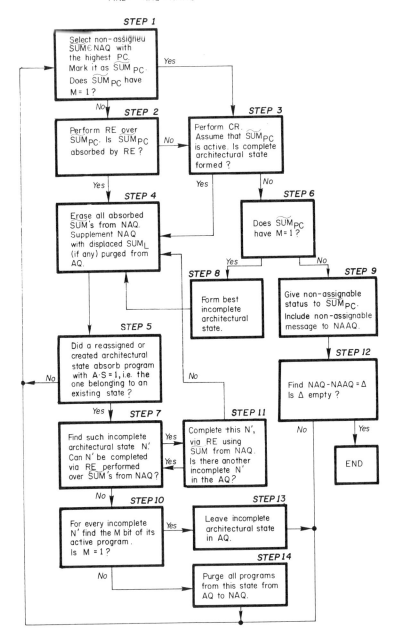

GIVEN: AQ AND NON-EMPTY NAQ
FIND: NAQ = NAAQ

STEP 1
Select non-assigned $\widetilde{SUM} \in$ NAQ with the highest PC. Mark it as $\widetilde{SUM}_{PC}$. Does $\widetilde{SUM}_{PC}$ have M = 1 ?

STEP 2
Perform RE over $\widetilde{SUM}_{PC}$. Is $\widetilde{SUM}_{PC}$ absorbed by RE ?

STEP 3
Perform CR. Assume that $\widetilde{SUM}_{PC}$ is active. Is complete architectural state formed ?

STEP 4
Erase all absorbed $\widetilde{SUM}$'s from NAQ. Supplement NAQ with displaced SUM_L (if any) purged from AQ.

STEP 6
Does $\widetilde{SUM}_{PC}$ have M = 1 ?

STEP 8
Form best incomplete architectural state.

STEP 9
Give non-assignable status to $\widetilde{SUM}_{PC}$. Include non-assignable message to NAAQ.

STEP 5
Did a reassigned or created architectural state absorb program with A·S = 1, i.e. the one belonging to an existing state ?

STEP 12
Find NAQ−NAAQ = Δ Is Δ empty ?

STEP 7
Find such incomplete architectural state N.' Can N' be completed via RE performed over $\widetilde{SUM}$'s from NAQ?

STEP 11
Complete this N', via RE using $\widetilde{SUM}$ from NAQ. Is there another incomplete N' in the AQ?

END

STEP 10
For every incomplete N' find the M bit of its active program. Is M = 1 ?

STEP 13
Leave incomplete architectural state in AQ.

STEP 14
Purge all programs from this state from AQ to NAQ.

FIGURE III.33 Algorithm of the absorption process aimed at absorbing a nonassigned queue of SUMs with assigned one

absorption is incomplete, AQ − NAQ = NAAQ, where NAAQ is a nonassignable queue made of those SUMs that can no longer be assigned to the architectural states of the reconfiguration flow chart without a considerable deterioration in the utilization factor of the used equipment. In the latter case, this nonassignable queue must wait until it will be filled with new arriving $\widetilde{SUM}$s that can change the assignment status of some (if not all) of nonassignable SUM messages.

The absorption process includes the two consecutive subprocesses, RE and CR, performed at Steps 2 and 3 and aimed at reassignment and creation of architectural states. All the programs are divided into the two classes, M and $\overline{M}$. The programs of class M are processed by the CR process (Step 3). The programs of class $\overline{M}$ are processed by the sequence RE → CR (Steps 2 and 3).

Typically, a nonassigned program of class M (bit M = 1) is (1) either very important, or (2) much shorter or longer in time than other programs from the same program mix, so the computer system can execute this program with the degree of underutilization of used resources which exceeds the admissible tolerances on idle equipment if a complete resources utilization cannot be achieved.

Therefore, any such program skips RE and starts CR by first attempting to create a complete architectural state (Step 3). If, however, it is found that this program cannot create a complete architectural state (test *no* for Step 3), then bit M = 1 guarantees that the architectural state will be formed immediately, no matter whether or not this state is complete. Therefore, for the programs with M = 1, the CR iteration is repeated again, resulting in forming incomplete architectural states that are ready for computation (Step 8). Since programs with bit M = 1 are always active, bit M = 1 also characterizes the architectural state that is formed by such program. Thus, M = is stored in the A header.

The programs of class $\overline{M}$ are processed by the sequence RE → CR, where CR is executed only if a selected message $\widetilde{SUM}_{PC}$ cannot be absorbed with RE (Steps 2 and 3). Both RE and CR may create displaced SUM_Ls that should be purged from AQ to NAQ, where RE always creates displaced SUM_Ls by definition, and CR may create displaced SUM_Ls if it absorbs programs already assigned to other architectural states.

Therefore, after each iteration of RE and/or CR, a nonassigned queue, NAQ, is purged of all the SUMs that become absorbed into assigned queue, AQ, via their integration into existing or new architectural states, whereas assigned queue, AQ, is purged of all displaced SUM_L that go back to NAQ because of such absorption (Step 4). Since CR may absorb not only nonassigned $\widetilde{SUM}$s but those previously assigned to other architectural states N and passive in these states (S = 1), each such N', when deprived of its passive program(s), becomes incomplete (Step 5). Every incomplete N' initiates RE to be completed again (Steps 7 and 11). If no RE can complete an incomplete N', N' is tested for its bit M, where the meaning of M in N' is equal to that of its active program (Step 10). If M = 0, this state is purged from the reconfiguration flow chart because the resulting undcrutilization of the equipment is not tolerated; all programs of the purged state become nonassigned and purged from AQ to NAQ (Step 14). If M = 1, the incomplete architectural state N' remains in the AQ.

Since the absorption process always erases the absorbed $\widetilde{\text{SUM}}$ from the NAQ, using Step 4), in the end of NAQ remainder will contain *currently nonassignable* SUMs.

Therefore, the current stage of the absorption process ends when the nonassigned NAQ and currently nonassignable NAAQ coincide. This occurs with both queues become either empty for the case of complete absorption or totally coincident for incomplete absorption. Thus, each new iteration of the absorption process is triggered by the rival of new nonassigned $\widetilde{\text{SUM}}$, which may change the status of the NAQ remainder (NAAQ) if it is not empty.

The above absorption algorithm will be illustrated with the example that follows.

Example. Given the two nonempty queues, AQ and NAQ [Fig. III.34(a)]. Let us try to absorb the NAQ into the AQ. First we fetch SUM_7 from NAQ (highest $\widetilde{\text{PC}}$

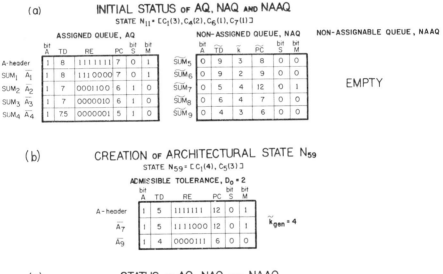

FIGURE III.34 Creation of architectural state N_{59}: (a) initial status before the creation; (b) the act of creation; (c) status following the act of creation

= 12). Since, for the $\widetilde{SUM}_7$, M = 1, $\widetilde{SUM}_7$ should not be absorbed by the RE process. Instead, $\widetilde{SUM}_7$ is processed by Step 3, which assumes that $\widetilde{SUM}_7$ is active. Thus, $\widetilde{SUM}_7$ forms the header followed by the active program $\overline{A}_7$ [Fig. III.34(b)].

We now start to find program joiners for this state. The order of selection will depend on the program priorities. First, we test programs having PC = 9. Numerical value test 2 of $\widetilde{SUM}_6$ is negative since $TD_6 > TD_7$ (9 > 5).

Next we test programs with PC = 8. Numerical value test 2 of $\widetilde{SUM}_5$ is negative since $TD_5 > TD_7$ (9 > 5). We now test programs with PC = 7. Assignment test of SUM_1 is negative since $\overline{A} \cdot S = 1$ (it is assigned and active). Numerical value test 4 of $\widetilde{SUM}_8$ is negative since $k_7 + k_8 = 8 > n$, where $n = 7$.

Let us test programs with PC = 6. For SUM_3 and SUM_2, test 2 is negative since $TD_3 > TD_7$ (7 > 5) and $TD_2 > TD_7$ (7 > 5). For $\widetilde{SUM}_9$, all the assignment and numerical value tests are positive; $\widetilde{SUM}_9$ is the program joiner. The created state is $CR(N) = N_{59}$. It is complete [Fig. III.34(b)]. The original NAQ is purged of SUM_7 and SUM_9 [Fig. III.34(c)]. Since NAAQ is empty, the absorption process continues.

Fetch $\widetilde{SUM}_6$. Since M = 0, it is processed by Step 2. Since PC_6 is larger than that in the A header of N_{11}, $\widetilde{SUM}_6$ cannot be absorbed by N_{11}. The incompatibility of $\widetilde{SUM}_6$ and N_{59} was established before. Thus, $\widetilde{SUM}_6$ is tested for the CR process. The A header formed by $\widetilde{SUM}_6$ is shown in Fig. III.34(d). We now try to create new CR(N). Test programs with PC = 8. For SUM_5, all the assignment and numerical value tests give positive results. Thus $\widetilde{SUM}_5$ is the program joiner. The remaining equipment after joining $\widetilde{SUM}_5$ is specified with $\Delta = n - (k_6 + k_5) = 7 - (2 + 3) = 2$. Therefore, the join process may continue.

For PC = 8, SUM_8 cannot join since created delays are intolerable (test 2 is negative since $9 - 5 > D_0 = 2$). For PC = 6, SUM_2 can join, since $TD_6 - TD_2 = D_0$ (9 − 7 = 2, and $D_0 = 2$ is admissible delay). The new architectural state is $CR(N) = 010010 = N_{18}$. It is shown in Fig. III.34(d). The new status of NAQ is shown in Fig. III.34(e). ■

Note. During formation of N_{18}, the program SUM_2 formerly belonging to N_{11} and specified with $A \cdot S = 1$ (assigned and passive) has been absorbed by N_{18}. Thus, the state N_{11} which has contained it in the AQ becomes incomplete. Let us try to make N_{11} complete using nonassigned SUMs. The only nonassigned SUM remained in NAQ is SUM_8. It cannot be absorbed into the incomplete N_{11} since it requires 4 CE ($k_8 = 4$) for its dynamic computer, whereas the number of CEs that are free in N_{11} is $k_2 = 2$. Thus, SUM_8 is nonassignable since it is incompatible with other states, and it has M = 0. Therefore, NAAQ = {SUM_8}. The incomplete state N_{11} is tested for M = 1. Since M = 1, N_{11} can be computed incomplete. Therefore, the new status of AQ includes incomplete N_{11}, complete N_{59}, and complete N_{18}. NAAQ includes nonassignable SUM_8 [Fig. III.34(e)].

Several Observations about the Nature of Programs with M = 1. A program, P_M, having M = 1 is always active. Let us show that this program cannot be a (passive) program joiner in CR, nor can it be absorbed via RE as a passive program. Assume the opposite, that the program P_M with M = 1 is passive and it is absorbed by N. Sup-

(d)   CREATION of NEW ARCHITECTURAL STATE N_{18}

STATE N_{18} = $[C_1(2), C_3(3), C_6(2)]$

	bit A	TD	RE	PC	bit S	bit M	
A-header	1	9	1111111	9	0	0	
$\overline{A_6}$	1	9	1100000	9	0	0	N_{18}
$\overline{A_5}$	1	9	0011100	8	1	0	
$\overline{A_2}$	1	7	0000011	6	1	0	

(e)   STATUS of AQ, NAQ and NAAQ

FOLLOWING CREATION OF N_{18}

ASSIGNED QUEUE, AQ

	bit A	TD	RE	PC	bit S	bit M	
A-header	1	8	1111111	7	0	1	
$\overline{A_1}$	1	8	1110000	7	0	1	
$\overline{A_3}$	1	7	0000010	6	1	0	N_{11}- Incomplete
$\overline{A_4}$	1	7.5	0000001	5	1	0	
A-header	1	5	1111111	12	0	1	
$\overline{A_7}$	1	5	1111000	12	0	1	N_{59} Complete
$\overline{A_9}$	1	4	0000111	6	0	0	
A-header	1	9	1111111	9	0	0	
$\overline{A_6}$	1	9	1100000	9	0	0	N_{18} Complete
$\overline{A_5}$	1	9	0011100	8	1	0	
$\overline{A_2}$	1	7	0000011	6	1	0	

NON-ASSIGNED QUEUE, NAQ

	bit A	$\widetilde{TD}$	$\tilde{k}$	$\widetilde{PC}$	bit S	bit M
$\widetilde{SUM}_8$	0	6	4	7	0	0

NON-ASSIGNABLE QUEUE, NAAQ

	bit A	$\widetilde{TD}$	$\tilde{k}$	$\widetilde{PC}$	bit S	bit M
$\widetilde{SUM}_8$	0	6	4	7	0	0

Since for N_{11}, bit M = 1, it can be computed incomplete.
Since NAQ = NAAQ, the absorption ends.

FIGURE III.34(d, e)   Creation of new architectural state N_{18}

pose that such N absorbs P_M that the active program of N is characterized by M = 0. Also, assume that N becomes incomplete in some dynamic situation by being deprived of a program P' not coincident with P_M (P' ≠ P_M). Because incomplete state N is characterized by M = 0, the underutilization of resources cannot be tolerated and all programs of N are purged to NAQ (Steps 10 and 14). Thus P_M is also purged to NAQ and is denied its privileged status of guaranteed assignment and computation even in an incomplete N, which contradicts the functions that are assigned to bit M. Therefore, bit M becomes useless and there is no need for programs to be characterized with M = 1 or 0.

On the other hand, if P_M is active, state N that contains P_M is always specified with M = 1, which guarantees that this state will never be eliminated. This establishes the active status of any program that has M = 1.

5.6.4 Creation of the Architectural Sequences for Long and Tasked Programs

The creation process introduced so far has dealt only with the dynamic formation of a single architectural state. This required that all programs to be integrated into each such state be time compatible with one another in order not to create unwarranted idleness in the hardware equipment which exceeds D_0.

However, this is a severe restriction, since programs in the program mix may be characterized by a diversified spectrum of durations. To lift this restriction requires dynamic creation of a sequence of architectural states. Such a sequence will be called a t sequence. Generally, a t sequence, S, is made of t architectural states $S = N^{(1)} \rightarrow N^{(2)} \rightarrow \ldots \rightarrow N^{(t)}$ and is created during t iterations of the *noninterrupted process CR*.

Therefore, the general motivations behind dynamic creation of the t sequence are:

1. To lift a severe restriction on compatibility in program durations.
2. To allow a minimal time execution for multiple task active programs with the highest priority since each t sequence is created in its entirety with no interruption.

There are two types of t sequences: (1) a t sequence constructed for a long and single-tasked program, and (2) a t sequence constructed for a multiple-tasked program. Consider the differences and similarities between these two types of t sequences.

5.6.4.1 Long programs

If the t sequence is constructed for a *long* program, this program is 1-tasked and lasts all t states. † Therefore, the resources of this program are not requested for reconfiguration in each state $N^{(i)}$ ($i = 2, \ldots, t$) of the t sequence, other than the initial state $N^{(1)}$ (see Fig. III.35). The long program of the t sequence is always passive and all active programs of the t sequence must be assigned with the same priority in the monitor in order to have a noninterrupted creation and, if possible, a noninterrupted execution whenever the active program of the initial state $N^{(1)}$ is the highest in priority among all others available.

Once the long program of the t sequence is selected, the creation of each state, $N^{(i)}$, of the t sequence is similar to the one considered above using the system resources that are left for the assignment, after the assignment of the long program. The advantage of such creation is that it eliminates any restriction on the compatible duration of programs, because any long program can last t states, where $t > 1$, and state-to-state switches can be performed by active and short programs.

5.6.4.2 Tasked programs

A t sequence is constructed for a multiple-tasked program if the following conditions are satisfied:

---

†By introducing a simple *join* operation between two t sequences $S^{(1)}$ and $S^{(2)}$, we may form the sequence $S^{(1,2)} = S^{(1)}S^{(2)}$ that contains two long programs. By iterating the join operation r times, we obtain the sequence $S^{(1, \ldots, r)}$ that contains r long programs, etc.

a. This program is specified with the sequence made of t tasks, $TA_1 \rightarrow TA_2 \rightarrow \ldots \rightarrow TA_t$, where each task requires an individual computer size.

b. This program initiates all architectural transitions of the t sequence; i.e., it is active during the entire t-sequence execution.

For instance, in Fig. III.35, dynamic program P_1 is 3-tasked; i.e., it is partitioned into three tasks requiring, respectively, (1) a 32-bit computer, $C_1(2)$, (2) a 64-bit computer, $C_1(4)$, and (3) a 48-bit computer, $C_1(3)$. Also, program P_1 performs all the architectural transitions in $S = N_{42} \rightarrow N_{11} \rightarrow N_{24}$. Therefore, the t sequence, S, is constructed for P_1, where $t = 3$.

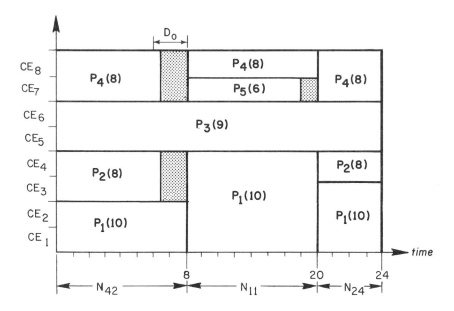

$$N_{42} = [C_1(2), C_3(2), C_5(2), C_7(2)]$$
$$N_{11} = [C_1(4), C_5(2), C_7(1), C_8(1)]$$
$$N_{24} = [C_1(3), C_4(1), C_5(2), C_7(2)]$$

FIGURE III.35 Handling long and tasked programs by a sequence of created states

In general, if a dynamic program is t tasked, each task must be represented with a separate $\widetilde{\text{SUM}}$ message and assigned to a separate architectural state, since any two tasks may have different and conflicting resource requirements on time of duration, TD, computer size, k, etc.

The next question to be solved is to find out when each $\widetilde{\text{SUM}}$ of the t-tasked program should be received in the monitor. There are two alternatives in this receipt.

Alternative 1. Each $\widetilde{\text{SUM}}_i$ for task TA_i is received in the monitor upon completion of the preceding task TA_{i-1}.

Alternative 2. For t-tasked program messages, the monitor receives the entire $\widetilde{\text{SUM}}$ *package* containing all t $\widetilde{\text{SUM}}$s of this program.

Let us show that alternative 2 is better since it minimizes the resulting program delays. Indeed, assume the opposite, i.e., the monitor receives every $\widetilde{\text{SUM}}_i$ only upon completion of the preceding task TA_{i-1}. In this case, the execution of task TA_i cannot start following completion of TA_{i-1}, since $\widetilde{\text{SUM}}_i$ is incomplete a priori inasmuch as it knows only of the individual resource needs of task TA_i. Therefore, between tasks TA_{i-1} and TA_i there is an inserted and sequential program delay aimed at dynamic assignment of $\widetilde{\text{SUM}}_i$ to a new architectural state even if the program priority warrants a noninterrupted execution of TA_i and TA_{i-1}.

To prevent this from happening, for a dynamic, active t-tasked program, the entire sequence of architectural states $S = N^{(1)} \rightarrow N^{(2)} \rightarrow \ldots \rightarrow N^{(t)}$ must be also created during a single noninterrupted process CR iterated t times, where each iteration creates one state of the sequence. This requires that the monitor receive an entire $\widetilde{\text{SUM}}$-package for creating the t sequence (Fig. III.36).

5.6.4.3 Similarities and Differences between Two Types of *t Sequences*

We can specify the following similarities and differences between the two types of t sequences introduced above.

Similarities

1. Each t sequence is created during a noninterrupted process, CR, iterated t times, where t is the number of architectural states.

2. All active programs of the t sequence are assigned the same priorities in order not to interrupt the creation of S and, if possible, not to interrupt computation of S.

3. Computation of the t sequence can be interrupted depending on the current priority situation.

Differences

1. If the t sequence is constructed for one long program, all architectural transitions in this sequence can be made by differing active programs which are assigned with the same priorities in the monitor. The long program is always passive in the t sequence and it is always 1-tasked.

PROGRAM P₁

	A	TD	k	PC	SEN	
SUM₁	O	8	2	10	1	...
SUM₁	O	12	4	10	2	...
SUM₁	O	4	3	10	3	...

PROGRAM P₂

	A	TD	k	PC	SEN	
SUM₂	O	8	2	8	I	...
SUM₂	O	4	1	8	2	...

PROGRAM P₄

	A	TD	k	PC	SEN	
SUM₄	O	6	2	8	1	...
SUM₄	O	14	1	8	2	...
SUM₄	O	4	2	8	3	...

FIGURE III.36   SUM packages for tasked programs

2.   If the *t* sequence is constructed for a *t* tasked program, this program is always active for the entire sequence; i.e., it activates all the transitions in this sequence. The $\widetilde{SUM}$ messages of this program are provided with special sequence codes, SEN (where SEN = 1, 2, ..., *t*), since they appear simultaneously in the monitor and the monitor must know about task precedence for this *t* sequence (Fig. III.36).

Note: The SEN code is introduced only in the SUM messages of *t*-tasked dynamic programs to provide sequential assignment of SUMs to architectural states. That is, for any pair of SUMs (SUM_i and SUM_j) representing TA_i and TA_j of the same program such that TA_j follows TA_i (not necessarily immediately), the two architectural states $N^{(i)}$ and $N^{(j)}$ that will integrate TA_i and TA_j must also be sequential in dynamic (noninterrupted) creation and computation (interrupted or noninterrupted); i.e., $N^{(i)}$ must be created before $N^{(j)}$ and must be executed before $N^{(j)}$. Without the SEN codes, the precedence rules in execution may be violated; i.e., SUM_j may be assigned to an earlier state $N^{(i)}$, since SUM_i and SUM_j are specified with the same priority and they appear concurrently in the monitor.

5.6.4.4 Combining the two types of t sequences

The two types of t sequences can be *combined* if the total duration of the t tasks for one type of t sequence is compatible with that of the long program for another type of t sequence.

Example. In Fig. III.35 there is a combined t sequence (where $t = 3$) constructed for the 3-tasked program P_1 and long program P_3, since these two programs are time compatible. Two other programs (P_2 and P_4) assigned to this 3 sequence are also multiple-tasked, whereas program P_5 is a single tasked. Programs P_2, P_3, P_4, and P_5 are passive. (In this figure, integers in parentheses show program priorities.)

The SUM packages of all multiple-tasked programs received by the monitor are shown in Fig. III.36. For program P_1, the SUM package contains three SUM_1 having the same priority code ($PC = 10$) and distinguished by three sequence codes $SEN = 1, 2$, and 3, and other codes (TD and k). Since during t-sequence creation, P_1 is nonassigned, bit $A = 0$. Similarly, one can form other SUM packages for P_2 and P_4, where P_2 is 2-tasked and P_4 is 3-tasked. The dynamic creation of this 3 sequence is initiated with the receipt of the SUM_1 package, provided other SUM packages are also available in the monitor. ■

We conclude this subsection with several observations about the completeness of active and passive programs in the t sequence. A t sequence accommodates the entire program only if this program is active and/or it is long. Therefore, if the program is passive and multiple tasked, it does not need to be absorbed into the same t sequence. Indeed, in every state of the t sequence a passive multiple-tasked program is always a program joiner with the priority not higher than that of some other programs of this state, since the active program of this state has a higher priority than any passive one. Therefore, a potential requirement that all tasks of the same passive program be assigned to the same t sequence of architectural states may violate the priority rules that are used in such an assignment and introduce the unwarranted program delays for high-priority programs because of this violation. Thus, a passive multiple-tasked program is not required to be assigned to the same t sequence.

Note: The noninterrupted creation of a t sequence, S, for long and/or active programs does not mean the noninterrupted execution of S. As a matter of fact, the execution of S may be interrupted if a dynamic program arrives with a higher priority than that of the executing architectural state. Such interrupt occurs only when a complete architectural state that integrates this higher-priority dynamic program is available. If this state is available because the arriving program requests the entire hardware resources, the architectural interrupt occurs immediately. Otherwise, the architectural interrupt follows the software creation process aimed at creating a new architectural state that can accommodate as active the arriving dynamic program with the highest priority among those currently available.

5.7 Program Start-up in the New Architectural State[†]

In general, program start-up is the last step of the architectural reconfiguration (see Step 10, multicomputer reconfiguration algorithm, Fig. II.2). For static programs, it starts immediately following establishment of new interconnections in the interconnection network since the required start-up state M(N) is stored in the monitor. For dynamic programs, the program start-up may follow the process of dynamic assignment aimed at either creation of a new architectural state, CR(N), or reassignment of the existing state RE(N), if the respective SUM message is nonassigned. For both types of programs, static and dynamic, the program start-up is reduced to execution of:

Action 1.   Organization of the one-to-one correspondence between the reconfiguration flow chart and the assigned queue of SUM messages.

Action 2.   Providing each dynamic computer of the new architectural state with all the necessary start information in order that this computer can start its independent and asynchronous computations.

5.7.1 Organization of the One-To-One Correspondence between the Reconfiguration Flow Chart and the Assigned Queue of SUM Messages

As was described in Chapter II, Sec. 3.2 (Resolution of Reconfiguration Conflicts), the reconfiguration flow chart is maintained in the monitor with the use of two registers, R1 and R2, that store current and the next allowed reconfiguration request messages, RRM, and denied resource handler that stores all denied RRMs [Fig. II.5(a, b, c)]. The monitor also maintains the assigned queue, AQ of SUM messages, in which each architectural state N is represented with the set of SUM messages, called the *start-up state* M(N).

Therefore, to organize the one-to-one correspondence between the reconfiguration flow chart and the assigned queue AQ, it is sufficient to let each allowed RRM fetch the respective start-up state from the assigned queue [Fig. III.34(e)]. Thus, the assigned queue must be maintained as a table, in which each start-up state can be fetched using the address $E = ID - PUC - N$ stored in the RRM, where ID is the

---

[†]The material of this subsection is closely related to Section 3 in Chapter II.

program identification code, PUC is the program user code, and N is the code of the architectural state [Fig. II.4(a)].

To maintain the computational overlap of dynamic assignment with the execution of the reconfiguration flow chart, it is necessary that each arriving RRM perform concurrently two independent processes:

a. Conflict resolution
b. Checking availability of the start-up state, M(N)

If for the arriving RRM the start-up state can be fetched from the assigned queue, then action 2 is carried out as the last part of Step 10 (Fig. II.2). It is aimed at the distribution of the start-up information among individual dynamic computers.

Otherwise, RRM is put on *hold* operation as H-RRM, whereby it initiates the architectural creation or reassignment. To this end, it generates either an individual SUM message or a SUM package. Next, it sends a newly created SUM into the nonassigned queue, NAQ, and triggers the absorption process aimed at absorption of the nonassigned queue, NAQ, with the assigned queue, AQ (Fig. III.33).

During the hold action for the H-RRM, the reconfiguration flow chart continues execution of other allowed RRM messages (RRM ≠ H-RRM) that are specified with complete start-up states. For static programs, the required start-up states are always available in the AQ queue. Thus, the hold operation may occur only for nonassigned dynamic programs.

For any such program, its H-RRM messages has an empty N field designated for the architectural state [Fig. II.4(a)], since an H-RRM represents only the individual computer(s) that it must use in computations and does not know of any other dynamic computers that can be integrated into the same architectural state. If an H-program is single tasked, the H-RRM messages forms a single SUM message (Fig. III.27). If an H program is t tasked, the H-RRM message forms the entire SUM package made of t SUMs (Fig. III.36). Therefore, in addition to the codes shown in Fig. II.4, an H-RRM message of every dynamic program must store other codes (TD, PC, and k) that allow execution of creation and reassignment processes for a single architectural state or t sequences. The Hold operation ends when the held H-RRM forms either CR(N) or RE(N).

In general, each such completion signals stripping H-RRM of its hold status to become $\overline{\text{H}}$-RRM. Specific actions to be executed in the monitor depend on what type of dynamic state has been formed by this $\overline{\text{H}}$-RRM. If $\overline{\text{H}}$-RRM has generated a dynamic state CR(N) that wins the current reconfiguration conflict, there follows an architectural interrupt (current or next) triggered by this CR(N).

If $\overline{\text{H}}$-RRM has generated a denied dynamic state CR(N), this $\overline{\text{H}}$-RRM is sent to the denied resource handler, DRH. When $\overline{\text{H}}$-RRM is accessed again, it no longer needs dynamic assignment, since a required dynamic architectural state has already been created.

If $\overline{\text{H}}$-RRM has reassigned dynamic state RE(N), this state can never win the reconfiguration conflict at the moment of reassignment, since the priority of $\overline{\text{H}}$-RRM is not higher than that of the active program assigned to RE(N). Therefore, $\overline{H}$-RRM loses its active status and no longer needs to be remembered in the DRH unit. It acquires the status of a passive program whose reconfiguration needs will be represented by the only active program of RE(N). Thus the $\overline{H}$-RRM which generates RE(N) can be destroyed. The same is true about the reconfiguration request messages of all dynamic joiners of any CR(N). Since they have also lost their active status during creation of CR(N), their $\overline{H}$-RRM messages can be destroyed.

5.7.2 Distribution of Start-Up Information among Dynamic Computers

This process starts when the required start-up state is fetched from the assigned queue [Fig. III.34(e)]. Using the requested equipment code of every dynamic computer of this state, the monitor sends to this computer all the individual information associated with the basic address, BA, of the program and the address of the memory element, ME, that stores a current program segment in the new architectural state. Therefore, in its $\overline{A}$ zone, each SUM message must store the individual start-up information that allows an individual program start-up in the next architectural state.

6 CONCLUSIONS TO CHAPTER III

This chapter has dealt with the material dedicated to the software design of a reconfiguration flow chart. It was established that such a design is reduced to the resource assignment of programs to the available resources, since any reconfiguration flow chart can be obtained automatically from the resource (assignment) diagram which is constructed by the assignment process.

6.1 Optimization Criteria Used in Resource Assignment for Different Computing Structures

It was shown that different computing structures may require application of different optimization criteria during resource assignment. For dynamic multicomputer systems, an optimal assignment must minimize possible program delays and execute each program (member of the program mix) in the dynamic computer required by this program and at the earliest moment of time which is possible under circumstances.

For the reconfigurable binary tree, an optimal resource assignment is associated with the minimization of communication delays in node-to-node communications, since only this type of optimization allows each local program consumer not to be delayed due to the nonavailability of the required data words produced by other node(s) producer(s). Therefore, for reconfigurable binary trees, the multicomputer optimization criteria work on the level of separate nodes that act as independent multicomputers, since it is the objective of local resource assignments to minimize program delays and shorten possible moments of program completion (i.e., to apply the optimization criteria of multicomputer assignment).

The introduced techniques of resource assignment have shown that reconfiguration is an extremely powerful factor aimed at achieving the criteria of the respective resource assignment. For instance, as will be shown in Chapter 5, dedicated to *algorithm development,* the use of reconfiguration for multicomputer resource assignment achieves a 42% speed-up in the total program execution time in comparison with that afforded by static computer systems for the same program mixes. The nature of this speed-up is in the capability of dynamic architecture to execute each program in the minimal-size computer and to maximize the number of concurrent programs that can be executed in the system.

The performance improvement for the reconfigurable binary tree established with the use of contributed assignment algorithms is even more dramatic and constitutes 370%. Namely, a reconfigurable binary tree may execute the same assortment of node-to-node data exchanges 370% faster than that afforded in any static binary tree. The nature of this improvement is associated with the capability of reconfiguration to minimize path durations and maximize path concurrency, by computing each critical (main) data exchange in the best tree configuration and assigning this tree configuration with other concurrent exchanges that do not increase the time of the critical exchange.

6.2 Static and Dynamic Assignments

Another division which is applied in this chapter to the overall problem of resource assignment for an arbitrary computing structure is to divide a resource assignment into static and dynamic.

A *static resource assignment* is applied to program mixes for which all the resource needs of the individual programs (members of these mixes) are known before the assignment process. These programs are called *static.* Therefore, any static assignment is capable of handling the needs of static programs in a nonconflicing manner by constructing an optimal resource assignment diagram which uniquely specifies the static reconfiguration flow chart.

A *dynamic resource assignment* is applied to program mixes which include static and dynamic programs.

If the resource needs of a static program are taken into account in the construction of the static reconfiguration flow chart, the resource needs of a dynamic program are not, since a dynamic program may arrive when the static reconfiguration flow chart is executing in the system.

Thus, it is the task of the monitor to modify a static reconfiguration flow chart with either a newly created architectural state(s) or a reassigned architectural state(s) which takes into account the resource needs of dynamic programs. Such modification is performed concurrently with system execution by an independent absorption process triggered by the reconfiguration request message of the dynamic program.

Therefore, dynamic assignment creates no idleness in the computer resources since dynamic architecture may interrupt a current or next architectural state only upon availability of the newly created state

This segment of the chapter has introduced the optimal techniques of static and dynamic assignment for dynamic multicomputer systems. The optimization criteria for both dynamic assignments are the same and are aimed at minimization of program delays and fulfillment of the program resource needs, aimed at creation of the dynamic computer(s) needed by each program.

Therefore, the major role of any dynamic assignment in overall performance optimization is in its capability to modify a static reconfiguration flow chart created by static assignment by introducing such techniques of this modification that reflect the resource needs of dynamic programs which have not been considered in the construction of the static reconfiguration flow chart. Therefore, without dynamic assignment a static reconfiguration flow chart will remain unmodified and will thus be unable to meet the new challenging and unpredictable computational requirements of dynamic programs.

Also, it is only a dynamic assignment that introduces reconfiguration conflicts, whereby a dynamic program is assigned to a newly created architectural state which is in reconfiguration conflict with either the current or next architectural state of a reconfiguration flow chart. As was indicated above, there are no conflicts for static resource assignments, since it is always possible to plan future reconfigurations in a nonconflicting manner using ordered program priorities if all request needs of participating programs are known before the assignment. On the other hand, for dynamic assignment it is fundamentally impossible to perform such nonconflicting planning, since it is impossible to predict the priority of any arriving program without violation of the spontaneity and dynamic nature of its arrival.

Therefore, the significance of this chapter in the overall volume is in its capability to focus the reader's attention on different types of resource assignments characterized by different optimization criteria (multicomputer and binary tree) and to signify the role, distinctions, and application areas of static and dynamic resource assignments.

Chapter IV

Dynamic Compiler

The objectives of this chapter are as follows:

1. To outline the effect of dynamic reconfiguration on some popular ADA constructs, such as packages, task rendezvous, and exceptions handling.
2. To give memory management techniques for some data structures created dynamically.

This chapter contains only preliminary research results. Continuation of research in the area is the subject of future research by these authors. Also, some of the material of this chapter depends on material discussed in other chapters. To avoid repetition, the reader is referred to those chapters.

Below is a description of the topics that fall under categories 1 and 2.

1   THE EFFECT OF DYNAMIC RECONFIGURATION ON ADA LANGUAGE CONSTRUCTS

In general, dynamic reconfiguration greatly simplifies the compilation of ADA-oriented programs since it allows the creation of a dynamic match between an ADA construct and the hardware structure created dynamically that supports this construct.

Before describing the effect of reconfiguration on Ada constructs we will introduce some basic concepts of Ada language which will be used in our discussion. Thereafter, we will show how the power and performance of these constructs are improved in the dynamically reconfigurable hardware environment epitomized by dynamic architectures, since these architectures create a natural modular base for dynamic implementation (creation) of Ada constructs in hardware

In presenting basic Ada concepts (package, task rendezvous, and exception handling), we will adopt basic definitions and programming examples that illustrate them from the book, *Ada, An Introduction,* † because of their lucidity and succinctness. The readers of this book are referred to this publication if they would like to enrich their understanding of and experience in Ada.

1.1 ADA Packages

As shown in the literature [10-13, 25, 26], an ADA package covers a wide range of uses, including named collections of common data, groups of related subprograms that collectively carry out some activity, and definitions of private types with specialized operations. In general, by a package we mean a language construct that warrants a separate compilation independent of other packages.

1.1.1 Visible Part

Every package is specified by giving a list of declarative information. This declarative information can be made accessible to a user and is called its *visible part.* While a package defines a collection of information, the information is not directly visible to other program units. One way to refer to an identifier declared in a package is with a name in the dot notation form:

package-name.declared-identifier

For example, consider the package *WEATHER__DATA* introduced as follows:

package WEATHER__DATA is
      ALTITUDE   :   *array (-90 .. 90, -90 .. 90) of Fixed;*
      TEMPERATURE :   *array (-90 .. 90, -90 .. 90) of Fixed;*
      WIND__SPEED :   *array (-90 .. 90, -90 .. 90) of Fixed;*
end;

Array *WIND__SPEED* can be denoted with the name

WEATHER__DATA.WIND__SPEED

and thus have the assignment

WEATHER__DATA.WIND__SPEED (I,J)   := *WIND__READING;*

Therefore, using the dot notation we may reference a selected portion of the package. If, on the other hand, the entire visible part should be referenced, we are using a *use* clause at the beginning of the unit. For example, we may have the subprogram

---

†Henry Ledgard, *ADA, An Introduction*, 2nd ed. (Springer-Verlag, 1983).

```
procedure UPDATE_WEATHER_DATA is
    use WEATHER_DATA;

    I, J: INTEGER range -90 .. 90;
    ALT_READING, TEMP_READING, WIND_READING: FLOAT;

begin

    GET_ZONE_COORDINATES (I,J);
    GET_SENSOR_VALUES (ALT_READING, TEMP_READING, WIND
    READING);

    ALTITUDE      (I,J)   := ALT_READING;
    TEMPERATURE   (I,J):= TEMP_READING;
    WIND_SPEED    (I,J):= WIND_READING;

end;
```

The effect of the use clause is to make the identifiers declared in WEATHER_DATA directly visible in the program unit containing the use clause. Thus, we see that the information in a package is made visible on a selective basis.

1.1.2 Private Information

Consider the following package:

```
package SIMPLE_I_O IS
    type FILE_NAME is private;
        procedure CREATE  (F:  out FILE_NAME);
        procedure READ    (F:  in FILE_NAME;  ITEM:  out INTEGER);
        procedure WRITE   (F:  in FILE_NAME;  ITEM:  in  INTEGER);
private
    type FILE_NAME is the range 0 .. 50;
end;

package body SIMPLE_I_O is
    — implementation of file handling procedures
end;
```

A user of this package can declare variables of type FILE_NAME and can pass these variables to the procedures CREATE, READ, and WRITE. However, because the type FILE_NAME is declared as private, the user cannot make use of the fact that this type is internally defined as an integer; that is, the user cannot perform arithmetic on variables of type FILE_NAME. The only language defined operations that can be used are assignment and comparison for equality or inequality.

If we wish, even these operations can be forbidden by declaring FILE_NAME as a *limited* private type, as in:

```
type FILE_NAME is limited private;
```

In either case, the visible part of the package is followed by a *private part,* in which the full type definition of each private type is given. This form is characteristic of situations where we want complete control over the operations of a type.

1.1.3 Creation of ADA Packages in Dynamic Architecture

Dynamic architecture greatly facilitates creation of ADA packages inasmuch as reconfiguration may create additional links among such information arrays that in static computer systems are totally disjoint. [By a disjoint pair $(IA_i IA_j)$ of two information arrays IA_i and IA_j, we mean those that can be used together only following a data transfer $ME_i \rightarrow ME_j$ or $ME_j \rightarrow ME_i$, where ME_i stores IA_i and ME_j stores IA_j.]

If an ADA package contains only a data part and no functional part, it identifies a data structure created out of participating MEs. If an ADA package contains the two parts functional and data it identifies a computing structure created out of participating CEs. Both structures can be made reconfigurable using the reconfiguration mechanisms implemented in hardware. The assignment of memory and processor resources that support reconfigurable memory structures and reconfigurable computing structures identifiable with the two types of packages is similar to the one discussed in Secs. 3.3.2 to 3.6, Chapter III and dedicated to the reconfiguration flow chart that was constructed for the general-purpose program mix.

Example.   Consider the Weather__Data package introduced above. It includes only a data part consisting of three two-dimensional data arrays A_1, A_2, and A_3 that store information on altitude, temperature, and wind speed received from the sensors. Suppose that we are dealing with 48-bit sensors that give 48 bits of fixed-point digital information transformed from the continuous form. Then we will store A_1, A_2, and A_3 arrays in parallel cells of ME_1, ME_2, and ME_3 [Fig. IV.1(a)]. That is, each 48-bit memory word is made of three 16-bit bytes stored in ME_1, ME_2, and ME_3 under the same relative address, A_p. The major advantage of such data storage is in parallel word access of variable-size data words, since a $16 \cdot k$-bit data word may be accessed in parallel when all k ME receive the same relative address A_p of the byte location in the memory. For our case, $k = 3$ and a 48-bit data word is read in or read out in parallel during one interval of memory access. Another advantage is in implementing the universality of the programs principle, since the vertical size of each data array becomes independent of the computer word size. For instance, if A_1, A_2, and A_3 arrays are received from 64-bit sensors, then the vertical sizes of these arrays remain unchanged, provided the same number of coordinates is used. What is changed, however, is the horizontal word size, since a 64-bit data word will be stored in a parallel cell made of four 16-bit bytes requiring four MEs for storage [Fig. IV.1(b)].   ■

1.1.4 Access to a Visible Part of the Package

This can be done conventionally using the base address of the entire package array in the memory; or when the dot notation form of access is used, only one array out of many is accessed. For instance, for the procedure *Update__Weather__Data* that

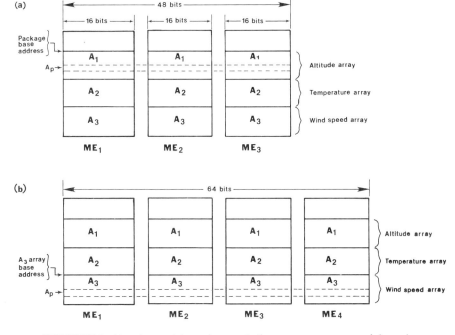

FIGURE IV.1 Mapping an Ada package onto the memory resources of dynamic architecture

is using the Weather__Data package, to access this package is sufficient to specify the package base address, 100 (see Fig. IV.1). To access Wind__Speed array in the Weather__Data package is sufficient to specify the base address of the A_3 array.

1.1.5 Selective Access to a Private Part of the Package

Since an ADA package may contain private information, this must be accessed on a strictly selective basis. That is, some users should be given a privilege to use this information. Others are not. (If no users can have such privilege, the private information becomes useless and there is no sense in storing it in the memory.)

To provide such selectivity of accessing for package private parts and independent compilation of package visible parts, private parts must be stored in separate locations other than visible parts. Only then can visible parts be compiled separately and independently.

Next, a special private table must be built and updated by the operating system which shows what user programs are allowed privileged information contained in all private parts of all packages. When each such program requires privileged information, it executes a special instruction that fetches the current program status regarding accessing a particular private file. If this accessing is allowed, then the private file is accessed. Otherwise, the accessing is prohibited.

Therefore, to implement the independence of compilation for package visible parts and selective accessing for package private parts the following memory management for private parts will be used. All private parts of all ADA packages stored in the primary memory are assigned a special memory array whereby each private part is given a separate memory space, MS. Thereafter, a special *private table* is created in which rows are marked with program user codes, PUC, and the columns are marked with memory spaces, MS. The intersection (PUC, MS) shows the base address for the given PUC and the number of words which are allowed access. If no access is allowed, the intersection (PUC, MS) is filled with zeros.

Example. Consider selective access to private information shown in Fig. IV.2. Suppose that we have five memory spaces MS_1 to MS_5 assigned to store five private parts of all ADA packages (Fig. IV.2). Suppose that the system with dynamic architecture executes four user programs assigned with user codes from PUC_1 to PUC_4. A private table for selective accessing of private portions of ADA packages is shown in Fig. IV.2.

As seen, this table consists of four rows PUC_1 through PUC_4 and five columns MS_1 through MS_5. The intersection (PUC_i, MS_j) shows a base address and the number of memory words from MS_j which are allowed to be accessed by PUC_i. If no access is allowed, the intersection is empty. For instance, (PUC_1, MS_1) intersection stores base address 500 of MS_1 and the number of words, 100, that PUC_1 can access from this MS_1. This means that PUC_1 is privileged to access the entire private file. Other programs are not allowed to access MS_1. Thus, their (PUC_i, MS_1) intersections are

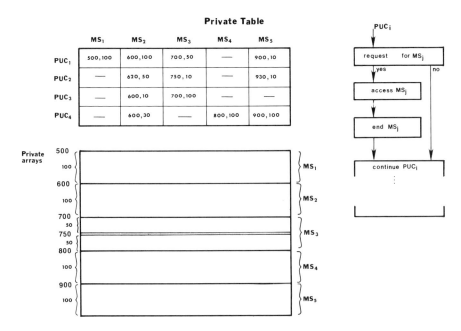

FIGURE IV.2 Selective access to a private part of an Ada package

empty. The private space MS_2 is allowed to be accessed by all current users. However, PUC_1 may access the entire array made of 100 words; PUC_2 may access only 50 words of MS_2, beginning with base address 620; PUC_3 may access only 10 words of MS_2, beginning with base address 600; etc. Other entries of this private table are self-explanatory.

When the user program PUC_i enters the phase when it needs private file MS_j, it executes special instruction "Request for MS_j" (Fig. IV.2). Execution of this instruction consists of forming the effective address, PUC_iMS_j, and fetching the array of entries specified with this address. If this array is empty, the access is prohibited and PUC_i branches to the next executable portion. If this array is not empty, it contains the allowable base address of MS_j and the number of words from MS_j that can be accessed. Program PUC_i performs the access specified and executes a subroutine aimed at processing the data words fetched from the private file MS_j. This subroutine is a part of privileged information fetched during accessing MS_j. This subroutine is ended with the special *End* MS_i instruction that specifies the end of privileged processing specified by the operating system. Thereafter, PUC_i continues execution which it would have entered otherwise should no privileged access be allowed. ∎

1.1.6 Conclusions

As described above, dynamic architecture greatly enhances the creation of ADA packages, i.e., those compiling items that can be compiled independently of other packages. Accessing the totality or a portion of a visible part of the package is performed with the use of the base address of the qualified visible part of the entire package array. Selective accessing of the private part of the package is performed with the use of a special private table whose construction and use were described above. The advantage of such organization is that the operating system may fill up this table with entries that reflect a current status of privileged access for a given set of user programs. Also, the techniques introduced support independence of compilation for visible and private parts of ADA packages.

1.2 Task Rendezvous

An ADA task is a program unit that can be executed concurrently with other program units. In the environment of a reconfigurable parallel system, one must organize such communication among tasks that support ADA-oriented *task rendezvous.*

1.2.1 Description of Task Rendezvous Construct

A task that calls for communication will be specified as a *calling task*. A calling task issues an entry call. A task that accepts communication will be specified as a *called task*. It issues an accept statement, whereby it is prepared to accept the entry call made by a calling task. Thus the calling and the called tasks may be considered meeting in a *rendezvous.*

Example. Consider the task for the three tasks GENERATE__CODES, DECODE, and PRINT__MESSAGES, given by the following task bodies:

Task 1

```
task body GENERATE__CODES is
    NEXT__CODE: CHARACTER;
begin
    loop

        --statements for receiving data
        --and generating a value for NEXT__CODE

        DECODE.SEND__CODE (NEXT__CODE); --entry call
    end loop;
end;
```

Task 2

```
task body DECODE is
    CODE, CHAR: CHARACTER;
begin
    loop
        accept SEND__CODE (C: in CHARACTER) DO
            CODE : = C;
        end;

        --statements for decoding the value of CODE
        --and producing the decoded value in CHAR

        accept RECEIVE__CHAR (C: out CHARACTER) do
            C : = CHAR̄;
        end;
    end loop;
end;
```

For the task PRINT MESSAGES:

Task 3

```
task body PRINT__MESSAGES is
    LINE__SIZE       :  constant INTEGER   := 72;
    NEXT__CHAR     :  CHARACTER;
    LINE__POSITION:  INTEGER;
    LINE             :  STRING (1 .. LINE-SIZE);
begin
    LINE__POSITION : = 1;
    loop
        DECODE.RECEIVE__CHAR (NEXT__CHAR); -- entry call
        LINE (LINE__POSITION) := NEXT__CHAR;
```

```
        if LINE__POSITION < LINE__SIZE then
          LINE__POSITION := LINE__POSITION + 1;
        else
            PRINT (LINE);
            LINE__POSITION := 1;
        end if;
      end loop;
   end;
```

The relationship between these tasks is shown in Fig. IV.3. Task 1 generates codes out of input characters. Task 2 receives codes issued by task 1 and decodes them into characters. Task 3 receives characters generated by task 2 and prints messages. Also, since tasks 1 and 3 issue entry calls, they are calling tasks. Since task 2 accepts both entry calls, it is a called task. When task 2 accepts the entry call of task 1, this means that it accepts each code generated by task 1. When task 2 accepts an entry call of task 3, this means that it sends to task 3 each character it generates. ■

There are two possibilities for a rendezvous according to whether the calling task issues a calling statement before or after a corresponding accept statement is reached by the called task. Whichever gets there first waits for the other, with some qualifications described below. When the rendezvous is achieved, the arguments of the entry call are passed to the called task if the calling task *produces* data words and the called task *consumes* these data words. Otherwise, the accept statement of the called task generates the parameters of data array, which are then passed to a calling task that in this case consumes these data words.

The accept statement of the called task is embraced by *do* and *end*, which delimit the actions of the called task in response to an entry call. When the rendezvous occurs, both tasks proceed independently of each other. We thus see the three basic notions achieved with a rendezvous.

* *Synchronization:* The calling task must issue an entry call, and the called task must reach a corresponding accept statement.

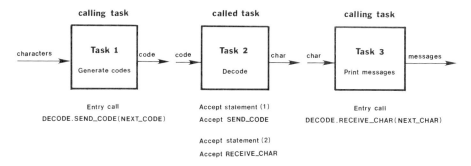

FIGURE IV.3 Task rendezvous illustration

- *Exchange of information:* The entry can have parameters and thus receive or transmit values.
- *Mutual exclusion:* If two or more tasks generate the same entry, only one entry can be accepted at a time.

Notice that the rendezvous is named in one direction only. The calling task must know the name of the called task (containing the accept statement). The called task, on the other hand, will accept calls from any task. However, it must know the source of each entry call. Thus, in general, we have a many-to-one pattern of communication whereby several calling tasks may call the same called task. As a consequence, a called task may have a queue of tasks calling it. Any such calls are processed in the order of arrival.

1.2.2 Organization of Task Rendezvous in Dynamic Architecture

Both the detailed organization of the bus structure and basic software solutions for the operating system that supports the task rendezvous are discussed in Chapter V, Sec. 3. Here we discuss the major software organizations involved. The assessment of the adopted software organization is discussed in Sec. 1.2.3 of this chapter.

In dynamic architecture, the task rendezvous is accomplished by the two processor operating systems, POS, residing in two PEs designated to compute a calling task, B and a called task, A, respectively. Assume that a calling task B is computed by processor element, PE_B. Thus local POS_B is calling for exchange. The POS_B is activated by the communication request instruction, CR, issued by calling task B. (The organization of this instruction is described in Chapter V, Sec. 3.1.2.2).

1.2.2.1 Request message issued by the calling task

Having executed CR-instruction, POS_B forms a request message, RM_B, with the format shown in Fig. IV.4. It contains the identification part, ID, and the control part. The ID is the position code of the destination PE that computes the called task. The control part includes the following codes:

1. Two program user codes, PUC_B and PUC_A, for calling task B and called task A.
2. Priority code PC_B of calling task B and the tentative duration (optional) of exchange TDE (these codes are used for priority analysis provided a requested page is being used).
3. The (optional) requested page address, RPA, if the calling task is producer.
4. A special status bit, SB = P or C, where SB = P means that the calling task produces data and SB = C means that the calling task consumes data.

1.2.2.2 Deposit table

Since the basic data array parameters (array dimension, d, base address of the array, BA, and page address, PA, of the array) are known only to a task producer (called

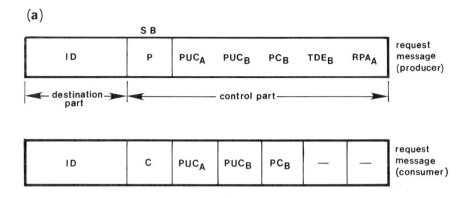

FIGURE IV.4   Formats of two request messages for the task producer and the
task consumer

or calling), the major problem of any task rendezvous is in passing these parameters
to a task consumer (called or calling).

Below, one organization is described that totally eliminates the waiting time involved in task rendezvous if the task producer produces data words before they can
be consumed. That is, if a task producer, either calling or called, generates the respective statement (entry call or accept) before the task consumer (called or calling) consumes the data array, no delay in rendezvous is involved, even if both statements issued
by the two tasks are separated in time. When this organization is used, the only source
of delay in this organization of rendezvous is when a task consumer issues a call for
request or acceptance of task rendezvous before the task producer produces data words
involved in data exchanges.

The basic idea that supports this organization is in constructing a *deposit table*
that resides in the destination PE_A computing a called task. Below is a justification of
why a deposit table should be stored in the destination (and not source) PE.

Most of the time a called task is a task producer which generates a data array that
can be consumed by several calling tasks consumers. Since each calling task consumer
may reside in a separate source, PE, an alternative organization of storing a deposit

table in a source PE (rather than the destination PE) would have required duplication of the same deposit table in all sources which may require rendezvous with the same destination, which is totally unwarranted.

The deposit table stores the following parameters of an accessed data array: array dimension, d; base address, BA; and page address, PA. † These parameters are always deposited to the deposit table by the task that *produces* data. The task that *consumes* data always reads d, BA, and PA from the deposit table. Therefore, if calling task PUC_B consumes data to be produced by the called task PUC_A, then PUC_A supplies d, BA, and PA. Otherwise, they are supplied by PUC_B.

Therefore, the deposit table is organized as follows. Its rows are marked by calling tasks, PUC_B, its columns are marked by called tasks, PUC_A; the intersection (PUC_A, PUC_B) is either empty or filled with d, BA, and PA. If it is empty, then d, BA, and PA have not yet been deposited or tasks A and B do not meet in a rendezvous. If (PUC_A, PUC_B) is not empty, then d, BA, and PA have been deposited by the task producer (either called or calling) [Fig. IV.4(b)].

Such organization of the deposit table allows convenient programming flexibility for the case when the same called task producer must generate one data array for several calling consumers. Different consumers may not need the whole array but only certain portions specified with different base addresses (BA_i), array dimensions (d_i), and even page addresses (PA_i) if the array occupies several pages. This flexibility in organizing all the specific needs of the consumers of the same data array can be easily accomplished by writing specific entries d_i and BA_i into the same producer column, PUC (A), and different consumer rows specified by the calling consumers.

1.2.2.3 Actions of the destination operating system

In this section we will discuss the actions of the destination operating system POS_A in response to either an entry call issued by the calling task B or an accept statement issued by the called task A.

Case 1: Handling a Request for Rendezvous

As was indicated above, an entry call for rendezvous is equivalent to execution of the communication request instruction that forms the request message RM_B shown in Fig. IV.4(a). When the request message RM_B is received by the destination operating system POS_A, it executes the following algorithm (Fig. IV.5).

Algorithm for Arranging a Rendezvous. The essence of the algorithm is to arrange the rendezvous between a calling task B that resides in CE_B and a called task A that resides in CE_A. Depending on the content of the (PUC_A, PUC_B) entry of the deposit table and the meaning of the SB bit of the request message RM_B received in the destination POS_A, the following types of rendezvous will be distinguished:

---

†Sometimes the d parameter is not known since it is determined by the task consumer. For this case, the end of the array is ended with a special *end-word*, and the task consumer accesses only a needed portion of the entire array.

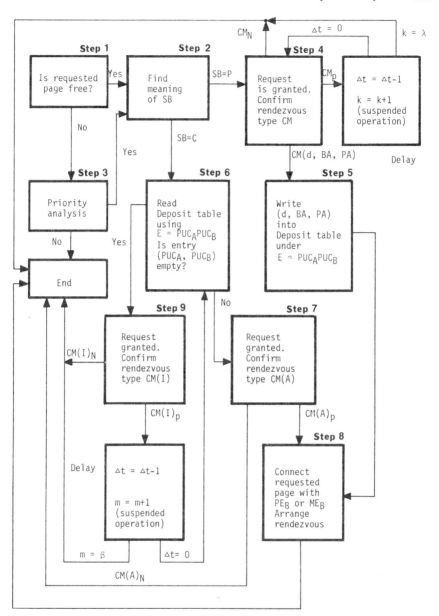

FIGURE IV.5 Algorithm for arranging a task rendezvous in dynamic architecture

a. Type CM(A), when data array parameters are available; i.e., $(PUC_A, PUC_B) \neq 0$.

b. Type CM(I), if $SB = C$ and $(PUC_A, PUC_B) = 0$; i.e., the calling task is the consumer, and the data array is not yet produced by the producer-called task.

c. Type CM, if SB = P and (PUC$_A$, PUC$_B$) = 0; i.e., the calling task is the producer and it did not yet produce the data array.

The algorithm starts with the common part and then branches into three different types, CM(A), CM(I) or CM, depending on the type of rendezvous. The common part is triggered into execution by the arriving RM$_B$.

First, the algorithm finds if a requested page of its local memory, ME$_A$, is free (Step 1). If it is not, the priority analysis is performed (Step 3). Otherwise, the SB bit of the RM$_B$ message is analyzed (Step 2). If the priority analysis is positive, SB bit is found, too (Step 2). Thereafter, the algorithm branches into rendezvous of different types introduced above.

Rendezvous Type CM(A). Because this type of rendezvous is characterized by the availability of d, BA, and PA in the deposit table, they can be written to the (PUC$_A$, PUC$_B$) location by either a calling task for the case B is a producer or by a called task A for the case B is a consumer. Since RM$_B$ requests this array, B cannot be its producer and its SB = C.

Therefore, this rendezvous type starts with Step 6, which fetches data array parameters (d, BA, PA) from the (PUC$_A$, PUC$_B$) location of the deposit table. Thereafter, POS$_A$ sends the acceptance statement to POS$_B$ and requests that POS$_B$ send one of two types of confirmation messages: CM(A)$_P$ (positive), confirming rendezvous, or CM(A)$_N$ (negative), denying rendezvous (Step 7). Upon receipt of CM(A)$_P$, the requested page in ME$_A$ is connected to either PE$_B$ or ME$_B$ (Step 8). Upon receipt of CM(A)$_N$, the algorithm ends.

Rendezvous Type CM(I). This type of rendezvous occurs if the calling task is a consumer but the array parameters (d, BA, PA) have not yet been deposited by the called task A (Step 6). Therefore, POS$_A$ requests POS$_B$ to confirm the intended rendezvous (Step 9) using either negative confirmation CM(I)$_N$ or positive confirmation CM(I)$_P$. If CM(I)$_N$, the algorithm is ended. If CM(I)$_P$, delay Δt is introduced whereby POS$_A$ suspends operation until $\Delta t = 0$. When $\Delta t = 0$, the iterative loop (6, 9) is repeated. If (PUC$_A$, PUC$_B$) is empty, the total number of iterations is restricted by integer β selected by the programmer; then the algorithm ends. If the (PUC$_A$, PUC$_B$) entry becomes nonempty (i.e., it has been deposited with the called task), the rendezvous is transformed into type CM(A), which is characterized by the availability of the data array.

Rendezvous Type CM. Rendezvous type CM occurs if calling task B is a data producer (Step 2) and array parameters are not available. This means that B must send three array parameters, d, BA, and PA, to processor element PE$_A$ and deposit the data array to ME$_A$. Thus, in Step 4, POS$_A$ requests from POS$_B$ one of the three types of confirmation messages: CM$_N$ negative confirmation, meaning that B called off the rendezvous; CM$_P$, positive confirmation without array parameters; CM (d, BA, PA)$_P$, positive confirmation with (d, BA, PA). If CM$_N$, the algorithm ends. If CM$_P$, then the algorithm performs a delay phase whereby the operating system suspends involvement until $\Delta t = 0$. Again, it executes a new iteration of Step 4 and requests confirmation of type CM. Step 4 iterates until either positive confirmation CM (d, BA, PA)$_P$

with array parameters is received, or the number of iterations k becomes λ ($k = \lambda$, where λ is chosen by the programmer).

If array parameters (d, BA, PA) are issued by the calling task, then they are written to the deposit table under address $E = \text{PUC}_A \text{ PUC}_B$ (Step 5), and the algorithm performs transition to Step 8 aimed at connecting a requested page residing in ME_A to either PE_B or ME_B, depending on the request type.

Case 2: Handling an Acceptance for Rendezvous

When a called task generates an accept statement, this is similar to execution of the accept instruction that generates an accept message for the local operating system (Fig. IV. 6). The format of the accept message for the consumer and producer case is similar to that of the request message considered above. The only difference is in the absence of the ID code for the accept message, since it is designed for the local operating system. The algorithm performed by the operating system, POS_A, is similar to the one performed by POS_A when it handles request message RM_B.

Example. Suppose that calling task PUC_3 computed by CE_3 requests to produce 50 data words into memory page 7 of ME_5. Suppose that this data array will be consumed by called task PUC_5, computed by CE_5. We assume that the entry call made by PUC_3 occurs at moment $t = 50$, and the accept statement issued by PUC_5 occurs at the moment $t = 70$. We also assume that the called task PUC_5 will be using page 7 only when it issues the accept statement. [Fig. IV.7 (a)]. Thus, when 50 data words are deposited into page 7, it is free.

Let us show that with the use of the deposit table neither task PUC_3 nor task PUC_5 need to wait for rendezvous. It occurs automatically, since task PUC_3 deposits data words into page 7 shortly after the moment $t = 50$ when it issues an entry call, and task PUC_5 consumes these data words when it issues the accept statement at moment $t = 70$. Indeed, when task PUC_3 executes an entry call, it is equivalent to executing a communication request instruction, CR, which forms the following request message RM_3 [Fig. IV.7 (b)].

a. ID $= 5$, since destination CE_5 has position code $i = 5$.

b. Status bit SB $= $ P, since PUC_3 is a producer.

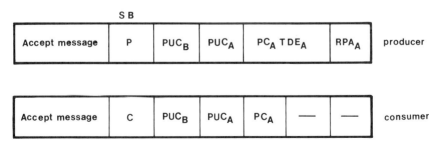

	S B				
Accept message	P	PUC$_B$	PUC$_A$	PC$_A$ TDE$_A$	RPA$_A$	producer

Accept message	C	PUC$_B$	PUC$_A$	PC$_A$	—	—	consumer

FIGURE IV.6   Format of the accept message for the task producer and task consumer

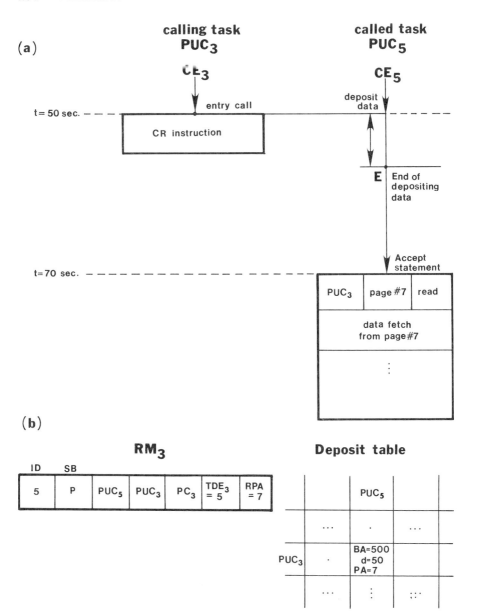

FIGURE IV.7 One example of the adopted task rendezvous organization

c. Since PUC$_3$ needs to arrange a rendezvous with PUC$_5$, it writes user code PUC$_5$ into message RM.

d. PC$_3$ is the priority code of PUC$_3$ to use page 7 of ME$_7$. Assume that priority code PC$_3$ is high to grant this request.

When the request message RM_3 is received by POS_5, it performs the following steps:

Step 1. Find if page 7 is free? (Assume it is free.)

Step 2. Find SB = P.

Step 4. Notify POS_3 that page 7 is granted. POS_3 is requested to confirm rendezvous type CM. Suppose that when PUC_3 issues the entry call it already knows array parameters $d = 50$, BA = 500, and PA = 7. Thus POS_3 sends confirmation: CM(d, BA, PA) = CM(50, 500, 7).

Step 5. Array parameters (50, 500, 7) are written into the deposit table. Page address 7 is written to a page address register that connects PE_3 or ME_3 with ME_5 using the DC bus (see Chapter V, Sec. 3.1.1).

Step 8. Page 7 of ME_5 is connected with, say, ME_3. Using $ME_3 \rightarrow ME_5$ instruction, calling task PUC_3 begins depositing 50 words into 50 data locations of page 7. Suppose all 50 data words are deposited at point E. Therefore, the data words were deposited into page 7 of ME_5 without interrupting called task PUC_5.

The task PUC_5 begins using these data deposited by PUC_3 when it issues the accept statement, which is similar to execution of the accept instruction, organized as follows:

The instruction stores the following codes: PUC_3 and page address 7 (optional). When the instruction is fetched, the effective address (PUC_5, PUC_3) is formed and the deposit table is read out. Therefore, the called task PUC_5 now has all the array parameters it needs to fetch 50 data words deposited by PUC_3.

Therefore, the organization that was discussed has organized task rendezvous without interrupting called task A. The time of interruption for calling task B was also reduced to the minimum required to send a RM message to POS_A and then to wait for a reply in order to deposit the produced data words. ■

1.2.3 Assessment of Adopted Organizations for Task Rendezvous

The adopted organization of task rendezvous is optimal since it minimizes the waiting time that usually occurs in conventional rendezvous organizations when the moments of request and acceptance for communication do not coincide. In the organization that has been discussed, no waiting time is incurred if data words are produced before they can be consumed. This is accomplished with the use of a deposit table which acts as a conventional mail box. A task producer deposits to the mail box parameters of the data array that are later fetched by the task consumer. Having performed this fetch, a task consumer begins accessing the data array. The algorithms that have been introduced make no distinction as to who is assigned the producer and consumer functions—a calling task or called. They are applicable for both situations, thus achieving a great flexibility in communications.

1.3 Exceptions Handling

In every application errors may arise. There are many sources of error, and many do not result from an incorrect program. Input data may contain values that are out of range, a hardware unit may fail, a tape may have a parity error, or a transmission line may be sporadically faulty. Often, a message is reported to the user and the program stops. The simple termination of a program is not always desirable and in some cases can be disastrous.

1.3.1 ADA Exceptions

In this section we discuss the ADA facilities for dealing with such situations. These facilities center on the concept of an *exception*. An exception is an event that causes suspension of normal program execution. Bringing an exception situation to attention is called *raising* the exception. Responding to the exception is called *handling* the exception.

The language itself defines situations that cause exceptions. These exceptions are the result of errors encountered during program execution. All such runtime errors are treated as predefined exceptions. These are the exceptions:

NUMERIC__ERROR   When the result of a predefined numeric operation does not lie within the implemented range or accuracy for the numeric type.

CONSTRAINT__ERROR   When a range constraint, index constraint, or discriminant constraint is violated, or when an attempt to dereference a null access value is made.

PROGRAM__ERROR   When all alternatives of a select statement with no else part are closed, when a program unit is invoked but its body has not been elaborated, and in various implementation-dependent situations.

STORAGE__ERROR   When the dynamic storage allocated to a task is exceeded, when the available space for objects of an access type is exhausted, or when a subprogram or declarative part is elaborated and storage is insufficient.

TASKING__ERROR   When an exception arises during communication between tasks.

The most important are numeric errors, because constraint errors, program errors, and tasking errors are a sole result of poor programming. On the other hand, numeric errors do not belong to this category since sometimes a programmer (however well qualified) is incapable of anticipating in advance that either the range or computational errors for computed results can exceed those which should be maintained in a given computer system for the given application. As for storage errors, these become of minor importance for modern computer systems because of the huge memory capacities (primary and I/O) they now possess.

Below we consider how numeric errors are handled by conventional and dynamic computers.

1.3.2 Two Types of Numeric Errors

The basic source of numeric errors originates from the following factors: insufficient range and insufficient accuracy. *Insufficient range* means that a computed number is larger (smaller) than the maximal (minimal) number that can be stored in computer data registers. *Insufficient accuracy* means that for a given application the computational error obtained by a computer system exceeds the maximal one that can be tolerated.

1.3.3 Insufficient Range

Two types of insufficient range should be distinguished: for additions and multiplications, respectively, since all other computer operations are implemented as subroutines that include additions (subtractions) and/or multiplications (divisions).

For additions, the insufficient range is recognized by fixed- and floating-point overflows. For multiplications, the insufficient range problem is handled differently for single- and double-precision computers.

Below we discuss the problem of insufficient range for additions and multiplications.

1.3.3.1 Insufficient range for additions

For fixed-point addition, the insufficient range is recognized by a fixed-point overflow (underflow) issued by the processor each time the size of a computed sum exceeds the size of the data register.

For floating-point computation, the insufficient range is recognized by a floating-point overflow (underflow) issued by the processor each time the size of a computed exponent exceeds the number of bits assigned for its storage in a floating-point data register. A conventional computer system equipped with a fixed- and floating-point operation handles a fixed-point overflow by switching into a floating-point operation. That is, a special subroutine is invoked that transforms all initial data words into a floating-point form and a computer begins floating-point computations.

A floating-point overflow cannot be handled at all in a conventional computer system because, if a computed exponent size exceeds that of a data register assigned for its storage, no floating-point operation can be maintained, because the bit size of computed exponents exceeds that of all logical circuits and data registers assigned for exponent handling. Therefore, a program with a floating-point overflow stops computation.

1.3.3.2 Insufficient range for multiplications

The problem is handled differently for single- and double-precision computers. Since multiplication may double the bit size of a computed result (product), and a single-precision computer is not provided with the capacity to handle double-precision words, each time a double-precision result is obtained, a computer switches into floating-point operation.

For a double-precision computer, a double-precision product is stored in two data registers and is given two consecutive memory words in the memory. Therefore, no switch to floating-point computation is required when a double-precision product is the final result.

However, if a double-precision word is an intermediate result, then this switch is required. Indeed, consider what happens if the computer executes C = A + B, where A is a double-precision word. The result C is also a double-precision word. To handle C requires two time intervals in the adder and two words in the memory for its storage. Therefore, a special addition instruction should be devised that handles both single- and double-precision words. Next, the situation is even worse when C = A $*$ B and A and B are double-precision words. Then C may become four-precision; i.e., it may require four words for storage and four time intervals to perform addition in the adder.

Therefore, if the number of double-precision temporary results is large, the computer may be confined to a byte type of operation, whereby it loses its capacity to perform a parallel operation over full data words that match its size. Thus, to prevent this from happening, again a switch into floating-point operation is required.

1.3.3.3 Conclusions

Summarizing the above, for conventional computers the problem of insufficient range for fixed-point computation is handled by performing a switch into a floating-point computation. For floating-point computation, the problem of insufficient range cannot be handled at all. The program stops computing since it requires a larger-size computer.

1.3.4 Insufficient Accuracy

There are two cases of insufficient accuracy that require different handling in conventional computer systems:

Case 1.   Insufficient accuracy because of truncated results

Case 2.   Insufficient accuracy caused by a switch into floating-point operation.

Both cases cannot be remedied and require abandoning of computation in a given computer system.

1.3.5 Comparative Assessment of Floating-Point Versus Fixed-Point Performance from the Viewpoint of Conventional Exception Handling

As seen from the analysis introduced above, a conventional remedy for some of the numeric errors consists of switching the computation into a floating-point form. However, any such switch leads to the following undersirable consequences:

1. *Inferior Precision:* The quality of floating-point computation measured by committed computational errors expressed in percent is much inferior to that of the fixed-point computation. Indeed, a floating-point data register having n bits (signs are excluded for simplicity) is partitioned into two portions, the exponent (p bits) and mantissa (k bits), where $n = p + k$. Of these bits, the accuracy bits are only the mantissa bits; the exponent bits do not contribute to the precision of computation. On the other hand, a fixed-point data register having n bits will have the entire n bits assigned for precision. Therefore, precision or accuracy of fixed-point computation is much better than that of floating-point computation, because $n > k$ since $p > 1$.

2. *Inferior Time:* The time of executing a floating-point operation at least doubles that of executing a fixed-point operation. The reason for this is that each floating-point operation includes two time intervals aimed at handling mantissas and exponents, respectively. For floating-point additions, handling exponents and mantissas is performed sequentially, since mantissas should first be aligned before they can be added. For floating-point multiplications, even in spite of the fact that mantissa and exponent operations can be performed concurrently, there arise two additional sequential steps aimed at mantissa normalization and exponent correction, which are absent in fixed-point multiplications. Therefore, the time of any floating-point operation at least doubles that of a fixed-point operation. Since the time of addition is an average time of a machine instruction, the entire exection time of the same program in a floating-point form at least doubles that in a fixed-point form.

Therefore, handling fixed-point overflow by transforming computation into a floating-point form, which is accepted in conventional systems, results in inferior computations from the viewpoint of accuracy and time. The accuracy is diminished by p bits, where p is the number of bits assigned for exponents, and the time of program execution increases at least twice in comparison with a similar fixed-point computation.

1.3.6 Handling Numeric Errors by Dynamic Architecture

Dynamic architecture provides additional means for handling numeric exceptions which are beyond the reach of static architectures. Most of the numeric errors can be handled by assuming architectural states that call for larger computer sizes so that the respective errors are circumvented. As for other types of errors that are the sole result of poor programming, dynamic architecture will treat them using conventional means.

We consider now the new capabilities of dynamic architectures that allow overcoming most of the numeric errors.

1.3.6.1 Insufficient range

For a fixed-point operation, the problem of insufficient range does not require a switch into a floating-point operation. Instead, it can be remedied by reconfiguring into a larger-size computer by switching into operation one or two spare CEs out of the available bank of spare CEs. Other programs are not affected by this switch since they continue computation in the same computers that computed them before.

Example. Suppose that a current dynamic architecture functions as two computers, a 32-bit computer $C_1(2) = \{CE_1, CE_2\}$ and a 48-bit computer $C_3(3) = \{CE_3, CE_4, CE_5\}$ (Fig. IV.8). Suppose that a fixed-point overflow occurred during addition $A + B$ in the 48-bit computer, $C_3(3)$. When the fixed-point overflow signal is generated, it causes the transition of the instruction sequencer into a special exception handling state that (1) stops execution of the current program, (2) saves a current program address, and (3) writes a special fixed address (say, 1000) into a program counter (Fig. IV.9).

For our case address 1000 stores a current address, Ad(Sub), of the exception handling subroutine which performs the following actions. It forms the next architectural state N_f using a current architectural state N_d and informs the monitor that new CE is added to the system. Formation of N_f in our case is reduced to adding a least significant zero to current state $N_d = 0100$, since computer $C_3(3)$ is transformed into com-

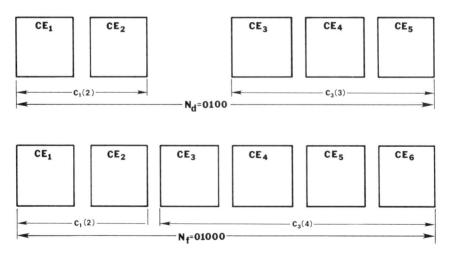

FIGURE IV.8 Dynamic organization of numeric exceptions

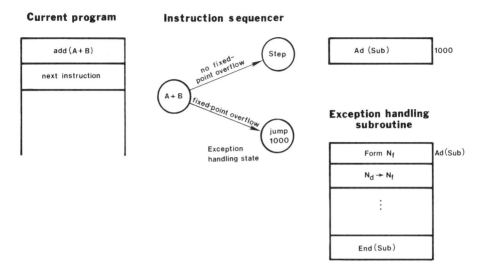

FIGURE IV.9 Exception handling subroutine for numeric exceptions

puter $C_3(4)$ giving $N_f = 01000$. Thereafter, this subroutine performs $N_d \rightarrow N_f$ architectural switch, forming a larger computer $C_3(4)$ and some other actions not considered here.

All other programs are not affected with this switch since their resources are not requested for reconfiguration. The end instruction of the subroutine resumes computation of the current program by writing an incremented saved address to the program counter. Therefore, computation is resumed in a fixed-point form, requiring no switch to floating point and thus causing no unpleasant consequences of such a switch for computations, as is done in conventional systems. ■

The problem of insufficient range for multiplication is handled similarly. For a floating-point operation, insufficient exponent range is also handled by either adding a new computer element and performing transition into a new architectural state that incorporates this element or activating exponent operation in the next less significant CE of the given dynamic computer $C_i(k)$. Therefore, contrary to conventional systems that cannot handle an exponent overflow, dynamic architecture does handle the exceptions caused by the exponent overflow. The reason for this is as follows. Each computer element CE has 16 bits which may function as follows:

a. Precision bits in their entirety
b. p exponent bits and k mantissa bits, where $p + k = 16$

When we are having a dynamic computer $C_i(k)$ assembled from k CE, then a data register in k CE may function as:

a . $16k$-bit fixed-point data register (Fig. IV.10).
b. Floating-point data register having p exponent bits and $(16k - p)$ mantissa bits.

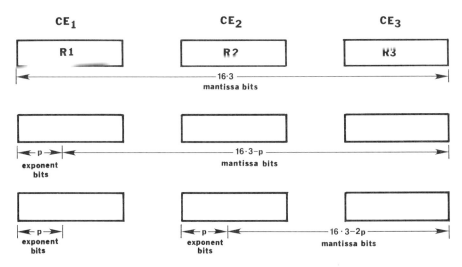

FIGURE IV.10 Dynamic handling of exponent overflow

c. Floating-point data register having $p \cdot \ell$ exponent bits and $(16k - p \cdot \ell)$ mantissa bits, where ℓ is selectable by a programmer and $\ell \leq k$. Therefore, if a floating-point overflow occurs in computer $C_i(k)$, a special exception handling subroutine is invoked that changes the format of a floating-point data register in the given computer $C_i(k)$ by assigning for new exponent $p(\ell +1)$ bits, i.e., activating the next less significant CE for exponent and mantissa operations (Fig. IV.10).

1.3.6.2 Insufficient precision

As was indicated above, the major causes of insufficient precision are in truncation of double-precision products (quotients with remainders) and in switching the computation into a less precise floating-point form. In conventional systems, there is no other remedy for handling the case of insufficient precision but selecting a new computer with a larger word size. That is, if the program suffers from insufficient precision, then its computation in a given computer stops.

For dynamic architectures, the exception of insufficient precision can be effectively handled by the available dynamic architecture using the following technique. First, there is no need to truncate a double-precision product if such a truncation leads to a computational error that exceeds an admissible error threshold. Instead, if in critical computations it is found that possible mantissa truncation may lead toward an inadmissible error, then a special exceptions handling routine is invoked that changes the size of the dynamic computer using the technique presented above for handling an insufficient range.

As for the loss of precision because of a possible switch into floating-point operation, there is no need to perform this switch at all. Far more beneficial is to switch the system into a larger dynamic computer and continue fixed-point operation in this computer.

1.3.7 Handling Numeric Errors in Dynamic Architectures: Assessment

As follows from the above analysis, the use of dynamic architecture greatly expands the area of applications for a computer system. The major factors that contributed to the unsuitability of a given computer system for application was (1) its insufficient range whereby a system overflows in producing intermediate results, and (2) its insufficient accuracy whereby the difference between actual results and computed results exceeds the threshold which is admissible for an application.

The past way of handling these problems was by selecting a new larger-size computer and abandoning the old computer. Dynamic architecture, however, does not require abandonment of the old computer. The problems of insufficient range and accuracy are handled by reconfiguring the system into concurrent computers that continue to maintain the required range and accuracy of application. Also, no switches from fixed to floating-point form are required and thus there are no negative consequences for computations that such switches may cause. Therefore, dynamic architectures provide an effective solution to all numeric types of errors, greatly expanding the area of application for a computer system.

2   MEMORY ALLOCATION IN RELATIONAL DATA BASES

While the objective of the preceding section of this chapter was to show how some typical ADA language constructs can be interpreted by dynamic architecture, the objective of this section is to give memory-management techniques for some data structures created dynamically. Therefore, the relationship of this section to the general dynamic compiler topic discussed in this chapter is in offering specific memory-management methodology that can be used by a dynamic compiler for the dynamic data structures that are described by relational data bases. That is, in this section we will restrict ourselves to memory allocations for relational data bases. The extensions of these and other memory-allocation techniques to other dynamic data structures that can be represented in ADA language is the subject of future research.

2.1 Motivation

The material presented in this section is organized as follows: First, we outline the meaning of relational data bases and content addressable memories that are used for their storage. Second, we justify the usefulness of relational data bases for typical real-time applications. Thereafter, we will give the architecture of a reconfigurable multiprocessor system designated to store and manage a real-time, high-performance relational data base. This will complete the motivation of the research that has been performed and dedicated to memory management for real-time relational data bases. The rest of the section will concentrate on describing concrete memory-management algorithms and forming optimal data files for real-time relational data bases. *Note:* The reconfigurable (dynamic) relational data base described in this section can be treated as an I/O for the system, with dynamic architecture designated for high-performance real-time processing. That is, data files stored and updated in this data base can be regarded as the input information files used by dynamic architectures in computing those real-time algorithms which warrant representation of the input information as a relational data base.

2.1.1 Usefulness of Content-Addressable Memories for Handling High-Performance Relational Data Bases

A *content-addressable memory* (CAM memory) accesses the word on the basis of its content, rather than its address, as is true for random-access memories (RAM memory). The word access of a content-addressable memory is described by the following simple algorithm:

Step 1.   Fetch the *output word, w*, in a word queue (Fig. IV.11).

Step 2.   Compare w with the key word, k.
If $w \neq k$, go to Step 1.
If $w = k$, end.

A typical content-addressable memory of size ($h \times T^*$), where h is the word size and T^* is the number of words functions as a shift-register memory formed out of h T^*-bit shift registers. At each clock period, it is possible to have the two memory accesses in parallel: (1) to fetch information from the current *output word* and (2) to write information into the current *input word*. This is either a shifted output word or a new updated word. At the next clock period, the memory shifts its content by moving new data words into its output and input words, respectively, so that they can be accessed again.

As will be shown in the next section, the proliferation of content-addressable memories is for storage of relational data bases [72], i.e., those that are represented by tables.

In this section we discuss various memory-allocation algorithms that allow storage of a relational data base in a content-addressable memory that is connected with several processors. The section discusses a simple extension of the techniques developed to several content-addressable memories. Thus, it is possible to form a reconfigurable multiprocessor system having T processors connected with g content-addressable memories to organize efficient data-base performance in the system with dynamic architecture.

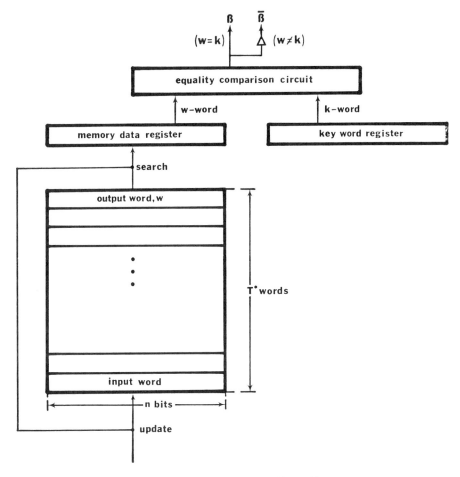

FIGURE IV.11   Diagram of a content-addressable memory

All allocation schemes introduced in this section are described by a Diophantine equation † whose solution, x, shows the distance between any two processors that are not in conflict when they access the same content-addressable memory. The section presents a technique for finding a maximal set of noninterfering processors and conflict-free allocation techniques for various structures of data files. These techniques achieve very high performance characteristics since:

a. They allow the entire memory space of a CAM memory either to be completely filled with data files or to be filled with minimal memory overhead created to exclude interference between any pair of noninterfering processors.

---

†In general, by a Diophantine equation [73], we mean a linear equation $ax + by = c$, where a, b, and c are integers.

b. All the memory allocations developed are conflict free.

c. During one memory revolution, the entire content of each content-addressable memory can be completely fetched by a set of noninterfering processors that perform processing of data-base entries.

The relationship of this research to other works in the area is as follows:

1. Since it deals with the file allocation for content-addressable memories, it is connected with the literature on associative processing. Associative parallel processors for file searching are discussed in [74] and [75], and a survey of associative and parallel processors is found in [76]. The most recent publication is a comprehensive description made by H. Love [61] of industrial associative processors (ALAP, STARAN, etc.), which are also used extensively for data-base operations. Reference [77] discusses the use of bubble memories for supporting associative data-base architectures.

2. By creating noninterfering sets of processors that may access the same content-addressable memory in a conflict-free manner and by forming various structures of data files for the noninterfering sets of processors, this paper contributes to the theory of shift-register sequences, since to form such processor sets and to find the data-file structures for them requires application of interesting circular properties exhibited by shift-register sequences. Basic concepts of shift-register sequences are represented in [35-39], where [35] is a pioneering work that first represented shift-register sequences in the form of autonomous linear sequential networks, while [38] contains the most complete treatment of shift-register sequences ever published. Papers [41, 42] contain some ideas on shift-register sequences that are closely related to this research, which extends them to memory-allocation schemes and noninterfering data files.

3. Finally, by developing conflict-free memory-allocation techniques for a multiprocessor system that includes content-adressable memories, this research is connected with the literature on conflict-free and parallel memory access [78-82]. Paper [78] introduced the concept of a multidimensional access memory which can be accessed in several accessing modes (word slice, bit slice, multibyte single record, single-byte multirecord, etc.). Papers [79-82] have developed conflict-free and concurrent memory-access techniques for the RAM memories interconnected into a multiprocessor system. This section develops techniques for a conflict-free and parallel memory access for the case of a multiprocessor system that incorporates several content-addressable memories. The results of this research are published in [83, 84].

Section 2.2 describes the benefits of using relational data bases and makes an assessment of the research results presented in this section.

2.2 Relational Data Base

In this section, we describe the meaning of a relational data base. Next, we outline the problem of file allocation for CAM memories when they are used in a relational data base and classify various data files that can be stored in them.

2.2.1 Definition of a Relational Data Base

Typically, large data bases are represented by tables and they are called relational data bases [72]. In these tables, rows are marked by *items* and columns are marked by *attributes* (Table IV.1). The intersection of one row and one column shows the meaning acquired by a specific attribute for a specific item. For instance, Table IV.1 shows a data base having four rows (items: object 1 through object 4) and five columns that specify five attributes related to the statuses of their observation made by radar. The main objective of any feasible and veritable data base is to maintain the correct and current meanings of all its attributes for all the items. Thus, each attribute is processed separately, since its different meanings which fill in one column are determined by the same attribute algorithm. For instance, for Table IV.1 there are five different algorithms that specify five attributes (columns) of the table, where algorithm I specifies for all rows a current altitude maintained by the object, algorithm II specifies its current velocity, etc. Therefore, for data bases represented by tables, it is expedient to form a separate data file, DF, out of all the entries belonging to same column, since they are obtained sequentially using the same real-time processing algorithm.

2.2.2 The Use of RAMs for Storing a Relational Data Base

As was shown in [77] and demonstrated by past experiences, random-access memories become extremely ineffective for storage of a relational data base because of the following factors:

1. Since any RAM memory can have only one access at a time (write or read), it is impossible to execute two data-base operations concurrently over two different data-base entries (such as *search* and *update* or *search* and *delete*, etc.). Instead, these two operations must be executed only sequentially.

TABLE IV.1

RELATIONAL DATA BASE

Attributes (items)	Current Altitude (km)	Current Velocity (km/hour)	Predicted Corrections in Altitude per 10 Minutes (m)	Predicted Corrections in Velocity per 10 Minutes (km/hr)	Total Number of Measurements Used to Find a Trajectory
Object 1	1000	2000	50	—	25
Object 2	2000	5000	100	20	38
Object 3	2000	8000	200	30	44
Object 4	3000	6000	300	10	39

2. Since the size of each data file can be extremely large, a data file is moved to a main RAM by portions from a secondary memory. Thus, a considerable time overhead is created by such movements when no data-base operations can be performed, since each RAM cannot read (i.e., search) any of its words while it is writing information from a secondary memory.

3. For RAM memories, the cost of addressing software becomes expensive since it is necessary to introduce complex addressing procedures for maintaining extensive directories and complex search routines.

2.2.3 The Use of Content-Addressable Memories

By storing a relational data base in a content-addressable memory, all these drawbacks of RAMs can be eliminated. Indeed, since a typical content-addressable memory allows execution of two opearations at one time (read and write), it can perform two data-base operations at a time: search and update, or search and delete. Drawback 2 of the RAM is also eliminated, since a content-addressable memory can receive a new block of data by executing an update-write operation concurrently with the search-read operation when it fetches the output word and compares it with the key word. Finally, the addressing software of content-addressable memories become exceedingly simple, since it is reduced to equality comparison between a current output word with the key word (Fig. IV. 11). Thus, all extensive directories can be maintained very easily by simply writing a new key word to a key word register.

Therefore, as follows from the above, a sequential content-addressable memory is a viable alternative for storing relational data bases. It will have T separate data files, DF, if a relational data base is represented by T attributes (T columns). Each data file, DF, will be represented by all values acquired by a single attribute.

2.2.4 Reconfigurable Multiprocessor Architecture for Handling a Relational Data Base

Since each data file stored in the CAM-memory is processed sequentially (word by word) by a separate algorithm, to improve concurrency of data-base operations, it is expedient to process each file in a separate processor. Therefore, a multiprocessor system having T processors connected to a single content-addressable memory (Fig. IV.12) becomes an attractive implementation diagram for storage of a relational data base represented by T attributes.

At each moment of time, this architecture performs the following actions in parallel: (1) it fetches the current output word to the processor, P, whose address is stored in the processor counter (this transfer is performed via the connecting elements MSE), and (2) it either updates the current input word with the one stored in the buffer registers or transfers the current output word to its input word location if no update is required. Buffer registers are a register stack that is connected with the processors P_1, P_2, ..., P_T via connecting elements CME_1, CME_2, ..., CME_T, respectively.

Updating the input word of the memory with a new data word is performed as

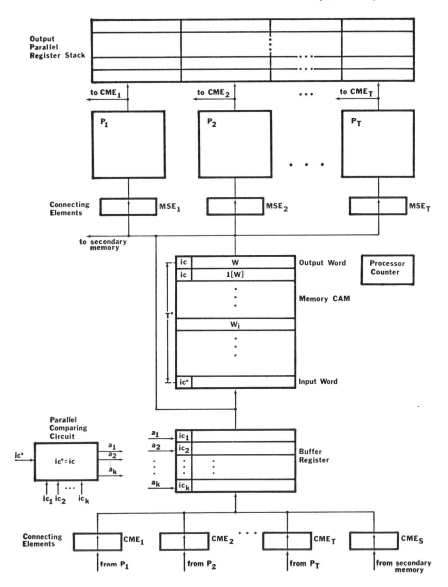

FIGURE IV.12   A multiprocessor system with content-addressable memory

follows. Since the content-addressable memory is already filled with data files, its current input word stores some file identification code, ic*. This code is sent to a parallel comparing circuit that performs equality comparison of the current ic* received by the memory input word with all the ic's of the data words stored in buffer registers. A buffer register for which ic* = ic transfers its word to the current input word. If several buffer registers store the same ic such that ic* $=$ ic, then the equality signal, a_i, generated as a result of ic* $=$ ic transfers to the input word a data word stored in the buffer register with the smallest address. As for the remaining registers with the same ic, their contents are shifted, so that one register with the largest address is released and cleared in order to receive a new incoming word from one of the processors.

Since sometimes a relational data base must print a tabular representation of its current attributes for particular items, the processors P_1 , P_2 , ..., P_T are connected with the output parallel register stack that receives in parallel updated data entries computed by P_1 , P_2 , ..., P_T . The parallel output registers are connected with the I/O terminal, which prints updated data-base information as specified by the user.

2.2.5 Problem of Memory Allocation

In this section, we outline a problem of file allocation for a content-addressable memory (CAM) serving T processors. In general, to take into account various delays introduced by the processors performing an update operation over data-base entries, assume that each data file may take nonconsecutive words of the CAM memory, and the total number of words in the CAM is T^*. Assume that at each clock period the output word issued by the CAM will go to a separate processor. This assumption will minimize the total time required to fetch T^* words by T processors, since this time will coincide with the time of one revolution of the CAM memory. (On the other hand, an alternative organization whereby each processor fetches its data file alone following the fetches completed by another processor will lead to a situation in which each data file will be fetched during one memory revolution. Therefore, if the memory stores T data files, they will be fetched only after T revolutions of the CAM memory.)

To perform a minimization of the total time to access a queue made of T data files and stored in one circulating memory, the following problem has to be solved:

Given T processors, P_0 , P_1 , ..., P_{T-1} , connected with the CAM memory that has T^* data words (Fig. IV.12). Generally, $T \neq T^*$. Assume that the CAM memory stores T data files, DF, where each data file may consist of nonconsecutive memory words of the CAM memory. File storage techniques have to be developed such that the following conditions are satisfied:

C1. No file interference arises, such that if two data files DF_i and DF_j are accessed by the two processors P_i and P_j their intersection is empty. ($DF_i \Omega DF_j = \Lambda$); i.e., for each data file, every memory word contained in it is accessed only by one processor.

C2. Minimal time access to all data files is achieved, whereby a minimal number of dummy clock periods is created during memory revolutions when no data words are fetched by the processors.

C3. Independence of allocation techniques of the memory revolutions is achieved, whereby if a data file is accessed by the processor during consecutive memory revolutions, the relative address of every word, w, contained in this file must remain unchanged in order to be accessed only by the same processor. This processor, however, may fetch an updated word w if memory CAM updates its content at this address.

(Indeed, if no independence-of-revolutions principle is implemented in memory allocation, then the memory addressing procedures will become revolution dependent, which will entirely preclude their use in viable memory-allocation techniques.)

2.3 Classification of Allocation Schemes

If the entire memory space is allocated to data files in such a way that all memory words are included in noninterfering data files, then the allocation will be called *noninterfering.* For noninterfering allocation, no dummy clock periods are created since the entire memory space is occupied with data words.

If, on the other hand, there are *s* common words in a pair of data files that are marked with a special bit (C = 1) to exclude their access by two processors, these two files become noninterfering. However, in accessing them, memory loses *s* clock periods during each revolution. This allocation will be called *s-interfering.* If *s* is the least possible integer, then the allocation becomes *least interfering.*

2.3.1 Minimal and Nonminimal Data Files

It should be noted that the use of principle C3 implemented in allocation leads to the appearance of a *minimal data file,* MF(P), accessed by processor P and defined as follows: MF(P) includes those memory words that are connected with P during consecutive memory revolutions. That is, if P fetches word w' during one memory revolution and word w'' during another revolution, then, to make the allocation strategy independent of memory revolutions, words w' and w'' must be included into the minimal file handled by P. Obviously, to implement principle C3, any nonminimal file, NF(P), accessed by P must include MF(P) as its nucleus; i.e., MF(P) $\leq$ NF(P).

Since in our scheme the entire memory content made of T^* words may be updated during one revolution, assume that each processor P fetches either a minimal file, MF, or a nonminimal file, NF, during one memory revolution. This assumption will define the following two types of allocation that will be discussed in this section: *minimal file allocation,* whereby each qualified processor accesses its minimal data file, MF(P), during each memory revolution, and *nonminimal file allocation,* whereby each qualified processor accesses a nonminimal data file, NF(P), during each revolution.

2.3.2 Classification of Files That Can Be Stored in the CAM Memory

In this section, we will perform classification of files for minimal and nonminimal file allocations. For minimal file allocation, the size of a minimal file, MF, is determined as $f = T^*/\beta$, where $\beta = \gcd(T, T^*)$ and gcd is the greatest common devisor of T and T^*.

For nonminimal file allocation, we find the structure of each nonminimal file, NF, that must necessarily include a *primitive file,* PF, consisting of *j* words called the *allocation index,* selected by the programmer. The size of the nonminimal file is then determined as $j \cdot f = j \cdot T^*/\beta$. Thus, if $j = 1$, the nonminimal allocation becomes a minimal one (Fig. IV.13).

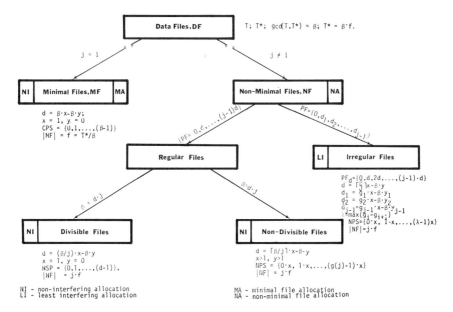

FIGURE IV.13 Classification of files stored in a content-addressable (circulating) memory

As follows from Fig. IV.13, each nonminimal file can be further classified as either *regular* or *irregular*. A regular file is specified by the same distance d between any two consecutive memory words belonging to the primitive file. An irregular file is specified by a variable distance d (w_i, w_{i+1}) between any two consecutive words w_i and w_{i+1}. We will denote each primitive file (regular or irregular) as an ordered set of distances between a current output word w_0 and all other words. Since $d(w_0, w_0) = 0$, 0 is always a member of a primitive file. Thus, a regular primitive file is PF = $\{0, d, 2d, \cdots, (j-1)d\}$; an irregular primitive file is PF = $\{0, d_1, d_2, \cdots, d_{j-1}\}$, where d_i is the distance between the output word w_0 and w_i and $d_1 \leq d_2 \leq \cdots \leq d_{j-1}$, since all the distances are from the same output word w_0 and they are ordered. For instance, in Fig. IV.14 we have a regular primitive file, PF, that includes words, w_0, w_1, w_2 and w_3, such that distance, d, between any two consecutive words is the same and $d = 2$. Thus, PF = $\{0, d, 2d, 3d\}$ = $\{0, 2, 4, 6\}$. In Fig. IV.14 we have the irregular primitive file with distances $d(w_0, w_1) = 2$ and $d(w_1, w_2) = 3$, giving primitive file PF = $\{0, 2, 5\}$, and $5 = d (w_0, w_1) + d(w_1, w_2) = 2 + 3$. Regular nonminimal files are further subdivided into divisible files if $\beta = \gcd(T, T^*) = d \cdot j$ and non-divisible files if $\beta = \gcd (T, T^*) > d \cdot j$, as shown in Fig. IV.13.

Here we study conflict-free allocations for all data files of the classification in Fig. IV.13. This section shows that for all files but the irregular ones the allocation creates no memory overhead if it is described by the following Diophantine equation:

$$d = g(j) \cdot x - \beta \cdot y$$

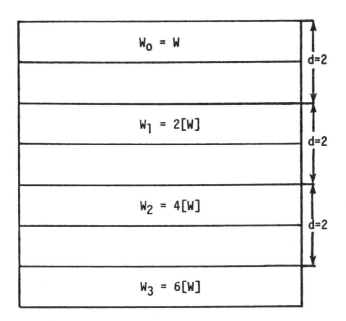

Regular Primitive File PF = {0, 2, 4, 6}

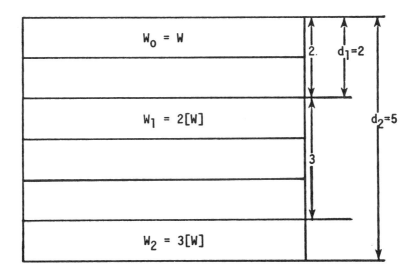

Irregular Primitive File PF = {0, 2, 5}

FIGURE IV.14   Two types of primitive files: (a) regular with permanent $d = 2$ and (b) irregular with $d_1 = 2$ and $d_2 = 5$

where d is the permanent distance between two consecutive memory words belonging to the file of the same type (minimal and nonminimal regular); $g(j) = \lceil \beta/j \rceil$ is the number of processors that fetch noninterfering files and $\lceil \ \ \rceil$ is an operation of rounding to the least integer that is $\geq$ the fraction β/j. The processors that fetch noninterfering files form the noninterfering processor set NPS $= \{P^{(0)}, P^{(1 \cdot x)}, P^{(2 \cdot x)}, \ldots, P^{(g(j)-1) \cdot x}\}$ and x is the processor displacement which equals the shifting distance between two consecutive processors from the NPS set; j is the allocation index, selected by the programmer. For minimal files, $j = 1$ and $d = \beta \cdot x - \beta \cdot y$. This implies that the only solution of the Diophantine equation is $x = 1$, $y = 0$. Thus the noninterfering processor set contains $g(1) = \beta$ processors with the displacement $x = 1$ from each other.

For nonminimal divisible files, $j \neq 1$ and $d = g(j) \cdot x - \beta \cdot y = \beta/j \cdot x - \beta \cdot y$. This equation has also only one solution, $x = 1$, $y = 0$, because β is divided by j and $d = \beta/j$ by definition. Thus, the noninterfering processor set contains $d = \beta/j$ processors with the shifting distance $x = 1$ from each other.

For the nonminimal, nondivisible files, since $d \cdot j < \beta$, the Diophantine equation has a nontrivial solution, $x > 0$, $y > 0$, provided $\gcd(\lceil \beta/j \rceil, \beta) = 1$ and $\gcd(\beta, x,) = 1$. Thus the noninterfering processor set, NPS, will have $g(j)$ members, where $g(j) = \lceil \beta/j \rceil$ and the shifting distance between any two consecutive processors from NPS is $x > 1$.

For irregular files, the allocation creates a minimal memory overhead; i.e., it is the least interfering because of the following factors. First, for a given irregular primitive file PF $= \{0, d_1, d_2, \ldots, d_{j-1}\}$, a closest regular file PF$' = \{0, d, 2d, \ldots, (j - 1)d\}$ is found that provides a solution x, y of the Diophantine equation $d = \lceil \beta/j \rceil \cdot x - \beta \cdot y$ formed for this file (Fig. IV.13). Thereafter, each difference d_i of the irregular file is presented by its own Diophantine equation $d_i = g_i \cdot x - \beta \cdot y_i$ ($i = 1, \ldots, j - 1$), where x is found for the regular file PF$'$. Therefore, we obtain a set of integer solutions $(g_1, y_1), (g_2, y_2), \ldots, (g_{j-1}, y_{j-1})$. Next, the numbers $g_1, g_2, \ldots, g_{j-1}$ are ordered as $g_1' > g_2' > \ldots > g_{j-1}'$ and $\lambda = \max(g_i' - g_{i+1}')$ is found. This λ gives the number of members in the NPS set of processors, and x gives the displacement among two consecutive processors from the NPS set:

$$\text{NPS} = \{0 \cdot x, 1 \cdot x, \ldots, (\lambda - 1)x\}$$

Therefore, since a displacement x is selected among processors which maintains the maximal regularity of the allocation that can be accomplished under the circumstances, the minimal number of words in each data file becomes common with other data files. Thus, the irregular allocation becomes least noninterfering. Indeed, it is best approximated by the closest regular allocation which is noninterfering by construction, since for the selected regular allocation the Diophantine equation does have a solution.

The section shows that all allocation techniques are completely deterministic and described by the strict algorithmic procedures presented.

2.3.3 Parallel Operation of Several CAM Memories

Since a noninterfering processor set, NPS, that allows obtaining noninterfering data files includes only $g(j)$ processors, the remaining $T - g(j)$ processors do not participate in file fetches from the same CAM memory. To prevent their idleness, a procedure is described for connecting these processors with other CAM memories so that all processors will be fetching data files and all the memories will be provided with either noninterfering or the least interfering allocations (Fig. IV.15).

As a result, the allocation techniques presented in this section achieve very high performance characteristics since:

a. They allow obtaining either noninterfering or least interfering memory allocation in which the entire memory space of each CAM memory is either completely filled with noninterfering files accessed by $g(j)$ processors or a minimal number of memory words is not used.

b. T processors can be partitioned into $T/g(j)$ groups, each of which is served by one CAM memory. Therefore, instead of T CAM memories that serve T processors provided by conventional techniques, we obtain $T/g(j)$ CAM memories serving the same number of processors, where T, T^*, j, and d are selectable by the programmer.

2.4 Structure of a Minimal File and File Interference Problem

In this section, we will find the size of a minimal file, MF, and outline the problem of file interference. The appearance of a *minimal file* originates from the following observations.

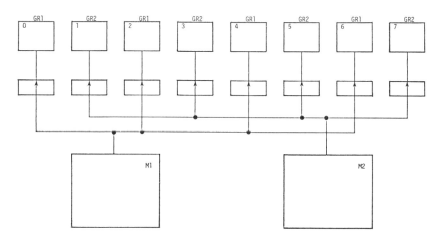

FIGURE IV.15 A multiprocessor system having two content-addressable memories

Let processor P fetch word w. Since the period T^* of CAM is not the same as the number of processors, T, during each revolution of CAM, one processor, P, will fetch a new word of CAM. We find the number of such words and their relative locations with respect to the original word w. Obviously, all these words should be included into the minimal file of P.

Another problem that will be solved is finding out what processors fetch the same word w during consecutive revolutions of CAM. The importance of these findings is in developing algorithmic procedures of file allocation that will eliminate the file-interference problem by including all minimal files into a single data file.

2.4.1 Structure of the Minimal File

As was indicated in Section 2.2.5, the following rule of accessing will be used: If processor P accesses word w, then the next word $w' = 1[w]$ will be accessed by the next processor $P' = 1[P]$. Since there are T^* words in the CAM, memory that are fetched by T processors, processors are forming *processors sequence*, PS, of period T and memory words are forming memory sequence, MS*, of period T^*:

$$PS = \{P, 1[P], ..., (T - 1)[P]\}$$

$$MS^* = \{w, 1[w], ..., (T^* - 1)[w]\}$$

Iterative application of the sequentiality rule leads to processor $i[P]$ accessing word $i[w]$, where i shows the displacement or the shifting distance between P and $i[P]$ or w and $i[w]$, respectively.

Obviously, for processors $T[P] = P$; i.e. after T shifts, the same processor will fetch word $T[w]$. Likewise, for memories $T^*[w] = w$, i.e., after T^* shifts, the same memory location, w, is accessed by processor $T^*[P]$.

For convenience of notation, we denote the event of P fetching word w as $P \rightarrow w$, where P is called *source* and w is called *destination*.

Let us find the least common multiple of T and T^*, lcm (T, T^*), and denote $f = $ lcm $(T, T^*)/T$, and $f^* = $ lcm $(T, T^*)/T^*$. The f integer shows the minimal number of different words that are connected with processor P during consecutive revolutions of the CAM memory. That is, if P accesses w, or $P \rightarrow w$, then during cyclic revolutions of memory, CAM, P accesses only f different words, where $f = $ lcm $(T, T^*)/T$. To implement the independence of allocation of memory revolutions, these words must be included into the *minimal file of* P, MF(P).

These words are found as follows:

$$\text{If } P \rightarrow w, \text{ then:}$$

$$T[P] \rightarrow T[w],$$

$$2T[P] \rightarrow 2T[w],$$

$$\vdots$$

$$(f - 1)T[P] \rightarrow (f - 1)T[w]$$

For these fetches, all sources are the same since T is the period of the processor sequence. Thus $P = T[P] = 2T[P] = \cdots = (f - 1)T[P]$.

As for destinations, they are not the same, since, in general, T^*, the period of memory sequence, does not divide T. Thus $T[w] \neq 2T[w] \neq \cdots \neq (f - 1)T[w]$ and these are different words of memory M. Therefore, if $P \rightarrow T[w] = w^{(1)}$, $P \rightarrow 2T[w] = w^{(2)}$, ..., $P \rightarrow (f - 1)T[w] = w^{(f-1)}$. Note, since $f \cdot T = f^* \cdot T^* = \text{lcm}(T, T^*)$, after $f \cdot T$ fetches the same processor, P will fetch the same word; i.e., $f \cdot T[P] \rightarrow f \cdot T[w] = P \rightarrow w$. Thus, the minimal file of P, MF(P), contains the following words:

$$MF(P) = \{w, T[w], 2T[w], \ldots, (f - 1) \cdot T[w]\} \tag{1}$$

As follows from the constructing procedures used in finding MF(P), this is a minimal set since the only assumption that was made in the construction of MF(P) was that a processor P fetches only one word, w, from this file. All other members of MF(P) have been found by iterative application of the $T[w]$ rule.

Therefore, if it is required that processor P fetch j words such that each word w_i initiates a separate minimal file, $MF_i(P) = \{w_i, T[w_i], \ldots, (f - 1)T[w_i]\}$, then the total number of words that will be accessed by P is $j \cdot f$.

2.4.2 File Interference Record

Let us now find the significance of the f^* integer, where $f^* = \text{lcm}(T, T^*)/T^*$. The f^* integer shows how many processors forming an interfering processor set (IPS) access the same word w during consecutive memory revolutions. The processors that belong to IPS can be found via similar techniques used in finding the minimal file of P, MF(P). In other words,

$$IPS = \{P, T^*[P], \ldots, (f^* - 1) \cdot T^*[P]\} \tag{2}$$

As follows, all processors of the set IPS access the same word w, since T^* is the period of memory CAM. However, since T^* is not the period of the processor sequence, all these processors are different. Thus, the allocation strategies that are to be developed must prevent a word w from being accessed by any pair of processors belonging to the same IPS set.

2.4.3 Fetches of Minimal File During One Memory Cycle

To provide that all words from the minimal file of P be fetched during one memory revolution, it is necessary to find values for their relative positions $T, 2T, \ldots, (f - 1)T$ that do not exceed T^*; i.e., it is necessary to reduce them by mod T^*. This can be easily done using the following well-known properties of congruences given in reference [73]: "when each member of a complete set of residues $\{0, 1, 2, \ldots, p - 1\}$ is multiplied by an integer k (p and k are relatively prime) which is not a multiple of p to yield $\{0, k, 2k, \ldots, (p - 1) \cdot k\}$, and when these numbers are reduced mod p, the resulting remainders are precisely the numbers in the set $\{0, 1, 2, \ldots, p - 1\}$ except possibly for the order."

In our case, we reduce all numbers $\{0, T, 2T, \ldots, (f - 1) \cdot T\}$ by mod T^*. Since $f \cdot T = f^* \cdot T^* = \mathrm{lcm}(T, T^*)$, $T = f^* \cdot \beta$, $T^* = f \cdot \beta$, where $\beta = \gcd(T, T^*)$. All members of the minimal file are then reduced by mod $T^* = f \cdot \beta$ and not mod T as states the property of congruences formulated for $\beta = 1$. Since for the general case $\beta \geq 1$, the result of mod T^* reduction will be an integer including two factors: β and i. Thus, the minimal file of P, MF(P), will be given as

$$\mathrm{MF(P)} = \{w, \beta[w], 2 \cdot \beta[w], \ldots, (f - 1) \cdot \beta[w]\} \qquad (3)$$

where $\beta = \gcd(T, T^*)$.

A similar reduction procedure extended to IPS leads to

$$\mathrm{IPS} = \{P, \beta[P], 2 \cdot \beta[P], \ldots, (f^* - 1) \cdot \beta[P]\} \qquad (4)$$

Example. Let processors and memory words form two sequences, PS and MS, with periods $T = 15$ and $T^* = 35$, respectively, We find $\beta = \gcd(15, 35) = 5$; $f^* = T/\beta = 15/5 = 3$ and $f = T^*/\beta = 35/5 = 7$. First, let us form the minimal processor file, MF(P), in which the relative locations of the words are not reduced mod $T^* = \mathrm{mod}\ 35$. $\mathrm{MF(P)} = \{0, 1 \cdot 15, 2 \cdot 15, 3 \cdot 15, 4 \cdot 15, 5 \cdot 15, 6 \cdot 15\}$. Let us reduce all members of MF(P) by mod $T^* = 35$. Since $15 = 3 \cdot 5 \equiv 3\beta$, $2 \cdot 15 = 6 \cdot 5 \equiv 6\beta$, $3 \cdot 15 = 35 + 2 \cdot 5 \equiv 2\beta$, $4 \cdot 15 = 35 + 5 \cdot 5 \equiv 5\beta$, $5 \cdot 15 = 2 \cdot 35 + 1 \cdot 5 \equiv 1\beta$, and $6 \cdot 15 = 2 \cdot 35 + 4 \cdot 5 \equiv 4\beta$, we obtain the following reduced MF(P) $= \{0, 1\beta, 2\beta, 3\beta, 4\beta, 5\beta, 6\beta\}$, which corresponds to eq. (3). Therefore, during one revolution of CAM, all words of MF(P) can be accessed by P. Using Eq. (2), let us find the interfering processor set for each word w: $\mathrm{IPS} = \{0, 1 \cdot 35, 2 \cdot 35\}$, where $f^* - 1 = 3 - 1 = 2$. Let us reduce IPS mod 15. $1 \cdot 35 = 2 \cdot 15 + 5 \equiv 1\beta$; $2 \cdot 35 = 4 \cdot 15 + 2 \cdot 5 \equiv 2\beta$. Therefore, $\mathrm{IPS} = \{0, 1 \cdot \beta, 2\beta\}$, which corresponds to Eq. (4). ■

2.5 Noninterfering File Allocation for Minimal Processor Files

In this section, we will discuss the procedures for noninterfering file allocation of minimal processor files, MF(P): $\mathrm{MF(P)} = \{0, \beta, 2\beta, \ldots, (f - 1) \cdot \beta\}$. Since each word w is accessed by the processors forming the set $\mathrm{IPS} = \{P, \beta[P], 2\beta[P], \ldots, (f^* - 1) \cdot \beta[P]\}$, let us find the set of *noninterfering processors*, i.e. those whose minimal files do not interfere or have empty intersections. This can be done by applying shift iterations to the set MF(P) as follows: a 1-bit shift, 1[MF], of MF is the minimal file accessed by the processor $P^{(1)} = 1[P]$. This file has the following form: $\mathrm{MF(P^{(1)})} = 1[\mathrm{MF}] = \{1, \beta + 1, 2\beta + 1, \ldots, (f - 1)\beta + 1\}$.

Similarly, one can obtain a 2-bit shift, 2[MF], of MF accessed by the processor $P^{(2)} = 2[P]$, etc. The number of noninterfering processors is β. Their relative locations to the P processor are

$$P, 1[P], 2[P], \ldots, (\beta - 1)[P].$$

These locations form a noninterfering processor set.

$$\text{NPS} = \{P, 1[P], 2[P], \ldots, (\beta - 1)[P]\}.$$

Indeed, for the processor $P^{(\beta)} = \beta[P]$, we obtain the following minimal processor file: MF $(\beta) = \beta[\text{MF}] = \{\beta, 2\beta, \ldots, f \cdot \beta\}$. Since $f \cdot \beta = T^* \equiv 0$, we obtain a complete coincidence of these two files. Therefore, processors P and $P^{(\beta)} = \beta[P]$ access the same minimal files. Thus, there exists a noninterfering file allocation if the CAM memory is accessed by precisely β processors forming a noninterfering processor set, NPS $= \{P, 1[P], \ldots, (\beta - 1)[P]\}$.

Memory accesses performed by these processors are described by the following *noninterfering minimal file allocation matrix*, MAM, containing β rows and f columns. Each row i of the MAM matrix contains words belonging to the minimal processor file that are accessed by the processor $P^{(i)} = i[P]$.

	MF($P^{(i)}$) $0 \cdot \beta$	$1 \cdot \beta$	$2 \cdot \beta$	...,	$(f - 1) \cdot \beta$
$P^{(i)}$					
$P^{(0)}$	0,	β,	2β,	...,	$(f - 1) \cdot \beta$
$P^{(1)}$	1,	$\beta + 1$,	$2\beta + 1$,	...,	$(f - 1) \cdot \beta + 1$
$P^{(2)}$	2,	$\beta + 2$,	$2\beta + 2$,	...,	$(f - 1) \cdot \beta + 2$
$\bullet$					
$\bullet$					
$\bullet$					
$P(\beta - 1)$	$(\beta - 1)$,	$\beta + (\beta - 1)$,	$2\beta + (\beta - 1)$,...,		$(f - 1) \cdot \beta + (\beta - 1)$

MAM = $\qquad\qquad$ (5)

By construction, the intersection of two different rows is empty. The MAM matrix contains $f \cdot \beta$ entries, where $f \cdot \beta = T^*$ and T^* is the number of words in the CAM memory. Therefore, the processors of the NPS set access all locations of memory CAM without file interference.

Example. Let us construct the noninterfering processor set, NPS, using the data of the preceding example. Since $T = 15$, $T^* = 35$, $\beta = \gcd(15, 35) = 5$, and $f = T^*/\beta = 7$, we obtain the following allocation: The noninterfering processor set NPS = {P, 1[P], 2[P], 3[P], 4[P]}, where these processors are allocated with the following minimal data files: since $f = 7$, $f - 1 = 6$, and

MF(P) $= \{0, 5, 2 \cdot 5, 3 \cdot 5, 4 \cdot 5, 5 \cdot 5, 6 \cdot 5\} = \{0, 5, 10, 15, 20, 25, 30\}$

MF($P^{(1)}$) $=$ MF(1[P]) $= \{1, 6, 11, 16, 21, 26, 31\}$

MF($P^{(2)}$) $=$ MF(2[P]) $= \{2, 7, 12, 17, 22, 27, 32\}$

MF($P^{(3)}$) $=$ MF(3[P]) $= \{3, 8, 13, 18, 23, 28, 33\}$

MF($P^{(4)}$) $=$ MF(4[P]) $= \{4, 9, 14, 19, 24, 29, 34\}$

Therefore, there is no interference between minimal data files accessed by the processors from the noninterfering processor set. Also, memory CAM is completely filled with information. Therefore, the allocation is noninterfering. ■

2.6 Nonminimal Files

In this section, we will discuss a noninterfering file allocation for nonminimal data files. Each nonminimal file is specified as follows: Since for each word w fetched by P there exists a minimal processor file, $MF_w(P) = \{w, \beta[w], 2\beta[w], \ldots, (f-1)\beta[w]\}$, to give a nonminimal file $NF(P)$ is

   a. to give only j *primitive words,* i.e., those words any pair of which are not in the same $MF(P)$, and
   b. to construct the minimal data file for each primitive word.

   The total number of words in $NF(P)$ is $j \cdot f$. It then follows that each nonminimal file accessed by P is specified by primitive file $PF(P)$ made of j primitive words: $PF(P) = \{w, d_1[w], d_2[w], \ldots, d_{j-1}[w]\}$, where d_i is the shifting distance between a current output word w and another primitive word. Obviously, it is possible to select primitive words such that each $d_i < \beta$, inasmuch as the distance between each primitive word and its derivatives in the minimal file originated by this primitive word is a multiple of $\beta(1 \cdot \beta, 2\beta, \ldots, (f-1)\beta)$. Also, for notational convenience, all d's are ordered as $d_i < d_{i+1}$ $(i = 1, \ldots, j-1)$ since they are taken from the same output word w. Therefore, the nonminimal file $NF(P)$ can be expressed in the following form. Given words w, $d_1[w], d_2[w], \ldots, d_{j-1}[w]$, that must be accessed by P. Then all the words accessed by P during consecutive memory revolutions are given as follows:

$$NF(P) = \begin{vmatrix} 0, & \beta, & 2\beta, & \ldots, & (f-1)\beta \\ d_1, & d_1 + \beta, & d_1 + 2\beta, & \ldots, & d_1 + (f-1)\beta \\ d_2, & d_2 + \beta, & d_2 + 2\beta, & \ldots, & d_2 + (f-1)\beta \\ \cdot & & & \cdot & \\ \cdot & \cdot & \cdot & \cdot & \\ \cdot & & & \cdot & \\ d_{j-1}, & d_j + \beta, & d_j + 2\beta, & \ldots, & d_j + (f-1)\beta \end{vmatrix} \quad (6)$$

As follows, the first column of $NF(P)$ contains all the primitive words that must be fetched by P. The rows show the minimal files formed by each primitive word. The procedure of obtaining NF from PF is called a β-*expansion,* where $\beta = \gcd((T, T^*)$.

   Example.   Let $T = 30$ processors be connected with the CAM memory containing $T^* = 105$ words. Let us find gcd $(T, T^*) = \gcd(30, 105) = 15$, and $f = 105/15 = 7$. Suppose that a processor P must fetch the following primitive words: $PF(P) = \{w, d_1[w], d_2[w]\}$, where $d_1 = 2$ and $d_2 = 5$. Thus, during each revolution, it fetches a nonminimal job file, NF(P), that includes the following words given by their relative positions with respect to *w:*

$$
NF(P) = \begin{vmatrix} 0, & 15, & 2 \cdot 15, & 3 \cdot 15, & 4 \cdot 15, & 5 \cdot 15, & 6 \cdot 15 \\ 2, & 2 + 15, & 2 + 2 \cdot 15, & 2 + 3 \cdot 15, & 2 + 4 \cdot 15, & 2 + 5 \cdot 15, & 2 + 6 \cdot 15 \\ 5, & 5 + 15, & 5 + 2 \cdot 15, & 5 + 3 \cdot 15, & 5 + 4 \cdot 15, & 5 + 5 \cdot 15, & 5 + 6 \cdot 15 \end{vmatrix}
$$

This file will contain $3 \cdot 7 = 21$ words. Thus, for a noninterfering file allocation, the memory can be accessed by not more than five processors ($5 = 105/21$). However, as will be shown below, since this allocation is irregular, it is the least interfering allocation, and the noninterfering processor set will contain six processors separated by displacement $x = 8$ (see Sec. 2.6.2.1).   ■

In the following sections we will study noninterfering and least interfering file allocations for nonminimal data files (regular and irregular). Before developing some results for the general case whereby $j > 1$ and d_1 does not divide any d_i, let us consider a particular case of regular files whereby the primitive file PF(P) is given as

$$
PF\ (P) = \{0, d, 2d, \ldots, (j - 1)d\}
$$

where $j \cdot d \le \beta = \gcd(T, T^*)$.

A nonminimal file handled by processor P is called a *regular nonminimal file, NF,* if its primitive file is made of all equally distant primitive words; i.e., PF = $\{0, d, 2d, \ldots, (j - 1)d\}$.

2.6.1 Regular Nonminimal Files

Using β-expansion procedure, one obtains the following regular nonminimal file.

$$
NF = \begin{vmatrix} 0, & \beta, & 2\beta, & \ldots, & (f - 1)\beta \\ d, & d + \beta, & d + 2\beta, & \ldots, & d + \beta(f - 1) \\ 2d, & 2d + \beta, & 2d + 2\beta, & \ldots, & 2d + \beta(f - 1) \\ \bullet & & & & \\ \bullet & & & & \\ \bullet & & & & \\ (j - 1)d, & (j - 1)d + \beta, & (j - 1)d + 2\beta, & \ldots, & (j - 1) \cdot d + \beta(f - 1) \end{vmatrix} \quad (7)
$$

As was shown in Fig. IV.13, one can have two types of regular nonminimal files:

1. *Divisible regular files,* where $j \cdot d = \beta$ and $\beta = \gcd(T, T^*)$
2. *Nondivisible regular files,* where $j \cdot d < \beta$

The next two sections will discuss the noninterfering allocation for these two files.

2.6.1.1 Divisible regular files

For divisible regular files, there exists a noninterfering file allocation. A noninterfering processor set consists of d processors given by the following relative distances to each other: NPS = {0, 1, 2, ..., d − 1}. Indeed, for the closest processor $P^{(d)} = d[P]$ that does not belong to NPS, its nonminimal file $NF(P^{(d)}) = d[NF(P)] = NF(P)$; i.e., there is a complete coincidence in two nonminimal files acquired by processors P and d[P].

Example. Let us construct divisible regular files for the following processor-memory interconnection scheme: $T = 27$, $T^* = 45$, $j = 3$. This means the following: since $\beta = \gcd(T, T^*) = \gcd(27, 45) = 9$, $f = T^*/\beta = 45/9 = 5$, and $d = \beta/j = 9/3 = 3$, one can select a noninterfering nonminimal file allocation. Each nonminimal file NF contains $|NF|$ members, where $|NF| = f \cdot j = 5 \cdot 3 = 15$. The set of noninterfering processors is given as NPS = {0, 1, 2} = {P, 1[P], 2[P]}. This allocation is noninterfering since it introduces no dummy clock periods in accessing and achieves a complete filling of the available memory space. Each nonminimal file is given as follows:

$NF^{[0]} =$

$\beta \cdot \ell$ \ $d \cdot m$	$0 \cdot \beta$	$1 \cdot \beta$	$2 \cdot \beta$	$3 \cdot \beta$	$f - 1 = 4 \cdot \beta$
0,	0,	9,	18,	27,	36
1d	3,	12,	21,	30,	39
2d	6,	15,	24,	33,	42

$\ell = 0, \ldots, f - 1$
$m = 0, \ldots, j - 1$

$NF^{[1]} =$

$\beta \cdot \ell + 1$ \ $d \cdot m$	$0\beta + 1$,	$1\beta + 1$,	$2\beta + 1$,	$3\beta + 1$,	$4\beta + 1$
0	1,	10,	19,	28,	37
$1 \cdot d$	4,	13,	22,	31,	40
2d	7,	16,	25,	34,	43

$NF^{(2)} =$

$d \cdot m$ \ $\beta \cdot \ell + 2$	$0\beta + 2$	$1\beta + 2$	$2\beta + 2$	$3\beta + 2$	$4\beta + 2$
0	2,	11,	20,	29,	38
$1 \cdot d$	5,	14,	23,	32,	41
$2d$	7,	17,	26,	35,	44

As follows,

$NF^{(3)} =$
$NF^{(4)} =$

$d \cdot m$ \ $\beta \cdot \ell + 3$	$0\beta + 3$	$1\beta + 3$	$2\beta + 3$	$3\beta + 3$	$4\beta + 3$
0	3,	12,	21,	30,	39
$1 \cdot d$	6,	15,	24,	33,	42
$2d$	9,	18,	27,	36,	$45 \equiv 0$

and $NF^{(3)}$ coincides with $NF^{(0)}$. ∎

2.6.1.2 Nondivisible Regular Files

As follows, from Sec. 2.6.1. this chapter, by a nondivisible regular file, NF, we mean a nonminimal file accessed by processor P and specified with the following parameters:

1. Its primitive file is PF = $\{0, d, 2d, \ldots, (j - 1)d\}$, where d is the equal shifting distance parameter.
2. $d \cdot j < \beta$, where $\beta = \gcd(T, T^*)$, T is the number of processors, and T^* is the number of words of the content-addressable memory CAM.

Since $d \cdot j < \beta$, j may not be a divisor of β. Thus, the distance d will be presented as the following equation:

$$d = [\beta/j] \cdot x - \beta \cdot y \tag{8}$$

We obtained a linear Diophantine equation also called the *modular equation*. Generally, as was shown in [73], a Diophantine equation $ax + by = c$ has a solution (x, y) only if $gcd(a, b)$ is a divisor of c. For our case, we obtain that the modular equation (8) has a solution if and only if $gcd([\beta/J], \beta)$ is a divisor of equal distance d. Therefore if β, j, and d are given, not all d's are allowed to have an x and y solution of the modular equation. However, if for β, j, and d, there is an integer solution, there exists a noninterfering file allocation whereby no dummy clock periods are introduced in file fetches. Otherwise, one can find the least interfering file allocation whereby the number of dummy clock periods lost in file fetches is minimal. The interesting theorem below establishes the conditions of noninterfering file allocation. Its validity and significance are established via examples that follow.

> ***Theorem 1.***   If there exists an integer solution x and y of the modular equation $d = g(j) \bullet x - \beta \bullet y$, where $g(j) = [\beta/j]$ and $gcd(\beta, x) = 1$, then there exists a noninterfering file allocation whereby a noninterfering processor set is NPS = $\{P^{(0)}, P^{(x)}, P^{(2x)}, \ldots, P^{(g-1)x)}\}$, where $P^{(ix)} = ix[P^{(0)}]$, and x is the root of the modular equation. Each processor, $P^{(ix)}$, but the last one, $P^{(g-1)x}$, accesses a standard nonminimal file, $NF^{(ix)}$, containing $j \bullet f$ members, where j is the index of allocation. In other words, if $P^{(0)}$ accesses $NF^{(0)}$, then any $P^{(ix)}$ but $P^{(g-1)x}$ accesses $NF^{(ix)}$ = $ix[NF^{(0)}]$. The last processor, $P^{(g-1)x}$, fetches a smaller nonminimal file, $NF_L^{(g-1)x}$ obtained from the standard file, $NF^{(g-1)x}$, by erasing the last L words, where $L = g \bullet f \bullet j - T^*$, since these words are included in $NF^{(0)}$.

> ***Corollary.***   For the modular equation $d = g(j) \bullet x - \beta \bullet y$ having $g(j) = \beta/j$, there exists the trivial solution $x = 1$, $y = 0$. Therefore, for minimal ($j = 1$) and nonminimal divisible files ($d = g(j) = \beta/j$), the noninterfering processor set includes $g(j)$ members with displacement $x = 1$: NPS = $\{P, 1[P], 2[P], \ldots, (g(j) - 1)[P]\}$.

Example.   Let memory CAM have $T^* = 42$ words. Suppose that this memory is attached to $T = 28$ processors. Suppose that $d = 3$ and $j = 3$; i.e., for each nonminimal file NF, its primitive file contains $j = 3$ primitive words with the same relative distance $d = 3$ from each other: PF = $\{0, d, 2d, \ldots, (j - 1) \bullet d\} = \{0, d, 2d\} = \{0, 3, 6\}$. Since $\beta = gcd(T, T^*) = gcd(28, 42) = 14$ and $d \bullet j = 3 \bullet 3 = 9$, we have $\beta > d \bullet j$. Let us find $f = T^*/\beta = 42/14 = 3$. In accordance with Theorem 1, there exists a noninterfering file allocation for which $L = 3$; i.e., $L = g \bullet f \bullet j - T^* = [\beta/j] \bullet f \bullet j - T = 5 \bullet 3 \bullet 3 - 42 = 3$. Thus, only three members of two nonminimal file sets are common. Let us find the x and y roots: since $gcd([\beta/j], \beta) = gcd([14/3], 14) = gcd(5, 14) = 1$, there exists an x and y solution of the modular equation (8): $d = [\beta/j] \bullet x - \beta \bullet y = 5x - 14y = 5 \bullet 9 - 14 \bullet 3 = 45 - 42$. Therefore, processor displacement $x = 9$ and the noninterfering processor set is given as NPS = $\{0, x, 2x, \ldots, ([\beta/j] - 1)x\} = \{0, x, 2x, 3x, 4x\}$. Each processor of the NPS accesses the nonminimal file given below and in Fig. IV.16, where each memory word is marked by the unique processor that fetches this word.

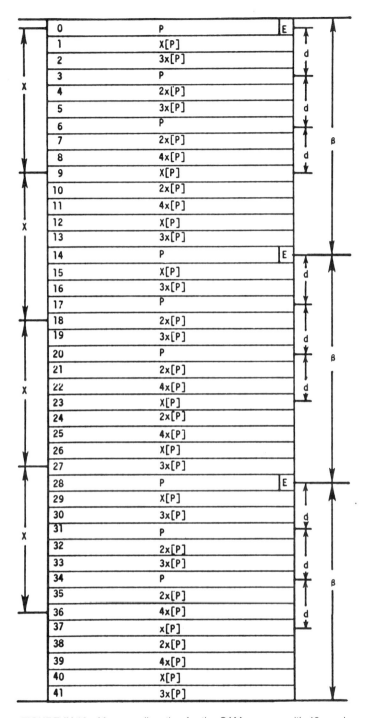

FIGURE IV.16 Memory allocation for the CAM-memory with 42 words

295

NF(P) =

	0	$\beta \cdot 1$	$\beta \cdot 2$
0	0	14	28
d	3	17	31
2d	6	20	34

, $\mathrm{NF}^{(x)}$ =

	$0 + x$	$\beta \cdot 1 + x$	$\beta \cdot 2 + x$
0	9	23	37
d	12	26	40
2d	15	29	1

$\mathrm{NF}^{(2x)}$ =

	$0 + 2x$	$\beta \cdot 1 + 2x$	$\beta \cdot 2 + 2x$
0	18	32	4
d	21	35	7
2d	24	38	10

$\mathrm{NF}^{(3x)}$ =

	$0 + 3x$	$\beta \cdot 1 + 3x$	$\beta \cdot 2 + 3x$
0	27	41	13
d	30	2	16
2d	33	5	19

$\mathrm{NF}^{(4x)}$ =

	$0 + 4x$	$\beta \cdot 1 + 4x$	$\beta \cdot 2 + 4x$
0	36	8	22
d	39	11	25
2d	0	14	28

As follows, the only common words are words 0, 14, and 28 in files $\mathrm{NF}^{(0)}$ and $\mathrm{NF}^{(4x)}$. Assume that 0, 14, and 28 belong only to $\mathrm{NF}^{(0)}$. They will be marked with a special bit E in Fig. IV.16. Thus, $\mathrm{NF}_L^{(4x)}$ is obtained from $\mathrm{NF}^{(4x)}$ by erasing words 0, 14, and 28 from it. The file allocation is noninterfering, since no memory words are empty. ■

2.6.1.3 Generation of processor addresses for nonminimal file allocation

In this section, we will devise the procedures for finding the address of a processor that has to fetch a current output word w issued by the memory. Since for the minimal and divisible regular files, the noninterfering processor set is given as NPS = {0, 1, 2, ..., $(d - 1)$}, each dth word of the memory goes to the same processor. Thus, generation of the processor addresses may be obtained with mod-d counter that shows the address of a processor that has to receive a current output word.

For the nondivisible regular files, the procedure of finding a processor address becomes more complicated since two adjacent words w and one $1[w]$, should be fetched by the two processors which may not be adjacent in the multiprocessor system. For instance, in the example above, if word 3 is in $\mathrm{NF}^{(0)}$ and is accessed by $\mathrm{P}^{(0)}$, then the next word 4 should be accessed by $\mathrm{P}^{(2x)} = \mathrm{P}^{(18)}$ since it belongs to $\mathrm{NF}^{(2x)}$, where 2 • x = 18 (Fig. IV.16.).

Therefore, one must devise procedures for generating processor addresses for non-divisible regular files because only then can one take advantage of the elegant and attractive attributes of the allocations that are developed.

Address Generation Table To develop addressing procedures for the nondivisible regular files, we will construct the *address generation table* containing $g \cdot j$ rows and f columns, where $g = [\beta/j]$ and $f = T^*/\beta$. The table is partitioned into g squares so that each ith square is occupied by the nonminimal file, $NF^{(ix)}$, where $i = 0, ..., g - 1$.

Example. Table IV.2 shows the address generation table built for the data of the previous example. It contains f columns, where $f = T^*/\beta = 42/14 = 3$ and $j \cdot [\beta/j] = 3 \cdot 5 = 15$ rows. It is partionied into $g = 5$ squares marked by respective files, $NF^{(ix)}$ ($i = 0, 1, ..., 4$) and the address $i \cdot x$ of the processor that fetches all entries of this file. ∎

TABLE IV.2
ADDRESS GENERATION TABLE

Processor Address	0	1·β	2·β	
0x	0	14	28	
0x	3	17	31	$NF^{(0x)}$
0x	6	20	34	
1x	9	23	37	
1x	12	26	40	$NF^{(1x)}$
1x	15	29	1	
2x	18	32	4	
2x	21	35	7	$NF^{(2x)}$ $f=3$, $g=[\frac{\beta}{j}]=5$
2x	24	38	10	
3x	27	41	13	
3x	30	2	16	$NF^{(3x)}$
3x	33	5	19	
4x	36	8	22	
4x	39	11	25	$NF^{(4x)}$
0x	0	14	28	

$g \cdot j$, j, j_L

$\longleftarrow f \longrightarrow$

As follows, from the construction of each $NF^{(ix)}$, each processor address $i \cdot x$ $(i = 0, ..., g - 1)$, includes two factors: *variable factor i* and the *displacement factor x*, where x is the root of the modular equation. Thus, to find the effective processor address ix, we have to find i, since x may be stored in a register for a given allocation. Thereafter, $i \cdot x$ is obtained via simple multiplication.

One can examine the following obvious properties of the address generation table: All words from the same column k ($k = 0, ..., f - 1$) are fetched by such processors whose addresses are changed as follows:

1. *Variable factor i* of each processor address grows from 0 to $g - 1$ and then assumes again the 0 value for the L common words belonging to $NF^{(0)}$ and $NF^{(gx)}$.

2. j consecutive words from the same column and the same square $NF^{(ix)}$ are specified with the same processor address.

3. The shifting distance between any two consecutive words, w and w', from the same column is d; i.e., $w' = D[w]$.

Processor Counter   These three properties are crucial for the processor address-generating procedures that follow. Since for all consecutive memory words belonging to the same column the variable factor i changes consecutively from $i = 0$ to $i = g - 1$, it may be generated by a processor counter, PCO, with the following properties:

1. PCO increments the variable factor i of the processor address, ix, from 0 to $g - 1$.

2. The same value i of the variable factor is maintained for j consecutive words. Thereafter, $i = i + 1 \pmod{g}$.

3. The highest value $(g - 1)$ of the variable factor i is maintained for the number of words j_L that is smaller than j, where $j_L = j - L/f$; L is the number of common words attributed to $NF^{(0)}$, and f is the number of columns.

4. Since one PCO may generate processor addresses for memory words only from the same column and the distance between two consecutive memory words from the same column is d, one must have d PCO numbered as PCO_0, PCO_1, ..., PCO_{d-1} so that PCO_m computes the variable factor i of processor addresses for all memory words with distance d and residue $m = 0, 1, ..., d - 1$.

Example.   For the address generation table of the previous example having $d = 3$, it is sufficient to have $d = 3$ processor counters, PCO_0, PCO_1, and PCO_2, so that PCO_0 counts the variable factors i of processor addresses for the following memory words: 0, 3, 6, 9, 12, 15, 18, 21, 24, 27, 30, 33, 36, 39. All these words are multiples of $d = 3$ with residue $R = 0$. The processor counter PCO_1 counts processor addresses for the following memory words with residue 1: 1, 4, 7, 10, 13, 16, 19, 22, 25, 28, 31, 34, 37, 40. Each such word has the following representation: $w = d \cdot p + 1$ where $p \geq 0$ and $d = 3$. Finally, PCO_2 counts processor addresses for the remaining memory words with residue 2: 2, 5, 8, 11, 14, 17, 20, 23, 26, 29, 32, 35, 38, 41. Therefore, together PCO_0, PCO_1, and PCO_2 generate processor addresses for all memory words.

To find out the processor counter that shows the variable factor i of a current processor address, $i \cdot x$, one must have a mod-d counter, MCO, that at any moment of time shows the PCO that must send its value i to activate the memory word fetch to the processor with the address $i \cdot x$.

Therefore, each PCO is represented by the transition table that contains $g \cdot j - L/f$ states (Fig. IV. 17). Each state of the transition table identifies the variable factor i of the processor address $i \cdot x$, where $i = 0, \ldots, g - 1$, inasmuch as there are g processors, $P^{(0)}$, $P^{(ix)}$, ..., $P^{(g-1)x}$, whose nonminimal files are noninterfering.

In the PCO transition table, each variable factor but the highest one, $g - 1$, is represented by j consecutive states. The highest one, $g - 1$, is represented by j_L states, where $j_L = j - L/f$. ∎

Example. Figure IV.17 shows three transition tables for PCO_0, PCO_1, and PCO_2 built for the address generation table (Table IV.2). Since each column of this table contains 14 different words ($14 = g \cdot j - L/f = [14/3] \cdot 3 - 3/3$, the counter transition table contains 14 states. Since the variable factor i of the processor address ix changes from 0 to $g - 1 = 4$, the states of the transition table represent integers ranging from 0 to 4. Since the allocation index j is 3, each integer i ($i = 0, \ldots, 3$) is represented by three consecutive states. The highest, $i = 4$, is represented by j_L states, where $j_L = j - L/f = 3 - 3/3 = 2$. ∎

Concurrent Operation of Processor Counters As follows from the previous discussion, d, processor counters, PCO_0, ..., PCO_{d-1}, may generate variable factors i of processor addresses, $i \cdot x$, for all memory words. The i factor of the processor address $i \cdot x$ for a current memory word is generated by a PCO_ℓ whose position ℓ is determined by the mod-d counter MCO.

Thus, the procedure of processor address generation starts with MCO counting mod d, indicating which PCO_ℓ ($\ell = 0, \ldots, d - 1$) should issue its current content i in order that the processor identified with address $i \cdot x$ fetch the current output memory word (Fig. IV.18).

Each clock period the mod-d counter MCO issues one signal, 0_ℓ (mod d), indicating that it stores integer ℓ. The 0_ℓ signal activates the respective processor counter, PCO_ℓ, into the following parallel actions.

Action 1. Sending its current content i to the processor address multiplier, PAM.

Action 2. Making transition to the next state of its transition diagram.

The initial setting of the counters is determined as follows. Since each PCO_ℓ counts the processor addresses for memory words with residue ℓ ($\ell = 0, \ldots, d - 1$), and the smallest word with residue ℓ is ℓ, in the beginning of the address generation,

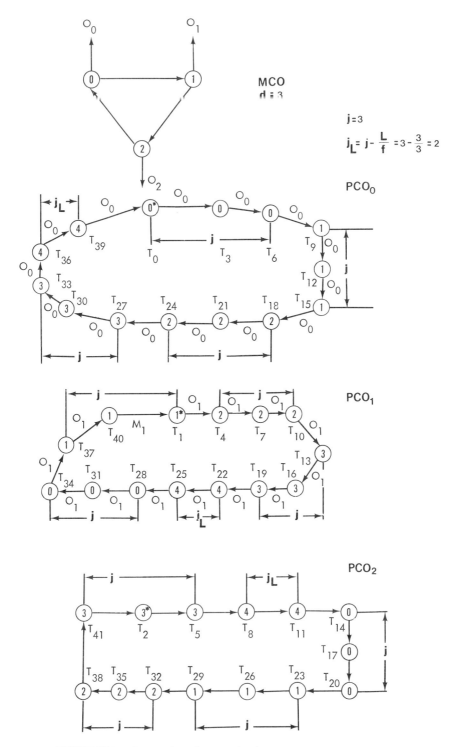

FIGURE IV.17 Sequencing diagrams for the processor counters that generate processor addresses

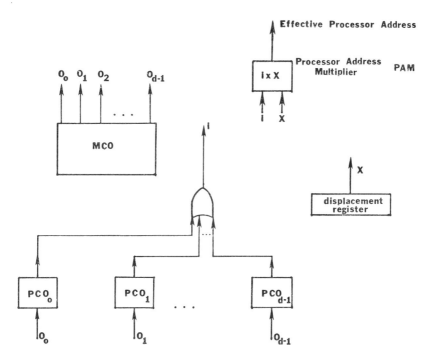

FIGURE IV.18 Block diagram of the processor address generation

each PCO_ℓ should store a variable factor i such that memory word ℓ is a member of the nonminimal file, $NF^{(ix)}$. For instance, in Fig. IV. 17 the initial settings of PCO_0, PCO_1, and PCO_2 are (they are marked with asterisks) PCO_0 stores 0^*, since the smallest word with residue 0 is 0 and $0 \in NF^{(0)}$; PCO_1 stores 1, since it counts processor addresses for all memory words with residue 1 and $1 \in NF^{(1x)}$; PCO_2 stores 3^*, since $2 \in NF^{(3x)}$.

The next problem is to determine the position of the initial variable factor i^* among j or j_L states marked with i of the PCO transition diagram. This is determined by the following procedure.

For each PCO_ℓ find the $NF^{(ix)}$ that contains residue ℓ. Find the row m that contains ℓ $(m = 0, ..., j - 1)$. Then m gives the position of initial variable factor i^* among j or j_L consecutive states that represent i in the PCO diagram. Once we establish the initial settings of the PCO counters, it is possible to start the automatic procedure of processor address generation.

Example. Consider generation of processor addresses for nonminimal files constructed in the example of Sec. 2.6.1.2 for the memory with $T^* = 42$ and accessed by $T = 28$ processors. For the noninterfering processor set $NPS = \{0, x, 2x, 3x, 4x,\}$, $\beta = \gcd(T, T^*) = 14, x = 9, d = 3, j = 3$. Since $d = 3$, the processor address generation procedure is performed by three processor counters, PCO_0, PCO_1, and PCO_2, and one mod-3 counter, MCO. Earlier we constructed the transition diagrams of these counters (Fig. IV.17).

Let us now find their initial settings. PCO_0 stores the first 0 marked as 0^*, since 0 is in the first row of $NF^{(0)}$; PCO_1 stores the third 1 (1^*), since 1 is in the third row of $NF^{(1x)}$; PCO_2 stores the second 3(3^*), since 2 is in the second row of $NF^{(3x)}$.

At the moment T_0 memory outputs word 0, MCO stores 0 and issues signal 0_0. Under signal 0_0, counter PCO_0 transfers its initial state 0^* to the PAM multiplier (Fig. IV.18) and performs the $0^* \rightarrow 0$ transition to the next state of its diagram (Fig. IV.17). Therefore, the PAM multiplier issues $0 \cdot x = 0$ processor address for memory word 0.

At the moment T_1, memory outputs word 1, MCO stores 1 and issues signal 0_1 (Fig. IV. 18). Under this signal, the PCO_1 counter transfers initial state 1^* to the PAM multiplier and makes the $1^* \rightarrow 2$ transition (Fig. IV.17). Thus, PAM generates $1 \cdot x = 9$ processor address for the memory word 1.

At the moment T_2 memory outputs word 2, MCO stores 2 and issues 0_2 (Fig. IV.18). Under this signal, the PCO_2 counter transfers its initial state to the PAM and makes the $3^* \rightarrow 3$ transition (Fig. IV.17). Thus, PAM generates processor address $3 \cdot x = 27$ for memory word 2.

At the moment T_3 memory outputs word 3, MCO stores 0 and issues 0_0. The PCO_0 broadcasts its current value 0 to PAM and makes the $0 \rightarrow 0$ transition. Thus, the processor addresses $0 \cdot x = 0$ for word 3, etc. ∎

2.6.1.4 Comparative Evaluation of the Minimal and Nonminimal Regular File Allocations

As follows from the procedures of file allocation introduced for nonminimal regular files, NFs there exists a noninterfering file allocation for $g = \lceil \beta/j \rceil$ files, where $\beta = \gcd(T, T^*)$ and j is the number of primitive words in each NF. Therefore, the noninterfering processor set NPS contains g processors with distance x from each other: NPS $= \{0, x, 2x, \ldots, (g - 1)x\}$, where x is the solution of the modular equation $d = \lceil \beta/j \rceil x - \beta \cdot y$, and d is the distance between two consecutive primitive words of each nonminimal file of NF.

If $x = 1$, then $y = 0$ and $d = g = \beta/j$. This means that the NPS includes consecutive processors: NPS $= \{0, 1, \ldots, d - 1\}$. Thus, all nonminimal files are divisible by d and contain $j \cdot f$ members. If $x \neq 1$, then $y \neq 0$, and $d \neq g$, where $g = \lceil \beta/j \rceil$. Therefore, NPS includes nonconsecutive processors $P^{(0)}, P^{(x)}, \ldots, P^{(g-1)x}$. Each of these processors (but the last one) fetch a nonminimal file containing $j \cdot f$ members; the last processor, $P^{(g-1)x}$, fetches a nonminimal file with $j \cdot f - L$ words, where $L = g \cdot j \cdot f - T^*$. The allocation is noninterfering.

Therefore, from the time viewpoint, the nonminimal regular allocation loses no dummy clocks in accessing each file and is as good as the minimal file allocation. Here, however, one can obtain a better time of accessing each data file compared to the minimal allocation, since during each revolution $f \cdot j$ words from each file are fetched rather than f words, as is true for the minimal file allocation. However, minimization in the total time of file access by j is accompanied by reducing by j, the concurrency identified as the number of files accessed during each memory revolution.

2.6.2 Irregular Files

A file is called irregular if (1) it is nonminimal, and (2) its primitive file PF is given as PF $= \{0, d_1, d_2, \ldots, d_{j-1}\}$, where shifting distances $d_1, d_2, \ldots, d_j$ are not consecutive multiples of the same interger d.

In this section we will study a file allocation of irregular files. As follows from Theorem 1, generally there exists no noninterfering file allocation of irregular files. Indeed, the modular equation $d = \lceil \beta/j \rceil x - \beta \bullet y$ has no integer solutions, x and y, by definition, because $d_1 \neq d$ and $d_2 \neq 2d, \ldots, d_{j-1} \neq (j-1)d$. Thus, no d can be found, not to mention other conditions, such as gcd $(\lceil \beta/j \rceil, \beta) = 1$ and $\gcd(x, \beta) = 1$.

However, if we find the closest approximation of PF $= \{0, d_1, d_2, \ldots, d_{j-1}$ with some set $PF_d = \{0, d, 2d, \ldots, (j-1)d\}$ of equal distances, it is possible to find a least interfering file allocation. This means that it is possible to construct such a noninterfering processor set, NPS, that (1) each P ϵ NPS fetches a nonminimal file, NF, given by Eq. (6), and (2) between different files fetched by members of NPS there exists a minimal interference (i.e., the minimal number of common words). Thereafter, each common memory word is marked with a special bit C to exclude its fetch by a processor.

Therefore, a dummy clock will be introduced into a file access each time a memory word with bit C is the output word, since no processor will fetch this word. The number of such dummy clocks will be minimal, since a given irregular allocation is represented with the best regular approximation that allows a noninterfering allocation in accordance with Theorem 1.

As will be shown below, the procedures for obtaining a noninterfering processor set, NPS, are deterministic and described with the use of the irregular allocation algorithm that ends with marking common words belonging to more than one data file with bit C = 1.

Before presenting an irregular file-allocation algorithm, we will introduce an example of irregular file allocation and establish the least interference of this allocation.

2.6.2.1 Example of Irregular File Allocation

Example. Let memory CAM contain 105 words ($T^* = 105$) and it is connected with $T = 30$ processors. Suppose that processor $P^{(0)}$ fetches the following primitive file: $PF^{(0)} = \{0, 2, 5\}$; i.e., $d_1 = 2$, $d_2 = 5$, and $j = 3$. Since d_1 does not divide d_2, $PF^{(0)}$ is irregular. The resulting nonminimal file, $NF^{(0)}$, will contain $j \bullet f = 21$ words, where $j = 3$, $f = T^*/\gcd(T, T^*) = 105/15 = 7$. Using Eq. (6), let us construct this file.

$NF^{(0)} =$

d_i \ $\beta \bullet \ell$	0	$\beta \bullet 1$	$\beta \bullet 2$	$\beta \bullet 3$	$\beta \bullet 4$	$\beta \bullet 5$	$\beta \bullet 6$
0	0	15	30	45	60	75	90
d_1	2	17	32	47	62	77	92
d_2	5	20	35	50	65	80	95

$\ell = 0, 1, 2, 3, 4, 5, 6$

If we select a noninterfering processor set as NPS = $\{0, x, 2x, 3x, 4x, 5x\}$, where $x = 8$, then we will have a file allocation with the least interference. (A formal procedure for finding this x will be given in the example in Sec. 2.6.2.2.) Indeed, if processor $P^{(0)}$ accesses $NF^{(0)}$, given above, then processor $P^{(x)} = x[P]$ will access the following $NF^{(x)}$:

$$NF^{(x)} = \begin{vmatrix} 8 & 23 & 38 & 53 & 68 & 83 & 98 \\ 10 & 25 & 40 & 55 & 70 & 85 & 100 \\ 13 & 28 & 43 & 58 & 73 & 88 & 103 \end{vmatrix}$$

The processor $P^{(2x)}$ will access the following $NF^{(2x)}$:

$$NF^{(2x)} = \begin{vmatrix} 16 & 31 & 46 & 61 & 76 & 91 & 1 \\ 18 & 33 & 48 & 63 & 78 & 93 & 3 \\ 21 & 36 & 51 & 66 & 81 & 96 & 6 \end{vmatrix}$$

The remaining processors, $P^{(3x)}$, $P^{(4x)}$, and $P^{(5x)}$, will access $NF^{(3x)}$, $NF^{(4x)}$, and $NF^{(5x)}$, respectively, where

$$NF^{(3x)} = \begin{vmatrix} 24 & 39 & 54 & 69 & 84 & 99 & 9 \\ 26 & 41 & 56 & 71 & 86 & 101 & 11 \\ 29 & 44 & 59 & 74 & 89 & 104 & 14 \end{vmatrix}$$

$$NF^{(4x)} = \begin{vmatrix} \boxed{32 \quad 47 \quad 62 \quad 77 \quad 92 \quad 2 \quad 17} \\ 34 \quad 49 \quad 64 \quad 79 \quad 94 \quad 4 \quad 19 \\ 37 \quad 52 \quad 67 \quad 82 \quad 97 \quad 7 \quad 22 \end{vmatrix}$$

$$NF^{(5x)} = \begin{vmatrix} \boxed{40 \quad 55 \quad 70 \quad 85 \quad 100 \quad 10 \quad 25} \\ 42 \quad 57 \quad 72 \quad 87 \quad 102 \quad 12 \quad 27 \\ \boxed{45 \quad 60 \quad 75 \quad 90 \quad 0 \quad 15 \quad 30} \end{vmatrix}$$

As seen, the allocation is 21-interfering. Indeed, $NF^{(0)}$, $NF^{(x)}$, $NF^{(2x)}$, and $NF^{(3x)}$ have no common words at all; as for $NF^{(4x)}$, it has a common row of seven words with $NF^{(0)}$; $NF^{(5x)}$ has one common row with $NF^{(0)}$ (seven words) and one common row with $NF^{(x)}$ (seven words). The common rows of $NF^{(4x)}$ and $NF^{(5x)}$ are squared. In all, 21 words are common.

The minimal interference of this allocation is established as follows. If, for the same memory containing 105 words, a noninterfering allocation exists, it requires $105/21 = 5$ processors, where each processor fetches $j \cdot f = 3 \cdot 7 = 21$ memory words. However, in accordance with Theorem 1, no noninterfering allocation exists. Our allocation requires six processors instead of five, i.e., only one processor more than is required by a noninterfering allocation. For this allocation, since each processor fetches 21 words, six processors will fetch $21 \cdot 6 = 126$ words. Since the memory stores 105 words, $126 - 105 = 21$ words are common. The number of common words is minimal, since the memory is accessed only by one processor more than is required by such a noninterfering processor set that can be constructed for the noninterfering allocation. ■

2.6.2.2 Irregular File Allocation Algorithm

Given irregular primitive file PF $= \{0, d_1, d_2, \ldots, d_{j-1}\}$. Find the noninterfering processor set NPS such that the resulting allocation includes all memory words and introduces the least interference or the minimal memory overhead between various nonminimal files accessed by individual processors from the set NPS.

Step 1. For a given irregular primitive file, PF $= \{0, d_1, d_2, \ldots, d_{j-1}\}$, find a set, PF$_d = \{0, d, 2d, \ldots, (j-1)d\}$, of equal distances such that intersection PF $\cap$ PF$_d$ contains maximal number of members. The set PF$_d$ is called the *maximal approximation* of PF.

Step 2. Find $[\beta/j] = g(j)$, where $\beta = \gcd(T, T^*)$ and T is the number of processors, T^* is the number of memory words, and j is the number of words in PF$_d$.

Step 3. Construct the modular equation $d = [\beta/j]x - \beta y = gx - \beta y$. Find its solution, x and y, such that $\gcd(\beta, x) = 1$ and $\gcd(g, \beta) = 1$. If no integer solution, x, y, can be found, then either change j in PF$_d$ or select another PF$_{d'}$, etc., until such d' and/or j' are found that $d' = g' \cdot x' - \beta \cdot y'$ has the integer solution x' and y'.

Step 4. For each shifting distance, d_i, that is a member of the irregular primitive file PF, form the following equations: $d_1 = g_1 \cdot x - \beta \cdot y_1$; $d_2 = g_2 \cdot x - \beta \cdot y_2$; $\ldots$; $d_{j-1} = g_{j-1} \cdot x - \beta \cdot y_{j-1}$, where x is the fixed root of the modular equation $d = g \cdot x - \beta \cdot y$ found in Step 3. All these equations have solutions g_i, y_i ($i = 1, \ldots, j - 1$), respectively, since $d_i < \beta$ and $\gcd(x, \beta) = 1$; i.e., $\gcd(x, \beta)$ divides d_i ($i = 1, \ldots, j - 1$).

Step 5. Order numbers $g_1, \ldots, g_{j-1}$, obtained in Step 4 as $g'_1 > g'_2 > \ldots, > g'_{j-1}$. The noninterfering processor set NPS will contain λ members, where λ is the maximal difference between two *consecutive* g'_i and g'_{i+1}, i.e., $\lambda = \max(g'_i - g'_{i+1})$. NPS $= \{P^{(0)}, P^{(x)}, P^{(2x)}, \ldots, P^{((\lambda-1)x)}\}$, where x is the shifting distance between two consecutive members of NPS.

Example. Using the irregular file-allocation algorithm, let us find a noninterfering processor set for the previous example, whereby the CAM memory with $T^* = 105$

words is connected with $T = 30$ processors and primitive file PF $= \{0, 2, 5\}$; i.e., $d_1 = 2$, $d_2 = 5$, and $j = 3$. Since $\beta = \gcd(30, 105) = 15$, let us select PF$_d = \{0, 2, 4\}$, leading to $d = 2$ and $g = \beta/j = 15/3 = 5$. However, since $\gcd(\lfloor \beta/j \rfloor, \beta) = \gcd(5, 15) = 5 \neq 1$, the modular equation $d = \lceil \beta/j \rceil x - \beta \cdot y$ has no integer solution x, y. Therefore, the maximal approximation, PF$_d = \{0, 2, 4\}$, has to be modified by selecting such j that $\gcd(\lceil \beta/j \rceil, \beta) = 1$. Suppose that $j = 4$; then PF$_d = \{0, 2, 4, 6\}$ and $g = \lceil \beta/j \rceil = \lceil 15/4 \rceil = 4$. Therefore, $d = 4 \cdot x - 15 \cdot y$ or $2 = 4 \cdot x - 15y$. This equation has solution $x = 8$, $y = 2$, because $2 = 4 \cdot 8 - 15 \cdot 2 = 32 - 30$. Therefore, we obtain processor displacement $x = 8$ for the irregular allocation with PF $= \{0, 2, 5\}$. Let us now find how many members will be in the NPS processing set.

Since the primitive file PF has $d_1 = 2$ and $d_2 = 5$, we find numbers g_1 and g_2 by constructing the following equations:

$$2 = 8 \cdot g_1 - 15y_1, \qquad g_1 = 4, y_1 = 2$$

$$5 = 8 \cdot g_2 - 15y_2, \qquad g_2 = 10, y_2 = 5$$

Therefore, the noninterfering processor set NPS contains λ members, where $\lambda = g_2 - g_1 = 10 - 4 = 6$; NPS $= \{P^{(0)}, P^{(1 \cdot 8)}, P^{(2 \cdot 8)}, P^{(3 \cdot 8)}, P^{(4 \cdot 8)}, P^{(5 \cdot 8)}\}$. The minimal interference of this allocation was established in Sec. 2.6.2.1.

As follows from the material of this section, the irregular file allocation is entirely algorithmic because one can find both x and λ for the noninterfering processor set NPS $= \{P^{(0)}, P^{(1x)}, \ldots, P^{((\lambda - 1)x)}\}$, via the algorithmic procedures specified above.

If common words are then eliminated entirely from all interfering files, one obtains irregular file allocation with the least interference when memory introduces a minimal number of dummy clocks in file accessing. Therefore, if possible, one should use either minimal or regular file allocations which are specified by a permanent distance $d \geq 1$ and allocation index $j \geq 1$. ■

2.7 Conclusions: Assessment of the Allocation Methodology Presented

This section has shown that if T processors are connected with one circulating memory having T^* words then the following cases of allocation can be distinguished:

I. *Regular allocation,* whereby a single memory is accessed by $g(j)$ processors with the following processor addresses: 0, 1x, 2x, ..., $(g(j) - 1)x$, where $g(j) = \{\lceil \gcd(T, T^*) \rceil/j\}$, and the processor displacement x is the root of the modular equation $d = g(j) \cdot x - \beta \cdot y$. The regular allocation is called *minimal* if allocation factor $j = 1$ and *divisible* if allocation factor j divides $\gcd(T, T^*)$. In both cases, $x = 1$ and $y = 0$. If allocation is *not divisible,* we obtain a nontrivial displacement x of the processor address, $i \cdot x$. As follows, all regular allocations (minimal, nonminimal divisible, and nonminimal nondivisible) are noninterfering; i.e., circulating memory is completely filled with information and loses no clock periods during each file access.

II. *Irregular allocation,* whereby a single memory is accessed by λ processors, where $\lambda = \max(g_i - g_{i+1})$ and the addresses of participating processors are 0, x, $2x$,

..., $(\lambda - 1) \cdot x$. The allocation described is the least interfering since a minimal number of words of memory CAM are empty. Thus, during memory circulation a minimal number of clock periods are wasted.

Therefore, to provide either noninterfering or minimal interfering file allocation, one must connect only $g(j)$ or λ processors with one content-addressable memory. The remaining processors are idle. To eliminate their idleness, it is necessary for a regular allocation to have NM circulating memories serving T processors, where NM $= T/g(j)$, and $g(j)$ processors are connected with one memory (Fig. IV.15).

Similarly, one finds that the number of memories for irregular allocation is NM $= T/\lambda$. In Fig. IV.15, we have two circulating memories, CAM_1 and CAM_2, storing files for eight processors partitioned into two groups, GR1 and GR2, where GR1 includes processors P_0, P_2, P_4, and P_6 and GR1 includes P_1, P_3, P_5, and P_7.

Generally, the addresses of the processors connected with the same memory are 0, $1x$, $2x$, ..., $(g - 1)x$ and they are determined via the solution of the modular equation, $d = gx - \beta y$, where 0 address is assigned to the processor that fetches the first output word, w, of the memory M. Therefore, to exclude intersection among any two groups of processors, GR_1 and GR_2 connected to two different circulating memories, CAM_1 and CAM_2, respectively, allocations should be selected which are characterized by the same displacement x and the same number, $g(j)$ or λ, of processors included into each group, GR_i. In Fig. IV.15, $x = 6$ and $g(j) = 4$. Thus, group GR1 is formed of the noninterfering processor set $NPS_1 = \{0, 6 \cdot 1, 6 \cdot 2, 6 \cdot 3\} = \{0, 6, 4, 2\}$ and group GR2 is formed of noninterfering processor set $CPS_2 = \{1, 1 + 6, 1 + 12, 1 + 18\} = \{1, 7, 5, 3\}$. In this case, we will obtain a very effective utilization of processor and memory resources, and either no or a minimal number of clock periods are wasted in each allocation.

Therefore, for regular files one obtains a high-performance memory allocation in which each circulating memory is completely filled with the information. In addition, each memory will fetch $g(j)$ files to $g(j)$ processors, and T processors will be served by $T/g(j)$ circulating memories. The allocation is noninterfering.

For irregular files a very high performance is also achieved whereby in each memory a minimal number of cells is empty and each memory fetches files for λ processors. The number of circulating memories serving T processors will be T/λ. Since λ is greater than $g(j)$, the performance of irregular allocations is not as good as for the regular ones. Therefore, whenever possible, it is preferable to use regular allocations.

In all, the importance of developed allocations for real-time data bases is that they allow concurrent and efficient maintaining of large data bases in a multiprocessor system that incorporates several CAM memories. Each CAM can now serve several processors. This greatly enhances concurrency of the data-base handling, since each data file can be handled and updated in a separate processor concurrently with other files. Due to the fact that each CAM memory is much cheaper than RAM, and it possesses considerable advantages over RAM in storing a relational data base, the proposed architecture can accommodate a huge data base without any sacrifice for the concurrency of the operation in handling data files that are stored in one CAM. Furthermore, the major capability of the allocations developed, that all data files stored in one CAM can be searched and updated during one memory revolution, provides an indisputable justification for using these allocations for all large data bases in which speed, concurrency, and convenience of data file handling become a major characteristic of the application. This is true for all real-time data bases and other nonreal-time, high-speed, data-base applications.

3 CONCLUSIONS TO CHAPTER IV

Chapter IV has presented research results accomplished for the topic, dynamic compiler, which is understood as follows:

1. Development of compilation techniques that allow execution of an ADA language construct by a dynamically reconfigurable system.
2. Development of memory-allocation techniques for the hardware structures that support ADA dynamic data structure.

As shown in this chapter, generally dynamic reconfiguration drastically improves and optimizes compilation, since an ADA high-level language construct finds its natural match in the hardware structure created dynamically, requiring no long interpretation process and no additional time overhead introduced with such interpretation. For instance, once the system with dynamic architecture has reconfigured into a new hardware structure that supports an ADA dynamic data structure, no further interpretation is required since the new hardware structure has been completely created during reconfiguration, and it is now ready to perform execution of the respective ADA construct. Therefore, the new hardware structure can be announced the same way as its language analogue in ADA.

For task rendezvous, both the reconfigurable memory-processor bus (DC bus) and the software organization presented in this chapter totally exclude any waiting time that is present in conventional rendezvous organizations, provided that the task producer (called or calling) generates its data array before this data array is needed by the task consumer of an opposite function. As shown in Chapter III, implementation of such organization becomes possible only with the use of dynamic reconfiguration, whereby both a calling task and a called task have easy access to the parameters of data array stored in the deposit table and deposited by the task producer (called or calling).

As for the contribution of completed research to topic 2 (memory allocation), as shown in this chapter, the system ability of reconfiguration encourages proliferation of optimal memory allocation strategies that improve system performance by achieving a better concurrency and reducing memory overhead in time and space. Therefore, the major result accomplished by this chapter is in establishing the fact that, generally, dynamic reconfiguration optimizes compilation and allows creation of optimal memory-allocation techniques for dynamic data structures.

Chapter V

Algorithm Development

1 INTRODUCTION

In Chapter I we outlined general areas of applications for dynamic architectures; the objective of this chapter is to give a detailed technical description of performance demonstrated by dynamic architecture in the execution of several classes of popular parallel algorithms. These algorithms belong to the following classes:

1. *General-purpose parallel algorithms.* Two such applications are described:

    a. General-purpose program mix

    b. Parallel construct fork-join

The general-purpose program mix describes a mix of 14 programs given by their resource requirements on the processor and memory resources. It is shown that a dynamic architecture achieves a 42% speedup in comparison with a conventional multicomputer system having the same complexity of resources in executing this program mix.

For the fork-join construct, performance gains accomplished by dynamic architecture also show a 42% improvement in comparison with conventional systems.

2. *Producer-consumer algorithms,* whereby one instruction sequence *(producer)* produces data words consumed by another instruction sequence *(consumer).* Four such data dependencies are analyzed: memory-memory, processor-memory-processor, memory-processor-memory, and processor-processor.

Memory-memory data exchange is understood as a conventional long-range data exchange whereby one program writes into its local memory M_i data words that are

309

fetched (consumed) by another program and written into its local memory, M_j, where $i \neq j$. In order not to interrupt the main program run in the processor, P_i, processor P_i should not participate in such exchanges.

Processor-memory-processor exchange is equivalent to the store-fetch data exchange SF used in conventional parallel programming whereby data words computed by one processor P_i are stored in its local memory M_i before being fetched by another processor P_j [71], where $i \neq j$.

Memory-processor-memory exchange is equivalent to the *fetch-store* data exchange FS used in parallel programming whereby processor P_i fetches data words either from its own memory M_i or from nonlocal memory M_j and then sends computed results for storage either to M_i, M_j, or M_k, where $i \neq j \neq k$.

Processor-processor exchange, whereby one processor P_i that computes one program loop is sending its data to another processor P_j; P_j is using these data for another loop computation.

It is shown that for dynamic architectures all these exchanges (which are quite popular for all algorithms featuring data dependencies) can be organized practically instantaneously, introducing practically no time overhead and performance degradation into data-dependent programs.

3. *Array computations* used in relaxation problems and pulse deinterleaving. The last group of algorithms is aimed at formation of pulse trains out of interleaved pulses received in real time. The performance of dynamic architectures in the execution of such algorithms is ideal, since a required array structure is created practically instantaneously with the use of only one program instruction.

4. *Data management* in data bases organized as binary trees. It is shown that if dynamic architectures assume architectural configurations equivalent to reconfigurable binary trees, these hardware structures will greatly improve the performance of data bases created dynamically. Thus, dynamic architectures may reconfigure into such states that support *dynamic data structures* constructs of ADA-oriented programs.

5. *Real-time sorting* aimed at sorting real-time data words into classes whereby each class characterizes the behavior of one or several real-time objects. It is shown that, by reconfiguring a dynamic architecture into an architectural configuration which includes several multirooted trees or stars, we can create ideal hardware structures for execution that adapt to the following variable characteristics of sorting algorithms:

a.   The number of sorting classes, which is equivalent to the number of trees or stars created dynamically.

b.   The number of stages in a sorting algorithm, which is equivalent to the number of levels in a tree or star created via reconfiguration.

c.   The number of sorting outcomes, which is equivalent to the number of immediate successors for each node of the star created via reconfiguration.

The performance of dynamic architectures in real-time sorting is close to the ideal, because each sorting structure can be created during one clock period, since it takes only one control code and one mod-2 addition for such reconfiguration.

6. *Divide-and-conquer* or tree structured algorithms executed by dynamic architecture in multicomputer networks organized as reconfigurable binary trees. It is shown that reconfiguration into each such tree can be organized practically instantaneously using one mod-2 addition and one control code. Thus, the performance of dynamic architectures in such executions is ideal, since the required reconfiguration into the ideal hardware structure is made with no reconfiguration overhead.

2 GENERAL-PURPOSE PARALLEL ALGORITHMS

In this section, we will evaluate the performance of dynamic architectures in the execution of the following two general-purpose parallel algorithms: (1) general-purpose program mix and (2) fork-join construct.

2.1 General-Purpose Program Mix

In Section 3.3.2, Chapter III, we introduced a general-purpose program mix consisting of 14 noninterruptible and interruptible programs whose requirements on processor and memory resources were shown in Fig. III.10 (for eight noninterruptible programs) and Fig. III.11 (for six interruptible programs). (How to find program requirements on the processor and memory resources is shown in Section 3.2, Chapter III.)

In the same section, we introduced a technique of mapping program resource requirements onto the available resources of dynamic architecture. Using these techniques, we constructed the scheduling diagram (called CE resource diagram) for dynamic architecture having 5 CE and executing this program mix having eight noninterruptible and six interruptible programs (Fig. III.12). As follows from this figure, the total time of executing this program mix by the dynamic architecture having 5 CE is 167.5 sec.

For comparison, consider execution of the same program mix made of 14 programs by conventional static architecture, which does not change the word sizes of its computers and which has the same resource complexity, $n = 5$. To minimize the number of floating-point operations for this program mix, we will compute it in two computers having 48-bits, where $48 = 3 \cdot 16$, and 32-bits, where $32 = 16 \cdot 2$, respectively, thus realizing partition $3 + 2 = 5$ of the total resources made of 5 CE. If other partitions are used [for instance, $(1 + 4)$CE or $(1 + 2 + 2)$CE], then for partition $(1 + 4)$CE, all programs requiring 32-bit data words will be computed by 16-bit computers. This means that their executions will be significantly delayed due to the necessity of computing all operations in a floating-point form. Similar argument is true for a $1 + 2 + 2$ partition.

On the other hand, the partition of the resources into 48- and 32-bit computers [or $(3 + 2)$CE partition] requires that only two tasks (TA_1 and TA_4) of program P_3 and two tasks (TA_1 and TA_3) of program P_4 requiring 64-bit computers be computed in floating-point form by a 48-bit computer. Thus, only execution of these tasks will be delayed. All the remaining programs will be computed in a fixed-point form, introducing no additional delays to their minimal times of computation.

Since each floating-point operation lasts much longer than its fixed-point analog, and the time of addition is an average time to execute one computer instruction, assume that the floating-point addition takes at least twice as long as the fixed-point addition. Thus, execution of each task in floating-point form will be at least twice as delayed as compared to that in a fixed-point form.

Partitioning $(3 + 2) \cdot$ CE of the architecture into 48- and 32-bit computers requires that P_3 and P_4 be assigned to the 48-bit computer. Consequently, two tasks of P_3 and P_4 that require 64-bit data words will be computed in floating-point form when they are executed in a 48-bit computer. Let us find new execution times for P_3 and P_4 caused by the floating-point way of computation. For P_3 the time of its execution in a dynamic computer, as shown in Fig. III.12, is

$$T_3(\text{dyn}) = t(TA_1) + t(TA_2) + t(TA_3) + t(TA_4) = 10 + 7.5 + 5 + 7.5 = 30$$

where TA_1 and TA_4 require 64 bits, TA_2 requires 48 bits, and TA_3 requires 32 bits. Concurring with our assumption, new times for TA_1 and TA_4 by a conventional 48-bit computer will be

$$t'(TA_1) = 20 \quad \text{and} \quad t'(TA_4) = 15$$

This gives the following T_3 (conv) for a conventional 48-bit computer:

$$T_3(\text{conv}) = 20 + 7.5 + 5 + 15 = 47.5 \text{ sec}$$

For P_4, the execution time by a dynamic computer is

$$T_4(\text{dyn}) = t(TA_1) + t(TA_2) + t(TA_3) = 5 + 7.5 + 7.5 = 20 \text{ sec}$$

Since TA_1 and TA_3 require 64 bits, then $T_4(\text{conv}) = 10 + 7.5 + 15 = 32.5$ sec. The remaining programs have minimal execution time unchanged when they are computed in a system consisting of two computers.

Furthermore, to minimize the overall time of executing 14 programs by conventional architecture, let us assume that the objective of the resource scheduling is aimed at increasing the concurrency of execution only. Program priorities are thus ignored whenever they delay execution. This requires that the 48-bit computer execute programs P_2, P_3, P_4, P_5, P_6, P_9, and P_{12} and the 32-bit computer executes P_1, P_7, P_8, P_{10}, P_{11}, P_{13}, and P_{14}.

As follows from Figure V.1, the total time of execution is 237.5 sec. On the other hand, the total time of executing the same program mix by dynamic architecture with the same complexity of resources (5 CE) is 167.5 sec. Therefore, achieved performance improvement is 70 sec. or about 42%. The origin of this improvement is only due to dynamic reconfiguration, which is capable of creating a minimal-size computer for each task of the program and improve system concurrency by using the resources that are freed for additional parallel computations.

2.2 Parallel Construct Fork-Join

This algorithm is one of the fundamental constructs in general-purpose parallel processing. It is used as an ingredient of a majority of parallel application algorithms.

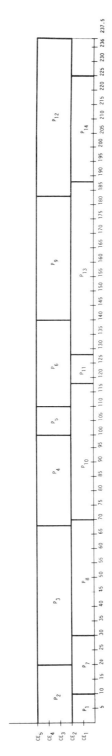

FIGURE V.1 Execution of the program mix made of 14 programs by a conventional static architecture.

313

Therefore, it is desirable to illustrate how dynamic architecture executes this algorithm and in what way its performance in such execution is comparable with those of traditional parallel systems with static configurations.

2.2.1 Definition of Fork-Join Construct

By the **fork-join** algorithm, we mean a concurrent process whereby one sequential program P_1 initiates execution of several other sequential programs P_2, ..., P_k, concurrently with P_1. The initiating program (P_1) will be called the *program starter*. The spawned programs P_2, ..., P_k will be called *program-offsprings* (Fig. V.2). Usually, the *fork construct* is concluded by the synchronization construct, *join*, which indicates the end of this particular forking process. The objection of join is to provide the synchronization point for all programs (starter and offsprings) that are participating in forking; i.e., to ensure that they complete their execution during forking.

Example.   Consider the following fork-join process:

Fork S_7

DO S_1, $I \to 1$, $N + 1$

S_1 A(I) $\to 2 * I + 3$

Join

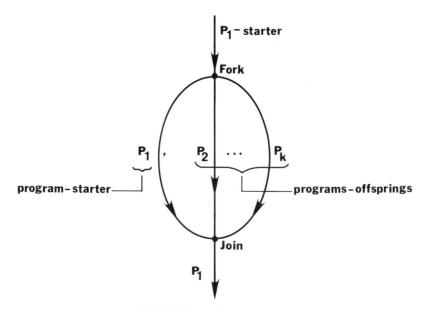

FIGURE V.2   Fork-join construct

Here the program-starter is S_7. The program offspring is DO S_1. Therefore, there are two programs (S_7 and DO S_1) in this fork-join process, which is concluded by synchronization statement join. ■

2.2.2 Execution of the Fork-Join Construct

Since fork-join is a concurrent process, it is executed by a parallel system (multicomputer or multiprocessor). In the beginning, it is assumed that all but one processor assigned for P_1 starter are either idle or their programs are interrupted. The fork begins when P_1 initializes all other program offsprings. Two cases of such execution should be considered:

Case 1.   The available configuration of the parallel system matches the resource requirements of the forking programs, P_1, P_2, ..., P_k.

Case 2.   The available configuration of the parallel system does not match the resource requirements of the forking programs.

Below we will perform a detailed analysis of how dynamic architecture executes cases 1 and 2 and how its performance in such execution compares with that of traditional systems.

2.2.3 Match between Program Resource Requirements and System Configuration

Given a dynamic architecture containing four CE (Fig. V.3). Program starter, P_1, is executed on CE_1. Spawned programs, P_2, P_3, and P_4, are executed on CE_2, CE_3, and CE_4, respectively.

Assume that before the fork instruction starts execution, past programs run on CE_2, CE_3, and CE_4 have been interrupted. When program P_1 begins execution of the fork instruction, it sends this instruction to the local operating system, POS_1, which forms three 16-bit start messages, MES.

Each message MES is designated to initialize the respective program offspring. It is partitioned into two parts: identification code, ID, and the program user code, PUS (Fig. V.4), where ID is the identification code of the computer element which will be used for running the respective program offspring P_i. Each message is sent via a shift bus and received by the destination CE during one clock period. Therefore, it takes three clock periods to transfer three messages.

In the destination CE, the message is received by the local processor operating system. Its PUS part is sent to the local lookup table to fetch the jump address of the offspring program P_i. Therefore, each offspring P_i is initiated following not more than four clock periods after the fork instruction finished its execution in CE_1. As a matter of fact, four clock periods is the longest time that it takes to initiate P_4; P_2 is initiated after two clock periods and P_3 is initiated after three clock periods following completion of the fork instruction by program P_1.

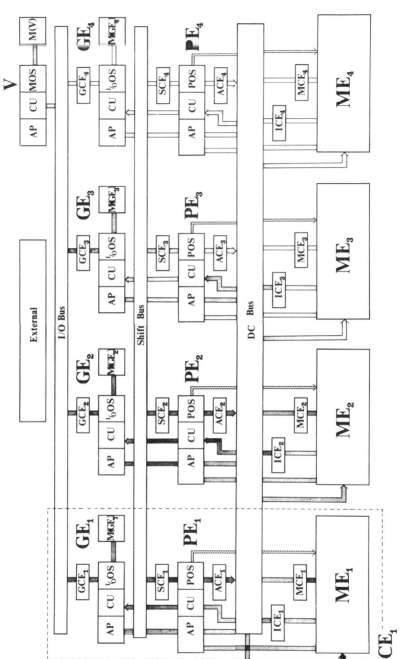

FIGURE V.3 One dynamic architecture with four CEs.

Message

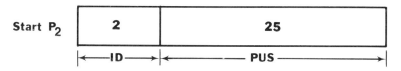

FIGURE V.4   Format of the start message, MES

2.2.4 Mismatch between Program Resource Requirements and System Configuration

It should be noted that a match between resource requirements and system configuration considered in the previous section can happen very rarely, due to the variability and unpredictability of the resource requirements of the running programs. Therefore, the case of mismatch (case 2) is a typical case in programming whose execution by dynamic architecture and traditional systems must be evaluated with great care.

There are three cases of such a mismatch:

1. *Bit-size mismatch,* which is understood as a mismatch between bit sizes of running programs and the available bit sizes of processors working in the system.
2. *Concurrency mismatch*, which is understood as a mismatch between the number of offspring programs and the number of processors in the system.
3. *Mixed mismatch,* which includes bit-size and concurrency mismatches.

Most typical is the mixed mismatch whose execution will be evaluated below. The other two mismatches (bit size and concurrency) can be considered particular cases of the more general mixed mismatch.

Our evaluation will proceed as follows. First, we will give initial conditions of the fork-join process that fall under the category of the mixed mismatch. Thereafter, we will consider the execution of this fork-join process by the two systems, dynamic and static architectures, respectively, having the same complexity of hardware resources, i.e., the same number of computer elements. We will then perform performance comparison of two system computations in terms of incurred program delays, since the resource complexities of the systems under comparison are assumed to be the same.

2.2.5 Fork-Join Requirements for the Mixed Mismatch

Given eight programs P_1, P_2, ..., P_8 represented by their resource requests shown in Fig. V.5. Program P_1 needs a 16-bit computer during 5 minutes. Program P_2 needs a 32-bit computer during 3 minutes. Other program needs on the computer resource are shown in Fig. V.5.

Let these eight programs form the following fork-join construct:

Fork P_1

Compute P_2, P_3, P_4, P_5, P_6, P_7, P_8 (P_8 must follow P_6)

Join

As follows, P_1 is the starter; P_2 through P_8 are offsprings. Also, P_8 should be executed only after program P_6.

Therefore, P_1 must initiate P_2 through P_8 and, upon completion of all these programs, P_1 must execute the join instruction. That is, it must inform the monitor that the fork-join operator has completed its execution. Consider the execution of this program mix by the two systems having six computer elements. One of the systems is equipped with dynamic architecture; the other one is not. Since for both systems, the resource requirements of eight programs are 20 CE, they exceed the total number of available computer elements. Therefore, this program mix should be executed sequentially.

2.2.6 Execution of the Mixed Mismatch Fork-Join by the System with Dynamic Architecture

2.2.6.1 Scheduling Diagram

Before this execution can start, the monitor operating system performs resource assignment whereby it maps the resource needs of executing programs onto the available processor and memory resources. The techniques for such scheduling were discussed in Sec. 3.3, Chapter III. Figure V.6 shows the scheduling diagram for the program mix of Fig. V.5.

As seen, this scheduling diagram has two axes: horizontal (time) and vertical (CE resources). It shows how the available resources of CE_1 through CE_6 are assigned in time for executing P_1 through P_8, whereby each of these programs is run on an individual dynamic computer $C_i(k)$ having k CE. Program starter P_1 is executed by a 16-bit computer, $C_1(1) = \{CE_1\}$, that includes one CE_1. Programs P_2 and P_3 are executed by a 32-bit computer, $C_5(2) = \{CE_5, CE_6\}$, made of CE_5 and CE_6. Program P_4 is executed by a 48-bit computer, $C_2(3) = \{CE_2, CE_3, CE_4\}$. Program P_5 is executed by a 64-bit computer, $C_1(4) = \{CE_1, CE_2, CE_3, CE_4\}$; programs P_6, P_7, and P_8 are executed by $C_5(2)$, $C_4(3)$, and $C_1(3)$, respectively.

2.2.6.2 Reconfiguration Flow Chart

Construction of this scheduling diagram is equivalent to construction of the reconfiguration flow chart shown in Fig. V.6(b). As seen, the system passes through three architectural states N_{18}, N_2, and N_4 in executing P_1 through P_8. State N_{18} is characterized by three concurrent computers $C_1(1)$, $C_2(3)$, and $C_5(2)$ that execute P_1, P_4 and P_2, P_3. State N_2 is characterized by two dynamic computers, $C_1(4)$ that executes P_5 and $C_5(2)$ that executes P_6. Transition from N_{18} to N_2 is performed by program P_1 that executes the architectural switch instruction $N_{18} \rightarrow N_2$, etc. As shown above, the time of

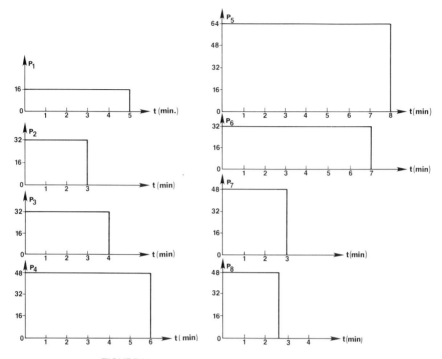

FIGURE V.5   Resource requests of eight programs

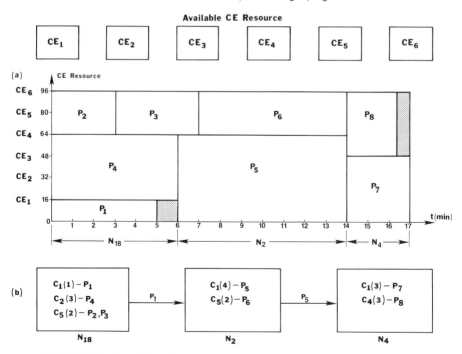

FIGURE V.6   Scheduling diagram and reconfiguration flow chart for the program mix of Fig. V.5

multicomputer reconfiguration does not exceed the time of 64-bit addition if the requested resources are available and there are no conflicts in the system. Thus, the architectural reconfiguration is performed practically instantaneously and introduces no reconfiguration overhead.

Similarly, transition $N_2 \rightarrow N_4$ is performed by program P_5 that includes instruction $N_2 \rightarrow N_4$.

Note: For static programs, to provide better programming flexibility, the active program performing transition $N \rightarrow N^*$ may be assigned to states N and/or N^*.

In our case, program P_1 is active by performing the $N_{18} \rightarrow N_2$ transition. However, it is not assigned to state N_2. Similar assignment is true for P_5, which is active for $N_2 \rightarrow N_4$ and not assigned to N_4. This is very easy to accomplish using the sequencing rules for static assignment described in Sec. 3.6.2, Chapter III.

For dynamic programs, such programming flexibility is fundamentally impossible since one dynamic program cannot know and thus represent a priori the resource needs of other programs. Therefore, any active dynamic program P_D performing transition $N \rightarrow N^*$ must be necessarily assigned to N^*, since N^* is always the state created dynamically on the request of dynamic program P_D and N^* contains a dynamic computer(s) requested by P_D. The monitor assigns N^* with other programs to provide full utilization of the system resources in state N^* (see Sec. 5.6.2, Chapter III).

2.2.6.3 Fork-Join Start

Let us now consider how this fork-join is executed by the dynamic architecture which includes six CEs. Since P_1 is the starter, before it can start its own execution, it must start all other programs.† To this end, it forms seven *Start P* messages shown in Fig. V.7. Each message *Start P* contains two parts:

a. The ID part, which is the identification code of the most significant CE_i of the dynamic computer $C_i(k)$ assembled from k CE that is destined to compute program P.

b. The program user code PUS(P) of program P.

Consider how IDs are selected. Since program P_2 is assigned to $C_5(2) = \{CE_5, CE_6\}$, ID = 5, since CE_5 is most significant for $C_5(2)$. Since P_4 is executed by $C_2(3) = \{CE_2, CE_3, CE_4\}$, CE_2 is the most significant. Thus, code ID = 2, etc.

Therefore, each of the CE receives the following message queue (Fig. V.8): CE_1 has a queue of two messages that start P_5 and P_7, respectively; CE_2 has a single message to start P_4; CE_3 receives no messages, since CE_3 is not most significant in any dynamic computer of this reconfiguration flow chart; CE_4 receives one message to start P_8; CE_5 forms a queue of three messages to start P_2, P_3, and P_6, respectively. CE_6 receives no messages.

---

† The start-up for fork-join differs from conventional start-up performed by the monitor (see Sec. 5.7, Chapter III), since *for fork-join it is the program starter and not the monitor which must start all other forking programs.* The task of the monitor for the fork-join case is to send simplified start messages, which just prepare respective computers for computation, since the actual start-up will be performed by the program starter.

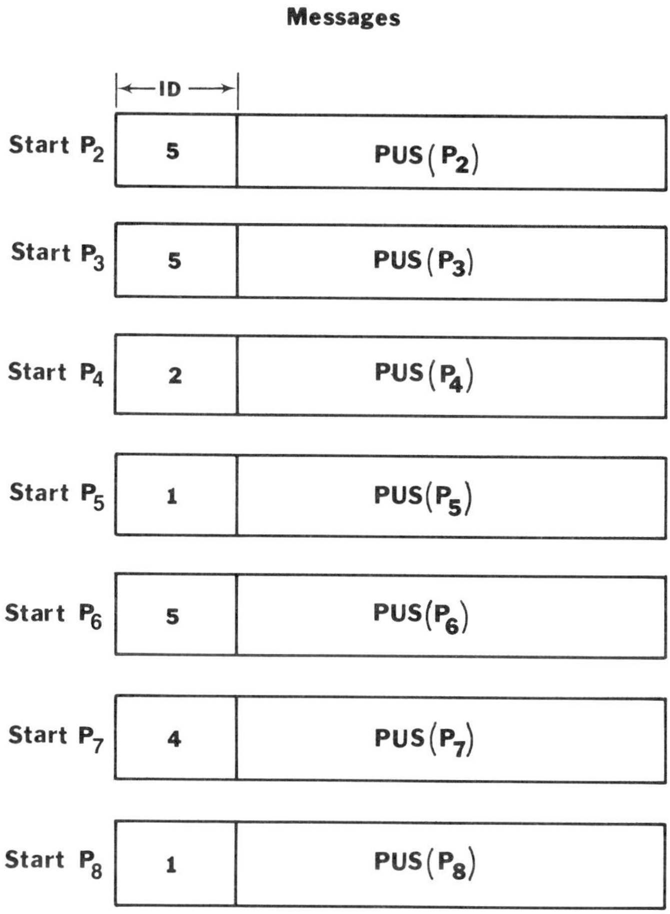

Messages

FIGURE V.7   Start P messages

Upon receipt of the queue of start messages, each dynamic computer begins computation of the first program from the message queue. Therefore, execution of P_1, P_2, and P_4 is begun. Other programs will wait until resources they need become available.

2.2.6.4 Problems of Synchronization and Architectural Reconfiguration during Fork-Join

In order that the system with dynamic architecture execute the reconfiguration flow chart of Fig. V.6, the following problems have to be solved:

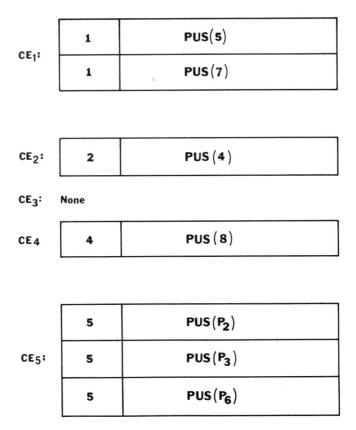

FIGURE V.8 Message queues in computer elements

a. Fork-join task synchronization
b. Execution of the reconfiguration flow chart in the system for fork-join

Fork-Join Task Synchronization. Fork-join task synchronization includes two types of synchronization:

a. Architectural task synchronization
b. Join task synchronization

The objective of the architectural task synchronization during the $N_i \rightarrow N_j$ transition from state N_i to state N_j is to guarantee that all asynchronous programs assigned to N_i have completed their execution in N_i if their CE resources are requested to form new computers of N_j.

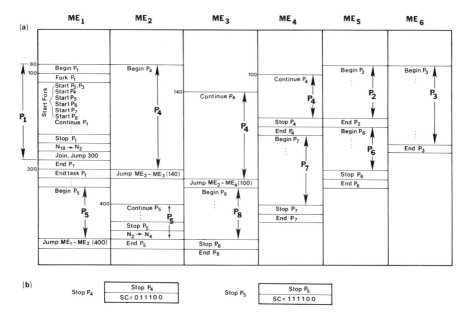

(a)

(b)

	Stop P_4			Stop P_5	
Stop P_4	SC = 011100		Stop P_5	SC = 111100	

FIGURE V.9 Memory allocation for the fork-join process

On the other hand, if no such requests are made, no such synchronization is required. This means that each such program is run in the same computer which exists both in N_i and N_j, and this program ignores architecural reconfiguration.

As for the join task synchronization, the *join* instruction is executed by the program starter (P_1). Offspring programs may take a longer time than the program starter. Thus, such synchronization techniques should be developed that allow all offspring programs to inform the program starter of the end of their execution in order that the program starter can end its join instruction.

For dynamic architecture, the architectural synchronization will be accomplished with instruction *Stop P*; the Join synchronization will be accomplished with instruction *End P*.

Case 1: Architectural task synchronization. The *Stop P* instruction format is as follows: it consists of two words where the second word is occupied with the stop code, SC, which shows the positions of CEs that are included into a given dynamic computer. For instance, if P_4 is executed by $C_2(3) = \{CE_2, CE_3, CE_4\}$ in state N_{18}, then the *Stop P_4* instruction stores the stop code SC = 011100, having (1) $n = 6$ binary positions, because of 6 CE in the system, and (2) three ones in positions 2, 3, and 4 corresponding to CE_2, CE_3, and CE_4 [Fig. V.9(b)]. For program P_5, Stop P_5 has SC = 111100, since program P_5 is executed by $C_1(4) = \{CE_1, CE_2, CE_3, CE_4\}$ in state N_2, etc.

When instruction *Stop P* † is fetched to the processor, its SC code is sent to the monitor, which stores the current idle equipment code in its H register. Upon receiv-

---

† In Sec. 3.3, Chapter II, a similar instruction was called Stop N, where N is a current architectural state.

ing new SC code, the monitor performs logical addition SC V H → H; i.e., its H register is updated on new idle equipment which is being created in the system.

During execution of the architectural reconfiguration instruction, N_i → N_j, the monitor receives requested equipment code RE from the program that performs reconfiguration. If RE $\wedge$ H = RE, reconfiguration is allowed. If RE $\wedge$ H ≠ RE, the system waits until all programs that need architectural synchronization have completed their execution.

Case 2:   Join Task Synchronization. During execution of the fork-join, the task synchronization is performed conventionally. That is, in the beginning of forking, the program starter sends to the monitor the list of all program offsprings. Upon completion, each program offspring executes instruction *End P* that informs the monitor that program P had ended its execution. Upon receiving all the completion signals from all the programs from the list, the monitor, on request of the program starter, informs this program that all program offsprings have completed computations.

Consider how both types of synchronization are accomplished for the program mix of Fig. V.6(a). Since program P_1 is executed in CE_1, its instruction array is stored in memory element ME_1 [Fig. V.9(a)]. First, it executes the fork P_1 instruction, whereby it sends to the monitor the list of all program offsprings P_2, ..., P_8 and its own user code identifying P_1 for the monitor as the program starter. Next, it forms seven start messages to start P_2 - P_8. Having started all program offsprings, P_1 begins its own execution, which ends with the instruction *Stop P_1* that stores stop code SC = 100000, since P_1 is executed by $C_1(1) = \{CE_1\}$. Thus, the H register of the monitor now stores H = 100000, since only CE_1 is idle.

Similarly, program P_4 also needs architectural synchronization, since its dynamic computer $C_2(3) = \{CE_2, CE_3, CE_4\}$ is used to form the new dynamic computer of the next state N_2 (Fig. V.6). Therefore, P_4 (which is stored in three memory elements, ME_2, ME_3, ME_4) is concluded by *Stop P_4* which stores SC = 011100. Programs P_2 and P_3 do not need architectural synchronization, since they are executed by the same computer $C_5(2)$ in two states. Thus, they ignore reconfiguration, and execution of P_3 starts following the End instruction of P_2, *End P_2* (Fig. V.6). The remaining programs P_5, P_6, P_7, and P_8 need architectural synchronization, because P_5 and P_6 resources are used to form new computers of state N_4, and P_7 and P_8 are the end programs of state N_4 [Fig. V.6(a)].

Execution of Reconfiguration Flow Chart for the Fork-Join Construct.   In general, architectural reconfiguration is performed by the instruction N_i → N_j, which follows the architectural synchronization instruction *Stop P,* provided P is the active program that initiates reconfiguration. If reconfiguration is requested during execution of fork-join, then the program that requests this reconfiguration must be either the program starter or a program offspring which is on the list sent earlier by the program starter during execution of the fork instruction. If a conflicting reconfiguration is requested by a program which is neither of these two, such program must compete with the entire set of forking programs (starter and all offsprings); i.e., its priority must warrant interruption of the entire fork-join process.

Consider execution of the system reconfigurations during our fork-join process. The first reconfiguration $N_{18} \rightarrow N_2$ is performed by the program starter P_1. Thus, its *Stop P_1* instruction is followed by $N_{18} \rightarrow N_2$ instruction [Fig. V.9(a)]. The second system reconfiguration is performed by program P_5 [Fig. V.6(b)]. Thus, its Stop P_5 is followed by the $N_2 \rightarrow N_4$ instruction [Fig. V.9(a)].

Consider execution of $N_{18} \rightarrow N_2$ by program P_1. The second instruction $N_2 \rightarrow N_4$ is executed similarly. Instruction $N_{18} \rightarrow N_2$ stores $(n-1)$ bit code $N_2 = 00010$ of the next architectural state, requested equipment code RE $= 111100$, and some other control codes which will not be discussed here, since they have already been discussed in Sec. 3, Chapter II.

When $N_{18} \rightarrow N_2$ is fetched to the processor of P_1, codes N_2 and RE are sent to the monitor. Code N_2 is used for priority analysis. Code RE is used for finding the moment of readiness for requested equipment. Since for our case there is only one reconfiguration request made by P_1, it is granted and no priority analysis is necessary. The next action performed by the monitor is to check the readiness of requested equipment. Since only CE_1, CE_2, CE_3, and CE_4 are requested to form new computers of the next state N_2, RE $= 111100$.

When program P_1 is completed, it sends SC $= 100000$. Therefore, the H register of the monitor stores H $= 1000000$. Thus, H $\wedge$ RE $= 100000 \wedge 111100 \neq 111100$ and the program P_1 waits [shaded areas mean waiting time in Fig V.6(a)]. When P_4 ends, it sends synchronization code SC $= 011100$ to the monitor. Therefore, the H register in the monitor now stores H $\vee$ SC $\rightarrow$ H $= 100000 \vee 011100 = 111100$. Again, the monitor performs the readiness test, RE $\wedge$ H $= 111100 \wedge 111100 = 111100$. Since this test is positive, the monitor begins reconfiguration. It performs writing of several new control codes to requested computer elements CE_1, CE_2, CE_3, and CE_4 in order that they function as new dynamic computer $C_1(4)$. Computer elements CE_5 and CE_6 are not touched since they are integrated by the same dynamic computer in the predecessor state N_{18} and the successor state N_2.

Execution of the Join Instruction by the Program Starter. As was indicated above, the fork-join process is concluded by the *Join* instruction executed by the program starter, P_1. In our case, the *Join* instruction immediately follows the architectural reconfiguration $N_{18} \rightarrow N_2$, performed by P_1, because, by condition, it is program P_1 which must conclude this fork-join process [Fig. V.9(a)].

Since, in the beginning of fork-join computation, P_1 has sent to the monitor the entire list of program offsprings, the task of the *Join* instruction is to request the monitor about the completion status of all the program offsprings. If all program offsprings have ended their executions, the monitor sends to the program starter the completion message which allows this program to finish the entire fork-join process by executing the *End P_1* instruction. If not all program offsprings ended their executions, the *Join* instruction saves a current program address where it is stored and jumps to a jump address which shows what to do next.

In our case, the jump address is 300. It stores instruction *End task P_1*, which means the following: The entire P_1 is not completed, since its join construct did not finish.

However, its current task does. Thus, the next program P_5 stored in the program queue of CE_1 may proceed with execution. (Without such organization, execution of the fork-join reconfiguration flow chart halts inasmuch as P_5 cannot start, since P_1 did not finish. However, to end P_1 means to end the entire fork-join. Therefore, to prevent this deadlock situation from happening, we are using the two *End P* modifications: *End, task P,* and *End, P_1* where *End, task P* means the end of the current task of P. This allows other executions and reconfigurations provided by the fork-join reconfiguration flow chart of Fig. V.6(b). Instruction *End-P* means the end of the entire fork-join initiated by program starter P.

The entire execution of this fork-join process ends when all the programs inform the monitor of their completion using their *End P* instructions and the monitor sends the completion message to CE_1 which executed P_1. This completion message stores the user code of P_1. When received in CE_1, it fetches the current saved address of P_1, which stores *Join* instruction. Thus, P_1 can execute its instruction *Join* again. Since all forking programs have completed their processes, the instruction *Join* obtains a true step condition. Therefore, it is followed by the last instruction, *End P_1*, which signifies the end of the entire fork-join process.

As follows from Fig. V.6(a), the entire execution takes 17 minutes, where shaded areas show idle resources. These are equivalent to one CE not working during 1 minute and three CE not working during 36 sec.

2.2.7 Execution of the Mixed Mismatch Fork-Join by the Conventional System

For comparison, let us execute the same mixed mismatch fork-join by a conventional nonreconfigurable system having 6 CE. Since the system maintains fixed configuration during the entire computation, let us find the best computer sizes and the best number of computers that can be formed out of six CE. Since P_5 is the longest program (8 min) requiring 64 bits, we must have 64-bit computer in this system (Fig. V.10). The remaining 2 CE should form a 32-bit computer for computing 32-bit programs P_2, P_3, and P_6 during 14 minutes. Thus, the system with fixed configuration will achieve an ideal performance in executing only P_2, P_3, P_5, and P_6 (Fig. V.10). In execu-

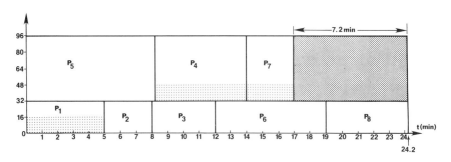

FIGURE V.10   Execution of the fork-join process in a static multicomputer architecture

tion of other programs, the system will create redundancy of the resources. Indeed, program P_1 will execute in a 32-bit computer creating 16-bit redundancy during 5 minutes, which cannot be freed for other computations. Similarly, programs P_4 and P_7 that require 48 bits will be executed by a 64-bit computer creating 16-bit equipment redundancy during 9 minutes.

Also, since P_8 must be executed after P_6, it is data dependent on P_6. Therefore, it must be executed by the same computer that executed P_6 in order to be capable of using data words computed by P_6. Since the system has two different-size computers, 32 bit and 64 bit, and P_6 was computed in a 32-bit computer, P_8 must be also computed by the same computer. But P_8 requires a 48-bit processor (Fig. V.5). Thus, it must be computed in floating-point form in the 32-bit computer. It then follows that its execution in floating-point form will be slowed at least twice, in comparison with fixed-point execution. Usually, the add instruction measures an average instruction time. Inasmuch as floating-point addition is described by a sequential algorithm containing at least two consecutive steps (mantissa alignment and mantissa addition), it takes at least twice as long to compute as its conventional fixed-point analog. Therefore, the entire program in floating-point form is slowed twice in comparison with execution of the same program in fixed-point form. Therefore, program P_8 will be executing not during 2.6 minutes, but during 5.2 minutes following program P_6†). Thus, the entire fork-join process ends after 24.2 minutes.

For comparison purposes, remember that dynamic architecture executes the same process during 17 minutes, or 7.2 minutes faster than the conventional system. Therefore, what is achieved is 42% speedup in comparison with conventional computation.

3 PRODUCER–CONSUMER ALGORITHMS

As was indicated above, producer–consumer algorithms denote a wide class of algorithms with data dependencies, whereby one instruction sequence produces data words consumed by another instruction sequence. Below, we will make a detailed analysis aimed at finding out how a dynamic architecture performs the following types of data exchanges:

1 Memory–memory
2 Processor–memory–processor
3 Memory–processor–memory

where the significance of these exchanges was given in Sec. 1, this chapter.

---

† Another source of slow-down for P_8 not considered here is as follows. Since P_8 is executed in a floating-point form and it uses 32-bit data words computed by P_6 in a fixed-point form, it must transform the used data array of 32-bit words received from P_6 into a 32-bit floating-point format before it can perform any computations over this array. This slow-down is valid only for a static system. For dynamic architecture, P_8 is slowed neither by the slower floating-point computations nor by additional floating-point transformations, since P_8 is computed in a fixed-point form.

Note: Processor–memory and memory–processor are particular cases of exchanges 2 and 3. Thus, they will be considered in this more general context.

Organization of these exchanges will be exemplified by the system with dynamic architecture which we have built for ballistic missile defense (BMD) applications, although the concepts to be used allow a more general treatment. The reason for this is that this is the dynamic architecture with a well-developed instruction set. We will use concrete instructions to show how we accomplish each of the data exchanges indicated above. We believe that this approach is much more realistic than an alternative one consisting of developing these exchanges for a theoretical dynamic architecture.

The material below on producer–consumer algorithms will be organized as follows. First, we will present a general bus structure adopted in the system with dynamic architecture for BMD which allows organization of all data exchanges of the three types introduced above. Second, we will introduce instructions that implement these data exchanges. Third, we will consider the effectiveness of using these instructions in concrete producer–consumer algorithms.

3.1 General Bus Organization

A dynamic architecture is assembled from building blocks called dynamic computer groups. Each DC group contains n 16-bit computer elements CE, where each CE includes a 16-bit processor element, PE, a 16-bit memory element, ME, and a 16-bit I/O element, GE (Fig. V.3).

In Fig. V.3, the DC group includes 4CE; i.e., $n = 4$. The DC group may form dynamic computers $C_i(k)$. Each dynamic computer handles $16 \cdot k$-bit words; it is assembled from k consecutive CE (CE_i, CE_{i+1}, . . ., CE_{i+k-1}), and the i subscript shows the position code of its significant CE.

The data exchanges between dynamic computers of the DC group are organized as follows. If computer B needs a data array stored in a memory page of computer A, then this page is connected with computer B. By loaning its page(s), computer A does not interrupt its program, whereas computer B begins to work with the loaned page as if it had belonged to its own memory. Loaning the memory resource for temporary use by another computer requires interference of the local operating system, which resolves conflicts arising each time two or more computers request the same memory page of another computer.

As was indicated above, memory conflicts are not the only type of conflicts that must be resolved by the operating system for dynamic architecture. Another type of conflict is reconfiguration conflict when two computers existing concurrently in a current architectural state N request transition into two different next states N' and N", which cannot merge into a single state N* = N' ∪ N" (Chapter III, Sec. 3.2.1). A third type of conflict is associated with the use of I/O resources. The I/O conflicts may arise if memory-memory data exchange is performed via an I/O bus or if there are conflicts for the I/O terminals or several I/Os make concurrent communications with the system monitor.

To solve the three types of conflicts outlined above (memory, reconfiguration, and

I/O), the OS must be functionally or *vertically* distributed; i.e., it must include three subsystems:

1. The processor operating system, POS, which resolves memory conflicts.
2. The I/O operating system, I/O OS, which resolves all types of I/O conflicts.
3. The monitor operating system, MOS, which resolves conflicts during system reconfiguration.

To be most efficient, these three OSs must reside in functionally oriented units with matching dedication; i.e., the POS must reside in the processor of a dynamic computer, the I/O OS must reside in its I/O unit, and the MOS must reside in the system monitor (Fig. V.3).

In addition to vertical or functional distribution, the operating system must feature horizontal distribution among separate CEs of the dynamic computer. Indeed, since dynamic computer $C_i(k)$ consists of k CE and minimal $k = 1$, then the same POS and I/O OS must reside in every CE. Therefore, not only is the entire OS vertically distributed because of the three types of conflicts that should be resolved; it becomes horizontally distributed to resolve memory and I/O conflicts because of the modular structure of a dynamic computer.

3.1.1 Data Exchanges between Dynamic Computers

Since each dynamic computer $C_i(k)$ is assembled from k CEs, to organize a parallel data exchange between two dynamic computers, it is necessary to organize concurrent exchanges between respective pairs $CE_A \rightarrow CE_B$, where CE_A belongs to computer A and CE_B belongs to computer B. Assume that in each type of A-B exchange the exchange is requested by computer B, whereas A loans its equipment; therefore, the direction of exchange is $A \rightarrow B$.

Furthermore, the DC group is provided with three system buses (Fig. V.3): (1) a DC bus that connects all the PEs with all the MEs via separate instruction and data paths; (2) a shift bus that connects all PEs; and (3) the I/O bus, which connects all I/O elements, GE. Therefore, the four types of exchanges between CE_A and CE_B which are possible are as follows (Fig. V.11):

1. Memory-processor exchange, $ME_A \rightarrow PE_B$, performed via the DC bus
2. DC memory-memory exchange, $ME_A \rightarrow ME_B$, performed via the DC bus
3. Processor-processor exchange, $PE_A \rightarrow PE_B$, performed via the shift bus
4. I/O memory-memory exchange, $ME_A \rightarrow ME_B$, performed via the I/O bus

To increase a system's throughput, it is essential to provide maximal concurrency in all the possible data exchanges listed above. Furthermore, since some programs require minimal time of execution without interrupts, it is necessary to discuss such organizations that do not interrupt currently executing programs.

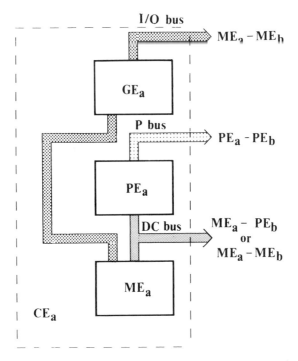

FIGURE V.11   Four types of data exchanges between two computer elements

Since there are three dedicated buses in the DC group, any two dynamic computers may perform up to three concurrent data broadcasts. Indeed, it is possible to organize the following types of exchange concurrency in a system:

Type 1 exchange concurrency: (a) $ME_A \rightarrow PE_B$ (DC) via the DC bus; (b) $PE_A \rightarrow PE_B$; and (c) $ME_A \rightarrow ME_B$ (I/O) via the I/O bus.

Type 2 exchange concurrency: (a) $ME_A \rightarrow ME_B$ (DC) via the DC bus; (b) $PE_A \rightarrow PE_B$; and (c) $ME_A \rightarrow ME_B$ (I/O) via the I/O bus.

Since each exchange is requested by computer B, computer A does not interrupt its program for all exchanges, but $PE_A \rightarrow PE_B$. For the latter case, the A computer computes an A operand for computer B, whereas a B operand is computed by computer B. In addition, one modification of the $ME_A \rightarrow PE_B$ exchange provides that the program computed in computer B fetch one of the operands from the memory of computer A. This fetch takes the same time as the fetch of an operand from the B memory. The result of the computation can be written to the memory of computer A, computer B, or both (Fig. V.12).

Realization of concurrent data exchanges from dynamic computer A to dynamic computer B without interrupting the programs that are computed by these two computers requires implementation of the following features:

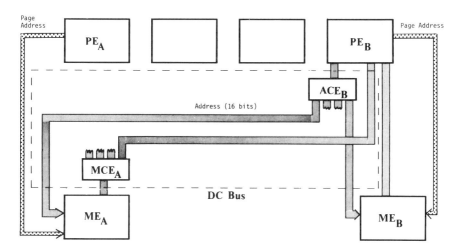

FIGURE V.12 $ME_A \rightarrow PE_B$ exchange

1. For a dynamic computer, every memory element, ME, of its primary memory must be multiport and reconfigurable; i.e., ME should be provided with four information ports and be capable of connecting all its pages to the four ports (Fig. V.13). These ports are as follows:

   a. A local data port that provides fetch of the local data word for the program computed by the dynamic computer A.

   b. An instruction port that fetches instructions to all PEs of the dynamic computer. Since instructions may be stored in any ME of a dynamic computer, every ME must have a separate instruction port.

   c. A DC port that fetches a data word stored in this ME to another dynamic computer.

   d. An I/O port that transfers a data word stored in this ME to another dynamic computer, using an I/O bus.

2. Every computer element CE_A of the dynamic computer A must be provided with two operating systems: POS and I/O OS. Furthermore, to speed up conflict resolution, it is essential to implement these two OSs via hardware. The POS will resolve memory conflicts for the pages of this ME_A, and I/O OS will find what dynamic computer B will participate in the memory-memory exchange $ME_A \rightarrow ME_B$ with ME_A via the I/O bus.

3.1.1.1 Multiport and Reconfigurable Memory ME

As was indicated above, each CE is equipped with a reconfigurable multiport ME that can access up to four 16-bit data words concurrently. One ME has f pages: $ME\text{-}P_1$, $ME\text{-}P_2$, ..., $ME\text{-}P_f$ (Fig. V.13). In the system, DCA-2, that has been implemented $f = 32$; i.e., each ME has 32 pages, each of which has 64K words. The memory, ME,

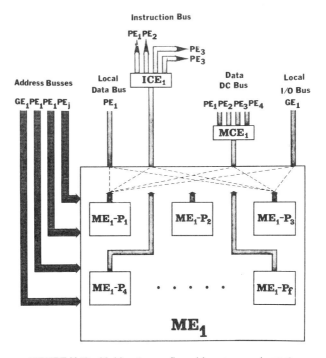

FIGURE V.13   Multiport reconfigurable memory element

is provided with four ports, each of which consists of a 24-bit address bus and a 16-bit data bus. There are four data buses.

Let us discuss the designation of each of them.

1. The local data bus provides 16-bit word exchange between the local ME and PE. A dynamic computer handles 16 · k-bit words in parallel. Since a 16 · k-bit word is stored in a parallel cell of k ME specified with the same address, A_P, an access to this cell (read or write) is specified by concurrent broadcast of the same address, A_P, by k PEs of the dynamic computer. This allows a concurrent fetch of k 16-bit bytes of the same data words via the respective local data buses to k PEs of the dynamic computer.

2. The instruction bus provides fetch of consecutive 16-bit words of one instruction that is stored in one ME. One instruction may be two-word (32-bit instruction) or three-word (48-bit instruction). Furthermore, it must be fetched to all k PEs of the dynamic computer. The instruction broadcast to k PEs of the computer is performed via a connecting element, ICE.

3. The DC bus provides broadcast of a 16-bit word from the given ME to any PE or ME of the DC group. For ME_A, belonging to computer A, any of its pages may be connected with any PE_B (Fig. V.12) or ME_B belonging to computer B (Fig. V.14).

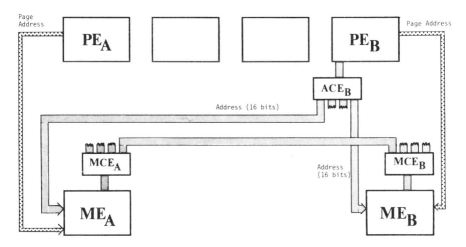

FIGURE V.14 Memory-memory exchange $ME_A \rightarrow ME_B$ via DC bus

4. The local I/O bus provides broadcast of 16-bit data between local ME and I/O (GE), belonging to the same CE.

Therefore, multiport reconfigurable memory ME provides for concurrent connection of any four-page combination of its pages with the four buses mentioned above. It may be fed with up to four addresses, leading to concurrent accesses of up to four data words transferred to local PE and GE and nonlocal PE_B or ME_B of another computer element CE_B .

As was mentioned above, each address bus is a 24-bit. It is formed of two parts: the 8-bit page address and the 16-bit relative address within one page. Each ME_A receives its addresses from the followng sources. All four 8-bit page addresses are received from the local POS_A belonging to the local PE_A; 16-bit relative addresses for local data words and instructions that must be fetched to local PE_A are broadcast from the local control unit CU(PE) of this PE_A. If a 16-bit data word must be broadcast to a nonlocal PE_B of another computer, its 16-bit relative address is broadcast from this nonlocal PE_B (Fig. V.12).

Local GE_A broadcasts a 16-bit address for the data to be transferred via the local I/O bus (Fig. V.15). The same 8-bit page address is fed to the memory continuously during program computation from the same page, whereas 16-bit relative addresses are sent to the memory only during the clock period of data word fetch. A change in an 8-bit page address is performed either via special instruction or via POS_A.

3.1.1.2 Memory-Processor Data Exchange, $ME_A \rightarrow PE_B$

Let us discuss the memory-processor data exchange of the data word stored in ME_A and fetched to PE_B. Suppose that a PE_B of computer B needs a data array stored in the page ME_4-P_1 of the ME_A of the A computer. In this case, computer A connects page

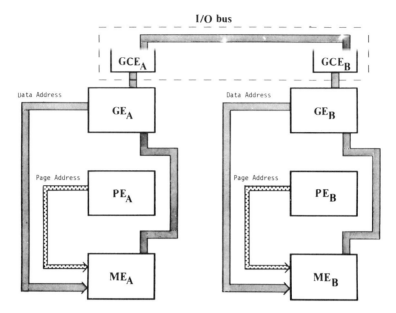

FIGURE V.15   Memory-memory exchange via I/O bus

ME_A-P_1 with the DC bus. The 8-bit page address is generated by the operating system POS_A in PE_A of computer A and continuously fed to ME_A during the entire exchange (Fig. V.12).

Computer B sends a 16-bit relative address to the ME_A via its connecting element ACE_B that belongs to the address portion of the DC bus. The data word fetched via an effective 24-bit address is sent via connecting element MCE_A to the data portion of the DC bus that connects MCE_A with PE_B.

It should be noted that the delay introduced by the DC bus in transferring addresses and data words is very insignificant and equivalent to two gates delay. In addition, these delays are permanent and independent of the location of ME_A and PE_B in the resource. This allows organization of new types of instructions. Each such instruction executed in computer B may fetch one operand from ME_A and the second operand from ME_B and write the result either to ME_B or ME_A. This instruction is organized as follows: computer B sends concurrently two 16-bit addresses; one via the DC (address) bus is fed to ME_A, and another via the local (address) bus is fed to ME_B. Thus, PE_B receives two operands concurrently: one fetched via the DC (data) bus, another via the local (data) bus. The page address for ME_B is generated by PE_B. The result of the operation can be written either to ME_A or ME_B.

Note that the fact that computer A loans its page, ME_A-P_1, to computer B does not prevent A from executing its program because a loaned page, ME_A-P_1, is connected with the DC bus, whereas program instructions computed in computer A are stored in another page connected with the instruction bus. If there are no conflicts for the page ME_A-P_1 of computer A, then to transfer a data array made of d words from

ME_A to PE_B takes $(d + t)$ clock periods, where t is a small number of clock periods required to generate the page address by POS_A; thereafter, each word may be transferred during one clock period.

Another advantage of such organization is as follows: Since the DC bus is connected with all computer elements, it may be used by computer B for fetching one of its operands from the local ME_B; the second operand may be fetched concurrently from another page of the same ME_B via a local data bus. This results in a concurrent fetch to two operands, which leads to a significant speed-up in data fetches.

3.1.1.3 Memory-Memory Exchange, $ME_A \rightarrow ME_B$

As was indicated above, there are two types of memory-memory exchange between computers A and B, organized via a DC bus and an I/O bus, respectively (Figs. V.14 and V.15). Both types of exchanges do not interrupt programs run on computers A and B. The most typical use of both exchanges occurs when the data array stored in computer A is transferred to computer B before the program run in computer B actually needs this array.

$ME_A \rightarrow ME_B$ *Exchange via the DC Bus.* Since the DC bus is connected with each element, MCE, the $MCE_A \rightarrow MCE_B$ connection will establish a data path for data words fetched from ME_A and to be written to ME_B (Fig. V.14). Since the program run on computer B requests this exchange, computer B generates 16-bit address for ME_A and ME_B. In addition, computer B generates the page address (8 bits) for ME_B. This address connects the respective page in ME_B to the DC bus. The page address for ME_A is generated by computer A.

Two 16-bit addresses that define, respectively, the source and destination of a data word in ME_A and ME_B are generated in two clock periods ($T_0^{[1]}$ and $T_0^{[2]}$), and one data word is transferred during the second clock period, $T_0^{[2]}$, from ME_A to ME_B. The same page addresses are fed continuously to ME_A and ME_B during the entire broadcast of the data array from the page of ME_A to the page of ME_B.

$ME_A \rightarrow ME_B$ *Exchange via the I/O Bus.* Since the DC bus is often occupied by $ME_A \rightarrow PE_B$ exchanges, and the program on computer B may often need data words computed by computer A in the past, it is desirable to organize another type of $ME_A \rightarrow ME_B$ exchange via the I/O bus. Since each ME may connect its pages to the local I/O bus, one can organize $ME_A \rightarrow ME_B$ exchange via I/O elements GE of computers A and B (Fig. V.15). The page addresses in ME_A and ME_B are generated by PE_A and PE_B, respectively. Therefore, the following data path is established: During the first clock period, $T_0^{[1]}$, a data word is fetched from ME_A to GE_A; during $T_0^{[2]}$ it is transferred via the I/O bus to GE_B; during $T_0^{[3]}$ it is written to ME_B. This transfer is overlapped, so that each clock period features one fetch of a new data word from ME_A, and the entire transfer of a data array having d words from ME_A to ME_B takes $d + 2$ clock periods.

This concludes the description of all data exchanges that involve the operating system.

3.1.2 Distributed Operating System

If the same page of computer A is requested by two or more other computers, the POS_A residing in PE_A has to decide which computer request for $ME_A \rightarrow PE_B$ or $ME_A \rightarrow ME_B$ exchanges should be granted. Similar conflict resolution must be provided by the I/O OS_A to decide which computer may use $ME_A \rightarrow ME_B$ (I/O) exchange via an I/O bus. To solve these conflicts, each program is assigned the priority code, PC, that shows the relative importance of this program among all others that are being computed by the system. Also, each request for a page is provided with another important characteristic — the tentative duration of a data exchange, TD†.

These two codes will provide the user with much better quality of service, since the programs with low PCs and small TD may be granted requests because the requested exchange will take a short time. Should a page request be characterized by the PC code alone, it would be impossible for a program of low priority or priorities to request data exchanges of short durations.

Thus, if a page of computer A is requested, either POS_A or I/O OS_A receive two characteristics of each page request: the priority code, PC, of the requesting program and the tentative duration, TD, of the exchange. The POS_A receives PC and TD if a requested data exchange will use the DC bus; the I/O OS_A receives PC and TD if the exchange will use the I/O bus.

POS_A controls all four buses of ME_A; i.e., it alone connects memory pages to the buses. Therefore, if I/O OS_A has a request on $ME_A \rightarrow ME_B$ (I/O) exchange, it requests the POS_A on the possibility of connecting a requested page to the local I/O bus (Fig. V.15).

Other functions of the I/O OS_A include finding the terminal that should be connected with GE_A, communication with the V monitor, and similar functions. These functions of the I/O OS_A will not be considered in this chapter.

3.1.2.1 Communication Between Different POSs

Since a dynamic computer A includes k CEs, it has k POSs. Each POS_A makes decisions concerning the pages of the local ME_A only. As will be shown below, such horizontal distribution of functions allows parallel data exchanges both with full $16 \cdot k$-bit data words and with $16 \cdot f$-bit bytes, where $1 \leq f < k$. Indeed, if two computers, A and B, are assembled from the same number k of CEs, then parallel $16 \cdot k$-bit data exchanges mean concurrent communication by each CE of computer A with the respective CE of computer B. In Fig. V.16 this communication is shown for 32-bit computers A and B, assembled from CE_1 and CE_2 for A and CE_3 and CE_4 for B. Thus, POS_4 of PE_4 communicates with POS_2 of PE_2, and POS_3 of PE_3 communicates with POS_1 of PE_1.

This means that each CE_A of computer A generates the same page address to connect this page with the DC bus in the local ME_A. This will lead to a concurrent fetch of a $16 \cdot k$-bit word from the same page of k ME_A, so that each ME_A will produce

† It is worth noting that similar codes (PC and TD) are used for resolving reconfiguration conflicts in a dynamic situation characterized by unpredictable arrival of dynamic programs (see Sec. 5, Chapter III).

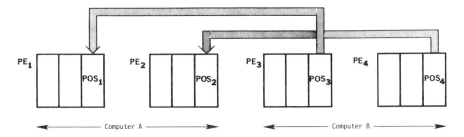

FIGURE V.16 Communication between the two processor operating systems

1 byte of this word. The decision on what page should be connected with the DC bus is performed by the local POS_A when it receives the page address from the respective POS_B of computer B. Thus, if computers A and B have the same number of CEs, then k communicating pairs POS_A, POS_B are formed, where each POS_B sends the request to the respective POS_A. This request is organized with a special communication request instruction, CR instruction, whose organization is described below.

3.1.2.2 Organization of Communication Request Instruction

The CR instruction is fetched by all CEs of computer B. It stores the following codes: w_B, y_A, and x_B, where:

1. w_B is the position code of the most significant CE (CE_w) of computer B which requests communication with its analog of computer A.
2. y_A is the position code of the most significant CE (CE_y) of computer A which receives requests from CE_w.
3. x_B is the position code of the least significant CE (CE_x) of computer B which participates in communication.

Let i_B be a current position code of a CE_B of computer B, where $w_B \leq i_B \leq x_B$. Then position code j_A of CE_A of computer A, which communicates with this CE_B, is given as follows:

$$j_A = i_B + (y_A - w_B) \tag{1}$$

The execution of this instruction is organized as follows: Having received a communication request instruction, each CE_B of computer B compares its position code i_B with w_B and x_B. If $w_B \leq i_B \leq x_B$, CE_B finds j_A of the CE_A via Eq. (1). Otherwise, the CR instruction is not executed.

It should be noted that this instruction can organize both parallel byte and full word exchanges. For a byte exchange, w_B and x_B show positions of the most and least significant bytes for every data word to be exchanged. For full data word exchanges, there is no need to store x_B, since the instruction is received by all CEs of computer B and every CE_B of computer B will thus find the position code j_A of its communication pair in the A computer.

Example.   First, consider parallel exchange with $16 \cdot f$-bit bytes. Let a dynamic computer $B = C_5(3)$ assembled from CE_5, CE_6, and CE_7 require that CE_5 send a request to CE_1, and CE_6 send a request to CE_2, where CE_1 and CE_2 belong to computer A and $A = C_1(3) = \{CE_1, CE_2, CE_3\}$ (Fig. V.17). The CR instruction stores the following codes: $w_B = 5$, since CE_5 is the most significant slice of computer B that needs the exchange; $y_A = 1$, since CE_1 is the most significant slice of computer A; $x_B = 6$, since CE_6 is the least significant slice of computer B that needs exchange.

Each CE_B of computer B compares its position code, i_B, with w_B and x_B; for CE_5, $i_B = 5$; therefore, $w_B \le i_B \le x_B$ is true $(5 \le 5 \le 6)$. For CE_6, $i_B = 6$, $w_B \le i_B \le x_B$ is also true $(5 \le 6 \le 6)$. For CE_7, $i_B = 7$; therefore, $w_B \le i_B \le x_B$ is false $(5 \nleq 7 \nleq 6)$. Therefore, $j_A = 5 + (1 - 5) = 5 - 4 = 1$; i.e., CE_5 sends a request to CE_1. For CE_6, $i_B = 6$. Therefore, $j_A = 6 + (1 - 5) = 2$; i.e., CE_6 sends a request to CE_2. CE_7 sends no communication request since it did not pass via the conditional test.

For full data word exchanges, the CR instruction stores only w_B and y_A codes; i.e., field x_B is empty and each CE_B of computer B executes Eq. (1).

In Fig. V.17(b), let computer B, $C_5(4)$, assembled from CE_5, CE_6, CE_7, and CE_8, need 64-bit data words stored in a computer, $C_1(4)$, assembled from CE_1, CE_2, CE_3, and CE_4. The CR instruction stores $w_B = 5$, $y_A = 1$, and $x_B = 0$. In CE_5 the following j_A is obtained: $j_A = 5 + 1 - 5 = 1$; i.e., CE_5 communicates with CE_1. For CE_6, $j_A = 6 + (1 - 5) = 2$; i.e., CE_6 communiates with CE_2. For CE_7, $j_A = 7 + (1 - 5) = 3$; i.e., CE_7 communicates with CE_3. Similarly, CE_8 communicates with CE_4.

The power of the CR instruction is such that it can organize data exchanges between different-size computers, A and B, when the size of B may be either smaller or larger than the size of computer A. If the size of B is smaller than that of A, then B may receive

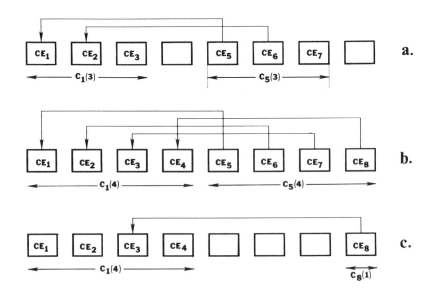

FIGURE V.17   Parallel data exchanges with $16 \cdot f$-bit data bytes

16 • f-bit bytes from computer A that match the size of B. If the size of B is larger than that of A, only a portion of the CEs in the B computer will establish communication connections with their pairs from the A computer. In this case, computer A, assembled from f CE, will send full 16 • f-bit data words, which will be received only by f slices of computer B assembled from k CE, where $f < k$. The data exchange between different-size computers is exemplified by Fig. V.17(c) in which 16-bit computer B = $C_8(1)$, assembled from CE_8, requests an array of 16-bit bytes stored in CE_3; CE_3 belongs to computer A, $C_1(4)$, assembled from CE_1 through CE_4.

Computer B fetches the CR instruction that stores $w_B = 8$, since CE_8 is the most significant in $C_8(1)$; $y_A = 3$, because CE_3 is the most significant CE in computer A that receives communication requests, and $x_B = 0$. Thus, $j_A = 8 + (3 - 8) = 3$, and CE_8 communicates with CE_3. ■

3.2 Data Exchange Instructions

Once the POS_A grants the communication request made by POS_B, it connects a selected memory page to either the DC bus or I/O bus by sending the page portion of the effective address. Thereafter, each qualified PE_B of computer B executes a dedicated data-exchange instruction which specifies what type of data exchange has to be performed. Thus, all data-exchange instructions are divided into four groups, each of which is specified by the type of data exchange that will be executed: $ME_A \rightarrow PE_B$, $ME_A \rightarrow ME_B$ (DC), $PE_A \rightarrow PE_B$, $ME_A \rightarrow ME_B$ (I/O). Consider execution of a typical instruction from the group $ME_A \rightarrow PE_B$.

An $ME_A \rightarrow PE_B$ Instruction. An instruction $ME_A \rightarrow PE_B$ is executed by PE_B. It can be a two-word or three-word, where the first word always stores control codes (Fig. V.18). A three-word instruction stores two relative addresses, $A(ME_A)$ and $A(ME_B)$, in ME_A and ME_B, respectively. A two-word instruction stores one relative address $A(ME_A)$.

Since an actual data exchange can be performed only if processor operating system

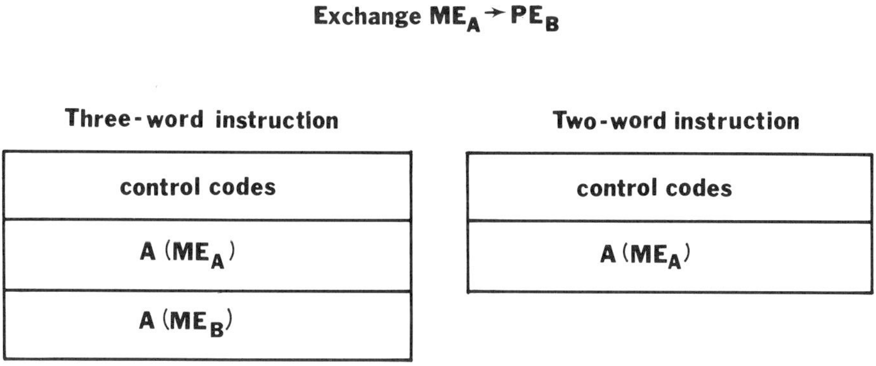

Exchange $ME_A \rightarrow PE_B$

Three-word instruction

control codes
$A(ME_A)$
$A(ME_B)$

Two-word instruction

control codes
$A(ME_A)$

FIGURE V.18 Format of $ME_A \rightarrow PE_B$ instruction

POS$_A$ grants communication request, a ME$_A \rightarrow$ PE$_B$ instruction always follows a CR instruction (not necessarily immediately for the case of long anticipated requests).

Thus, each processor element PE$_B$ always has the position code i_A of ME$_A$ found by the CR instruction. PE$_B$ uses this code to select the address channel in the local address connecting element ACE$_B$ (Fig. V.12) that transfers relative address A(ME$_A$) to ME$_A$. Thus, ME$_A$ receives the full 24-bit effective address and fetches to PE$_B$ a 16-bit byte stored under this address. If it is a three-word instruction, then, concurrently, PE$_B$ fetches the second operand from its own memory, since it uses for the purpose the local data bus for fetches of the second operand. If it is a two-word instruction, then the second operand is stored in a processor register of PE$_B$.

Therefore, a three-word instruction ME$_A \rightarrow$ PE$_B$ may fetch two operands for execution concurrently during one clock period, of which one operand is from nonlocal ME$_A$ and the second operand is from local ME$_B$. Thus, the instruction works with a nonlocal page as if it is a local page; this means that fetches of nonlocal data words produced by other programs take the same time as those of local data words. It then follows that adopted organizations of data exchanges are optimal, since they introduce the minimal time overhead into computations.

3.3 Organization of Programming Construct Fetch-Store

Below we will describe how the data exchanges developed for the system with dynamic architecture support such popular ingredients of producer-consumer algorithms as programming constructs, fetch-store, and store-fetch. As was indicated above, in general, the fetch-store algorithm, FS, means the following: for input operands A$_f$ (that have to be fetched) and computed results A$_s$ (that have to be stored) A$_s$'s are sent to the memory only following the fetch of A$_f$'s [71]. The SF construct means just the opposite: every computed result A$_s$ has to be sent to the memory before the next operand A$_f$ is to be fetched.

Therefore, FS means memory-processor-memory exchange whereby A$_f$ is fetched from memory, and A$_s$ is obtained in the processor and then sent back to the memory. On the other hand, SF means processor-memory-processor, whereby A$_s$ is computed in the processor and sent to the memory. Only following this act, the next A$_f$ is sent to the processor.

Consider how one can organize the FS construct; execution of the SF can be organized similarly. Given the following FS construct that has to be executed 100 times:

$$\text{FS}[A_s \leftarrow 3 * C_f/B_f, \ B_s \leftarrow C_f * 5, \ C_s \leftarrow 7 + E_f + C_f]$$

Consider execution of this construct by the dynamic architecture having three PEs working cooperatively [Fig. V.19(a)].

Since realistic programming situations may feature modifiable and nonmodifiable data arrays, local or nonlocal with engaged PEs, assume that for this FS (1) two data arrays B and C are modifiable, i.e., their input variables B$_f$ and C$_f$ are stored in the same arrays as computed results B$_s$ and C$_s$, and (2) arrays C and A are stored nonlocally, i.e., the PEs and MEs that compute and store arrays C$_s$ and A$_s$ are not local. With

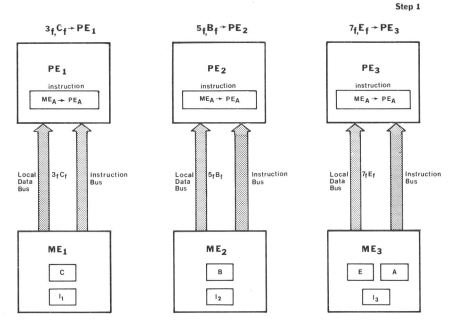

FIGURE V.19(a)   Step 1 of the fetch-store execution

these assumptions in mind, suppose that ME_1 stores C array, ME_2 stores B array, and ME_3 stores E and A arrays. Also, PE_1 computes A_s, PE_2 computes B_s, and PE_3 computes C_s. Processors PE_1, PE_2, and PE_3 store all the necessary instructions for such computations in arrays I_1, I_2, and I_3.

As will be shown below, to execute this FS, one has to use the DC bus only once, to send computed variable A_s from PE_1 to ME_3. Thus, we assume that before this FS starts the operating system POS_3 residing in PE_3 has already given its permission to use the A page for storing A_s variables. This means that POS_3 has already formed the page address of this array. Relative addresses for A_s variables will be found during FS execution.

Using the data-exchange instructions considered above, the system with dynamic architecture may execute each iteration of this FS algorithm during four steps, where each step is equivalent to one instruction in one processor.

3.3.1 Four-Step Computation of FS

Step 1.   Each of the processors PE_1, PE_2, and PE_3 fetches one operand and one constant from its local page(s) using a three-word data fetch instruction, $ME_A \rightarrow PE_B$. Thus, PE_1 fetches 3_f, C_f; PE_2 fetches 5_f, B_f; PE_3 fetches 7_f, E_f. The buses used in each PE are the local data bus and the instruction bus [Fig. V.19(a)].

Step 2.   Using the shift bus that connects all the processors of the system (Fig. V.3), C_f is sent from PE_1 to PE_2 and PE_3; B_f is sent from PE_2 to PE_1. Therefore, PE_1

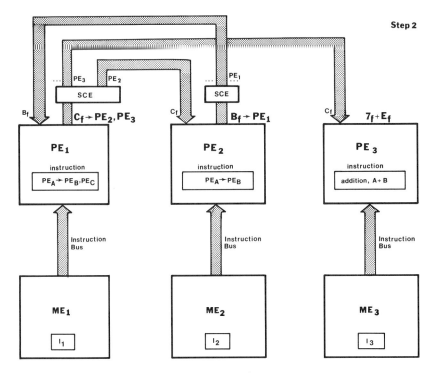

FIGURE V.19(b)   Step 2 of the fetch-store execution

uses $PE_A \rightarrow PE_B$, PE_C instruction; PE_2 uses $PE_A \rightarrow PE_B$ instruction; PE_3 executes addition instruction $7_f + E_f$ [Fig V.19(b)].

Step 3. PE_1 executes multiplication $3 * C_f$ using multiplication instruction $X *$ Y, which leaves the result in the same processor; PE_2 executes a two-word multiplication instruction with the result B_s being sent to local memory; PE_3 executes an addition instruction with the result sent to ME_1 via PE_1 [Fig. V.19(c)].

Step 4. PE_1 executes division $(3 * C_f)/B_f$ using division instruction $X_A \div Y_A \rightarrow$ ME_B that sends computed variable $A_s \leftarrow (3 * C_f)/B_f$ to ME_3 using DC bus [Fig. V.19(d)].

As was indicated above, the page address PA for the A array was obtained in the processor operating system POS_3 before the FS construct started computation. The basic relative address RA is stored in the division instruction and then iteratively incremented during each iteration of the FS construct.

3.3.2 Performance Evaluation

Let us analyze the performance of dynamic architectures in the execution of the FS construct considered above. To organize one iteration of FS requires data fetches from six arrays and sending computing result to the seventh array. These arrays are three arrays of constants in ME_1, ME_2, and ME_3; C array in ME_1, B array in ME_2,

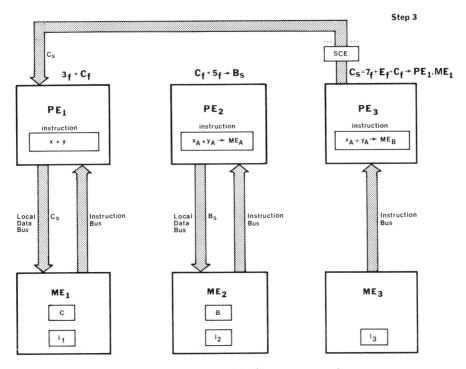

FIGURE V.19(c) Step 3 of the fetch-store execution

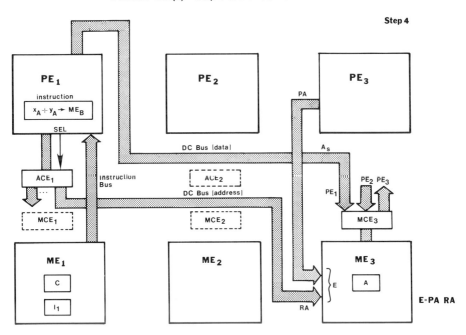

FIGURE V.19(d) Step 4 of the fetch-store execution

and A and E arrays in ME_3. Furthermore, the longest expression $(A = 3 \cdot C/B)$ takes two steps, multiplication and division. Yet to access seven arrays and to compute three arithmetic expressions requires execution of not more than four instructions in three participating processors PE_1, PE_2, and PE_3, i.e., only two instructions more than that required for two consecutive operations in one of the expressions, which can be organized only if one assumes that all data words are available.

Also, the operating system has to intervene only once before execution of this FS in order to connect the page for the A array. Because of the variety of different types of data exchanges, no interference of the operating system is required in the process of execution of this FS, although PE_1, PE_2, and PE_3 must fetch nonlocal variables, B_f and/or C_f, for computing their expressions; and PE_1 and PE_3 must send their results also to nonlocal memories. Therefore, the data exchanges for dynamic architectures are optimal from the following viewpoints:

1. Because of the variety of alternative routes, the interference of operating systems can be reduced to a minimum.
2. Each data exchange takes the minimal time since it takes only a few levels of gates (t_d) in the memory-processor bus.
3. All data exchanges are made in parallel for variable-size data words.

The combination of these three factors leads to an extreme amenability of dynamic architectures in the execution of the entire class of producer-consumer algorithms.

4 ARRAY COMPUTATIONS

The material in this section will be organized as follows: First, we will briefly outline general principles of dynamic array architecture. Second, we will show how the array configurations of the system with dynamic architecture compute the following typical array tasks:

a. Relaxation equations
b. Pulse deinterleaving

Finally, we compare the performance of dynamic array systems with that of conventional dedicated arrays.

4.1 Dynamic Array Architecture

The DC group may form a variable number of concurrent arrays A. Each A array contains d processors, each of which may process $16k$-bit words, i.e., contain k processor elements PE (Table V.1). One of the processors in the A array assumes the function of processor supervisor P*. This means that it generates addresses of program instructions stored in its local primary memory.

Since P* contains k PEs, its local primary memory contains k MEs. Thus, P* may store instructions in any of its k MEs and broadcast them to all PEs of the array. That is, all PEs of the array store the same program selection code PSC $= j$, which shows position j of the ME_j where a currently executed program segment is stored. This ensures that an instruction fetched from ME_j be broadcast to all PEs of the array and be prevented from going to other arrays or computers. A change in PSC leads to a change in a memory element, from which a new program segment is fetched. This is accomplished by a special jump $ME_i \rightarrow ME_j$ instruction, which by writing a new PSC code to all PEs of the array organizes instruction fetches from a new memory element.

Example.   Table V.1 shows some of the array states assumed by the DC group containing $n = 4$ computer elements. These states are distinguished by the number of concurrent arrays and the number and sizes of processors working in each array. For each array, a current position of the processor supervisor is marked with (*); i.e., a switch in supervisors requires no architectural reconfiguration since it is accomplished by writing a new PSC to all PEs of the array. For state N_1, one array A is formed. It contains three processors, $P_1(1)$ made of PE_1, $P_2(2)$ made of PE_2 and PE_3, and $P_4(1)$ made of PE_4. This means that each instruction handles a three-dimensional data vector (a_1, a_2, a_3), where a_1 and a_3 are 16-bit words and a_2 is a 32-bit word. The current position of the supervisor is $P_1(1)$ coincident with PE_1; i.e., PE_1 broadcasts instructions to (PE_2, PE_3) and PE_4:$PE_1 \rightarrow (PE_2, PE_3)$, PE_4. For the N_7 state, two concurrent arrays are formed. Each of them handles a two-dimensional vector (a_1, a_2) made of two 16-bit operands. Current positions of processor-supervisors are PE_1* for the first array and PE_3* for the second, etc.   ■

It then follows from the above discussion that the following parameters of dynamic array architecture are selectable by the programmer:

a.   *The number of concurrent arrays* being formed in the system. This specifies the number of data vectors executed at a time by the entire array system. For instance, an array system containing three arrays computes three data vectors at a time.

b.   *The number of processors in each array.* This specifies the dimension of the data vector computed in each array. For instance, consider the system that is now reconfigured into two arrays A_1 and A_2 of which one array includes three processors, i.e., $A_1 = [P_{11}, P_{12}, \text{and } P_{13}]$, and the second array includes five processors, i.e., $A_2 = [P_{21}, P_{22}, P_{23}, P_{24}, P_{25}]$. The first array computes a three-dimensional data vector $\vec{V}_1$ at a time with a single instruction; $\vec{V}_1 = (a_{11}, a_{12}, a_{13})$; and the second array computes a five-dimensional data vector $\vec{V}_2$ at a time with a single instruction, $\vec{V}_2 = (a_{21}, a_{22}, a_{23}, a_{24}, a_{25})$. Here each P_{1i} of the array A_1 computes one component a_{1i} of the $\vec{V}_1$ vector ($i = 1, 2, 3$), and each P_{2j} of the array A_2 computes one component a_{2j} of the $\vec{V}_2$ vector ($j = 1, \ldots, 5$).

c.   *The word size of each processor in each array.* This is specified by the number

TABLE V.1

Code of	Architectural	Symbolic Notation
N_0		$PE_1 \rightarrow PE_2, PE_3, PE_4$
N_1		$PE_1 \rightarrow (PE_2, PE_3), PE_4$
N_2		$PE_1 \rightarrow PE_2 (PE_3, PE_4)$
N_3		$PE_1 \rightarrow (PE_2, PE_3, PE_4)$
N_4		$(PE_1, PE_2) \rightarrow PE_3, PE_4$
N_5		$(PE_1, PE_2) \rightarrow (PE_3, PE_4)$
N_6		$(PE_1, PE_2, PE_3) \rightarrow PE_4$
N_7		$PE_1 \rightarrow PE_2; PE_3 \rightarrow PE_4$
N_8		$PE_1 \rightarrow PE_2, PE_3$
N_9		$PE_1 \rightarrow PE_2, PE_4$
N_{10}		$PE_1 \rightarrow PE_3, PE_4$
N_{11}		$PE_2 \rightarrow PE_3, PE_4$
N_{12}		$(PE_1, PE_2) \rightarrow PE_3$
N_{13}		$PE_1 \rightarrow (PE_2, PE_3)$
N_{14}		$(PE_1, PE_2) \rightarrow PE_4$
N_{15}		$PE_1 \rightarrow (PE_3, PE_4)$
N_{16}		$PE_2 \rightarrow (PE_3, PE_4)$
N_{17}		$(PE_2, PE_3) \rightarrow PE_4$
N_{18}		$PE_1 \rightarrow PE_2$
N_{19}		$PE_2 \rightarrow PE_3$
N_{20}		$PE_3 \rightarrow PE_4$
N_{21}		$PE_1 \rightarrow PE_3$
N_{22}		$PE_1 \rightarrow PE_4$
N_{23}		$PE_2 \rightarrow PE_4$

k of PE included in each processor. For instance, a system that computes two data vectors $\overline{V}_1$ and $\overline{V}_2$ at a time, where vector $\overline{V}_1 = (a_1(16), a_2(32), a_3(32))$ and $\overline{V}_2 = (b_1(16), b_2(16))$, has two arrays A_1 and A_2. The A_1 array includes three processors, P_{11}, P_{12}, and P_{13}; the 16-bit processor P_{11} computes a 16-bit word $a_1(16)$; P_{11} is assembled from one PE; the 32-bit processor P_{12} computes a 32-bit word $a_2(32)$; P_{12} is assembled from two PE; the 32-bit processor P_{13} computes $a_3(32)$. It is assembled from two PEs. In all, the A_1 array is formed of 5 PE. Similarly, one can find the number of PEs in the A_2 array.

4.2 Selected Array Algorithms

In this section we consider how the dynamic architecture performs the following array computations:

a. Relaxation equations
b. Pulse deinterleaving

4.2.1 Relaxation Equations

This is a class of algorithms aimed at performing the following steps during each algorithm iteration.

Step 1. Basis: Concurrent evaluation of a relaxation function (temperature, heat distribution, etc.) at each set of neighboring points of a plane. (Location of the neighbors in every set is determined by each relaxation algorithm.)

Note: Each set of the neighboring points is assigned to one of two categories: *internal* and *boundary*. For an internal set of points, the median point of the set is always internal. For a boundary set of points, the median point of the set is always boundary. Also, for some relaxation algorithms there are special boundary points in which evaluation of a relaxation function is prohibited since it may distort the relaxation process carried out in other points of the plane. These points will be called *prohibited points* (Fig. V.20).

Step 2.   Iterative step: Finding the average of the relaxation function for each such evaluation and assigning this average as the meaning of the median point of each set of neighboring points for the next iteration.

*Step 3.   * Do Step 2 until the changes in the relaxation function between two consecutive evaluations do not fall within a specified pair of limits, L (low) and H (high).

As follows from Steps 1 through 3, the best array system that computes a relaxation equation(s) possesses the following attributes:

Task 1: Heat Relaxation
Time : 20 min.

Task 2: Temperature Relaxation
Time : 30 min.

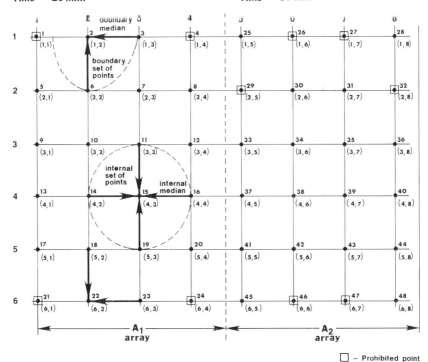

☐ – Prohibited point

FIGURE V.20   Two relaxation processes

1. The number of PEs in the array equals the number of functional points that must be evaluated.

2 . All PEs of the system are divided into internal PEs for evaluating internal functional points and boundary PEs for evaluating boundary functional points.

3. Some PEs of the system may be idle if their locations coincide with prohibited boundary points.

4 . Each internal PE evaluates a *complete relaxation function;* each boundary PE evaluates a *boundary relaxation function,* which is either a subfunction of a complete function or a special function specified by a given relaxation algorithm.

5. A typical relaxation function for an internal set of points is specified as follows (Fig. V.20):

$$x_{i,j}(k) = [x_{i-1,j}(k - 1) + x_{i+1, j}(k-1) + x_{i,j-1}(k-1) + x_{i,j+1}(k - 1)]/4 \quad (1)$$

where $x_{i,j}(k)$ is the meaning of the relaxation function for the ith row, jth column, and kth iteration.

As follows, a typical set of neighboring points includes four members which are orthogonal to the set median. Their functions are averaged to give the one assigned to the median for the next iteration.

Example. Consider the A_1 array designated to compute the heat relaxation. Assume that for the functional plane shown in Fig. V.20 there are 24 functional points. These are represented by the following two notations: (1) an i notation is specified by the position code i of the respective PE assigned for computation and (2) an i, j notation, where i is the row and j is the column number of the PE in the functional plane. Also, square boxes represent prohibited boundary functional points which must be excluded from evaluation. Using the i, j notation, let us give several examples of internal and boundary sets of points and find the values of the relaxation function for these sets.

The internal sets of points $\text{ISP}_{i, j}$ for this functional plane, where i, j is the median location, have the following ranges for i and j: $i = 2, \ldots, 5$ and $j = 2, 3$, since $i = 1$ and 6 specify the boundary rows and $j = 1$ and 4 specify the boundary columns. The values of relaxation function $x_{i, j}(k)$ assumed for each internal ISP_{ij} are shown in Table V.2.

Any boundary set of points, BSP_{ij}, is specified by the boundary median i, j, where either i or j is boundary. For our example, if both i and j are boundary, the point is prohibited. Table V.2 specifies the boundary sets of points, BSP, and the values of the relaxation equation assumed for each BSP. As follows, if a boundary median (i, j) is adjacent to the prohibited point, then the relaxation equation is made of two addends, since the third one is a prohibited point which is excluded from evaluation. Otherwise, the relaxation equation is made of three addends. ■

4.2.1.1 Computation of Relaxation Equations by Dynamic Array Architecture

Given a dynamic array architecture consisting of 48 computer elements CE, assume that this architecture has to compute three relaxation tasks specified by the following parameters: During the time $T = 24$ minutes, task 1 computes the heat relaxation on the functional plane having 24 functional points (Fig. V.20). During the time $T = 30$ minutes, task 2 computes the temperature relaxation algorithm on the functional plane having 24 functional points. During the time $T = 30$ minutes, task 3 computes the next temperature relaxation algorithm on the functional plane having 48 functional points (Fig. V.21). Figure V.22 shows computation of tasks 1, 2, and 3 by the dynamic array architecture consisting of 48 CE. As seen, the system forms two array states, $N_1(A)$ and $N_2(A)$, in computation. State $N_1(A)$ is characterized by the formation of the two arrays A_1 and A_2 designated to compute tasks 1 and 2, respectively. The next state $N_2(A)$ forms a single array from the entire available resources destined to compute task 3. The whole computation takes 60 minutes (Fig. V.22). Let us consider the computation of task 1 in more detail. Tasks 2 and 3 are executed similarly.

Basis step: All nonprohibited PEs execute the same subroutine aimed at finding

TABLE V.2

INTERNAL SET OF POINTS $\text{ISP}_{i,j}$ $(t = 2, \ldots, 5, j = 2, 3)$

$\text{ISP}_{i,j}$	Internal Median Point, i, j	Relaxation Equation
$\text{ISP}_{22} = \{(1, 2), (2, 1), (2, 3), (3, 2)\}$	(2, 2)	$x_{22}(k) = [x_{12}(k - 1) + x_{21}(k - 1) + x_{23}(k - 1) + x_{2}(k - 1)]/4$
$\text{ISP}_{23} = \{(1, 3), (2, 2), (3, 3), (2, 4)\}$	(2, 3)	$x_{23}(k) = [x_{13}(k - 1) + x_{22}(k - 1) + x_{33}(k - 1) + x_{2}(k - 1)]/4$
$\cdot$	$\cdot$	$\cdot$
$\cdot$	$\cdot$	$\cdot$
$\cdot$	$\cdot$	$\cdot$
$\text{ISP}_{53} = \{(5, 2), (6, 3), (5, 4), (4, 3)\}$	(5, 3)	$x_{53}(k) = [x_{52}(k - 1) + x_{63}(k - 1) + x_{54}(k - 1) + x_{4}(k - 1)]/4$

Boundary Set of Points $\text{BSP}_{i,j}$, where $i, j = \begin{cases} (1, j) \text{ or } (6, j) \text{ and } j \neq 4 \\ (i, 1) \text{ or } (i, 4) \text{ and } i \neq 1 \end{cases}$

BSP$_{i,j}$	Boundary Median Point i, j	Relaxation Equation
BSP$_{12}$ = {(2, 2), (1, 3)}	(1, 2)	$x_{12}(k) = [x_{22}(k - 1) + x_{13}(k - 1)]/2$
BSP$_{13}$ = {(1, 2), (2, 3)}	(1, 3)	$x_{13}(k) = [x_{12}(k - 1) + x_{23}(k - 1)]/2$
BSP$_{21}$ = {(3, 1), (2, 2)}	(2, 1)	$x_{21}(k) = [x_{31}(k - 1) + x_{22}(k - 1)]/2$
BSP$_{24}$ = {(2, 3), (3, 4)}	(2, 4)	$x_{24}(k) = [x_{23}(k - 1) + x_{34}(k - 1)]/2$
BSP$_{31}$ = {(2, 1), (3, 2), (4, 1)}	(3, 1)	$x_{31}(k) = [x_{21}(k - 1) + x_{32}(k - 1) + x_{41}(k - 1)]/3$
.	.	.
.	.	.
.	.	.
BSP$_{63}$ = {(6, 2), (5, 3)}	(6, 3)	$x_{63}(k) = [x_{62}(k - 1) + x_{53}(k - 1)]/2$

351

Task 3: Temperature Relaxation
Time : 30 min.

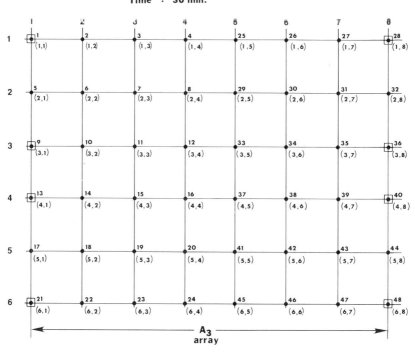

FIGURE V.21   Temperature relaxation process

the initial value of every nonprohibited functional point. The result is all the possible values $x_{ij}(0)$ for the zero iteration.

Iterative step: Using Eq. (1), this step finds $x_{i,j}(k)$ for the kth iteration, given all the nonprohibited $x_{i,j}(k-1)$ for the $(k-1)$ iteration, where $k = 1, 2, \ldots$.

Finding each $x_{i,j}(k)$ is performed with two processes I_1 and I_2 where process I_1 sends $x_{ij}(k-1)$ to all neighboring locations and process I_2 finds $x_{i,j}(k)$ for the next iteration.

Process I_1. Process I_1 is equivalent to one instruction executed in each PE: Each nonprohibited PE of the functional plane receives a special instruction $PE_A \rightarrow PE_B$, PE_C, PE_D, PE_E shown in Fig. V.23 (A prohibited PE is excluded from computation.) Each nonprohibited PE_A stores its row-column notation code $A = (i, j)$ that specifies its row i and column j in the functional plane.

The instruction $PE_A \rightarrow PE_B$, PE_C, PE_D, PE_E stores the following codes (Fig. V.23): low and high row bounds $i_L{}^*$ and $i_H{}^*$ and low and high column bounds $j_L{}^*$ and $j_H{}^*$. These codes are defined as follows:

$$i_L{}^* = i_L - 1, \text{ and } i_L \text{ is the lowest (boundary) row}$$

$$i_H{}^* = i_H + 1, \text{ and } i_H \text{ is the highest (boundary) row}$$

Similarly, $j_L{}^* = j_L - 1$ and $j_H{}^* = j_H + 1$.

Computation of Tasks 1, 2 and 3 by dynamic array architecture

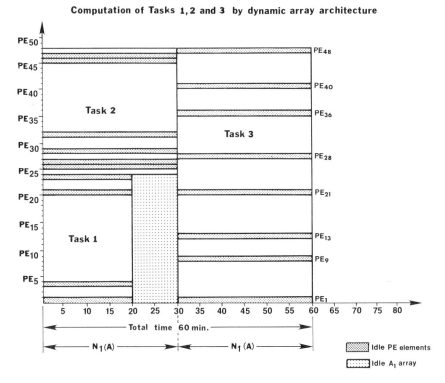

FIGURE V.22　Computation of three relaxation algorithms by dynamic array architecture

For our example, since $i_L = 1$, $i_H = 6$, $i_L^* = 0$, and $i_H^* = 7$. Similarly, since $j_L = 1$, $j_H = 4$, $j_L^* = 0$, and $j_H^* = 5$. When the instruction is fetched to each PE_A of the array, this PE_A performs the following actions:

Action 1.　Each processor element PE_A finds destination addresses B and C, where $B = (i - 1, j)$ and $C = (i + 1, j)$, and $A = (i, j)$ is the local address.

op code	row bound		column bound	
$PE_A \rightarrow PE_B, PE_C, PE_D, PE_E$	$i_L^* = 0$	$i_H^* = 7$	$j_L^* = 0$	$j_H^* = 5$

$A = (i, j)$
$B = (i-1, j)$
$C = (i+1, j)$
$D = (i, j-1)$
$E = (i, j+1)$

FIGURE V.23　Format of the instruction that represents Process 1

Action 2.   Each processor element PE_A forms two *row-bound* addresses, $R_L^* = (i_L^*, j)$ and $R_H^* = (i_H^*, j)$, where i_L^*, i_H^* are row bounds stored in the instruction, and j is the local column address taken from $A = (i, j)$.

If $R_L^* < B$, the B destination is allowed. If $R_L^* = B$, the B destination is prohibited. Similarly, if $R_H^* > C$, the C destination is allowed. If $R_H^* = C$, the C destination is prohibited.

Action 3.   Each processor element PE_A forms two *column-bound* addresses $C_L^* = (i, j_L^*)$ and $C_H^* = (i, j_H^*)$, where j_L^* and j_H^* are column bounds stored in the instruction, and i is the local row address taken from $A = (i, j)$.

If $C_L^* < D$, the D destination is allowed; if $C_L^* = D$, the D destination is prohibited. If $C_H^* > E$, the E destination is allowed; otherwise, it is prohibited.

Action 4. PE_A sends concurrently the local relaxation value $x_{ij}(k - 1)$ to all allowed destinations.

Process I_2.   This process executes Eq. (1) and finds $x_{ij}(k) - x_{i, j}(k - 1) = \Delta$. If $L \leq \Delta \leq H$, the iterative process stops; otherwise, it continues for the next iteration.

Example.   Consider execution of the instruction $PE_A \rightarrow PE_B, PE_C, PE_D, PE_E$ in several PEs of the A_1 array (Fig. V.20). Our objective is to show that the same instruction $PE_A \rightarrow PE_B, PE_C, PE_D, PE_E$ executed in a boundary PE_A and/or an internal PE_A will correctly identify all the other PEs that must receive the relaxation value computed in PE_A. To achieve this objective, we will consider two PE_A: *boundary* having $A = (2, 1)$, and *internal* having $A = (3, 3)$.

Case 1:   Boundary PE_A, where $A = (2, 1)$. For $A = (2, 1)$, $i = 2$ and $j = 1$. First PE_A finds B and C addresses: $B = (i - 1, j) = (1, 1)$ and $C = (i + 1, j) = (3, 1)$. Since $B = (1, 1)$ is a prohibited location, it is excluded, inasmuch as $PE_{1,1}$ receives no instructions. Next PE_A forms two row-bound addresses:

$$R_L(i_L^*, j) = R_L = (0, 1) \quad \text{and} \quad R_H = (i_H^*, j) = (7, 1)$$

where $i_L^* = 0$ and $i_H^* = 7$ (Fig. V.23). $R_L = (0, 1)$ is not compared with B, because $B = (1, 1)$ is a priori prohibited. Since $R_H = (7, 1) > C = (3, 1)$, destination C is allowed.

Second, PE_A finds D and E addresses. $D = (i, j - 1) = (2, 0)$; $E = (i, j + 1) = (2, 2)$. Thereafter, PE_A forms two column-bound addresses.

$$C_L = (i, j_L^*) = (2, 0) \quad \text{and} \quad C_H = (i, j_H^*) = (2, 5)$$

where $j_L^* = 0$ and $j_H^* = 5$ (Fig. V.23). Since $C_L = D$, D is prohibited. Since $C_H > E$, E is allowed. Therefore, PE_A sends its local value only to PE_C and PE_E, where $C = (3, 1)$ and $E = (2, 2)$ (Fig. V.20).

Case 2:   Internal PE_A, where $A = (3, 3)$. Since $A = (3, 3)$, $B = (2, 3)$, $C = (4, 3)$, $R_L = (0, 3)$, and $R_H = (7, 3)$. Since $R_L < B$, B is allowed; since $R_H > C$, C is allowed. Next PE_A finds $D = (3, 2)$, $E = (3, 4)$ and $C_L = (3, 0)$, $C_H = (3, 5)$. Since

C_L < D, D is allowed; since C_H > E, E is allowed. Therefore, the relaxation value found in $PE_{(3,\ 3)}$ is sent concurrently to B, C, D, and E. ∎

4.2.1.2 Computation of Relaxation Equations by Static Array

As follows from the previous section, the total time of executing tasks 1, 2, and 3 by the dynamic array architecture consisting of 48 PE is 60 minutes. For comparison, consider execution of the same tasks by the static array system consisting of 48 PE. Since the most complex task 3 requires a single array made of 48 PE, the entire static array system must function as a single array consisting of 48 PE (Fig. V.21). As follows, tasks 1, 2, and 3 must be executed sequentially, since the system functions as a single array. Execution of task 1 is shown in Fig. V.24. Only 24 PEs of the resources are involved. Other PEs are idle. The engaged PEs (active or prohibited) form the A_1 array. Similarly, task 2 is executed in the A_2 subarray also consisting of 24 PEs (Fig. V.25). Finally, Fig. V.21 shows the engagement of the system in execution of the A_3 array. The entire scheduling diagram of execution is shown in Fig. V.26. As follows, the same computation takes 80 minutes, i.e., 20 minutes more than the one performed by the dynamic array system. Therefore, accomplished speed-up is (80 - 60)/60 = 33%.

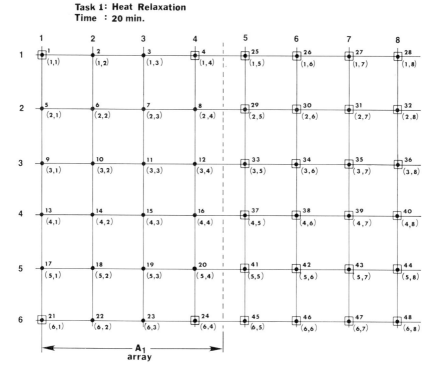

FIGURE V.24   Execution of task 1 in a conventional array system

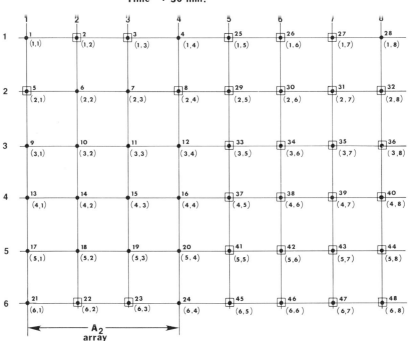

Task 2: **Temperature Relaxation**
Time   : 30 min.

FIGURE V.25   Execution of task 2 in a conventional array system

4.2.1.3 Resume

As follows from this analysis, in computing a typical relaxation algorithm, a dynamic array system can accomplish a 33% speed-up in comparison with the static array system having the same complexity of the resources. The only source of this speed-up is in dynamic reconfiguration aimed at releasing redundant resources into additional computations.

Note: We did not consider here other sources of speed-up that can be accomplished in a dynamic array system due to flexible data changes. For instance, as was shown by Love [61] in conventional array systems, all the processor-to-processor transfers required by Eq. (1) take four instructions, $PE_A \rightarrow PE_B$ where the first instruction $PE_A \rightarrow PE_B$; the second instruction performs $PE_A \rightarrow PE_C$, the third instruction performs $PE_A \rightarrow PE_D$; and the fourth instruction performs $PE_A \rightarrow PE_E$.

In contrast, the dynamic array architecture executes all four of these transfers with a single instruction whose computation was considered in the preceding section. Therefore, availability of well-developed data exchanges will reduce even further the time of execution of tasks 1, 2, and 3 in comparison with conventional array systems.

Computation of Tasks 1, 2 and 3 by conventional static array system

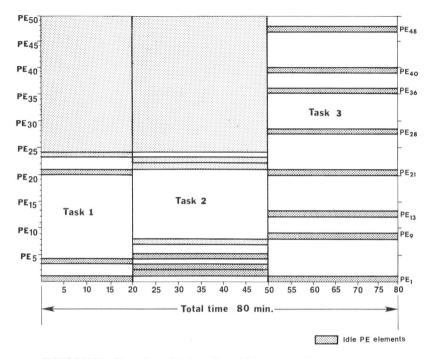

FIGURE V.26   Execution of tasks 1, 2, and 3 in a conventional array system

4.2.2 Pulse Deinterleaving

The objective of the pulse deinterleaving process is to form various pulse trains where each pulse train defines a sequence of pulses with identical pulse characteristics. Each established pulse train is represented by a file, which maintains matching characteristics for the pulse train.† These characteristics are as follows [61]:

1. The upper and lower limits of several important pulse parameters such as:
   a. Pulse time of arrival TOA_h and TOA_ℓ, where TOA shows the moment of time a given pulse was acquired (Fig. V.27).
   b. Pulse width W_h and W_ℓ, where W measures the time interval of a short burst of high-frequency carrier signals that are included in one pulse envelope.
   c. Pulse frequency F, which measures the frequency of the carrier signal included in a single pulse.

† Throughout this section we will base our description of the execution of the pulse deinterleaving algorithm by dynamic architecture on the information about this algorithm given by H. Love in [61].

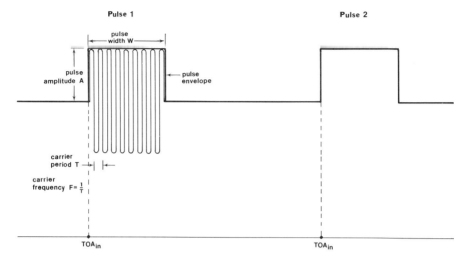

FIGURE V.27 Important pulse parameters

    d. Pulse amplitude, A_ℓ and A_h, which is understood as the amplitude of the carrier signal included in a pulse.

2. The number of missed pulses. It is expected that some pulses are acquired with insufficient amplitude to be recognized as legitimate pulses. The algorithm must take such missed pulses into account.

3. The number of accumulated pulses in the pulse train, NS. This will be needed for analyzing the final pulse train data.

4. W_s and F_s, the cumulative sums of W and F, respectively, for all pulses in the train. These are also needed for final analysis of the pulse trains.

5. The "active flag," AF. The state of this flag indicates that the pulse train is either active (AF is set) or else is inactive or lost (AF is reset).

4.2.2.1 Rules of Pulse Acquisition

Let TOA_{in}, W_{in}, F_{in}, and A_{in} be the parameters of the current input pulse just received from the antenna. The current input pulse is considered matching an established pulse train if the following conditions are satisified:

    a. $TOA_\ell \leq TOA_{in} \leq TOA_h$
    b. $W_\ell \leq W_{in} \leq W_h$
    c. $F_\ell \leq F_{in} \leq F_h$
    d. $A_\ell \leq A_{in} \leq A_h$

Therefore, in order to acquire a new pulse to an established train, it is necessary to find low and upper bounds of the four train parameters, TOA, W, F, and A. For the

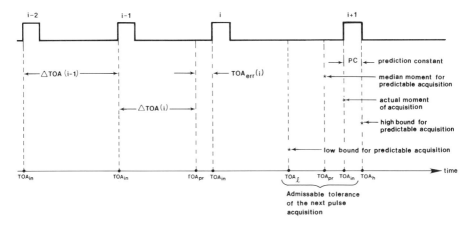

FIGURE V.28   Finding a predictable TOA parameter

following pulse parameters such as width W, frequency F, and amplitude A, the high and lower bounds remain constant for the entire train and are established in the beginning of the train formation with the acquisition of the first pulse of the train.† As for the TOA parameter, TOA_ℓ and TOA_h are variable and may change with acquisition of each new pulse to an established pulse train. New meanings of TOA_ℓ and TOA_h for the next pulse i are computed by the following prediction algorithm that varies an admissible tolerance $TOA_h(i) - TOA_\ell(i)$ in acquiring the next pulse i dependent on the error committed in predicting the time of arrival for the previous pulse $i - 1$.

4.2.2.2 Prediction Algorithm for Variable TOA_ℓ and TOA_h

Given: (a) $TOA_{in}(i - 2)$ and $TOA_{in}(i - 1)$ for the acquired pulses $(i - 2)$ and $(i - 1)$ (Fig. V.28). (b) Predicted $TOA_{pr}(i - 1)$ for the pulse $(i - 1)$.

Find: Predicted high and low bounds $TOA_h(i)$ and $TOA_\ell(i)$ for the next pulse i that has to be acquired. (*Note:* The algorithm assumes that an *established pulse train* contains at least three pulses. Otherwise, a pulse train belongs to the category of a *train candidate*. To form an established train from a train candidate, a special start-up algorithm will be used which uses standard tolerances for the four pulse parameters.)

Step 1. For the two consecutive pulses $(i - 1)$ and $(i - 2)$ already acquired, find $\Delta TOA(i - 1) = TOA_{in}(i - 1) - TOA_{in}(i - 2)$.

Step 2. Find median predicted $TOA_{pr}(i)$ for the next pulse i: $TOA_{pr}(i) = TOA_{in}(i - 1) + \Delta TOA(i - 1)$.

---

† We do not consider here deliberate jittering of the basic pulse parameters, since our objective is not to propose various complex signal processing algorithms that allow one to overcome the problem of jittering. Rather, our objective is to demonstrate how a typical pulse deinterleaving algorithm is executed by dynamic architecture and in what way its performance in such execution is comparable with that of conventional systems having the same complexity of resources.

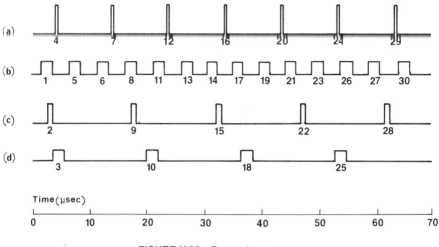

FIGURE V.29 Four pulse trains

Step 3. Find the error in prediction of the previous pulse, $i - 1$: $TOA_{err}(i - 1)$ $= |TOA_{pr}(i - 1) - TOA_{in}(i - 1)|$.

Step 4. Find $TOA_h(i) = TOA_{pr}(i) + TOA_{err}(i - 1) + PC$: $TOA_\ell(i) = TOA_{pr}(i)$ $- TOA_{err}(i - 1) - PC$.

Here PC is a prediction constant selectable by the programmer. Its purpose is to prevent the admissible tolerance $TOA_h(i) - TOA_\ell(i)$ from becoming 0 for the case $TOA_{err}(i - 1) = 0$, i.e., when there is no error in prediction. As follows, this prediction algorithm varies the interval of admissible tolerance for acquisition of the next pulse dependent on the error $TOA_{err}(i - 1)$ made in predicting the time of arrival of the previous pulse. The greater $TOA_{err}(i - 1)$, the greater admissible tolerance of the next acquisition.

4.2.2.3 Pulse Train Start-Up

In the beginning the system has to execute a special start-up algorithm aimed at forming an established pulse train, i.e., the one that has at least three pulses.

The operation of the start-up algorithm can be illustrated by the following example. This is the case when system operation is just beginning and there are, as yet, no candidates or acquired pulse trains.

Figure V.29† shows sequences of pulses from four pulse trains displayed on a common time line. For convenience in the discussion, the pulses are numbered in order of arrival (at the receiver). Table V.3 is a list of the 30 pulses from Fig. V.29 and the values of their three parameters. The fourth parameter (amplitude) is omitted for simplicity of discussion. Table V.3 shows the average values of the three pulse parameters

† This figure as well as Tables V.3 and V.4 are taken from [61].

TABLE V.3

PULSE PARAMETER VALUES

Pulse	TOA	W	F	Train
1	1.0	0.6	795	b
2	2.0	0.35	1010	c
3	3.0	0.6	790	d
4	3.7	0.15	600	a
5	6.0	0.65	795	b
6	11.0	0.65	798	b
7	13.8	0.1	610	a
8	16.0	0.6	805	b
9	17.0	0.3	1007	c
10	20.0	0.65	800	d
11	21.0	0.7	803	b
12	23.8	0.15	605	a
13	26.0	0.65	805	b
14	31.0	0.7	800	b
15	32.0	0.35	1007	c
16	33.7	0.15	607	a
17	36.0	0.65	798	b
18	37.0	0.7	797	d
19	41.0	0.6	800	b
20	43.7	0.1	605	a
21	46.0	0.6	802	b
22	47.0	0.35	1000	c
23	51.0	0.6	800	b
24	53.8	0.15	605	a
25	54.0	0.65	807	d
26	56.0	0.65	795	b
27	61.0	0.7	798	b
28	62.0	0.3	1005	c
29	63.8	0.15	603	a
30	66.0	0.7	798	b

TABLE V.4

Assignment of First 12 Pulses

Candidate File	Contents (Pulse Numbers)											
	Step 1	Step 2	Step 3	Step 4	Step 5	Step 6	Step 7	Step 8	Step 9	Step 10	Step 11	Step 12
1	1	1	1, 3	1, 3	1, 3		7	7	7	7	7	
2		2	2	2	2	2	2	2	2, 9	2, 9	2, 9	2, 9
3			1	1	1, 5		4	4	4	4	4	
4			3	3	3, 5				2	2	2	2
5				4	4	4	4, 7	4, 7	4, 7	4, 7	4, 7	
6					1				9	9	9	9
7					3	3	3	3	3	3, 10	3, 10	3, 10
8					5					3	3	3
9										10	10	10
Train File												
1					1, 5	1, 5 6	1, 5 6	1, 5 6, 8	1, 5 6, 8	1, 5 6, 8	1, 5 6, 8 11	6, 8 11
2												4, 7, 12

for each of the four pulse trains. (In the table, instead of the TOA parameter, we use an average $\Delta TOA = TOA_{in}(i) - TOA_{in}(i - 1)$, since ΔTOA is one of the characteristics that distinguishes one pulse train from another.)

For our evaluation, we will use predicted TOA values (TOA_ℓ and TOA_h) found with the use of the predictor algorithm.

Table V.4 shows the assignments of the first 12 pulses to candidates and pulse trains, as they would be made by the start-up and maintenance algorithms. In this table, each step $i(i = 1, \ldots, 12)$, corresponds to the processing of the pulse with matching number i, and it shows the status of files following completion of the pulse processing.

For example, after Step 7, during which pulse 7 is processed, there are five candidates and one established pulse train. The deletion of candidates occurs at Steps 6 and 12, each of which establishes a single new pulse train. The enormous proliferation of candidates is apparent in this example. The pulse widths and carrier frequencies for pulse trains b and d were deliberately made the same to illustrate the way in which "false" candidates can multiply when there are many pulse trains in the input having similar characteristics.

4.2.2.4 Selection of the Best Architecture

The best architecture for solving the pulse-deinterleaving problem is an array architecture having the number of PEs matching the number of established trains. The reason for this is as follows. As was shown above, both the formation of new pulse trains and the maintenance of existing pulse trains are reduced to execution of simple parallel comparisons and parallel sequences of additions and subtractions aimed at finding out whether or not a newly arrived pulse belongs to any of the established or candidate trains.

While comparison operations find whether or not the pulse parameters are within the admissible tolerances of matching train parameters, additions and subtractions are aimed at finding predicted train parameters, (TOA_ℓ and TOA_h, etc.) for the case in which they are not permanent for the given train.

Further, the same sequence of operations [comparisons and additions (subtractions)] should be performed in parallel in each pulse train.

Since a complete match may occur only in one *established* pulse train, only this train out of many others will acquire the next newly arrived pulse. (As for candidates, in the beginning we may have a large number of possible candidates. Later on, however, all but true trains will be eliminated.)

The speediest way of executing identical parallel comparisons and other parallel arithmetic operations is to have a single array having the number of processors matching the number of possible trains. Certainly in realistic situations when the number of actual pulse trains N_{PT} cannot be predicted precisely, we may have the number of processors N_{AP} in the array either larger or smaller than the number of actual trains. In the case of case $N_{AP} > N_{PT}$, all the redundant processors can be released from computation once the actual number of pulse trains is found. This is accomplished by reconfiguring dynamic array architecture into the array state in which there is a precise match between the parameters of the array and those of the pulse deinterleaving algorithm.

If $N_{AP} < N_{PT}$, which means that new pulse trains will appear in the process of computation, the dynamic architecture may reconfigure into a new architectural state in which the new number of established pulse trains will correspond again to the new number of processors in the array. Again, the architecture will be able to match its characteristics with those of the pulse deinterleaving algorithm creating maximal possible concurrency under the circumstances.

4.2.2.5 Three Algorithms of Pulse Deinterleaving

Suppose that a dynamic array architecture made of 10 processor elements has to execute the following three algorithms of pulse deinterleaving:

Algorithm 1: Four pulse trains must be distinguished with permanent tolerances for TOA, W, F, and A. The total time of execution in the array system consisting of four processors is 30 minutes.

Algorithm 2: Ten pulse trains must be distinguished with permanent tolerances for W, F, and A and a predictable (variable) tolerance for TOA. The total time of execution in the array system consisting of ten processors is 40 minutes.

Algorithm 3:   Five pulse trains must be distinguished with predictable (variable) tolerances for all the pulse parameters, W, F, A, and TOA, i.e., high and low values for each of the parameters for the next pulse are computed on the basis of current input value, found error for previous prediction, and prediction constant. The total time of execution in the array system consisting of five processors is 50 minutes.

It should be noted that the initial condition of having (a) no variable tolerances for Algorithm 1, (b) permanent tolerances for W, F, and A, and variable tolerance for TOA for Algorithm 2, and (c) variable tolerance for W, F, A, and TOA for Algorithm 3 requires that each of the algorithms (1, 2, and 3) be computed with a separate instruction sequence. Therefore, dynamic architecture must form three separate arrays A_1, A_2, and A_3 aimed at execution of algorithms 1, 2, and 3, respectively.

4.2.2.6 Execution of Algorithm 1 in Dynamic Architecture

As an example, consider execution of Algorithm 1 in the Array A_1 formed of four processors. Algorithms 2 and 3 are executed similarly. The only distinction in their executions is in more complex arithmetic computations aimed at finding predictable values of TOA (Algorithm 2) and those for all the other pulse parameters (Algorithm 3).

Assume that for Algorithm 1, the pulse trains that have to be recognized are shown in Fig. V.29. The actual pulse parameters received in real-time are shown in Table V.3 and the train start-up algorithm is shown in Table V.4. The configuration of the A_1 array in execution of Algorithm 1 is shown in Fig. V.30. As seen, the A_1 array consists of four PEs aimed at maintaining four pulse trains: a, b, c, and d, respectively. Therefore, ME_1 stores the data files necessary to maintain pulse train a; ME_2 through ME_4 store data files for pulse trains b, c, and d, respectively. The instruction and data arrays for Algorithm 1 are stored in ME_1, since PE_1 is the processor-supervisor. Consecutive steps for executing this algorithm are shown in Table V.4, where each step consists of all actions in our PEs aimed at processing one arriving pulse. All data parameters of each pulse are received by all PEs which perform concurrent comparisons with high and low values of TOA, W, F, and A parameters, respectively, fetched locally from the arrays a, b, c, and d, respectively.

For pulse 1 received during Step 1, a complete match occurs in PE_2 which forms a candidate-train (1) out of a single pulse.

During Step 2, aimed at broadcasting the parameters of pulse 2, match occurs in PE_3. Thus, PE_3 forms a candidate-train (2) from the single pulse 2 (Fig. V.30).

For Step 3, pulse 3 has matching characteristics with pulse 1. Thus, PE_2 forms a candidate-train (1, 3). Since pulse 1 may belong to a separate train, PE_2 maintains a separate candidate-train (1). PE_3 continues to maintain candidate-train (2) acquired during Step 2, and PE_4 forms a separate candidate-train (3) since it also features a match with file d. For Step 4, pulse 4 is used to form a separate candidate-train (4) in PE_1. The status of the remaining candidate-trains remain unchanged. For Step 5, the following new candidate-trains are formed, in addition to those existing during Step 4: new candidate-train (5) in PE_2; new candidate-train (1, 5) in PE_2; and new candidate-train (3, 5) in PE_4.

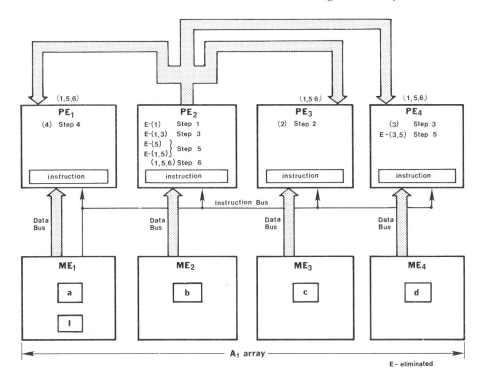

FIGURE V.30 Execution of Algorithm 1 in the A_1-array

For Step 6, we are in a position to form an established train "b" out of three pulses (1, 5, 6) and to eliminate all train candidates that have a nonempty intersection with (1, 5, 6). The (1, 5, 6) train is formed in PE_2. The eliminated candidates are (1), (1, 3), (5), and (1, 5) in PE_2 and (3, 5) in PE_4. This elimination is performed when PE_2 which has formed a three-pulse train first sends the (1, 5, 6) data information to all other PEs that use this information for elimination of their false one- and two-pulse candidates, etc.

As follows, the A_1 array consisting of four PEs is an ideal architecture for this algorithm for the following reasons:

a. Each PE maintains one established train. Therefore, when all trains are established, all the comparison operations aimed at acquisition of the next pulse by one of the available trains can be performed concurrently. Therefore, the rate of new pulse acquisition is the time of one step aimed at executing the following four comparisons in each PE:

$$W_\ell \leq W_{in} \leq W_h$$

$$F_\ell \leq F_{in} \leq F_h$$

$$A_\ell \leq A_{in} \leq A_h$$

$$TOA_\ell \leq TOA_{in} \leq TOA_h$$

Note: No other alternative architecture can provide such a rate of pulse acquisition, since no other architecture can perform four parallel comparisons at a time with a single instruction.

b. During each pulse train start-up, some PEs may maintain several one- and two-pulse candidates. However, no degradation in performance occurs since

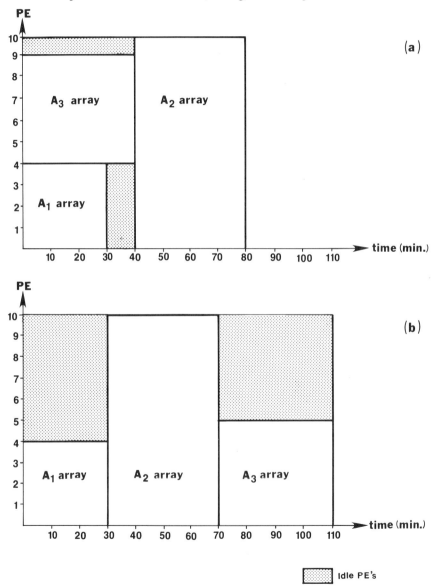

FIGURE V.31 Comparative executions of three pulse deinterleaving algorithms in dynamic and static array architectures

each eligible PE still takes four time intervals (eight clock periods) to perform four comparisons with high and low values stored locally and then during one clock period this PE forms all the new combinations of one- and two-pulse candidates.

For instance, consider execution of Step 5 in PE_2 (Fig. V.30). First, PE_2 compares the four parameters of pulse 5 brought with the instruction with those stored locally. Since a match is established, PE_2 forms two new trains (1, 5) and (5) concurrently during one clock period. Therefore, an increase in the number of possible candidates does not degrade the performance of the array.

4.2.2.7 Comparative Evaluation of Algorithms 1, 2, and 3 by Dynamic Array Architecture and Static Array System

In this section we will perform comparative evaluation of executing Algorithms 1, 2, and 3 by dynamic and static array architectures having 10 PE, since it is the complexity required by the most complex Algorithm 2 (Fig. V.31).

Executions of Algorithms 1, 2, and 3 by Dynamic Architecture.   A dynamic array architecture that executes Algorithms 1, 2, and 3 will consist of 10 CE. First, it forms the architectural state ($1 \times 4CE$, $1 \times 5CE$) which is equivalent to two separate arrays, A_1 and A_3, aimed at computing Algorithm 1 and Algorithm 3 concurrently. Upon completion of the two algorithms, dynamic architecture reconfigures into the A_2 array designated for Algorithm 2. The entire execution takes 80 minutes.

Execution of Algorithms 1, 2, and 3 by Static Array Architecture.   Since Algorithms 1, 2, and 3 are specified by different instruction sequences, they require sequential execution in a static array system consisting of 10 PE. The system executes Algorithm 1 in 30 minutes in 4 PE of the available resources. The remaining 6 PE where 6 PE = (10 − 4) PE are idle.

Upon completion of Algorithm 1, the system begins execution of Algorithm 2 in 10 PE of the resources. The entire execution takes 40 minutes. Having completed Algorithm 2, the system executes Algorithm 3 in 5 PE. The remaining five PE are idle. As follows from Fig. V.31, the total execution time is 110 minutes, which compares with 80 minutes of execution in dynamic array architecture. Therefore, accomplished speed-up is 30 minutes, or 37%. The origin of this speed-up is only due to dynamic reconfiguration which releases redundant resources into additional computations.

5 DATA-BASE MANAGEMENT IN TREE DATA BASES

In this section we will describe the performance of dynamic architectures in the execution of typical data-base management algorithms for a binary tree network data base. The performance of dynamic architectures in executing this type of tree management exchange will be compared with that of static tree architectures.

Typical data-base management involves node-to-node information transfer, whereby one tree node, called the *source node,* broadcasts an information array to another tree node, called the *destination node.* In a static data base, since node positions within the tree remain fixed, a pair of communicating nodes may be connected via the minimal communication path of length greater than 1 where the length of the path shows the number of other nodes the message must pass to reach the destination node. For instance, for the tree data base in Fig. III.18(a), to reach the destination (node 4), a message issued by the source (node 7) must pass through the path $7 \rightarrow 6 \rightarrow 4$ that contains two other nodes. Therefore, this path is of length 2. For the $7 \rightarrow 5$ communication, the following path should be formed: $7 \rightarrow 6 \rightarrow 4 \rightarrow 2 \rightarrow 5$. The length of the path is 4.

Let T_0 be the time of a message transit via one node. Then, for the $7 \rightarrow 5$ communication, the total time of one word broadcast will be $4T_0$. If 20 words are to be broadcast, then the total time T of communication becomes $T = 4 \cdot 20T_0 = 80T_0$.

In a reconfigurable data base, it is always possible to select a tree configuration that minimizes the path length, PL, between a pair of exchanging nodes leading to a reduction in the time of exchange, TE, among them, where $TE = DAN \cdot PL \cdot T_0$, and DAN is the number of words that are transferred.

Therefore, introduction of reconfiguration into a binary tree data base dramatically improves data-base performance as illustrated by the example discussed in Sec. 4.1, Chapter III. As was established, reconfiguration effects about 370% improvement in performance in comparison with the static and nonreconfigurable data base. The nature of this improvement lies in (1) minimization of the TE parameter at the expense of PL minimization, and (2) maximization in the number of concurrent data exchanges.

6 REAL-TIME SORTING

6.1 Motivation

Real-time systems compose a class of extremely stressing computational problems [59-61]. These systems may be characterized as having a sensing device that collects data, a processing device to extract information from the data, and a reactive device to make use of the information. In the case of defense systems the problem is complicated by the extremely short times in which a system must respond, as well as the large dynamic variations of data to which a processing system must be able to react. This places a premium on the processing system's having high throughput as well as a great degree of flexibility.

A typical real-time application is described in Fig. II.13, where the four stages indicate a sequence of processing stages performed by the system. The main system sensor is a phased array radar which can generate a pencil beam that changes directions in a few microseconds. The objective of the second stage is to eliminate most non-threatening targets from consideration via crude first checks. This may be done through special-purpose hardware dedicated to signal processing.

After this initial filtering operation, the radar objects that are potentially threatening are reported to a computer, which initiates a separate file on each object. The computer communicates with the radar by making requests to collect additional information about every object. Each target is then followed, and the computer computes its velocity, trajectory, current position, and other important information. After the target has been in the precision track for a short interval, discrimination routines are used to discriminate among targets.

6.2 Computation Requirements

Each stage of Fig. II.13 requires the following type of processing. Since computer processing starts with stage 2, it receives input prepared by stage 1, which ends with the arrival of multiple data streams requiring the same operation over multiple data items. Thus, stage 2 is characterized by the MIMD mode of opeation since it is specified by several instruction streams, each of which operates over a vector of data items.

Once most of the unthreatening objects are filtered out from consideration, the objects that are left are subjected to a more detailed check. Most of the typical computations in stage 3 are sorting and arithmetic pipelined computations. Sorting is aimed at forming classes of threatening objects, whereas pipelining is directed at quick organization of a separate data file for each object of the same class. These files are then updated with new information received from the radar.

Finally, stage 4 is aimed at very precise computation of trajectories of several high-priority objects that are still threatening after stage 3 and at predicting the points of their interception with the killer mechanisms that are going to be launched. The most effective computations of stage 4 are of an asynchronous MIMD type, performed over data words with long sizes to maintain a required level of accuracy.

6.3 Most Useful Configurations of a Multicomputer Network

As was shown in [59], heavy computer involvement in a computational process of real-time application begins with stages 3 and 4. The nature of the application supports distributive and reconfigurable computer resources, which are understood as a collection of computer elements interconnected by an interconnection network. Let us show which are the most efficient configurations that can be assumed by the resources.

Stage 3 involves (1) sorting and discrimination aimed at partitioning the incoming data items into categories, and (2) pipelining aimed at performing identical computations over the items of the same category. During execution of sorting and discrimination routines, the most efficient configurations of the system are either binary trees or stars. Once all the necessary classes of data words have been formed, the system must execute pipeline computations over the data words belonging to the same class. The most efficient configurations for this are rings of different periods, whereby each node of a ring fetches one operand from its local memory and receives the second operand from its predecessor in the ring. The task of reconfiguration is thus reduced to forming rings with various periods in order to organize pipelined computations of various complex arithmetic expressions, requiring a variable number of arithmetic operations (Fig. II.14).

Because tracking and discrimination processing, realized via sorting and pipelining, are performed over continuously arriving input data words, trees, stars, and rings should coexist in the same system. Since binary trees are characterized by two outcomes for each nonleaf node, they are useful configurations for tests with two outcomes: true, T, and false, F. If the number of true outcomes is greater than 1, then it is more cost efficient for the network to assume a star configuration (Fig. II.14).

Trees and stars can be singly or multiply rooted. For a multirooted tree or star, roots form a ring and specify the number of real-time classes that must be distinguished. Each class is specified by an m-step test procedure, where $m = 1, 2, \ldots$, and each step is described by a specific sorting algorithm aimed at distinguishing specific qualifications of the class. The tree or star structure will then contain m levels, where the root(s) is of the highest level and the leaves are of the lowest level (0). The task of the leaves is to accumulate data words with identical test qualifications.

Concurrency is understood here as the continuous acquisition of real-time data streams by the roots $R_1, R_2, \ldots, R_k$, which execute concurrent test algorithms. A tested data word is either forwarded to the true node of the next $m - 1$ level distinguished by the test result T_i, or the next root R_{j+1} (mod k) if the result of the test is F. Similar procedures are performed by all other lower-level nodes except leaves that perform no tests and merely maintain object files, where each file stores data words with identical test outcomes.

Figure II.14(a) shows a six-rooted two-level binary tree configuration assumed by the multicomputer network performing concurrent two-step sorting of continuously arriving data into six classes, R_1 through R_6. True data words for each class are then accumulated in true leaves.

Once all the necessary classes of data words have been formed, a computer reconfigures into rings with selectable periods to execute pipeline computations over the data words belonging to the same class. Or, if the response requirements are particularly demanding, trees, stars, and rings may coexist in the same system. In this case, sorting and tracking (pipelining) realized via trees/stars and rings can be performed over continuously arriving input words [Fig. II.14(a)].

As follows from this analysis, the most cost-efficient configurations during stage 3 are trees, stars, and rings to adapt to specific sorting and discrimination algorithms and the number of real-time objects that must be analyzed in a timely manner. Therefore, a dynamic architecture performing very fast reconfigurations into various types of k-rooted trees, stars (where $k \geq 1$), and rings becomes extremely cost efficient in sorting and evaluation of data words that specify k real-time classes. Each such class can be described by d different data files, so that each data file contains data words with the same test characteristics. Techniques for the reconfiguration of dynamic architecture into such structures are described in Sec. 4, Chapter II.

As was established there, each computing structure can be established practically instantaneously with the use of two control codes (bias B and reconfiguration code RC) and taking the time of mod-2 addition. Therefore, the introduced reconfiguration methodology carries no reconfiguration overhead and allows a considerable performance improvement because of computing each real-time algorithm in the best computing structure.

7 DIVIDE-AND-CONQUER OR TREE-STRUCTURED ALGORITHMS

Performance of dynamic architecture in executing this class of algorithms is similar to the one demonstrated for classes 4 and 5 and dedicated to computations in reconfigurable binary trees (class 4, see Sec. 5) and network computations (class 5, see Sec. 6, this chapter).

CONCLUSIONS TO THE BOOK

As has been demonstrated in this book, the benefits of using dynamic architectures for mission-critical applications are twofold:

1. They allow a significant performance improvement of mission-critical computers in comparison with conventional systems having similar complexity of hardware resources.

2. Their use in mission-critical computers leads to a substantial reduction in the overall software costs, since the same software can be used with no modification in all the architectural configurations that can be assumed by dynamic architecture to meet the very stringent requirements of mission-critical applications.

As demonstrated by this book, the major source of performance improvement attained by dynamic architectures is through the extensive use of reconfiguration, which allows minimization of the hardware resources involved in computing each algorithm and freeing all the unused resources into additional computations. This resource minimization assigned to each algorithm leads to maximization in the number of algorithms that are computed by the available resources.

No other architecture, either general purpose or dedicated, can accomplish such a performance improvement for such a large spectrum of applications. Indeed, to achieve a comparable throughput, a general-purpose architecture must be equipped with dynamic reconfiguration, since only reconfiguration allows fitting the architecture to an individual application algorithm other than the one the system has been designed for. Conversely, without dynamic reconfiguration, any static architecture creates resource redundancy in the execution of an algorithm, because a computer designer is incapable of anticipating all the resource needs that can be encountered in all the programs that are designated for present and future use of a given static computer system.

Furthermore, since no static architecture is provided with the architectural means of releasing redundant resources created in each execution into additional computations, the throughput figures for static architectures are lower than those for dynamic architectures that possess the same complexity of resources.

For dedicated architectures provided with dedicated hardware circuits, high throughput figures can be obtained only for the algorithms they have been designed for. Therefore, these architectures possess the following important drawbacks from the viewpoint of mission-critical applications:

D1. Since their areas of applications are narrow, they become totally unsuitable for an ever-increasing class of mission-critical applications (space, satellite, etc.) that are characterized by:

a. Extreme versatility of possible missions specified by demanding timing characteristics,

b. Inability of human interference in computer systems that are operable,

c. Continuous increases in throughput requirements for mission-critical computers that reflect a continuous improvement of defense weapon systems in detecting, following, homing, and destroying a target.

D2. In view of dedicated hardware solutions, dedicated mission-critical computers have already led to exponential cost increases in the software systems that also become dedicated. Thus, the following dead circle is created with the use of dedicated computers:

To meet particularly rigorous timing requirements of a real-time application algorithm(s), a dedicated computer is being built. To develop its software requires incurring significant software costs. Soon this computer becomes unsuitable for applications in view of any combination of factors a, b, and c noted above. As a result, the cycle starts again with building a new dedicated mission-critical computer and incurring new software costs for this computer, leading to a further heightening of the software cost spiral to higher and higher cost figures.

The way out of this circle is to apply to the architecture of mission-critical computers the same concepts of modularization, standardization, and reconfiguration that are now applied to mission-critical software systems in order to reduce their cost.

This means that mission-critical computers must be equipped with dynamic architectures in order to solve the following two problems at once:

1. To meet the variable requirements of each present and future mission from a broad spectrum of mission-critical applications (i.e., to have an enhanced life cycle),

2. To reduce the software costs of system development.

This book was dedicated to solving these two problems by discussing the reconfiguration software for dynamic architecture and presenting an *extensive algorithm development* of their most effective application areas. In the domain of reconfiguration software, this book concentrated on reconfiguration methodology and the recon-figuration flow chart.

Conclusions: Reconfiguration Software. The major findings of this book in the area of *reconfiguration software* demonstrate the following results:

A1. It is possible to create a software design methodology aimed at finding a flow chart of reconfigurations to be assumed by dynamic architectures in the execution of a given program mix. As was illustrated in this book, such design methodology has already been created by the authors for a general-purpose program mix of indepen-dent programs presented in FORTRAN and designated for multicomputer dynamic architectures and for reconfigurable data bases than can assume a sequence of tree configurations.

A2. It is possible to create concurrent and fast reconfiguration algorithms that allow swift reconfigurations to be performed by dynamic architectures in executing a reconfiguration flow chart that can be constructed using automatic software design procedures. Therefore, the reconfiguration techniques that have been presented in this book (for multicomputer, network, and fault-tolerant reconfigurations) create prac-tically no reconfiguration overhead and can be organized via one program instruction whose time does not exceed the time of 64-bit addition. (For network reconfigura-tions, the reconfiguration time is made even shorter, since it takes the time of one mod-2 addition and is affected by only two control codes.)

Therefore, the task of future research for reconfiguration software is:

P1. To extend the reconfiguration flow chart methodology to true dynamic pro-gram mixes of mission-critical programs presented in ADA and characterized by data dependencies, changeable priorities, program requirements on response time, concur-rency of observation, and exception handling.

P2. To develop the reconfiguration methodology for a comprehensive set of ar-chitectural and fault-tolerant reconfigurations, where architectural reconfigurations are understood as reconfiguration techniques into five dynamic architectures and fault-tolerant reconfigurations are understood as the techniques of either dynamic replace-ment of a faulty module via a matching spare or graceful degradation of a given dynamic configuration achieved via turning off faulty modules from the operations.

Conclusions: Algorithm Development. The most essential results of this book in the area of algorithm development demonstrate that the performance of dynamic architecture is superior to that of conventional systems in the execution of the follow-ing classes of algorithms:

I. *General-purpose algorithms,* which included a general-purpose program mix and a parallel programming construct fork-join. It is shown that for both these classes, the performance gains were above 40% in comparison with conventional multicom-puters having similar complexity of the resources. Such performance improvement was accomplished because of system reconfiguration, which allowed the creation of the minimal-size computer for each program of the program mix and formation of freed redundant resources into additional computations.

II. *Producer-consumer algorithms,* which included a sampled execution by dynamic architecture of the popular programming construct fetch-store (FS), which is equivalent to the execution of memory-processor-memory data exchange. Such FS was considered which required data fetches from six arrays, computing three arithmetic expressions and sending computing results to the seventh array. These arrays were stored in ME_1, ME_2, and ME_3, requiring considerable interaction between respective PE_1, PE_2, and PE_3 in accessing local and nonlocal variables.

It is shown that to access seven arrays and to compute three arithmetic expressions assigned to PE_1, PE_2, and PE_3, respectively, requires execution of not more than four instructions in three participating processors, i.e., only two instructions more than that required for two consecutive operations in one of the expressions, which can be organized only if all data words are available. Also, the operating system has to intervene only once before execution of this FS in order to connect the page of ME_3 with PE_1. Because of the variety of different types of data exchanges, no interference of the operating system was required in the process of execution of this FS, although PE_1, PE_2, and PE_3 must have fetched nonlocal data variables for computing expressions assigned to them.

Therefore, the data exchanges for dynamic architecture are optimal because of:

a. Variety of alternative routes for data words that can be organized via reconfiguration,

b. Ability of dynamic architectures to maintain parallel data exchanges with variable-size data words.

III. *Array computations,* which included sampled execution of three relaxation equations and one pulse deinterleaving algorithm. In computing a typical relaxation algorithm, a dynamic array system can accomplish a 33% speed-up in comparison with a static array system having the same complexity of resources. The only source of this speed-up is dynamic reconfiguration, which allowed the creation of a minimal-size array required by each relaxation equation and the formation of released resources in computing the second relaxation algorithm in the second array concurrent with the first one. Contrary to such execution, a static array system of the same complexity required three time intervals for executing three relaxation equations sequentially. This accounted for the obtained speed-up in 33%.

In computing a typical pulse-deinterleaving algorithm, which consists of forming separate pulse trains out of the arriving interleaved pulses, the performance improvement accomplished is 37% in comparison with conventional static arrays having similar complexity of resources. Again, this performance gain was due to the architectural capability in organizing more concurrent computations than it is possible to organize for static arrays.

IV. *Data-base management* in tree data bases, which included execution of the same table of required data exchanges among tree nodes by (1) the several binary tree configurations that can be assumed by dynamic architecture and (2) the static tree data base.

It is shown that performance improvement achieved via reconfiguration is especially dramatic and is 370% (!!) in comparison with static data bases. The only source of such performance improvements is in a capability of reconfigurable binary trees to organize a far shorter communication path among exchanging nodes, via reconfiguration, than it is possible to have in a static tree data base which has the positions of nodes in a tree fixed.

V. *Real-time sorting in multiple trees and stars structures.* The performance of dynamic architecture in the execution of real-time sorting algorithms is ideal because a system with dynamic architecture may assume a network structure that totally adapts to the following parameters of real-time sorting:

a. The number of sorting classes that have to be distinguished, which is equivalent to the number of concurrent trees or stars that have to be formed via reconfiguration.

b. The number of steps in a sorting algorithm, which is equivalent to the number of levels in each tree or star of a given network structure.

c. The number of outcomes for each sorting step, which is equivalent to the number of the adjacent nodes of the next level in a tree or star (for a tree the number of such outcomes is 2, i.e., true or false; for a star the number of such outcomes is greater than 2).

As follows from these findings, the task of future research on algorithm development is:

P1. To perform further algorithm development for a comprehensive spectrum of mission-critical application algorithms that includes popular algorithms described in the literature and new algorithms from the same categories that have much higher performance requirement figures.

P2. To perform the evaluation and comparison of executions attained in dynamic architecture with those demonstrated by conventional systems, both dedicated and general purpose. The expected outcomes are:

a. Finding the most efficient areas of mission-critical applications for dynamic architectures.

b. Evaluating these areas quantitatively.

c. Forecasting expected performances that can be obtained for new and more demanding mission-critical algorithms.

Appendix

Finding Bit Sizes
of Computed Variables

1 BIT SIZES OF INTEGERS

We will determine the bit sizes of integers involved in operations leading to an increase in bit sizes (additions and multiplications). The formulas for divisions and subtractions that as a rule reduce the bit size of the variables are conceived of as a simple extension of additions and multiplications. The next section will extend this analysis to real and floating-point variables.

1.1 Addition

We distinguish three possible options for addition, $X = A + B$: nonrecursive addition, recursive addition with nonrecursive addends, and recursive addition with recursive addends.

I. Nonrecursive Addition. X is assigned neither to A nor B, i.e., is not of the form $X = X + A$ or $X = X + B$; then

$$\text{BS}(X) \leq \max \left[\text{BS}(A), \text{BS}(B) \right] + 1 \tag{A1}$$

where $\text{BS}(A)$ and $\text{BS}(B)$ are maximal bit sizes of the computed variables A and B, respectively, obtained after Z iterations.

II. Recursive Addition with Nonrecursive Addends. X was assigned either A or B, i.e., $X = X + A$ (or $X = X + B$) where this addition iterates Z times.
The bit size of a computed variable X is bounded above by

$$BS(X) \leq \max [BS(X_0), BS(A)] + \log_2 (1 + Z) \tag{A2}$$

where $BS(X_0)$ is the bit size of variable X before the iterative process. If A is a constant, $BS(A)$ is its bit size; if A is a computed variable, then $BS(A)$ is its final bit size found after iteration.

III. Recursive Addition with Recursive Addends (RARA). By RARA we mean an addition in which each addend is an arithmetic expression consisting of one or several recursive sums obtained during earlier iterations. For instance, $S_i = S_{i-1} + S_{i-2}$ is a RARA, since to find sum S_i for the ith iteration one needs to know sums S_{i-1} and S_{i-2} obtained during iterations $i - 1$ and $i - 2$, respectively.

One can distinguish two types of RARA that lead to a bit-size increase:

1. Additive RARA:

$$S_i = a_1 \cdot S_{j_1} + a_2 \cdot S_{j_2} + \cdots + a_p \cdot S_{j_p} = \sum_{j=1}^{j=p} a_j \cdot S_{k_j} \tag{A3}$$

where $a_1, a_2, \ldots, a_p$ are nonrecursive coefficients, and $S_{j_1}, S_{j_2}, \ldots, S_{j_p}$ are recursive sums formed by RARA during earlier iterations; i.e., $j_1, j_2, \ldots, j_p < i$, where i is the index of the current iteration.

2. Multiplicative RARA:

$$S_i = \sum_{j=1}^{j=p} a_j \cdot [S_{\ell_{1j}} \cdot S_{\ell_{2j}} \cdot \cdots \cdot S_{\ell_{dj}}] \tag{A4}$$

For instance, if $p = 2$, $a_1 = a_2 = a_3 = 1$, $d = 2$, $\ell_{11} = i - 1$, $\ell_{21} = i - 2$, $\ell_{12} = i - 2$, and $\ell_{22} = i - 3$, we obtain the following multiplicative RARA: $S_i = S_{i-1} \cdot S_{i-2} + S_{i-2} \cdot S_{i-3}$; i.e., each recursive sum, S_i, for the ith iteration is the sum of products, where the factors in each product are recursive sums obtained during earlier iterations.

For bit-size analysis it is essential to consider the case in which all recursive sums grow monotonically; i.e., $S_1 < S_2 < \cdots < S_i < S_{i+1}$. Otherwise, if $S_i < S_{i-1}$, we obtain a bit-decreasing operation. Our objective is to find an upper bound on S_i for the additive and multiplicative RARA.

Upper Bound on Sum S_i for Additive RARA

$$S_i = a_1 \cdot S_{j_1} + a_2 \cdot S_{j_2} + \cdots + a_p \cdot S_{j_p} \tag{A5}$$

In Eq. (A5) all recursive sums are distinct; otherwise, if $S_{j\ell} = S_{j_k}$, then $a_\ell \cdot S_{j\ell} + a_k \cdot S_{j_k} = S_{j\ell} (a_\ell + a_k) = b_\ell \cdot S_{j\ell}$, and we obtain a distinct sum, $S_{j\ell}$, with a new coefficient b_p. Since coefficients $a_1, a_2, \ldots, a_p$ are non-RARA sums, we may evaluate their values using the techniques of bit-size analysis developed for other additions or multiplications. As a result, we obtain $A = \max[a_1, \ldots, a_p]$ and Eq. (A5) will be bounded by

$$S_i \leq A \cdot [S_{i-1} + S_{i-2} + \cdots + S_{i-p}] \leq A \cdot p \cdot S_{i-1}$$

Find upper bounds for $S_1, S_2, \ldots, S_i$:

$$S_1 \leq A \cdot p \cdot S_0$$

$$S_2 \leq A \cdot p \cdot S_1$$

$$S_3 \leq A \cdot p \cdot S_2 \leq A \cdot p \cdot A \cdot p \cdot S_1 = A^2 \cdot p^2 \cdot S_1$$

$$S_4 \leq A^3 \cdot p^3 \cdot S_1$$

$$\vdots$$

$$S_i \leq A^{i-1} \cdot p^{i-1} \cdot S_1$$

Therefore, the bit size, S_i, for the additive RARA, $BS(S_i)$, is bounded above by

$$BS(S_i) \leq (i - 1) \, log_2 \, A + (i - 1) \log_2 p + \log_2 S_1 \qquad (A6)$$

Example. A popular case of additive RARA is exemplified by the Fibonacci sequence:

$$S_1 = 1$$

$$S_2 = 1$$

$$S_3 = S_2 + S_1 = 2$$

$$S_4 = S_3 + S_2 = 2 + 1 = 3$$

$$\vdots$$

$$S_i = S_{i-1} + S_{i-2}$$

Let us find A and p. Since a_1 and a_2 are constant and $a_1 = a_2 = 1$, $A = \max(a_1, a_2) = 1$, and $p = 2$. Since $S_1 = 1$, $\log_2 S_1 = \log_2 1 = 0$. Therefore, $BS(S_i) \leq (i - 1) \log_2 1 + (i - 1) \log_2 2 + \log_2 1 = 0 + (i - 1) \cdot 1 + 0 = i - 1$.

Let us check this bound for a concrete i. If $i = 13$, the precise meaning of S_{13} is $S_{13} = S_{12} + S_{11} = 233$. $BS(S_{13}) = 8$, since to store 233 one needs 8 bits. The upper bound obtained is $BS(S_{13}) \leq (13 - 1) = 12$. Thus a correct upper bound is found which exceeds the actual bit size by 4 bits. ∎

Upper Bound on Sum S_i for Multiplicative RARA

$$S_i = a_1 \cdot S_{\ell_{11}} \cdot S_{\ell_{21}} \cdot \cdots \cdot S_{\ell_{d1}} + a_2 \cdot S_{\ell_{12}} \cdot S_{\ell_{22}} \cdot \cdots \cdot S_{\ell_{d2}}$$
$$+ \cdots a_p \cdot S_{\ell_{1p}} \cdot S_{\ell_{2p}} \cdot \cdots \cdot S_{\ell_{dp}} \tag{A7}$$

In view of the monotonic growth of sums $S_1, S_2, \cdots, S_i, S_{i+1}$, Eq. (A7) is upper-bounded as follows: Each addend of the sum S_i is not greater than $A \cdot S_{i-1}^d$, where $A = \max(a_1, \cdots, a_p)$ and d is the number of factors in each addend. Since the number of addends in Eq. (A7) is p, then

$$S_i \leq A \cdot p \cdot S_{i-1}^d \tag{A8}$$

and

$$S_1 \leq A \cdot p \cdot S_o^d$$

$$S_2 \leq A \cdot p \cdot S_1^d$$

$$S_3 \leq A \cdot p \cdot S_2^d \leq A \cdot p \cdot (A \cdot p \cdot S_1^d)^d = A \cdot p \cdot (A^d \cdot p^d) \cdot S_1^{d^2}$$

$$S_4 \leq A \cdot p \cdot S_3^d \leq A \cdot p \, [(A \cdot p) \cdot (A^d \cdot p^d) \cdot S_1^{d^2}]^d = A \cdot p \, (A \cdot p)^d \cdot S_1^{d^3}$$

$$\bullet$$
$$\bullet \tag{A9}$$
$$\bullet$$

$$S_i \leq (A \cdot p) \cdot (A \cdot p)^d \cdot (A \cdot p)^d \cdot \cdots \cdot (A \cdot p)^{d^{i-2}} \cdot S_1^{d^{i-1}}$$

Therefore, the bit size $BS(S_i)$ is restricted as follows: $BS(S_i) \leq [\log_2 (A \cdot p)]$ $(1 + d + d^2 + \cdots + d^{i-2}) + d^{i-1} \cdot \log_2 S_1 \leq d^{i-1}(\log_2 (A \cdot p) + \log_2 S_1)$ and

$$BS(S_i) \leq d^{i-1}[\log_2 A + \log_2 p + \log_2 S_1] \tag{A10}$$

where d is the number of recursive factors, S_j, in each addend of RARA addition; p is the number of addends; S_1 is the value of multiplicative RARA for the first iteration, $A = \max(a_1, a_2, \cdots, a_p)$.

As follows from Eq. (A10), $BS(S_i)$ grows exponentially for each iteration. Thus multiplicative RARA should be computed as a floating-point operation. In this case, the growth of the exponent bit size, $BS(EXP_i)$ for the ith iteration will be restricted by a linear function, $B \cdot (i - 1)$; i.e., $BS(EXP_i) \leq B \cdot (i - 1)$, where i is a current index of iterations and

$$B = \log_2 d + \log_2[\log_2 A + \log_2 p + \log_2 S_1] \tag{A11}$$

1.2 Multiplication

Consider three possible options for multiplication $X = A * B$:

I. Nonrecursive Multiplication with Complex Changeable Factors A and B: At least one of the values, A or B, is described by expressions containing more than one arithmetic operation. (For instance, $A = C^2 - D + E$, or $B = K * D + C$, etc.) For this case,

$$BS(X) \leq BS(A) + BS(B) \tag{A12}$$

where $BS(A)$ and $BS(B)$ are maximal bit sizes of the computed variables A and B, respectively, obtained after Z iterations.

II. Nonrecursive Multiplication with Simple Changeable Factors: In $X = A * B$, X assumes neither A nor B; factors A and B are described by arithmetic expressions containing not more than one operation.

Suppose that A and B are variables involved in bit-increasing operations (addition and multiplication).

1. *A and B are changed via addition;* i.e., $X = (A + \Delta_1) * (B + \Delta_2)$, where Δ_1 and Δ_2 increment A and B during each iteration. For this case,

$$BS(X) \leq 2BS(\max[A_0, B_0, \Delta_1, \Delta_2]) + 2 \log_2 (1 + Z) \tag{A13}$$

where $\max [A_0, B_0, \Delta_1, \Delta_2]$ is the maximal value among four meanings A_0 and B_0 (before iterative process) and Δ_1 and Δ_2.

2. *A and B are changed via multiplication;* i.e., $X = (A * \Delta_1) * (B * \Delta_2)$, where Δ_1 and Δ_2 are multiplicative factors which change A and B during each iteration. The bit size of the product is upper bounded as

$$BS(X) \leq BS(A_0) + BS(B_0) + Z \cdot [BS(\Delta_1) + BS(\Delta_2)] \tag{A14}$$

Indeed, after the first iteration, $X_1 = A_1 * B_1 = A_0 * B_0 * \Delta_1 * \Delta_2$; after the second iteration, $X_2 = A_2 * B_2 = A_0 * B_0(\Delta_1 * \Delta_2)^2$; ...; after the Zth iteration, $X_z = A_z * B_z = A_0 * B_0 * (\Delta_1 * \Delta_2)^z$. Taking the bit size of this expression leads to (A14).

Note: Equations (A13) and (A14) assume that in the product $X = A * B$ both values A and B change via bit-increasing operations. If only one value, say A, changes, whereas B_0 remains constant, then $\Delta_1 \neq 0$, $\Delta_2 = 0$, and Eq. (A13) is transformed into

$$BS(X) \leq 2BS(\max[A_0, B_0, \Delta_1]) + \log_2 (1 + Z) \tag{A15}$$

Likewise Eq. (A14) is transformed into

$$BS(X) \leq BS(X_0) + BS(B_0) + Z \cdot BS(\Delta_1) \tag{A16}$$

Equations (A15) and (A16) can be used in case product $X - A * B$ grows, although Δ_1 is a bit-increasing increment (addend or multiplier) and Δ_2 is bit-decreasing increment (subtrahend or divisor). For this case we may assume that $\Delta_2 = 0$; i.e., the value of B is a constant. Then Eqs. (A15) and (A16) will give a correct upper bound.

If both A and B are changed via division or subtraction during Z iterations, then the bit size of the product $BS(X)$ after Z iterations will be smaller than that before iterations. As a result, there is no need to specify BS(X) at all, since we will have a bit-decreasing operation.

*III. **Recursive Multiplication:*** X was assigned either A or B; i.e., $X = X * A$ (or $X = X * B$), and multiplication iterates Z times. Then the bit size of the X variable is upper bounded as

$$BS(X) \le BS(X_0) + Z \cdot BS(A) \tag{A17}$$

Example. Let $X = X * A$ iterate $Z = 3$ times and during each iteration A also changes as $A = A + B$. Assume that in the beginning $X_0 = 3$, $A_0 = 7$, and $B = 3$. First find BS(A) after three iterations. Since A changes via recursive addition with constant addend B, we use Eq. (A2) to find BS(A) $\le$ max[BS(A_0), BS(B)] + $\log_2 (1 + 3)$ = max[3, 2] + $\log_2 (1 + 3)$ = 3 + 2 = 5 bits. Then, using Eq. (A17) and substituting BS(A) into Eq. (A17), we obtain BS(X) $\le$ BS(3) + 3 $\cdot$ 5 = 2 + 15 = 17 bits. The actual value of the product is 2730. To store it takes 13 bits. ∎

Above we considered bit sizes of integers participating in bit-increasing operations (additions and multiplications). Similar formulas can be obtained for integers involved in bit-decreasing operations (subtractions and divisions). For instance, for subtractions we have to subtract $\log_2 (1 + Z)$ in Eq. (A2), whereas Eq. (A1) is transformed into BS(X) $\le$ max[BS(A), BS(B)], where $X = A - B$. For divisions, $X = A \div B$, Eq. (A12) is transformed into BS(X) $\le$ BS(A) − BS(B). Similar transforms can be extended to Eqs. (A13) to (A16).

2 BIT SIZES OF REAL AND FLOATING-POINT VARIABLES

Let us show that the techniques introduced above can be extended to real and floating-point variables.

2.1 Real Variables

The bit size of a real variable, BSR, is

$$BSR = BSI + BSF \tag{A18}$$

where BSI and BSF are the bit sizes of the integer and fractional portions; BSI may be obtained via the same techniques considered above for integers; BSF is determined in advance by the user, since for most fractions there exist no exact conversions to the binary form. Therefore, the number of bits a fractional number will take for its storage is determined by required accuracy of computation. It then follows that BSF must be given in advance. Having found BSI and substituting it into Eq. (A18), one finds the bit size of a real variable. Thus analysis presented above is extendable not only to integers but also to real numbers.

2.2 Floating-Point Variables

The bit size of a floating-point number is determined as follows. Since the mantissa is a fraction, its bit size is specified in advance by the required accuracy of computation; as for exponents they may be treated as integers and their bit sizes may be determined using the formulas developed above for operations over integers.

For instance, for multiplication of two floating-point numbers, the bit size of the mantissa product remains the same or it doubles the precision of the multiplicand; the bit size of the exponent of the result is determined using the formulas which give the bit size of a sum of two integers because, during multiplication, exponents of operands are added.

Example. Suppose that for a recursive floating-point multiplication $X = X * A$, where product $X = XE \times XM$; XE is the exponent, and XM is the mantissa. Similarly, $A = AE \times AM$. Let a required accuracy of the mantissa operation be 10 bits; multiplication iterates $Z = 10$ times; the exponent AE of the multiplier is a constant and $AE = 5$; and initial value XE_0 of the XE exponent is $XE_0 = 3$. Since $XE_i = XE_{i-1} + AE$ ($i = 1, \ldots, Z$), the exponent operation is reduced to recursive addition. Thus, using Eq. (A2) we may find the bit size of the exponent result, XE: $BS(XE) \leq \max[BS(XE_0), BS(AE)] + \log_2 (1 + Z) = \max[BS(3), BS(5)] + \log_2 (1 + 10) = \max(2, 3) + 4 = 7$ bits. The actual value of XE is found as follows. After the first iteration, $XE_1 = XE_0 + AE = 8$; after the second iteration, $XE_2 = XE_1 + AE = XE_0 + 2AE = 13; \ldots$; after the ten's iteration, $XE_{10} = XE_0 + 10AE = 3 + 50 = 53$. To store $XE = 53$ takes 6 bits. Therefore, a correct upper bound is found. The overall size of the floating-point number $X = XE \times XM$ after 10 iterations is 16 bits. Our analysis gives it as 17 bits, since we obtained 7 bits for XE, and the bit size of the mantissa is fixed and takes 10 bits. ■

References

1. KARTASHEV, S. P., "Supersystems: Current State-of-the-Art Guest Editor's Introduction," *IEEE Trans. on Computers,* May 1982, Vol. C-31, No. 5, pp. 345-349.

2. AMDAHL, G., "The Validity of the Single Processor Approach to Achieving Large Scale Computing Capabilities," *AFIPS Conference Proceedings,* Vol. 30, 1967, SJCC, pp. 483-485

3. AMDAHL, G., "Tempered Expectations in Massively Parallel Processing and Semiconductor Industry," Keynote address, Second International Conference on Supercomputing, Santa Clara, CA, May 3-8, 1987.

4. KARTASHEV, S. P. and KARTASHEV, S. I., "Distribution of Programs for a System with Dynamic Architecture," *IEEE Trans. on Computers,* June 1982, pp. 488-514.

5. KARTASHEV, S. P., and KARTASHEV, S. I., Guest Editor's Introduction, Special issue, *Computer,* "Design for Adaptability," Feb. 1986, 19, 2, pp. 9-16.

6. DAVIS, CARL, KARTASHEV, S. P., and KARTASHEV, S. I., "Reconfigurable Multicomputer Networks for Very Fast Real-Time Applications," *1982 National Computer Conference Proceedings,* AFIPS Press, *51,* pp. 167-184.

7. KARTASHEV, S. I., KARTASHEV, S. P. and VICK, C. R., "Adaptable Architectures for Supersystems," *Computer,* Nov. 1980, Vol. 13, pp. 17-35.

8. KARTASHEV, S. I., and KARTASHEV, S.P., "Designing and Programming Supersystems with Dynamic Architectures," Series: *Designing and Programming Modern Computer Systems,* Vol. 1, Chapter III, *LSI Modular Computer Systems,* Englewood Cliffs, N.J., Prentice-Hall, Inc., 1982, pp. 245-385.

9. KARTASHEV, S. I., and KARTASHEV, S. P., "Dynamic Architectures: Problems and Solutions," *Computer, 11,* July 1978, pp. 26-40.

10. STENNING, V., and others, "The Ada Environment: A Perspective," *Computer, 14, 6,* June 1981, pp. 26-37.

11. WOLFE, MARTIN I., and others, "The Ada Language System," *Computer, 14, 6,* June 1981, pp. 37-47.

12. LEDGARD, HENRY, *Ada, An Introduction,* 2nd ed., Springer-Verlag, New York, 1983, 135 pages.

13. BRENDER, RONALD F., and NASSI, ISAAC R., "What Is Ada," *Computer, 14, 6,* June 1981, pp. 17-26.

14. KARTASHEV, S. I., and KARTASHEV, S. P., "Multicomputer System with Dynamic Architecture," *IEEE Trans. on Computers, C-28, 10,* Oct. 1979, pp. 704-721.

385

15. KARTASHEV, S. P., and KARTASHEV, S. I., "Reconfiguration of Dynamic Architectures into Multicomputer Networks," *Proceedings of the 1981 International Conference on Parallel Processing,* Aug. 1981, IEEE Computer Society, Belle Aire, Mich., pp. 133-140.

16. KARTASHEV, S. P., and KARTASHEV, S. I., "Fault-Tolerant Reconfigurable Multicomputer Network," *1983 National Computer Conference Proceedings,* AFIPS Press, *52.*

17. KARTASHEV, S. I. and KARTASHEV, S. P., "Distributed Dynamic Hardware Operating System for Reconfigurable Multiport Memory," *The 3rd International Conference Proceedings on Distributed Computing Systems,* IEEE Computer Society, Miami/Ft. Lauderdale, Fla., Oct. 18-22, 1982, pp. 122-127.

18. KARTASHEV, S.I., and KARTASHEV, S. P., "Distributed Operating System for a System with Dynamic Architecture," *1982 National Computer Conference Proceedings,* AFIPS Press, *51.*

19. *Department of Defense Requirements for High Order Computer Programming Languages,* "TINMAN," High Order Language Working Group, U. S. Dept. of Defense, June 1976.

20. CLAPP, J. A., LOEBENSTEIN, E., and RHYMER, P., *A Cost/Benefit Analysis of Higher Order Language Standardization,* Bedford, Mass., Mitre Corp., Sept. 1977.

21. FOX, J. M., *Benefit Model for High Order Language,* Decisions and Designs, Inc., March 1978.

22. *Department of Defense Requirements for High Order Computer Programming Language "Revised IRONMAN",* High Order Lanaguage Working Group, U. S. Dept. of Defense, July 1977.

23. CARLSON, W. E., and others, "Introducing Ada," *Proceedings ACM Annual Conference,* Oct. 1980.

24. DRUFFEL, L. E., "Ada—How Will It Affect College Offerings," *Interface,* Sept. 1979, pp. 58-61.

25. FISHER, D. A., "DoD's Common Programming Language Effort," *Computer, 11, 3,* March 1978, pp. 24-33.

26. ICHBIAH, J. D., "Ada and the Development of Software Components," *Proceedings 4th International Conference on Software Engineering,* IEEE Computer Society, Orlando, Fla., Sept. 1979.

27. WHITAKER, W. A., "The U. S. Department of Defense Common High Order Language Effort," *Sigplan Notices,* Feb. 1977.

28. *Requirements for Ada Programming Support Environments "STONEMAN",* U. S. Dept. of Defense, Feb. 1980.

29. ROCHKIND, M. J., "The Source Code Control System," *IEEE Trans. on Software Engineering, SE-1, 4,* Dec. 1975, pp. 364-370.

30. ZEIGLER, S., and others, "Ada for the Intel 432 Mircocomputer," *Computer, 14, 6,* June 1981, pp. 47-57.

31. KARTASHEV, S. I., and KARTASHEV, S. P., "LSI Modular Computers, Systems and Networks," *Computer, 11,* July 1978, pp. 7-15.

32. KARTASHEV, S. I., and KARTASHEV, S. P., "Evolution in Dynamic Architectures," *Microprocessors and Microsystems, 3, 6,* July 1979, pp. 249-256.

33. KARTASHEV, S. P., and KARTASHEV, S. I., "Analysis and Synthesis of Dynamic Multicomputer Networks That Reconfigure into Rings, Trees and Stars," *IEEE Transactions on Computers, 7, C-36,* July 1987, pp. 823-844.

34. KARTASHEV, S. P., KARTASHEV, S. I., and VICK, C. R., "Historic Progress in Architectures for Computers and Systems," Chapter I, pp. 3-100, *LSI Modular Computer Systems,* Vol. 1 in series *Designing and Programming Modern Computers and Systems* (S. P. Kartashev and S. I. Kartashev, eds.), Englewood Cliffs, N.J., Prentice-Hall, Inc., 1982.

35. ELSPAS, B., "The Theory of Autonomous Linear Sequential Networks," *IRE Trans. on Circuit Theory,* January 1959, pp. 45-60.

36. ZIERLER, N., "Linear Recurring Sequencer," *J. SIAM, 7, 1,* 1965, pp. 31-48.

37. KAUTZ, W. H. (ed.), *Linear Sequential Switching Circuits,* San Francisco, Holden-Day, Inc., 1965.

38. GOLOMB, S. W., *Swift Register Sequences,* San Francisco, Holden-Day, Inc., 1967.

39. BOOTH, T. L., *Sequential Machines and Automata Theory,* New York, John Wiley and Sons, Inc., 1967.

40. KARTASHEV, S. I. and KARTASHEV, S. P., "The Effect of LSI Technology on Computation and Computer Organization," Infotech State of the Art Report (invited paper), Series 8, Number 2, Maidenhead, Berkshire, England, Infotech, Limited, pp. 220-258.

41. KARTASHEV, S. P., "Theory and Implementation of p-Multiple Sequential Machines," *IEEE Trans. on Computers,* May 1974, pp. 500-523.

42. KARTASHEV, S. P., "State Assignment for Realizing Modular Input-free Sequential Logical Networks without Invertors, " *Journal of Computer and System Sciences, 7, 5,* Oct. 1973, pp. 522-542.

43. KARTASHEV, S. P., and KARTASHEV, S. I., "On Modular Networks Satisfying the Shift-Register Rule," *IEEE Trans. on Computers, C-27,* Dec. 1978, pp. 1153-1176.

44. McMILLAN, R. J. and SIEGEL, H. J., "The Hybrid Cube Network," *Proceedings of the Distributed Data Acquisition, Computing, and Control Symposium,* IEEE Computer Society, Miami, Fla., 1980, pp. 11-22.

45. PEASE, M. C., "The Indirect Binary n-Cube Microprocessor Array," *IEEE Trans. on Computers, C-26, 5,* May 1977, pp. 458-473.

46. PAXER, Y., and BOZYGIT, M., "Variable Topology Multicomputer," *Proceedings of the Second Euromicro Symposium on Microprocessing and Microprogramming,* North-Holland Publishing Company, Venice, 1976, pp. 141-149.

47. WITTIE, L. D., and VAN TILBORG, A. M., "MICROS, A Distributed Operating System for MICRONET, A Reconfigurable Network Computer," *IEEE Trans. on Computers, C-29,* Dec. 1980, pp. 1144-2233.

48. DESPAIN, A., and PATTERSON, D., "X-Tree: A Tree Structured Multi-Processor Computer Architecture," *Proceedings Fifth Annual Symposium on Computer Architecture,* Boston, IEEE Computer Society, 1978, pp. 144-150.

49. GOYAL, A., and LIPOVSKI, G. J., "Reconfigurable Hierarchical Rings," *Proceedings of the Distributed Data Acquisition, Computing, and Control Symposium,* 1980, Miami, Fla., IEEE Computer Society, pp. 3-10.

50. DeGROOT, D., and MALIK, M., "Resource Allocation for Macropipelines," *Proceedings of the Distributed Data Acquisition, Computing, and Control Symposium,* 1980, Miami, Fla., IEEE Computer Society, pp. 23-27.

51. GARCIA-MOLINA, H., "Elections in a Distributed Computing System," *IEEE Trans. on Computers, C-31, 1,* January 1982, pp. 48-60.

52. GARCIA-MOLINA, H., "Performance of Update Algorithms for Replicated Data in a Distributed Database," *Department of Computer Science, Stanford University,* Stanford, Calif., Rep. STAN-CS-79-744., June 1979.

53. LAMPORT, L., "The Implementation of Reliable Distributed Systems," *Computer Networks, 2,* 1978, pp. 95-114.

54. LAMPSON, B. W., and STURGIS, H. E., "Crash Recovery in a Distributed Data Storage System," Xerox, Palo-Alto, Xerox Corporation, PARC, Rep., 1979.

55. MENASCE, D. A., POPECK, G. J., and MUNTZ, R. R., "A Locking Protocol for Resource Coordination in Distributed Databases," *ACM Trans. on Database System, 5,* June 1980, pp. 103-138.

56. McMILLEN, R. J., and SIEGEL, H. J., "Routing Schemes for the Augmented Data Manipulator Network in an MIMD System," *IEEE Trans. on Computers, C-31,* Dec. 1982, pp. 1202-1214.

57. LAWRIE, D. H., "Access and Alignment of Data in an Array Processor," *IEEE Trans. on Computers, C-24,* Dec. 1975, pp. 1145-1155.

58. KARTASHEV, S. I., and KARTASHEV, S. P., "Problems of Designing Sypersystems with Dynamic Architectures," *IEEE Trans. on Computers, C-29,* Dec. 1980, pp. 1114-1132.

59. DAVIS, CARL G., and COUCH, ROBERT L., "Ballistic Missile Defense: A Supercomputer Challenge," *Computer, 13,* 1980, pp. 37-48.

60. ARNOLD, R. G., BERG, R. O., and THOMAS, J. W., "A Modular Approach to Real-Time Supersystems," *IEEE Trans. on Computers, C-31,* May 1982, pp. 385-398.

61. LOTL, H. H., "Reconfigurable Parallel Array Systems," Chapter II in the book, Vol. 1, *LSI Modular Computer Systems,* in series, *Designing and Programming Modern Computers and Systems,* Englewood Cliffs, N.J., Prentice-Hall, Inc., 1982, pp. 99-241.

62. KARTASHEV, S. P., and KARTASHEV, S. I., "Memory Allocations for Multiprocessor Systems That Incorporate Content-Addressable Memories," *IEEE Trans. on Computers, C-33, 1,* January 1984, pp. 28-44.

63. KARTASHEV, S. P., and KARTASHEV, S. I., "Data Exchange Optimization in Reconfigurable Binary Trees," *IEEE Trans. on Computers, C-35, 3,* March 1986, pp. 257-274.

64. KARTASHEV, S. P., and KARTASHEV, S. I., "Performance Optimization in a Reconfigurable Binary Tree," *Advances in Microprocessing and Microprogramming, Tenth Euromicro Symposium on Microprocessing and Microprogramming,* Copenhagen, August 27-30, 1984, pp. 305-315.

65. KARTASHEV, S. P., and KARTASHEV, S. I., "Efficient Internode Communications in Reconfigurable Binary Trees," *IEEE Trans. on Computers, C-33, 11,* November 1984, pp. 977-991.

66. CHU, W. W., LEE, D., and IFFLA, B., "A Distributed Processing System for Naval Data Communication Networks," in *Proceedings of the 1978 National Computer Conference,* AFIPS, 1978, *47,* pp. 783-793.

67. MARIANI, M. P., and PALMER, D. F., *Tutorial: Distributed System Design,* IEEE, New York, 1979.

68. STONE, H. S., "Multiprocessor Scheduling with the Aid of Network Flow Algorithms," *IEEE Trans. on Software Eng., SE-3,* January 1977, pp. 85-93.

69. STONE, H. S., and BOKHARI, S. H., "Control of Distributed Processes," *Computer,* July 1978, pp. 97-106.

70. CHU, W. W., and others, "Task Allocation in Distributed Data Processing," *Computer, 13,* November 1980, pp. 57-70.

71. KUCK, DAVID J., *The Structure of Computers and Computations,* Vol. 1, New York, John Wiley & Sons, 1978, 611 pp.

72. DATE, C. J., *An Introduction to Database Systems,* 2nd ed., Reading, Mass., Addison-Wesley, 1977, pp. 51-66, 73-79.

73. BARNETT, I. A., *Elements of Number Theory,* Boston, Prindle, Webber and Schmidt, 1969, 213 pp.

74. ANDERSON, G. A., and KAIN, R. Y., "A Content-Addressed Memory Designed for Database Applications," *Proceedings of the 1976 International Conference on Parallel Processing,* August 1976, IEEE Computer Society, Belle Aire, Michigan, pp. 191-195.

75. LEA, R. M., "An Associative Parallel Processor for Efficient and Flexible File Searching," *Proceedings of the International Symposium on Technology for Selective Dissemination of Information,* September 1976, pp. 73-78.

76. THURBER, K. J., "Associative and Parallel Processors," *Computing Surveys,* December 1975, pp. 215-255.

77. DOTY, K. L., GREENBLATT, J. D., and SU, S. Y. W., "Magnetic Bubble Memory Architectures for Supporting Associative Searching of Relational Databases," *IEEE Trans. on Computers, C-29, 11,* November 1980, pp. 957-970.

78. BATCHER, K.E., "The Multi-Dimensional Access Memory in STARAN," *IEEE Trans. on Computers, C-26, 2,* February 1977, pp. 174-177.

79. LAWRIE, D. H., "Access and Alignment of Data in an Array Processor," *IEEE Trans. on Computers, C-24, 12,* December 1975, pp. 1145-1155.

80. SIEGEL, H. J., KEMMERER, F., and WASHBURN, M., "Parallel Memory System for a Partitionable SIMD/MIMD Machine," *Proceedings of the 1979 International Conference on Parallel Processing,* IEEE Computer Society, Belle Aire, Michigan, August 1979, pp. 212-221.

81. SIEGEL, H. J., "Interconnection Networks for SIMD Machines," *IEEE Computer, 12, 6,* June 1979, pp. 57-65.

82. LAWRIE, D. H., and VORA, C., "The Prime Memory System for Array Access," *IEEE Trans. on Computers,* May 1982, pp. 435-443.

83. KARTASHEV, S. P., and KARTASHEV, S. I., "Conflict-free Memory Allocation for Associative Data Files," *AFIPS Conference Proceedings 1983, 52,* National Computer Conference, pp. 579-595.

84. KARTASHEV, S. P., and KARTASHEV, S. I., "Adaptable Software for Dynamic Architectures," *Computer,* February 1986, *19, 2,* pp. 61-78.

Glossary
of Definitions Used
in the Book

Absorption Process. The absorption process is a process of dynamic assignment aimed at absorption of a nonassigned queue NAQ of startup messages SUM's with an assigned queue, AQ. It can lead to either complete or incomplete absorption. If absorption is complete, AQ − NAQ = 0. If absorption is incomplete, AQ − NAQ = NAAQ, where NAAQ is a nonassignable queue made of SUM's that can no longer be assigned to the architectural states of a reconfiguration flowchart without a considerable deterioration in the utilization factor of the used equipment.

Active and Passive Programs. A program may be *active* by executing a reconfiguration request N → N* or *passive* by granting execution of personal reconfiguration requests to other program(s).

Ada Exception. An Ada exception is an event that causes suspension of normal program execution. Bringing an exception situation to attention is called *raising* the exception. Responding to the exception is called *handling* the exception. There are the following types of Ada exceptions:

- Numeric Error: When the result of a predefined numeric operation does not lie within the implemented range or accuracy for the numeric type.
- Constraint Error: When a range constraint, index constraint or discriminant constraint is violated or when an attempt to dereference a null access value is made.
- Program Error: When all alternatives of a select statement with no else part are closed, when a program unit is invoked but its body has not been elaborated, and in various implementation dependent situations.
- Storage Error: When the dynamic storage allocated to a task is exceeded, or the available space for objects of an access type is exhausted, or when a subprogram or declarative part is elaborated and storage is insufficient.

- Tasking Error: When an exception arises during communication between tasks.

Ada Package. Ada package covers a wide range of uses, including named collections of common data, groups of related subprograms that collectively carry out some activity, and definitions of private types with specialized operations. In general, by a package we mean a language construct that warrants a separate compilation independent of other packages. Every package is specified by giving a list of declarative information. This declarative information can be made accessible to a user and is called its *visible part.* (See also Use Clause of an Ada Package.)

Adaptable Supercomputing Architecture. A Supercomputing architecture is called adaptable if it adapts to the algorithms in order to compute them within the minimal times which are needed.

Adaptable Supercomputing Systems Rationale. Major motivation behind the use of Adaptable Supercomputing Systems is twofold:

- By reconfiguring the system into the structure(s) that most closely approximate(s) the executing algorithm(s), one gains the performance improvement at the expense of added executional concurrency and data exchange optimization.
- By developing fast and concurrent reconfiguration techniques, an additional performance improvement is achieved at the expense of minimization or total elimination of any reconfiguration overhead that accompanies a nonoptimal reconfiguration process.

Adaptable Supercomputing System Speed-up. This is achieved by maximizing the time Δ $= \Delta T - \Delta t$, where ΔT is the time of program speed-up because of the Supersystem reconfigurability; Δt is the reconfiguration overhead, measured as the time lost during reconfiguration when no computation can be performed.

Available reconfiguration methodology improves Δ by the minimizing Δt. The program speedup, ΔT, is maximized at the expense of the following factors:

1. *Creation of additional concurrency:* accomplished via its dynamic reconfiguration into closely fitted (minimal) hardware structures of which the parameters match those of executing algorithm(s). This is accompanied by a release of redundant computer elements into additional computations; such a release always creates an additional parallelism in execution with respect to nonreconfigurable systems having the same complexity of resources.

2. *Data exchange optimization:* accomplished via its dynamic reconfiguration into hardware structures (particularly trees and stars) in which node pairs with a large number of data exchanges are connected via communication paths of minimal length.

Ada Task. A program unit that can be executed concurrently with other program units.

Adaptive Assignment of System Resources. Includes:

1. *CE resource diagram* which charts the computer elements assigned to each task and defines the flow chart of architectural transitions.

2. *ME resource diagram* which indicates the allocation of the primary memory among various user programs.

Adaptive Assignment Rationale. For dynamic architectures, the adaptive assignment achieves minimization of the amount of processor and memory resources involved in computations. Such a minimization realizes the capability of dynamic architectures to maximize the number of programs executed concurrently.

Adaptive Resource Assignment for a Computer System. An adaptive assignment is applicable for a computer system that has the following features:

1. Its bus structure introduces a permanent communication delay either internal (between local processor and memory belonging to the same computer) or external (between processor and memory of two different computers that are available in the system) and

2. A computer system may adapt to executing algorithms via reconfigurable and/or dynamic adaptations.

For such systems, the resource assignment must reflect specific attributes of the respective architectures, (i.e., be adaptive rather than be minimal cost) since due to the permanency of communication delays within a system there is no sense in their minimization.

Address Code of Node N in a Reconfigurable Binary Tree. In general, by the address code AC_N of the node N, we define a binary word which contains all the routing information such that it allows a data word to reach node N from the current root R of TS_i using the minimal communication path. The length, ℓ, of AC_N is restricted by n, the number of levels in the tree, where $\ell = n$ for leaves located on the level 0 and for a tree node of level i, $\ell = n - i$.

A-Header. Since each assigned SUM is specified with the two zones A and $\overline{A}$ where A stores the necessary attributes of the architectural state N, and $\overline{A}$ stores the individual startup attributes of the respective program P, each startup state M(N) is made of SUM messages that are identified with the same A-zone, called the A-header. Thus, M(N) is understood as a set consisting of one A zone (A-header), which specifies the architectural state N, and $m\,\overline{A}_i$ zones, which identify m program P_i assigned to N.

Alignment of Bit Size Diagram. Alignment of a bit size diagram of a program graph means aligning graph nodes to dominant computer sizes in order to exclude excessive reconfigurations in the system. This means that, for a sequence of nodes requiring approximately the same bit size, a statistically dominant bit size is found. It is then accepted as the size of the computer which will compute the sequence. If a node in the sequence requires an exceptionally large bit size for a fixed point operation it is necessary to replace it using a floating point operation.

Architectural Flow Chart. Architectural flow chart is a directed graph in which a node means an architectural state and an arrow is marked by a program, which is allowed execution of the transition. This program is found on the CE resource diagram and it is conceived as the highest priority program that needs to form a new dynamic computer. The architectural states should be assigned with binary codes using the assignment techniques that minimize the time of architectural reconfiguration (See Reconfiguration Flow Chart).

Architectural Interrupt of the Current State. This occurs when the $N \rightarrow N^*$ transition of static reconfiguration flow chart is switched into $\widetilde{N} \rightarrow N \rightarrow N^*$ where $\widetilde{N}$ is a dynamically created state.

Architectural Interrupt of the Next State. This occurs when the $N \rightarrow N^*$ transition of static reconfiguration flow chart is changed into $N \rightarrow \widetilde{N} \rightarrow N^*$ where $\widetilde{N}$ is a dynamically created state.

Architectural Reconfiguration. Any architectural reconfiguration includes the following steps:

1. Conflict resolution aimed at resolving reconfiguration conflicts among independent programs.

2. Task synchronization aimed at finding the moment of finish for the tasks run on hardware resources, which are requested for reconfiguration.

3. Fetch of variable control codes by the hardware resources requested for reconfiguration.

4. Activation of new interconnections in the interconnection networks caused by the control codes that are fetched.

5. Start up of all programs assigned for the next architectural state.

Architectural State of the Reconfiguration Flow Chart. Each state of the reconfiguration flow chart is understood as a set of nonconflicting computing structures (dynamic computers, trees, stars, pipelines, arrays, etc.) formed in the system by reconfiguration. Every $N_i \to N_j$ transition of the reconfiguration flow chart from the current architectural state N_i to the next architectural state N_j is performed by the active program with the highest priority, which either needs a new computing structure included into N_j or represents a set of other concurrent and non-conflicting programs assigned to N_j. Therefore, to construct a reconfiguration flow chart is to assign reconfigurable hardware resources to the programs of the program mix. Henceforth, the problem of Reconfiguration Flow Chart is equivalent to the problem of the Resource Assignment in which the resources can perform dynamic reconfigurations.

Assignable Resources of Dynamic Architecture. If dynamic architecture executes p concurrent and sequential programs during the total execution time T, then the total assignable resource R that is distributed among programs is

$$R = n \cdot \mathrm{CE} \cdot T$$

Assigned and Nonassigned Programs for Dynamic Architectures. There are two types of programs represented with their SUM messages: *assigned* (bit $A = 1$) and *nonassigned* ($A = 0$). An assigned SUM is assigned to the architectural state N. A nonassigned SUM is free. It is the task of the monitor to select an architectural state N that can execute a nonassigned SUM.

A program belongs to the A class, if it is static (S) or it requests the total system resource (T) for its reconfiguration into state N. This defines $A = S \vee T$. Otherwise a program is attributed to the $\overline{A}$-class. Therefore, the $\overline{A}$-class is made of those user programs that are dynamic ($\overline{S}$) and request a portion (not totality) of the available CE resources, giving $\overline{A} = \overline{S \vee T} = \overline{S} \,\&\, \overline{T}$.

Assigned and Non-Assigned Queues of Start-Up Messages. To start each program assigned to the architectural state N, the monitor must possess its Start-Up Message, SUM, which must be sent from the monitor to the hardware resources assigned to this program whenever the computation of N is allowed. For static programs an Assigned Queue AQ, of start up messages, assigned to the architectural states, is stored in the monitor. Dynamic programs are also represented by a queue, NAQ, of nonassigned messages, otherwise called, *Non-Assigned Queue.*

Assigned Queue Attributes. An assigned queue, AQ, is understood as a sequence of start states M(N), where each state M(N) is represented by such a set of SUM messages that are assigned to the same architectural state N.

Any assigned queue, AQ, must possess the following attributes:

A1. *Synchronization attribute:* Since each start-up state M(N) is one-to-one with the architectural state N, the system must perform the M(N) → M(N*) transition synchronously with the N → N* transition of reconfiguration flow chart.

A2. *Restructuring attribute:* To implement the Minimal Delay condition of the dynamic assignment any assigned queue must be capable of restructuring itself perennially by performing continuous reassignment of existing architectural states and continuous creation of the new architectural states.

(See Assigned and Non-Assigned Queues of Start-Up Messages).

Bias Distance. Bias Distance, a_i $(i = 1, ..., t)$, represents the number of shifts between two generating positions, GP_i and GP_{i+1} of the Bias *B*. That is, $GP_{i+1} = a_i[GP_i]$.

Bias Modifiable Positions. Bias modifiable positions are those that are modified with the MC code to yield A_0^*, which is the generic state of a new ring.

Bias Parameters. *Bias weight* shows the number of ones in the bias; *bias distance* shows the number of shifts between two consecutive ones positions (generating positions) in the bias; *bias period* shows the sum of consecutive and periodical bias distances; *bias dimension* shows the number of bias distances included into the bias period; finally, *bias index* shows the number of bias periods contained in the bias.

Bias Weight. Bias weight is the number of ones contained in the bias.

Bit Size of a Computer for a Computed Variable. For bit size increasing operations, the bit size of the computer coincides with the maximal bit size of a final result. For bit size decreasing operations, it coincides with the maximal bit size of an intermediate result.

Bit Size Diagram of a Program Graph. Having found bit sizes for all nodes in a program graph, one constructs a bit size diagram in which the horizontal axis specifies the nodes of the program graph. The vertical axis shows the two bit size parameters, BSN and BSN*, found for each node (See Two Bit Size Parameters for a Computing Variable). The bit size diagram of a program graph serves as a basis for finding the computer size diagram required by a program (See Program Graph).

Bit Size Diagram of One Program. For each node of the program graph, one finds a minimal computer size in which a node may be executed. Next, one constructs a diagram of bit sizes for all graph nodes, which serves as a basis for finding a diagram of the computer sizes, required for executing a given user program. This diagram will partition the program into tasks, where each task is composed of the sequence of nodes that require the same computer size (See Program Graph).

$BL_i(GP_i)$ - sum. $BL_i(GP_i)$ - sum is $BL_i(GP_i) = GP_i + 1[GP_i] + \cdots + (a - 1)[GP_i]$ where $a_i[GP_i] = GP_{i+1}$, i.e., a_i defines a bias distance.

Circuit and Module Level Fault-Tolerant Reconfigurations. The fault-tolerant reconfiguration can be performed at the following levels:

    1. *circuit-level:* aimed at isolating faulty computing devices inside a computing module;

2. *module-level:* aimed at isolating a faulty computing module from other fault free modules of the computer system.

The module-level reconfiguration is performed if and when (1) all circuit-level reconfigurations fail, in that they are incapable of restoring correct computations inside the faulty module, and/or (2) a faulty circuit inside the module is or becomes unique, thus non-reconfigurable, and so prevents a fault free performance of the entire module. To sustain a fault free operation of a computing module in the presence of faults requires considerable duplication of all its circuits. Thus, if a fault occurs in a unique nonduplicated circuit, or all duplicates of this circuit have been exhausted through the previous circuit reconfigurations, this module becomes faulty; it must be isolated from the system operation using a module-level reconfiguration.

Classification Among Different SRVB Types. Each shift register SRVB is classified as follows:
1. It can be either single or composite, where a composite SRVB consists of $k > 1$ single SRVB's.
2. Each component shift register of a composite SRVB may perform either circular or non-circular shifts, denoted as $1[N]_1$ and $1[N]_0$ respectively.

Closest Intermediate Root, CIR. Closest intermediate root, CIR, is the tree node that connects two terminal nodes, source node N_s, and destination node N_d with the minimal communication path $N_s \to CIR$, $CIR \to N_d$.

Closure of Succession Between P_i and P_{i-1}. For any two structures P_i and P_{i-1} in the source tree, where P_i is made of leaves and P_{i-1} is any other structure of dimension $i - 1$ that does not necessarily succeed P_i in this tree, it is possible to find a bias $B(r)$ that generates a reconfigured tree $TS(r)$ in which P_{i-1} immediately succeeds P_i and P_i retains its leaf-status (See Recursive Structure P_i).

Complemented Level Value, CL. Complemented Level Value (CL) of the size $\log_2 n = \log_2\log_2 K$ shows which bit of the address code must be selected to find the route from the given node N to the next node N* in the path, where n is the size of SRVB and K is the number of nodes in the tree. To find CL, each node (N) finds its individual recursive sum. $RS_i = R + N$ where R is the root. N then shifts RS_i to the LSB until LSB = 1 and counts the number of shifts, k; $CL = n - (k - 1)$, where n is the number of levels in the tree.

Complete and Incomplete Reconfiguration Request Messages. A Complete Reconfiguration Request Message requests the architechural reconfiguration N $\to$ N*, such that a Non-Requested Equipment, NRE is not idle for the duration of state N*, where NRE = $\overline{SR \wedge RE}$, and SR is the system resource. The SR code is the n-bit code consisting of all ones, where n is the number of CE's in the system, and RE is the code of Requested Equipment. Therefore, a complete RRM requests either the entire system resource for forming N* (SR = RE), or no idleness in the non-requested equipment is created, if RE is a subset of SR. An Incomplete Reconfiguration Request Message requests the architectural reconfiguration, N $\to$ N*, in which a portion or the totality of nonrequested equipment is idle for the duration of N*.

Typically, an incomplete RRM can be issued by a dynamic program, which does not know in advance the nonconflicting needs of other programs capable of being executed concurrently with the incomplete RRM.

Composite Structures. Composite Structures are:

- composite rings,
- composite stars,
- composite multiple trees,
- composite multiple stars.

Computed Variables. Computed variables are those assigned by the program to changeable values.

Computer Size Code k for Dynamic Programs. This code is stored only in the non-assigned $\overline{\text{SUM}}$. When this $\overline{\text{SUM}}$ becomes assigned to the architectural state N, the code is exchanged with the matching $\text{RE}(\overline{\text{A}}_L)$ of the displaced $\overline{\text{A}}_L$-zone; the displaced $\overline{\text{A}}_L$ zone will receive $\tilde{\text{k}}$ from $\overline{\text{SUM}}$ before going back to the non assigned queue.

Concurrency of Two Communicating Pairs of Tree Nodes. Two communicating pairs (N_s, N_d) and (N'_s, N'_d) are concurrent if their data exchanges can be performed in parallel via non-shared communication paths. Here N_s is the source node and N_d is the destination node.

Conditions of Dynamic Assignment. If there arrives a dynamic program (P_D) with nonassigned SUM (bit A = 0) the task of the monitor is to perform a dynamic assignment of this SUM to the archtectural state N so that the following conditions are satisfied:

- **C1.** *Fulfillment of the program resource needs.* A selected architectural state N must contain the dynamic computer(s) needed by dynamic program P_D .
- **C2.** *Minimal delay in computations.* A selected architectural state N must be assumed by the system earlier than any possible alternative state N′ which may also satisfy the resource needs of program P_D .

Implementation of the C2 principle requires that dynamic programs be assigned to architectural states using their priority codes.

Conflict Resolution During Reconfiguration. Programs computed in the same architectural state are asynchronous and independent. Thus, they may feature conflicting needs for the next architectural state N*. The monitor must resolve these conflicts on the basis of priorities assigned to the programs. Therefore, during each reconfiguration, the monitor initiates the procedure for conflict resolution when it allows or denies an architectural reconfiguration requested by a program.

Conflicts in a System with Dynamic Architectures. There are three types of conflicts in a system with dynamic architecture:

- *Memory conflicts* when two or more computers request the same memory page either local or nonlocal with one requesting computer;
- *Reconfiguration conflicts* when two computers existing concurrently in a current architectural state N request transitions into two different next states N′* and N″*, which cannot merge into a single N* = N′*UN″*;
- *I/O conflicts* when two computers request the same I/O terminal (for instance, for organization of memory-memory data exchange via I/O bus), or when two I/Os request concurrent communication with the monitor, etc.

Connection N → N*. Connection N → N* means activation of the data path between nodes N and N*. During such activation the following are performed:

1. N generates the position code of N* and establishes a data path between N and N*, and
2. The data path between N and N* is bidirectional: either from N to N* or from N* to N. It can be one of the four types— PE-ME*, PE-PE*, ME-PE*, ME-ME* —where the first element belongs to node N, the second element belongs to code N*, PE stands for the processor element and ME stands for the memory element.

Control Algorithms Yielding a Tree or Star Implementation. These typically describe a tree or a star hierarchical management configuration in which each higher level node (a) manages and distributes information among all lower level nodes that follow it in a tree or star, and (b) receives completion signals from all lower level nodes indicating that all jobs assigned for execution have been completed.

Control Codes During Reconfiguration. Each architectural state is characterized by its own set of control codes. For instance, to reconfigure into a new multicomputer state requires writing four control codes with changeable values into each computer element of the requested resources.

On the other hand, to establish a new network state (rings, trees, and stars) requires only two invariant control codes to be written to all CE's of requested resources.

Therefore, required control codes can be stored as an array in the memory, or, if their number is small (as is true for network reconfigurations), it is beneficial to store them in the architectural switch instruction, N → N*. For the first case, storage of the array of control codes should be organized so that the time of their sorting and accessing to requested computer elements would be minimized. For the second case, organization of the architectural switch instruction should be developed so that these codes can be sent (possibly via monitor) to requested computing resources that will be using these codes for formation of N*.

Control Codes. (See Variant and Invariant Control Codes.)

Control Codes for the DMN that Use the SRVB Techniques. Each reconfiguration is concurrent and carried out by all affected network nodes with the use of only two codes; reconfiguration code (RC), and bias (B), where RC reconfigures an SRVB into a specific shifting format and B generates a unique successor N* of N in the new network structure that will be formed.

Creation and Reassignment Processes. The task of the dynamic assignment is reduced to the *absorption* of the nonassigned queue NAQ with the assigned queue AQ. (See Assigned and Non-Assigned Queues) This absorption can be implemented via the following two operations.

- *creation*, aimed at creation of a new architectural state, and
- *reassignment*, aimed at reassigning a new high-priority program to an existing architectural state, while deleting from this state an old program with a lower priority status and compatible time and resource needs. This deleted program acquires a status of nonassigned program and its startup message is sent back to the nonassigned queue, NAQ.

Cross-CIR of the Two Paths in a Reconfigurable Binary Tree. By a cross-CIR of the two paths, PA1 = N_{s1} → N_{d1} and PA2 = N_{s2} → N_{d2} , we mean the closest intermediate root of a cross-path (C-PA) that has a source node identified with one of the terminal nodes from PA1

(N_{s1} or N_{d1}) and the destination node identified with one of the terminal nodes (N_{s2} or N_{d2}) from PA2.

Since PA1 and PA2 have two terminal nodes each, it is possible to construct four cross-paths for them that are specified with four cross-CIRs (C-CIR). These paths are:

$$C\text{-}PA_{ss} = N_{s1} \to N_{s2} \; ; \; C\text{-}PA_{sd} = N_{s1} \to N_{d2} \; ; \; C\text{-}PA_{ds} = N_{d1} \to N_{s2} \text{ and } C\text{-}PA_{dd} = N_{d1} \to N_{d2} \; .$$

This gives four cross CIRs for these paths: ss cross CIR, C-Cir$_{ss}$ for C-PA$_{ss}$; sd cross CIR, C-CIR$_{sd}$ for C-PA$_{sd}$; ds cross CIR, C-CIR$_{ds}$ for C-PA$_{ds}$ and dd cross CIR, C-CIr$_{dd}$, for C-PA$_{dd}$.

Data Exchange Optimization. Data exchange optimization achieved with the use of reconfiguration in a reconfigurable binary tree is an extremely powerful source of improving performance of the binary tree because, by using reconfiguration, one can minimize the duration and maximize the concurrency of requested data exchanges relative to those performed in a static tree configuration.

Deposit Table in a Task Rendezvous. The Deposit Table is organized as follows. Its rows are marked by calling tasks, PUC$_B$; its columns are marked by called tasks, PUC$_A$. The intersection (PUC$_A$, PUC$_B$) is either empty or filled with d, BA, and PA, where d is array dimension, BA is base address and PA is page address. If it is empty, then d, BA, and PA have not yet been deposited or Tasks A and B do not meet in a rendezvous. If (PUC$_A$, PUC$_B$) is not empty, then d, BA and PA have been deposited by the task producer (either called or calling).

Dot Notation in an Ada Package. Dot notation in an Ada Package allows referencing of the selected portion of the package specified with the dot.

Dynamic Assignment Rules. For any two architectural states N and N', where N' follows N in the architectural flow chart (not necessarily immediately), none of the programs assigned to N' has a higher priority than any of those assigned to N if:

- N can satisfy the resource needs of each such program;
- The reconfiguration flow chart can assume N and N' with such an assignment (i.e., none of the existing architectural states becomes unreachable or dead because of a particular dynamic assignment);
- Unwarranted idleness of equipment during computation of N is not created with such an assignment.;
- All programs to be assigned to N and N' are available before the system assumes N and N'.

Dynamic Computer. A dynamic computer $C_i(k)$, where k shows the number of integrated CE's and i shows the position of its most significant CE, is formed via software. This computer handles 16 • k-bit words and has a primary memory 16 • k-bit wide; thus each word is stored in a single parallel cell made of k 16-bit bytes. To reduce the complexity and increase the speed of the reconfigurable processor bus destined to transmit processor signals (such as carries, overflows and equalities among PEs), each $C_i(k)$ *must include only adjacent* CEs, for which positions are fixed as CE$_i$, CE$_{i+1}$, ..., CE$_{i+k-1}$. For example, dynamic computer $C_3(3)$ contains CE$_3$, CE$_4$ and CE$_5$ and it handles 16 • 3-bit words. Its CE$_3$ is the most significant; its CE$_5$ is the least significant.

Dynamic Multicomputer Network. A dynamically reconfigurable interconnection network defines a dynamic multicomputer network, DMN, that can assume a set of configurations during execution time and improve performance by executing the algorithm(s) in the most appropriate network configuration or sequence of configurations.

Dynamic Multicomputer Network, Analysis. Means finding and quantification of all possible network structures that can be generated with the use of particular reconfiguration methodology.

Dynamic Multicomputer Network, Synthesis. Means finding specific control codes that can generate a given network structure, describing a particular application.

Dynamic Program Computation. To be executed, a dynamic program must first be assigned to the architectural state. This means that the monitor must either (a) find other concurrent and compatible nonassigned programs that can be assigned to the same architectural state, or (b) swap a nonassigned higher priority dynamic program with one having a lower priority assigned to the existing architectural state. The (a) action leads to the creation, and the (b) action leads to the reassignment of architectural states. Therefore, any nonassigned program becomes ready for computation only following the state of dynamic assignment, which includes creation and reassignment of architectural states.

Dynamic Program for Adaptable Architectures. A Dynamic program P_D is the one which possesses the following attributes.

- Its assignment to hardware resources proceeds during system execution;
- Program P_D represents only the individual resource needs. It does not represent the resource needs of the other programs that may be executed concurrently in the same architectural state;
- Program P_D , as a rule, is non assigned with respect to architectural state, if its resource needs form a portion (not totality) of the system assignable resource.

Dynamic Reconfiguration and Ada Compilation. Dynamic reconfiguration greatly simplifies the compilation of Ada-oriented programs since it allows creation of a dynamic match between an Ada construct and the hardware structure (created dynamically) that supports this construct.

Dynamic Reconfiguration and Ada Packages. Dynamic architecture greatly facilitates the creation of Ada packages in that reconfiguration may allow concurrent computation of informatin arrays that, in static computer systems, are totally disjoint. By a disjoint pair (IA_i , IA_j) of two information arrays IA_i and IA_j we mean those that can be used together only following a data transfer $ME_i \rightarrow ME_j$ or $ME_j \rightarrow ME_i$, where ME_i stores IA_i and ME_j stores IA_j .

If an Ada package contains only a data part and no functional part, it identifies a data structure created out of participating MEs.

If an Ada package contains the two parts - functional and data - it identifies a computing structure created out of participating CEs. Both structures can be made reconfigurable using the reconfiguration mechanisms implemented in hardware. The assignment of memory and processor resources that support reconfigurable memory structures and reconfigurable computing structures (identifiable with the two types of packages) is similar to the one used for the Reconfiguration Flow Chart.

Dynamic Replacement Strategy. Aimed at replacing each faulty module with a spare from the available bank without any decrease in the system throughput.

Dynamic Resource Assignment. By dynamic resource assignment, we identify an assignment process for which all resource needs of participating programs are not given in advance. For dynamic assignment, the entire program mix consists of two types of programs: *static* with stored requests on reconfigurable resources (processor and/or memory) and *dynamic* or *arriving programs,* with requests on reconfigurable resources that have not been considered during static assignment. The arrival of such programs may change the constructed (static) reconfiguration flow chart since the priorities of dynamic programs may be higher than those for static ones.

Therefore, dynamic assignments, as a rule, feature reconfiguration conflicts since a dynamic program may compete for the reconfigurable resources assigned to a static program during static assignments or to another dynamic program during a previous dynamic assignment.

Even-Composite Ring Structure. Even-Composite Ring Structure is represented by the shifting format $SF_1 E = [1^{r_1}, 2^{r_2}, \ldots, t^{r_t}]$ that is specified by the characterization format $CF = [E_1, E_2, \ldots E_t]$, which means that each bias component fed to a respective single register of SF_1 is even-weighed.

Even-Single Ring Structure. Even-Single Ring Structure is generated by the SRVB receiving an even-weighed bias and is described by a single and circular shifting format such that $SF_1 = [n^1]$.

Even-Weighed and Odd-Weighed Bias. Bias B is called even-weighed if its weight is an even integer and odd-weighed if its weight is an odd integer.

Execution Time of One Task in a Dynamic Computer. The adaptive assignment of the resources of a dynamic architecture among independent programs must be based on the execution time of each task in a given size computer. Indeed, since a system with dynamic architecture may compute several concurrent programs, one architectural state may feature several independent tasks computed in concurrent computers. If reconfiguration is done by the longest task, shorter tasks will finish their executions earlier and await the end of the longest task leading to a performance deterioration. Therefore, the longest task must be executed in several states using the same computer. The shorter tasks may switch architecture and continue their execution without waiting for the end of the longest task. The system will perform correctly because the resource of the longest task will not be requested for reconfiguration.

Fault-tolerant Reconfiguration in a Reconfigurable Binary Tree. The objective of the best fault-tolerant reconfiguration is to assemble as many fault nodes as possible into end subtrees that can be disconnected from the system.

The procedure for finding the maximal i-dimensional faulty end tree starts by finding a completely faulty structure P_i formed of leaves, where i is a maximal integer. The next step is iterative; it consists of finding a complete faulty structure P_{i-1} somewhere in the tree and performing a tree reconfiguration that allows P_{i-1} to become the immediate successor of P_i. If P_{i-1} is partial, the process stops (See Recursive Structure P_i). Otherwise it continues with finding P_{i-2}, etc.

Floating Point Computation Assessment. Any switch into floating point computation leads to the following undesirable consequences:

1. *Inferior precision:* The quality of floating point computation measured by committed computational errors expressed in percent is significantly inferior to that of the fixed point computation.

2. *Inferior time:* The time of executing a floating point operation is at least double that of executing a fixed point operation. Since the addition is an average time of a machine instruction and the time of a floating point addition doubles that of a fixed point one, the entire execution time of the same program in a floating point form at least doubles that of a fixed point form.

Fork-Join Algorithm. By fork-join algorithm, we mean a concurrent process whereby one sequential program P_1 initiates execution of several other sequential programs P_2 , ..., P_k , concurrently with P_1 . The initiating program (P_1) will be called the program-starter. The spawned programs P_2 , ..., P_k will be called *program offsprings*. Usually, the *Fork-Construct* is concluded by the synchronization construct, *Join*, which indicates the end of this particular forking process. The objective of Join is to provide the synchronization point for all programs (starter and offsprings) that are participating in forking, i.e., to insure that they complete their execution during forking.

Fork-Join Task Synchronization in a Reconfigurable Computer System. Fork-join task synchronization in a reconfigurable computer system includes two types of synchronization:

1. Architectural task synchronization, and
2. Join task synchronization.

The objective of the architectural task synchronization during the $N_i \rightarrow N_j$ transition from state N_i to state N_j is to guarantee that all asynchronous programs assigned to N_i have completed their execution in N_i , if their RE resources are requested to form new computers of N_j .

As for the Join task synchronization, the *Join* instruction is executed by the program-starter (P_1). Offspring programs may take longer time than that of program-starter. Thus, Join task synchronization features the synchronization techniques that allow all offspring-programs to inform the program-starter of the end of their execution so that the program-starter can end its Join instruction.

Generating Position of a Bias. Since bias B is a binary number, it can be given by its ones' positions, hereafter called generating positions, GP, as in the following:

$$B = GP_1 + GP_2 + ... + GP_t$$

where t is called the bias weight.

Generic Ring. A generic ring is generated by a circular SRVB ($SF_1 = [n^1]$), storing bias B. Thus, bias B is always the first node of GRI and 0, its last node because 0 is succeeded by B. In other words, GRI = $\{A_0 = B, A_1 , ..., A_{T-1} = 0\}$, where T is the period of GRI.

Graceful Degradation Strategy. Such a strategy is aimed at turning off each faulty module from computation and maintaining adequate performance using the fault-free modules that remain in the system.

Horizontal Distribution of Operating System Functions for Dynamic Architecture. (See Vertical and Horizontal Distribution of Operating System Functions for Dynamic Architecture.)

i-Dimensional End Subtree. By the i-dimensional *end subtree*, we mean a tree formed of structures P_i , P_{i-1} , ..., P_0 , where P_i includes only leaves and P_{i-1} , P_{i-2} , ..., P_0 are all j-successors of P_i ; in this tree (j =1, 2, ..., i). Since $P_0 = N*$, P_0 is the unique i-successor of P_i (See Recursive Structures, P_i).

Incomplete Reconfiguration Request Messages. (See Complete and Incomplete Reconfiguration Request Messages.)

Insufficient Accuracy. There are two cases of accuracy degradation in conventional computer systems.

- Loss of accuracy because of truncated results.
- Loss of accuracy caused by a switch into a less precise floating point operation.

If computational errors caused by such accuracy losses exceed the maximal admissible tolerances, the accuracy becomes insufficient and requires abandoning of the computation in a given computer system.

Insufficient Precision and Dynamic Architectures. The major causes of insufficient precision are in

- truncation of double-precision products (quotients with remainders) and in
- switching computation into a less precise floating point form.

For dynamic architectures, there is no need to truncate a double-precision product or to switch into a floating point operation. It is far more beneficial to switch the system to a larger dynamic computer and continue the operation of this computer over larger data words.

Insufficient Range. Insufficient range means that a computed number is larger (smaller) than the maximal (minimal) number, which can be stored in a data register. The insufficient range is recognized either by an adder overflow (for additions) or by obtaining double-precision intermediate results (for multiplications). The problem of insufficient range for fixed point computation is remedied by a switch into a floating point computation. For floating point computation, the problem of insufficient range simply cannot be remedied. The program stops computing since it requires a larger size of data registers for exponent storage.

Insufficient Range and Dynamic Architectures. For a fixed point operation, the problem of insufficient range does not require a switch to a floating point operation. Instead, it can be remedied by switching into operation one or two spare CEs out of the available bank of spare CEs thus reconfiguring to a larger size computer.

Other programs are not affected by this switch since they continue computation in the same computers that computed them before.

For a floating point operation, insufficient exponent range can also be handled either by adding a new computer element and performing transition into a new architectural state which incorporates this element, or activating exponent operation in the next less significant CE of the dynamic computer C(k)

Invariant Control Codes. (See Variant and Invariant Control Codes.)

Iterative and Noniterative Nodes in the Program Graph. Nodes in the graph may be *iterative* and *noniterative*. Each *iterative node* is specified with the parameter Z, which is the maximal number of iterations it may go through in a program loop. Parameter Z may be given as follows:

1. It can be presented explicitly in the program.
2. It can be defined via analysis of a control statement, which specifies an exit from the program loop.
3. In cases where Z cannot be defined via **1** or **2**, its statistical value can be given based on experiences with the past computations of the same program (See Program Graph).

Left Prefix Operation for the Address Codes of Two Nodes in a Reconfigurable Binary Tree. If the two tree nodes N and N', having levels i and i', where i < i' are on the same communication path from the root R, then their address codes AC_N and $AC_{N'}$, are related as follows:

* AC_N has $l = n - i$ binary digits; $AC_{N'}$ has $l' = n - l'$ binary digits, where $n - i > n - i'$.
* $AC_{N'}$ is a left prefix of AC_N, because to reach N from a root, R, a communication message must pass node N' in transit. Thus, it must use the address information of $AC_{N'}$ before it reaches N. We will denote the operation of left prefix as LP, meaning that $AC_{N'} = LP(AC_N)$.

Left and Right Prefixes in a Dynamic Computer. Dynamic computer C(k) is called a *right prefix* of dynamic computer C'(k'), if C(k) is formed of k least significant CE belonging to computer C'(k'), where $k \le k'$. It is obviously assumed that C(k) and C'(k') do not exist concurrently.

Similar definition can be made for a *left prefix*; the only requirement is that C(k) be made of k most significant CE belonging to computer C'(k') and $k \le k'$.

Left and Right Prefixes Rule During Assignment. For any two sequential tasks of the same P-resource diagram (See P-Resource Diagram) requiring the dynamic computers C(k) and C'(k') where k < k', the resource assignment will provide that C(k) be a left or right prefix of C'(k') (See Left and Right Prefixes in a Dynamic Computer). Such an assignment will eliminate any memory contentions that arise each time C'(k') should access the primary memory of another concurrent computer, say C"(k"), for the data words computer by C(k) that existed earlier. Each such accessing would have required activation of the local operating system of C"(k"), which is designated to check the priority of a program run on C'(k') to perform a nonlocal memory access to the primary memory or separate MEs of the computer C"(k").

Memory Management for Dynamic Architectures.
Principle 1: In any dynamic computer that includes k CEs, one 16 • k-bit data word is stored in a single parallel cell of k MEs, all having the same address. Consequently, a data array containing d 16 • k-bit words will take d parallel cells for its storage in different size computers. This results in independence of the data array size d from the computer size k, and, also, leads

to the independence of a data address from the computer size and a concurrent fetch of all k 16-bit bytes comprising a single data word.

Principle 2: Since the minimal size computer is equivalent to one CE, the instruction size has been made coincident with that of one CE. The instruction sequences are stored in consecutive cells of one ME and complex programs may be stored in several MEs. The instruction fetched from one ME would then be sent concurrently to all modules of the C(k) computer. The same program occupies the same number of cells in any size computer, therefore achieving independence of the sizes of instruction arrays from computer sizes. This leads to the independence of the instruction address (jump address, etc.) from computer size.

ME Resource Diagram. Constructing the ME resource diagram is equivalent to distributing the primary memory of dynamic architecture among various user programs. To construct the ME resource diagram, one must use the memory size portions of all the P-resource diagrams and the Reconfiguration flow chart (See P-resource diagram). Since the ME resource diagram shows the scheduling of primary memory for accessing in different states of the Reconfiguration flow chart the memory mapping finds two memory spaces which store (respectively) the data and instruction arrays of one user program for each architectural state.

Mismatch Between Resources Needed by the Program and Parameters of a Computer System that Executes this Program. Three types of such a mismatch are possible:

1. *Bit size mismatch* is understood as a mismatch between bit sizes of data words used by running programs and the available sizes of processors computing these programs.
2. *Concurrency mismatch* is a mismatch between the number of concurrent instruction sequences in a program and the number of processors in the system.
3. *Mixed mismatch* includes bit size and concurrency mismatches.

Mission-Critical Supercomputing System. A Supercomputing system whose performance is based on successful execution of its mission, specified by concrete mission-critical requirements and defined quantitatively. This is now called a *mission-critical Supersystem.*

Mixed-Composite Ring Structure. Mixed-Composite Ring Structure is represented by the shifting format $SF_1 = [1^{r_1}, 2^{r_2}, ..., t^{r_t}]$, identified by the characterization format $CF = [m_1, m_2, ..., m_t]$, $m_1, m_2, ..., m_t \in \{O, E\}$. O and E stand, respectively, for odd weighed and even weighed bias components fed to a single shift register of SF_1.

Mixed Reconfiguration. By mixed reconfigurations ($X_{j1}, X_{j2}, ..., X_{jk}$ reconfigurations) we mean reconfigurations that are determined by the mapping code $MC = X_{j1} + X_{j2} + ... + X_{jk}$. The $X_{j1}, X_{j2}, ..., X_{jk}$-reconfigured tree can be found by applying concurrently $X_{j1}, X_{j2}, ..., X_{jk}$-level reconfigurations to the source tree.

Module-level Reconfiguration. (See Circuit-level and Module-level Reconfiguration.)

Monitor Approach for Tree Reconfiguration. All fault-tolerant reconfigurations are performed by a system monitor, which is connected with each tree node. The major advantage of this approach is that it can be performed very rapidly since, when the monitor obtains a status of each node, it finds the best bias B that restores connectivity in the tree. It then sends this bias to each tree node, thus effecting the tree reconfiguration into a new connected tree structure. Major disadvantages of this approach include the following:

1. It requires that the monitor be connected with every tree node. This requires a complex network to perform these connections.
2. The monitor may become faulty, making the monitor approach totally inapplicable.

m-Reducible Bias. Bias of size n is called m-reducible if m is the size of its period. That is, $m \cdot p = n$.

Multicomputer Network. A Multicomputer network is a collection of computer elements connected via an interconnection network.

Multistaged and Single Staged Interconnection Networks Trade-off. The difference between multistaged and single staged interconnection networks is in (a) the time of message transit between two adjacent nodes, $N \rightarrow N^*$, of the communication path and (b) the overall complexity of realization, expressed by the number of connecting elements in the network. If all network nodes are interconnected, with an interconnection network that interfaces the entire processor resource (made of K PE) with the entire memory resource (made of K ME), then for a more complex and faster single staged network, a message transit between every pair of nodes of a communication path will be delayed by a pair of consecutive connecting elements in the path. For a multistaged interconnection network, this transit will be delayed by $2n = 2 \log_2 K$ consecutive connecting elements. At the same time, a single staged network will require K^2 connecting elements with a single-port bidirectional broadcast, whereas a multiple staged network will take $K/2 \cdot \log_2 K$ connecting elements with a four-port bidirectional broadcast or $2K \cdot \log_2 K$ connecting elements with single-port bidirectional broadcast.

Network Analysis and Synthesis in the Context of SRVB Methodology. When we apply the shift-register theory for generating multicomputer networks, the following problems of consequence must be solved.

Network Analysis - Given a type of SRVB and bias B, find the network structure that is generated with this SRVB.
Network Synthesis - Given the configuration of a network structure, find the SRVB and bias B that can generate either this structure or a larger one that contains the given structure as a substructure.

Network and Multicomputer Reconfigurations. In general, for a Dynamic Multicomputer Network (DMN), the sequence of reconfiguration steps remains the same as for a multicomputer reconfiguration since this sequence is determined by the requirement to provide correct computations in the environment of (a) conflicts and (b) reconfigurable and distributed computing resources joined by an interconnection network (single staged or multistaged). Indeed, for a DMN to implement feature (a) of multicomputer reconfiguration requires the conflict resolution process and its implied outcomes, consisting of an architectural interrupt (current or next) or no interrupt. If there are no conflicts or no architectural interrupts caused by conflicts, there is the task synchronization step, aimed at finding the moment of completion for programs computed in a previous computing structure.

To implement (b) requires accessing an array of control codes and writing this array to the requested resource modules of the DMN, in order to establish required interconnections in the interconnection network which will then identify a new computing structure created with the use of reconfiguration.

Network versus Multicomputer Reconfigurations. The distinction is not made in the overall sequence of steps to be performed in a general reconfiguration algorithm but, rather, in the set of control codes that must be accessed and the techniques of data path activations.

To form a new dynamic computer takes a specific set of control codes for multicomputer reconfiguration. However, to form a new network structure requires not only a node reconfiguration aimed at formation of dynamic computers, but also the network reconfiguration for the formation of a new topology of activated interconnections among separate dynamic computers.

Therefore, the network reconfiguration is accomplished using an additional set of control codes and special techniques for data path activations in the used interconnection network.

New Interconnections in the Interconnection Network during Reconfiguration. They are activated following the access of variable control codes.

This activation finalizes the act of forming new computing structures of the next architectural state. Such interconnections should be activated that allow correct formation of (a) *reconfigurable instruction busses,* which broadcast each instruction only to the modules of a newly formed computing structure and prevent this broadcast to all other computing structures that coexist concurrently; (b) *reconfigurable data busses,* that allow fast and concurrent data exchanges within each newly formed computing structure, and between different computing structures, existing either concurrently or sequentially.

No Conflict Reconfiguration. If the system features no reconfiguration conflicts, it either executes a static reconfiguration flow chart, in which each current state is succeeded with the unique next state, or the system is idle. Therefore, the arriving $\overline{RRM}$ message is either the one that requests the only next state $\tilde{N}$ or the one that requests the current state N in the event of the total system idleness.

Nodes in a Program Graph. There exist two types of nodes in the program graph: *simple* and *complex.* A *simple node* has one outgoing arrow, which means unconditional transition to its immediate successor. A *complex node* has several outgoing arrows. Selection of its immediate successor depends on a conditional test executed by the control statement in this node (See Program Graph).

Nonassigned Programs for Dynamic Architectures. (See Assigned and Nonassigned Programs for Dynamic Architectures.)

Non-Interruptible and Interruptible Programs. Computed programs may be divided into two classes, *noninterruptible* and *interruptible*. Program P is *noninterruptible* if it cannot be interrupted because of the specificities of its algorithm (for instance, real-time control), or due to a requirement that its computational time be kept minimal demanding that it not tolerate delays caused by program interrupts. All the remaining programs will be called *interruptible*.

Noniterative Nodes in the Program Graph. (See Iterative and Noniterative Nodes in the Program Graph.)

Numeric Errors and Dynamic Architecture. Dynamic architecture provides additional means for handling numeric exceptions that are beyond the reach of static architectures. Most of the numeric errors can be handled by assuming architectural states that call for larger computer sizes, so the respective errors are circumvented.

Odd-Composite Ring Structure. Odd-Composite Ring Structure is represented by shifting format ($SF_1 = [1^{r_1}, 2^{r_2}, ..., t^{r_t}]$) with the characterization format $CF = [0_1, 0_2, ..., 0_t]$, which means that each bias component fed to a respective single register of SF_1 is odd weighed.

Odd Representation of m. Expression of m via d addends will be called an *odd representation of number m*, ORS(m) if d is an odd number. In other words, if d is odd, ORS(m) = $b_1 + b_2 + ... + b_d$.

Odd-Single Ring Structures. Odd-single ring structure is generated by the SRVB receiving and odd weighed bias and described by a single and circular shifting format $SF_1 = [n^1]$.

One Graph Node Time and One Task Time. Having found the times to execute all instructions of the instruction set, one constructs a special table in which rows correspond to machine instruction. An entry in a row shows the number of clock periods required for the execution of that instruction. A processor dependent instruction is assigned n rows, each showing the instruction time in a computer of given size ranging from 16 to 16 • n-bits, respectively. A processor independent instruction is assigned a single row since its execution time does not depend on the computer size. If a node of the Program Graph is interpreted as f machine instructions, then its time is found as the sum of the times of all its instructions. If this statement belongs to a node with iteration parameter Z, then the number of clock periods thus obtained is multiplied by Z. Having obtained the time of each statement, one may find the time of the node and the time of the task.

Optimal Static Tree Configuration. The best static tree configuration can be found via the following assignment process. Let AC be the address code from the root to the node N of level $n-i$. Obviously, AC contains i binary positions because the communication path to N from the root R_a has i edges. The n-bit code N is found as follows:

$$N = \underbrace{rot\ (AC)}_{i}\ \underbrace{00\ ...\ 0}_{n-i}$$

where rot is a simple logical operation called *rotation* extended to AC made of *i* positions. The remaining $(n - i)$ positions of *N* are filled with 0's.

Optimization Criteria During Resource Assignment for Different Computing Structures. For dynamic multicomputer systems an optimal assignment minimizes possible program delays and executes each program, a member of the program mix, in the dynamic computer required by this program. This should occur at the earliest moment of time possible under circumstances. For the reconfigurable binary tree, an optimal resource assignment is associated with the minimization of communication delays in node-to-node communications, since only this type of optimization allows each local program consumer to avoid delay due to nonavailability of the required data words produced by some other node(s) producer(s).

Parameters of Dynamic Array Architecture. The following parameters of dynamic array architecture are selectable by the programmer:

1. *The number of concurrent arrays* being formed in the system. This specifies the number of data vectors executed at a time by the entire array system. For instance, an array system containing three arrays computes three data vectors at a time.

2. *The number of processors in each array.* This specifies the dimension of the data vector computed in each array. For instance, consider the system that is now reconfigured into two arrays, A_1 and A_2, of which one array includes three processors, $A_1 = [P_{11}, P_{12}, P_{13}]$ and the other includes five processors, i.e., $A_2 = [P_{21}, P_{22}, P_{23}, P_{24}, P_{25}]$. The first array computes a three dimensional data vector V_1 at a time with a single instruction; $V_1 = (a_{11}, a_{12}, a_{13})$; and the second array computes a five-dimensional data vector V_2 at a time with a single instruction, $V_2 = (a_{21}, a_{22}, a_{23}, a_{24}, a_{25})$. Here, each P_{1i} of the array A_1 computes one component a_{1i} of the V_1 vector ($i = 1, 2, 3$) and each P_{2j} of the array A_2 computes one component a_{2j} of the V_2 vector ($j = 1, ..., 5$).

3. *The word size of each processor in each array.* This is specified by the number k of PE included into each processor. For instance, a system that computes two data vectors V_1 and V_2 at a time where vector $V_1 = (a_1(16), a_2(32), a_3(32))$ and $V_2 = (b_1(16), b_2(16))$, has two arrays, A_1 and A_2. The A_1 array includes three processors; P_{11}, P_{12}, P_{13}; 16-bit processor P_{11} computes 16-bit word $a_1(16)$; P_{11} is assembled from one PE; 32-bit processor P_{12} computes 32-bit word $a_2(32)$; P_{12} is assembled from two PE; 32-bit processor, processor P_{13} computes $a_3(32)$. It is assembled from two PE. In all, the A_1 array is formed of five PEs. Similarly, one can find the number of PEs in the A_2 array.

Parameter of Iteration for Each Node. The parameter of iteration for each node shows the maximal number of iterations this node can execute. To find this parameter one has to mark all of the nodes in the graph, which belong to one program loop. For each such node, i, one finds the maximal number of iterations, Z_i, of the respective loop, and this number is assigned to all nodes included into the loop. If node b belongs to several program loops which iterate Z_a, Z_c, ..., Z_n times, respectively, then the paramenter of iteration, Z_b, of this node is:

$$Z_b = Z_a \cdot Z_c \cdot ... \cdot Z_n .$$

Passive Program. (See Active and Passive Programs.)

Path Duration in a Binary Tree. Given a data exchange path (N_s, N_d) assigned to tree structure TS_i. Find the duration of this path in TS_i, where duration of the path is understood as the duration of a data exchange that is performed via this path.

Priority of a Dynamic Program for Creating CR(N). The creation of a new architectural state, CR(N), is performed by the nonassigned program P (represented with its SUM) whose priority is either higher or lower than those of all other programs already assigned to the architectural states. The program P that creates CR(N) will be called the *program generator*, $P = P_{gen}$. Its SUM will be denoted SUM_{gen}.

P-Resource Diagram. P-resource diagram is the diagram of individual needs of program P. Its horizontal axis shows the time of functioning of each task and the vertical axis contains two portions; the upper portion shows computer sizes, and the lower portion shows dimensions of data arrays.

Private Information in an Ada Package. Since an Ada package may contain private information, this must be accessed on a strictly selective basis. Namely, some users are given a privilege to use this information. Others are not. (If no users can have such privilege, the private information becomes useless and there is no sense of storing it in the memory.)

Private Part of a Package. The visible part of the package is followed by a *private part,* in which the full type definition of each private type is given. This form is characteristic of situations, which warrant a selected access for each private type.

Private Table for Accessing Private Information in a Package. The private table updated by the operating system shows what user programs are allowed privileged information, contained in all private parts of all packages. When each such program requires privileged information, it executes a special instruction that fetches the current program status regarding accessing a particular private file. If this accessing is allowed, then the private file is accessed. Otherwise, the accessing is prohibited.

Therefore, to implement the independence of compilation for package visible parts and selective accessing for package private parts the following memory management for private parts is used. All private parts of all Ada packages stored in the primary memory are assigned a special memory array whereby each private part is given a separate memory space, MS. In a *private table,* rows are marked with program user codes (PUC) and the columns are marked with memory spaces (MSs). The intersection (PUC, MS), shows the base address for the given PUC and the number of words which are allowed access. If no access is allowed, the intersection (PUC, MS) is filled with zeros.

Producer-Consumer Algorithms. Producer-consumer algorithms is a class characterized by data dependencies, in which one instruction sequence (*producer*) produces data words consumed by another instruction sequence (*consumer*). Four such data dependencies can be organized: memory-memory, processor-memory-processor, memory-processor-memory and processor-processor.

Memory-memory data exchange is understood as a conventional long-range data exchange whereby one program writes into its local memory M_i data words that are fetched (consumed) by another program and written into its local memory M_j , where $i \neq j$.

Processor-memory-processor exchange is equivalent to store-fetch data exchange SF, used in conventional parallel programming in which data words computed by one processor P_i are stored in its local memory M_i before being fetched by another processor P_j , where $i \neq j$.

Memory-processor-memory exchange is equivalent to *fetch-store* data exchange FS, used in parallel programming whereby processor P_i fetches data words either from its own memory M_i or from nonlocal memory M_j and then sends computed results for storage either to M_i , or to M_j or M_k , where $i \neq j \neq k$.

Processor-processor exchange characterizes the following typical data dependency: one processor P_i computes one program loop and sends its data to another processor P_j ; P_j uses these data for another loop computation.

Program Graph. A Program Graph is a graph constructed for a high level program in which each node includes one or more high level statements and the arrows show sequencing.

Program Graph Formation. Formation of the Program Graph depends on the following types of statements:

1. A noncontrol statement that is not referenced by any other statement.
2. A statement that is referenced by another control statement.

3. All control statements (*except* the DO statement).
4. The DO statement.
5. The DO reference statement or the DO object.

Program Priorities. Program priorities are integers assigned to the programs by the operating system based on their relative importance.

Program Startup During Reconfiguration. Each program must start its execution in the next architectural state N*. The following cases of this startup are distinguished:

1. Program P is assigned to both states current N and next N*, and
   (a) P requests transition N → N*, or in other words, P is *active*
   (b) P does not request N → N* transition (P is *passive*)
2. Program P is assigned only to N* and
   (a) It is *active* by performing transition N → N*;
   (b) It is *passive* by not performing transition N → N*.

Program Startup in the New Architectural State. Program startup in the new architectural state is the last step of the architectural reconfiguration. For static programs it starts immediately following establishment of new interconnections in the interconnection network since the required startup state M(N) is stored in the monitor. For dynamic programs, the program startup may follow the process of dynamic assignment aimed either at creation of a new architectural state CR(N), or at reassignment of the existing state RE(N) if the respective SUM message is nonassigned. For both types of programs, static and dynamic, the program startup is reduced to

- Organization of the one-to-one correspondence between the reconfiguration flow chart and the assigned queue of SUM messages, and
- Providing each dynamic computer of the new architectural state with all of the necessary start information so that this computer can start its independent and asynchronous computations.

Pulse Deinterleaving Process. The objective of the pulse deinterleaving process is to form various pulse trains such that each defines a sequence of pulses with identical pulse characteristics. Each established pulse train is represented by a file, which maintains matching characteristics for the pulse train.

Quantative Characterization of a Ring Structure. Quantative characterization of a ring structure consists of:

- a set of ring periods, and
- the number of rings with the same period

Readiness Test. A readiness test is aimed at checking the readiness of equipment requested to participate in reconfigurations. If the equipment is ready the monitor allows execution of the next step of the Reconfiguration Algorithm. If it is not ready the monitor initiates a waiting loop which is ended by the new iteration of the readiness test. This loop is repeated until the RT test gives a positive result.

Real Time Sorting. Real time sorting is aimed at sorting real time data words into classes such that each class characterizes the behavior of one or several real time objects.

Reassigned and Created Architectural States. The state N of Assigned Queue AQ that accepts an arriving $\widetilde{\text{SUM}}$ from nonassigned queue NAQ belongs to one of the following categories: it is either an *existing state* or it is a *newly created state*.

If state N is an existing state of AQ and it accepts new $\widetilde{\text{SUM}}$, this state becomes reassigned as RE(N).

If state N is a new state of AQ, the assignment of one or several nonassigned $\widetilde{\text{SUM}}$'s to this state means *creation*, CR(N). Thus, a new state has been created that did not exist in the original queue, AQ.

Reassignment of Architectural States. This is an important ingredient of dynamic assignment process, since it allows a high-priority dynamic program P_H to be reassigned to an existing architectural state N_H with higher priority while purging from this state a lower priority program P_L with compatible resource needs. Thus, because of reassignment, the execution of P_H will not be delayed, as would have happened otherwise had the Monitor not been provided with the procedure. Conditions for reassignment are: Let $\widetilde{\text{SUM}}$ and SUM_L be startup messages that represent P_H and P_L, respectively. A qualified $\widetilde{\text{SUM}}$ can be executed in the architectural state N assigned with other programs having higher priorities, provided SUM_L exists, already assigned to N,

1. whose priority is lower than that of $\widetilde{\text{SUM}}$ and,
2. whose resource needs match those of $\widetilde{\text{SUM}}$.

If these conditions are true, the startup message, SUM_L, exchanges its location with $\widetilde{\text{SUM}}$. Namely, SUM_L, becomes nonassigned and goes back to nonassigned queue NAQ, while $\widetilde{\text{SUM}}$ takes its location in architectural state N.

Reconfiguration Code for the SRVB. Reconfiguration of any SRVB into a given type (single, composite, circular, non-circular) is performed with the special reconfiguration code (RC) brought to each network node requested for reconfiguration, with the special reconfiguration instruction.

Reconfiguration Conflicts. Reconfiguration conflicts arise during reconfiguration requests of independent programs that cannot be met in the same architectural state. If two concurrent programs P_i and P_j request transitions into two different architectural state, N_i and N_j such that N_i and N_j cannot merge into a single architectural state, N, as $N = N_i \cup N_j$, then P_i and P_j are said to be in a conflict.

Reconfiguration Flow Chart. A sequence of configurations assumed by an adaptable supercomputing system in execution of a set of programs.

Reconfiguration Flow Chart Methodology. This is a set of software tools that allows automatic construction of the sequence of architectural configurations, given the resource request of participating programs, which form a program mix executed by the system.

Reconfiguration Instruction $N \rightarrow N^*$. This belongs to a program that needs a new dynamic computer and/or executes reconfiguration requests on behalf of other programs.

Reconfiguration Methodology. The problem of reconfiguration methodology is divided into two planes:

- Architectural reconfiguration, and
- Fault tolerant reconfiguration

The task of architectural reconfiguration is to organize an architectural transition from one state to another in the flow chart of architectural transitions, otherwise called Reconfiguration flow chart.

The task of fault tolerant reconfiguration is either (a) to organize a dynamic replacement of the faulty module(s) with the identical spare(s), or (b) to organize graceful degradation by turning off all faulty modules from computations and forming a connected and gracefully degraded architectural state from the set of remaining fault free modules.

Reconfiguration Software. For adaptable supercomputing systems the adaptable software must take advantage of the additional performance gains that can be achieved via reconfiguration. We will call this type of adaptable software *reconfiguration software.*

Reconfiguration Software for Adaptable Supercomputing Systems. This is a collection of software tools that possess the following attributes:

1. They provide for extensive use of reconfigurability concepts implemented in the hardware of any such system, and
2. They must be included in a software package of adaptable supercomputing system to enable it to complete mission critical programs written in ADA programming language.

Reconfiguration of the SRVB into Any Given Shifting Format. Reconfiguration of the SRVB into any given shifting format will be performed with the reconfiguration code, RC. The code RC is stored in the reconfiguration instruction and is described as follows: RC is a $(2n-1)$ bit code where n is the size of each SRVB. It consists of $(n-1)$ 2-bit zones, Z_i , each consisting of bits F_i and S_i , and one 1-bit zone, Z_0 , including only one bit, F_0 . Thus, RC $= (Z_{n-1} , Z_{n-2} , ..., Z_1 , Z_0)$, where $Z_i = (F_i , S_i)$ if i $\neq$ 0 and $Z_0 = F_0$.

For each zone $Z_i = (F_i , S_i)$ the values of F_i and S_i show what type of path is activated for each pair of consecutive bits, b_i and b_{i-1} . If $F_i = 1$, the respective feedback input FI is activated. If $F_i = 0$ feedback input is deactivated. Bit $S_i = 1$ of zone Z_i stands for left shift from b_{i-1} to b_i and $S_i = 0$ stands for no shift from b_{i-1} . Therefore, together F_i and S_i show what type of path is activated between b_i and b_{i-1} : shift path ($F_i = 0$, $S_i = 1$), or feedback path to b_i and no shift from b_{i-1} ($F_i =$ Ov1, $S_i = 0$). Therefore, for zone Z_i, if $S_i = 1$, $F_i = 0$; if $S_i = 0$, $F_i = 0$ or 1.

Recursive Structure $P_i = (P_{i-1} , P_{i-1} + X_i)$. Recursive Structure $P_i = (P_{i-1} , P_{i-1} + X_i)$ is a simple tool for describing all possible reconfigurations in a binary tree with the use of SRVB. It is defined recursively for i $-$ 1, ..., n using the following rules.

- *Basis i* =1: $P_1 = (N_o , N_0 + X_1)$, where N_0 is an arbitrary tree node and $X_1 = 2^{n-1}$.
- *Inductive step:* $P_i = (P_{i-1} , P_{i-1} + X_i)$ where P_{i-1} is obtained during previous iteration and $P_{i-1} + X_i$ is obtained from P_{i-1} by complementing the X_i variable in all nodes that are included into P_{i-1} .

most typical problem of nonreconfigurable pipeline systems: a mismatch in a variety of computations between the number of resource units that are connected into a pipeline and the number of operations in a pipelined arithmetic expression(s), creating time and resource overhead in pipelined computation.

Root Approach for Tree Reconfiguration. For the root approach, a fault-tolerant reconfiguration is performed by the root, the tree's connectivity having first been temporarily restored. However, this requires that some fault-free leaves change their position codes, or addresses, and assume the position codes or vacancies created by all faulty nonleaves. Such node reassignment should be temporary, since permanent reassignment requires extensive modifications in all program jump addresses for data exchanges with the nodes that have changed addresses, which becomes practically infeasible.

Once the tree's connectivity is temporarily restored, its temporary root receives all information on the status of tree nodes. Next, it finds the new tree's bias B and reconfigures this tree into one in which connectivity is restored for all fault-tree nodes. These nodes reassume the position codes that they had in the original or source tree.

Rotate Operation, rot(RS_i). Rotate Operation, rot(RS_i) is a logical operation which rotates consecutive bits of RS_i by moving the least significant bit $X_i = 2^{n-i}$ of RS_i to the most significant position, MSB; all the more significant positions that precede X_i in RS_i are moved into new locations in which they follow the MSB in a reversed order.

For instance, rot (01100010) = 10001100.

Routing Algorithmn for R → N_d Communication in a Reconfigurable Binary Tree. The algorithm routes the message issued by root R to a destination node N_d . The algorithm contains two steps, *root step* and *transit step*. The root step is aimed at finding the address code (AC_d) of the destination node, forming the routing information code RI for the communication message CM and passing CM to the only node of level n−1. The transit step is executed iteratively in each transit node of the communication path. It is aimed at finding the next transit node of the communication path and moving the CM message to this node.

Shifting Format of SRVB. Each SRVB can be either a single shift register or a composite shift register consisting of several single SRVB's. Thus, reconfiguration of an n-bit SRVB into a composite shift register is understood as partitioning into p single shift registers of size k_i (i = 1, ..., p). Therefore, each composite SRVB will be described with the shifting format

$$SF = [k_1 , k_2 , ..., k_p], \text{ where } n = k_1 + ... + k_p .$$

The shifting format (SF) may be divided into the following categories:

1. Circular SF_1 when all its single shift-registers perform circular shifts;
2. Non-circular SF_0 when all its single shift-registers perform noncircular shifts;
3. Mixed SF_{10} when single shift-registers described by it perform circular and noncircular shifts.

Shift Register with the Variable Bias, SRVB. A reconfiguration tool that can be used for generating rings, trees and stars during the time of one logical operation of mod 2 addition.

Single and Composite Network Structures. The network structures are divided into single and composite as they are generated by single and composite SRVB's, respectively.

Single structures are further subdivided into single trees, STS, generated by single SF_0 and single rings, SRS, generated by singe SF_1 .

Composite structures are divided into composite rings (CRS) generated by composite SF_1 ; composite stars (CSS) generated by composite SF_0 and mixed structures generated by mixed $SF_{10} = SF_1 \cup SF_0$. The mixed structure is a composite multiple tree structure (CMTS) if SF_0 is single; it is a composite multiple star structure CMSS if SF_0 is composite.

Single Tree Structure. Single Tree Structure is generated by a single and noncircular SRVB.

Stars. (See Trees and Stars Application).

Start-Up Messages. Every user program is started up in a new dynamic computer of the next architectural state with the use of special Start-Up Message SUM. Therefore, to start all programs assigned to the allowed architectural state N, this state should fetch the respective start-up state, $M(N)$, $(N \rightarrow M(N))$, which is understood as a set of SUM messages assigned to N. (See also Assigned and Non-Assigned Queues of Start-Up Messages; Assigned Queue of Start-Up Messages.)

Static and Dynamic Flow Charts Combination. The flow chart executed by the system with dynamic architecture is a combination of static and dynamic reconfiguration flow charts. A static reconfiguration flow chart created during preprocessing is modified by new architectural states created dynamically and included into the dynamic reconfiguration flow chart.

Static and Dynamic Reconfiguration Flow Charts, Architectural States. For *static reconfiguration flow chart*, each architectural state represents a collective reconfiguration request made by an active program on behalf of several passive programs with nonconflicting resource needs. The formation of an architectural state is performed during the preprocessing aimed at construction of a static resource assignment diagram.

For a *dynamic reconfiguration flow chart,* such a formation is triggered with the arrival of an individual reconfiguration request message, issued by the dynamic program. Since a dynamic program cannot know in advance about nonconflicting reconfiguration needs of other passive programs that might be concurrent with the arriving request, the new architectural state is formed by the monitor during computations in the system.

Static Programs for Adaptable Architectures.

- For a static program P_s, its assignment to hardware resources is made during compilation, i.e., during preprocessing, and not during computation.
- Any qualified static program P_s, represents the reconfiguration needs of other programs, which can be satisfied in the same architectural state. Static programs can be *active* and *passive*, where an active program requests an architectural reconfiguration $(N \rightarrow N^*)$ and a passive program does not request any architectural reconfiguration.
- Any static program P_s is always assigned to the architectural state N by the static assignment process, which precedes computation.

Static Resource Assignment. By static resource assignment, we mean an assignment process for which all reconfiguration needs of participating programs are given in advance, before the assignment starts. For static assignment it is always possible to assign these programs to the available system resources in a nonconflicting manner, since all reconfiguration request and program priorities are known. This leads to the total absence of conflicts in execution.

Static Resource Assignment Rationale. For dynamic multicomputer systems, the major objective of the static resource assignment is to minimize possible program delays, via enhanced resource utilization, and to complete each program of the program mix at the earliest moment of time possible under the circumstances.

Static Resource Assignment for Reconfigurable Binary Trees. For reconfigurable binary trees, the major objective of the static resource assignment is to minimize the total time of node-to-node data exchanges. This can be accomplished by minimizing the path durations and maximizing path concurrencies for all node-to-node communications assigned to each tree configuration.

Storage of Assigned Queue of Startup Messages. Stored in the monitor as a table of states in order to (a) maintain the 1-1 correspondence with the reconfiguration flow chart and, (b) uphold a possible restructuring of the assigned queue for dynamic programs. Each startup state of the assigned queue is available in the startup table for static programs or is created dynamically for dynamic programs.

Task Rendezvous. A task that calls for communication will be specified as a *calling* task. A calling task issues an entry call. A task that accepts communication will be specified as a *called* task. It issues an accept statement whereby it is prepared to accept the entry call made by a calling task. Thus the calling and the called tasks may be considered meeting in a *rendezvous.*

Task Rendezvous Accept Statement of the Called Task. The accept statement of the called task is embraced by *do* and *end*, which delimit the actions of the called task in response to an entry call. When the rendezvous occurs, both tasks proceed independently.

Task Rendezvous Basic Steps.

- *Synchronization:* The calling task must issue an entry call and the called task must reach a corresponding accept statement. Synchronization means reaching the latest of these two events.
- *Exchange of Information:* The entry or accept statements can have data parameters, and thus receive or transmit values.
- *Mutual Exclusion:* If two or more calling tasks call the same called task it can accept only one call at a time.

Task Rendezvous for a Dynamic Architecture. In dynamic architecture, the task rendezvous is accomplished by the two processor operating systems POS residing in two PEs designated to compute a calling task, B and a called task, A, respectively. Assume that a calling task B is computed by processor element PE_B. Thus, local POS_B is calling for exchange. The POS_B is activated by the communication request instruction CR issued by the calling task B.

Task Synchronization During Reconfiguration. The objective of the task synchronization is to establish the moment of time when the computer resources requested by a reconfiguration request message (RRM) are ready for reconfiguration.

The task synchronization step is performed under the following circumstances:

1. If there are no conflicts in the system, it is initiated with each arriving RRM message;
2. If there are conflicts in the system, it is performed following the stage of successful conflict resolution.

Task Synchronization During Reconfiguration Conflicts. The task synchronization is warranted only for a reconfiguration conflict that causes the next architectural interrupt. Indeed, for the next interrupt, the anticipated $N \rightarrow N^*$ transition of a static reconfiguration flow chart is replaced with the $N \rightarrow \tilde{N} \rightarrow N^*$ transition, where $\tilde{N}$ is the dynamically assigned state. Therefore, computation of $\tilde{N}$ should wait for completion of N. This requires the task synchronization to determine the moment of this completion and the associated readiness of requested equipment.

Reconfiguration conflict that causes the current interrupt never requires any task synchronization, by definition, because the requested equipment becomes ready as a result of this interrupt.

Tentative Duration Code TD. In the A zone this code shows the tentative duration of state N which is identical to that of the highest priority program that is computed in N. In the $\overline{A}$-zone, this code shows the tentative duration of the individual program, which is represented with this $\overline{A}$ (See A-Header).

Time for a Processor Dependent Operation. Time for a processor dependent operation is determined as $T = p \cdot t_o$, where p is the number of clock periods t_o that a processor dependent operation requires to execute in a given size computer.

Time for Executing a Task in a Dynamic Computer. Since all computers of dynamic architecture use the same clock period t_o the time to execute a task may be expressed in terms of t_o . One first finds the number of clock periods t_o required for each node included in the task. This is done with due regard to iterative execution, as specified by the iteration parameter Z of the node (See Program Graph).

Having found the time for each node, one finds the time of the task as the sum of times for the nodes included in the task. Therefore, to find the time of a single task, one has to find the time to execute one node. This may be accomplished if one finds the time to execute one machine instruction since each statement in the node may be interpreted as a sequence of machine instructions.

Trees and Stars Application. Trees and stars are convenient structures for a variety of computational algorithms of the "divide and conquer" type (sorting, evaluation of arithmetic expressions, inference algorithms for knowledge-based data bases, etc.) in which the entire computation can be partitioned into portions assigned to nodes of a tree or star.

t-Sequence of Architectural States. Generally, a t-sequence S is made of t architectural states $S = N^{(1)} \rightarrow N^{(2)} \rightarrow \ldots \rightarrow N^{(t)}$ and is created during t iterations of the noninterrupted creation process CR. General motivation behind dynamic creation of the t-sequence includes:

- They lift a severe restriction on compatibility in program durations.

420   *Glossary*

- They allow a minimal time execution for multiple task active programs with the highest priority, since each t-sequence is created in its entirety with no interruptions.

Type-1 or 1-Truncated GDT. Type-1 or 1-truncated GDT is a gracefully degraded tree in which all faulty nodes are reconfigured into leaves. This tree will have $(n-1)$ levels of fault free nodes, where n is the number of levels in the original tree.

Type-2 or i-Truncated GDT. Type-2 or i-truncated GDT is a gracefully degraded tree in which $i > 1$ and all faulty nodes are reconfigured into i-level tree branches, otherwise called i-end trees. Each i-end tree is made out of $(2^i - 1)$ faulty nodes. A gracefully degraded tree will then have $(n-i)$ highest levels, composed entirely of fault free nodes. As for i lowest levels, since all faulty end trees are disconnected via reconfiguration, there remain only fault free i-end trees that contain no faulty nodes.

Universality of Programs for Dynamic Architecture. Universality of programs for dynamic architecture is achieved with memory management that provides for the independence of a data address and an instruction address of the computer sizes. This accomplishes the independence of programs of computer sizes such that, during relocations, all the relative addresses inside instruction arrays (jump addresses and data addresses) remain the same, requiring no modifications.

Use Clause of an Ada Package. The use clause of an Ada Package allows referencing the entire visible part of this package by other program units.

Variant and Invariant Control Codes. Control codes stored in each CE are divided into two categories: variant and invariant.

The variant codes are reconfiguration dependent; that is, they change during each system reconfiguration.

The invariant codes are written to each CE forever, during the assembly stage. Their origin is due to the modular nature of dynamic architectures and the necessity to minimize the number of module types that are used in system implementation.

Vertical and Horizontal Distribution of Operating System Functions for Dynamic Architecture. To solve the three types of conflicts (memory, reconfiguration, and I/O), the OS must be functionally or vertically distributed; i.e., it must include three subsystems:

1. The processor operating system POS, which resolves memory conflicts.
2. The I/O operating system I/O OS, which resolves all types of I/O conflicts.
3. The monitor operating system MOS, which resolves conflicts during system reconfiguration.

To be most efficient, these three OSs must reside in functionally oriented units with matching dedication; i.e., the POS must reside in the processor of a dynamic computer, the I/O must reside in its I/O unit, and the MOS must reside in the system monitor.

In addition to vertical or functional distribution, the operating system must feature horizontal distribution among separate CEs of the dynamic computer. Indeed, since dynamic computer, $C_i(k)$, consists of k CE and minimal k = 1, then the same POS and I/O must reside in every CE. Therefore, not only is the entire OS vertically distributed because of the three types of conflicts that should be resolved; it becomes horizontally distributed to resolve memory and I/O conflicts because of the modular structure of a dynamic computer.

X_i -Level Reconfiguration. By the X_i-level reconfiguration or X_i reconfiguration, we mean the reconfiguration determined by mapping code $MC = X_i$ ($i = 1, \ldots, n$). The X_i reconfiguration is performed on the level of all structures $P_i = (P_{i-1}, P_{i-1} + X_i)$ in the tree. It consists of exchanging P_{i-1} with $P_{i-1} + X_i$ as $(P_{i-1} \rightleftharpoons P_{i-1} + X_i)$. Each reconfigured structure $P_i(r)$ obtained as a result of this reconfiguration is specified as follows:

$$P_i(r) = (P_{i-1} + X_i , P_{i-1}).$$

In a new reconfigured tree the root $R(r)$ becomes: $R(r) = R + X_i$. All sources nodes of the level $n-i$ specified with level variable X_i, become the reconfigured nodes of level $n, n-1, n-2, \ldots, n-(i-1)$. On the other hand, all the source nodes of higher levels of $n, n-1, \ldots, n-(i-1)$ become the reconfigured nodes of level $n-i$. Thus, the change in levels occurs only for source nodes with levels $n, n-1, \ldots, n-i$. All source nodes of lower levels $n-(i+1), n-(i+2), \ldots, n-n = 0$, described by structures $P_{i+1}, P_{i+2}, \ldots, P_n$ retain their levels. Instead, in each P_{i+k}-structure, each reconfiguration exchange is performed on the level of P_i, whereby each left element P_{i-1} of P_i is exchanged with its right element $P_{i-1} + X_i$ (See Recursive Structure P_i).

Index

423

F